HANDBOOK OF EVALUATION

HANDBOOK OF EVALUATION

Policies, Programs and Practices

Edited by

Ian F. Shaw, Jennifer C. Greene,
Melvin M. Mark

SAGE Publications

London ● Thousand Oaks ● New Delhi

First published 2006

Reprinted 2007

SAGE Publications Ltd
1 Oliver's Yard
55 City Road
London EC1Y 1SP

SAGE Publications Inc.
2455 Teller Road
Thousand Oaks, California 91320

SAGE Publications India Pvt Ltd
B 1/I 1 Mohan Cooperative Industrial Area
Mathura Road, New Delhi 110 044
India

SAGE Publications Asia-Pacific Pte Ltd
33 Pekin Street #02-01
Far East Square
Singapore 048763

British Library Cataloguing in Publication data
A catalogue record for this book is available from the British Library

ISBN 978-0-7619-7305-8

Library of Congress Control Number 2005935244

Typeset by C&M Digitals (P) Ltd., Chennai, India
Printed on paper from sustainable resources
Printed in Great Britain by The Cromwell Press Ltd, Trowbridge, Wiltshire

CONTENTS

ABOUT THE EDITORS

Jennifer C. Greene is Professor of Educational Psychology at the University of Illinois, Urbana-Champaign. She served as the Co-Editor-in-Chief of *New Directions for Evaluation* from 1997 to 2004 and received the Lazarsfeld Award for distinguished contributions to evaluation theory from the American Evaluation Association in 2003. Dr Greene's evaluation scholarship probes the intersections of social science method with policy discourse and program decision making. She has contributed to works on qualitative, participatory, and mixed-method approaches to evaluation, including *New Directions* volumes on mixed-method and responsive evaluation designs. Her evaluation practice has emphasized the domains of education, community-based family services, and youth development.

Melvin M. Mark is Professor of Psychology at Penn State University. He has served as Editor of the *American Journal of Evaluation*, and is now Editor Emeritus. He is President of the American Evaluation Association in 2006. Dr. Mark's interests include the theory, methodology, practice, and profession of program and policy evaluation. He has been involved in evaluations in a number of areas, including prevention programs, federal personnel policies, and various educational interventions. Among his books are *Evaluation: An integrated framework for understanding, guiding, and improving policies and programs* (Jossey-Bass, 2000; with Gary Henry and George Julnes) and forthcoming books *Exemplars of Evaluation* (Sage; with Jody Fitzpatrick and Tina Christie) and *Social Psychology and Evaluation* (Guilford; with Stewart Donaldson and Bernadette Campbell).

Ian F. Shaw is Professor of Social Work at the University of York. He is founder and co-editor of *Qualitative Social Work*. His more recent evaluation work has focused on practitioner evaluation, the kinds and quality of social work research, and an evaluation of several pilot sites pending the UK government's introduction of an Integrated Children's System in 2006/7. His books include *Qualitative Evaluation* (Sage), *Qualitative Research in Social Work* (Sage; with Nick Gould), *Evaluation and Social Work Practice* (Sage; with Joyce Lishman), and *Evaluating in Practice* (Ashgate).

INTERNATIONAL ADVISORY BOARD

We wish to acknowledge the work of the Handbook's International Advisory Board, the members of which acted as consultants for the structure and content of the handbook and gave extensive peer review contributions on the text of the Handbook

Howard S. Bloom is Chief Social Scientist at MDRC, New York

Robert Burgess is Vice Chancellor of the University of Leicester, England.

Eleanor Chelimsky was, before her retirement, Director of the Institute for Program Evaluation at the U.S. General Accounting Office (now Government Accountability Office) and latterly Assistant Comptroller General and Director of the GAO Program Evaluation and Methodology Division. She is a former president of the American Evaluation Association

Sue Funnell is Director of Performance Improvement Pty Ltd, New South Wales, Australia, and a former president of the Australasian Evaluation Society.

Yvonna S. Lincoln is Professor, Educational Administration & Human Resource Development, at the College of Education & Human Development, Texas A&M University and a former president of the American Evaluation Association.

Arnold Love is an international independent evaluation consultant based in Toronto, Canada, and a former president of the Canadian Evaluation Society.

Ulf Lundgren is Professor of Education at Uppsala University and also works with the Swedish Research Council.

Gill McIvor is Professor of Criminal Justice and Co-Director of the Scottish Centre for Crime and Justice Research, University of Stirling, Scotland.

Michael Quinn Patton, a former president of the American Evaluation Association, directs an organizational development consulting business, Utilization-Focused Evaluation.

Michael Scriven is Professor of Philosophy and Associate Director of The Evaluation Centre, Western Michigan University, Michigan, and former President of the American Evaluation Association.

CONTRIBUTORS

Tineke A. Abma is senior researcher at the University of Maastricht, Healthcare Ethics and Philosophy in the Netherlands. Areas of interest are responsive evaluation, dialogue, storytelling and patient participation in health research. She has conducted evaluation projects in the fields of healthcare (psychiatry, palliative care and rehabilitation). Publications include an issue on 'dialogue' in evaluation (*Evaluation*, 7, 2, 2001), a volume on *Responsive Evaluation* (*New Directions for Evaluation*, 92, 2001) and a volume on narrative in evaluation (*Telling Tales*, JAI Press, 6, 1999). Recent projects focus on patient participation in health research, coercion in mental healthcare and moral deliberation.

Marvin C. Alkin is an emeritus professor in the Social Research Methodology Division in the Graduate School of Education and Information Studies at University of California, Los Angeles. Recent publications include: *Theorists' Models in Action*, co-edited with Christina A. Christie (*NDE* Number 106, Summer 2005), and *Evaluation Roots: Tracing Theorists' Views and Influences* (Sage, 2004). Interested in education evaluation theory and practice, Dr Alkin heads the SRM Evaluation Group at UCLA, where he devotes much of his time to mentoring students. The group contributes to the advancement of program evaluation as a field in three specific ways: *academic study*, *evaluation practice*, and *research*.

Tony Beck has a Ph.D. in Geography from the University of London, and a BA and MA in English Literature from the University of Cambridge. He worked in India for four years carrying out research and as administrator for an India NGO, and since 1990 has been a consultant to over 20 organizations working on evaluation and evaluation design, humanitarian and development issues. He is the author of two books and 22 academic articles and book chapters on development and evaluation issues.

Holli Burgon, University of Illinois at Urbana-Champaign, has primary interests in evaluation, qualitative research, and philosophy of inquiry. She is working with Jennifer Greene, Lizanne DeStefano, and Jori Hall to develop the Values-Engaged Evaluation Approach, an NSF funded project featured in *New Directions for Evaluation*. Additionally, she is working with Thomas Schwandt to examine conceptions and transfer of professional judgment in evaluation and the helping professions.

Eleanor Chelimsky has had a career in evaluation practice, economic planning, policy analysis, and the critical review of program, budget, audit and evaluation processes. Following work for the U.S. Mission to NATO, and positions of increasing responsibility with the MITRE

Corporation, she was Director of the Institute for Program Evaluation at the U.S. General Accounting Office (now Government Accountability Office) and latterly Assistant Comptroller General and Director of the GAO Program Evaluation and Methodology Division. She was granted several distinguished honors including the Comptroller General's Award (the GAO's top honor) and the Donald Campbell Award for Methodological Innovation in Public Policy Studies.

Matthew Jacob Chinman, Ph.D. is a Behavioral Scientist at the RAND Corporation. His focus has been to develop and assess strategies to enhance the capacity of community-based prevention practitioners. He is co-developer of the Getting To Outcomes (GTO) system and the lead author of the RAND Corporation Technical Report, 'Getting to Outcomes 2004: Promoting Accountability through Methods and Tools for Planning, Implementation, and Evaluation.' GTO won an award for the best self-help manual from the American Evaluation Association. He is currently the principal investigator of a grant from the Centers for Disease Control and Prevention to examine how the Getting To Outcomes system helps improve community capacity in substance abuse prevention practitioners. Dr Chinman has published on such topics as program evaluation methodology, empowerment evaluation, adolescent empowerment, coalition functioning, and peer support.

Christina A. Christie is an Assistant Professor, Director of the Masters of Arts Program in Psychology and Evaluation, and Associate Director of the Institute of Organizational and Program Evaluation Research in the School of Behavioral and Organizational Sciences at Claremont Graduate University. Christie has published on evaluation use, social justice in evaluation, and teaching evaluation. Her publications also include empirical studies of evaluation (Christie, C.A. 2003. The practice-theory relationship in evaluation. *New Directions for Evaluation*, 97 and Alkin, M.C. & Christie, C. A. (2005). Theorists' models in action. *New Directions for Evaluation*, 106). She has received funding from a variety of sources, including the U.S. Department of Education, the Hewlett-Carnegie Foundation, and the Haynes Foundation to evaluate social, education, and health behavior programs targeting high-risk and underrepresented populations.

Alan Clarke is Professor of Criminology in the Department of Law at the University of Wales, Aberystwyth. He has a general interest in evaluation research methodology and is the author of *Evaluation Research: An Introduction to Principles, Methods and Practice*, (Sage, 1999). His main evaluation research projects have been in the field of crime and criminal justice. He has been involved in evaluating numerous intervention programmes including treatment for offenders with drug misuse problems, cognitive behaviour programmes for adult male prisoners and mentoring schemes for young people at risk of offending.

Ross Conner is director of the Center for Community Health Research and Professor, School of Social Ecology, at the University of California, Irvine. He received his Ph.D. and M.A. from Northwestern University (social psychology/evaluation) and his B.A. from The Johns Hopkins University. He is President of the International Organization for Cooperation in Evaluation and a past president of the American Evaluation Association. His research focuses on community health promotion/disease prevention programs and their evaluation. He is currently collaborating with and studying two such programs: cancer control with Korean and Chinese communities and HIV prevention with Latino men. He also is conducting an assessment of California's largest community-initiated health promotion programs, the CommunitiesFirst initiative of The California Endowment.

J. Bradley Cousins is Professor of Educational Administration at the Faculty of Education, University of Ottawa and Editor-in-chief of the *Canadian Journal of Program Evaluation*. Professor Cousins' main academic interests are in program evaluation including participatory and collaborative approaches, utilization issues and capacity building. He is author of several articles, international handbook chapters and books on evaluation related topics including 'Use effects of participatory evaluation' (2003, *International Handbook of Educational Evaluation*) and 'Integrating evaluative inquiry into the organizational culture' (2004, *Canadian Journal of Program Evaluation*). He has received several awards and distinctions for his research which now centers on evaluation capacity building in governmental and not-for-profit sectors in Canada.

Peter Dahler-Larsen, Ph.D., is professor at the Department of Political Science and Public Management, University of Southern Denmark. His main research interest is institutional, organizational and cultural aspects of evaluation and definitions of quality. From this perspective, he is also interested in variants of theory-based evaluation models, which he has helped develop for two ministries in Denmark. He works with good friends and colleagues in the U.S., in Europe, Scandinavia, and Denmark. He is the president of European Evaluation Society in 2006–07.

Lois-ellin Datta's work has focused on the intersect of policy, practice and methodology. A Past President of the Evaluation Research Society, recipient of the American Evaluation Association Myrdal Award, and former Editor-in-Chief of *New Directions for Evaluation*, she has served as Director of the U.S. GAO's Human Services in Evaluation/Program and Methodology Division, Director of national research in Teaching, Learning, and Assessment, and as National Director of Project Head Start/Children's Bureau evaluation. Her publications include articles such as 'Easier Trekking: some pathways to combining and integrating qualitative and quantitative approaches' and books, such as (co-authored with Patrick Grasso) *Evaluating Tax Expenditures: Tools and Techniques for Assessing Outcomes*.

Philip Davies is with the Government Social Research Unit, UK Cabinet Office, London. His overriding area of interest at the present time is in research utilization and getting research into policy and practice. He has particular interests in developing systematic review methods for public policy purposes and in developing capacity within government and UK social science to undertake high-quality experimental and quasi-experimental research. His substantive areas of interest and expertise are in health and health care, education, crime and justice and social welfare. His recent publications have been on the potential of systematic reviews and other forms of research synthesis for policy making, and on what policy makers want from social researchers. His current research project, entitled *Analysis for Policy*, addresses what policy makers in central government understand by evidence, where they go for evidence, and what they expect from the research community.

Stewart I. Donaldson is Professor and Chair of Psychology, Director of the Institute of Organizational and Program Evaluation Research, and Dean of the School of Behavioral and Organizational Sciences, Claremont Graduate University. Dr. Donaldson leads one of the most extensive and rigorous graduate programs in evaluation. He has published a wide range of articles and chapters on theory-driven evaluation and applied psychology. His recent books include *Evaluating Social Programs and Problems: Visions for the New Millennium* (2003; with Michael Scriven) and *Applied Psychology: New Frontiers and Rewarding Careers* (in press; with Dale E. Berger and Kathy Pezdek).

Osvaldo N. Feinstein retired in November 2004 from the World Bank (former Adviser and Manager at the Operations Evaluation Department), having also worked at the UN-IFAD and with other UN organizations and international development banks. He lectured at several universities and published various books (including one on 'poverty reduction and evaluation') and articles (e.g., 'Use of evaluation and the evaluation of their use' and 'Neostructuralism and paradigms of economic policy'). He is currently working as an evaluation consultant with the World Bank and the African Development Bank, and plans to continue writing and lecturing on evaluation, development and economics.

Irene Guijt is an independent advisor and researcher focusing on learning processes and systems (including monitoring and evaluation) in rural development and natural resource management, particularly where this involves collective action. She is completing her Ph.D. on the contribution of monitoring to trigger learning. Key publications include *Participatory Learning and Action: A Trainer's Guide* (co-author) and *The Myth of Community: Gender Issues in Participatory Development* (with M. K. Shah).

Gary T. Henry is a professor in the Andrew Young School of Policy Studies, Department of Political Science at Georgia State University and the Department of Public Policy at Georgia Institute of Technology. Professor Henry has authored and co-authored several books and articles including *Evaluation: An Integrated Framework for Understanding, Guiding, and Improving Policies and Programs* (Jossey-Bass 2000), 'Competition in the Sandbox: A Test of the Effects of Preschool Competition on Educational Outcomes' in the *Journal of Policy Analysis and Management* (2006), and 'Beyond Use: Understanding Evaluation's Influence on Attitudes and Actions' in the *American Journal of Evaluation*. Currently, Dr Henry serves on the systemic and broad-based reform scientific peer review panel for the Institute of Education Sciences, U.S. Department of Education and on a National Research Council/National Academy of Science panel assessing the effects of 'green schools' on the health and productivity of teachers and students.

Pamela S. Imm, Ph.D., received her doctorate degree in Clinical and Community Psychology from the University of South Carolina in 1996. Her strongest area of interest is working with community-based organizations to help them integrate evaluation and research-based concepts into their work. She has published in the areas of alcohol and drug abuse prevention, evaluation research, and models of effective programming. She is a co-author of 'Getting to Outcomes: Methods and Tools for Planning, Self-assessment, and Accountability,' published by the RAND Corporation. She and her colleagues have recently collaborated with the Search Institute to write *Getting to Outcomes with Developmental Assets* which should be available in January, 2006.

Mark W. Lipsey is the Director of the Center for Evaluation Research and Methodology and a Senior Research Associate at the Vanderbilt Institute for Public Policy Studies. His research interests are in the areas of public policy, program evaluation, social intervention, field research methodology, and meta-analysis. Recent research has focused on risk and intervention for juvenile delinquency, early childhood educational programs, and issues of methodological quality in program evaluation research. His published work includes *Evaluation: A Systematic Approach* (7th edition, 2004; with Peter Rossi and Howard Freeman) and *Practical Meta-Analysis* (with David Wilson).

Andrew Long is Professor of Health Systems Research at the School of Healthcare, University of Leeds. His specialist interests lie in methodology (quantitative and qualitative, evaluation and critical appraisal), outcome measurement and effectiveness of health and social care, and complementary and alternative medicine (CAM) interventions. His research programme includes: development of an evaluation tool for appraising qualitative research studies; conceptualizing and developing appropriate outcome criteria and measures, in particular in the CAM field; generating evidence on patient perceptions and experiences of services; and exploring models of patient-centred care and empowerment within interventions centred on behavioural change.

Donna M. Mertens is a Professor in the Department of Educational Foundations and Research at Gallaudet University in Washington DC. Dr. Mertens teaches program evaluation to deaf and hearing students in an international development program for people with disabilities. Her publications include *Research and Evaluation in Education and Psychology: Integrating Diversity with Quantitative and Qualitative Designs* (Sage, 2005), *Research and Evaluation in Special Education* (with John McLaughlin, Corwin, 2004), and *Parents and their Deaf Children* (with Kay Meadow Orlans and Marilyn Sass Lehrer, Gallaudet Press, 2003). Dr. Mertens' work is rooted in the transformative paradigm, with a specific focus on accurate inclusion of underrepresented groups and a conscious awareness of the role of evaluators as being integral to the achievement of social justice.

David Nevo is Professor and Head of the School of Education at Tel Aviv University, with professional interests in evaluation theory, program evaluation, school-based evaluation and student assessment. His current research is focused on Dialogue Evaluation, combining internal and external evaluation and working with schools and teachers to improve their evaluation capabilities and their ability to cope with external evaluation requirements and accountability. Dr. Nevo is author of *Evaluation in decision making* (with Glasman, Kluwer, 1988), *School-based evaluation: A dialogue for school improvement* (Pergamon, 1995), editor of *School-based evaluation: An international perspective* (Elsevier, 2002) and Editor-in-Chief of *Studies in Educational Evaluation*.

Kathryn Newcomer is Director of the School of Public Policy and Public Administration at the George Washington University where she teaches public and non-profit program evaluation, research design, and applied statistics. She conducts research and training for federal and local government agencies on performance measurement and program evaluation. Dr. Newcomer has published five books, including *The Handbook of Practical Program Evaluation* (1994, 2004), and *Getting Results: A Guide for Federal Leaders and Managers* (2005), and numerous articles in journals. She is a Fellow of the National Academy of Public Administration, and currently serves on the Comptroller General's Educators' Advisory Panel. She is Vice President of the National Association of Schools of Public Affairs and Administration, will serve as president in 2006. She has received two Fulbright awards, one for Taiwan (1993) and one for Egypt (2001–04).

Patricia Rogers is Associate Professor in Public Sector Evaluation and Director of CIRCLE (Collaborative Institute for Research, Consulting and Learning in Evaluation) at the Royal Melbourne Institute of Technology, Australia. Her main interests are improving the impact of evaluation through developing the evaluation capacity of organizations and the use of program theory and systems thinking. Her publications include a co-edited *New Directions in Evaluation* volume on program theory (Rogers, Hacsi, Petrosino and Huebner, 1999), and papers on building evaluation capability (McDonald, Rogers and Kefford, 2003), and internationalizing evaluation (Rogers, 2001). Recent evaluation projects include community capacity-building, family strengthening, Indigenous housing, and community corrections.

Mike Rose is a professor in the Social Research Methodology Division of the UCLA Graduate School of Education and Information Studies. His research interests are primarily in the areas of literacy, cognition, and teaching, with more recent publications in the areas of work and cognition, research methodology, and the training of graduate students in education. His books include *Lives on the Boundary: The Struggles and Achievements of America's Underprepared, Possible Lives: The Promise of Public Education in America, The Mind at Work: Valuing the Intelligence of the American Worker*, and the forthcoming *An Open Language: Selected Writing on Literacy, Learning, and Opportunity*.

Thomas A. Schwandt is University Distinguished Teacher/Scholar and Professor of Education at the University of Illinois at Urbana-Champaign. His scholarship focuses on interpretive methodologies and evaluation theory. He is the author of *Evaluation Practice Reconsidered* (Peter Lang); the *Dictionary of Qualitative Inquiry* (Sage), and with Edward Halpern, *Linking Auditing and Meta-evaluation* (Sage); with his Norwegian colleague Peder Haug he has co-edited *Evaluating Educational Reforms: Scandinavian Perspectives* (Information Age Press) and with Katherine Ryan, *Exploring Evaluator Role and Identity* (Information Age Press, 2002). In 2002 he received the Paul F. Lazarsfeld Award from the American Evaluation Association for his contributions to evaluation theory.

Lyn Shulha is a Director of the Assessment and Evaluation Group, Queen's University at Kingston, Canada. She is currently a Canadian member of the Joint Committee for Standards in Educational Evaluation (JCSEE) and a writer and editor for the forthcoming, *Program Evaluation Standards, 3rd Edition*. Lyn is a continuing member of the editorial boards for both the *Canadian Journal of Program Evaluation* and the *American Journal of Evaluation*. Being primarily a participatory evaluator and collaborative researcher, she continues to examine the challenges of evaluation use and collaborative mixed-methods research (*Handbook of Mixed Methodology*, A. Tashakkori and C. Teddlie Eds., 2003).

Helen Simons is Professor of Education and Evaluation at the University of Southampton, UK, where she specializes in evaluation and research training, particularly in qualitative methodologies. Her research interests are in democratic evaluation, ethics, programme, policy and institutional self-evaluation, evaluation and the creative arts. Helen's publications include numerous papers (e.g. 'Utilizing Evaluation Evidence to Enhance Professional Practice', 2004, *Evaluation*; 'Whose Data is it Anyway: Ethics in Qualitative Research' 2005, *Malaysian Journal of Qualitative Research*), and several books including *Getting to Know Schools in a Democracy: the politics and process of evaluation* (1987) Lewes: Falmer Press, which won an international book award.

Professor Simons is an elected academician of the Academy of Social Sciences. She was a key author of the ethical guidelines of British Educational Research Association and the UK Evaluation Society (of which she is President 2005–6).

Haluk Soydan has a Ph.D. in sociology from Uppsala University, Sweden. His research experience includes intervention and evaluation studies, systematic research reviews, qualitative studies of how human services organizations work, service delivery among ethnic clients and patients, and core theoretical issues in social work research. He is co-founder and co-chair of the international Campbell Collaboration.

Robert E. Stake is a specialist in the evaluation of educational programs and case study methods. He is director of the Center for Instructional Research and Curriculum Evaluation at the University of Illinois. Stake has authored *Quieting Reform*, a book on Charles Murray's evaluation of Cities-in-Schools and four books on research methods, *Multiple Case Study Analysis, Standards-Based and Responsive Evaluation, Evaluating the Arts in Education*, and *The Art of Case Study Research*. His three major clients have been the National Science Foundation, the Chicago Teachers Academy for Mathematics and Science, and the international Step by Step early childhood education program.

Elliot Stern is an independent evaluation consultant and until retirement a Director of the Tavistock Institute. He edits the journal *Evaluation* (for Sage UK); has recently edited *Evaluation Research Methods* – Sage Benchmarks in Social Research Methods; and contributed to *Understanding Research for Social Policy and Practice* (Eds Becker and Bryman, Policy Press, 2004). He is interested in evaluator education; evaluation of international development; and methods for the evaluation of polices. He is past President of both UK and European evaluation societies and currently a member of the governing council of the UK Academy of Social Sciences.

John F. Stevenson, Ph.D. is a Professor of Psychology and chairs the Psychology Department at the University of Rhode Island. He teaches evaluation methodology at the graduate level and has conducted many workshops on evaluation for practitioners. His research has examined such questions as the measurement of outcomes in psychiatric inpatient care, the effectiveness of graduate training in clinical psychology, and the effectiveness of alcohol, tobacco, and other drug abuse prevention programs in a variety of community settings including the college campus. At present his research focuses on state-level evaluation of coalition-driven prevention using evidence-based interventions. Recent publications include: 'Cultivating capacity: Outcomes of a statewide support system for prevention coalitions' (*Journal of Prevention and Intervention in the Community*, 2004); 'Community level collaboration for substance abuse prevention' (*Journal of Primary Prevention*, 2003); and 'Building evaluation capacity in human service organizations: A case study' (*Evaluation and Program Planning*, 2002).

David Thomas is Professor of Social and Community Health in the School of Population Health at the University of Auckland, New Zealand. He teaches social science research methods and evaluation. His current areas of research include evaluation of health and education services and family intervention programs. He has a specific interest in culture, ethnicity and health. Recent publications include: 'Evaluating the cultural appropriateness of service delivery in multi-ethnic communities' (*Evaluation Journal of Australasia*, 2002); and 'A general inductive approach for analysing qualitative evaluation data' (2006, *American Journal of Evaluation*, in press). His publications include 60 journal articles and book chapters and two edited books.

Nick Tilley is Professor of Sociology at Nottingham Trent University and Visiting Professor at the Jill Dando Institute of Crime Science, University College London. His main interests lie in program evaluation methodology, policing and crime prevention. Books include *Realistic Evaluation* (with Ray Pawson, Sage 1997), *Evaluation for Crime Prevention* (Criminal Justice Press 2002) and a *Handbook of Crime Prevention and Community Safety* (Willan, 2005). Current research projects relate to volume crime investigation, the prevention of fly-tipping, methods of policing antisocial behavior, traveling victims of crime, and notions of program fidelity.

Ove Karlsson Vestman is professor of education, Associate Dean of the Department of Social Sciences at Mälardalen University, Sweden, where he directs the Mälardalen Evaluation Academy. He is Associate Dean of the Faculty Board and Vice-President of the Swedish Evaluation Society. His work concentrates on participatory and mixed-method approaches. He has published on dialogue methods and critical theory, and has written about the role of values and social justice in evaluation, for example: Critical Dialogue: Its Value and Meaning, *Evaluation*, 7 (2); Program Evaluation in Europe: Between Democratic and New Public Management Evaluation, *International Handbook of Educational Evaluation* (Kellaghan & Stufflebeam, eds.); Democratic Evaluation: An Arena for Dialogue and Learning? *Evaluating Educational Reforms: Scandinavian Perspectives* (Schwandt & Haug, eds.).

Robert Walker is Professor of Social Policy at the University of Nottingham and a Research Fellow at the Institute for Fiscal Studies. He formerly directed the Centre for Research in Social Policy at Loughborough University where he managed around 50 research projects including direction of international consortia engaged on large scale, multi-method evaluations. His latest books include *Social Security and welfare* (2005, Policy Press); *Welfare to Work: New Labour and the US experience* (with Andreas Cebulla, Karl Ashworth and David Greenberg, 2005, Ashgate) and *The Welfare We Want: The British challenge for American reform* (with Michael Wiseman, 2003, Policy Press).

Abraham Wandersman Ph.D. is a Professor of Psychology at the University of South Carolina-Columbia. Dr. Wandersman performs research and program evaluation on citizen participation in community organizations and coalitions and on interagency collaboration. He is a co-editor of two books on empowerment evaluation, and a co-author of *Getting To Outcomes*. In 1998, he received the Myrdal Award for Evaluation Practice from the American Evaluation Association. In 2000, he was elected President of the Society for Community Research and Action (SCRA). In 2005, he was awarded the Distinguished Theory and Research Contibutions Award by SCRA.

Elizabeth Whitmore is Professor (Emerita) from Carleton University School of Social Work, in Ottawa, Canada. Her areas of interest include participatory approaches to research and evaluation, and international social development. She edited a volume entitled *Understanding and*

Practicing Participatory Evaluation (1998), and has co-authored two books: *Seeds of Fire: Social Development in an Age of Globalism* (2000), and *Globalization, Social Justice and Social Work* (2005). Current projects include an examination of the effectiveness of advocacy by organizations engaged in social justice work.

Bob Williams is self-employed and based in New Zealand. He is widely known throughout the evaluation world for his contributions to Evaltalk and promoting the use of systems-based approaches in the evaluation field. Bob has written extensively on the relationship between evaluation use, evaluation usefulness, and organizational development. He is the co-editor of the AEA Monologue on systems and evaluation, a member of the Editorial Board of the *American Journal of Evaluation*, and helped develop the revised *Evaluation Journal of Australasia*. Bob is a qualified snowboard and windsurfing instructor.

Michael Wiseman is Research Professor of Public Policy, Public Administration, and Economics at The George Washington University and a Visiting Scholar in the Office of Policy of the U.S. Social Security Administration and the Office of the Assistant Secretary for Policy and Evaluation in the U.S. Department of Health and Human Services. He has served as consultant on public assistance management and program evaluation for various U.S. government agencies, the World Bank, several states, and various program evaluation contractors. His publications include *The Welfare We Want: the British Challenge to American Reform* (co-authored/edited with Robert Walker) (2003).

We also wish to acknowledge additional contributions to the Handbook from:

- Professor Hazel Qureshi (York, UK) and Professor Carol T. Mowbray (University of Michigan). (Chapter 22, "Social Work and the Human Services".)
- Alison Mathie (Coady Institute for International Development, St. Xavier University, Canada) and Ana Coghlan (independent consultant on international development evaluation). (Chapter on humanitarian and development evaluation.)

Professor of Social Work and Associate Professor of Psychology, **Carol T. Mowbray** died in August, 2005. She was the Co-Director of the School of Social Work's Center for Poverty, Risk, and Mental Health. From 1996 to 2001, she was the University of Michigan School of Social Work Associate Dean of Research. Her nationally and internationally cited research and many publications focused on community integration and recovery for adults with serious mental illnesses, especially homeless persons, and those with co-occurring substance use disorders. She also helped to develop a special emphasis on women who are mentally ill (especially those who are mothers and their children). She developed and evaluated the effectiveness of interventions for disadvantaged mentally ill populations, focusing especially on consumer-run and supported education programs in various locations.

INTRODUCTION

THE EVALUATION OF POLICIES, PROGRAMS, AND PRACTICES

Melvin M. Mark, Jennifer C. Greene, and Ian F. Shaw

Introduction to the Handbook

A handbook is an ambitious enterprise, but one that also needs delimiting and framing. There are simply too many good ideas and useful perspectives to include in any one volume. The commitments and framework that informed the development of this Handbook are introduced in this chapter. We also offer an overview of and perspective on evaluation.

Evaluation as a Human Activity

Evaluation is a natural part of humans' everyday life. People make evaluations, in the form of judgments of how good or bad, how desirable or undesirable something is, almost nonstop in the ordinary course of their daily lives. How good was breakfast at the restaurant? How did the meeting with a client go? How good was the play, symphony, or disk jockey last night? Not only is evaluation commonplace. It also appears to be fairly fundamental. Evidence from psychology indicates that, when asked to make an evaluative judgment about some object, people respond more quickly than when asked to make a descriptive statement about the same object (Maio and Olson, 2000; Musch and Klauer, 2003). This may indicate that making evaluative judgments about the world is even more basic than making sense of the world descriptively. Emerging evidence from neuroscience also indicates that making evaluative judgments involves different parts of the brain than making descriptive judgments (Maio and Olson, 2000; Musch and Klauer, 2003). Humans may be hardwired to look at the world evaluatively.

Even though it is natural for humans to make evaluations as part of their everyday lives, both personally and professionally, this kind of everyday, informal evaluative judgment often does not suffice. It has long been known that an individual's informal evaluations can be affected by her or his expectations and preferences (e.g., Shaw, 1984). With everyday, informal evaluation, it usually is not clear to others (and perhaps not even to the individual making the judgment) what has led to a particular evaluative conclusion. Systematic, formal evaluation can, at the very least, make explicit the evidence and criteria on which evaluative judgments are based. Systematic methods of evaluation also can, if not completely eliminate biases, at least help make it clearer or easier to detect what the sources of possible judgmental or evaluative biases are.

In addition, everyday, informal evaluations are typically made by individuals. And any given individual may not have as much information as one would like for making an evaluative judgment that could inspire confidence in others. For instance, staff members working in a social program almost certainly make evaluative judgments about it. But they often don't see what happens to the clients who drop out of the program; they probably don't know what happens to most clients a year after they have completed the program; and they rarely have a good way to gauge what would have happened to clients if they had not been in the program. Systematic evaluation can offer a way to go beyond the evidence available to any individual, as well as to facilitate evaluative processes that are collective and not simply individual.

Disciplined and systematic means of evaluation also allow for evaluative processes to be designed so as to achieve different ends. As is demonstrated throughout this Handbook, systematic evaluation can be aimed at a variety of purposes, including policy making and public accountability, program and organizational improvement, knowledge development, advancement of social justice, and the enhancement of practical wisdom and good practice judgments. The ideas, first, that systematic

evaluation can be directed towards different purposes and, second, that the choice of a specific purpose can have implications for how evaluation should be done, permeate this Handbook. Indeed, parts of the Handbook, in particular Part 1 and some of Part 3, are organized around alternative evaluation purposes.

Having made a distinction here between everyday, informal evaluation, on the one hand, and more formal, systematic evaluation, on the other, we should recognize that there is no consensus in the evaluation or the wider social science communities about the relationship between the different kinds of knowledge that are entailed in more formal and more informal evaluative judgments. Some would claim that one is based on the logic of science and the other on the fundamentally different logic of everyday reasoning (e.g., Hammersley, 2003; Polkinghorne, 2000). Others, while developing and emphasizing the significance of alternative forms of knowledge, see them as potentially complementary (e.g., Schmidt, 1993). We do not mean to suggest a chasm between these two forms of evaluation. Everyday evaluation and more systematic evaluation can and should have much in common. To the extent that there are differences between the two, they are differences of degree. And, whenever more formal, systematic evaluation is done, it inevitably rests on and interacts with everyday evaluation activities. To take but one example, the findings reported from a systematic evaluation almost certainly are interpreted in the context of the evaluation users' pre-existing, everyday evaluations of the policy, program, or practice in question.

More generally, we think there are perhaps three different ways in which informal and formal evaluation have been related. First, many see formal evaluation as an improvement, strengthening and offering more explicit and usable knowledge than informal evaluations.

In general form, this position is similar to that held by advocates of critical thinking and evidence-based policy and practice. Second, some would regard informal and formal knowledge as different but, potentially at least, *complementary* (e.g., Schmidt, 1993). Third, some have seen these as essentially *interactive* forms of knowledge, such that informal and formal evaluations mutually challenge and question the other in a non-hierarchical way.

In spite of such complexities, the distinction between everyday, informal evaluation and more formal, systematic evaluation is useful. In particular, readers should recognize that this Handbook focuses, albeit not exclusively, on more formal, systematic approaches to evaluation, rather than on informal, everyday evaluation. To those who make their living as evaluators, and to others aware of the professional activity of evaluators, this focus is not surprising. Regardless, keeping in mind the distinction between everyday evaluation and more formal evaluation is important. Professional evaluators should remember that everyday, informal evaluation takes place without them, that their systematic evaluation work occurs in a world filled with natural evaluative judgments, and that it is but a small fraction of that larger evaluative world.

The Scope of the Handbook

In focusing on more formal evaluation, the Handbook describes and critiques the kind of evaluation carried out by professional evaluators and others who may not label themselves as "evaluators" but who do similar work. We have aimed throughout to respect the diversity of evaluators' social roles and to avoid unquestioningly treating the evaluation history of any one country or discipline as normative or regulative for any others. Evaluation, whether more formal and systematic or more informal and everyday, can be

applied to almost anything. Michael Scriven (1991, 1999), a major figure in the evaluation literature, has referred to evaluating the "six Ps": programs, policies, performance, products, personnel, and proposals. Indeed, evaluation itself can be evaluated – evaluators have come to call this meta-evaluation.

This Handbook focuses on the evaluation of programs, policies, and practices. We believe it is infeasible to discuss in detail the evaluation of everything in a single handbook. Personnel evaluation, for instance, is a sufficiently specialized area to have its own handbooks (e.g., Anderson, 2001; Evers, Anderson, & Voskuijl, 2005; Lombardi, 1988). The present Handbook addresses "three Ps" – programs, policies, and practices – largely because there is enough commonality across these three in terms of the purposes, methods, and uses of evaluation and because a narrower focus could contribute to a kind of myopia. A secondary reason for focusing on programs, policies, and practices is that the communities of evaluators that examine these three categories have considerable overlap. For example, evaluative activities designed to improve programs often actually involve the evaluation of specific practices being carried out by program staff. As another example, policies are often important precisely because of the programs they stimulate. Policies, programs, and practices are often intertwined.

To achieve greater coherence, the Handbook's focus is restricted to directly *people-related* programs, policies, and practices. It does not address, for example, energy policies, space exploration programs, defence policy, or animal husbandry practices. Programs, policies, and practices that are not directly people-related can of course be evaluated. Indeed, there are evaluators who specialize in such areas of work. But that is not the focus of the current Handbook.

In this Handbook, we broadly consider policies as legislative and political statements of governmental or organizational intent. A policy sets direction for how resources in a given domain (e.g., education) will be allocated and what substantive foci will receive priority (e.g., a policy promoting the inclusion of diverse people in science and mathematics careers). A program then is a particular enactment of a policy. It offers one concrete representation of *how* a given policy can be realized, in terms of particular activities and materials provided to a particular target population (e.g., a program designed to attract diverse students to a university campus for scientific laboratory training). And a practice refers to the specific professional interactions that take place within programs (e.g., the teaching or mentoring that diverse students receive during their laboratory training).

Aspirations for the Handbook

This Handbook is written for practicing evaluators, academics, advanced post-graduate students, and evaluation clients. It is intended to offer a definitive, benchmark statement on evaluation theory and practice for the first decades of the twenty-first century. In developing this Handbook, we strove to offer a coherent picture of the nature and role of evaluative inquiry in contemporary twenty-first century societies around the globe. The resulting picture is necessarily pluralistic, because evaluation has many countenances, multiple vested audiences, and diverse ideologies. The picture of evaluation presented in this Handbook is also necessarily dynamic – tracing historical evolutions and projecting future pathways – because evaluation is changing and evolving. The end chapters in each of the four parts specifically address the implications of these issues. This dynamic nature exists partly because evaluation is intrinsically linked to changing societal and scientific ideas and ideals. And the picture of evaluation

painted in this volume is of necessity targeted, for even a relatively comprehensive Handbook must leave out some perspectives, some ways of knowing, and some domains of evaluation.

Despite the need to be targeted, this Handbook is also intended to be reasonably comprehensive. The volume includes many diverse evaluation stances. But these are directed toward greater theoretical coherence and practical value than is typical of independent descriptions of alternative perspectives. To achieve a comprehensive statement, the Handbook aspires to an integration of theory, research and practice within each chapter (although the relative mix of theory, research and practice varies from chapter to chapter). Contributors were asked to discuss the strengths and weaknesses of alternative perspectives, including their own – a tough act, requiring them to avoid the Scylla of blandness and the Charybdis of partisanship. Contributors were also asked to consider how evaluation practice is part of a changing social and political context. They look backward as well as forward as they overview the field. They also explore linkages with other disciplines and fields of practice.

While reflecting the highly pluralistic field of evaluation, the Handbook also strives for coherence. Coherence is enhanced through the Handbook's organizing framework (with four parts that address, respectively, the role and purpose of evaluation in society; evaluation as a social practice; the practice of evaluation, including methods; and a relatively full sampling of evaluation in various people-related domains). Moreover, in each of the four parts, a final chapter offers a critical synthesis of key ideas related to the contents of that part. These synthesis chapters are not intended as summaries or reviews of the chapters within each part; rather, they are relatively independent assessments of key issues related to the concerns raised.

Another decision made in service of coherence was the limitation of the Handbook's coverage to the evaluation of people-related policies, programs, and practices. The policies, programs, and practices discussed in the Handbook may be international or local in scope, public or private in origin, established or innovative in demeanor. However, they share the commonalities of involving people as participants and of somehow seeking a valued improvement in the life quality of these participants.

Development of the Handbook

The process by which this project has been developed reflects these aspirations for a Handbook which, while reflecting the diversity of the field of evaluation, is both coherent and comprehensive. The three editors represent different disciplinary backgrounds, various domains of evaluation practice, alternative methods proclivities, and different theoretical stances. A relatively small but international and eminent Editorial Advisory Board was constituted, again reflecting a range of perspectives and experiences. If anything, the cast of chapter authors is even more diverse, on several dimensions, than the editorial team or the Board. That many chapters are co-authored is no mere pragmatic solution, but rather incorporates our intention to represent multiple perspectives and backgrounds. The Handbook in a sense represents a conversation – in part between chapters, and in several instances within chapters.

The three editors developed a detailed outline of the Handbook, including a list of possible authors for each chapter. The Editorial Board provided comments on the overall outline, as well as suggestions about contributors. A detailed "Briefing" was then developed for contributors (running to 14 single-spaced pages). The briefing included an overall description of the project, an introduction to each of the four parts, and suggestions about the content of most chapters. Contributors were encouraged to include exemplars where possible, and to avoid national or other forms of ethnocentrism. We also asked contributors to include critical, reflexive assessments of the viewpoints they described, including positions with which they themselves are associated. They were asked to consider the overall gains and deficits in the area about which they wrote and, where appropriate, to set out their aspirations as to what developments would make for substantial gains in the near and medium-term future.

Contributors first submitted an abstract outlining the expected content of their chapters. The three editors responded collectively to the abstracts, aiming to support the development of a first chapter draft that would both represent the intended scope and tone of the chapter, and also ensure completeness for the overall Handbook "map." A lead editor was appointed for each chapter. In most cases, draft chapters were reviewed by a member of the Editorial Advisory Board and the lead editor. Feedback in most instances was considerable. Of course, contributors varied somewhat in the extent to which they complied with the initial briefing or were responsive to the editorial feedback. In some cases they responsively enriched the editors' original concept for that chapter. In general, we believe the contributors' work has resulted in a picture of evaluation that is definitive, diverse, comprehensive, and coherent.

Perspectives on Evaluation

In this Handbook, systematic evaluation is conceptualized as a social and politicized practice that nonetheless aspires to some position of impartiality or fairness, so that evaluation can contribute meaningfully to the well-being of people in that specific context and beyond.

What is Evaluation?

Paraphrasing an old joke, if you ask 10 evaluators to define evaluation, you'll probably end up with 23 different definitions. Given that evaluation is diverse, with multiple countenances, it should not be surprising that varying definitions exist.

"Evaluate," or at least its root word "value," finds its origin in the Old French *value* and *valoir* and the Latin *valére*, which had the sense of "to be worth (something)" and "to work out the value of (something)." Even in present everyday usage this has a double meaning, of finding a numerical expression for, and estimating the worth of. And of course, "worth" carries several distinct meanings, including personal worthiness, status, how we personally estimate someone, judgments of importance, and intrinsic worth.

The merit/worth distinction has sometimes been pressed into service to make distinctions by evaluation writers. Lincoln & Guba, for example, use the term "merit" to refer to the intrinsic, context-free qualities that accompany the evaluand from place to place and are relatively invariant. For example, a curriculum may have a value independent of any local application. "Worth" refers to the context-determined value, which varies from one context to another. For example, a curriculum may have a certain value for teaching a particular child in a given setting. Based on these distinctions they define evaluation as:

> a type of disciplined inquiry undertaken to determine the value (merit and/or worth) of some entity – the evaluand – such as a treatment, program, facility, performance, and the like – in order to improve or refine the evaluand (formative evaluation) or to assess its impact (summative evaluation). (Lincoln & Guba, 1986a, p. 550)

One key way that definitions of evaluation differ is in terms of the components they include. Some definitions of evaluation focus on the general *function* evaluation serves. The most common functional definition would indicate that evaluation involves judgments of value, determinations of the merit, worth or significance of something. This kind of definition is associated with Michael Scriven, among others. It is a kind of definition that bridges the more systematic and the more everyday forms of evaluation. Scriven's definition follows:

> Evaluation refers to the process of determining the merit, worth, or value of something, or the product of that process... . The evaluation process normally involves some identification of relevant standards of merit, worth, or value; some investigation of the performance of the evaluands on these standards; and some integration or synthesis of the results to achieve an overall evaluation or set of associated evaluations. (Scriven, 1991, p. 139)

Other definitions of evaluation include as a core aspect of the definition a specification of evaluation *purpose* (e.g., providing information for policy making or for program improvement). Given the multiplicity of evaluation purposes, several variations on this theme exist. Michael Patton's commitment to evaluation use in multiple forms (that is, to multiple purposes, depending on user's intentions) is evident in his definition:

> Program evaluation is the systematic collection of information about the activities, characteristics, and outcomes of programs to make judgments about the program, improve program effectiveness, and/or inform decisions about future programming. (Patton, 1997, p. 23)

This can be contrasted with Barry MacDonald's democratic commitment to evaluation as providing important information about educational programs to multiple, diverse audiences, each with a different stake in the program.

> Democratic Evaluation is an information service to the community about the characteristics of an educational program. . . . The democratic evaluator recognises value pluralism and seeks to represent the range of interests in his [or her] issue formulation. The basic value is an informed citizenry, and the evaluator acts as a broker in exchanges of information between groups who want knowledge of each other. (MacDonald, 1987, p. 45)

Further, at least some historically important definitions have also specified evaluation *methods*, as illustrated by Peter Rossi and Howard Freeman's definition:

> Evaluation research [considered the same as evaluation] is the systematic application of social research procedures in assessing the conceptualization and design, implementation, and utility of social intervention programs. In other words, evaluation research involves the use of social research methodologies to judge and to improve the planning, monitoring, effectiveness, and efficiency of health, education, welfare, and other human service programs. (Rossi & Freeman, 1985, p. 19)

Given the many faces of evaluation, and given its dynamic nature, it is not surprising that no single definition has taken hold among all evaluators.

Different Kinds of Approaches to Evaluation

Definitions of evaluation provide one way of thinking about what evaluation involves. Yet another way of trying to gain a sense of what the field encompasses is to look instead at evaluation theories, approaches, and models (these terms are often used interchangeably in the evaluation literature). While it is not feasible here to recount a wide range of evaluation theories, we will glance in passing at one or two selected "meta-models" that aspire to capture some of the key similarities and differences across evaluation theories. This may be helpful in understanding some aspects of the "lay of the land" of contemporary evaluation, and links with Stevenson and Thomas's review of the intellectual contexts of evaluation in Chapter 9.

For example, Shadish, Cook & Leviton (1991), in a comprehensive review of the work of seven program evaluation theorists, offered a stage model meant to describe the development of major evaluation theories to that point in time. During the first stage, according to Shadish et al., "Evaluation started with theories that emphasized a search for truth about effective solutions to social problems" (p. 67). In other words, Stage 1 theorists emphasized the use of procedures to get valid, unbiased answers to questions about the performance of social programs (Donald Campbell and Michael Scriven represent Stage 1 theorists, according to Shadish et al.). During Stage 2, evaluation theorists "generated many alternatives predicated on detailed knowledge of how organizations in the public-sector operate, aimed at producing politically and socially useful results" (p. 67). That is, Shadish et al.'s Stage 2 theorists (Carol Weiss, Joseph Wholey, and Robert Stake) attempted to go beyond previous work by examining the details of organizational processes and decision-making, and trying to shape evaluation to fit these organizational realities. Stage 3, represented by Lee Cronbach and Peter Rossi, "then produced theories that tried to integrate the alternatives generated in the first two stages" (p. 67).

Shadish et al.'s (1991) stage model has limits, as does any attempt to capture the complex and multifaceted state of evaluation theory (or practice) with a simple system. For example, it tends to over-individualize evaluation theory, and to underemphasize structural and societal factors. It is a "great man" approach. Indeed, the term great *man* generally applies, with Carol Weiss being the only female included. The model thus discloses (without explicit discussion) the gendered nature of evaluation's development, at least in the USA. And this is its third limitation – it is a North American model and history. However, Shadish et al.'s stage model is valuable in several ways. For example, it helpfully demonstrates that evaluation is dynamic and changing, and successfully avoids overemphasizing differences. Their model also reminds us that some perspectives on evaluation are less comprehensive than others. For example, the Stage 3 theorists attempted to build on selected developments from the previous stages. Stage 1 theorists, in contrast, tended to emphasize a single approach to evaluation. In addition, Shadish et al.'s stage model reminds us that different approaches to evaluation have varying emphases. A more recent framework concentrates even more on this point.

In a book entitled *Evaluation Roots: Tracing theorists' views and influences*, Marvin Alkin (2004b) asked a number of evaluation theorists both to summarize their own views and to describe which evaluators and other sources have most influenced their work. In an effort to capture the historical and conceptual relationships among these evaluation theorists, Alkin & Christie (2004) developed the "evaluation theory tree," a graphical representation modeled after a tree with three main branches. Each theorist was placed on one of the three branches, to indicate his or her *relative degree of emphasis* on three issues: "(a) issues related to the methodology being used; (b) the manner in which data are to be judged or valued; and (c) the user focus of the evaluation effort" (Alkin, 2004a, p. 8; the tree diagram is reproduced in Chapter 2).

In other words, Alkin & Christie (2004) suggest that there are three distinguishable streams, or traditions, in evaluation theory. One has focused on evaluation methods, another on values or valued judgments, and the third on users and use. These three streams, as Alkin & Christie acknowledge, have intersected at times, and many evaluation theorists address all three issues, methods, values, and use, to some extent. Again, though, placement on one or another branch of the evaluation tree is intended to reflect the "relative degree of emphasis" on these three concerns. Contributors to the *Evaluation Roots* book were asked to comment on the tree itself. Many reported finding the evaluation tree useful and were satisfied with their placement on it. Others offered criticism of the tree model, their placement on it, or both.

The evaluation tree, in our view, is useful in highlighting some of the major conceptual emphases in the field of evaluation, as well as in capturing how many major figures in evaluation have influenced or been influenced by others. At the same time, a unidimensional model with three categories cannot capture all of the important aspects of the diversity of the field. For example, there are broader intellectual traditions that have influenced evaluation that are not reflected in the evaluation tree (to take but one example, see the discussion in Chapter 4 of the influence of continental philosophy).

Our own view is that any attempt to classify alternative approaches to evaluation will necessarily have shortcomings, especially so with simpler frameworks. Nevertheless, these frameworks do provide alternative views of the "big picture" of the field of evaluation. At the very least, readers of this Handbook may find it useful, as they read various chapters, to think about how a given approach would fall in terms of Shadish et al.'s stage model and Alkin & Christie's evaluation tree.

Histories of Evaluation

It seems almost a requirement in a *Handbook of Evaluation* to discuss the history of evaluation. However, we find it important to avoid taking a stance that appears (usually implicitly) in most of the brief discussions of history one finds in evaluation textbooks and elsewhere. That is, most often these presentations suggest that there is *a* history of evaluation. To the contrary, we believe there are *multiple histories* of evaluation. There are somewhat different histories depending upon one's discipline and domain of evaluation work. For example, in the United States, discussions of educational evaluation often suggest a pivotal historical role of the work of Ralph Tyler; in contrast, discussions of non-educational social programs often ignore Tyler completely and emphasize the explosion of evaluation activity during the 1960s and 1970s, often referring to the Johnson administration's "Great Society." Moreover, the work of Stafford Hood (1998) and others shows that most histories of evaluation in the United States ignore the contributions of African American evaluation scholars, likely due to the discrimination endemic to US society.[1]

The history of evaluation also varies, to a greater or lesser extent, with geography and governments. The Great Society stimulated program evaluation in the United States, but not worldwide. Other sources of influence exist elsewhere. For example, one stream that has contributed to evaluation in the United Kingdom is the policy research tradition that goes back to the Fabian impact on British welfare state policy after the Second World War, with the associated presence of social policy as a distinct discipline in the social sciences. More recently, the development of the European Union has had important impacts on the presence and nature of evaluation in many countries. In so-called developing countries, the growth and style of evaluation has drawn heavily on liberation ideology, such as the writings of Paolo Freire (1970). Again, there are multiple histories of evaluation, which collectively have contributed to the growing diversity in the field. This diversity is reflected in several of the co-written Handbook chapters, where the range of issues often lies beyond any individual writer. It is also reflected in the substantive scope of the Handbook, as, for example, in Chapter 25, which deals not only with development but also with the rapidly growing experience of evaluation in the context of complex humanitarian emergencies.

Despite the multiplicity of evaluation histories, we believe it is possible to offer at least a tentative assessment of the current status of evaluation, as follows. In less than one generation, evaluation has become an internationally recognized practice that is positioned at the intersection of broad social and economic aspirations, contested political ideologies, and individual life quality. Evaluations of people-related policies, programs, and practices can and do contribute to the betterment of life for individual people and to the defensibility and effectiveness of varied national policy decisions and directions. Evaluation *is* a player on the world stage of debate about how best to address contemporary critical concerns of the international community – concerns such as extreme poverty, inadequate health care, environmental degradation and global warming, ethnic and religious strife and warfare, access to education, and fair distribution of resources.

The developing history of evaluation, and the emergence of social and cultural forces that will influence evaluation, continues. We mention but a few of the relevant forces here. Major economic shifts, political watersheds, the emergence of faith-based governments, the characteristics of late modernity – each of these has fundamental consequences for nature and very existence of evaluation. Politically, the dissolution of the USSR, and more recently the emergence on the world stage of China, both presage the diversification and probably the expansion of evaluation in association with national policies, programs and practice. The characteristics of late modernity are also shaping evaluation. For instance, the contemporary "evidence-based practice" movement has increased pressure for evaluation, and also has tended to shape evaluation in some directions and against others. This widespread force is mentioned by several of the Handbook contributors, most obviously in Part 4. Rationality in policy making is also the leading edge of the Cochrane Collaboration in medical practice and the Campbell Collaboration in social and educational programs and practice. Both involve the use of meta-analysis, or quantitative synthesis of comparative evaluations, with the goal of identifying effective courses of action. Both are about evaluation for decision-making. And they both represent a social organization that goes beyond individual evaluators or evaluation organizations, as well as a striking preference for some kinds of evaluation designs and evidence over others (a preference that is not without controversy; see, e.g., Lipsey, 2000a, 2000b; Schwandt, 2000a, 2000b). The long-term consequences of these endeavors, especially the Campbell Collaboration, are yet to be seen. Widespread preoccupations with information use and application also show little sign of abating. For instance, Carol Weiss and her colleagues have recently identified what they see as a new form of evaluation use, which they call "imposed use" (Weiss et al., 2005). Imposed use occurs, for example, when local schools believe (accurately or not) that they will receive state funding for a particular kind of program only if they adopt a program from the state's approved list. To the extent that imposed use becomes more common, it may change the nature of evaluation's influence – and with possible implications for evaluators' standards of evidence.

Our discussion here of contemporary forces that may affect the future history of evaluation is necessarily brief and selective, although sufficient to illustrate that, for evaluation, "all the world's a stage."[2] But a stage on which the evaluation community is merely a player with its exits and entrances, and playing many parts. Additional attention to such forces occurs in many of the chapters in this Handbook, is the primary focus of Chapter 6, and recurs through Parts 2 and 3.

Having addressed the definitions, shape, and histories of evaluation in this section, in the next section of this introductory chapter we highlight our perspectives on some of the critical facets of contemporary evaluation theory and practice.

Critical Dimensions and Issues in Evaluation

We have observed that the character and import of evaluation's contributions to social betterment remain necessarily pluralistic, as evaluation has many countenances, multiple vested audiences, and diverse ideologies. Part of this pluralism is indeed ideological, as evaluation has been at the center of a generation of controversy on the meanings of defensible social inquiry. Part of this pluralism is temporal, as evaluation is intrinsically linked to changing societal and international ideals and aspirations. And part of this pluralism is spatial, as evaluation is inherently embedded in its contexts, which themselves vary in multiple ways, both within a given program and more dramatically around the globe.

In this Handbook, we intentionally engage the pluralism of social policy, program, and practice evaluation today. We engage this pluralism by featuring diverse evaluation traditions, methods, and practices throughout the Handbook. We engage this pluralism by respecting and highlighting critical differences, as well as commonalities, among different approaches to and rationales for evaluation. And we engage this pluralism by aspiring to counter ethnocentrism of various kinds. The field of evaluation has often been limited by boundaries of discipline, professional interest and paradigmatic location. National boundaries also have often served to introduce an unnecessary parochialism into the development of the field. We seek to resist such ethnocentric tendencies through the cultivation of a critical (rather than polemical) and open stance. The Handbook contributors stand against naïve pragmatism on such matters and have included in their chapters critical, reflexive assessments of positions with which they themselves are associated.

We further engage the pluralism of the field of evaluation today in this introductory essay, though in doing so we regard "pluralism," to borrow Karl Popper's term, as a "bucket word." In its strict philosophical meaning it refers to a system of thought which recognizes more than one ultimate principle, over against philosophical monism. Reflecting back, our mention of strong ways of distinguishing between formal and informal evaluation, and our subsequent discussion of contingency models, can both be read as more strictly pluralist in this sense.

But more commonly, reference to pluralism seems to refer to the distribution of power in (western) society. Lee Cronbach and Ernie House have offered sharp examples of this sense of pluralist. Cronbach's pluralism echoed his conception of the policy context in which evaluation is located. He and his colleagues complained that evaluation theory has "been developed almost wholly around the image of command" and the assumption that managers and policy makers have a firm grip on the control of decision making. However, "most action is determined by a pluralist community not by a lone decision maker" (Cronbach et al., 1980, p. 84). Hence, evaluation enters a context of government which is typically one of accommodation rather than command, and "a theory of evaluation must be as much a theory of political interaction as it is a theory of how knowledge is constructed" (1980, pp. 52–3). Cronbach drew on this form of pluralism to attack goal-setting and accountability models of evaluation, and to portray the role of the evaluator as adopting "a critical, scholarly cast of mind" to serve the cause of relatively piecemeal, multi-partisan advocacy (1980, pp. 67, 157).

Cronbach's position is quite different from a tendency to soft relativism that is present in some forms of the pluralist argument. House, for example, criticizes pluralism on the grounds that in essence it "confuses issues of interests with conflicts of power. It can balance only those interests that are represented – typically those of the powerful" (House, 1991, p. 240). The risk not only of relativism but also of political conservatism may be evident when Lincoln & Guba some time ago concluded that "all ideologies should have an equal chance of expression in the process of negotiating recommendations" (Lincoln & Guba, 1986b, p. 79), and when Guba says "it is the mind that is to be transformed, not the real world" (Guba, 1990, p. 27).

The editors represent different positions in the field and we have crafted this essay to reflect our own differences, as well as commonalities. These are captured in various stances presented throughout the chapter. Yet, our highlighting of the pluralistic character of evaluation today does not signal a purely relativistic stance. We do not believe that any evaluation practice is as good as any other. Further, we all agree that good evaluation practice engages important societal concerns along with the political controversies that usually accompany such concerns, is methodologically and ethically defensible, is responsive and useful to key stakeholders both inside and external to the context being evaluated, and contributes to some form of social betterment. Yet, as the old adage suggests, the devil is in the details. And we do not fully agree on all details, as signaled within this introductory essay.

In the remainder of this section, we address four sets of questions that roughly parallel the four main sections of the Handbook:

1. What are the purposes of evaluation today? What are the most important questions that evaluation can address?

2. Who conducts and who participates in evaluation, and what is the character of that participation in varied evaluation contexts?

3. What methodologies characterize evaluation practice?

4. Who are the audiences for evaluation in varied domains of practice? What uses do they make of evaluative work?

We do not attempt to provide definitive answers to these questions. Indeed, given the many faces of evaluation, no single answer could be adequate. Instead, we provide and discuss these questions for three reasons. First, they serve as a kind of "advance organizer." That is, they provide a framework and a set of issues that readers can apply as they examine and respond to the various chapters in the Handbook. In other words, we think it beneficial if readers, in examining each of the chapters, ask themselves what evaluation purpose or purposes the author is emphasizing, who would participate in the evaluation and how, what methodologies would be employed, and who the intended audience would be. Second, as noted, the questions correspond roughly to the four parts of the Handbook. Thus, addressing the questions provides us an opportunity to overview very briefly the contents of each part. Third, as we consider this set of questions, it allows us as editors to highlight various issues. Many of these

are issues that have been raised by one or more of the contributors to the Handbook, but that warrant more focused attention.

That said, let us turn to the four sets of questions.

(1) What Are the Purposes of Evaluation Today? What Are the Most Important Questions that Evaluation Can Address?

A striking characteristic of contemporary evaluation theory and practice is the recognition that there are alternative purposes toward which evaluation can be directed. Put differently, evaluators and evaluation can fill various roles. Is the purpose of evaluation to generate information that can contribute to improved decision-making by those in policy positions? Should evaluation instead have as its purpose improvement of everyday program operations and practices? Or is the evaluator's role, not unlike that of the social researcher, to develop and test general knowledge about social problems and their solutions? Should evaluators strive to enhance democratic processes and help achieve democratic ideals? Or is the purpose of evaluation to improve the wisdom of practitioners to engage wisely in the practice choices they face?

The chapters in Part 1 explicitly examine a set of alternative evaluation purposes. The contributors of the first five chapters were briefed to regard the chapters as organized around distinctive intellectual traditions and ways of thinking and knowing within evaluation, with each tradition representing a particular role or purpose for evaluation in society. For each tradition, contributors were asked to consider:

■ *Philosophy and paradigm.* What is the philosophical framework justifying this intellectual tradition?

■ *Theory.* What major evaluation approaches characterize this intellectual tradition?

- *Practice.* What does evaluation practice within this intellectual tradition look like? Whose interests does it serve? What major questions does it answer?
- *Critique.* What are important critiques of this tradition in evaluation? What are its particular benefits and limitations? What are important future areas for refinement and development?
- *Exemplars.* What do exemplars of this approach look like?

The authors were also asked to concentrate on the broad, macro picture of evaluation practice, rather than try to detail all specific methods for that tradition. Of course, the authors of these chapters responded in different ways to the complex request facing them. Thus, the chapters in Part 1 vary in their relative emphasis on the five considerations listed above.

We invited Eleanor Chelimsky to discuss evaluation for decision-making and public accountability. In Chapter 1, she addresses these interrelated evaluation purposes, but casts a broader net by examining the role of evaluation in democracies. In that context, she describes three purposes of evaluation, two of which overlap in part with Chapters 2 and 3. However, Chelimsky's attention to knowledge development and organizational improvement is narrower than in the subsequent chapters. She always frames these other purposes in ways that ultimately serve accountability and decision-making. Regardless, Chelimsky's chapter reminds us that the boundaries between evaluation purposes are not fixed or rigid, and that an evaluator can have an overarching mission and role but still needs to address different evaluation purposes at times.

In Chapter 2, Stewart Donaldson and Mark Lipsey address evaluation that has as its purpose the generation or advancement of knowledge about social problems and their solutions. Although they address other approaches, they focus primarily on the role of theory in efforts to facilitate knowledge development through evaluation. Patricia Rogers and Bob Williams, in Chapter 3, consider practice improvement and organizational learning as closely related purposes of evaluation. After discussing a set of general issues related to these evaluation goals, they describe and critique nine approaches that evaluators have used toward these ends.

Chapter 4 focuses on evaluation as an enterprise concerned with representing the experience of those involved in a program or practice. In that chapter, Thomas Schwandt and Holli Burgon discuss and illustrate approaches to evaluation that attend to lived experience and to engagement in practice. Jennifer Greene, in Chapter 5, discusses evaluation approaches intended to contribute to democracy, not primarily by infusing good information into existing decision-making processes; rather, these approaches take evaluation itself as a way of enhancing and even constituting democratic processes and ideals. Finally, in Chapter 6, Peter Dahler-Larsen begins by describing the current state of evaluation in terms of three characteristics. He then discusses five issues that he suggests may help shape the nature of evaluation in the future.

Although evaluation purposes are most explicitly related to the organization of Part 1, they appear elsewhere in this volume. Notably, the same set of purposes also helps organize some of Part 3. In Chapters 14 and 15, a range of evaluation methods are discussed. The authors of these chapters were asked to focus on methods that can be used in service of two or three of the evaluation purposes addressed in Part 1. Thus, these Part 3 chapters complement the corresponding Part 1 chapters, and offer more detail regarding method. In addition, the chapters in Part 4 include numerous examples of evaluation aimed at alternative purposes, insofar as professions and services are associated with alternative social arguments. The Handbook is in part an exploration of how the range of issues about contexts, methods, and domains of practice in evaluation can be pictured when evaluation purposes are made the gateway.

Forces Influencing Preferences Among Evaluation Purposes

The contents of the Part 1 chapters, along with the rest of the volume, should be helpful to readers as they deal with the question of which evaluation purpose(s) to emphasize, under what conditions. However, because we asked the Part 1 authors to focus on a specific tradition in evaluation, they may not have gone into as much detail as possible about why alternative evaluation approaches have developed that emphasize different purposes. Nor have they gone into great detail about what an evaluator or evaluation client might want to consider as they choose which particular purpose to emphasize in a given evaluation. Given the diversity of the field, we do not expect that evaluators would always agree about their role or about an evaluation's purpose in a particular case. Perhaps we would agree more about the fit and congruency between purpose and the context, method or domain in a given evaluation.

Presumed Leverage Points. Historically, we believe, much of the divergence across evaluation traditions has been based on judgments, sometimes implicit, about where leverage exists for evaluation to make a contribution. Cronbach and colleagues in their influential book, *Towards the Reform of Program Evaluation* (1980), employed the idea of leverage. "*Leverage* is the bottom line. Leverage refers to the probability that the information – *if* believed – will change the course of events" (p. 265). Let us take as examples of different

presumptions about where leverage exists the contributions to evaluation of Donald Campbell and Joseph Wholey.

Campbell is best known among evaluators as an advocate of using quasi-experiments and randomized experiments, to assess the effect of a policy or program on various outcomes of interest while attempting to minimize various validity threats. Implicit in most of Campbell's writings on evaluation is the idea that an important leverage point exists when democracies or organizations make choices among program or policy alternatives. For example, schools face decisions about whether to implement a new math curriculum or retain the old one; cities face decisions about whether to ban smoking in public places; states face decisions about whether to adopt new welfare policies; and so on. Campbell's approach to evaluation assumed that such decisions – where there are forks in the road, so to speak – are an important leverage point for evaluative information.

Wholey, in contrast, has emphasized the benefits of providing program managers with information about program performance, to allow better decision-making on an ongoing basis. Wholey observed public sector managers who did not have the benefit of information on how their organizations were doing (versus, say, private sector managers who had access to information on sales, profits, and the like). In other words, Wholey emphasized a different leverage point than Campbell. Wholey focused on the potential of evaluative information, in the form of performance measurement systems, to influence the operations of ongoing programs and agencies.

Leverage can also be conceptualized as contingent upon context (a notion elaborated on subsequently). That is, from this view, determining what is an appropriate purpose for evaluation depends on the context at hand. Leverage, and therefore, choice of evaluation purpose and method, can be affected by considerations such as the character and longevity of the program, the political contentiousness of its ambitions, and the funding dynamics of the program and the evaluation. Highly context-sensitive evaluators may well shift purpose dramatically from one context to the next, as each presents different opportunities for and constraints on leverage.

The role of leverage in identifying an evaluation purpose seems most evident in the first three chapters of Part 1. Campbell's influence is visible in some of the work discussed in Chapter 1, for example, while Wholey's influence is present in the discussion of performance measurement in Chapter 3. In addition, Chapter 2, on knowledge development and theory testing, offers a relatively pragmatic justification for this approach, which could easily be translated into the language of leverage points.

Value Commitments. To make a judgment about where leverage exists for evaluation is to be rather pragmatic. Alternatively, the choice of evaluation purpose or evaluator role may be more heavily influenced by values, specifically values about the relationship evaluation should have in and with the world. It appears that advocates of some evaluation approaches are driven more by such values than they are by assumptions about where an effective leverage point exists. This is not to say that choice of evaluation purpose involves either leverage *or* values; rather we mean to suggest a difference across evaluation approaches in terms of the *relative* priority given to values (about evaluation's role in and with the world) and to assumed leverage points.

For example, what have come to be called democratic approaches to evaluation, as discussed in Chapter 5, appear to be driven largely by value positions regarding the role evaluation should have in democracies. Valuing some sort of system change also tends to characterize

several of these democratic evaluation approaches more than, say, the approaches of Campbell or Wholey. The furtherance and representation of certain values through evaluation also seems evident in the evaluation approaches discussed in Chapter 4, where some of the approaches to capturing lived experience are based on considerations of social power or transformation.

Of course, considerations other than leverage and values influence judgments about evaluation purpose and evaluator's role. For instance, much has often been made of philosophical differences across evaluators (including alternative assumptions about the nature of the world and about how evaluators and others can generate defensible claims about how things are). Indeed, such differences were often taken as central in the so-called paradigm war, or qualitative–quantitative debate that consumed much of the intellectual capital of evaluators for years (House, 1994).

Undoubtedly, philosophical assumptions and a host of other factors influence preferences for different evaluation purposes. Pluralism about such choices (and even, perhaps, in views about the forces that influence such preferences) is a fact of life in contemporary evaluation. Nevertheless, the importance of presumed leverage points and values, we feel, deserves highlighting.

Contingencies Among Alternative Purposes

Although the organization of Part 1 required authors to focus primarily on one evaluation purpose or another, some of the models that evaluators have developed instead emphasize, to some degree, ways of choosing among alternative evaluation purposes. These "contingency models" differ in important ways, and we cannot fully summarize them all here. Instead, we offer a selective review of three contingency models, which provide very different views of the primary reason for choosing one evaluation purpose versus another in a given evaluation. By way of overview, the three models we mention suggest, respectively, that the choice of an evaluation purpose should be based primarily on the preferences of intended users, or on program stage, or on a kind of policy analytic assessment of the likely contribution of alternative evaluation purposes to social betterment. Familiarity of these three kinds of "drivers" of contingent decision-making may be more advantageous than strict adherence to one model or another. Again, the three contingency models focus on different factors that may help guide choices about which evaluation purpose to emphasize in a given situation.

Michael Patton (1997) has long been a visible advocate of what he calls utilization-focused evaluation. According to Patton, "the *focus* in utilization-focused evaluation is on *intended use by intended users*" (p. 20). On other words, any purpose of evaluation, any evaluator role, is appropriate – if it satisfies the intended users' intended use of the evaluation (and if it is consistent with personal morality and professional standards; Patton, 1997, p. 364).

In contrast, several evaluation models have focused on how the stage of a program should influence the purpose of evaluation (see Cronbach et al., 1980). Chen (2005) has recently articulated a relatively thorough stage model. According to Chen, "Stakeholders' evaluation needs vary across the stages of program growth. . . . Evaluators can best understand stakeholders' evaluation needs if the evaluators are provided with information on the stage(s) the stakeholders are interested in evaluating" (p. 49). (Chen also provides a useful discussion of the trade-offs for evaluation design that can occur across timeliness, rigor, thoroughness, and cost.) A common, simple version of a stage model suggests that evaluation should emphasize program improvement and

organizational learning early in a program's life, and shift toward a more summative, accountability focus later on.

Yet a third kind of contingency model exists in the work of Mark, Henry, & Julnes (2000), who suggest that evaluators (with stakeholders) should scan the policy environment, and assess the likely contribution of different evaluation purposes to social betterment. Mark and colleagues suggest, in essence, an analysis of the extent to which leverage exists for each of the alternative evaluation purposes that might be considered.

In practice there often may be more overlap across these three approaches to contingent selection of evaluation purpose than the simplified descriptions here would suggest. More importantly, we suggest that these should be seen not as competitors, but as complementary ways of thinking about choices among evaluation purposes. Each may be more useful in some situations than others, and there is considerable value in evaluators being "multilingual." In addition, all three of these contingency models have limitations, though we will not attempt to list them all here. But there is a shared limitation that should be acknowledged: almost by definition, none of the three deals with value-driven choices of evaluation purpose to the degree represented, say, in Chapters 4 and 5.

Responding to the Diversity Among Evaluation Approaches

There are various ways that evaluators respond to the multiplicity of evaluation purposes, approaches, and roles. Some evaluators endorse (and advocate) a given approach to evaluation. In essence, they argue for a "winner" among the diversity of evaluation approaches. Others suggest we embrace diversity within the field of evaluation as but one characteristic of the essential uncertainty of postmodernity. Still others suggest that flexibility may not be adequate, that something is needed to guide efforts to choose which approaches might best apply under different circumstances, and thus prefer integrative models such as the contingency models just described.

Donaldson and Lipsey, in Chapter 2, have captured this state of affairs nicely, as they discuss a symposium (Donaldson & Scriven, 2003) in which a set of prominent evaluation theorists described their vision for the future of evaluation, along with a set of responses:

> [One] major theme that emerged from this discourse on future evaluation practice was the challenge posed by the vast diversity represented in modern evaluation theories. Mark (2003) observed that each vision for the future of evaluation gave a central place to one theory of evaluation practice and left scant room for others. One way out of the continuous polarization of perspectives that results from these diverse theoretical allegiances is the development of higher order frameworks that integrate evaluation theories (Mark, 2003). Another option presented for achieving a peaceful and productive future for evaluation involved a strategy for embracing diversity in evaluation theory, recognizing that fundamental differences cannot be reconciled or integrated, and that clients may benefit most from having a diverse smorgasbord of options to choose from for evaluating their programs and policies.

But how well can clients choose from a "smorgasbord of options"? How effectively can evaluators truly embrace diversity of perspectives, without giving way to skirmishes or outright resumption of updated versions of the paradigm wars? We may not completely agree about the answers to these questions, but the reality is that there is likely to continue to be a multiplicity of ways that evaluators react to the diversity in our field. And in our view, tolerance, and acceptance – yet with deliberative dialog among our different ideas – will do

more to further the visibility and potential reach of evaluation than skirmishes and debates about winners and losers.

Research on Evaluation. Evaluations can contribute to democratic governance, to social betterment, to organizational learning, and more. But how do we know which types of evaluation are more likely to make what kinds of contributions? The idea that it would be helpful to increase the evidence base about evaluation practices and their consequences is not new. For example, Shadish et al. (1991), state that "In the long run, . . . evaluation will be better served by increasing the more systematic empirical evaluation of its theories, by treating evaluation theory like any other scientific theory, subjecting its problems and hypotheses to the same wide scientific scrutiny to which any theory is subjected. We do not lack for hypotheses worth studying" (p. 483). More recently, Marvin Alkin and Christina Christie have in several publications argued for empirical assessments of the theoretical claims of evaluators. With such empirical data, the evaluation community could construct a "descriptive theory" of evaluation, or an empirically based assessment of what evaluation looks like, under different conditions, and what kind of consequences result from various approaches to evaluation (e.g., Alkin, 2003).[3] Viewed from this perspective, a growing evidence base about evaluation could help answer questions such as: Which approaches to evaluation, implemented how, and under what conditions, lead to what kind of improvements in policy deliberations, program operations, or client outcomes?

In addition to providing better advice for evaluation practitioners (Shadish et al., 1991), a larger evidence base about evaluation might have several other benefits (Mark, in press). For instance, increasing the evidence base of evaluation might:

- improve the terms of debate among evaluators, by helping to substitute some degree of empirical evidence for rhetorical style;
- allow us to document and understand evaluation's current and past contributions;
- facilitate appropriate claims about what evaluation can do, perhaps most often by moving evaluators in the direction of modesty (Weiss, 1991);[4]
- stimulate efforts to improve evaluation practice, in part by identifying circumstances in which evaluation demonstrably fails to meet its promise;
- increase a sense of professionalism among evaluators, by making it clear that evaluation itself is a worthy of systematic study; and
- help move the field past generic and relatively abstract standards and guiding principles, to more empirically supported guidance about the relative benefits of different evaluation practices.

Research on evaluation will not be a magic bullet. It will not immediately transform the field. It will not replace all judgments about wise evaluation practice – but instead can aid such judgment to a significant extent. Research on evaluation, like evaluation itself, will raise questions about generalizability, contextuality, and applicability to specific situations. Research on evaluation will at least some of the time be ignored – even in cases where it could be useful. In short, the various problems and limits we know about regarding evaluation (and research) itself and its use will also arise in the context of research on evaluation.

(2) Who Conducts and Who Participates in Evaluation, and What Is the Character of that Participation in Varied Evaluation Contexts?

Evaluation is a social practice. This notion has shaped the Handbook to the considerable extent that Part 2 brings together the social,

relational, political and ethical dimensions of evaluation as a practice engaged with people and their programs, policies, and own practices. Indeed, one early anonymous reviewer of the Handbook proposal took the view in this regard that we had majored on participatory approaches at all costs! Just how we interpret the scope, importance and indeed meaning of the social character of evaluation is itself one of the centrally recurring conversations within the evaluation community. But social, intellectual, political, ethical matters and issues of use, voice, and audience will be inescapable, whether we align ourselves with a strict accountability model of evaluation or with a dialogical and hermeneutical stance.

In Chapter 7 we asked Phil Davies, Kathryn Newcomer, and Haluk Soydan to focus on evaluation and government. These authors examine why governments fund evaluations and how they use them, and also examine alternative structural arrangements and processes through which evaluation is carried out. Other structural contexts are dealt with fully elsewhere in the Handbook, for example, in Chapter 16 and throughout Part 4. In Chapter 8, Tineke Abma explores the relational dimensions of evaluation as a social practice. She probes the ways in which internal stakeholder relationships and stakeholder–evaluator relationships matter in different approaches to evaluation practice and for different aspects of our work, most notably, the character of our knowledge claims.

John Stevenson and David Thomas paint a large canvas for their comprehensive review of the intellectual contexts of evaluation in Chapter 9. We asked these writers to set evaluation in its intellectual contexts and discuss what the evaluator brings to those contexts. There are various disciplinary frames that impinge on evaluation, including sociology, social policy, psychology, economics, education, and political science. The editors and writers recognize that the intellectual contexts are wide, and that they include intellectual contexts that are not narrowly disciplinary in nature (e.g., evaluation draws upon intuition and common sense, and follows with attention to shared experience, education, history, philosophy, and of course, literary and arts criticism). We have dealt in part with this wider intellectual context in this editorial essay.

In Chapter 10, Ove Karlsson Vestman and Ross Conner analyze the nature and role of politics and related values, both as critical contextual features of evaluation practice and as intertwined with epistemological claims of knowledge. They examine varying conceptions of politics, and describe and critique alternative models which they believe characterize the differing views evaluators have about the relationship between evaluation and politics. This chapter links closely with Chapter 5 in its relevance to questions of social justice as a purpose of evaluation. In Chapter 11, Helen Simons brings her experience and interest to bear on the professional, personal, and public dimensions of ethics in evaluation practice. This discussion traces the development of ethical standards and guidelines in evaluation communities; describes and critiques the different purposes, theoretical links and political stances associated with ethical guidelines in evaluation; and offers an elaborated discussion of ethics as inscribed in evaluation practice. In Chapter 12, Brad Cousins and Lyn Shulha review work on evaluation utilization as compared to its "cognate fields," particularly of research and knowledge utilization. They aspire in this chapter to "situate current trends in the study of evaluation use within the broader intellectual landscape of research and knowledge utilization." And they focus this comparative discussion around six themes common to various domains of inquiry on utilization: (1) epistemological challenges, (2) emphasis on context for use,

(3) focus on user characteristics, (4) linking knowledge production and use, (5) utilization as process, and (6) methodological challenges. This chapter is thus related to the discussion on evaluation and utilization in Chapter 3, but offers a very different lens on the issues.

Elliot Stern, in writing the forward-gazing chapter for Part 2 (13), describes and reflects on the complex contextual landscape of evaluation as a profession, occupation, community, and discipline. He touches on discussions of standards, the role of journals, and professional associations in the field. He also addresses challenges of teaching and learning for evaluation, demands for evaluation competencies, and challenges of building evaluation capacity. But more interestingly than this, he writes in a way that opens up the sense of "context" and that both portrays the texture of context while crossing local frontiers and exploring a globalizing world.

Part 2 poses some big and complex issues, issues that are embedded in the very fabric of evaluation as a human endeavor. These issues are *invoked* in significant part by the topics that constitute this section – evaluation's structural contexts, social relationships, disciplinary legacies, politics and values, ethical considerations, and utilization. But the issues do not reside within these topics; rather they permeate all other aspects of evaluative thinking and evaluation practice. These issues significantly include the plurality and diversity of contemporary evaluation theory and practice and the challenges this diversity presents to considerations of what constitutes "good" evaluation practice. Related are the challenges of forging respectful and constructive engagement with the differences of intellectual persuasion and political commitment that sometimes still polarize the evaluation community, and then signaling this respectful engagement to our clients. And there are the continuing challenges of utilization and dissemination of what is learned from evaluation studies. Paralleling the integrated character of these issues in evaluation practice, our own engagement with these issues is not separated out in this Part 2 discussion but rather permeates this introductory essay. In this way we seek to mirror our view that the social dimensions of evaluation powerfully influence its character and its potential reach.

(3) What Methodologies Characterize Evaluation?

As a member of the social science family, evaluation integrally involves the systematic and defensible use of methods for gathering or generating, analyzing and interpreting, and representing – usually in written and oral form – information about the quality of the program, practice or policy being evaluated. In the United States and other western countries, in fact, early evaluators were disciplinary social scientists (sociologists, economists, educators, psychologists) who endeavored to apply their methodological expertise to real world, social policy settings. And while the challenges of this form of applied social science were substantially greater than anticipated (Cook, 1985), evaluation remains a method-driven field, especially in its public perception and in the formal training many evaluators receive.

Part 3 of the Handbook engages discussions about the methods that evaluators use in their work. However, the Handbook as a whole represents our view that methodology is but one facet of the practice of evaluation. This view is evident, not only in Part 3, but also in the inclusion of Part 2 of the Handbook – which highlights the complex contexts and contours of evaluation that both shape its character as a social practice and are, in turn, reshaped by the particular conduct of an evaluation study. As just described, other facets highlighted in Part 2

include the socio-political and economic characteristics of the context in which evaluation is conducted, the character of the interactions and relationships that take place among stakeholders and evaluators, the intellectual traditions that inform an evaluation study, the politics and values embedded in a given evaluation approach, as well as the ethical considerations and the varied commitments to utilization that importantly guide evaluation practice.

Part 3 was envisioned as the Handbook location for discussions of the actual practice of evaluation, or "how to" do evaluation and why. Again, given our conceptualization of evaluation practice as more than methodology, the six chapters in Part 3 encompass practical issues related to evaluation management, communication, and quality in addition to issues of method within various evaluation traditions. Specifically, the Part 3 chapter authors were guided by the following suggested themes:

- How evaluation practice is shaped by evaluative purpose.
- The role of the evaluator.
- Important practice-ethics decisions in the field.
- How practical exemplars demonstrate evaluation practice in the field.
- Reasoning about evaluation method, or where methods decisions are located in the evaluation process and what influences methods decisions.

As with every part, chapter authors in Part 3 differentially responded to this guidance, resulting in a diverse set of discussions on evaluation practice.

As noted above, the first two chapters in Part 3 explicitly connect evaluation methodology with evaluation purpose. In Chapter 14, Melvin Mark and Gary Henry present contemporary methodological approaches to evaluations conducted for purposes of decision-making, accountability, and knowledge generation (corresponding to Chapters 1 and 2 in Part 1). In Chapter 15, Elizabeth Whitmore, Irene Guijt, Donna Mertens, Pamela Imm, Matthew Chinman, and Abraham Wandersman present methodologies for evaluations conducted for purposes of improving practice, understanding lived experience, and enhancing democratization or social justice (corresponding to Chapters 3, 4, and 5 in Part 1). To fulfill such an ambitious agenda, the authors of Chapter 15 offer three different case examples of evaluation as well as an analysis of the themes and commitments common to all. Then in Chapter 16, Robert Walker and Michael Wiseman offer perspectives on and examples of how to manage evaluation, especially within complex policy contexts. Interestingly, these authors echo the relational themes of Part 2, especially the concentrated focus on evaluative relationships presented in Chapter 8. Chapter 17, by Marvin Alkin, Christina Christie, and Mike Rose, surveys the considerable evaluation literature on communications in evaluation. Among the topics engaged in this chapter are when and how to communicate with stakeholders during the course of an evaluation and how to structure and write an evaluation report for maximum impact. Chapter 18, by Robert Stake and Thomas Schwandt, addresses matters of the recognition and representation of quality in evaluation – the quality of that which is being evaluated and the quality of evaluation itself. As evaluation is at root an enterprise dedicated to discerning quality, this chapter is an integral part of a conceptualization of evaluation practice. Finally, in Chapter 19, Lois-ellin Datta offers wise and thoughtful reflections on evaluation practice in the three-part form of challenges met, unfinished business, and new challenges ahead.

The thoughtful discussions in the Part 3 chapters offer a rich and multihued portrait of evaluation practice. In this introductory essay,

we briefly take up three issues commonplace in discussions of methodology: (1) the intellectual traditions that have informed and shaped evaluation methodologies; (2) what, if anything, is distinctive about the methodologies and methods evaluators employ; and (3) implications for evaluation training.

The Intellectual Traditions that Have Informed Evaluation Methodologies

Evaluation is generally understood, both within and outside the evaluation community, as an "applied" social science. The intellectual traditions that have informed evaluation methodologies are thus (a) the disciplinary perspectives of sociology, economics, and psychology and also, more recently, anthropology, women's studies, and cultural studies, and (b) the accompanying perspectives of various philosophies of science, often referred to as scientific paradigms.[5] While our disciplinary legacies are more implicitly embedded in our practice than is usually acknowledged explicitly or discussed (although see Chapter 9), our varied philosophical or paradigmatic allegiances have been at the center of considerable controversy and debate throughout the last quarter of the twentieth century.

During the 1970s and 1980s in particular, evaluators were engaged in a broad debate that permeated all corners of the social scientific community regarding the primary rationales, roles, and character of social science in society. Most popularly dubbed the "quantitative-qualitative debate," this controversy centered around the legitimacy and relative superiority of "quantitative" versus "qualitative" methodologies for evaluation. Prior to this debate, most evaluation practice had followed the standard social science conventions of the era, which were largely "quantitative." Evaluation practice at that time, like most social research, focused largely on assessing the strength of causal relationships (in evaluation, between treatments and outcomes) via experimental or quasi-experimental designs and standardized measurements. The debate surrounding social science methodology first arose within the philosophy of science, where prior commitments to extreme versions of objectivity and remaining notions of methodological infallibility were seriously challenged, and where convictions about the relevance and applicability of objectivist and realist frameworks (or paradigms) for the study of *human* phenomena had gradually eroded during the twentieth century (Schwandt, 2000c). In evaluation, the debate also arose because the initial use of conventional methodologies had demonstrated mixed success, at best, in assessing the quality and effectiveness of public policies and programs. The door was thus opened to alternative ways of understanding human phenomena and their accompanying alternative paradigms.

Thus entered a variety of "qualitative" paradigms and methodologies, collectively under the banner of the "interpretive turn" in social science.[6] "Qualitative" paradigms emphasize the interpreted and constructed (often versus real) nature of the social world, and thus emphasize the value-laden and contextual nature of social knowledge (versus quantitative approaches' emphasis more on the objective and generalizable). Qualitative methodologies generally focus on the meaningfulness of human activity, while quantitative methods usually address its frequency or magnitude (such as estimates of the size of a program's effects). Qualitative methods represent human phenomena in words or images or symbols, rather than in numbers and ordered dimensions.[7]

As revealed by its moniker, this "quantitative-qualitative" debate was centered on social-scientific inquiry designs and methods, but it was especially charged because it also involved politics and values and thereby fundamental definitions and understandings of the role of (social science and) evaluation in society. That is, "quantitative" and "qualitative" philosophical traditions generally take different stances on the place of values in social inquiry. In "quantitative" traditions, a long-standing view was that values can be empirically studied but are otherwise outside the boundaries of science and more properly in the domains of ethics, morality, religion, and politics: Scientists provide the facts; politicians and priests debate their significance. In contrast, in "qualitative" traditions, values have always been seen as inherent in all human action and all knowledge generated about that action. Values inevitably and for many properly refract the lens of the scientist and that which he or she is studying. There is no value-free knowledge nor any value-free methodology, argue proponents of "qualitative" traditions (a position with which many if not most contemporary quantitatively oriented evaluators agree, though often to somewhat different effect). And because the debate was as much about underlying values and commitments as about the right methodology, the stakes of this debate were high and passions were engaged as often as reasoned argument.[8]

The debate was most intense in evaluation during the 1980s, followed by a period of rapprochement in the 1990s, signaling an acceptance of the legitimacy of multiple methodological traditions in the evaluation community with attendant turns to multiplism and to mixed methodological thinking (Greene, Caracelli, & Graham, 1989). Yet, controversy about what constitutes legitimate or "good" practice still persists in many domains of social science, including evaluation, as underscored by the pluralist stance taken in this Handbook.

We endorse the rapprochement that characterized the end of the "quantitative–qualitative debate" and support a vibrant evaluation community filled with different ways of knowing and different ways of practicing our craft. We believe that this debate, in the end, was educative in important ways, as evaluators of all stripes had to engage seriously with their own assumptions, stances, and beliefs, *and* had to learn how to assume responsibility for making thoughtful and informed choices among the multiplicity of approaches to evaluation that emerged during this era. That is, this was a richly generative era in evaluation that yielded multiple, diverse evaluation theories and practices – a diversity which remains today.

Amidst this diversity, as stated above, we also believe that continued dialog and even debate on our differences – *and* on our commonalities – can and should help to quiet worries about a wildly relativistic community of practice. In the tradition of the "quantitative-qualitative debate," but with greater civility and acceptance of others' viewpoints, we encourage continued conversation about just what constitutes good evaluation practice.

What is Distinctive About Evaluation?

The question of what is distinctive to evaluation may refer either to methods of inquiry, or to the fundamental nature of evaluation. As for the first, there are a few distinctive evaluation methods, strategies, and techniques, examples of which are sprinkled throughout this volume, including the "Most Significant Change" approach featured in Chapter 15. Other "methods" distinctive to evaluation[9] include the multi-utility attribution technique, log frames and logic models (e.g., United Way of America, 1996), values inquiry (Mark et al., 2000), and Scriven's (1991) version of the weight-and-sum technique. Mostly, however, evaluators make liberal use of methodologies and methods from other disciplines and traditions in the social sciences. These include large-scale statistical modeling methods like hierarchical linear modeling and on-site, up-close methods like participant observation and individual interviewing.

What is perhaps distinctive to evaluation practice is that we use methodologies and methods from multiple and diverse social sciences and that we unhesitatingly use them side-by-side, or in the best of mixed method evaluation practice, actually attain some kind of integration of originally quite different ways of making sense of human phenomena. In general, that is, the community of evaluators welcomes multiple ways of understanding the very complex phenomena we study. Our practice is thus quite multidisciplinary in character. This is especially so because the nature of our practice includes aspects of management, communication, and utilization, which draw on fields of research and practice outside the social science core.

What is perhaps also somewhat distinctive to evaluation practice is that the requirements of methods do not reign supreme but rather must be negotiated with other important features of our work. Notably, evaluation is fundamentally judgmental; we are charged with discerning and assessing the quality of the program, policy, or practice we are evaluating. Judgments of quality rest on particular conceptualizations of "goodness," "effectiveness," or "success," which themselves are often contested. Further, evaluation takes place in politicized contexts with multiple legitimate stakeholders and interests. Good evaluators skillfully honor and respectfully help to negotiate these multiple interests. And also, evaluation is fundamentally relational, anchored in the kinds of relationships established among stakeholders and with the evaluator in particular contexts. These characteristics of our practice place particular burdens on our methods. Our methods inevitably bump into the various commitments to quality, interests and values, and dynamic and complex relationships that inhabit a given evaluation context, and methods usually must accommodate these values, interests and relationships in service of the larger evaluative mission or purpose. Good evaluation practice thus involves a delicate and negotiated balance among the contours of a particular context, the public interests at hand, and the methodological requirements for rigor and defensibility.

When we explore the distinctive character of evaluation, it is important to recognize that we are compressing three different questions.

- First, can evaluation be distinctive?
- Second, is evaluation distinctive?
- Third, should evaluation be different from or similar to research?

The first question is theoretical, the second empirical, and the third is normative. We will end up in murky waters if we treat the question as if it were empirical when in fact it is usually normative or theoretical.

Some have concluded that research, evaluation, and policy analysis are different forms of disciplined inquiry. Hence, Lincoln (1990, p. 76) states that it makes "no sense to refer to 'evaluation research', save as research *on* evaluation methods or models." We acknowledge that, on average, there are important differences between evaluation and research, which follow from the differing clusters of purposes that direct each form of inquiry. Nevertheless, making over-simple generalizations about homogeneous entities of "research" and "evaluation" risks contributing to rhetoric rather than good practice. Thus, in the UK or the Nordic countries, for example, to talk of "evaluation research" or "policy research" may make good sense, and involve no confusion of categories, whereas for many – but certainly not all – in the USA it may be treated as involving some confusion of terms.

Implications for Evaluator Training

Many educational and training programs in evaluation include coursework or readings in evaluation theory, evaluation practice, and social science methods, both qualitative and quantitative. Training programs in the USA often also include an evaluation practicum, in which novice evaluators get invaluable experience in the field. There are, of course, many people who practice evaluation without any particular form of professional training. But, the important question here is, what should be included in such training for those who choose to participate?

A thorough answer to this question is well beyond the scope of this introductory essay. We wish to suggest, however, that, even in a relatively developed circumstance such as the USA, there are important gaps in current training programs for evaluators – gaps in such areas as management, communication, and ethics, as well as gaps in processes like negotiation, dialog, deliberation, and conflict resolution. We all recognize the contested character of the contexts in which we work. However, as evaluators we have yet to incorporate this recognition into our programs for training evaluators of the future. Finally, we also wish to encourage readers of this Handbook to consider issues of evaluator training as they pursue the chapters that follow. What implications do these various discussions have for how we should train new entrants into our field?

(4) Who Are the Audiences for Evaluation in Varied Domains of Practice? What Uses Do They Make of Evaluative Work?

In fundamental ways, the audiences of evaluation, or the stakeholder groups and individuals for whom the evaluation is being conducted, are connected to evaluation purposes. Generally speaking, evaluations intended to provide accountability or to support decision-making serve the interests of stakeholders responsible for policy and program decisions, including legislators and other policy makers. Evaluations designed to generate knowledge about the phenomena being studied speak to the interests of program developers and theoreticians with expertise in that area. Evaluations designed for program improvement or organizational learning serve the interests of stakeholders responsible for administering the program or managing the organization. Evaluations that seek critical insight into the professional practices of program staff or in-depth understanding of the lived experiences of participants likely engage staff and participant interests and concerns. And evaluations with an ideological agenda, like democratization or empowerment, are intended to address most directly the interests of those at the margins of society. These purpose–audience connections reflect, in part, different perspectives on critical leverage points and different value commitments, as discussed above.

The concept of evaluation audience is further connected to issues of utilization and dissemination of evaluation findings, which likely vary across domains of practice. For whom is evaluation conducted in various domains of practice? How does audience affect the conceptualization and implementation of evaluation in various domains of human professional practice?

Part 4 of the Handbook explores the conceptual, methodological, and practical issues of evaluation in different domains of professional and occupational practice, including attention to issues of audience and utilization. Contributors to this section were asked to include in their discussion:

- The history of evaluation in their field.
- Evaluation purposes, social and disciplinary contexts, and practice issues that have most powerfully influenced evaluation in their field.
- The descriptive character of evaluation in their field, and how evaluation has helped to shape key discussions in the field.
- Likely future developments in evaluation for their field.

We noted at the outset that this part is where the risk of ethnocentrism is at its greatest. It is for readers to judge how well we have avoided the danger. Representing a relatively comprehensive though not exhaustive sample of important human endeavors, Part 4 includes six chapters. David Nevo discusses evaluation in the field of education (Chapter 20), Andrew Long in the field of health (Chapter 21), Ian Shaw for human services and social work (Chapter 22), Nick Tilley and Alan Clarke for criminal justice (Chapter 23), and Osvaldo Feinstein and Tony Beck for the combined fields of humanitarian relief and international development (Chapter 24). Finally, in Chapter 25, Alan Clarke, in closing the Handbook, offers his perspectives on challenges and new directions for evaluation in occupational domains, including thoughts about interprofessional evaluation practice.

Part 4 is important for several reasons. First, more than elsewhere, the chapters flesh out the recurring *motif* of the Handbook, of "policies, programs, and practice." It is in these domains of evaluation practice that we see the enactment of legislative and political statements of governmental or organizational intent, and the evaluation of policies as setting the direction for how resources in a given domain will be allocated and what substantive foci will receive priority. For each domain we witness the evaluation of programs as particular enactments of a policy, which offer concrete representations of *how* a given policy can be realized, in terms of particular activities and materials provided to a particular target population. And we see diverse instances of practices – the specific professional interactions that take place within programs.

Second, and perhaps serendipitously as we did not plan it thus, Part 4 contains the Handbook's most sustained discussions and reflections on the place of evidence-based drivers in the evaluation of health, human services, education, and the like. Alan Clarke knits much of this together in his closing essay.

Third, and following from the first point, we witness the diversity and commonalities of contextual issues, which embody the important issues addressed in Part 2. In Part 4 we witness structural contexts, social relations, intellectual contexts, politics and values, evaluation ethics, and utilization practices working out in national, state or local domains. This introductory essay now briefly takes up the final issue of utilization and dissemination as relevant to evaluation audience. We again hope that these prefatory comments will help sensitize Handbook readers and encourage their own reflections on these issues as they read the chapters in Part 4.

Connections to Utilization

As is well discussed in this Handbook (see Chapters 3, 12, and 17), evaluators are deeply concerned about being useful. 'To whom and for what purposes?" are the questions that immediately come to mind. Audiences are multiple. Uses characteristically take instrumental, conceptual, or symbolic form. Instrumental uses involve direct, visible contributions to decisions about the evaluated program, policy, or practice. Conceptual uses take more educational form, contributing, for example, to the direction of a policy conversation or to enlightenment of heretofore unacknowledged dimensions relevant to this conversation

(Weiss, 1998). And symbolic uses are more political, for example, using evaluation primarily to signal attention to a particular program area.[10]

Some evaluators emphasize the need to plan for a particular form of use, by specific, identifiable users (e.g., Patton, 1997). Others believe that, in most cases, conceptual use is more likely to occur (e.g., Weiss, 1991). It may well be that when situated in and viewed from within particular domains of professional practice, evaluation uses become primarily conceptual and users or audiences become theorists, program developers, and other content experts in that field. Evaluations in the domain of health care, for example, may importantly inform other health care researchers and theorists about the specific ways in which and extent to which the intervention studied influenced the health outcomes of interest.

To the extent this is true, what distinguishes evaluation from other forms of social research? And does this matter? Moreover, what does this knowledge-oriented, conceptualization of use and audience suggest about the importance of generalizability in evaluation practice? Many evaluation studies are conducted with explicit, context-bound purposes and identifiable, local audiences in mind. A perspective that privileges conceptual and knowledge-oriented use and audiences may exert unwarranted pressure on evaluation studies for results that are applicable to other contexts. Does this reduce the likelihood of important local uses? Or does it increase the likelihood that evaluation is influential and contributes to social betterment?

We raise these issues, once again, not to provide answers, but instead to sensitize the reader to issues of audience and use – and their implications for evaluation design and methods – as they read the chapters about evaluation in professional practice in Part 4.

Connections to Dissemination

In recent years, many evaluators have expanded their efforts to disseminate findings. In the USA it is increasingly common for large evaluation firms to have specialists in communication, for instance. More generally, the interest in kinds of knowledge used by policy-makers and professionals (an issue touched upon in our opening discussion of evaluation as a human activity) stimulates and enriches the debate on how knowledge is utilized.

The kinds of dissemination efforts we have been seeing more in practice often include: multiple forms of reports, typically with at least a more user-friendly and a more technical version, as well as versions for peer-reviewed journals and perhaps releases for practitioner newsletters; press briefings, as well as briefings for identifiable decision-makers and major stakeholder groups; websites on the evaluation and its results. In addition, some evaluators are active in the "issues networks" that exist around various policy issues. One rationale for these extended dissemination efforts is that, given the costs of evaluations (including not only financial costs, but also the time and other burdens born by the study participants), those who conduct social experiments should try to facilitate use, at the very least through extensive dissemination (cf. Rosenthal, 1994).

Concern about effective dissemination is, of course, not new. Cronbach and his colleagues some time ago urged the importance of tellable stories. The evaluator faces a mild paradox. "All research strives to reduce reality to a tellable story", but "thorough study of a social problem makes it seem more complicated" (Cronbach et al., 1980, p. 184). Cronbach and his associates' resolution of this paradox lay in urging that evaluators should seek constant opportunity to communicate with the policy-shaping community throughout the evaluation.

They believed that "much of the most significant communication is informal, not all of it is deliberate, and some of the largest effects are indirect" (p. 174). Their recommendations – unnervingly contemporary – were:

- Be around.
- Talk briefly and often.
- Tell stories. Always be prepared with a stock of anecdotes regarding the evaluation.
- Talk to the manager's sources.
- Use multiple models of presentation.
- Provide publicly defensible justifications for any recommended program changes. These will be very different from scientific arguments.

Cronbach was strongly opposed to holding on until all the data are in and conclusions are firm. Influence and precision will be in constant tension, and Cronbach held that if in doubt we should always go for influence. Live, informal, quick overviews, responsiveness to questions, the use of film and sound clips, and personal appearances are the stuff of influence. On this view of things, the final report thus acts as an archival document.

> The impotence that comes with delay . . . can be a greater cost than the consequences of misjudgment. The political process is accustomed to vigorous advocacy . . . (and) is not going to be swept off its feet by an ill-considered assertion even from an evaluator. (Cronbach et al., 1980, pp. 179–80)

Of course, as with other concerns related to evaluation, we recognize that a diversity of views exists about dissemination. Once again, we invite the reader to consider this issue when engaging with the chapters to follow.

Conclusion

We began this chapter with the idea that evaluation is a natural human activity. Throughout this chapter we have also noted many of the challenges and complexities that arise in professional efforts to evaluate people-related programs, policies, and practices. Among these complexities is the reality that contemporary evaluation has many faces, histories, approaches and views on such issues as evaluation's purpose, the role of values, the most likely leverage points for evaluation influence, and the preferred form of use.

These multiplicities can pose challenges, for example, by overwhelming some evaluators' capacity to choose thoughtfully. Alternatively, these multiplicities can create opportunities, for example, by providing a rich array of options from which to choose, and by contributing to ongoing dialog and exchanges among evaluators that lead to even better approaches to practice. We hope this Handbook might contribute to such exchanges.

Notes

1. Perhaps because of these multiple and relatively early developments in the United States, and perhaps because of the relatively earlier creation of professional evaluation associations in the United States, American writers and practitioners for some time have had a disproportionate influence in the field.

2. Shakespeare, *As You Like It* Act 2 Sc VII 134–142.

3. Similar arguments for an empirical approach to issues like evaluators' epistemology and evaluation utilization have been advanced in the human services field by Kirk & Reid (2002).

4. For example, the word "transformative" has been bantered about by many evaluators in recent years, and it would be good either to have evidence that evaluation is indeed transformative or instead to embrace the value of more incremental consequences of evaluation.

5. Paradigms are constellations of inter-related assumptions about the nature of the social world, the nature of the knowledge we can have about that social world, what's most important to know, and how best to attain or generate this knowledge.

6. There are numerous accounts of this shift, perhaps most familiar in Norman Denzin's various incarnations of the historical "moments" of qualitative inquiry (Denzin & Lincoln, 2004). Clifford & Marcus's

book is often taken as the fulcrum of this shift (Clifford & Marcus, 1986).

7. We hasten to add that, in capturing the differences between qualitative and quantitative, it is possible to exaggerate differences, easy to ignore moderate voices from the center, and difficult to avoid language that may strike someone as favoring one "side" or the other.

8. See Cook & Reichardt (1979) and Reichardt & Rallis (1994) for additional discussions of the "qualitative–quantitative" debate in the evaluation community.

9. "Distinctive" in this context may mean methods stemming from and unique to the practice of evaluation, or, less strongly (and perhaps more likely), methods that the evaluation field has distinctively contributed to the wider family of social science methods.

10. Again, as noted above, uses may also now take an "imposed" form (Weiss et al., 2005).

References

Alkin, M. C. (2004a). Comparing evaluation points of view. In M. C. Alkin (ed.), *Evaluation Roots: Tracing theorists' views and influences*. Thousand Oaks, CA: Sage.

Alkin, M. C. (ed.) (2004b). *Evaluation Roots: Tracing theorists' views and influences*. Thousand Oaks, CA: Sage.

Alkin, M. C., & Christie, C. A. (2004). An evaluation theory tree. In M. C. Alkin (ed.), *Evaluation Roots: Tracing theorists' views and influences*. Thousand Oaks, CA: Sage.

Anderson, N. (2001). *Handbook of Industrial, Work and Organizational Psychology*. Thousand Oaks, CA: Sage.

Chen, H-T. (2005). *Practical Program Evaluation: Assessing and improving planning, implementation, and effectiveness*. Thousand Oaks, CA: Sage.

Clifford, J., & Marcus, G. E. (eds) (1986). *Writing Culture: the poetics and politics of ethnography*. Berkeley, CA: University of California Press.

Cook, T. D. (1985). Postpositivist critical multiplism. In R. L. Shotland & M. M. Mark (eds) *Social Science and Social Policy* (pp. 21–62). Thousand Oaks, CA: Sage.

Cook, T. D., & Reichardt, C. S. (1979). *Qualitative and Quantitative Methods in Evaluation Research*. Thousand Oaks, CA: Sage.

Cronbach, L., Ambron, S., Dornbusch, S., Hess, R., Hornik, R., Phillips, D., Walker, D., & Weiner, S. (1980). *Toward Reform of Program Evaluation.* San Francisco: Jossey-Bass.

Denzin, N. K., & Lincoln, Y. S. (2004). *Handbook of Qualitative Research,* third edition. Thousand Oaks, CA: Sage.

Donaldson, S. I., & Scriven, M. (2003). *Evaluating Social Programs and Problems: Visions for the new millennium.* Mahwah, NJ: Lawrence Erlbaum.

Evers, A., Anderson, N., & Voskuijl, O. (eds) (2005). *The Blackwell Handbook of personnel Selection.* Oxford: Blackwell.

Freire, P. (1970). *Pedagogy of the Oppressed.* New York: Continuum.

Greene, J. C., Caracelli, V. J., & Graham, W. F. (1989). Toward a conceptual framework for mixed-method evaluation designs. *Educational Evaluation and Policy Analysis,* 11(3), 255–274.

Guba, E. (1990), The alternative paradigm dialog, In E. Guba (ed.), *The Paradigm Dialog.* Newbury Park: Sage.

Hammersley, M. (2003). Social research today: some dilemmas and distinctions. in *Qualitative Social Work,* 2(1): 25–44.

Hood, S. (1998). Responsive evaluation Amistad style: Perspectives of one African American evaluator. In R. Davis (ed.), *Proceedings of the Stake Symposium on Educational Evaluation* (pp. 101–112). University of Illinois at Urbana-Champaign.

House, E. (1991). Evaluation and social justice: where are we now? In M. McLaughlin & D. Phillips (eds) *Evaluation and Education: At quarter century* (pp. 233–247). Chicago: Chicago University Press.

House, E. R. (1994). Integrating the quantitative and the qualitative. In C. S. Reichardt & S. F. Rallis (eds) *The Qualitative-Quantitative Debate: New perspectives. New Directions for Program Evaluation,* No. 61. San Francisco: Jossey-Bass.

Kirk, S., & Reid, W. (2002). *Science and Social Work.* New York: Columbia University Press.

Lipsey, M. W. (2000a). Meta-analysis and the learning curve in evaluation practice. *American Journal of Evaluation,* 21, 207–212.

Lipsey, M. W. (2000b). Method and rationality are not social diseases. *American Journal of Evaluation,* 21, 221–223.

Lincoln, Y. (1990). The making of a constructivist: a remembrance of transformations past. in E. Guba, (ed.), *The Paradigm Dialog.* Newbury Park: Sage.

Lincoln, Y., & Guba, E. (1986a). Research, evaluation and policy analysis: heuristics and disciplined inquiry. *Policy Studies Review,* 5(3), 546–565.

Lincoln, Y., & Guba, E. (1986b) But is it rigorous? Trustworthiness and authenticity in naturalistic evaluation. In D. D. Williams (ed.), *Naturalistic Evaluation. New Directions in Program Evaluation,* No. 30. San Francisco: Jossey-Bass.

Lombardi, D. N. (ed.) (1988). *Handbook of Personnel Selection and Performance Evaluation in Healthcare: Guidelines for hourly, professional, and managerial employees.* San Francisco: Jossey-Bass.

MacDonald, B. (1987). Evaluation and the control of information. In R. Murphy & H. Torrance (eds) *Issues and Methods in Evaluation* (pp. 36–48). London: Paul Chapman.

Maio, G. R., & Olson, J. M. (eds) (2000). *Why We Evaluate: Functions of attitudes.* Mahwah, NJ: Erlbaum.

Mark, M. M. (2003). Toward a comprehensive view of the theory and practice of program and policy evaluation. In S. I. Donaldson & M. Scriven (eds) *Evaluating Social Programs and Problems: Visions for the new millennium* (pp. 183–204). Hillsdale, NJ: Erlbaum.

Mark, M. M. (in press). Building a better evidence-base for evaluation theory. In P. R. Brandon & N. L. Smith (eds) *Fundamental Issues in Evaluation.* New York: Guilford.

Mark, M. M., Henry, G. T., & Julnes, G. (2000). *Evaluation: An integrated framework for understanding, guiding, and improving policies and programs.* San Francisco, CA: Jossey-Bass.

Musch, J., & Klauer, K. C. (eds) (2003). *The Psychology of Evaluation: Affective processes in cognition and emotion.* Mahwah, NJ: Erlbaum.

Patton, M. Q. (1997). *Utilization-Focused Evaluation: The new century text.* Thousand Oaks, CA: Sage.

Polkinghorne, D (2000). Psychological inquiry and the pragmatic and hermeneutic traditions. *Theory and Psychology,* 10(4), 453–479.

Reichardt, C. S., & Rallis, S. F. (eds.) (1994). *The Qualitative-Quantitative Debate: New perspectives. New Directions for Evaluation,* No. 61. San Francisco: Jossey-Bass.

Rosenthal, R. (1994). Science and ethics in conducting, analyzing, and reporting psychological research. *Psychological Science,* 5, 127–134.

Rossi, P. H., & Freeman, H.E. (1985). *Evaluation, a Systematic Approach,* third edition. Thousand Oaks, CA: Sage.

Schmidt, M. (1993). Grout: Alternative kinds of knowledge and why they are ignored. *Public Administration Review,* 53(6), 525–530.

Schwandt, T. A. (2000a). Further diagnostic thoughts on what ails evaluation practice *American Journal of Evaluation,* 21, 225–229.

Schwandt, T. A. (2000b). Meta-analysis and everyday life: The good, the bad, and the ugly. *American Journal of Evaluation,* 21, 213–219.

Schwandt, T. A. (2000c). Three epistemological stances for qualitative inquiry: Interpretivism, hermeneutics, and social constructionism. In N. K. Denzin & Y. S. Lincoln (eds), Handbook *of Qualitative Research,* second edition (pp. 189–213). Thousand Oaks, CA: Sage.

Scriven, M. (1991). *Evaluation Thesaurus,* fourth edition. Thousand Oaks, CA: Sage.

Scriven, M. (1999). The nature of evaluation part ii: Training. *Practical Assessment, Research and Evaluation,* 6(12). Retrieved September 12, 2005 from http://PAREonline.net/getvn.asp?v=6&n=12

Shadish, W. R., Cook, T. D., & Leviton, L. C. (1991). *Foundations of Program Evaluation: Theories of practice.* Newbury Park, CA: Sage.

Shaw, Ian F. (1984). Consumer evaluations of the personal social services. *British Journal of Social Work,* 14(3), 277–284.

United Way of America (1996). *Measuring Program Outcomes: A practical aproach.* Alexandria, VA: United Way of America.

Weiss, C. H. (1991). Evaluation research in the political context: Sixteen years and four administrations later. In M. W. McLaughlin & D. C. Phillips (eds), *Evaluation and Education: At quarter century* (pp. 211–231). Chicago: University of Chicago Press.

Weiss, C. H. (1998). *Evaluation,* second edition. Upper Saddle River, NJ: Prentice Hall.

Weiss, C. H., Murphy-Graham, E., & Birkeland, S. (2005). An alternate route to policy influence: How evaluations affect D.A.R.E. *American Journal of Evaluation,* 26, 12–30.

PART ONE

ROLE AND PURPOSE
OF EVALUATION
IN SOCIETY

1

THE PURPOSES OF EVALUATION IN A DEMOCRATIC SOCIETY

Eleanor Chelimsky

The evaluation of public policies, programs, and practices seems to be an intrinsic part of democratic government for four reasons. It reports information about government performance that the public needs to know. It adds new data to the existing stock of knowledge required for government action. It develops an analytical capability within agencies that moves them away from territoriality and toward a culture of learning. And, more generally, its spirit of skepticism and willingness to embrace dissent help keep the government honest. Evaluation thus serves many purposes, and it is common to find that what may have begun, say, as an accountability study of government performance, ends up dominated by a different purpose or at least includes other purposes as an integral part of the evaluation.

Many evaluators, however, disagree about the viability of the various purposes, often favoring one over another. Some evaluators say that evaluation is valuable only when it measures accountability, that is, when it maximizes tax resources by holding policy-makers and program managers accountable for the merit and worth of their policies and programs. Others see evaluation as valuable only when it generates knowledge, when it brings new or more profound understandings in some specific area of public endeavor. Still others believe that without evaluation capacity in government agencies, nothing good can happen: for them, evaluation is valuable only when it improves institutions, moving them from performance measurement and self-evaluation to the learning organization.

This would not be much of a problem if we evaluators took a more inclusive stance about why we do what we do. After all, these three perspectives are not mutually exclusive. But people who engage in one type of evaluation often condemn the work of others who engage in a different kind. There have been veritable battles in the literature between warriors claiming, on the one hand, that "the only real evaluation is ultimately a fundamental judgment of merit or worth," and, on the other, that there is a whole "menu of evaluation purposes" – seven and still expanding – that have equal importance with merit and worth (Patton, 1996).

Looking at evaluation only from an evaluator's perspective might cause us to underestimate, misinterpret, or rule out purposes for evaluation that we would recognize as valid if we saw them from a different, broader perspective. We're not unlike those ants, asked to write a zoology paper, who divided the animal kingdom into two classes: the kind, gentle beasts such as the lion, tiger or jackal, and the ferocious ones like the chicken, duck or goose.

Still, it's not really surprising that we have such disparate perceptions of evaluation's purpose, and that we have not spent much time examining where it fits in government. Government in the United States became a prime player in evaluation starting only in the 1960s, whereas evaluation itself developed incrementally over more than 100 years. That lengthy development, and especially the dissimilar paths through which it evolved, could not help but influence the distinctions we make when we look at evaluation purpose today.

Varieties of Public Policy Evaluation in the United States

A first strand of evaluative development can be traced to government agricultural research begun in the early 1900s. The purpose was knowledge enhancement, to find out which agricultural practices would lead to the largest crop yield. Experimental design and statistical analysis techniques were applied, with advances coming from social scientists and statisticians, many of whom worked in universities as well as government.

By the 1950s, large-scale retrospective evaluations of the merit-and-worth type were being performed, using survey and computer-assisted techniques. Carefully evaluated demonstration programs came along in the 1960s, responding to the government's efforts to examine social programs' effectiveness in, say, moving people out of poverty or reducing crime. This path of evaluative development, focusing also on education, public health, equality of opportunity and other areas, drew on learning from a wide array of fields, including psychology, sociology, economics, political science and anthropology.

A second evaluative strand began during the 1950s, with efforts to rationalize the resource allocation and management of defense programs. Born in a think tank (the Rand Corporation) but developed within government, this eventually grew into the Department of Defense's Planning, Programming, and Budgeting System (PPBS), and was later expanded to other agencies under Lyndon Johnson. Focused on management improvement and the development of institutional capability, PPBS also had an underlying concern with questions of merit and worth. The thrust was to plan for program cost-effectiveness, and then to evaluate whether this had been achieved. Developed largely by economists and political scientists, the system used techniques such as policy analysis, cost-benefit, cost-effectiveness and systems analysis (Rhoads, 1978). Over time, these techniques implanted themselves into general evaluation practice (Rossi & Freeman, 1985).

These two strands of evaluative inquiry are much less distinct today. It is common to find techniques from both strands used in a single study. Nevertheless, the differing purposes, settings, disciplines, and mindsets (not to mention differing evaluative questions, methods, and goals) have made for a climate in which it is easy for evaluators to claim exclusive value for one evaluation purpose over another.

When I first began evaluating weapons and military budget systems at NATO in 1966, however, I had no such exclusive views. My idea was to use any and all plausible theories, any and all proven methods, any and all types of analysis that could help answer the questions I was asked by Defense or State Department officials (USNATO was a combined mission of the two agencies). The purpose of my work was always perfectly clear, based on the policy or program need expressed in the question; the work itself, however, was not.

My biggest problem was that the data from NATO nations were often non-comparable. There were few standard definitions of categories and items; missing entries were common; costs depended on the sometimes wildly-varying currency rates used in the country calculations; and individual NATO ministries had a vested interest in keeping their defense figures as obscure as possible, often denying access to information I needed simply to adjust the data. Seemingly straight-forward questions that policy-makers needed answers to – like "Why do military pension costs appear to be spiking in some countries but not in others?" – turned into data-sifting nightmares simply to determine whether the differences were real.

Using a clunky, government-issue calculator, a closetful of columnar pads, and a stack of No. 2 pencils, I scratched my way, slowly and laboriously, tabulating the entries of 15 nations. I sat on the floor, surrounded by giant yellow spreadsheets, sharpening pencils and making adjustments. It was not a comfortable process, but at least we evaluators at NATO were always told why our information was needed and what management or policy-making purpose it was intended to serve.

After we finally published a few studies and our work gained some credibility within NATO, we began trying to spread our evaluation methods to other national offices. We had both the altruistic aim of developing a more widespread analytical capability across NATO and the unabashedly self-interested one of being able to count on better data to support our studies.

Eventually, our work led to some basic policy questions about the impacts of the real drawdown of forces and resources we had found (a drawdown that had hitherto been camouflaged under a welter of indecipherable data). We were asked to evaluate the effects of some of these reductive actions by individual NATO nations on the readiness of NATO as a whole. These were, in fact, accountability studies, intended to illuminate the results of covert decisions and unfulfilled responsibilities, to link cause and effect.

Because of this experience, then, it has always seemed sensible to me that evaluation should have at least these three purposes: to gain new knowledge (by performing studies to answer questions about unknowns in a program or policy area); to improve agency capability (by using evaluation to improve problem-solving, database development, analytical skills, management practices, and the like); and to determine accountability (by performing studies that measure policy or program effectiveness or efficiency, assign responsibilities for successes and failures, and lay out options for improvement and correction). Indeed, these three purposes arise even in organizations that have oversight responsibilities and might be expected by some observers to rely mostly on accountability evaluations. In practice, accountability evaluations often depend on or give way to evaluations with another purpose.

Later, after a symposium looking at how the Congress, seven federal agencies, and the

Office of Management and Budget had actually used evaluations, I saw the same three purposes emerge from the analysis of the proceedings (Chelimsky, 1977b, 1978). Again, in 1995, at the international Vancouver conference of five evaluation societies, a look at the evaluations presented gave rise to the same view: the three major purposes were still there, and no single purpose could account for the body of evaluations in the field (Chelimsky, 1996; Chelimsky & Shadish, 1997).

This is not, of course, to suggest that no other purposes exist or could exist (indeed, I believe other chapters in this part address alternative possible purposes for evaluation, such as social justice). My point is that claiming a unique purpose for evaluation flies in the face of past and current practice. Nor is it my argument that any of the three purposes just discussed is typically present in a pristine state within an evaluation. Rather, these purposes rely on, and are intertwined with, each other in many different ways. Yet claimants for a unique purpose rarely admit how much, say, accountability evaluations depend on the work of preceding knowledge or development evaluations that have built the databases and descriptions of prior experience needed to establish accountability. Likewise, proponents of knowledge or development purposes don't often recognize the extent to which earlier or pending accountability studies create the climate of interest or political pressure that make their recommendations more likely to be heard and used.

Because so many evaluations have multiple purposes, then (even though a single purpose may dominate the others), I have chosen not to focus on any one of them here, but instead to examine their intermingling. In my experience, this better reflects the reality of program and policy evaluation in the public sphere.

But before looking at how these purposes work together to answer evaluation questions and facilitate the use of their findings in that murky, complex and painful process known as public decision-making, it may be important to go beyond evidence from experience or practice to understand why these particular purposes have emerged. Is there a larger basis for their presence, a structural core from which they spring? Can we deduce some necessity for their existence and how they fit together? To try to answer these questions, we need to look again at evaluative purpose, but this time from a political or governmental viewpoint, including the principles that dictate the need for evaluation in a democracy. I address this largely from the vantage point of the United States, but later in the chapter examine generalizability to other countries.

Governmental Structure and Congressional Oversight

In most democracies, and certainly in the United States, we find a government whose functions are split across three branches (legislative, executive, and judicial). Such a structure has the political goal of keeping too much power from accumulating in any one place. At least in the US, it is a structure born of distrust: distrust based on past experience with a coercive autocracy.

Such a structure is not, of course, without its disadvantages. Walls generated by individual branches and agencies to protect their independence also generate suspicion and secrecy. Fragmentation carries a host of impediments; sharing of information across agencies, for example, is rare. Most democracies are far away from efficient government performance. But conversely, calls to improve performance, to "make the trains run on time," as in fascist Italy, often turn out to be little more than disguised attempts to weaken individual rights or freedom. So there is some tension between optimal performance in government and the preservation of liberty.

After the American Revolution, the framers of the US Constitution came up against this very tension: the need for a government to have enough power to govern, versus the distrust expressed by citizens and states of any overarching central authority that could become abusive or corrupt. The Constitution thus produced a divided governmental structure, featuring both a separation of powers among executive, legislative, and judicial branches, and a distribution of powers between federal and state levels of government. Although a far-reaching compromise between distrust and need had thus been achieved, it was so tenuous, vague, and ambiguous that the argument about it has never really been resolved (Ellis, 2002).

This architecture of "checks and balances" was, of course, intended to be an organizational bulwark – built on both external and internal controls – against too much centralized power. Madison wrote of "the necessary partition of power among the several departments" as part of an external control structure. He also called for internal controls to be established "by so contriving the interior structure of the government as that its several constituent parts may, by their mutual relations, be the means of keeping each other in their proper places." This is nothing less than a clarion call to agency independence. That is, "each department should have a will of its own; and consequently should be so constituted that the members of each should have as little agency as possible in the appointment of the members of the others" (Madison, 1788).

Yet the framers had few illusions about the dangers that could accompany too much agency independence, not to mention "the inevitable corruptions that could result when unseen rulers congregate in distant places" (Ellis, 2002). So they envisaged a check against agency autonomy in the form of congressional oversight, that is, the particular "authority to supervise the administration of government" which has led to so many confrontations over the years about accountability and secrecy in the executive branch (Jewell & Patterson, 1966).

Congress has oversight authority over the judicial branch, which it exerts, for example, through Senate approval of judicial appointments and the power to establish federal courts and prescribe their jurisdiction. Congress supervises the executive branch, through such mechanisms as the appropriations power, senatorial approval of nominations to executive office, and, notably, the investigation of how past legislation has been implemented (Jewell & Patterson, 1966). Through the Congressional Budget Control and Impoundment Act of 1974, Congress "greatly strengthened its resources for scrutiny and control of government programs and activities" (Bradshaw & Pring, 1981). Specifically, the Congress lodged within one of its own agencies (the General Accounting Office, or USGAO, now called the Government Accountability Office) the authority and responsibility to perform evaluations in support of congressional oversight.

In short, the US governmental structure builds in democratic protections through exterior and interior controls, agency independence, and congressional oversight. This structure is itself a careful equilibrium, a compromise arrived at between partisans of strong and limited government. Despite its apparent precarity, the framers believed their structure would stand against inevitable efforts to abuse or usurp power, but only if it could be vigorously supported by a well-informed public: that is, an electorate with enough distrust to sniff out problems in government, and also enough willingness and capability to correct them once they became known.

The People as Guarantors of Democracy, and the Information Function of Government

"One of the principal functions of a legislature is to inform the people about the activities of their government" (Bradshaw & Pring, 1981) – another idea that comes down to us from the framers. Madison recognized that organizational controls and the like were essentially adjuncts to the real power of the citizenry, which lies behind any governmental structure in a democracy: "A dependence on the people," Madison (1788) wrote, "is, no doubt, the primary control on the government." Jefferson went further in grappling with the issue of how even a vigilant population might become aware of a distant government's excesses or omissions and take steps to correct them. Writing to Abigail Adams in 1804, he noted the two political parties' disagreement about ensuring that the people should function as the best censor of government: "One side fears most the ignorance of the people; the other, the selfishness of rulers independent of them" (Jefferson, 1946).

Jefferson's view was that ignorance was curable:

> I am persuaded myself that the good sense of the people will always be found to be the best army. They may be led astray for a moment, but will soon correct themselves . . . . The way to prevent these [errors] of the people is to give them full information of their affairs through the channel of the public papers, and to contrive that these papers should penetrate the whole mass of the people . . . . I mean that every man should receive these papers and be capable of reading them. (Jefferson, 1946)

The press and education were thus the chief means through which Jefferson sought to involve the people. It is no accident that Jefferson considered his founding of the University of Virginia as one of the three main achievements of his life – along with the authorship of the Declaration of Independence and that of Virginia's statute for religious freedom (Bronowski & Mazlish, 1993). Jefferson put his faith especially in the spread of accurate information through science and research, and he believed knowledge should inform the activities of government: "Science is more important in a republican than in any other government" (Jefferson, 1946). As President, he conceived the Lewis and Clark expedition, which had as its primary purpose the acquisition of new knowledge (Hicks et al., 1964). Before that, under Vice President Jefferson's urging, the census – first begun only to inform on the size of the population – expanded its horizons to include details about the lifespan of Americans that could be used for social measures to improve longevity (Chelimsky, 1985). And it is no accident either that Jefferson so fervently championed a Bill of Rights that guaranteed, among other freedoms, freedom of the press, against the opinion of Hamilton.

Indeed, Hamilton wrote that he saw no need for a Bill of Rights, no need for concern about how to keep the citizenry well informed, and no need to guarantee freedom of the press, because individual state officials would take care "to apprise the community" of any government abuses that might be taking place. Also, nearby citizens could be trusted to warn those at a distance, "to sound the alarm when necessary, and to point out the actors in any pernicious project" (Hamilton, 1788).

Those of us who have experienced the impediments to the free flow of information brought by agency secrecy, or by general inattention or negligence, can have little confidence in Hamilton's view. His conception is so unrealistic – coming as it does from the most realistic of the framers – that it arouses suspicion it may have been put forward less to inform the public than to relieve the government of having to do so. Once again, this debate was part of the larger argument between advocates of strong versus limited government (resolved in this case in favor of the Bill of Rights).

To sum up, the democratic protections involving structure, independence, and control are joined by the ultimate protection of reliance on an informed public. These protections bring us a framework of issues that together delineate the form and function, the substance and shape of the governmental need for evaluation.

A Framework of Governmental Issues Relevant to Evaluation

These issues, five in number, are as follows:

- The structure of government is fragmented, with functions and powers divided between federal and state levels and among executive, legislative, and judicial branches to guard against over-centralization of political power.
- Each level and branch, and each department or agency within a branch, is expected to protect its allotted powers and independence against incursion by others.
- Walls, suspicion and secrecy co-exist around these divisions in government and around the prescribed independence of branches and agencies.
- As a check on too much executive independence and too little transparency, Congress uses its oversight authority to scrutinize and control executive branch activities.
- Because the people need knowledge to serve as the "primary control on government," a critical task for the legislative and other branches is to inform citizens about the activities of their government.

This framework sets up the principles and context from which we can infer the place of evaluation in government. Evaluation sits at the heart of the continuing tension between the need to govern and to be distrustful of government. As Joseph Ellis writes, the debate about strong versus limited government "was not resolved so much as built into the fabric of our national identity. If that means the United States is founded on a contradiction, then so be it . . . . We have been living with it successfully for over two hundred years" (Ellis, 2002). Indeed, it is that very contradiction which establishes the legitimacy of evaluation.

The Governmental Need for Evaluation

We can deduce, then, that a democratic government such as the US needs evaluation for four purposes:

(1) To support congressional oversight;

(2) To build a stronger knowledge base for policy-making;

(3) To help agencies develop improved capabilities for policy and program planning, implementation and analysis of results, as well as greater openness and a more learning-oriented direction in their practice;

(4) To strengthen public information about government activities through dissemination of evaluation findings.

How exactly does evaluation serve these purposes?

Supporting Congressional Oversight

Congressman Bolling of Missouri used to speak about oversight with knowledge and wit:

> The problem I've always found with congressional oversight is that most of the oversight done by congressional committees is the wrong kind. It's the kind that looks back and decides how many mistakes other people you disagree with have made. It very seldom involves dealing

with the skillful and knowledgeable monitoring of programs that committees have been responsible for. . . . I don't think that what I'm talking about is a little important; I think it's absolutely crucial. . . . In the long run, it's absolutely crucial to whether the democratic process will continue to work. This is the place where the democratic process in the United States is going to stand or fall, [based] on whether some day we are actually going to act as we talk on oversight. (Bolling, 1978)

Evaluation, of course, has a natural role in the "skillful and knowledgeable monitoring of programs," but also in the establishment of accountability within a jealous universe of competing priorities and prerogatives. Were legislative purposes appropriately served by a given executive branch policy or program? Were funds expended wisely, or at least efficiently? Evaluation in its retrospective mode can measure and account for the effectiveness and efficiency of an implemented policy or program. And it can also prospectively assess the likelihood, based on past performance and other data, that public funds will be usefully expended on some proposed new activity.

Indeed, in the Congressional Budget Control and Impoundment Act of 1974, Congress explicitly recognized the value of using evaluations in accountability assessments. As Senator Brock noted, "If these programs that we write, enact and administer are not subject to on-going oversight using evaluative techniques, they're just not going to do the job" (Brock, 1975).

Advancing Knowledge

Here the democratic purpose, derived from the information/education role of government, is to increase understanding about the factors underlying public problems, about the "fit" between these factors and the policy or program solutions proposed, and about the theory and logic (or lack thereof) that lie behind an implemented intervention. What are the different causes for homelessness? Why is a technology successful in Asia but not in Africa? Which policies and programs might best address problems of delinquency, based on which theory?

The importance of these evaluations to good government is incalculable. Without them, government takes high-stakes risks in moving ahead with large programs. We should not forget Patrick Moynihan, mourning the paucity of evidence brought to the plans and programs of the War on Poverty: "This is the essential fact. The government did not know what it was doing. It had a theory. Or rather a set of theories. Nothing more" (Moynihan, 1969). This lack of sound foundation not only hurt the success of the individual programs, but also caused the War on Poverty as a whole to be attacked on the grounds of imprudence and wastefulness (Moynihan, 1969).

Unfortunately, knowledge arrives according to its own timetable, and this timetable may not coincide with prevailing political winds. Still, the evidence brought by knowledge evaluations, when they are available, can be critical for the success of both ongoing and future government interventions.

Helping Agencies

Both accountability and knowledge evaluators draw on program data and other information available only within agencies. But for evaluators to collect and use that information, agencies must first allow them access to it. Also, if relevant actions are to be taken as a result of policy or program problems found by evaluators, it is often the agency managers who must take them. In other words, agencies need to possess an evaluative (and self-evaluative) capability and culture if accountability and knowledge evaluations are to be meaningful.

But agencies need evaluative capability for their own purposes, as we saw with PPBS, and also with the more recent Government Performance and Results Act (GPRA) of 1994. Alice Rivlin noted that, under GPRA, "every agency must present a clear picture of its goals, the links between those goals and how it spends its money, and its performance – what it produces for the American people. GPRA gives agencies the chance to tell their story in a credible way, to communicate the value of agency and program activities to OMB [the Office of Management and Budget], to Congress, and to the public" (Wholey, 1997).

Whatever the fate of GPRA, it seems clear that the ongoing development of institutional integrity and capability is as important a public need as the advancement of knowledge or the assessment of accountability. Indeed, from a practical viewpoint, given the evaluator's need for access to people and data, it will always be difficult to perform either knowledge or accountability evaluations without strong evaluative development within agencies.

Informing the People

Finally, insofar as evaluations are intended either to increase knowledge or to account for the activities of government, their publication contributes to the goal of an informed public. Evaluations report on the successes and failures of policies and programs. They speak to the probity and integrity of government practices. Importantly, they also enhance that transparency in government which allows accurate information to emerge. Evaluations that are credible, comprehensibly written, intelligently disseminated, and well reported by the press help make people aware of what is happening in government.

Development evaluations are less likely to be published or to be useful in informing the public. Such studies must walk a fine line between the twin goals of agency discretion and public service through improvements in practice. On the other hand, the information function served by accountability and knowledge evaluations means that, from the perspective of government need, the ultimate client or user of these evaluations is the public. This casts a slightly different light on the meaning of evaluation use. It also puts a premium on the independence of evaluators, on the accuracy and credibility of their product, on the free dissemination of their findings, and on the need for evaluators to fight barriers (such as denied access to data or unnecessary secrecy) which have the potential to distort their information.

Evaluation is not alone, of course, in the job of reporting about the government. Since the time of Madison and Jefferson, an enormous information industry has grown up – including a vastly expanded press, network and cable television, and the internet – whose predominant purpose is to inform the public. In the course of bringing the news, these media are often primary transmitters of evaluative information, frequently with evaluators briefing journalists on the scope and substance of their findings. There are also other forms of analysis, such as auditing or legal or budgetary analysis; while these may overlap with evaluation, they are not usually competitive. Evaluators are in a unique position to answer questions like, "What happened and why?" or "What difference did the policy or program make?" This work, properly disseminated, contributes powerfully both to transparency in government and to the overall democratic enterprise of informing the public.

In summary, there are four functions of government for which evaluation is needed (oversight, knowledge enhancement, agency development, and public information), demonstrating that determining merit or worth cannot be the sole purpose of public policy evaluation. From a governmental viewpoint, evaluation serves: to obtain accurate information for one branch of government on the activities and accountability of another; to increase knowledge about the underlying bases for legislating, as well as for implementing legislative mandates, in a vast array of subject areas; to inform the public about the successes and failures of government endeavors; and to help develop within agencies the orientation toward challenge and improvement that allows evaluations to be done and their recommendations implemented.

The purposes listed above, then, are not markedly different from the ones derived by analysis of the 1976 symposium and the 1995 international conference in Vancouver (i.e., accountability, knowledge, and development). But the public information function must be added. Still, informing the public is not a fourth purpose of evaluation at the same level as the others; rather, it concerns the requirement for publication and dissemination of the findings of accountability and knowledge evaluations. Further, in a democracy the three purposes can be seen to flow from a universe of checks and balances, and to fit together in relation to that universe. It's true, of course, as noted earlier, that these purposes may not be exhaustive. But it's also true that the integrated response offered to the political and information needs of a democratic government by these three evaluation purposes confers upon them both authenticity and legitimacy.

As I re-examine the evaluations we did at the Program Evaluation and Methodology Division (PEMD) of the GAO, I see a body of work that is entirely consistent with these three purposes. During our 14 years, we were privileged to perform nearly 300 evaluations of all three types, mostly at congressional request. Over time, it became increasingly apparent to us that the support of congressional

oversight is integrally tied to knowledge and development work, as well as to the dissemination of information to the public.

The Experience at PEMD

I arrived at GAO in 1980, invited by then-Comptroller General Elmer Staats, to lead the agency's new Institute for Program Evaluation. The GAO is a legislative agency established by the Budget and Accounting Act of 1921, which also created the Office of Management and Budget. This Act provided for considerable independence of the Comptroller General of GAO, who is appointed to a 15-year term by the President of the United States and can be removed only by resolution of both Houses of Congress. The original objectives of the agency had been mostly auditive and investigatory, but the Congressional Budget Control and Impoundment Act of 1974 broadened GAO's responsibilities in program evaluation while retaining its remarkable independence. During the period I worked there (1980–1994), I had many occasions to be grateful for that independence, and for the strength and determination with which the agency defended it. The unit I would organize and direct at GAO, which I staffed largely with social scientists, soon evolved from an "institute" to a regular GAO division in 1983, referred to as PEMD.

My original expectation, based on my fairly shallow grasp of congressional oversight needs at that time, was that the Congress would be more interested in accountability studies than in anything else. But as I look back over our work, I find at least as many examples of evaluations for development or knowledge as for accountability. It's also the case that many of our studies had more than one purpose, or else grew one from another (as in the case of accountability evaluations that had to be followed by knowledge or development work to remedy some of the problems or gaps in information we had uncovered). Nevertheless, looking at the overall body of work, a particular purpose typically dominated the others in most of our evaluations.

Accountability Studies

Although some evaluators seem to believe that accountability studies are rare, at PEMD we did a great many of them. This surely had something to do with the strength and determination of the opposition in Congress to many policies of the Reagan and G.H.W. Bush Administrations. Accountability may be the terrible swift sword of democracy, but it requires a vigorous Congress to wield it.

Accountability studies are taken seriously in government. At very least, the general climate for doing an accountability study will be strained and its progress slow; often the context is more like the fog of war surrounding a pitched battle. We did accountability studies at PEMD for the Congress in almost every imaginable subject area (health, defense, public assistance, education, transportation, the environment, and more). Perhaps the most important one, in terms of size, scope, quality, and enduring agony, was our study of the United States' strategic nuclear triad.

Evaluation of the Nuclear Triad

In April, 1990, Chairman Dante Fascell, of the House Committee on Foreign Affairs, asked us to evaluate the major modernization programs proposed by the Department of Defense (DOD) for the strategic nuclear triad. "Triad" refers to the three methods of delivering nuclear retaliation: by land, sea, or air.

The Policy Question. The Chairman asked the following basic policy question: "In the

face of the budget deficit and the changing context of East-West relations" (the Berlin Wall had fallen in November, 1989), "how can Congress best provide for the strategic security of the United States?" Fascell wrote further, "As the United States and the Soviet Union reach new agreements on strategic arms reductions, Congress will be making important decisions concerning the size and quality of the air/land/sea components of our strategic offensive force structure" (Fascell, 1992a). He asked us to focus on the effectiveness, cost, policy, and arms control implications for each component of the triad and any likely nuclear upgrades. The breathtaking nature of this request is apparent, but is even clearer considering that in 1990 the systems and their upgrades amounted to an estimated $350 billion. Difficulties also were immediately apparent, not least of which was the highly classified status of most of the documents needed for our work. (All of the following discussion is derived from unclassified source material.)

The Evaluation Questions, Design, and Measures. For the triad study, we decided to take some time to examine carefully the rationales underlying the various systems and upgrades before setting up our evaluation design. With the agreement of the Committee on Foreign Affairs, we translated the policy question into seven evaluation questions (around which we would structure separate reports, allowing us to have at least some findings ready for the coming congressional policy and budgetary debates). In summary, these questions involved assessing (1) the vulnerability of the sea leg's nuclear-powered ballistic missile submarines (SSBNS) and (2) the land leg's silo-based intercontinental ballistic missiles (ICBMs); (3) the relative effectiveness of ICBMs versus submarine-launched ballistic missiles (SLBMs); (4) the air leg's proposed upgrades in terms of improved capacity, relative to existing systems; (5) the comparative costs of the proposed upgrades; (6) existing capabilities for addressing the threat posed by strategic relocatable targets (SRTs); and (7) strategic capabilities in France and the United Kingdom. The nuclear weapons systems and proposed upgrades we eventually included in the evaluation were the major ones (e.g., for the air leg, we examined the B-52G and B-52H, B-lB and B-2 bombers, as well as the ALCM, ACM, SRAM A, and SRAM II missiles). We knew we would have to assess all systems under a full range of threat scenarios, moving from total surprise attack to strategic warning.

Our basic design strategy was to develop a framework for comparison. Because we found no earlier comparative studies by DOD or others on which to build, we had to develop our own set of measurements. Our approach was to examine DOD's own conclusions about: the performance of the various triad weapons systems; the costs of the upgrades being proposed; and the size and nature of the Soviet threat. We then looked for the qualitative and quantitative evidence needed to support and validate these DOD conclusions.

The quantitative data came from a wide variety of data sources – about 250 major technical reports in all. We collected our qualitative data through interviews. We visited field sites, military commands and bases, as well as program offices. In addition to the special advisory board we constituted, we consulted military and civilian experts in a range of agencies, universities, and think tanks. In all, we did more than 200 extensive interviews.

To compare system costs across strategic program upgrades, our unit of analysis was the 30-year life-cycle (i.e., we included not just R&D and procurement, but also operations and support costs for every system). To compare system effectiveness, we used seven different measures: (1) survivability against both offensive and defensive threats, for both platforms and weapons (e.g., submarines or bombers and their missiles); (2) delivery system performance (i.e., accuracy, range and payload, which is the number of weapons carried by a single platform); (3) warhead yield and reliability (i.e., the probability that the warhead will detonate as intended); (4) weapon system reliability (i.e., the combined reliability of all the component processes, from platform launch to warhead detonation); (5) flexibility across a number of dimensions, including retargeting, recall, and impact on arms control; (6) communications (e.g., connectivity between command authority and platforms; and (7) responsiveness (i.e., alert rate and time-to-target).

In short, this was not a simple evaluation in its conception, in its execution, or in its logistics. In addition, its accountability character raised hackles at DOD. Still, we managed to study performance and cost within weapons systems, between existing weapons systems and their proposed upgrades, across weapons systems within a leg, and across legs, thanks to a stellar staff that included Kwai-Cheung Chan, Brett Haan, Rob Orwin, Jim Solomon, Jonathan Turnin, and Winslow Wheeler. All of us, I think, realized the importance of this evaluation and felt quite comfortable when the time came to set down our findings and conclusions.

Study Conclusions. Our first conclusion was that, on balance, the sea leg and its weapons systems emerged as the most cost-effective of the legs and systems. Second, the air leg continued to have a vital role in the triad context. Because strategic bombers are recallable (as missiles are not), and because they are virtually incapable of effecting a surprise attack, they add a critically important stabilizing character to the overall nuclear force. We also concluded that, within DOD, there was a troubling dearth of the comparative studies needed to show whether a proposed system is justified in terms of the threat it faces, its performance capabilities vis-à-vis other systems, and its relative costs.

From an accountability perspective, this evaluation was successful in many ways. It showed Members of Congress where cost savings could be achieved, if they wanted to make them, and it confirmed the quality of the sea leg's platforms and missiles. It justified the continued existence and modernization of the air leg. And it illuminated DOD's planning and program processes in such a way as to reveal major weaknesses in congressional oversight.

Indeed, within DOD, we found many instances of dubious support for claims of weapons systems' high performance; insufficient and often unrealistic testing; understated cost; incomplete or unrepresentative reporting; lack of systematic comparison of new systems against the systems they were to replace; and unconvincing rationales for their development in the first place. Where mature programs were concerned, on the other hand, we found that their performance was often understated and inappropriate claims of obsolescence were made.

The study was very difficult to carry out, which is hardly unusual in accountability studies. DOD resisted our efforts, and we often had to work with missing or sketchy or unconvincing data in critical areas of the evaluation. Nevertheless, the work clearly corresponds to the framers' vision of checks and balances and, especially, oversight and accountability. It corresponded less well, however, with their idea of providing information about the workings' of government to the citizenry.

Informing the People. Here we ran into trouble from two directions. First, DOD decided to classify all our reports in their

entirety (a departure from past experience where only partial classification had been the norm). This meant the whole evaluation would be inaccessible to the press and the public. Second, the study's sponsor, Chairman Fascell, announced his intention to retire from Congress at the end of the year, apparently signifying there would be no hearing either. So it seemed the triad evaluation would be publicly inaccessible. Of course, the Congress itself would be informed, since all members had access to the classified briefings arranged by the Committee on Foreign Affairs (Fascell, 1992a).

After three months of steady negotiation, DOD officials agreed to an unclassified summary statement, 15 pages long. This had the heavy burden of standing in for several thousand pages of text. We then published all of our reports in classified format (USGAO, 1992a–h) and sent Chairman Fascell the unclassified summary statement, which he published in the Congressional Record (Fascell, 1992b).

Press interest began slowly, mostly by specialized trade papers like *Defense Week* or *The Navy Times*. Coverage spread across the country over the next few months, with some serious debate and editorial commentary in the major newspapers. Then, out of the blue, I received a letter from Chairman John Glenn of the Senate Committee on Governmental Affairs, quoting extensively from our summary statement. He invited me to testify at a hearing the Committee wanted to prepare on our report (to look into the management of government and its effectiveness, rather than at strategic nuclear retaliatory systems).

When this hearing occurred, in June, it triggered a nationwide explosion of interest in our evaluation, for and against, in the best tradition of defense debate. From a public information viewpoint, it would be hard to imagine better coverage. However, the hearing also changed the way our study was perceived, to some degree, because its focus was on oversight and accountability issues rather than the policy and budgetary concerns that had inspired the evaluations. This did mean a new look at our data, and perhaps a slightly different presentation of the findings, but it distorted none of the findings and brought a richer public debate than would have occurred otherwise.

Two final points on the triad evaluation. First, despite the fact that DOD differed strenuously with us on many findings, the first Bush Administration's actions in fact mirrored some of the major recommendations in early drafts of our general summary report. To take but two of several examples, we questioned the need for either SICBM or Peacekeeper Rail Garrison: Both were cancelled by President Bush. We noticed that insufficient tests of the Minuteman IIs precluded any confidence in estimates of the missile's reliability: President Bush decommissioned the entire Minuteman II force. Second, by the time of Senator Glenn's hearing, the Clinton Administration had come to power, Les Aspin had replaced Dick Cheney, and Deputy Secretary of Defense William Perry testified along with me at the hearing. I was stunned to hear Perry say: "Now let me comment briefly on the GAO report. It is a very formidable, substantial undertaking, and it will be used – it is being used – as a very important input to our own planning of strategic forces. On balance, we think it is an excellent report, objectively done, and agree with most of the conclusions in the report" (Perry, 1993).

Drawing on the triad study and other experience, I conclude that accountability evaluations are not merely needed; they are absolutely essential for the effectiveness of congressional oversight. They can be performed, no matter how resistant the agency; and they may even, with help and luck, have extremely happy outcomes.

Development Studies

As I mentioned earlier, we often did developmental work in PEMD to help agencies strengthen their evaluation capabilities after one of our own studies showed that there were, say, technical skill areas or data problems that needed attention. In looking at how DOD assessed operational effectiveness using computer simulations, for example, we had observed problems in evaluating the credibility of results. So we developed a framework for use by DOD analysts to aid in assessing simulation strengths and weaknesses (USGAO, 1987a).

In the same way, a 1986 study sought to determine whether the construction grants program (on which $39 billion had been spent) was making improvements in the quality of the nation's waters. It turned up a staggering absence of effectiveness evaluations at EPA. We therefore undertook some developmental research to come up with guidelines that could help EPA determine whether the program was doing any good. Our method used only the data and software already available within EPA, and we not only developed the method but also tested it in case studies that measured the effects of upgrades in four wastewater treatment plants (USGAO, 1986a).

Having criticized the Department of Health and Human Services' process of initiating new rules for Medicare (in this case, the prospective payment system changes involving fixed per-case payments for diagnosis-related groups) without evaluating them, we developed for agency use a two-part evaluation plan for determining the effects of the prospective payment system on patients in post-hospital care (USGAO, 1986b). This effort began a close PEMD relationship with Senator John Heinz, Chairman of the Senate Special Committee on Aging, and started us on a continuing series of reports about the effectiveness of various medical treatments, processes and practices. In particular, this body of work, led by Lois-ellin Datta and supported by Senators John Heinz, George Mitchell, John Glenn, and David Pryor, helped bring about the creation in 1989 of the Agency for Health Care Policy and Research (now called the Agency for Health Quality Research), which has since made a distinguished contribution to the spread of effectiveness evaluations in medicine.

Another developmental endeavor of ours (begun in 1982, based on what we were coming to see as a basic need in some agencies) was the preparation of papers on evaluation methodology. These were essentially "how-to" reports, and they included volumes on evaluation design, questionnaire development, statistical sampling, structured interview techniques, quantitative data analysis, case study evaluation, and methods for synthesis research. Although we had designed these for agency use and published them with discretion, we were soon overwhelmed by requests for these papers, not only from agencies (both national and international), but also from universities here and abroad.

Finally, we put steady pressure: on agencies, to develop their evaluation capabilities and report on the effectiveness of their programs (USGAO, 1982, 1987b); on the Office of Management and Budget to demand strong evaluations from the agencies (USGAO, 1990); on individual congressional oversight committees, to insist on better evaluations from the agencies (USGAO, 1988a, 1991, 1993); and on the Congress as a whole to recognize the importance, for both legislative policy-making and oversight, of a thoughtful, vigorous, and courageous evaluation function in the executive branch (USGAO, 1988b, 1992i).

Overall, we spent considerable time and effort in PEMD doing development work, not just in pursuit of some abstract idea of general excellence in government, but because it was an integral part of every other kind of evaluation. More profoundly, perhaps, our experience with the triad study shows what a forceful tool accountability evaluations can be in opening agencies to public scrutiny. But sometimes force equates to overkill. Developmental evaluations act more softly to achieve transparency, and they encounter fewer obstacles to acceptance and use.

Knowledge Studies

Public policy evaluations also need to fulfill the Jeffersonian concept of bringing a better knowledge base to government. These kinds of evaluations not only examine the effects of programs, policies, and practices; they also assess their underlying assumptions, that is, those beliefs enshrined in the hearts and minds of officials and practitioners that may not stand up under examination. This testing of underlying assumptions turns out to be a very important part of knowledge evaluation. It is that component of skeptical observation Max Weber called *Entzauberung*, the demystification of dominant ideas and theories by means of empirical testing and analysis.

We did this kind of work often for congressional committees. In fact, a good example can be found in my testimony on the triad evaluation for Senator Glenn. A matrix at the end shows prevailing assumptions or beliefs about each of the triad legs (on issues like performance, vulnerability, and ease of communications) and compares them with the findings that emerged from a serious look at the data (Senate Committee on Governmental Affairs, 1993). Some studies, however, were entirely Weberian in nature. The one I discuss here is a 1987 evaluation (led by Richard Barnes and Roy Jones) which examined the idea that raising the minimum drinking age improves highway safety (USGAO, 1987c).

Evaluation of the Effects of Drinking Age Laws

In October, 1985, we received a letter from Congressman James Oberstar, Chairman of the Subcommittee on Oversight for the Committee on Public Works and Transportation. The Subcommittee wanted to know whether existing research supported the idea that raising minimum drinking-age laws improved highway safety. The Subcommittee noted "the frequency with which evaluations that are submitted for the record support opposing conclusions, even though they use similar data bases and assumptions" (USGAO, 1987c). This was a fascinating question, with an *Entzauberung* of its own, demolishing the hallowed belief that legislators are uninterested in research data and methods. The Subcommittee was actually asking us to tell them "what constitutes a 'good' evaluation."

The Policy Question. Of course, the Subcommittee came to us not only because they wanted to acquire knowledge, but also because they were in the middle of a political battle. This battle was part of a much longer war, with recent roots in the 1933 Repeal of Prohibition, but going back to the unresolved constitutional debate about state versus federal power. Repeal granted the states substantial power to regulate the purchase and possession of liquor, though The Highway Safety Act of 1966 returned some of that power to the federal government. Then, in the early 1970s, the 26th Amendment extended the right to vote to 18-year-olds, prompting 29 states to lower their minimum drinking age from 21 to 18.

By the 1980s, a documented increase in alcohol-related fatal crashes among younger drivers led to congressional enactment of the 1984 Uniform National Minimum Drinking-Age Law. This law included a controversial provision reducing the amount of federal highway aid to states that did not enact a legal minimum drinking age of 21. Although many states then passed "age 21" laws to avoid losing federal highway funds, others remained reluctant to do so. In September 1984, South Dakota brought suit against the Secretary of Transportation, asking that the Uniform National Drinking-Age Law be declared unconstitutional on the grounds that it violated states' rights. South Dakota also asserted there was no scientific evidence showing that raising the minimum age reduced alcohol-related traffic accidents. This lawsuit was being watched with passionate interest by lobbying groups on both sides of the issue. Many state legislatures, intensively jawboned by the liquor and restaurant lobbies and by college students, reportedly were planning again to repeal their age-21 laws.

This was the context in which we were asked to do our study. The policy question was "Does raising the minimum drinking age improve highway safety?" A corollary question was of equal policy importance: "How good is the research supporting each side of the issue?" The ability to distinguish a "good" evaluation from a "bad" one had taken on immense political significance.

The Evaluation Question, Methods, and Measures. We derived a number of evaluation questions from our discussions with the Subcommittee, but the main one was more or less the same as the policy question: Does raising the minimum drinking age result in a change in alcohol-related motor vehicle fatalities, injuries and crashes among the age group affected by the law? (Other questions related to effects on consumption, as well as displacement effects in other age groups.)

Given the large body of evaluation studies to be examined, we decided, in accord with the Subcommittee, to use the evaluation synthesis method, which had been one of the fruits of our development work (USGAO, 1983). The literature search uncovered 400 documents, of which 82 were evaluations of the effects of changing the minimum drinking age. Of these 82, 33 were directed at lowering the drinking age, leaving us with 49 evaluations as the basis for beginning our work.

We formed a review panel, including independent experts along with our staff, to develop rating criteria and review studies of direct relevance to the evaluation questions. The panel developed criteria for two generic types of studies: cross-sectional (comparing two or more defined groups at a single point in time) and pre–post (comparing groups at two or more points in time). We rated all studies in terms of five criteria: (1) the existence and adequacy of comparison groups; (2) the source data used; (3) the appropriateness and comparability of measures used; (4) the appropriateness of methods for taking chance into account; and (5) the extent to which a study controlled for other factors and provided quantitative measures of difference. For pre–post evaluations, we also looked for: (6) data that were comparable; and (7) controls for the non-independence of measures (autocorrelation, seasonality, and the like).

To assess the quality of the 49 evaluations, three raters reviewed each study independently, and then met to reconcile differences in individual ratings of "acceptable," "questionable," or "unacceptable." An unacceptable rating was typically given to evaluations failing to meet two or more criteria. Among the 49 studies, 28 thus dropped out, leaving us with 21 on which we based our findings. Every step in this process was carefully documented (because of past experience with a synthesis in which some evaluators were unhappy with our ratings).

Study Conclusions.   We finished our study in the summer of 1986. The most important conclusion was that raising the drinking age

does have direct, sizable effects on reducing traffic accidents among 18- to 20-year-olds, on average, across the states. We found statistically significant reductions ranging from 5% to 28% in "driver-fatal" crashes.

The Subcommittee held a hearing in September 1986, in which we were praised for our industry and grilled on our methodology (House Committee on Public Works and Transportation, 1986). Why did we throw out this evaluation or that one, for example, which found no effect? What is a cause-and-effect question and why do you need comparison groups to answer it? What are the advantages of cross-sectional versus time-series types of studies?

The four-hour hearing delved into questions of methodology and the foundations of conclusions to a degree I would never see again in any other hearing. Overall, the report was well received and the whole experience was positive in many ways: using a new method successfully, working well and easily with the Subcommittee, enduring little or no political pressure during the course of the work, answering a major policy question, and – critically important in this case – delivering the work on time. Also, with respect to disseminating the findings publicly, we turned out to be luckier than we could ever have imagined.

Informing the People.   The hearing, transmitted nationwide on television (C-Span broadcast it twice a day for more than a week), brought in a large response from viewers. But the debate was far from over. While we were doing our work, the South Dakota lawsuit was moving up to the Supreme Court calendar for the October term of 1986. When the Supreme Court issued its ruling in 1987, it went against South Dakota. Our congressional hearing of September 1986 was one of the "legislative materials" used by the Court, and our work was examined both for its conclusion on the effect of raising the minimum drinking age, and for its judgments about the methodological soundness of the various studies (Supreme Court of the United States, 1987).

The press and television coverage was extensive in every state. Editorials proliferated. As a result of the Supreme Court decision, by 1989 all 50 states had a minimum drinking age of 21. The Department of Transportation credited our evaluation with saving an estimated 1000 youthful lives in 1988, and a follow-on study of Tennessee showed a 38% decline in the death rate among 19- to 20-year-olds as a result of the legal increase in the drinking age (USGAO, 1989).

In summary, this knowledge evaluation fits well into the Jeffersonian vision of research as support for policy-making – though Jefferson probably would have been less than happy about the defeat handed to state sovereignty. Still, there is little doubt that the dissemination of information was exemplary. In this case, at least, the people knew what their government was doing.

Overall, the cumulative experience – not just with the illustrative cases presented above, but with accountability, development, and knowledge studies generally, as well as the evidence furnished by national symposia and by the international Vancouver conference – shows clearly that these different kinds of evaluations are all needed, and that together they derive legitimacy from their function of support to open democratic government. But to what degree is this experience transferable to countries with different types of government?

Issues of Generalizability

In considering whether these questions of form, function, and legitimacy are applicable to other nations, two issues appear germane:

- whether the nation is a democracy;
- if it is, whether its government is structured so as to oblige officials and politicians to tolerate dissent.

My own experience of evaluation in countries other than the US is not as extensive as I would wish, but what I have grasped – in working with NATO, the European Commission, the World Bank, and national audit offices of many authoritarian countries – is that non-democratic societies furnish sometimes insuperable obstacles to serious evaluation. This is largely because strong studies can threaten regimes. Evaluations showing improvement in the GDP or in the unemployment rate, for example, tend to strengthen the position of those in power; conversely, unfavorable conclusions may bring calls for change and/or reform. Where political controversies are the norm, this is merely a passing problem. But when there are no free newspapers, only a single political party, and a belief that citizens exist to serve the state (not vice versa), then calls for change and reform are usually unacceptable to those in power.

In one case (China, after the Hundred Flowers of 1958), the routine development of a statistical series brought down the agency that generated it. When critics of the new regime were able to point out that per capita income had undergone a long decline after the advent of the People's Republic in 1949, the carefully run State Statistical Bureau, which had developed both the data and their evaluation, fell into disfavor. For many years after 1958, aggregated data were not regularly produced in China (Chelimsky, 1977a; Chen & Galenson, 1969).

When I gave a talk in Beijing about evaluation practice (in December, 1988, under the auspices of the Chinese Auditor General, Lu Peijian), I was asked by one of the state planning economists present what I thought the chances were for developing a PEMD-like evaluation shop in China. I responded with another question: Could an evaluator really examine the short- and long-term effects of the single-child-per-family policy in China, without putting his or her freedom in jeopardy? Those seemed like pretty high stakes for evaluators. Yet, as we learned at the Vancouver conference, China is moving toward a national evaluation function.

Again, in Colombia (which was creating a legislatively mandated system of evaluation in 1991, when I spoke at their Santa Marta conference), I was startled to hear how Colombian justice officials planned to use evaluations: to prosecute and punish evaluators when ex-post results didn't square with ex-ante estimates. Such a mismatch, they claimed, showed the evaluators had "either cheated or made mistakes" in their analysis. In vain, I pointed out that this might create something of a chill in the evaluation profession if you could end up in jail for making an error in your cost-benefit calculations.

The truth is that authoritarian leaders don't, as a rule, think they have much to learn from research; the ability to express opinions or to publish is in short supply in their countries; and Machiavellian lion-and-fox tactics don't typically accommodate a lot of challenge from social scientists.

On the other hand, I have a more nuanced view today than I did in 1988. Thinking about the work in PEMD, I remember how much courage it took to pursue certain kinds of studies (like that of the nuclear triad). But would we really have wanted to tackle an evaluation of, say, the short- and long-term effects of Roe versus Wade (the Supreme Court decision that legalized abortion)? The ideological nature of the abortion debate and the consequent doubt that anyone could dispassionately examine the data from such an evaluation, make it unlikely that I would have recommended doing it. Still, if we had been

asked by the Congress, we would certainly have made an effort to find an entry into the issue that could have illuminated some part of the debate. But we were not asked, and that is the essential point here: Even in a democracy, some questions simply will not be posed. This may be because the legislature is intimidated by the executive, or because opinion is too evenly divided to make winning a political victory possible, or because a policy is so deeply entrenched that re-examining it seems like a waste of time and money, or because evaluating outcomes risks uncovering the shakiness of assumptions in some policies or programs and embarrassing the officials who believed in them, or for whatever reason.

But if this is true, then the extreme case – that is, the ability to do evaluations on the most highly sensitive of subjects – is not the best measure of the applicability of an evaluation function. After all, most evaluation situations are necessarily imperfect to some degree, given the unequal balance of power between researchers and politicians. So a better measure of applicability might be whether there is a clear recognition in government of the need to improve institutions, along with the will to do it. The goal of "better value for money," for example, is certainly a worthwhile accountability purpose, and has for many years inspired the evaluation of public policies and programs throughout the world. However, the more profound knowledge and accountability purposes of evaluation, with their essential characteristic of following wherever the evidence leads, are likely to be dangerous and difficult under authoritarian regimes. Further, when regimes consider themselves to be above the law, they feel no special compulsion to be accountable to the people.

In democracies, however, all evaluative things are possible, although they may not always materialize optimally. In France, for example, the Cour des Comptes (the French national audit agency) has done some excellent evaluations under the leadership of Pierre Joxe. I recall, in particular, a study presenting strong supporting data on the growing disparities between policy and practice in the management of France's highways (Cour des Comptes, 1992). Another impressive piece of work was an evaluation (performed under France's National Commission on Evaluation) of the RMI welfare program. RMI stands for "Revenu Minimum de l'Insertion," or the minimum income believed necessary to facilitate the integration of disadvantaged people into the society. This was a complex study seeking to measure not only what proportion of the real need had been addressed by the program (involving problems of identifying hidden populations, and of accounting for different concepts of need), but also to what degree improvements in integration had occurred, as viewed by the program's clients (Commission Nationale d'Evaluation, 1992).

Although the capacity and courage certainly exists in France for performing high-quality evaluations, there is a political problem that restricts the number and funding of evaluations likely to be done. That is the weakness of France's legislature. Power, largely centralized in Paris, has always resided preponderantly in the executive. Vigorous parliamentary oversight of government initiatives, never a very realistic possibility, was diminished even further by the French constitutional changes of 1958. However, the Cour des Comptes, with its considerable independence and its power to plan its own evaluations, can usually be counted on to do the kinds of studies needed to serve democratic government in France.

In Switzerland, a similar capacity exists, but again a political problem slows the development of the evaluation function: the extraordinarily lengthy process that precedes the implementation of government initiatives.

Because of the division of powers between the individual cantons and the Swiss Confederation, debate may take many years to be sufficiently resolved to permit legislation. As a result, when a policy or program is finally agreed to and put in practice, it may be almost impossible, politically, to pose serious questions about actual outcomes and effectiveness.

In the United Kingdom, evaluators not only have a strong evaluation capability, but also political institutions that have supported and facilitated the development of national models to assess government services and performance. Mawhood (1997) described the large-scale efforts of the "new public management" to examine programs and services by "setting specific output measures, performance indicators and targets," using these to evaluate achievements, and then following up, year after year. In Australia, a reasonably workable system has been established that links evaluation to the budget process (something we tried for many years to do in the US, without success). And Canada has developed a multi-pronged evaluation function which has much in common with that of the US.

Finally, the World Bank (under the evaluative leadership, first, of Mervyn Wiener, and later of Yves Rovani and Robert Picciotto) has promulgated a policy of evaluation for institutional improvement among all its nation-members, which makes very good sense as an evaluative common denominator in democratic and non-democratic governments alike. Also, the European Commission, the International Atomic Energy Agency (whose evaluation function used to be headed by David Kay), the International Monetary Fund, and many international foundations have adopted sound principles in evaluation design and practice, and have produced some thoughtful and courageous studies.

It seems reasonable to believe, then, that the evaluative work we did in PEMD – in support of knowledge, oversight, agency development, and public information – is largely generalizable to other democratic countries, when there is a national appetite to learn about what the government is doing, and when evaluators can count on adequate independence and protection for their work. In non-democratic societies, however, the evaluative menu is more likely to be restricted to "value for money" studies and institutional improvement, rather than knowledge and accountability evaluations that question the true bases for policies and programs. Still, the important point is that at least some useful evaluations can be done almost anywhere in the world. Indeed, the Vancouver conference gives tangible evidence that this has already begun to happen.

A Final Thought on Change and the Political Climate for Evaluation

In the United States, we continue to live under the same carefully balanced, 200+-year-old government which evaluation serves in so many ways. Quite a few things have changed in our thinking, but that balance still prevails. Other things that are important to evaluation have not changed at all, and this is as true internationally as it is in America. Evaluators still face closed administrations, and the more difficult it is to deal with agency walls and secrecy, the more important it is to do so, because people still need to know about the inner workings of their government. The war among different public sectors rages on (in varying degrees and distributions, of course), but the sectors also work together when the focus of their battle shifts, and this furnishes opportunities for evaluators (as we saw in our evaluation of drinking-age laws). Ineffective policies and programs continue to be implemented, poorly tested assumptions didn't die with the War on Poverty, and wasteful

spending is always with us, so the playing field for evaluation widens each day.

Yet evaluation is a fragile reed to send up against all those giant oaks – against entire agencies sometimes, as happened in our nuclear triad study – and evaluators need to be ingenious, lucky, and much better protected than they currently are if they are to survive in any government. Alas, we make a lot of enemies, although we try hard not to, and our bosses sometimes prefer being "part of the team" to defending the independence of evaluators and their often unwelcome and inconvenient findings.

Nevertheless, for most agencies, for legislatures, and for citizens everywhere, evaluation is a pretty good bargain, accomplishing a remarkable amount with just a few people. We help to keep a healthy balance of power across sectors and agencies. We improve the government's products and services. We hold down expenditures (in Fiscal Year 1992, for example, GAO's work saved taxpayers more than $36 billion). And, with the aid of the press, we tell the public the results of government initiatives.

It goes without saying that evaluators don't do all that alone. In democratic societies, we can count on institutions, like a determined legislature, service-oriented agencies, and a knowledgeable, persevering, imperturbable press. But we count even more on a watchful population that, in and of itself, creates the right climate for evaluation.

Some have expressed concern today about public distrust of government. This is seen as a very bad thing in France and Germany as well as in the United Kingdom and the US. Polls have shown, for example, that the American electorate is disenchanted with politics and politicians, and that citizen confidence in government is low. But there is nothing new about this, as we realize from reading Dickens' *American Notes* of 1842: "One great blemish," he wrote, "in the popular mind of America, and the prolific parent of an innumerable brood of evils, is Universal Distrust. Yet the American citizen plumes himself upon this spirit, even when he is sufficiently dispassionate to perceive the ruin it works, and will often adduce it . . . as an instance of the great sagacity and acuteness of the people, and their superior shrewdness and independence."

What Dickens discounted, however, in his irritation with "universal distrust" is that it was precisely this distrust on which the American framers relied to control the excesses of "unseen rulers in distant places." And it was this same distrust which brought to the British their Magna Carta and 1689 Bill of Rights, to the French, their Declaration of the Rights of Man, and to the US, its government of checks and balances. It is distrust, once again, that generates the deepest constituency for evaluation. After all, a trusting population is not likely to ask searching questions about cozy arrangements, wasted resources, or data-free policies in government.

Put another way, public distrust is, by its function and modalities, a positive, not a negative element in a democratic society. In that larger sense, the search for political balance and open government makes evaluators of us all.

References

Bolling, R. (1978). In *Proceedings of a Three-day Workshop on Congressional Oversight*, US House of Representatives, pp. 29–30.

Bradshaw, K. & Pring, D. (1981). *Parliament and Congress*. London: Quartet Books, pp. 479, 358.

Brock, B. (1975). In Chelimsky, E., Program evaluation and appropriate governmental change. *Annals, American Academy of Political Science*, 466 (March 1983), 106.

Bronowski, J. & Mazlish, B. (1993). *The Western Intellectual Tradition*, Barnes and Noble, p. 390.

Chelimsky, E. (1977a). The need for better data. *Evaluation Quarterly*, 1(3), 439–440.

Chelimsky, E. (1977b). *Proceedings of a Symposium on the Use of Evaluation by Federal Agencies*, Vols. I and II, MITRE Corp., VA.

Chelimsky, E. (1978). Differing perspectives of evaluation. *New Directions for Program Evaluation*, No. 2, 1–18.

Chelimsky, E. (1985). Budget cuts, data and evaluation. *Society*, 22(3), 67.

Chelimsky, E. (1996). Thoughts for a new evaluation society. *Evaluation*, 3(1), 97–109.

Chelimsky, E. & Shadish, W. R., Jr. (1997). *Evaluation for the 21st Century*. Sage Publications, pp. 10–18.

Chen, N. R. & Galenson, W. (1969). *The Chinese Economy Under Communism 1969*. Aldine Publishing Co, pp. 159–161.

Commission Nationale d'Evaluation (1992). *RMI: Le Pari de l'Insertion* (2 volumes). Paris: La Documentation Francaise.

Cour des Comptes (1992). La Politique Routiere et Autoroutiere, Evaluation de la Gestion du Reseau National (Report to the President of the Republic, May 1992).

Ellis, J. J. (2002). *Founding Brothers: The revolutionary generation*. Random House, Vintage Books, pp. 7, 9, 15, 16.

Fascell, D. B. (1992a). *Congressional Record*, July 21, p. E2179.

Fascell, D. B. (1992b). *Congressional Record*, September 29, pp. H9861–9864.

Hamilton, A. (1788). The Federalist, No. 84: On a bill of rights and freedom of the press." *Selected Federalist Papers*, Dover Publications, 2001, pp. 199–200.

Hicks, J., Mowry, G., & Burke, R. (1964). *The Federal Union*. Houghton Mifflin, p. 314.

House Committee on Public Works and Transportation (1986). Hearing Before the Subcommittee on Oversight, The National Minimum Drinking Age Law, USGPO, pp. 1–40.

Jefferson, T. (1946). *Thomas Jefferson on Democracy* (ed. S. K. Padover). Mentor Books, New American Library, pp. 44, 89, 90, 92–97.

Jewell. M. E. & Patterson, S. C. (1966). *The Legislative Process in the United States*. Random House, p. 131.

Madison, J. (1788). The Federalist No. 51: The structure of the government must furnish the proper checks and balances between the different departments. *Selected Federalist Papers*. Dover Publications, 2001, pp. 120–122.

Mawhood, C. (1997). Performance measurement in the United Kingdom, 1985–1995. In E. Chelimsky & W. R. Shadish, Jr. (eds) *Evaluation for the 21st Century*. Sage, pp. 134–144.

Moynihan, D. P. (1969). *Maximum Feasible Misunderstanding*. The Free Press, MacMillan Company, p. 170.

Patton, M. Q. (1996). *A world larger than formative and summative. Evaluation Practice*, 17(2), 132–142.

Perry, W. (1993). Evaluation of the U.S. strategic nuclear triad. Hearing Before the Committee on Governmental Affairs, U.S. Senate, June 10, USGPO, p. 16.

Rhoads, S. E. (1978). Economists and policy analysis. *Public Administration Review*, March/April, p. 114.

Rossi, P. H. & Freeman, H. E. (1985). *Evaluation: A systematic approach*, third edition. Sage Publications, pp. 321–356.

Senate Committee on Governmental Affairs (1993). Hearing on the Evaluation of the U.S. Strategic Nuclear Triad Testimony of Eleanor Chelimsky, USGPO, pp. 39–48.

Supreme Court of the United States (1987). The State of South Dakota Versus The Honorable Elizabeth H. Dole, Secretary, U.S. Department of Transportation, March 16.

USGAO (1982). A Profile of Federal Program Evaluation Activities (GAO/IPE, Special Study I, September).

USGAO (1983). The Evaluation Synthesis (GAO/PEMD-10.1.2, Revised March 1992).

USGAO (1986a). Water Quality: An Evaluation Method for the Construction Grants Program Vol. I, Methodology, Vol. II, Case Studies (GAO/PEMD-87-4B).

USGAO (1986b). Post-Hospital Care: Efforts to Evaluate Medicare Prospective Payment Effects Are Insufficient (GAO/PEMD-86-10).

USGAO (1987a). DOD Simulations: Improved Assessment Procedures Would Increase the Credibility of Results (GAO/PEMD-88-3).

USGAO (1987b). Federal Evaluation: Fewer Units, Reduced Resources, Different Studies from 1980 (GAO/PEMD-87-9).

USGAO (1987c). Drinking Age Laws: An Evaluation Synthesis of Their Impact on Highway Safety (GAO/PEMD-87-10).

USGAO (1988a). Children's Programs: A Comparative Evaluation Frame work and Five Illustrations (GAO/PEMD-88-28BR).

USGAO (1988b). Program Evaluation Issues (GAO/OCG-89-8TR).

USGAO (1989). *GAO Management News*, 16(36).

USGAO (1990). Improving Program Evaluation in the Executive Branch: What OMB Could Do (GAO/PEMD-90-19).

USGAO (1991). Child Support Enforcement: A Framework for Evaluating Costs, Benefits and Effects (GAO/PEMD-91-6).

USGAO (1992a). U.S. Strategic Triad: Vulnerability of Strategic Ballistic Missile Nuclear Submarines (C-GAO/PEMD-92-1).

USGAO (1992b). U.S. Strategic Triad: ICBM Vulnerability (C-GAO/PEMD-92-2).

USGAO (1992c). U.S. Strategic Triad: A Comparison of ICBMs and SLBMs (C-GAO/PEMD-92-3).

USGAO (1992d). U.S. Strategic Triad; Modernizing Strategic Bombers and Their Missiles (C-GAO/PEMD-92-4).

USGAO (1992e). U.S. Strategic Triad: Strategic Relocatable Targets (C-GAO/PEMD-92-5).

USGAO (1992f). U.S. Strategic Triad: Costs and Uncertainties of Proposed Upgrades (C-GAO/PEMD-92-6).

USGAO (1992g). U.S. Strategic Triad: Current Status, Modernization Plans and Doctrine of British and French Nuclear Forces (C-GAO/PEMD-92-7).

USGAO (1992h). U.S. Strategic Triad: Final Report and Recommendations (C-GAO/PEMD-92-8).

USGAO (1992i). Program Evaluation Issues (GAO/OCG-93-6TR).

USGAO (1993). Public Health Service: Evaluation Set-Aside Has Not Realized Its Potential to Inform the Congress (GAO/PEMD-93-13).

Wholey, J. S. (1997). Trends in performance measurement: challenges for evaluators. In E. Chelimsky & W. R. Shadish, Jr. (eds) *Evaluation for the 21st Century*. Sage Publications, p. 128.

2

ROLES FOR THEORY IN CONTEMPORARY EVALUATION PRACTICE: DEVELOPING PRACTICAL KNOWLEDGE

Stewart I. Donaldson and Mark W. Lipsey

Relative to many professions, evaluation has a brief but interesting history. Evaluation scholars often note the work of Ralph Tyler and his "Eight Year Study" of progressive education in the 1940s as one of the first landmarks in the development of the modern profession and discipline of evaluation (see, e.g., Alkin, 2004a). However, the first major boom in evaluation seemed to occur in the United States in late 1960s and 70s under the Kennedy and Johnson Administrations, when social programs were developed on a grand scale and heavily supported by federal funding under the policies of the "War on Poverty" and the "Great Society" (Rossi, Lipsey, & Freeman, 2004). Many of our most sophisticated experimental methods, quasi-experimental designs, and data analytic techniques for generalized causal inference were developed in response to the challenges of determining the net impact of these and subsequent large-scale government social programs and policies (Shadish, Cook, & Campbell, 2001).

Donaldson & Scriven (2003a) noted that we are now experiencing what could be called the "Second Boom in Evaluation," which is more global and has notably different characteristics than our first growth spurt. For example, in the past decade, we have witnessed societies all around the world embracing the values of accountability and professionalism. This has led organizations and agencies of all shapes and sizes to commission professional evaluations at a dramatically increasing rate. While these evaluations still include federally funded and other types of program and policy evaluations, interest in evaluating non-governmental programs, personnel, proposals, performance, technology, research, theory, and even evaluation itself fall under the growing domain of contemporary evaluation practice (American Evaluation Association, 2005). One indicator of the increasing demand for evaluation practice is the number of professionals now participating as members of organized evaluation associations and societies. In 1990, there were approximately five major evaluation professional associations, whereas today there are more than 50 worldwide (see Donaldson & Christie, 2006; Mertens, 2003), as well as an international alliance to link them together to share knowledge about how to improve the practice of evaluation (Mertens, 2005; Russon, 2004).

Another characteristic of the second boom is that new theories of evaluation practice, new evaluation methods, and new evaluation tools are being developed and refined to address a much broader and diverse range of evaluation practice challenges. Donaldson & Christie (2006) and Scriven (2003) describe some of these new challenges under the rubric of evaluation as a "transdiscipline" that supplies essential tools and techniques for a wide range of other disciplines, while retaining an autonomous research effort of its own, focused on advancing knowledge about how best to practice evaluation.

General organizing frameworks have been called for, and are beginning to emerge, as a way to recognize the new challenges faced by evaluators today (Mark, 2003). Mark, Henry, & Julnes (2000) provided a framework to guide the evaluation of programs and policies aimed at promoting social betterment. They proposed that four main evaluation purposes have now evolved in the program and policy evaluation domain:

1. Program and organizational improvement;
2. Oversight and compliance;
3. Assessment of merit and worth;
4. Knowledge development.

Keeping these purposes in mind, we will attempt to address in this chapter new and emerging roles for theory in "second boom" program evaluation practice. We will pay particularly close attention to those parts of the practice of evaluation that aspire to contribute to social programming and policy-making *by contributing to the knowledge and theoretical base* – in large part by using, developing, testing, or otherwise enhancing relevant theory.

Theory for Evaluation Practice

Reference to theory is widespread in the contemporary evaluation literature, but what is meant by "theory" encompasses a confusing mix of concepts related to evaluators' notions about how evaluation should be practiced, explanatory frameworks for social phenomena drawn from social science, and assumptions about how programs function or are supposed to function. A newcomer to evaluation, and even a grizzled veteran, could have a difficult time sorting through the closely related and sometimes interchangeable terms that litter the evaluation landscape – theories of practice, theory-based evaluation, theory-driven evaluation, program theory, evaluation theory, theory of change, logic models, and the like.

Aside from considerable potential for confusion, the nature and role of theory in evaluation is often a contentious matter. On the one hand, such distinguished evaluators as Scriven (1998, 2004a, 2004b) and Stufflebeam (2001, 2004) have asserted that there is little need for theory or, at least, some forms of theory, in evaluation. Scriven (2004a, 2004b), for instance, claimed "it's possible to do very good program evaluation without getting into evaluation theory or program theory," and declared that "the most popular misconception amongst currently politically correct program evaluators is the evaluation of a program (a) requires that you have, or (b) is much benefited by having, a logic model or program theory." Similarly, Stufflebeam (2001), in a review of evaluation models and theories of evaluation practice, remarked that "there really is not much to recommend theory-based evaluation, since doing it right is usually not feasible and since failed or misrepresented attempts can be counterproductive." More recently, Stufflebeam (2004) described the "now fashionable advocacy of 'theory-based evaluation'" as a situation

> . . . wherein one assumes that the complexity of variables and interactions involved in running a project in the complicated, sometimes chaotic conditions of the real world can be worked out and used a priori to determine the pertinent evaluation questions and variables . . . . Braybrooke & Lindblom (1963) discredited this notion 40 years ago, and their message clearly needs to be revisited. (p. 253)

In contrast, other eminent evaluators have argued that program theory, evaluation theory, and social science theory all do, and should, play important roles in modern program evaluation (e.g., Alkin, 2004a; Chen, 1990; Donaldson, 2003; Fetterman, 2003; Lipsey, 1990; Mark, 2003; Rossi et al., 2004; Shadish, Cook, & Campbell, 2004; Weiss, 2004a, 2004b). For example, in the case of evaluation theory, Shadish (1998) introduced his presidential address to the American Evaluation Association, entitled "Evaluation Theory Is Who We Are," with the following assertion:

> All evaluators should know evaluation theory because it is central to our professional identity.

It is what we talk about more than anything else, it seems to give rise to our most trenchant debates, it gives us the language we use for talking to ourselves and others, and perhaps most important, it is what makes us different from other professions. Especially in the latter regards, it is in our own self-interest to be explicit about this message, and to make evaluation theory the very core of our identity. Every profession needs a unique knowledge base. For us, evaluation theory is that knowledge base. (Shadish, 1998, p. 1)

One purpose of this chapter is to attempt to sort out some of the different meanings of theory in evaluation and the utility the different forms of theory might have for evaluation practice. This will be done in service of the larger purpose of discussing evaluation work that is carried out in an effort to generate knowledge and theory for program practice and policy-making. We will first distinguish the three most common types of theories encountered in evaluation – evaluation theory, social science theory, and program theory – and discuss their respective roles and limitations. We will then describe one way in which these different forms of theory intersect that defines a widespread and, we believe, especially fruitful approach to evaluation – where the theory of evaluation involves integration of social science theory in the development and use of program theory to guide evaluation practice and expand knowledge about how programs bring about social change. We suggest that, while both program theory and social science theory can enhance program planning and evaluation, the cause of knowledge development as a pathway to evaluation influence is particularly likely when both kinds of theory are integrated. Finally, we conclude the chapter by considering the implications of that perspective for the future of evaluation.

Evaluation Theory

Chen (1990) described theory as a frame of reference that helps humans understand their world and how to function within it. In program evaluation, he emphasized that it is important to distinguish between descriptive and prescriptive theories. Simply stated, descriptive theories characterize what is and prescriptive theories articulate what should be. *Evaluation theories* are largely prescriptive and "offer a set of rules, prescriptions, prohibitions, and guiding frameworks that specify what a good or proper evaluation is and how evaluation should be done" (Alkin, 2004a). They are thus theories of evaluation practice that address such enduring themes as how to understand the nature of what we evaluate, how to assign value to programs and their performance, how to construct knowledge, and how to use the knowledge generated by evaluation (Shadish, 1998).

In one sense, evaluation theories are less important than social science theories or program theories for a discussion of knowledge development as a purpose of evaluation. In another sense, evaluation theory is quite important in this regard: Contemporary evaluation theories differ in terms of their views of the appropriateness of and their emphasis on the four main purposes of evaluation. In particular, evaluation theories disagree about whether, and to what extent, priority should be given to theory building and testing, and more generally, to knowledge development, as a pathway to improving programs and policies. For this reason, and because our discussion of theory would be incomplete without some attention to evaluation theory, we give some attention to it in this chapter.

The Evolution of Evaluation Theory

Shadish, Cook, & Leviton (1991) characterized the history of theories of evaluation as a series of stages. Stage I theories emphasized the discovery of truth (e.g., the evaluation theories of Michael Scriven and Donald Campbell). Stage II focused on the way evaluation was used and its social utility (e.g., the theories of Joseph Wholey, Robert Stake, and Carol Weiss). In Stage III, theory development addressed the integration of inquiry and utility (e.g., the theories of Lee Cronbach and Peter Rossi).

It is only fitting that evaluation theories themselves be evaluated, and there is no shortage of critique in the writings and discussions among evaluators. The criteria Shadish et al., used specified that a good theory of evaluation practice should give a full account of the appropriate principles and practices relating to:

1. Knowledge: What methods to use to produce credible knowledge;

2. Use: How to use knowledge about social programs;

3. Valuing: How to construct value judgments;

4. Practice: How evaluators should practice in "real world" settings;

5. Social programming: The nature of social programs and their role in social problem solving.

In their final evaluation of these theories of evaluation practice, Shadish et al., (1991) concluded that only the Stage III integrative theories addressed all five criteria. However, they recognized the contributions of many perspectives to the evolution of theories of practice and argued that evaluators should not follow the same evaluation procedures under all conditions.

While the Shadish et al., framework has been widely cited and used to organize theories of evaluation practice for over a decade, it is controversial in a number of ways. Whatever

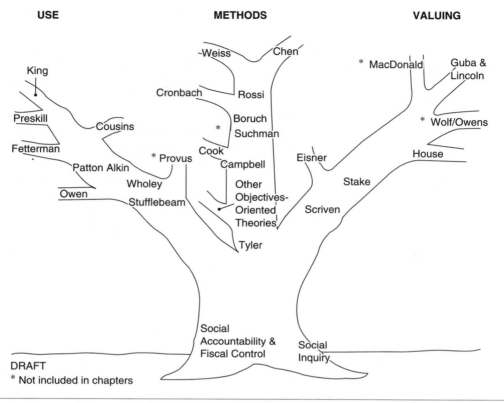

USE · METHODS · VALUING

Weiss · Chen · * MacDonald · Guba & Lincoln
King
Cronbach · Rossi
Preskill · Cousins · Boruch · * Suchman · * Wolf/Owens
Fetterman · Cook
Patton Alkin · * Provus · Campbell · Eisner · House
Wholey · Other · Stake
Owen · Stufflebeam · Objectives-Oriented Theories · Scriven
Tyler

Social Accountability & Fiscal Control · Social Inquiry

DRAFT
* Not included in chapters

Figure 2.1 Evaluation theory tree (Alkin, 2004).

criticisms the theorists evaluated, omitted, and their respective followers might have, however, it provides one of the most fully developed perspectives available on the nature of evaluation theory.

In a more recent attempt to trace the roots of modern theories of evaluation practice, Alkin & Christie (2004) developed a different scheme for classifying evaluation theories (see Figure 2.1). Their "Evaluation Theory Tree" has a trunk built on the dual foundation of accountability and social inquiry and branches of use, methods, and valuing. They placed 26 evaluation theorists on this tree and then gave them an opportunity to reflect on their theory of practice and to suggest

revisions to their classification. The resulting scheme promises to help evaluators understand fundamental differences and points of connection between some of the most common theories of evaluation practice, as well as illustrate how theorists' views change over time in light of experiences from evaluation practice. This process of reflection also underscores the point that the originators of ideas, evaluation theorists in this case, often disagree with how others interpret, describe, or classify their original works. This very different approach for understanding the history of evaluation provides a unique window on the development of the discipline and profession of evaluation.

The Role of Evaluation Theory

Many of those participating in evaluation do so within the confines of one theory of practice, often a general social science research paradigm, without much apparent reflection or concern about the underpinnings of that theory or the challenges posed by competing theories. Shadish (1998) provided at least six reasons why practicing evaluators should be thoughtful about evaluation theory:

- Evaluation theory provides a language that evaluators can use to talk with each other about evaluation;
- Evaluation theory encompasses many things in our field about which evaluators seem to care most deeply;
- Evaluation theory defines the themes of the majority of evaluation professional conferences;
- Evaluation theory provides evaluators with an identity that is different from the identity of other professionals.
- Evaluation theory provides the face that evaluators present to the outside world;
- Evaluation theory is the knowledge base that defines the profession.

Taken together, these points suggest that evaluation theory has become a central thread in the social fabric of the evaluation profession. Evaluation theory can facilitate communication amongst evaluators practicing across the globe, help evaluation practitioners understand and share best practices, and provide the rationale for the various procedures evaluators recommend and use in practice.

Knowledge of evaluation theory can also help evaluators become better ambassadors for the profession of evaluation and educators of potential clients. Because professional evaluation now offers a range of acceptable approaches and perspectives, it is critical that sponsors and users understand that there are variations and how they differ. Evaluation approaches and services may differ rather dramatically across evaluation teams. Finding an optimal fit between an evaluation team and the needs and interests of evaluation sponsors and stakeholders could arguably be one the most important factors in determining whether an evaluation will ultimately be useful (Donaldson, 2004).

In general, effective evaluation practice has the potential to help prospective clients and other stakeholders dramatically improve their work. For example, professional evaluation can help stakeholders make better decisions about service, policy, and organizational direction; build knowledge and skills, and develop a capacity for evaluative thinking; facilitate continuous quality improvement and organizational learning; and provide accountability or justify a program, policy, or organization's value to investors, volunteers, staff, and prospective funders.

Beyond the general benefits of evaluation, however, is the question of how appropriate a particular evaluation is for a particular program at a particular time. It is important to consider who could be negatively affected by an evaluation of a given sort, how much time and resources may be taken away from program services while the evaluation is being conducted, and the ways in which the evaluation process might be uncomfortable and disruptive for some project team members and other stakeholders (Donaldson, 2001b; Donaldson, Gooler, & Scriven, 2002). It must also be recognized that the questions a particular evaluation asks and the way in which it goes about answering those questions will have repercussions that will not always be constructive. When evaluators and stakeholders fully explore the potential benefits and costs of doing a specific evaluation and consider other options and approaches (based on other theories of practice), their expectations and plans become more realistic and the evaluation is much more likely to reach its potential (see Donaldson, 2001b).

Finally, evaluations are subject to critique, meta-evaluation, and even hostile attacks (most likely when negative findings surface – the "kill the messenger" phenomenon; Donaldson et al., 2002). Knowledge of evaluation theory can help evaluators better understand reactions to their work and help them defend against critics making different assumptions about evaluation design or unfairly using a fundamentally different theory of practice to discredit the work.

Of course, being knowledgeable about the history and "state of the art" of evaluation theory does not guarantee successful evaluation practice. Some theories of practice may not be effective or may even be harmful in certain circumstances. Moreover, every theory of practice is likely to be more effective in some settings than in others. Recognizing boundary conditions for the role of any one evaluation theory, and for the use of evaluation theories in general, is essential for good practice (Mark, 2003). In the end, logically consistent guiding frameworks for evaluation practice that are sensitive to the mainstream principles and standards in the field (e.g., American Evaluation Association, 2005; Joint Committee on Standards for Educational Evaluation, 1994) should play an important role in contemporary evaluation practice.

Social Science Theory

Social science theories are not especially concerned with methods or practices for evaluators. Rather, *social science theories* attempt to provide generalizable and verifiable knowledge about the principles that shape social behavior. When such theories address the social phenomena related to social programs and the social conditions they are intended to improve, however, they may be very relevant to evaluation.

Evidenced-based social science theories are often helpful for understanding the etiology of desired or undesired outcomes and for developing intervention strategies for influencing those outcomes. For example, social cognitive learning theory has been used effectively to design programs to promote positive social norms to prevent alcohol and drug use, risky sexual behavior, breast cancer, and a range of other social and behavioral problems (Bandura, 2006; Donaldson, Graham, & Hansen, 1994; Petraitis, Flay, & Miller, 1995). Indeed, many such social science theories have been, or might be, used for designing, improving, and evaluating programs: the theory of planned behavior (Ajzen, 2002; Bamberg & Schmidt, 1997), Prochaska & DiClemente's (1999) theory of health behavior change, Kram's (1985) theory of mentoring, Sternberg's (2003) theories of practical intelligence and leadership, theories of re-employment training (Price, van Ryn, & Vinokur, 1992), theories of learned helplessness (Seligman, 2003), and Rosenthal's (2006) theory of interpersonal expectations and self-fulfilling prophecies, just to name a few.

While it is true that the conceptual and empirical evidence base is sometimes thin for any given problem, we would argue it is misguided for evaluators to ignore potentially applicable prior research and empirically based social science theory when it is available (as has been suggested by, e.g., Scriven, 1998, 2004a, 2004b, and Stufflebeam, 2001, 2004).

The Role of Social Science Theory

Social science theory can play several important roles in evaluation practice. First, such theory and prior research can be very informative for initial needs assessment and program design. Many, if not most, social problems have been encountered by others, and sometimes research or evaluation exists on efforts to prevent or solve these problems. A careful examination of available literature, including primary studies, as well as syntheses such as meta-analyses, may turn up knowledge about effective strategies for dealing with the problems of concern, or just as important (and probably more likely), lessons learned about what does not work, which may save program designers and evaluators countless hours and resources. "Operating within a vacuum," when useful information exists, can be a very inefficient way to practice evaluation.

Another important role for social science theory and research is to help evaluators assess the likelihood that programs will be able to accomplish certain objectives. It is not uncommon to find stakeholders who have very unrealistic aspirations for their program, given what is known about the desired outcomes from prior research and evaluation. Such stakeholders might be best helped by a focus on program improvement rather than, say, a full-scale evaluation for outcomes they have little chance to produce. In other circumstances, stakeholders may believe there is something significantly different about their program, target population, and/or context relative to those evaluated previously. In this case, outcome evaluation might proceed, but findings from previous work could suggest important contextual or moderating factors to measure and include in the analyses (Donaldson, 2001a).

Finally, social science theory and research are sometimes useful for guiding evaluation measurement and design decisions, and can provide a context for interpreting evaluation findings. For example, it is sometimes possible to locate relevant and valid measures of constructs of interest or feasible designs that have lead to unequivocal findings, as well as measures and designs that are not likely to lead to valid results in your work. Previous theory and research can also provide a context, or suggest expectations for the range of effect sizes evaluators should expect. Estimated effect sizes in the current evaluation can be compared to previous findings in an effort to further explore the relative practical significance of the program under investigation (Donaldson et al., 2001; Lipsey, 1990).

One of the notable boundary conditions that must be acknowledged when using social science theory and research in evaluation practice is the limit of generalizability. Oftentimes the characteristics of previous research and evaluation are, to various degrees, different than those in the current investigation. It is very important not to assume, without serious critical reflection, that the results from previous work will necessarily generalize to the current application. Some evaluation theorists have suggested that evaluators should be much more concerned about producing local knowledge than concerning themselves with producing generalizable knowledge (e.g., Alkin, 2004b; Stake, 2004). While we agree with this prescription to a certain degree (i.e., it is important to meet contractual obligations and local needs first), examining local findings in relation to social science theory and research can be beneficial both for interpreting current findings and in adding to the knowledge base of how to prevent or solve societal problems more generally.

Scarcity of quality work is another common limitation encountered when trying to use social science theory and research in evaluation practice. That is, many areas of programming simply do not have much sound social science theory and research to draw upon. While somewhat related work might exist, it is important to be extremely careful not to overuse or generalize findings and lessons learned from only remotely similar efforts. However, testing the generalizability limits of related existing theory is another potential substantive benefit of incorporating social science theory in programs and their evaluation. As the discipline and profession of evaluation mature, our cumulative knowledge base in this area should expand and the scarcity problem is likely to be less common (Weiss, 2004b).

Program Theory

While evaluation theory is concerned with how to practice evaluation, *program theory* focuses on the nature of the evaluand itself (i.e., the program, treatment, intervention, policy, etc. being evaluated). Program theory should not be confused with social science theory, nor should it conjure up images of broad concepts about the nature of social problems (Donaldson, 2003; Weiss, 1997). Program theory is much more modest and deals with the assumptions that guide the way specific programs, treatments, or interventions are implemented and expected to bring about change (Donaldson, 2001b; Lipsey, 1993). The following definitions of program theory capture the essence of how program theory is typically defined in evaluation practice today:

- The construction of a plausible and sensible model of how a program is supposed to work (Bickman, 1987).
- A set of propositions regarding what goes on in the black box during the transformation of input to output, that is, how a bad situation is transformed into a better one through treatment inputs (Lipsey, 1993).
- The process through which program components are presumed to affect outcomes and the conditions under which these processes are believed to operate (Donaldson, 2001b).

Rossi et al., (2004) describe program theory as consisting of three main components:

1. *The organizational plan*: How to garner, configure, and deploy resources, and how to organize program activities so that the intended service delivery system is developed and maintained.

2. *The service utilization plan*: How the intended target population receives the intended amount of the intended intervention through interaction with the program's service delivery system.

3. *The impact theory*: How the intended intervention for the specified target population brings about the desired social benefits.

The organizational and service utilization plans together constitute the *program process theory* and the impact component is referred to as *program impact theory* (see Figure 2.2). This form of practical program theory is often referred to as the "program logic" and various logic modeling techniques and ways of depicting program logic have become commonplace in evaluation practice (Funnel, 1997; Gargani, 2003).

Program process theory must usually be developed from information that comes almost entirely from the program and its immediate context. Program impact theory, with its focus on the nature of the social, psychological, or behavioral change a program intends to bring about, however, may be informed by social science theory. This is a desirable circumstance; program impact theory gains plausibility if it is rooted in, or at least consistent with, behavioral or social science theory or prior research (Donaldson et al., 2001). Unfortunately, sound theory and research are not often available for the social problem of concern. The development of program impact theory must then rely on other sources of information such as the implicit theories held by those close to the operation of the program, program documents, observations of the program in action, and exploratory research to test critical assumptions about the nature of the program (Donaldson, 2001b; Rossi et al., 2004).

The Role of Program Theory

At the most practical level, a well-developed and fully articulated program theory can be very useful for framing key evaluation questions and designing sensitive and responsive

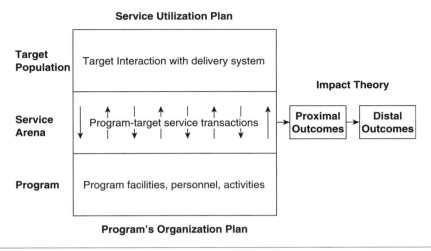

Figure 2.2   Program theory diagram (Rossi, et al., 2004).

evaluations. By indicating clearly what is assumed and expected in the operation and outcomes of a program, program theory helps the evaluator and program stakeholders identify the performance dimensions most critical to the program's success and, hence, those that may be most important to assess. For evaluation design, a detailed program theory informs the selection of variables, timing of measures and observations, identification of appropriate informants, and a host of other conceptual and procedural aspects of the evaluation plan. In many regards, it is the articulated program theory that links the evaluation design to the concerns and understandings of the stakeholders – it provides the common representation of the program that all parties can reference as the evaluation is planned and implemented, and its results interpreted.

As depiction of program theory has become more valued and common in evaluation practice, more and more clients and stakeholders are expecting evaluators to know how to develop and use it. Program theory is now playing an important role in needs assessment,

program planning and design, and evaluability assessment; in providing a basis for informed decisions about measurement and evaluation methods; in enabling evaluators to disentangle the success or failure of program implementation from the validity of the program's conceptual model; and for facilitating a cumulative wisdom about how programs work and how to make them work better (Donaldson, 2003, forthcoming).

The essential involvement of program stakeholders in the articulation of program theory has also emerged as one of the more significant aspects of an emphasis on theory as a tool for evaluation planning. Engaging stakeholders in discussions about the what, how, and why of program activities is often empowering for them and, additionally, promotes inclusion and facilitates meaningful participation by diverse stakeholder groups (see *Centers for Disease Control Program Evaluation Framework*, 1999; Donaldson, 2003). Involving stakeholders in this way can dramatically increase the chances that the evaluation will meet utility, feasibility, propriety, and accuracy evaluation standards (Joint Committee on Standards for Educational Evaluation, 1994). The engagement of stakeholders around developing program theory is a very important role for program theory to play in evaluation practice.

As with all evaluation tools and approaches, there are boundary conditions that evaluators must consider when developing and using program theory in evaluation. Some of the circumstances that can prevent program theory from reaching its potential in practice include lack of stakeholder cooperation, disagreements about program theory, highly dynamic programs and program theories, and lack of consensus about evaluation questions, what constitutes credible evidence, and how to use and disseminate evaluation findings (Donaldson, 2003, forthcoming; Donaldson et al., 2002; Mark, 2003). It is important for evaluators to assess project conditions carefully to determine if the stakeholders, and the project in general, are ready for the commitment necessary for the effective development and use of program theory to guide evaluation efforts.

Where They Come Together: Program Theory-Driven Evaluation Science

As the prior discussion has made evident, one widespread variant of evaluation theory is centered on the notion of articulating and using program theory to shape those aspects of evaluation practice that are related to conceptualizing social programs, designing evaluation studies, and interpreting evaluation findings. Program theory and evaluation research based on it, in turn, are enriched when they can draw on relevant social science theory and themselves enrich that theory when they contribute to knowledge about how social intervention brings about social change. This confluence of evaluation theory,

social science theory, and program theory constitutes a distinctive approach to evaluation one of us has recently broadly cast as "program theory-driven evaluation science" (Donaldson, 2005; forthcoming). We suggest that this integration of theory constitutes a (if not the) major way that evaluation contributes to social betterment by way of knowledge development.

As Gargani (2003) documented, the use of program theory in evaluation practice has a long history. He noted that the practice of articulating and testing program theory was introduced to evaluation by Ralph Tyler in the 1930s, but did not find widespread favor with evaluators at that time. It was in the 1990s that the notion of using program theory grounded in relevant substantive knowledge to guide evaluation practice took hold. The work of Chen & Rossi (1983, 1987) was especially instrumental in this development. They advocated for moving away from atheoretical, method-driven evaluation approaches to a "theory-driven" approach that they argued would both improve evaluation practice and make evaluation a more rigorous and thoughtful scientific endeavor.

Chen (1990) then provided the first text on theory-driven evaluation, which has been widely used and cited in the program evaluation literature. In their broad review of evaluation theory, Shadish et al., (1991) characterized the theory-driven evaluation approach as an ambitious attempt to bring coherence to a field in considerable turmoil and debate. In their view, this approach offered three fundamental concepts that facilitate the integration of concepts and practices in evaluation:

- *Comprehensive evaluation*: Studying the design and conceptualization of an intervention, its implementation, and its utility.
- *Tailored evaluation*: Evaluation questions and research procedures depend on whether the

program is an innovative intervention, a modification or expansion of an existing effort, or a well-established, stable activity.

- *Theory-driven evaluation*: Constructing models of how programs work, using the models to guide question formulation and data gathering; similar to what econometricians call model specification.

Some indication of the success of this perspective in providing an integrative framework for evaluation is its representation in contemporary evaluation textbooks. Most of the major texts in the field are based on or give significant attention to the role of program theory in evaluation practice (e.g., Posavac & Carey, 2003; Rossi et al., 2004; Weiss, 1998).

Serious dialog and applications of theory-driven or theory-based evaluation are now prevalent throughout most regions across the global evaluation landscape, and within most major evaluation associations. For example, recent volumes, papers, and visions for future applications of theory-driven evaluation have been discussed at length within the European Evaluation Community (e.g., Pawson & Tilley, 1997; Stame, 2004; Stern, 2004; Van Der Knaap, 2004). Published examples of theory-driven evaluations now exist from many parts of the world including but not limited to Taiwan (Chen, Wang, & Lin, 1997), Germany (Bamberg & Schmidt, 1997), Britain (Tilley, 2004), South Africa (Mouton & Wildschut, forthcoming), Canada (Mercier et al., 2000), as well as the United States (Bickman, 1996; Cook, Murphy, & Hunt, 2000; Donaldson & Gooler, 2002, 2003).

However, as mentioned earlier, there remains much confusion today about what is meant by theory-based or theory-driven evaluation, and the differences between using program theory and social science theory to guide evaluation efforts (Donaldson, 2003; Weiss, 1997). Rather than trying to sort out all the nuances of closely related or sometimes interchangeable terms in the evaluation literature, such as theory-oriented evaluation, theory-based evaluation, theory-driven evaluation, program theory evaluation, intervening mechanism evaluation, theoretically relevant evaluation research, program theory, program logic, and logic modeling, Donaldson (forthcoming) offers a broad definition in an attempt to be inclusive:

> *Program theory-driven evaluation science* is the systematic use of substantive knowledge about the phenomena under investigation and scientific methods to improve, to produce knowledge and feedback about, and to determine the merit, worth, and significance of evaluands such as social, educational, health, community, and organizational programs.

The phrase, *program theory-driven* (instead of theory-driven), is intended to clarify the meaning of the use of the word "theory" in this evaluation context. It specifies the type of theory (i.e., program theory) that is expected to guide the evaluation questions and design. The phrase, *evaluation science*, is intended to underscore the use of rigorous scientific methods (i.e., qualitative, quantitative, and mixed methods) to answer key evaluation questions. A renewed emphasis on the reliance of evaluation on systematic scientific methods is especially important for overcoming negative images of evaluation as unreliable, soft, or a second-class type of investigation (Donaldson, 2001b). *Evaluation science* signals the emphasis placed on the guiding principle of *systematic inquiry* (American Evaluation Association, 2005) and the critical evaluation standard of *accuracy* (Joint Committee on Standards for Educational Evaluation, 1994).

We view *program theory-driven evaluation science* as essentially method neutral within the broad domain of social science methodology. Its focus on the development of program theory and evaluation questions frees evaluators initially from having to presuppose use of one method or another. This simple view that the choice of methods is contingent on the nature of the question to be answered and the form of an answer that will be useful reinforces the idea that neither quantitative, qualitative, nor mixed method designs are necessarily superior or applicable in every evaluation context (cf. Chen, 1997). Whether an evaluator uses case studies, observational methods, structured or unstructured interviews, online or telephone survey research, a quasi-experiment, or a randomized experimental trial to answer the key evaluation questions is dependent on discussions with relevant stakeholders about what would constitute credible evidence in this context, and what is feasible given the practical and financial constraints (Donaldson, 2005).

In an effort to incorporate various lessons learned from the practice of theory-driven evaluation in recent years (e.g., Donaldson & Gooler, 2003) and make this approach more accessible to evaluation practitioners, Donaldson (2003, 2005) presented a simple three-step model for understanding the basic activities of program theory-driven evaluation science:

1. Developing program theory;

2. Formulating and prioritizing evaluation questions;

3. Answering evaluation questions.

Simply stated, evaluators work with stakeholders to develop a common understanding of how a program is presumed to solve the social problem(s) of interest, develop the implications and priorities for what aspects of program performance need to be examined, and design an evaluation that will provide information about those aspects.

Relevant social science theory and prior research (if available) are used to inform this process and to assess the plausibility of the relationships assumed between a program and its intended outcomes. Each program theory-driven evaluation also has the potential to contribute to an evolving understanding of the nature of the change processes programs bring about and how they can be optimized to produce social benefits. This orientation contrasts sharply with a history of evaluation practice that is filled with "method-driven," "black box," and "input/output" studies that reveal little about the mechanisms of change embodied in social programs. A program theory-driven approach focuses on which program components are most effective, the mediating causal processes through which they work, and the characteristics of the participants, service providers, settings, and the like that moderate the relationships between a program and its outcomes.

One of the best examples to date of program theory-driven evaluation science in action is embodied in the Centers for Disease Control's six-step Program Evaluation Framework. This framework is not only conceptually well developed and instructive for evaluation practitioners, it has been widely adopted for evaluating federally funded public health programs throughout the United States. The CDC framework extends the more concise three-step program theory-driven evaluation science model described above to guide to practitioners through six distinct evaluation steps:

1. Engage stakeholders;

2. Describe the program;

3. Focus the evaluation design;

4. Gather credible evidence;

5. Justify conclusions;

6. Ensure use and share lessons learned.

The second element of this framework is a set of 30 standards for assessing the quality of

ELEMENTS OF THE FRAMEWORK

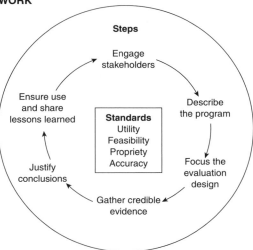

REFERENCE CARD

Steps in Evaluation Practice	Standards for Effective Evaluations
• **Engage Stakeholders** Those involved, those affected, primary intended users	
• **Describe the program** Need, expected effects, activities, resources, stage, context, logic model	• **Utility** Serve the information needs of intended users
• **Focus the evaluation design** Purpose, users, uses, questions, methods, agreements	• **Feasibility** Be realistic, prudent, diplomatic, and frugal
• **Gather credible evidence** Indicators, sources, quality, quantity, logistics	• **Propriety** Behave legally, ethically, and with due regard for the welfare of those involved and those affected
• **Justify conclusions** Standards, analysis/syntheses, interpretation, judgment, recommendations	• **Accuracy** Reveal and convey technically accurate information
• **Ensure use and share lessons learned** Design, preparation, feedback, follow-up, dissemination	

Figure 2.3   CDC framework (Centers For Disease Control Program Evaluation Framework, 1999).

the evaluation effort (adopted from Joint Committee on Standards for Educational Evaluation, 1994; see Figure 2.3). These standards are organized into categories relating to utility, feasibility, propriety, and accuracy. In addition, program theory-driven evaluations are designed to strictly adhere to the American Evaluation Association's Guiding Principles (American Evaluation Association, 2005):

- *Systematic inquiry:* Evaluators conduct systematic, data-based inquires about whatever is being evaluated.
- *Competence:* Evaluators provide competent performance to stakeholders.
- *Integrity/honesty:* Evaluators ensure the honesty and integrity of the entire evaluation process.
- *Respect for people:* Evaluators respect the security, dignity, and self-worth of the respondents, program participants, clients, and other stakeholders with whom they interact.
- *Responsibility for general and public welfare:* Evaluators articulate and take into account the diversity of interests and values that may be related to the general and public welfare.

Clearly we take issue with the notion that theory is not a useful tool for improving evaluation practice as has been asserted by, for example, Scriven (1998, 2004a) and Stufflebeam (2001, 2004). However, we should make it equally clear we are not claiming that program theory-driven evaluation science is a panacea for all that might ail evaluation practice. Nor do we wish to argue that this approach is right for all situations. Like most of the tools in an evaluator's toolkit, theory can be very useful under some conditions and not needed in others.

It is important to note here that theories of evaluation practice, other than explicitly theory-related ones, can also play an important role in knowledge development and theory improvement for social programming and policy-making (see Alkin, 2004a; Donaldson & Scriven, 2003a; Stufflebeam, 2001, for recent discussions about evaluation theories and approaches). Indeed, as Mark and Henry suggest elsewhere in this *Handbook*, an outcome evaluation can sometimes be seen as akin to a hypothesis test, with potential to contribute to

the knowledge base, even without any other of the characteristics of program theory-driven evaluation. Furthermore, a wide range of applied research applications and methods typically used in contemporary evaluation practice, such as needs assessment (Scriven, 2003), research synthesis and meta-analysis (Donaldson et al., 2001; Lipsey & Wilson, 1993), and a variety of qualitative approaches and methods (e.g., see Fetterman, 2003; Mertens, 2003, Patton, 1997), have much to offer for enhancing our knowledge and understanding of the effectiveness of social programs and policies.

Looking Toward the Future

While various perspectives on evaluation theory can provide important insights, practicing evaluators tend to be most concerned with current and emerging challenges for evaluation practice. To explore potential futures for evaluation practice, Donaldson & Scriven (2003b) invited a diverse group of evaluators and evaluation theorists to represent their own views at an interactive symposium. A "last lecture" format was used to encourage each participant to articulate a vision for "How We Should Practice Evaluation in the New Millennium." These evaluators were thus asked to give a "last lecture" passing on advice and wisdom to the next generation about how we should evaluate social programs and problems in the twenty-first century. In addition to six presentations of future visions, five prominent evaluators gave lectures in which they reacted to those visions. These reaction lectures were followed by responses from the initial visionaries and an audience of more than 300 participants.

This approach to exploring theories of evaluation practice and directions for the future led to an exceptionally diverse and provocative set of ideas about how to evaluate social programs and problems (Donaldson & Scriven, 2003b; Slater, 2006; Triolli, 2004). For present purposes, however, one aspect of this rich discourse was especially striking – program theory was an integral component of most of the visions and practice theories articulated (Crano, 2003). That is, in addition to being a relatively distinct stand-alone theory of evaluation practice, many elements of the theory-driven approach were incorporated into other theories of evaluation practice.

For example, Scriven (2003) described a transdisciplinary view of evaluation that included enlightened use of a tripartite set of program theories – the alleged program theory, the real logic of the program, and the optimal program theory. Fetterman (2003) described how the central process of empowerment evaluation creates a program theory and Mertens (2003) noted that inclusive evaluation encourages evaluators to prevent program theories from contributing to the negative stereotyping of marginalized groups. Results-oriented management incorporates logic models and program theory to guide performance measurement (Wholey, 2003) and Mark's (2003) integrative vision for evaluation theories suggested that theory-driven evaluation has a significant place in the toolkit for all evaluation approaches. In this regard, it is worth noting that recent presentations of "realist evaluation" focus on program mechanisms as part of program theory and evaluation practice (Mark et al., 2000; Pawson & Tilley, 1999) and that "utilization-focused evaluation" is highly compatible with a theory-driven approach (Christie & Alkin, 2003; Patton, 1997).

Another major theme that emerged from this discourse on future evaluation practice was the challenge posed by the vast diversity represented in modern evaluation theories. Mark (2003) observed that each vision for the future of evaluation gave a central place to

one theory of evaluation practice and left scant room for others. One way out of the continuous polarization of perspectives that results from these diverse theoretical allegiances is the development of higher-order frameworks that integrate evaluation theories (Mark, 2003). Another option presented for achieving a peaceful and productive future for evaluation involved a strategy for embracing diversity in evaluation theory, recognizing that fundamental differences cannot be reconciled or integrated, and that clients may benefit most from having a diverse smorgasbord of options to choose from for evaluating their programs and policies (Donaldson & Scriven, 2003b).

Developing the Evidence Base

Theories of evaluation practice are based more on philosophy and experience than systematic evidence of their effectiveness. Though exhortations to test the validity of claims made by these theories have been made (e.g., Mark, 2003), there is little likelihood that the diversity of practice theories in evaluation will be greatly influenced by any accumulation of research results. Evaluation theories remain largely prescriptive and unverified.

Program theory, on the other hand, is amenable to test by systematic research. Great advances can be made in the future if there is continuing development of evidence about the validity of the various program theories evaluators encounter. Birckmayer & Weiss (2000) examined a range of theory-driven evaluations conducted over the past decade and concluded that in almost every case some aspect of program theory was not supported by the resulting evidence. With sufficient information of this sort, misguided programs that rely on untenable concepts can be more readily identified without extensive empirical investigation. In addition, an expanded evidence base will allow programs based on sound theory to be more easily designed and the synthesis of research across evaluation studies will generate deeper understanding for evaluators, policy-makers, and social scientists about how social change can be brought about.

One purpose of program theory-driven evaluation science is to rigorously examine the validity of program theories. That is, once a program theory is developed and articulated, systematic, data-based evaluations would be used to determine if the program does bring about change in the manner theorized. Over time, program theory-driven evaluations will provide an expanding base of evidence about specific relationships that appear in the mechanisms of change assumed in social programs. This empirical evidence can be used to improve programs and program theories, as well as identify promising strategies for addressing problems in other program domains. Weiss (2004b) suggested it may well turn out, once the empirical evidence accumulates, that there are a limited number of effective change mechanisms that can be identified and applied to a wide range of social problems. A major goal of program theory-driven evaluation science, therefore, is to establish evidence-based program theories that can enhance efforts to promote social betterment.

Conclusion

While the following quote is dated and probably one of the most overused in the social sciences – we can't resist:

Nothing is so practical as a good theory (Lewin, 1945). This observation is widely accepted and valued in most social science disciplines and professions today. In this chapter, we have affirmed and extended the spirit of this observation to the emerging global transdiscipline of evaluation. Although evaluation has been frequently criticized for being atheoretical and method-driven, this chapter has illustrated how theory is playing, and should continue to play, important roles in evaluation practice. In particular, we argue that moving toward program theory-driven evaluation science will substantially increase the extent to which evaluation contributes to the purpose of knowledge generation and testing. More generally, well-supported evaluation theories, program theories, and social science theories are likely to be among the most useful and effective tools evaluators will have in their efforts to promote social betterment in the years ahead.

References

Ajzen, I. (2002). Perceived behavioral control, self-efficacy, locus of control, and the theory of planned behavior. *Journal of Applied Social Psychology*, 32(4), 665–683.

Alkin, M. C. (ed.) (2004a). *Evaluation Roots*. Thousand Oaks: Sage.

Alkin, M. C. (2004b). Context-adapted utilization: A personal journey. In M. C. Alkin (ed.) *Evaluation Roots* (pp. 293–303). Thousand Oaks: Sage.

Alkin, M. C. & Christie, C. A. (2004). An evaluation theory tree revisited. In M. C. Alkin (ed.) *Evaluation Roots*. Thousand Oaks: Sage.

American Evaluation Association (2005). *Guiding Principles for Evaluators*. Retrieved August 2, 2005, from http://www.eval.org.

Braybrooke, D. & Lindblom, C. E. (1963). *A strategy decision*. New York: Free Press.

Bamberg, S. & Schmidt, P. (1997). Theory driven evaluation of an environmental policy measure: Using the theory of planned behavior. *Zeitschrift für Sozialpsychologie*, 28(4), 280–297.

Bandura, A. (2006). Going global with social cognitive theory: From prospect to paydirt. In S. I. Donaldson, D. E. Berger, & K. Pezdek (eds) *Applied Psychology: New frontiers and rewarding careers*. Mahwah, NJ: Erlbaum.

Bickman, L. (1987). The functions of program theory. *New Directions for Program Evaluation*, 33, 5–18.

Bickman, L. (1996). A continuum of care: More is not always better. *American Psychologist*, 51(7), 689–701.

Birckmayer, J. D. & Weiss, C. H. (2000). Theory-based evaluation in practice. What do we learn? *Evaluation Review*, 24(4), 407–431.

Centers For Disease Control Program Evaluation Framework (1999). 48(RR11); 1–40.

Chen, H. T. (1990). *Theory-Driven Evaluations*. Newbury Park, CA: Sage.

Chen, H. T. (1997). Applying mixed methods under the framework of theory-driven evaluations. *New Directions for Evaluation*, 74, 61–72.

Chen, H. T. & Rossi, P. H. (1983). Evaluating with sense: The theory-driven approach. *Evaluation Review*, 7, 283–302.

Chen, H. T. & Rossi, P. H. (1987). The theory-driven approach to validity. *Evaluation and Program Planning*, 10, 95–103.

Chen H. T., Wang J. C. S., & Lin, L. H. (1997). Evaluating the process and outcome of a garbage reduction program in Taiwan. *Evaluation Review*, 21(1), 27–42.

Christie, C. A. & Alkin, M. C. (2003). The user-oriented evaluator's role in formulating a program theory: Using a theory-driven approach. *American Journal of Evaluation*, 24(3), 373–385.

Cook, T. D., Murphy, R. F., & Hunt, H. D. (2000). Comer's school development program in Chicago: A theory-based evaluation. *American Educational Research Journal*, 37(2), 535–597.

Crano, W. D. (2003). Theory-driven evaluation and construct validity. In S. I. Donaldson & M. Scriven (eds) *Evaluating Social Programs and Problems: Visions for the new millennium* (pp. 111–142). Mahwah, NJ: Erlbaum.

Donaldson, S. I. (2001a). Overcoming our negative reputation: Evaluation becomes known as a helping profession. *American Journal of Evaluation*, 22, 355–361.

Donaldson, S. I. (2001b). Mediator and moderator analysis in program development. In S. Sussman (ed.) *Handbook of Program Development for Health Behavior Research* and practice (pp. 470–496). Newbury Park, CA: Sage.

Donaldson, S. I. (2003). Theory-driven program evaluation in the new millennium. In S. I. Donaldson & M. Scriven (eds) *Evaluating Social Programs and Problems: Visions for the new millennium* (pp. 111–142). Mahwah, NJ: Erlbaum.

Donaldson, S. I. (2004). Using professional evaluation to improve the effectiveness of nonprofit organizations. In R. E. Riggio & S. Smith Orr (eds) *Improving Leadership in Nonprofit Organizations*. San Francisco, CA: Jossey-Bass.

Donaldson, S. I. (2005). Using program theory-driven evaluation science to crack the Da Vinci Code. In M. C. Alkin & Christina A. Christie (eds) Theorists' Models in Action. *New Directions for Evaluation*, 106, 65–84.

Donaldson, S. I. (forthcoming). *Program Theory-Driven Evaluation Science: Strategies and applications*. Mahwah, NJ: Erlbaum.

Donaldson, S. I. & Christie, C. A. (2006). Emerging career opportunities in the transdiscipline of evaluation science. In S. I. Donaldson, D. E. Berger, & K. Pezdek (eds) *Applied Psychology: New frontiers and rewarding careers*. Mahwah, NJ: Erlbaum.

Donaldson, S. I. & Gooler, L. E. (2002). Theory-driven evaluation of the work and health initiative: A focus on winning new jobs. *American Journal of Evaluation*, 23(3), 341–346.

Donaldson, S. I. & Gooler, L. E. (2003). Theory-driven evaluation in action: Lessons from a $20 million statewide work and health initiative. *Evaluation and Program Planning*, 26, 355–366.

Donaldson, S. I., Gooler, L. E., & Scriven, M. (2002). Strategies for managing evaluation anxiety: Toward a psychology of program evaluation. *American Journal of Evaluation*, 23(3), 261–273.

Donaldson, S. I., Graham, J. W., & Hansen, W. B. (1994). Testing the generalizability of intervening mechanism theories: Understanding the effects of school-based substance use prevention interventions. *Journal of Behavioral Medicine*, 17, 195–216.

Donaldson, S. I. & Scriven, M. (eds) (2003a). *Evaluating Social Programs and Problems: Visions for the new millennium*. Mahwah, NJ: Erlbaum.

Donaldson, S. I. & Scriven, M. (2003b). Diverse visions for evaluation in the new millennium: Should we integrate or embrace diversity? In S. I. Donaldson & M. Scriven (eds) *Evaluating Social Programs and Problems: Visions for the new millennium* (pp. 3–16). Mahwah, NJ: Erlbaum.

Donaldson, S. I., Street, G., Sussman, S., & Tobler, N. (2001). Using meta-analyses to improve the design of interventions. In S. Sussman (ed.), *Handbook of Program Development for Health Behavior Research and Practice* (pp. 449–466). Newbury Park, CA: Sage.

Fetterman, D. (2003). Empowerment evaluation strikes a responsive chord. In S. I. Donaldson & M. Scriven (eds) *Evaluating Social Programs and Problems: Visions for the new millennium* (pp. 63–76). Mahwah, NJ: Erlbaum.

Funnel, S. (1997). Program logic: An adaptable tool for designing and evaluating programs. *Evaluation News and Comment*, 5–17.

Gargani, J. (2003). The history of theory-based evaluation: 1909 to 2003. Paper presented at the American Evaluation Association annual conference, Reno, NV.

Joint Committee on Standards for Educational Evaluation (1994). *The Program Evaluation Standards: How to assess evaluations of educational programs.* Thousand, Oaks, CA: Sage.

Kram, K. E. (1985). *Mentoring at Work.* Glenview, IL: Scott Forseman.

Lewin, K. (1945). The Research Center for Group Dynamics at Massachusetts Institute of Technology. *Sociometry*, 2, 126–136.

Lipsey, M. W. (1990) *Design Sensitivity.* Newbury Park, CA: Sage.

Lipsey, M. W. (1993). Theory as method: Small theories of treatments. *New Directions for Program Evaluation*, 57, 5–38.

Lipsey, M. W. & Wilson, D. B. (1993). The efficacy of psychological, educational, and behavioral treatment: Confirmation from meta-analysis. *American Psychologist*, 48, 1181–1209.

Mark, M. M. (2003). Toward a integrative view of the theory and practice of program and policy evaluation. In S. I. Donaldson & M. Scriven (eds.) *Evaluating Social Programs and Problems: Visions for the new millennium* (pp. 183–204). Mahwah, NJ: Erlbaum.

Mark, M. M., Henry, G. T., & Julnes, G. (2000). *Evaluation: An integrative framework for understanding guiding, and improving policies and programs.* San Francisco, Jossey-Bass.

Mercier C., Piat M., Peladeau N., & Dagenais, C. (2000). An application of theory-driven evaluation to a drop-in youth center. *Evaluation Review*, 24(1), 73–91.

Mertens, D. M. (2003). The inclusive view of evaluation: Visions for the new millennium. In S. I. Donaldson & M. Scriven (eds.) *Evaluating Social Programs and Problems: Visions for the new millennium* (pp. 91–108). Mahwah, NJ: Erlbaum.

Mertens, D. M. (2005). The inauguration of the international organization for cooperation in evaluation. *American Journal of Evaluation*, 26(1), 124–130.

Mouton, J. & Wildschut, L. (forthcoming). Theory driven realist evaluation. In R. Basson,

C. Potter, & M. Mark (eds) *Internationalizing Evaluation: Reflections on evaluation approaches and their use globally using South Africa as a case example.*

Patton, M. Q. (1997). *Utilization-Focused Evaluation: The new century text*, 3rd edition. Thousand Oaks, CA: Sage.

Pawson, R. & Tilley, N. (1997). *Realist Evaluation.* Thousand Oaks, CA: Sage.

Petraitis, J., Flay, B. R., & Miller, T. Q. (1995). Reviewing theories of adolescent substance use: Organizing pieces in the puzzle. *Psychological Bulletin*, 117(1), 67–86.

Posavac, E. J. & Carey, R. G. (2003). *Program Evaluation: Methods and case studies,* 6th edition. Englewood Cliffs, NJ: Prentice-Hall.

Price, R. H., van Ryn, M., & Vinokur, A. D. (1992). Impact of a preventive job search intervention on the likelihood of depression among the unemployed. *Journal of Health and Social Behavior*, 33, 158–167.

Prochaska, J. O. & DiClemente, C. C. (1999). *The Transtheoretical Approach: Crossing traditional boundaries of change.* Homewood, IL: Dow Jones/Irwin.

Rosenthal, R. (2006). Applying psychological research on interpersonal expectations and covert communication in classrooms, clinics, corporations, and courtrooms. In S. I. Donaldson, D. E. Berger, & K. Pezdek (eds) *Applied Psychology: New frontiers and rewarding careers.* Mahwah, NJ: Erlbaum.

Rossi, P. H., Lipsey, M. W., & Freeman, H. E. (2004). *Evaluation: A systematic approach* (7th edition). Thousand Oaks, CA: Sage.

Russon, C. (2004). Cross-cutting issues in international standards development. In C. Russon & G. Russon (eds) International Perspectives on Evaluation Standards, *New Directions for Evaluation*, 104, 89–93.

Scriven, M. (1998). Minimalist theory: The least practice requires. *American Journal of Evaluation*, 19, 57–70.

Scriven, M. (2003). Evaluation in the new millennium: The transdisciplinary vision. In S. I. Donaldson & M. Scriven (eds) *Evaluating Social Programs and Problems: Visions for the new millennium* (pp. 19–42). Mahwah, NJ: Erlbaum.

Scriven, M. (2004a). *Practical Program Evaluation: A checklist approach.* Claremont Graduate University Annual Professional Development Workshop Series.

Scriven, M. (2004b). EvalTalk posting, April 26.

Seligman, M. E. P. (2003). *Authentic happiness: Using the new positive psychology to realize your potential for lasting fulfillment.* New York: Free Press.

Shadish, W. R. (1998). Evaluation theory is who we are. *American Journal of Evaluation,* 19(1), 1–19.

Shadish, W. R., Cook, T. D., & Campbell, D. T. (2004). *Experimental and Quasi-experimental Designs for Generalized Causal Inference.* Boston: Houghton-Mifflin.

Shadish, W. R., Cook, T. D., & Leviton, L. C. (1991). *Foundations of Program Evaluation: Theories of practice.* Newbury Park, CA: Sage.

Slater, J. K. (2006). Review of "Evaluation social programs and problems: Visions for the new millenium," *American Journal of Evaluation,* 27(1), 128–129.

Stake, R. E. (2004). Advocacy in evaluation: A necessary evil? In E. Chelimsky & W. R. Shadish (eds) *Evaluation for the 21st century: A handbook* (pp. 470–476). Thousand Oaks, CA: Sage.

Stame, N. (2004). Theory-based evaluation and types of complexity. *Evaluation: The International Journal of Theory, Research & Practice,* 10(1), 58–76.

Stern, E. (2004). What shapes European evaluation? A personal reflection. *Evaluation: The International Journal of Theory, Research & Practice,* 10(1), 7–15.

Sternberg, R. J. (2003). WICS: A model of leadership in organizations. *Academy of Management Learning and Education,* 2(4), 386–401.

Stufflebeam, D. L. (ed.) (2001). *Evaluation Models.* New Directions for Evaluation, No. 89. San Francisco, CA: Jossey-Bass.

Stufflebeam, D. L. (2004). The 21st-century CIPP model: origins, development, and use. In M. C. Alkin (ed.) *Evaluation Roots* (pp. 245–266). Thousand Oaks: Sage.

Tilley, N. (2004). Applying theory-driven evaluation to the British Crime Reduction Programme: The theories of the programme and of its evaluations. *Criminal Justice: International Journal of Policy and Practice,* 4(3), 255–276.

Triolli, T. (2004). Review of "Evaluating social program and problems: Visions for the new millennium." *Evaluation and Program Planning,* 26(3), 82–88.

Van Der Knaap, P. (2004). Theory-based evaluation and learning: Possibilities and challenges. *Evaluation: The International Journal of Theory, Research and Practice,* 10(1), 16–34.

Weiss, C. H. (1997). How can theory-based evaluation make greater headway? *Evaluation Review,* 21, 501–524.

Weiss, C. H. (1998). *Evaluation: Methods for studying programs and policies* (2nd edition). Upper Saddle River, NJ: Prentice Hall.

Weiss, C. H. (2004a). On theory-based evaluation: Winning friends and influencing people. *The Evaluation Exchange,* IX (4), 1–5.

Weiss, C. H. (2004b). Rooting for evaluation: A cliff notes version of my work. In M. C. Alkin (ed.) *Evaluation Roots* (pp. 153–168). Thousand Oaks: Sage.

Wholey, J. S. (2003). Improving performance and accountability: Responding to emerging management challenges. In S. I. Donaldson & M. Scriven (eds) *Evaluating Social Programs and Problems: Visions for the new millennium* (pp. 43–62). Mahwah, NJ: Erlbaum.

EVALUATION FOR PRACTICE IMPROVEMENT AND ORGANIZATIONAL LEARNING

Patricia J. Rogers and Bob Williams

One of the misconceptions of the performance movement is the notion that organizations are transformed by having information on how well they are doing. This optimism is rarely justified. . . . It requires sustained political and managerial will to reorient an organization in response to information on what it is doing or hopes to accomplish. In fact, genuine organizational change may be a pre-condition for effective use of performance information. (Schick, 2003)

Introduction

How does practice improve, and how can evaluation contribute to this improvement? There are many surprisingly different answers to these questions, each involving different types of evidence, different processes for gathering, analyzing, and using this evidence, as well as different roles for practitioners, funders,

researchers, customers, and evaluators. Practice improvement can come about, for example, through building knowledge about better ways to do things, or by accessing others' knowledge about better practice. It can come about through individual practitioners' reflection, peer review, or expert advice. Service beneficiaries can be simply a source of information about how well the service meets their needs, or they can provide suggestions for improvement, or even conduct and use the evaluation. Evaluation can be intended to find "the best way" to do things overall, or to discover a better way to do things in a particular situation – or to develop practitioners' abilities to respond and adapt in different ways to respond to the particular needs of individual service users.

Each of these approaches to evaluation is based on a different, and often implicit "theory of change", which links the evaluation with the intended improvements in practice. As the quote from Schick reminds us, these different theories of change involve assumptions, not only about the production of evaluative information or judgments, but also about the use that is made of this information and the impacts of the evaluation process. These processes are all heavily influenced by the learning processes of individuals and groups, as well as by the organizational context. Consequently, this chapter begins by discussing different types of learning and different aspects of organizational dynamics that may need to be addressed in order for this learning to happen.

The chapter then discusses in some detail nine different evaluation approaches and techniques. The first five approaches explicitly draw on research and thinking about learning and organizational change: action research; empowerment evaluation; appreciative inquiry; evaluative inquiry; and systemic evaluation. The remaining four are the success case method; evidence-based practice; program theory; and performance monitoring. We have selected these nine approaches for their intrinsic value and to highlight important issues in doing evaluation for practice improvement. Review of these approaches shows how thinking through the theories of change, practice improvement, different types of learning, and the influence of organizational context can be useful in selecting, adapting, and developing appropriate evaluation approaches for a given situation.

Finally, we discuss three overall challenges that emerge from these nine approaches: generating information about performance that is both timely and relevant; addressing the difficulty people have taking in information that does not match their implicit assumptions, or that underpins habitual behavior; and the consequent defensive routines that often arise.

We believe that these challenges must be adequately addressed before any evaluation approach, including ones not described in this chapter, can hope to contribute to practice improvement.

Aspects of Learning and Organizational Dynamics that Evaluation Needs to Address

There are many paths by which evaluation can contribute to practice improvement, but the end invariably involves stakeholders (staff, managers, funders, clients, other people and groups whose actions and decisions influence practice) who are expected to use the information or the process in some way. Attention to different types of learning, and to different ways of thinking about learning, can help us explore the different ways in which evaluation might contribute in a particular situation. We therefore begin by discussing some different types of learning important for evaluation aimed at practice improvement. We then explore the wider organizational settings within which this learning must be exercised.

From the rich and diverse literature on learning and organizational dynamics, we have identified three clusters of concepts we believe are especially important: learning; organizational learning; and organizational dynamics. Learning is essentially the way in which individuals develop meaning out of data they encounter. Organizational learning is a set of procedures and perspectives which allow that learning to be effectively transferred into the organizational or program setting. Organizational dynamics is a general description of what makes an organization behave in the way that it does; this includes both processes of organizational change and of organizational stability.

Learning

Among the many different theories of learning (e.g., http://tip.psychology.org/ describes 50 different theories of learning), two concepts that seem particularly useful for evaluation are single-loop/double-loop/deutero learning, and patterning/puzzling.

Single-Loop, Double-Loop, and Deutero Learning

Argyris & Schön (1996), building on the pioneering work of Bateson (1972), made a distinction between single- and double-loop learning:

- *Single-loop learning* – a response to an observation or event that is based on a person's, or an organization's, existing set of values, beliefs, and norms.
- *Double-loop learning* – a response to an observation or event that flows from a reflection on the dominant or stated values, beliefs, and norms.

For example, single-loop learning might help a practitioner improve a particular way of working with a particular client; double-loop learning would require a rethinking of whether this way was appropriate, or even whether the entire concept of the service was appropriate. Sometimes this is described as "doing things right" as compared to "doing the right thing." Double-loop learning is not necessarily more time-consuming, but it is more challenging to individuals and to their colleagues and therefore requires more institutional support. Thus, what might be an appropriate way to support single-loop learning (e.g., using teaching cases to practice classifying situations and applying appropriate techniques) might not support double-loop learning.

Much evaluation focuses on single-loop learning – that is, identifying errors and correcting them, but staying largely within the existing framework of world views, stated goals, and intended processes. While this can be useful, it can also be important to engage in double-loop learning that questions the assumptions about how the program works, how the environment works, and how the organization works. Not just "Did the program meet the stated goals?" but also "Do the goals of the project really suit the needs of the target group?" Not just "Were the prescribed procedures followed?" but also "Is the thinking behind those procedures appropriate?" Skilled facilitation will be required to balance inquiry with support for participants during the challenging process of examining their assumptions and misconceptions.

Argyris and Schön also identified a third type of learning, deutero learning, or learning to learn. It can also be important for an evaluation to help people in a program to learn more about how they learn, and how to improve their learning as well as their direct practice. This is particularly true for practice improvement that is intended to come about through increasing the adaptability and responsiveness of the practitioner.

Patterning and Puzzling

Vygotsky (1978) promoted the idea that we learn by two different processes: patterning and puzzling. Patterning is the process by which we develop current meanings and understandings by comparing them with and building on similar experiences. Essentially it is learning by generalization – adding incrementally to existing knowledge. Puzzling is the learning process we engage in when confronted with situations that have no reference point or with conditions that contradict each other, where we cannot reach back to previous experience or to existing generalizations. It is learning by exception, contradiction, or surprise. In both situations we can accept the learning opportunity or ignore it, although the latter requires more social support than the former.

The epistemological tradition in evaluation is to seek mostly for generalizations, or patterns. Indeed, the common quantitative statistical methods and the qualitative clustering methods often used by evaluators tend to guide towards treating "exceptions" as random noise rather than opportunities for potential learning. (See Williams, 2003, for an alternative that does promote "puzzling".)

Followers of Vygotsky's ideas also emphasize that context as well as content is important for learning. Lavé & Wenger (1990) called this "situated learning," and emphasized that the process of setting up (or scaffolding) is critical for learning to occur. For instance, learning can be inhibited if evaluators present their results using methods which assume the results are adding to existing knowledge (i.e., scaffolding for patterning), when in fact the results challenge current knowledge (i.e., require puzzling).

Disciplines of Organizational Learning

While Senge's (1990) book *The Fifth Discipline: The Art and Practice of The Learning Organization* introduced a wide audience to notions of organizational learning, the history of organizational learning is considerably longer. The first book with "organizational learning" in the title was published in 1978 by Argyris & Schön, but the history goes back even further, at least to the Second World War and the work of Lewin, Trist, and Revans.

Senge drew together the threads that had developed over the previous 50 years and organized them into five "disciplines" required to promote learning in organizations. The book has been criticized for its failure to tie these threads together (Flood, 1998), or to address emotional issues sufficiently (Long & Newton, 1997). However, few deny the importance of the ideas Senge promoted, their validity based on decades of practice, or how central

they are to informed and sustained organizational development. For this reason we explore the relevance to evaluation of Senge's five disciplines: mental models; personal mastery; systems thinking; shared vision; and team work.

Mental Models

The concept of mental modeling draws extensively on the work of Argyris and Schön. It suggests that, when confronted with challenging situations, we tend to view data using fixed yet unconscious theories of how the world works (i.e., assumptions). Individually and collectively we can be more innovative, and communicate more effectively, by surfacing our assumptions, values, and beliefs, and by being conscious about how they affect the way we engage with others. The concept of mental models also draws on notions of "reflection" – a questioning process by which we explore and challenge the assumptions that underpin our actions and behaviors. This is important for evaluation because it suggests that the *kinds* of evaluation questions posed can affect learning more than the actual subject matter of the question. Generally, questions that promote puzzling tend to promote more powerful reflection.

Personal Mastery

Personal mastery refers to people's need to live life from a creative rather than a reactive viewpoint. Evaluation methods that engage people's curiosity and their ambition to do a good (rather than a bad) job, or to be involved in a good (rather than a bad) program, are more likely to promote the discipline of personal mastery. This discipline suggests there is a risk with approaches to evaluation and practice improvement that are based on compliance with a centrally developed set of procedures, especially if this is done in a way that de-emphasizes that personal skill and mastery of practitioners, as in the notion of "teacher-proof curriculum." Even where evaluation works to develop a sense of personal mastery, the success of these attempts will depend on the extent to which other organizational processes and culture undermine personal mastery.

Systems Thinking

Systems thinking is a generic term for the application of approaches based on systems theories to provide insights into the way in which people, programs, and organizations interact with each other, their histories, and their environments. While system dynamics is perhaps the most widely known systems approach, it is a large field of inquiry with many different subfields (for an overview, see Williams, 2005). Different systems-based approaches have different roles – for instance, soft systems (exploring multiple perspectives), critical systems (exploring boundary conditions and conflict), complex systems (understanding emerging patterns), activity systems (exploring how people learn and respond to contradictions) and systems dynamics (the relationship between feedback, delay, and stocks and flows). Systems-based approaches provide a means of resolving many key issues about evaluation and program improvement, including the assumptions underpinning a program *and* its evaluation, establishing what lies inside and outside the boundary of the evaluation, problems of attribution, and more robust ways of exploring the behavior of programs and the mesh of causal relationships.

Shared Visions

Many argue that building a future orientation that is shared with others is a more powerful approach to organizational development than is problem solving based on past experience. The potential of vision-based rather than

problem-based approaches to inquiry flowed from the pioneering work of Lippett (1949). Lippett discovered that decisions based on imagined future states were far more creative and permanent than those based on a "problem solving" analysis of the past. Clearly this poses considerable challenges for evaluation theories and methods that envisage evaluation as a problem-oriented post-hoc analysis of past activities. This focus on envisioning the desired future is a strong feature of evaluation approaches such as "Appreciative Inquiry" and "Empowerment Evaluation" (see the sections on these below).

Team Work

The belief that teamwork is more productive, influential, and creative than individual work is not new, reaching back to the work of Lewin and Bion during the Second World War. Again, if we see evaluation for performance improvement at least partly as a learning process, then this provides further support for seeing teams that engage people in a spirit of joint inquiry as a core part of practice improvement, rather than as an optional element of evaluation. Evaluation approaches that focus on this aspect of organizational learning include various forms of participatory evaluation, including empowerment evaluation (Fetterman, 1996), deliberative democratic evaluation (House & Howe, 2000) action research approaches (e.g., Kemmis & McTaggart, 1988), reflective practitioner (e.g., Schön, 1983), collaborative enquiry (Wadsworth, 1997), and developmental evaluation (Patton, 1994).

Perspectives on Organizational Dynamics

Understanding how learning happens at the individual or collective level is necessary, but not sufficient to promote practice improvement. There is also the wider organizational context and how the program or organization works – the dynamics. To get to grips with the implications of this, it can be useful to draw on work on implementation (Elmore, 1978) and its implications for evaluation (Rogers & Hough, 1995) to explore six different perspectives on organizational dynamics, each focusing on different processes (Table 3.1).

Each perspective focuses on particular processes that occur within all organizations. Consequently, this framework suggests that evaluations are likely to have an impact on practice when they consider events through all six lenses rather than one or two. The *managerial hierarchy* perspective focuses on hierarchical, ordered delegation, and management control, including formal procedures, policies, decision-making, and monitoring of performance. The *street-level bureaucrat* perspective focuses on the firmly entrenched operating routines of largely unsupervised "street-level bureaucrats," or front-line workers. Staff, pressed between the needs of clients and the demands of management, develop coping routines which might work but not be in accordance with official policy. The *organizational development* perspective focuses on processes which encourage staff to exercise independent judgment in determining their own behavior, using small work groups for support and problem-solving, developing

ownership of the program, and influencing the development of an organization. The *conflict and bargaining* perspective focuses on conflict over scarce resources in organizations, and the resultant interactions between groups and individuals, including overt and covert conflict. Power over key resources, such as information, human resources, and advocacy is critical. The *external influence* perspective focuses on the impact that external stakeholders have on an organization through their action, reactions, resourcing, support, or lack of support. The *chance and chaos* perspective recognizes that practice can evolve by changes in context or program environment, the chance juxtaposition of events, or the unintended outcomes of deliberate actions. Complexity theory (Eoyang & Berkas, 1998) suggests that even well-understood and apparently predictable processes can have unexpected and seemingly chaotic outcomes.

This framework can be useful to an evaluator seeking to understand the political, social, and organizational dynamics within a program, or how to work out how an evaluation can have greater influence. It can be particularly useful for identifying other processes that may impede the intended practice change. For example, an evaluation that seeks to change formal

---

EXEMPLAR 3.1   Six different sets of processes involved in organizational dynamics

Label	Primary drivers of implementation
Managerial hierarchy	Formal procedures, guidelines, policies
Street-level bureaucrat	Informal operating routines
Organizational development	Bottom-up development of policy from small teams
Conflict and bargaining	Conflict over scarce resources and strategic alliances
External influence	Influence of external resource providers (e.g., customers, funders) or influencers (e.g., politicians, media)
Chance and chaos	Unpredicted events and outcomes and people's reactions to these

procedures and guidelines would benefit from considering the entrenched operating routines of street-level bureaucrats that might persist. Another evaluation that seeks to work through small teams developing better practice would do well to consider the formal organizational incentives to achieve particular targets, for example, and the strategic alliances and conflict that exist within the organization.

Culture and Organizational Dynamics

Intertwined with organizational dynamics is the issue of culture – the organizational culture, the ethnic culture, and the national culture. Our focus here is on organizational culture, although clearly other cultural dynamics have an effect.

Organizational culture, defined by Schein (1996) as "the basic tacit assumptions about how the world is and ought to be that a group of people share and that determines their perceptions, thoughts, feelings, and, their overt behavior," is clearly an important influence on people's willingness to use evaluation evidence and processes to influence their practice. Schein identified three layers of organizational culture: the obvious artifacts, the espoused values (formal and informal conscious strategies, goals, and philosophies) and basic values (tacit drivers of why an organization works the way it does).

Using these concepts, Davidson (2001, 2005) explored the aspects of organizational culture that have evaluation implications. An organizational culture that supports evaluation will have obvious artifacts, such as effective knowledge management systems and experimentation with new methods, as well as symbolic actions, such as rewarding near misses on high goals more than easily clearing low goals, along with tacit basic values, such as seeing that it is genuinely useful to distinguish good from bad performance and that

nothing is above being evaluated. While Davidson's full description of an organizational culture that supports evaluation may be a Utopian ideal, the extent to which the actual organizational culture differs from this ideal can be useful in identifying the scope for evaluation that can actually contribute to practice improvement. It can also help to identify cultural aspects of building evaluation capacity.

For instance, Harris & Williams (2001), in their discussion of organizational contexts for deep evaluative reflection, considered Edwards' (2001) study of Australian organizations where reflection (for which we might read "evaluation") was considered:

- a luxury which "gets in the way of work"
- something to be done in your own time and not the firm's
- not relevant because the firm is in perpetual chaos.

This view was held largely because:

- people weren't permitted to admit ignorance and were pressurized into providing quick fixes
- people were not confident about being reflective
- there was no place for formalized learning processes (as distinct from technical training)
- reflection tended to be individualized and occur off the work site
- the business must keep running at all costs.

Siebert & Daudelin (1999) identified the following aspects of organizational cultural contexts that promote reflection and learning in organizations:

- Autonomy and freedom to move within the task
- Feedback from others about the task
- Access to other people
- Support and stimulation from other people
- Pressure to deliver
- Clear focus.

Some Evaluation Approaches and Techniques for Practice Improvement

Bearing in mind the issues raised above, how can evaluation be done in ways that contribute to organizational learning and practice improvement of the types outlined above? If program evaluation is primarily focused on error correction within existing mental maps, then it will not contribute to double-loop learning. If it is primarily focused on increasing the incentives for good practice (through punitive accountability), this is not likely to encourage trust and collaboration, nor the identification of larger, troubling problems.

It would be a mistake to assume that learning, organizational development, and an appreciation of cultural factors will be simply achieved through collaborative approaches to evaluation (as discussed by Gregory, 2000), nor that all sorts of formative, problem-solving evaluation are effective in improving practice. Such evaluation, if not skillfully done, might tinker about with a few immediate problems, while leaving systemic problems and unsound assumptions intact or even reinforced.

We look now at nine specific evaluation approaches and consider their ability to influence practice improvement and organizational learning, drawing on the issues we have raised. The first five are strongly based on learning and organizational development principles; the other four are commonly or increasingly used in evaluation. Some reflect aspects of learning and organizational development, but do not draw explicitly from them.

Action research

Action Research (Reason & Bradbury, 2001, Dick, 2005) is becoming increasingly adopted and adapted into evaluation practice. It shares

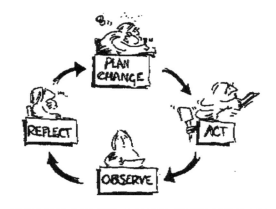

Figure 3.1   Action research cycle (from Wadsworth, 1997)

a parallel and often interconnected history with organizational learning ideas and is specifically focused on practice improvement.

There are several features that together distinguish action research from other improvement-oriented evaluation methods:

1. It is about action *and* research.

2. It is *cyclical* and *evolves*.

3. Each stage of the cycle is *rigorous*.

4. It is *critical*.

5. It tends to be *collaborative*.

6. It often starts with an *engaging question*.

It is about action and research. Action research is both about action that is intentionally researched, and research that is designed to inform subsequent actions.

It is cyclical and evolves. The classic action research cycle is shown in Figure 3.1. Each cycle can be short – maybe just a few hours, days, or weeks. There can be cycles within cycles. Over time, the purpose of a piece of action research may evolve into something quite different from its start. This is quite unlike "objectives"-oriented evaluation or applied research – unless those objectives are constantly under review.

Each stage of the cycle is rigorous. The cycle doesn't just happen. Accepted and appropriate methods of acting, observing, reflecting, and planning are used in each cycle.

Action Research is critical. Successful action research is based around shared curiosity, not individual certainty. Action research works less well if people seek to prove the correctness of their own ideas (or program objectives). Indeed, people are expected to put their practices, ideas, and assumptions to the test by gathering evidence which could convince them that those practices, ideas, and assumptions may be wrong.

Action research tends to be collaborative. There is no distinction made between those involved in the "action" and those involved in the "research." Everyone can be involved in both. The aim is to establish self-critical groups or communities participating in all stages of the cycle, although unlike some participative evaluation approaches, it allows for specialist roles within the endeavor.

Because action research is both action and research oriented, the inquiry starts best with an initial question that is action oriented. Those involved in a particular piece of action research will have many different perspectives and expectations. In order to engage them, this starting question needs to reflect some common ground between all those perspectives and expectations. An action-research-oriented addiction program will focus around the question "How can we improve the lives of those dependent on mind-altering drugs?" rather than "We will get people off amphetamines using a 12-step process."

Action research is attractive to evaluators seeking program improvement because of the link between action and research. Because the actual methods of observing, reflecting, planning, and acting are less important than the

way in which the methods are interlinked, action research is attractive to the method pluralism of evaluators. However, method pluralism doesn't mean that anything goes. The constraints on method are critical to the effectiveness of action research. This partly explains why action research appears easy in theory, but practitioners frequently find it a challenging approach in practice.

The most important challenge is that the "reflection" process primarily seeks to contest the existing mental models and assumptions that underpinned the previous "plans" and "actions." It is about double loop and deutero learning. It is about puzzling rather than patterning. Consequently, action-research-based evaluations can often be uncomfortable experiences for those involved – especially those who consider that action research is merely a systematic description of their own practice.

The other important challenge is that action research is usually, although not always, participative. Informed action requires the involvement of all actors in the reflection and planning process – although the nature and scale of that involvement can vary. Consistent with notions of situated learning, not everyone has to be involved in every aspect of the research and practice.

Descriptions of action research sometimes give the impression that collaboration is unproblematic and universally beneficial. However, collaboration tends to operate best within organizational dynamics that are devolved and uncontentious (e.g., those highlighted by street-level bureaucracy, organizational development perspectives) rather than within hierarchical and conflict orientations, as well as in cultures that can handle deep questioning.

Appreciative Inquiry (AI)

Appreciative inquiry (Elliott, 1999; Preskill & Coghlan, 2003) is built on the assumption that people are more motivated by focusing on achieving good outcomes than on avoiding or fixing problems. AI assumes the energy for organizational and program improvement is in focusing people on their aspirations and dreams of what could be. This releases energy to propel them towards doing an even better job than they are doing right now. In the practice of organizational development (and, by implication, evaluation), this means replacing the traditional problem-solving approach – as reflected in the question "What is going wrong and how do we fix it?" – by two simple questions: "What do we do well?" and "How can we do more of it?" AI seeks to exploit and build on what is going right (i.e., valuable in evaluation terms), rather than focusing on fixing what is going wrong (which is of little worth in an AI framework).

An appreciative inquiry will typically pass through four stages:

- Discovering periods and points of excellence within the program
- Dreaming an ideal program
- Designing new structures and processes
- Delivering the dream

AI gains its credibility by using many of the ideas discussed earlier in this chapter (e.g., shared visioning, team work, multiple perspectives on organizational change, and to some extent situated learning). It is inherently focused on program improvement. In its pure form, AI provides a coherent framework and robust suite of methods that drive a forward looking positive orientation through all stages of an organizational development and evaluation cycle. For that reason, AI is emerging as a significant new approach to evaluation. The first stage of an AI is clearly evaluative. As explained by Elliott:

> Through interviews and storytelling, participants remember significant past achievements

and periods of excellence. When was their organization or community functioning at its best? What happened to make those periods of excellence possible? By telling stories, people identify and analyze the unique factors – such as leadership, relationships, technologies, core processes, structures, values, learning processes, external relations, or planning methods – that contributed to peak experiences.

However, there are some important dimensions that are underdeveloped in many guides to using AI for evaluation. In particular, the descriptions of AI are often ambiguous on the nature and form of reflective practice. Some authors implicitly constrain reflection by the positive orientation of the inquiry (e.g., Whitney & Trosten-Bloom, 2003). From an evaluation perspective, this can be significant because it can lead to uncritical and incomplete assessments of program performance. Indeed, some versions of AI involve an exclusive focus on the positive, making AI only appropriate for situations where other evaluative activity has already identified problems and where AI is being used to gather the energy and commitment to make necessary changes (Rogers & Fraser, 2003). The assumptions about organizational dynamics and culture that underpin the use of AI are at best unclear and at worst naive. While AI refers to systems principles, some guides to AI muddle this with the concept of "wholeness" and promoting active participation of large range of stakeholders.

In the end, the weaknesses of AI (from a learning, evaluative, and practice improvement perspective) may be as much about the way in which it has sometimes been implemented as about the intrinsic principles of AI and its use in skilled hands. For instance, some in the AI field do place a strong emphasis on reflective practice, and on developing a deeper understanding of the program, which requires prolonged engagement, a commitment to empirical investigation, and progressive investigation of different perspectives.

> [A group using AI needs to be] continually asking itself and each other: How are we reading this? Is this the only way? What would another reading look like? If we rearrange the data we have from the appreciative interviews, what other sense can we make of what we are hearing? It is only when the data are interrogated in this way – and when the data themselves have been generated from a no less searching, restless, delving process of conversation – that they will yield all of which they are capable in terms of both information and perspective. (Elliot, 1999)

Empowerment Evaluation

Empowerment evaluation is designed to help people to help themselves and improve their programs using a form of self-evaluation and reflection (Fetterman, 1996, 2005).

The classic empowerment evaluation process has three steps. The first is establishing a mission or vision statement about the program. Some groups do not like the terms mission or vision and instead prefer to focus on results. They state the results they would like to see, based on the outcome of the implemented program and map, specifying the activities required to achieve those processes and outcomes.

The second step, taking stock, involves identifying and prioritizing the most significant program activities. Then program staff members and participants rate how well the program is doing in each of those activities, typically on a 1 (low) to 10 (high) scale, and they discuss the ratings. It is claimed that this helps to determine where the program stands, including strengths and weaknesses. More recent descriptions of empowerment evaluation pay more attention to both providing evidence to support these ratings, and to assessing the quality of this evidence, rather than accepting this assumed knowledge uncritically.

The third step involves charting a course for the future. The group states goals and strategies to achieve their dreams. Goals help program staff members and participants determine where they want to go in the future with an explicit emphasis on program improvement. Strategies help them accomplish program goals. These efforts are monitored using credible documentation. Empowerment evaluators help program staff members and participants identify the type of evidence required to document progress toward their goals. Evaluation becomes a part of the normal planning and management of the program, which is a means of institutionalizing and internalizing evaluation.

Empowerment evaluation therefore implicitly shares many features with organizational learning concepts and practice. In its pure form, it combines elements of collaborative strategic planning, visioning, reflection, and action research. The problems from a learning and improvement perspective lie in the practice – especially the quality of reflection and the assumption that "teams" are unproblematic and liberating.

Empowerment evaluation has also been criticized as being a method of teaching people about evaluation rather than being an evaluation method itself (Scriven, 1997). Although self-reflection is an important aspect of the empowerment evaluation, its stress on democratic decision-making also opens it up to criticism of being subject to majority pressure and the lowest common denominator. This is an inherent feature of the "patterning" orientation of most group-based inquiries, compared with the "puzzling" orientation of most expert-driven inquiries. However, the situated learning literature suggests that the problems can be overcome with adequate "scaffolding" of the learning situation. Thus, the nature and depth of reflection depends critically on the orientation and the skill of an expert facilitator.

Empowerment evaluation shares with appreciative inquiry and action research no particular perspective on how or why organizations or programs change. However, some (e.g. Scriven, 1997) have pointed to the fact that most empowerment evaluations seek to empower staff (e.g., the street-level bureaucrat), and suggested that this may actually work against putting clients' concerns and needs at the center of practice change (e.g., the external influence perspective). The label of the approach is also of concern if empowerment is understood to be something that an oppressed group must do for themselves, not something that an external facilitator, however well-intentioned, can do; empower is fundamentally not a transitive verb.

Evaluative Inquiry

Evaluative inquiry for learning in organizations (Preskill & Torres, 1999) draws directly from action science, action research, and the team learning concepts reflected in Senge's approach to organizational development. More specifically, the approach centers around four mechanisms by which people learn:

- Dialog (essentially a process of balancing advocacy with inquiry)
- Reflection
- Asking powerful questions (of the evaluative process as well as the program and its environment)
- Clarifying values, beliefs, assumptions, and knowledge

An evaluative inquiry follows a fairly traditional participative and collaborative evaluation process, but on its way it asks some tough questions of that process. These questions (just over a hundred of them) are really what distinguishes evaluative inquiry from other participative evaluation approaches. These questions reflect many of the features that promote individual and collective learning, and imply a range of perspective on organizational dynamics.

For example, Preskill & Torres (1999) suggested that evaluators should explicitly assess the organization's orientation towards learning to develop evaluations that are most likely to be able to be used. The questions they suggest posing include:

- What kinds of data does the organization typically respond to? What does it ignore?
- What incentives are there for organizational members to make the changes in their daily practices that it will require?
- To what extent will the organization's existing infrastructure (culture, leadership, modes of communication, other systems and structures) either support or undermine implementation of this action alternative?
- Conversely, what impact will it likely have on any elements of the infrastructure?

Thus, evaluative inquiry's approach to organizational development is eclectic rather than based on a single concept of organizational change. Also, unlike many evaluation approaches, evaluative inquiry strongly emphasizes the need to build up organizational development infrastructure before, during, and after the evaluation itself. It draws inspiration from a wide range of learning theories, compared with approaches specifically built on learning theory, although it is not clear how those theories underpin the selection of methods.

Evaluative inquiry is more structured than action research, and inherently more critically reflective than empowerment evaluation or appreciative inquiry. Unlike empowerment evaluation and appreciative inquiry, the issues of team building and team balance are not treated as unproblematic.

Systemic Evaluation

Systemic evaluation (Boyd et al., 2005) was developed within the field of Operational Research (OR) and thus implicitly draws on many of the ideas we have described earlier. It blends three different approaches to evaluation within a methodological framework drawn from a branch of systems theory known as critical systems thinking (CST) (e.g., Ulrich, 2000).

CST has at its core the notion that interventions to improve programs should be based on three principles.

The first principle of CST is, an appreciation of what lies inside and outside the system as it exists now and as it might exist in the future. In other words, CST is strongly focused on what happens at the boundary of an inquiry. A CST-based inquiry will create a debate around the program's purpose, values, activities, and intended actions.

The second principle is an acknowledgment that the observer (or evaluator) is part of the system being studied. So it will create a debate about the evaluation's purpose, values, methods, analysis, and conclusions. The result of this debate usually means that the evaluation not only contains a mixture of methods, but also a mixture of methodologies – different theoretical constructs are used.

The third principle is based on deeply exploring what people mean by "improvement." What freedom (ideologically and practically) does the system have to improve, and what are the possible unforeseeable and unforeseen consequences of any particular intervention? Over the past few years, systemic evaluators have developed a variety of different heuristics to help balance these principles and perspectives. (e.g., Urlich's critical systems heuristic). Practice improvement is therefore an inherent, core part of systemic evaluation. Indeed, its ethical stance about where to draw the boundary between who or what is "in" and "out" of the evaluation, poses some hard questions about the relationship between evaluation and practice improvement – improvement from whose point of view and for what benefit? Systemic evaluation consciously addresses most of the learning, organizational development, and cultural perspectives discussed in this chapter (including unusually the conflict and bargaining aspects of organizational dynamics).

We turn now to four approaches to evaluation which less explicitly address processes of learning and organizational change.

Success Case Method

The success case method (SCM; Brinkerhoff, 2003) was developed specifically to enable evaluation to contribute towards program and practice improvement through evaluating the impact of a particular intervention (e.g., a new process, a training program, an innovation). Although it was not developed explicitly from organizational learning or organizational development theories, it is based on some of the ideas already mentioned in this chapter – in particular, a rigorous focus on "what works," where it works, how it works, and how can this be built on.

The classic SCM approach has three key features. First, a logic model is developed that articulates how a particular intervention is expected to lead to a particular improvement. Then some "success" cases that demonstrate this relationship are selected, either through a survey or consultation. Sometimes "unsuccessful" cases are also selected. Finally, a sample of respondents making claims is interviewed in depth about the validity and accuracy of that claim.

Generally SCM assumes one of the more emergent models of organizational development (e.g., street-level bureaucrat), although it is often used in a managerial hierarchy reporting framework. Essentially, SCM is likely to promote learning because it is less likely than many evaluation methods to encounter *defensive* routines (see section on this below) because it avoids directly challenging people's mental models, whilst subtly delving into double-loop learning territory.

It also has a forward, visioning orientation rather than a retrospective problem-solving one. The questioning technique aims to explore the assumptions people make – by first developing a logic model, and then testing it out in the field. Its focus on personal experience will tend to evoke "single-loop learning" rather than "double-loop learning" responses, and the logic model is more akin to program logic approaches than to deep systemic approaches, but these could be incorporated relatively easily. For instance, interviews could also require people to justify their view of the link between the intervention and the improvement and could delve into people's mental models.

Evidence-Based Practice

While the term "evidence-based practice" is fairly recent, its roots go back at least to Taylor's (1911) scientific management approach. Taylor focused on identifying the best way to do things, and on helping others to use this information either through documenting it clearly or by redesigning the task. For example, having found the optimum weight of material that could be shoveled, he designed a shovel that could not carry more.

More recently there have been extensive efforts internationally to identify, document, and disseminate descriptions of best practice or "What works" in order to improve practice. Among the various versions of evidence-based practice and best practice, we have identified five broad clusters:

- *Meta-analysis*: Previous evaluations that meet particular methodological requirements are quantitatively synthesized to produce knowledge about "what works" in terms of implementation approaches, e.g., the Cochrane Collaboration for evidence-based medicine, and the similar Campbell Collaboration for human services such as education, criminal justice (Shadish et al., 2005).

- *Realist synthesis*: Previous evaluations using a range of methods and designs are synthesized analytically to produce knowledge about generative mechanisms that can be triggered by practice within particular contexts (i.e., what underlying assumptions works for whom in which programs in what contexts?) (Pawson, 2002; Farqhuar, 2003; Levine, 2004).
- *Proven practice*: A specific implementation package is developed, rigorously evaluated, and then replicated with sufficient fidelity – a franchise-like approach to improvement.
- *Corporate memory*: Information about previous practice within the organization is used to inform current practice. This could include organizational myths, shared histories, and performance data. Knowledge management techniques are used to gather, record, and access this information.
- *Reflective practice*: Practitioners use information about their current practice and its results, using techniques such as performance monitoring, learning logs, portfolios, and individual or group reflection.

Evidence-based practice is likely to have elements of *each* of these approaches, although the first three have received greater attention.

While evidence-based practice is an appealing approach, particularly for organizations seeking to reduce uncertainty, there are a number of challenges. The notion of "best practice," even in a realist sense, is highly problematic. It is only ever based on a review of a subset of existing practice, focuses on particular outcomes, and is based on the evidence available at the time. The generalizations produced by any study may decay over time. For instance, most of the companies showcased by Peters & Waterman's (1982) influential book *In Search of Excellence* experienced serious decline in subsequent performance. The designation of particular projects or approaches as "best practice" can stop further innovation and development, encouraging ossification.

Another danger is copying into an inappropriate context. Peters & Waterman's principles were adopted widely where they were not appropriate, including by small community-sector organizations. Some approaches to best practice try to identify the contexts within which particular approaches will be more or less successful. This can be controversial when these recommendations relate to different groups of clients, and can be at odds with the desire for equal access to services.

Meta-analysis and proven practice raise issues about applying a general pattern to a particular situation, and about the ability of an external authority to "identify and introduce a superior template" (Pascale & Sternin, 2005). Corporate memory and reflective practice, on the other hand, risks an excessively introverted and self-referential approach.

So how can evidence-based practice be made more valuable? Systems-based approaches provide a means to address the problems of timeliness and generalizability. The notion of mental models and organizational dynamics can overcome introspectiveness. The idea flowing from situated learning can help people synthesize evidence from their own practice and that of others.

Performance Monitoring

Performance monitoring works through providing information to check implementation during the program. The theory is that performance improvement comes about through data that "indicate" the overall behavior of the program. These indicators may be developed using a causal model or through trial-and-error. Much performance monitoring has focused on improving the accountability of government and non-government organizations, but it is also important as an approach to improving the quality of services and of practice (e.g., Luce & Thompson's (2005) recommendations for school districts).

While in theory, performance monitoring is a good idea, it has been remarkably difficult to enact successfully – historically so. Although some of the accounts of performance monitoring suggest that it is a recent development or emphasis (e.g., CGIAR, 2003), similar development of performance indicators was undertaken as part of the Planning–Programming–Budgeting System (PPBS) in the US in the 1960s (Lyden & Miller, 1967), and earlier in 19th-century England. There were contemporary criticisms of pay-for-performance systems in English school education in the 1880s based on meeting specific targets (Bullen, 1991; Rapple, 1994), and the difficulties in getting the PBBS system to actually contribute to practice improvement were discussed at the time (Rittell & Webber, 1973) in a history that seems to have been either forgotten or ignored in more recent discussions of performance monitoring.

What are these long-held concerns about the use of performance monitoring, and to what extent can they be addressed? (Propper & Wilson, 2003; Perrin, 2003) Clearly, this approach is dependent on having both valid and timely information about activities and results; it further depends on an accurate assessment of how these results contribute to the overall performance of the program. All of these can be difficult. For many programs, activities and results cannot be directly observed (Gregory, 1995; Wholey, 2003). There is a possibility that some of the short-term results that are easier to observe may not be directly related to the longer-term results – for example, easily corrected deviations from the performance indicator might not be the ones that are most important in improving the program.

Systems theory is rarely considered in the design or use of performance monitoring. In particular, there can be considerable challenges in terms of the timeliness of performance information, delayed feedback, and complex dynamics leading to emergent properties.

There is a considerable risk of mistaking interim feedback for final feedback and taking inappropriate action on that basis.

Performance monitoring is often based on a very shallow view of organizational dynamics – typically restricted only to the managerial hierarchy perspective. In doing so, it misses out on collecting key information on other ways in which organizations change and develop. The rise of network governance, where a single program is implemented by several organizations working together, raises further issues for performance monitoring (Uusikylä & Valovirta, 2002).

Another often ignored issue is the cultural and motivational assumption that publicly shaming or praising against specific measures leads to a behavioral response that improves performance. Many of the learning and cultural theories suggest that this risks the development of defensive routines (see below) – or goal displacement where people focus on achieving the measure rather than focusing on the wider vision of program improvement (Perrin, 2003; Winston, 1999).

Program Theory

Program theory involves developing a causal model of the program and then using this to guide the evaluation (Rogers et al., 2000). Program theory, also known as theory-based evaluation, theory-driven evaluation, and logic modeling, is an increasingly popular technique in evaluation that is used in very different ways to improve practice. It is sometimes used to develop large, theory-testing evaluations that try to answer the question "What works?" or "What works for whom in what circumstance?" (which are some of the evaluation types discussed previously under "evidence-based practice"). It is often used to develop indicators for performance monitoring, discussed previously. It is sometimes used to guide local evaluations that are aimed at improvement, by helping to identify important areas for data collection and for data analysis.

In addition to generating these three different types of information, program theory can contribute to practice improvement in two other ways – through helping to identify gaps in the causal chain that need to be filled in, and through developing a shared vision among staff and other stakeholders about what the program is trying to achieve and how.

Program theory can also contribute to practice improvements through helping program staff to be clearer about how their work links with broader organizational goals or changes, and increasing motivation to improve their practice (Huebner, 2000; Milne, 1993).

Program theory can expose and make explicit the tacit assumptions and mental models that underpin a program, and can then help people to use evidence to explore the validity and utility of these assumptions (van der Knaap, 2004). However, exposing these assumptions on their own is not enough. The challenge for those using program theory is to incorporate aspects of systems, group dynamic, learning, and cultural theories to help people reflect constructively and more deeply on the assumptions that underpin the theory as well as those that underpin the program. In particular, those using program theory need to explore systems-based alternatives to the traditional linear logic models used to demonstrate the program theory. There are also opportunities to combine the theories embedded within program with the theories embedded in the evaluation approach and to incorporate a finer appreciation of organizational dynamics.

Three Challenges to Using Evaluation for Practice Improvement

As we reviewed various approaches, three challenges for evaluation and practice improvement kept recurring. The first concerns the information that is produced through an evaluation, which must somehow be adequately relevant and comprehensive while also being timely. The second and third concern what happens in response to this information – the assumptions that can get in the way of taking in new information, and the defensive routines that can erupt in response to the emotions (such as shame, guilt, envy, and anxiety) generated by evaluations.

Balancing Timeliness and Relevance of Information About Current Performance

Many of the approaches to evaluation reviewed in this chapter depend on being able to provide information about current and past performance to people who can use this information to modify implementation. The notion of feedback comes from systems theory, where data about a current state in a particular context influence subsequent actions. Feedback can generate a reinforcing loop. For example, initial success may lead to greater engagement, which then leads to greater success. Or a balancing, or self-correcting, loop can occur. For example, a popular program on a fixed budget and staffing can get overwhelmed by clients, which reduces the quality of the service, which in turn reduces the number of clients, which then allows the quality of the service to improve.

There are two distinct but important reasons for evaluators to get a grip on the relationship between timeliness, delay, feedback, and practice improvement.

The first is to understand the relationship *within* the program, in order to understand its dynamics, and the appropriateness of people's responses to feedback. In program management, it is expected that a manager might adjust implementation to get the right balance between a set of performance indicators, for

example, shortening service duration to achieve throughput targets, or increasing it to achieve quality targets.

The timeliness of feedback is important. If delays exist between our action and getting information about the effects of that action, difficulties such as over-correction can result. But shortening the information cycle, by providing information on short-term outcomes that respond more quickly to actions, can create "misinformation," because we then risk interpreting interim feedback for the final feedback, making inaccurate judgments about whether things are working well or not, and taking inappropriate action. (These are known as "fixes that fail" in system dynamics jargon.)

The second reason is to understand the relationship *between* the program, its evaluation, and its environment. Programs and program environments have their own cycles – political, decision-making, budgeting, recruitment, service delivery. Evaluations have their own cycles. Matching the two in a way that allows the right information to be available at the right time is critical.

The wider adoption of systems-based methods may help to at least model the dynamics of processes – in particular, system dynamics with its sophisticated combination of logic models and scenario building. This allows exploration of the ultimate consequences of decisions and how different decisions interact with each other over time.

Assumptions About How Things Work

Taking in new information, developing meanings from that information, and using it to change behavior can be surprisingly difficult, particularly when the information does not match with deeply implicit assumptions, mental models, or habitual behavior. This was identified as a problem long ago (e.g., Epictetus (A.D. c.55–c.135) wrote "It is impossible for any one to begin to learn what he thinks that he already knows"). More recently, it has been extensively discussed in the organizational change literature. Tversky & Kahneman (1974) reported on the various ways in which people's initial assumptions influenced their ability to take in and use new information.

However, many evaluation approaches focus primarily on filling information gaps, and few have processes for checking the accuracy and continued relevance of assumed knowledge. Program theory can make some inroads into assumptions, but there is a risk that it can entrench previous assumptions about how things work. Evaluation approaches that promote puzzling or reflective practice may be a useful addition to expose and explore assumptions.

Defensive Routines and Emotional Responses

To avoid facing information that does not match our mental models, we often adopt defensive routines (Argyris & Schön, 1996), where we:

- Advocate our views without encouraging inquiry (hence, remaining in unilateral control and hopefully winning);
- Unilaterally save face – our own and other people's (hence, minimizing upsetting others or making them defensive);
- Design and manage situations unilaterally (in order to maintain control);
- Evaluate the thoughts and actions of others in ways that do not encourage testing the validity of the evaluation (and of our own thoughts and actions);
- Attribute causes for whatever we are trying to understand – without necessarily validating them;
- Engage in defensive actions such as blaming, stereotyping, and intellectualizing to suppress feelings.

According to Argyris & Schön, defensive routines arise as a result of situations where four rules are enacted:

- Craft messages that contain inconsistencies
- Act as if the messages are not inconsistent
- Make the ambiguity and inconsistency undiscussible
- Make the undiscussiblility undiscussible

Understanding how these defensive routines develop is critical to improving practice – especially in difficult situations.

Leaps of Inference

Argyris & Schön argued that people observe the world through a filtered continuum, which they called the Ladder of Inference. At one end of the continuum, people observe the world as it is and take action on that basis. At the other end of the continuum, people tend to view data using fixed yet unconscious theories of how the world works (i.e., assumptions, mental models). There is nothing inherently wrong in the latter decision-making, as long as we are aware of the impact of our beliefs on our analysis of the world. However, Argyris & Schön demonstrated that people generally fail to do this when feeling threatened or uncomfortable – precisely when they need to have as clear an understanding as possible.

Assumption-Based Behavior

If we base our own response to uncomfortable situations (e.g., evaluation data that challenges our idea of the program) on our beliefs, then we are also likely to interpret other people's behavior through our beliefs of them (e.g., the person who commissioned the evaluation wants the program terminated). Each party then starts communicating with the other, based less on what is said or written, but on our often unchecked ideas of where that person is coming from.

Advocacy for One's Point of View

If people fail to understand that their assessment of what is going on is filtered through unchallenged beliefs, then they are more likely to advocate or defend a position than to inquire reflectively. If they spend more time advocating for their own beliefs, rather than inquiring and engaging creatively with the puzzles and contradictions that challenge those beliefs, then learning opportunities are significantly inhibited.

Addressing Defensive Routines

The answer lies not only in careful facilitation of group and individual learning to help people move on (Donaldson et al., 2003, Schinker, 2005). It also requires the authority to do so, as well as deep understanding of what is going on. Argyris & Schön (1996) developed some techniques to help people notice their defensive routines, and move beyond them – such as the ladder of inference, where the evidence for assumptions and conclusions is carefully set out. Practitioners who use Vygotskyian approaches to learning have developed a range of tools that allow people to feel more comfortable exploring challenges to their mental models.

Other emotional responses to evaluation, such as anxiety, shame, guilt, and hostility (Kilburg, 1980; Brody, 1957), can inhibit processes of learning and improvement. Evaluation approaches vary considerably in the extent to which they address these emotional responses, as do individual evaluation practitioners. It may be that additional skills and experience are needed within a team undertaking evaluations that are aimed at learning and change.

Summary and Conclusion

Evaluations that seek to improve practice are premised on an (often implicit) theory of change linking the evaluation with such improvement. What this chapter has sought to do is to explore the assumptions that underpin the overall approaches to evaluation and program improvement, as illustrated in nine individual evaluation methods. We have done this by comparing these evaluation approaches and methods with what is known about learning, cultural orientations, and organizational dynamics.

Some of the most common approaches to evaluation often associated with practice improvement – performance monitoring, program theory, and evidence-based practice – have gaps in the implicit theory linking them with the intended change, and we suggest that anyone using these methods needs to focus on filling in these gaps in some way. We also conclude, unsurprisingly, that some of the approaches closely associated with learning and organizational development also have their blind spots that need coloring in.

In evaluation, as in practice, good intentions are not enough for improvement. Evaluators, people commissioning evaluations, and people evaluating their own work should consider their choices carefully when it comes to designing and implementing evaluations that are intended to contribute to practice improvement and organizational learning. These choices should be informed by an analysis of:

- the different types of learning that the evaluation requires (see pp. 77–80)
- the concepts of organizational and cultural dynamics that influence how those meanings are translated into practice (see pp. 80–82)
- ways to address the challenges of balancing timeliness and comprehensiveness; of going beyond assumptions, and of overcoming defensive routines. (see pp. 92–94)

Across all of these areas there is much to learn and apply in our evaluation work. We looked at some of the more promising approaches in current evaluation practice.

However, it is also wise to acknowledge Allen Schick's comments that opened this chapter. Whilst there are many things that we should do to increase the influence of evaluation on program performance, on their own they may not be sufficient. Perhaps there is another judgment to make – whether the program and the setting is capable of improving itself. We believe the analytical tools in this chapter also provide ways of addressing this.

Acknowledgments

Thanks to John Newton, Susan Long, Helen Goodman, Mike Faris, Dugan Fraser, Jerome Winston, Gerald Elsworth, Paul Cameron, Michael Patton, and Mel Mark for helpful comments on earlier and vastly different drafts.

References

Argyris, C. & Schön, D. (1996). *Organizational Learning II: Theory, method and practice.* Reading, Mass: Addison Wesley.

Bateson, G. (1972). *Steps to an Ecology of Mind.* New York: Ballantine Books.

Boyd, A., Geerling, T., Gregory, W. J., Kagan, C., Midgley, G., Murray, P., & Walsh, M. P. (2005) Systemic evaluation. *Journal of the Operational Research Society* (in press).

Brinkerhoff, R. (2003). *The Success Case Method: Find out quickly what's working and what's not.* San Francisco: Berrett-Koehler.

Brody, E. B. (1957). Discussion of anxieties associated with the conduct of research in a clinical setting. *American Journal of Orthopsychiatry,* 27, 327–330. (Cited in Kilburg, 1980.)

Bullen, P. (1991). Performance Indicators: New management jargon, political marketing, or one small element in developing quality services? *Caring, the Association of Children's Welfare Agencies Newsletter,* September.

CGIAR (Consultative Group in International Agricultural Research) Working Group on Performance Measurement (2003) *Towards Designing a Performance Measurement System for the CGIAR.* Report. Available at http://www.cgiar.org/pdf/agm03/agm03bus_wgpm_report.pdf.

Davidson, E. J. (2001). Mainstreaming evaluation into an organization's learning culture. Paper presented at the 2001 AEA Meeting St Louis, MO. Available at http://www.davidson consulting.co.nz/index_files/pres/olcult.pdf.

Davidson, E. J. (2005). *Evaluation Methodology Basics: The nuts and bolts of sound evaluation.* Newbury Park, CA: Sage.

Dick, B. (2005). *Action Research Resources.* http:// www.uq.net.au/action_research/arp/arphome. html.

Donaldson, S. I., Gooler, L. E., & Scriven, M. (2002). Strategies for managing evaluation anxiety: Toward a psychology of program evaluation. *American Journal of Evaluation,* 23(3), 261–272, 185–228.

Edwards J. (2001). The things we steal from children. Paper presented at the Ninth International Conference on Thinking. Auckland, New Zealand.

Elliott, C. (1999). *Locating the Energy for Change: An introduction to appreciative inquiry.* Winnipeg: International Institute for Sustainable Development. Available for download at http://iisd1.iisd.ca/pdf/appreciativeinquiry.pdf.

Elmore, R. (1978). Organizational models of social program implementation. *Public Policy,* 26(2), 185–228.

Eoyang, G. & Berkas, T. (1998). Evaluation in complex adaptive system. Available at http:// www.winternet.com/~eoyang/EvalinCAS.pdf.

Farquhar, S. (2003). *Quality Teaching Early Foundations: Best evidence synthesis.* Wellington, New Zealand. Ministry of Education. Available at http://www.minedu.govt.nz/web/down-loadable/dl8646_v1/qtef-bes-28-08.pdf.

Fetterman, D. (1996). *Empowerment Evaluation: Knowledge and tools for self assessment and accountability.* Thousand Oaks, CA: Sage.

Fetterman, D. (2005). Empowerment evaluation. http://www.stanford.edu/~davidf/empower mentevaluation.html.

Flood, R. (1998). *Rethinking the Fifth Discipline: Learning within the unknowable.* London: Routledge.

Gregory, A. (2000). Problematizing participation: A critical review of approaches to participation in evaluation theory. *Evaluation: The International Journal of Theory, Research and Practice,* 6(2), 179–199.

Gregory, R.J. (1995). Accountability, responsibility, and corruption: managing the 'public production process. In J. Boston (ed.) *The State Under Contract*. Wellington, NZ: Bridget Williams Books.

Harris, B. & Williams, B. (2001). Learning logs: Structured journals that work for busy people', In S. Sankaran, B. Dick, R. Passfield & P. Swepson (eds) *Effective Change Management Using Action Learning and Action Research*. Lismore, Queensland: Southern Cross University Press.

House, E. & Howe, K. (2000). *Deliberative Democratic Checklist*. Available at http://www.wmich.edu/evalctr/checklists/dd_checklist.pdf.

Huebner, T. A. (2000). Theory-based evaluation: Gaining a shared understanding between school staff and evaluators. In P. J., Rogers, A. J., Petrosino, T. A. Hacsi, & T. A. Huebner (eds). *Program Theory Evaluation: Challenges and Opportunities. New Directions in Evaluation*, No. 87. San Francisco: Jossey-Bass.

Kemmis, S. & McTaggart, R. (1988). *The Action Research Planner*, 3rd edition. Geelong: Deakin University.

Kilburg, R. (1980). Metaphysics and professional resistance to program evaluation. *Evaluation and Program Planning*, 3, 185–190.

Lavé, J. & Wenger, E. (1990). *Situated Learning: Legitimate Peripheral Participation*. Cambridge, UK: Cambridge University Press.

Levine, R., and the What Works Working Group with Molly Kinder (2004). *Millions Saved: Proven Success in Global Health*. Center for Global Development: Washington DC. Extracts available at http://www.cgdev.org/section/initiatives/_active/millionssaved.

Lippett, R. (1949). *Training in Community Relations*. New York: Harper and Row.

Long. S. & Newton, J. (1997). Educating the gut: Socio-emotional aspects of the learning organization. *The Journal of Management Development*, 16(4), 284–301.

Luce, T. & Thompson, L. (2005). *Do What Works: How proven practices can improve American schools*. Dallas, TX: Ascent Education Press.

Lyden, F. & Miller, E. (eds) (1967). *Planning Programming Budgeting: A systems approach to management*. Chicago: Markham.

Milne, C. (1993). Outcomes hierarchies and program logic as conceptual tools: Five case studies. A paper presented at the Australasian Evaluation Society International Conference, Brisbane.

Pascale, R. & Sternin, J. (2005). Your company's secret change agents. *Harvard Business Review* 83(5): 73–81.

Patton, M. Q. (1994). 'Developmental evaluation. *Evaluation Practice* 15(3), 311–319.

Pawson, R. (2002). Evidence-based policy: The promise of 'realist synthesis.' *Evaluation: The International Journal of Theory, Research and Practice*, 8(3), 340–358.

Perrin, B. (2003). Implementing the Vision: Addressing the challenges of results-based management. OCED. Available at http://www.oecd.org/dataoecd/4/10/2497163.pdf.

Peters, T. J. & Waterman, R. H. (1982). *In Search of Excellence: Lessons from America's best-run companies*. New York: Harper and Row.

Preskill, H. & Coghlan, A. (eds) (2003). *Appreciative Inquiry and Evaluation. New Directions for Evaluation*, No. 100 San Francisco: Jossey-Bass.

Preskill, H. & Torres, R. (1999) Building capacity for organizational learning through evaluative inquiry. *Evaluation: The International Journal of Theory, Research and Practice*, 5(1), 42–60.

Propper, C. & Wilson, D. (2003). The Use and Usefulness of Performance Measures in the Public Sector. CMPO Working Paper Series No. 03/073. Available at http://www.bris.ac.uk/Depts/CMPO/workingpapers/wp73.pdf.

Rapple, B. A. (1994). Payment by Results: An Example of Assessment in Elementary Education from Nineteenth Century Britain *Educational Policy Analysis Archive*, 2 (1), January 5. Available at http://epaa.asu.edu/epaa/v2n1.html.

Reason, P. & Bradbury, H. (eds) (2001). *Handbook of Action Research: Participative inquiry and Practice*. London: Sage Publications. Copy of 'Introduction' available at http://www.bath.ac.uk/~mnspwr/Papers/HandbookIntroduction.htm.

Rittell, H. & Webber, M. (1973). Dilemmas in a general theory of planning. *Policy Sciences*, 4, 155–169.

Rogers, P. J. & Fraser, D. (2004). Appreciating appreciative inquiry. In H. Preskill & A. Coghlan (eds) *Appreciative Inquiry and Evaluation. New Directions for Evaluation*, No. 100. San Francisco: Jossey-Bass.

Rogers, P. J. & Hough, G. (1995). Improving the effectiveness of evaluations: Making the link to organisational theory. *Evaluation and Program Planning*, 18(4), 321–332.

Rogers, P. J., Petrosino, A. J., Hacsi, T. A. & Huebner, T. A. (eds) (2000). *Program Theory Evaluation: Challenges and Opportunities New Directions in Evaluation*, No. 87. San Francisco: Jossey-Bass.

Schick, A. (2003). The performing state: Reflection on an idea whose time has come but whose implementation has not. *OECD Journal on Budgeting*, 3(2), 74–108.

Schein, E. H. (1996). Three cultures of management: The key to organizational learning. Sloan *Management Review*, 38(1).

Schinker, R. (2005). Managing extreme evaluation anxiety through nonverbal communication. *Journal of Multidisciplinary Evaluation*, 2, 76

Schön, D. (1983). *The Reflective Practitioner*. New York: Basic Books.

Scriven, M. (1997). Empowerment evaluation examined. *Evaluation Practice*, 18(2), 165–175.

Senge, P. (1990). *The Fifth Discipline: The art and practice of the learning organization*. New York: Doubleday.

Shadish, W. R., Chacon-Moscoso, S. & Sanchez-Meca, Julio. (2005). Evidence-based decision making: Enhancing systematic reviews of program evaluation results in Europe. *Evaluation: The International Journal of Theory, Research and Practice*, 11(1), 95–109.

Siebert, K. & Daudelin, M. (1999). *The Role of Reflection in Managerial Learning: Theory, research and practice*. London: Quorum.

Taylor, F. W. (1911). *The Principles of Scientific Management*.

Tversky, A. & Kahneman, D. (1974). Judgment under uncertainty: Heuristics and biases. *Science*, 185, 1124–1130.

Ulrich, W. (2000). Reflective practice in the civil society: the contribution of critically systemic thinking, *Reflective Practice*, 1(2): 247–268.

Also downloadable from http://www.geocities. com/csh_home/downloads.html.

Uusikylä, P. & Valovirta, V. (2002). Three spheres of performance governance: Spanning the boundaries from single-organisation focus towards a partnership network. Paper presented at the Conference of the European Group of Public Administration September 2004, Ljubljana, Slovenia. Available at www.soc. kuleuven.ac.be/pol/io/egpa/qual/ljubljana/ Valovirta%20Uusikila_paper.pdf.

van der Knaap, P. (2004). Theory-based evaluation and learning: Possibilities and challenges. *Evaluation: The International Journal of Theory, Research and Practice*, 10(1), 16–34.

Vygotsky, L. S. (1978). *Mind and Society* (M. Cole, V. John-Steiner, S. Scribner, & E. Souberman, eds). Cambridge, MA: Harvard University Press.

Wadsworth, Y. (1997). *Everyday Evaluation on the Run*, 2nd edition. St Leonards, NSW: Allen & Unwin Australia.

Whitney, D. & Trosten-Bloom, A. (2003). *The Power of Appreciative Inquiry: A practical guide to positive change*. Berrett-Koehler.

Wholey, J. S. (2003). Using policy evaluation to support decisionmaking and improve program performance. *The Japanese Journal of Evaluation Studies*, 3(2), 6–21. Available at http://www. idcj.or.jp/JES/JJESvol3no2.pdf.

Williams, B. (2002). *Evaluation And Systems Thinking*. Available at http://users.actrix.co. nz/bobwill/evalsys.pdf.

Williams, B. (2003). *A Data Analysis Tool*. Available at http://users.actrix.co.nz/bobwill/analysis. pdf.

Williams, B. (2005) *Systems Stuff*. Available at http://users.actrix.co.nz/bobwill/Resources. html#SYSTEMS.

Winston, J. A. (1999) Performance indicators – Promises unmet: A response to Perrin. *American Journal of Evaluation*, 20(1), 95–99.

4

EVALUATION AND THE STUDY OF LIVED EXPERIENCE

Thomas A. Schwandt and Holli Burgon

Scene: A municipality in northern Norway; municipal officials charged with the administration and coordination of rehabilitation services for individuals in the community are meeting with representatives of several medical and social services (hospital-based physicians, vocational rehabilitation workers, occupational health personnel, physiotherapists, nurses, social workers, etc.) and representatives of several advocacy groups for disabled people. This is the second in a series of several meetings organized by the municipality. The topic of discussion is how best to design an evaluation of rehabilitation. Norwegian policy has recently defined rehabilitation as a set of processes that are planned and limited in time, with well-defined goals and means; wherein several professions or social services cooperate in assisting individual users in their efforts to achieve the best possible functioning and coping capabilities, while also promoting their independence and participation in

society. Two external evaluators have been invited to participate in the conversation to offer their advice and assistance in the design of the evaluation that will eventually be commissioned by the municipality.

The conversation, often quite heated at times, and generally dominated by the powerful voices of the medical professionals, ranges over the concerns of various groups – for example, ensuring functional improvement, integration into the workforce, providing coordinated assistance, respecting the user's autonomy, tailoring services to individual needs, facilitating user empowerment, integration of disabled individuals into community life, and so on:

[Evaluator 1:] I think the best way to address the evaluation issues here is to look carefully at the definition of rehabilitation as a process for service provision that has well-defined characteristics and well-defined categories of beneficiaries. What I suggest is that we begin by defining the key dimensions of various types of rehabilitation processes, including who is (and ought to be) involved, and how. We work towards developing a set of criteria for planning processes that can, in turn, be used as a template to examine whether they are effective and efficient in achieving intended outcomes for different types of beneficiaries. We want to get at the facts of the matter here, so to speak – what does planning entail; what is an adequate measure of cooperation among professionals in planning; how do we judge whether the intended outcomes of planning were achieved; how is the process related to variables like available time, resource constraints, service location, professional responsibilities, user needs and values, and so forth. . .

[Evaluator 2:] I agree, in general, with the idea of looking at rehabilitation as a process. But I suggest we focus on portrayals of what various people involved in this "process" actually experience. In other words, we might attempt to grasp the various actors' understandings of the meaning of rehabilitation and the ways in which they attach value to it. I suggest that we think in terms of the ways people involved in rehabilitation make sense of their experience with it. In other words, focus on understanding rehabilitation as a lived reality; how it is felt, experienced, undergone, made sense of, accomplished, and valued. Rather than orienting the evaluation around such notions as planning processes, service providers and beneficiaries, means and outcomes, and goals and variables, we might think in terms of meanings, norms, routines, rituals, interactions, deliberations, dilemmas, paradoxes, issues, and so forth – ideas that draw our attention to the immediacy and particularity of the experience of rehabilitation. . .

This semi-fictionalized scenario is intended to convey a very wide-ranging sense of two different ways of approaching the task of evaluating educational and social programs. One way is focused on programs as objects or "thing-like" entities with identifiable properties that can be categorized and measured.

Robert Stake (2004) broadly characterized this way of thinking about evaluation as measurement-oriented and centered on matters of standards and criteria. The other way attends to programs as multifaceted compositions of lived human experiences permeated with meanings. Stake (2004, p. xv) has identified this way of thinking of evaluation as experience-oriented, building upon "experiential, personal knowing in real space and time and with real people" and "steadfastly responsive to the chronological activity, the perceptions, and the voices of people associated with [that which is being evaluated]." Of course, the evaluation task can be conceived in either way, and perhaps even in both ways to some degree simultaneously, but explaining and justifying that idea are not the purpose of this chapter. Rather, this chapter is devoted to an explication of evaluation that is experience-oriented, using two general notions – lived experience and practice – as general guides to understanding. As will become apparent in what follows, these two ideas are related but not identical and they provide a way of understanding some of the differences in ways of thinking about evaluation practice as focused on experience. The chapter unfolds as follows: First, it offers a characterization of some of the more prominent ideas that animate the focus on lived experience and practice. Second, it illustrates contemporary examples of evaluation approaches displaying variations in the meaning of experience-oriented evaluation. Third, it concludes with some thoughts on potentially fruitful avenues for further exploration and study.

Focus on Lived Experience: Intellectual Points of Reference

The primary sources of ideas about lived experience are found in the tradition of continental philosophy – in the intellectual movements of phenomenology, existentialism, hermeneutics, and critical theory – and not in the Anglo-American traditions of empiricism, logical positivism, and analytic philosophy. This is noteworthy in one important respect. The latter traditions are far more science-friendly, while the mood, so to speak, of continental philosophy was characteristically hostile to scientism (Cooper, 1996).[1] By calling attention to this well-known characteristic of these continental intellectual traditions, we do not mean to imply that all who currently value lived experience as a source for approaching the task of evaluation necessarily endorse this anti-scientism. Yet, healthy skepticism toward the claims of scientific evaluation (however conceived) is surely characteristic of many who do. Unquestionably, in the climate of evidence-based practice and science-based research in education and social services in which this chapter is now being written, criticisms of "scientific evaluation" have assumed special salience. However, our aim here is not to recount and discuss these criticisms, but simply to note that a focus on lived experience is often (but not always) partially motivated by criticism of some measurement-oriented alternative.

It is a truism that many evaluations draw, in some form or another, on stakeholders' experience as a source of evidence for making judgments about program value. One of the most important uses of interviews in evaluation is to learn what people have experienced – to draw out their descriptions of actions, activities, and feelings (Kvale, 1996; Patton, 2002; Stake, 2004). This information often is incorporated in frameworks for evaluation governed by measurement of goals, objectives, effects, outcomes, and the like. Yet, evaluations "oriented to experience" display more than a commitment to collecting data about stakeholders' opinions, perspectives, and experiences. These evaluations, in general, hold

that understanding and interpreting lived experience is *fundamental* to the activity of evaluation as social inquiry. The foundational nature of this commitment means that the primary task for the evaluator is to understand, portray, and interpret the meanings that actions and events have for those involved in a program. To grasp meaning, in turn, requires what Stake (1991) has called anthropological sensitivity and what fieldworkers (e.g., Emerson, 1983) have identified as appreciation of the distinctive concerns, forms of life, practices, and ways of speaking and behaving found in a particular setting. Appreciation is more than an attitude of respect; it is a kind of attunement to the particulars of experience, to its textures and concrete details, its situatedness in time and space. It is "situational appreciation" – the capacity to discern with clarity, imagination, and a quality sustained by embodied knowing and engagement with others the salient particulars of a situation (Pendlebury, 1995). This kind of attentiveness involves interpretive understanding – something more than the collection of facts and observation of events. Interpretive understanding is not simply an intellectual undertaking but a form of experiential, holistic learning.

It is beyond the charter of this chapter to explore the well-rehearsed, long, and complex history of an interpretive orientation to investigations of social phenomena (see, e.g., Bernstein, 1976; Hiley, Bohman, & Shusterman, 1991; Taylor, 1985). Here we only briefly mention a few points of reference for grasping the centrality of lived experience to this way of thinking. Many scholars trace the origins of the concern with life as it is experienced to the life philosophy of Wilhelm Dilthey that held that the only proper focus for human science is the concrete life – the experience of historically and culturally situated agents and their actions (Polkinghorne,

1983, p. 24ff.). Dilthey advanced this idea in opposition to two other prominent ways of thinking at the time – transcendentalism and (naïve) empiricism. Transcendentalism argued that there was some ultimate reality "behind" life that could explain it. Dilthey, on the contrary, maintained that there was no point outside of life on which to stand and observe it; all knowledge of life is an activity of life itself focused on itself. Naïve empiricism regarded "experience" to be nothing more than sensory input of disconnected sensations and impressions. Dilthey held that life experience is already full of meaning and understandable as it appears to us.

Another important reference point is the existential phenomenology of Martin Heidegger and Maurice Merleau-Ponty, among others, and its social science offspring – phenomenological sociology and ethnomethodology – inspired by the work of Alfred Schutz. Common to this intellectual development was a call for a return to the experience of the concrete, sensuous everyday life world. Again, this experience is not that of the British empiricists' "sense impressions" but of perceptions and understandings already shaped with schemes of interpretation and typifications in terms of objectives, values, meanings, and so on. This lived experience is embedded in and bears the imprint of a lifeworld – a world with historical dimensions extending backward in time and alluding to the future as well, a world which is continually changing (Alvesson & Sköldberg, 2000, p. 38). What matters for human science is understanding this world of lived experience. Many of us are familiar with a central phenomenological insight that has become common place in much sociological and anthropological inquiry, namely, the idea that any understanding of social action must begin with the social actors' own concepts, categories, and meanings in order to understand how they themselves conceive of what they are doing (Fay, 2003). Studying how actors in a given social situation invest objects, events, and experiences with meaning and then reconstructing (interpreting) those understandings is a mainstay of interpretive social science (Geertz, 1973; Flick, 1998).

Yet another significant influence on ways of thinking about the interpretation of lived experience is found in the hermeneutics of Hans-Georg Gadamer, Charles Taylor, and others. What is significant for our purposes here is that, from a hermeneutic point of view, the notion of the "meaning" of lived experience is not viewed as a private matter, something residing in the mind of the individual, subjective agent, but something that is intersubjectively constituted. In other words, as Brian Fay (2003) explains, the focus of social investigation is moved away from

> the conscious of the individual to the broader social world and its history on which the individual draws to be conscious in the first place. . . . To understand an individual consciousness one must situate it within the broader cultural and historical world in which it lives and breathes. This cultural world consists of language, of social rules and institutions, of cultural objects like houses and city streets and artworks, of ideologies, and so forth, all of which are situated within ongoing historical traditions. *Meaning is a broadly historical-cultural phenomenon, not an (individual) psychological one, and the interpretation of meaning (and the search for the source of meaning) must turn from the minds of people to the historically situated public world of shared practice.* (p. 51; emphasis added)

What we see here is an important turn to the "practical" – a movement away from understanding meaning in terms of inner motives, attitudes, and psychological states and toward grasping meaning in shared practices of concrete, socio-culturally, linguistically, and historically situated actors.

We pursue this line of thought in the next section.

This concern with understanding the meaning of experience as socially, historically, and linguistically *constructed* is echoed in a chief concern of ethnomethodologists who are highly critical of the assumption that lived experience is some kind of natural or authentic phenomena that can be taken at face value and relatively seamlessly represented in audiotapes, videotapes, photographs, and transcribed texts. Ethnomethodologists (e.g., Gubrium & Holstein, 1997; Silverman, 1997, 2001) argue that the bid to faithfully record the experience of others often neglects how cultural forms of representation shape experience itself. This contrast is evident in the way we think about using interviews in evaluation (Silverman, 2001). Some advocate in-depth interviewing that aims at accessing emotions, meanings, and inner experience via a kind of intersubjective communion of interviewer and interviewee resulting in an "an authentic gaze into the soul of another" (Silverman, 2001, p. 94). Others advocate using an active interview (Holstein & Gubrium, 2003) in which interviewer and interviewee are together engaged in the active construction of the meaning of experience and thus the respondent's comments and answers are "not treated as reality reports delivered from a fixed repository" of meaning (Silverman, 2001, p. 97).

A further criticism is directed at the shortcomings of the largely descriptive intent of capturing lived experience (i.e., with "what" – the subjective meanings of actors – or "how" – methods that actors use to produce social reality in everyday life). This kind of critique is most evident in work of critical theorists that endorse standpoint epistemology. To take but one example, feminist standpoint theory begins with a phenomenological approach to women's lived experience, but then analyzes that experience in terms of the structural conditions of power operative in a patriarchal society that shape women's emotions, goals, relations, feelings and

conceptions of self and subjectivity. As Dorothy Smith (1992, p. 88) explains: "The knowing subject is always located in a particular spatial and temporal site, a particular configuration of the everyday/every night world. Inquiry is directed toward exploring and explicating what she does not know – the social relations and organization pervading her world but invisible to it."

Taking the union of constructivist and critical concerns in a somewhat different direction in examining lived experience are those scholars who focus on the performance of experience (e.g., Denzin, 1997, 2003; Goodyear, 2001). They begin with the assumption that it is not possible to represent a life as it is actually lived or experienced. The link between lived experience and its expression is always problematic, and, thus, what we are able to access about lived experience are but various kinds of performances – spoken, told, and retold accounts. Moreover, these performances – narratives, stories, proverbs, and slices of conversation – are (as Smith noted above) shaped by politics of representation. Thus, those that study lived experience are naïve to assume that they can literally capture lived experience (e.g., via interviewing or observing), write it down, and unproblematically make it available to others as a source of knowledge and awareness. At best they are able to render their own performances of others' performances of their lived experience. Denzin (2002), echoing a significant trend in the "performance turn," explicitly links the performing of ethnography and of evaluation to critical and transformative agendas.

Focus on Practice: Intellectual Points of Reference

As noted above, a turn to the "practical" – that is to the situated, concrete, embodied actions and meanings of social actors – is foreshadowed in the focus on lived experience. The practical turn is a bit difficult to explain in an economical way because it takes up several sets of issues including the definitions of "practice," "practical reasoning," and "practical knowledge"; the importance of recovering practical knowledge as an antidote to technical rationality; the way in which practical knowledge (individual capacities for discernment, deliberation, and good judgment) is implicated in discussions of public, democratic participation in decision-making; and, how the cultivation of practical reason relates to matters of education and learning (e.g., Bourdieu, 1997; Dunne, 1997; Dunne & Pendlebury, 2003; Forester, 1999; Gadamer, 1981; Lave & Wenger, 1991; Molander, 1992; Pendlebury, 1990; Schön, 1983; Taylor, 1995; Toulmin, 1988, 2001; Wagenaar & Cook, 2003; Wenger, 1998; Wiggins, 1980). In what follows we single out a few salient features in what has been called the "practical turn" in the social sciences (Reckwitz, 2002; Schatzki, Knorr Cetina, & von Savigny, 2001; Stern, 2003) with implications for evaluation.

What is Practice?

Typically we think of practice in association with the idea of applying theory and science to everyday life: Theory and science is the realm of thinking and reflection, and practice – everyday life – is the realm of doing or action. In other words, theory and practice are defined in opposition to one another – theory is everything that practice is not. Thus, it is not uncommon to hear people talk about the theory of evaluation, on the one hand, and the actual practice of evaluation itself, on the other.

In the practical knowledge traditions, *practice* is not defined in terms of the theory-practice distinction; rather, *practice* is closer in meaning to the Greek term *praxis* that referred to a form of human activity concerned with the conduct of one's life as a member of society. Heidegger, for example, claimed that praxis was about our "concernful" dealings

with one another – our efforts to do the right thing and do it well in our everyday interactions with one another (McNeill, 1999). Dunne (1993) defines praxis as a:

> Type of human engagement that is embedded within a tradition of communally shared understandings and values, that remains vitally connected to peoples' life experience, that finds expression in their ordinary linguistic usage, and that, rather than being a means through which they achieve outcomes separate from themselves, is a kind of enactment through which they constitute themselves as person in a historical community. (p. 176)

The emphasis on *engagement* signifies that a practice is about one's transactions or dealings with others (and with material things). Teaching, counseling, providing health care of all kinds, social work, public administration, and so forth are all examples of these kinds of engagements. Each of these engagements or practices is simultaneously cognitive and emotive – conceptualizing and reflecting, feeling and action unfold together; each is based on shared understandings and values, connected to everyday experience, and expressed in language; each is a unique kind of purposeful, situated, flexible interaction with the world and others. Practices of all kinds are fluid, changeable, and dynamic. They are characterized by their alterability, indeterminacy, and particularity (Pendlebury, 1995).

Practice is not an object for examination on a par with terms like program or evaluand, rather, it is an analytic concept or theoretical perspective that provides a way of looking at and thinking about the meaning of lived experience that comprises a program being evaluated. As an analytic concept it directs attention away from mere doing (or behavior) and is associated with conceptual lenses such as habitus, constitutive meanings, configurations of human activity, activity systems, and so on (Wagenaar & Cook, 2003). Evaluations oriented to practice (praxis) *begin* with consideration of the realities of practice itself. The evaluator focuses on the lived reality of a program, especially the fact that practitioners are *always* facing contingencies, multiple demands on time and resources, competing conceptions of what is right to do, and so on as they make decisions. Thus, the evaluation is concerned with the deliberation of values (judging the merit, worth, or significance of various actions planned or taken) in terms of the practical activity and practical knowledge of actual daily practices (Flyvbjerg, 2001). This does *not* mean that a praxis-orientation denies the relevance of scientific thinking. What it does mean is that typically scientific considerations of valid, objective, and generalizable knowledge *follow from rather than lead* reflection on what practitioners actually perform and accomplish in their everyday knowing and doing.

Practical Reason

A significant aspect of the practical turn involves the explanation and defense of practitioners' knowledge. Central to this kind of knowledge is the idea of judgment, and judgment is different in kind than calculation or straightforward means–end, instrumental, or technical reasoning. As Dunne & Pendlebury (2003, p. 199) explain, the need for judgment in practical fields (like teaching, evaluating, administering, etc.) arises because of an "intricacy and frailty inherent in human affairs"; the practitioner is often presented with "a problematic situation where there is no discrete problem already clearly labeled as such" and hence, the practitioner faces something more like a difficulty or a predicament rather than a problem. These situations demand judgment that displays a characteristic set of elements: an open texture to the kind of deliberation involved; the need for perception or insight to meet the unique demands of each particular action-situation; an irreduciblity to general propositions,

rules, or formulas; its experiential character; and, it being directive not only of present action but itself shaped by the history of one's previous action as they have become part of one's character (Dunne & Pendlebury, 2003, p. 201). As we will show in the next section, this appeal to the importance of practical reason plays a role, albeit in different ways, in several approaches to evaluation, including the views of House and Schwandt.

Practice and Learning

A focus on practice is associated by some with socio-cultural and activity theories of learning, and we see this reflected in evaluations oriented toward organizational learning. Consider, for example, the following view offered by Lave & Wenger (1991):

> A theory of social practice emphasizes the relational dependency of agent and world, activity, meaning, cognition, learning and knowing. . . . Learning, thinking, and knowing are relations among people in activity in, with, and arising from the socially and culturally structured world. . . . One way to think about learning is as the historical production, transformation, and change of persons. (pp. 50–51)

From a "practice" perspective there is no knowledge apart from the active engagement or involvement of the knower with that which is to be known. Moreover, learning (or knowing) and application of that learning are not separate processes. Lave (1996, p. 12), for example, has argued that the separation of learning and doing is based on two questionable claims: (1) that practitioners' relations to their activity (practice) "are static and do not change except when subject to special periods of 'learning' or 'development'," and (2) that special institutional educational arrangements (e.g., workshops, professional development seminars and courses) are the circumstances for learning, separate from everyday practices of doing. In other words, we too readily assume that learning is some activity that takes place on a special occasion when a practitioner is not busy doing.

Learning in practical knowledge traditions emphasizes both participation and deliberation. Participation signifies that learning unfolds in collaborate endeavors in which new ideas, new ways of approaching problems, and new understandings are generated. Deliberation draws attention to the fact that in deciding on an effective and appropriate response to a situation, practitioners must act on what Forester (1999) describes as a "diverse, plural, and ill-defined set of concerns and values – values that may be, in any actual case, honored or ignored" (p. 230). Knowing what do in these situations cannot come from some easily applied procedure, technique, or cookbook; it cannot be a matter of "simply assessing, selecting, or recommending 'means' to well-defined and politically given ends. Instead, practice is inescapably deliberative, necessarily exploring and probing goals and ends as well as means" (p. 231).

Practical, Communicative Action

Collaborative, action-research-oriented, inclusive, participatory, and empowerment approaches to evaluation often portray evaluation less as a technical or scientific study and more as an arranged, organized event (ritual) in which participants encounter one another, listen to one another, learn about one another, and together deliberate a course of action. They often reflect the assumption that talk and dialogue are forms of practical, communicative action that change people and situations. It is through dialog and communication that we "move" one another as Shotter (1996) explains:

> For example, we "point things out" to people ("Look at this!"); give them "commands;" "remind" them ("Think what happened last

time"); "change their perspective" ("Look at it like this"); and so on. All these instructive forms of talk "direct" or "move" us, in practice, to do something we might not otherwise do: to relate ourselves to our circumstances in a different way, to look them over in a different manner. (pp. 338–339)

There are somewhat distinctively different emphases evident in these approaches to evaluation that feature the importance of communicative action. Some, for example, endorse a reflective pragmatism and democratic deliberation in which practitioners together with evaluators reflect in action. This framework is cooperative as well as deliberative and democratic. It is cooperative because evaluators and practitioners together generate problems to be solved and hunches to be tested. It is deliberative because this is a planned process for discovery, argumentation, and action. It is democratic because the process unfolds in view of a set of democratic norms or criteria for legitimate participation – for example, it must be possible for all to participate, each participant has an obligation not simply to put forth her or his own ideas but to help others contribute their ideas, all participants are equal, all arguments and points of view pertaining to the issue at hand are legitimate, the dialog must continually produce agreements that can provide the platform for practical action, and so forth.

Other evaluation approaches based in communicative action are more oriented to ideology critique and emancipation. They are more directly concerned with inequities of power and privilege that constrain or even invalidate a deliberative democratic process of reflection in action. They seek to move from participation to emancipation by focusing specifically on processes to ensure disenfranchised and traditionally powerless peoples' full participation. This often begins with critique of prevailing practices of power – who controls knowledge, whose definitions of problems and solutions dominate discussions, what role experts play (and should play), who has power (or is powerless) to speak, and so forth. Ensuring communicative action that is inclusive and empowering is a distinctive characteristic of this framework for evaluation. It is strongly attentive to often-overlooked structural positions of privilege in communication and to limitations in the norms of communication underlying reflective pragmatic-deliberative democratic approaches. These norms include privileging argument – an orderly chain of reasoning from premises to conclusion – over other forms of communication and dialog; holding forms of spoken expression that follow structures of well-formed written speech as more valuable than "circuitous, hesitant, or questioning expression"; prizing dispassionate and disembodied expression over expressions of emotion; valuing unity at all times over conflict and disagreement; holding to standards of civility of expression that rule as "out of order" forms of communication that aim to disrupt routines to call attention to unrecognized positions and issues, and so forth (Young, 2000, pp. 36–51).

A third orientation looks at the evaluation process more in terms of social and individual transformation (Prilleltensky, 2001). The aim is not simply to transform points of view, arguments, and actions through communication and dialog, but to transform persons. Forester (1999) explains:

> At the heart of this transformative account is a view of citizens' performances in safe rituals of participation in which citizens not only pursue interests strategically and display themselves expressively, but *reproduce and reconstitute their social and political relationships with one another* too. To understand participatory and deliberative encounters as social and political rituals means coming to see these as *organized forms of presenting and exploring value* rather than as going through meaningless motions, as forms of connecting past memory and obligation to

future strategy and possibility, and far more. Far from being empty containers in which dialog takes place, these deliberative rituals are laboratories, if not cauldrons, of political judgment. (pp. 130–131, emphasis added)

Contemporary Illustrations

In this section we illustrate how some of the ideas discussed above are apparent in different views of the nature and practice of evaluation. We first consider approaches to matters of practice and practical reasoning. Ernest House (1980, 1991, 1995; House & Howe, 1999) offers an explicit and sophisticated defense of evaluation as a form of practical reasoning that supports a cognitive democracy – one in which citizens rationally discuss facts, values, and interests. As a social institution, evaluation plays a supportive role in these deliberative democratic discussions by providing sound information and clarifying consequences of social programs and policies. However, in fulfilling this aim, evaluation is not limited to simply reporting the facts of the matter, so to speak. Evaluators ought to be advocates for democracy and the public interest and this requires that evaluators not simply promote the ideals of a deliberative democracy but demonstrate them in their work. Thus, evaluators must be adept at analyzing interests and values as well as facts; they must aim for inclusiveness – representing all relevant views of stakeholders; they must make every effort to insure sufficient participation of and dialog with relevant groups so that views are properly and authentically represented; and, they should take steps to establish conditions enabling adequate deliberation to arrive at findings (House & Howe, 1999, pp. 93–94). All of this places a premium on practical reasoning in evaluation. To design and manage the conditions of an evaluation in such a way that it supports deliberation on the value of social programs requires that evaluators have more than an ability to work with methods and bodies of scientific knowledge at stake in evaluating a program or policy. They must also have competence in practical reasoning – an ability to engage in argumentation and to themselves perform the act of deliberating values, interests, and facts to reach a wise judgment. Two things about House's vision of evaluation are significant for our purposes here. First, House is promoting a particular view of the evaluator as a person of wise judgment. Such a person must have several distinctive virtues of character – "reciprocity, mutual respect, openness, a willingness to give reasons and to listen to the reasons given by others in a deliberative interchange" (Dunne & Pendlebury, 2003, p. 208). Second, House's view of the centrality of practical reasoning to evaluation is a statement about the way evaluation knowledge is to be framed and understood. Because democracy is never a finished project, it demands a way of thinking and a kind of knowledge suitable for that kind of undertaking. Practical reasoning – a continuous, argumentative search for better answers – assumes that evaluation is always in a dialectic mode of inquiry.

Thomas Schwandt (1989, 2001, 2002, 2003) also emphasizes the centrality of practical reasoning to evaluation but in a different way. He draws broadly on the literature in the practical turn in the human sciences to criticize evaluation that is preoccupied with technical and instrumental rationality and to encourage evaluators to return to the site where evaluation action unfolds, namely, in the decisions made by practitioners in performing their practice. Unlike House's concern with evaluation as social institution, Schwandt focuses on the way evaluation is embedded and embodied in the everyday work of practitioners. He is concerned with the kinds of evaluative judgments that lie at the heart of professional practices – the

decisions about appropriate and effective action that a teacher makes facing a particular student, a nurse facing a patient, a social worker facing a client. In his view, these evaluative decisions are quite often matters of practical reason that require the exercise of deliberative judgment. Judgment, in turn, is a special kind of knowledge, "invested in action" and exhibiting a number of interrelated elements: "the open texture of the deliberation it sets in train; its need for fresh acts of perception or insight to meet the particularity of each action-situation; its irreducibility to general propositions and hence its inextinguishably experiential character; its being not only directive of present action but also itself shaped by the history of one's previous actions as those have become layered in one's character" (Dunne & Pendlebury, 2003, pp. 198, 201). The task of evaluation in Schwandt's view is pedagogical – to help practitioners understand the character and demands of this kind of knowledge that enables evaluative judgment, how this knowledge is neither a possession nor kind of capital one has at one's disposal but is constitutive of one's self-understanding as a practitioner, and how practitioners might enhance their ability to exercise judgment.

A profound concern for lived experience is manifest in a different way in those evaluation approaches that are broadly responsive to the issues and concerns of stakeholders. The work of Tineke Abma and Robert Stake is illustrative. Abma (1999a, 1999b, 2000, 2001, 2002) explores a postmodern, responsive approach to evaluation in which evaluators actively "(re)construct" the lived experience of participants into narrative. Narrative is defined as "the structure of a text and the way events are ordered in a meaningful whole" (Abma, 2002, p. 25). Abma argues that creating narrative is an everyday human endeavor for the purpose of meaning-making and understanding (Abma, 2001); it is the way in which people make sense of their lived experience as program participants (managers, service workers, beneficiaries, etc.). She aims to capitalize on this natural human capacity to relate stories of experience and incorporate it as the centerpiece of evaluation studies. Every evaluation participant has stories to share. In addition to presenting these stories, evaluators, Abma argues, ought to include their own voices as well as the voices of participants who are stereotypically marginalized. Throughout the evaluation activity, participants should be included as partners in the process of both crafting their own accounts of experience and engaging others' accounts.

Abma acknowledges that the process of constructing narrative accounts of others' lived experience is a complex activity because these accounts must accurately portray lived reality in all of its "polyvocal messiness" and capture people in their "fragmented" lives. Abma describes people as fragmented because they are multifaceted, they may present a "mask of success," but they also indicate or inadvertently reveal that, "behind the mask . . . a set of complex feelings lie hidden" (1999b, p. 249). She sees this untidy, often ambiguous, and contested character of lived experience as a point of departure for dialog with and among participants. Through coming to terms with others' stories (and specifically the meanings of experience reflected in those stories), both the evaluator and participants seek to better understand one another. However, the understanding that results from such a process need not necessarily take the form of a resolution to all ambiguities in meaning. In fact, Abma is skeptical of any strong sense of closure to such dialogs. She claims, "If our world is not simple and determined by natural laws, but rather complex and ambiguous, then we should not reduce its complexity and messiness to achieve a quasi-security" (2001, p. 274).

Evaluation should be a reflexive endeavor for participants, evaluators, and readers: "Such reflexivity is an attitude that suits the persuasion that researchers' constructions are inextricably part of a discourse that reproduces meanings and interdependence relations" (Abma, 2002, p. 9). These relations extend beyond those found within the written narrative of the evaluation report to responsively include the relations of the author to the subjects, the subjects to the reader, the author to the reader, and the entire narrative to the broader discourse of society.

Although sympathetic to a variety of approaches to evaluation, Stake (2004) is best known for his advocacy of responsive evaluation – an interpretive and qualitative approach that is both "episodic and holistic" and aims to determine and represent the quality of the evaluand "through subjective experience, using verbal description and vicarious experiencing of merit and shortcoming" (p. 2). This way of conducting evaluation "builds upon experiential, personal knowing [both of program stakeholders and the evaluator] in real space and real time and with real people" (p. xv). Hence, lived experience features prominently in this approach to evaluation. Stake stresses the importance of obtaining descriptions of experience of those involved with a program being evaluated. Stake "has promoted forms of reporting that appeal to the ways in which participants and stakeholders (indeed, all of us) ordinarily make sense of (our) selves, others, and the world" (Schwandt, 2001, p. 74). These include "stories and portrayals of people, places, and events . . . because their lifelikeness and concreteness is close to direct, personal experience" (Abma & Stake, 2001, p. 13) as presented, preferentially, in a case study (Abma & Stake, 2001; Stake 1995; Stake, 2004). The evaluator is a "portrayer of human experience" (Stake, 2004, p. 90), but does more than simply relate the lived experience of others; he or she interprets and synthesizes that experience thereby rendering a judgment of the meaning and value of the evaluand. Through the report he or she prepares, the evaluator plays a teaching role, providing information and vicarious experience for readers of the report. The responsive evaluator "seeks to facilitate audience understanding with considerable reliance on naturalistic generalization" (Stake, 2004, p. 248). Stake describes the process of naturalistic generalization by saying, "it may be that the essential understanding already exists, perhaps crudely shaped, in the mind of the reader, and that this new insight, this new set of findings [in the case study or report], gives him or her a basis for modifying, and hopefully improving it" (Abma & Stake, 2001, p. 14; see also Schwandt, 2001). The evaluator makes formal assertions but also uses vicarious experience to help readers make their own conclusions about program quality. These naturalistic generalizations then become the grounds for decisions and action that will affect future experience (Stake, 2004). In elaborating a responsive evaluation approach, in which the lived experiences of evaluator, stakeholder, participant, and reader mutually affect the individual understandings that these same parties come to and act upon, Stake advances an "interactive and social mode of inquiry" (Stronach, 2001, p. 63).

The avowedly social constructionist view of evaluation defended by Egon Guba and Yvonna Lincoln also places a premium on lived experience. Guba & Lincoln (1989) describe their fourth-generation model for evaluation as "a social construction, built on the stuff of experience – our own and that of others [stakeholders, other participants, and readers that has been] absorbed in the form of vicarious learning" (pp. 264–265). They argue that people construct their own sense of reality, their own ways of making meaning as they experience the

socio-political and material world. Although individuals create singular and unique constructions, agreement can be reached within a "local value context" (p. 102). Constructions are not generalizable beyond the local context because "the 'realities' to which one might wish to generalize exist in different minds, depending on different encountered circumstances in history, based on different experiences, interpreted with different value systems" (p. 236). Within a local context, the primary goal of the evaluation endeavor is to "devise joint, collaborative, or shared constructions" (p. 184), to agree (at least for a moment) on similar meanings despite the differences. Issues on which consensus cannot be reached are considered points of departure for further negotiation and study.

It is not only stakeholders that shape the shared constructions in an evaluation. The evaluator too, "rather than mere discoverer . . . is an active participant" (p. 261) as he or she teaches and learns along with stakeholders in the evaluation context. Most of the teaching and learning will occur as evaluators facilitate an iterative process of interview and discussion with multiple stakeholders in which the stakeholders share their constructions, respond to the constructions of others, and suggest additional contacts whose constructions may differ. By giving stakeholders a voice in the evaluation, the evaluator also empowers the stakeholders in the evaluation process. Empowerment, by giving voice to as many stakeholders as possible, is a secondary goal of the consensus-shaping evaluation process.

Saville Kushner (2000) sees evaluation, not as a consensus-shaping, but, as a discursive, reflexive process, part of the corpus of life experiences of program participants and the evaluator. In his way of thinking, participants' lived experiences are the context in which social/educational programs and their significance are to be understood instead of viewing the programs as the contexts in which participants' experiences with the program are read. The participants' and evaluators' lived experiences, past and present, prepare them to learn from, engage in, and respond to the program/ evaluation experience. Because each evaluation endeavor essentially contributes to lived experience, it will influence future programs, activities, and evaluations to the degree evaluators and participants are willing to let the experience motivate change. The extent to which a participant indicates that the program is important in his/her life is the extent to which the program is important. The program has no inherent value; the program's only value is that which participants give to the program by letting the program experience influence their life experience. Moreover, participants' experiences are not regarded equally. Kushner's is "among the evaluation approaches having a disposition toward human issues and aiding social action" (Stake, 2004, p. 48) and as such, it privileges the experience of young people and other participants traditionally marginalized (Kushner, 2000) over that of clients and other stakeholders.

Michael Patton's (1997) broad approach to process use of evaluation by client stakeholders is the key to understanding how lived experience figures in his utilization-focused perspective. It is the lived experience of the evaluation per se, particularly for the intended user, that is important to Patton. Process use means, "using the logic, employing the reasoning, and being guided by the values that undergird the [evaluation] profession" (p. 88). Because most stakeholders will have different logic, reasoning, and values that support their own professions, the introduction and implementation of evaluation becomes an educative process for the stakeholders. The evaluation process itself becomes an outcome of the evaluation because, in Patton's view, "learning to see the world as an evaluator sees it often has a lasting impact on those who

participate in an evaluation – an impact that can be greater and last longer than the findings that result from the same evaluation" (p. 88). He looks for intended user feedback that indicates intended users learned from and valued the evaluation experience, not just the evaluation report.

Patton views the evaluation itself as a lived experience that both teaches participants and enhances evaluation use. Greene (2002) argues that Patton's concerns with the utility and practicality of evaluation are grounded in a pragmatic rationale for judging the "quality of a study by its intended purposes, available resources, procedures followed, and results obtained all within a particular context and for a specific audience" (pp. 71–72); she calls this "situational responsiveness in the service of utility" (p. 65). To promote use, Patton recommends that key stakeholders, called "primary intended users," be identified and involved in the evaluation effort so that the evaluation "focuses on and is driven by the information needs of specific people who will use [both] the evaluation processes [as described above] and findings" (Patton, 1997, p. 56). This is so, in part, because that kind of engaged evaluation experience enhances ownership and commitment. Improved attitude, communication, and reflection fundamentally change the activities of a program, not just substantive changes that are made based on evaluation findings (p. 88).

Participatory evaluation is also oriented to fundamental program change through the inclusion of stakeholders/decision-makers in the evaluation process. In participatory evaluation approaches, professional evaluators use their expertise to guide stakeholders through every element of the evaluation. Although several stakeholder-oriented approaches suggest involving program funders, decision-makers and other participants during the planning and analysis stages, participatory approaches suggest involving them in activities usually conducted by the evaluation experts, including instrument development and data collection (Cousins & Earl, 1995a). But these efforts go beyond tools-centered activities to use "internal and external discourses, relationships, intuition, emotions, empathy, and experiences [of evaluation processes] as sources of knowledge that represent human experience" (Brisolara, 1998, p. 32). Engaging in a process with the "complementarity of [stakeholders'] program knowledge and [evaluators'] research expertise" (Cousins & Earl, 1995b, p. 178) can generate organizational learning (Cousins & Earl, 1995a) and build organizational capacity (Whitmore, 1998).

Participatory evaluation has pragmatic philosophical roots in the work of Pierce and Dewey who felt that inquiry should focus on an individual's participation in the activities/interactions of life (Brisolara, 1998). In her own practice, Greene (2002) focuses on these activities/interactions because "the meaningfulness of the lived experiences of members of the setting [being studied . . . is the] contextual meaningfulness that importantly guides human action" (p. 300). But the evaluators do not merely get close to the experiences of program participants, they must also be "willing and able to share experiences" (Whitmore, 1998, p. 98). This "participatory reflection on the dynamics and values inherent in the research process and context," Brisolara (1998) argues, "is a means of making sense of the world as it is, with all its contradictions, contingencies, tensions and indeterminacies" (p. 32).

Culturally responsive evaluation has emerged as a unique focus in American evaluation in the past few years (e.g., Hood, 2000; Stevens, 2000; Thomas & Stevens, 2004). Its major premise is that evaluators must understand the racial, ethnic, and linguistic contexts in which programs operate. However,

this understanding is not limited simply to describing and portraying these contexts, but more importantly in being responsive to them in the design and conduct of the evaluation (NSF, 2002). In short, an evaluation must take into account the culture of a program under investigation – the lived experience (actions, language, values, customs, norms, beliefs, etc.) of those involved. This can involve attending carefully to the multiracial and multiethnic composition of an evaluation team to increase the likelihood of genuinely hearing and listening to the voices of stakeholders; aggressively ensuring the representation of stakeholders typically least heard from in an evaluation; examining the program processes through culturally sensitive lenses so as not to misunderstand what is unfolding; selecting and/or designing means of collecting data that are sensitive to cultural and linguistic understandings, and so on.

Summary and Future Directions

The preceding pages only highlight a few significant concepts and developments that influence ways of thinking about the notions *lived experience* and *practice* in evaluation. We make no claim to understanding precisely how these ideas find their way into various evaluators' ways of theorizing and conducting evaluation. To fully understand that would require not only a fine-grained analysis of the writing of these evaluators but probably also something like an intellectual biography that offered personal understandings of the sources of important ideas (cf. Alkin, 2004). It should at least be apparent from the foregoing that these notions are multifaceted and fertile and, therefore, it is not surprising that they are subject to a variety of interpretations by evaluators who value these ideas as orientations for their inquiries.

As analytic concepts, lived experience and practice focus the evaluator's awareness in specific ways. Attention to lived experience reflects deep respect for the social world and invites careful consideration of participants' and stakeholders' ways of experiencing a program and how they invest actions with meaning. This concern is firmly grounded in the notion of naturalism that underlies qualitative sociology and some forms of cultural anthropology. As Gubrium & Holstein (1997, p. 19) explain, naturalism "presumes that reality exists in textured and dynamic detail in the 'natural' environment of the social world. The meaningful features of everyday life consist of participants' orientations to, and actions within, this world as they purposefully manage their realities." A commitment to grasping and documenting lived experience is evident in the significance attached to techniques (observation in natural contexts, studies of artifacts, interviews of various kinds) that yield empirical materials (transcripts, field notes, etc.) providing the grounds on which an authentic reconstruction of meaning can be had (Alvesson & Sköldberg, 2000).

Notions of practice also refocus the gaze of evaluators who employ them. The language of logic models, inputs, outcomes, service providers, service beneficiaries, and so on is a familiar enough vocabulary for framing the scientific study of a social or educational program as an object, but this kind of framing is inadequate to the task of examining and engaging programs as lived practices. For the latter, evaluators employ a set of analytical concepts that directs attention to the unfolding character of practice and its continuous accomplishment or performance; in other words, its processual and deliberative character. Thus, to grasp the practice of teaching, managing, providing social services or health care, and so on an evaluator will more likely think in terms of matters such as dilemmas, conflicts, common meanings, norms, and paradoxes as well as actions such as negotiating and deliberating rather than in terms of variables, barriers, factors, treatments, mechanisms, and the like. Grasping the kind of action that comprises practice involves examining how a given practice it is composed of an interlocking set of habits, routines, rituals, customs, intersubjectively shared understandings, language, and traditions. This foreground is likely evident in the simplest actions of a practice: For example, how are users of a particular rehabilitation service greeted when they arrive? What is the routine that is followed in intake and diagnosis? What typically transpires as the user of a service exits the clinic or office? How do professionals speak about the people they serve – for example, as patients, clients, service users, or citizens?

For some evaluators, a concern with practice involves paying particular attention to notions of practical reasoning and deliberation. They may be less focused on grasping the lived socio-anthropological character of a practice and more interested in understanding how the action we call evaluation is itself a form of deliberation (i.e., practical reasoning) about means and ends. They may attend specifically to evaluation as a form of practical, communicative action.

Criticisms of efforts that place lived experience at the center of evaluation come from both advocates and opponents of this view. As noted earlier, internal criticisms question the assumption that lived experience can be unproblematically captured and faithfully represented by the evaluator. While maintaining a respect for the empirical world, internal critics hold that too ready reliance on empirical material as providing confident access to meaning "misses the main part of the interpretive problematic, so that data appear as more or less unmediated, pure, and the research process is endowed with a naive character of gathering and threshing empirical material according to some sort of agricultural metaphor" (Alvesson & Sköldberg, 2000, p. 49). Criticisms from outside of the community of inquirers attentive to lived experience come in two forms. Strong forms of critique are based on some variant of the view that the understanding and knowledge characteristic of everyday life are unreliable. In this way of thinking, "insider," lived experience is a questionable source of knowledge because it is infected by intuition, habit, custom, tradition, social location, personal preferences, and the like. It must, in some sense, be redeemed by a more objective and valid "outside" knowledge perspective allegedly free of such biasing characteristics. Weaker forms of criticism hold that understanding meaning via the study of lived experience is a legitimate way of knowing, but it is only a partial view and must be complemented by forms of explanatory knowledge stemming from the study of social structures and causal mechanisms. One might read some of the efforts to develop mixed-methods approaches in evaluation as an outgrowth of this second view. As noted in the opening pages of this chapter, this controversy over the value and status of knowledge grounded in lived experience is endemic in the social sciences, and unlikely to be literally "resolved" in the field of evaluation. It is doubtful that some final genuine synthesis or blending of different ways of knowing (whether through mixed-methods approaches, social realist approaches, etc.) can be had in evaluation, for there is no "neutral," third place to stand from which one can effectively merge the two kinds of knowing. At best, we are likely to have at our disposal an amalgamation of different ways of grasping the merit, worth, and significance of social and educational programs, accompanied by unending criticism of the shortcomings of any single approach when viewed in terms of another.

The most fruitful lines of inquiry around the focus on lived experience and practice are thus probably not to be found in searching for ways of combining different types of knowledge. Rather, evaluators committed to examining lived experience and practices are perhaps best served by increasing the depth and breadth of their focus. Traditionally, evaluators interested in lived experience and everyday practice have looked to the ways in which these analytic concepts have been framed and studied in the fieldwork traditions of sociology and anthropology. Newer developments, most notably the growing interest in practice theories in sociology, and the ever-expanding literature in practical knowledge and practical reasoning (both of which have been already been noted) serve to expand ways of thinking about these concepts and related issues. Another potentially fruitful resource for investigation includes the literature on the communicative or argumentative turn in planning and policy analysis (e.g., Fischer & Forester, 1993; Forester, 1999; Innes, 1998) that offers ideas about the nature and status of information involved in decision-making, as well as insights into the process of deliberation involved in practice. Because a practice is not simply a matter of the action of individuals but a social, historical, material, and discursive process, several lines of inquiry into the constitution and transformation of practices are suggested by literature stemming from Habermas' notion of the public sphere (e.g., Kemmis, 2004), as well as the considerable literature on the impact of audit culture and the audit society on shaping lived experience, identity, and professional practices into auditable performances (e.g., Rose, 1996, 1999; Strathern, 2000).

Ideas surrounding lived experience and practice have particular value and currency in a climate that favors strong links between evaluation and notions of target-driven performance, science-based or evidence-based thinking, and consumerism versus citizenship. There is a tendency in this climate to dismiss the lived character of social and educational practices; to see little significance in emergent and negotiated understandings of program value; to disregard the diversity of experience and action (on the part of both service providers and service recipients); and, to assume that the ambiguity, uncertainty, and multiplicity inherent in professional social and educational practices ought to be minimized, if not all together eradicated. Evaluations that begin in lived experience and practice provide an antidote to these tendencies. They remind us that evaluation ought to be concerned with the multiplicity of ways in which program value is an existential, embodied, and constitutive experience.

Note

1. Scientism means "science's belief in itself: that is, the conviction that we can no longer understand science as one form of possible knowledge, but rather must identify knowledge with science" (Habermas, 1971, p. 4).

References

Abma, T. A. (1999a). Introduction: Narrative perspectives on program evaluation. In T. Abma (ed.) *Telling Tales: On evaluation and narrative. Advances in Program Evaluation*, 6, 1–27.

Abma, T. A. (1999b). Narrative stance, voice and tropes: A pastiche on evaluators as narrators. In T. Abma (ed.) *Telling Tales: On evaluation and narrative. Advances in Program Evaluation*, 6, 235–263.

Abma, T. A. (2000). Responding to ambiguity, responding to change the value of a responsive approach to evaluation. *Evaluation Program Planning*, 23, 461–470.

Abma, T. A. (2001). Evaluating palliative care: Facilitating reflexive dialogues about an ambiguous concept. *Medicine, Health Care and Philosophy*, 4, 261–276.

Abma, T. A. (2002). Emerging narrative forms of knowledge representation in the health sciences: Two texts in a postmodern context. *Qualitative Health Research*, 12(1), 5–27.

Abma, T. A. & Stake, R. E. (2001). Stake's responsive evaluation: Core ideas and evolution. In J. C. Greene & T. A. Abma (eds) *Responsive Evaluation. New Directions for Evaluation*, No. 92 (pp. 7–21). San Francisco: Jossey-Bass.

Alkin, M. (2004). *Evaluation Roots*. Thousand Oaks, CA: Sage.

Alvesson, M. & Sköldberg, K. (2000). *Reflexive methodology*. London: Sage.

Bernstein, R. J. (1976). *The Restructuring of Social and Political Theory*. Philadelphia, PA: University of Pennsylvania Press.

Bourdieu, P. (1997). *Outline of a Theory of Practice* (R. Nice, trans). Cambridge, England: Cambridge University Press.

Brisolara, S. (1998). The history of participatory evaluation and current debates in the field. In E. Whitmore (ed.) *New Directions for Evaluation*, No. 80 (pp. 25–41). San Francisco: Jossey-Bass.

Cooper, D. E. (1996). Modern European philosophy. In N. Bunnin & E. P. Tsui-James (eds) *The Blackwell Companion to Philosophy* (pp. 702–721). Oxford: Blackwell.

Cousins, J. B. & Earl, L. M. (1995a). The case for participatory evaluation: Theory, research, practice. In J. B. Cousins & L. M. Earl (eds.), *Participatory Evaluation in Education: Studies in evaluation use and organizational learning* (pp. 3–18). London: The Falmer Press.

Cousins, J. B. & Earl, L. M. (1995b). Participatory evaluation in education: What do we know? Where do we go? In J. B. Cousins & L. M. Earl (eds) *Participatory Evaluation in Education: Studies in evaluation use and organizational learning*, (pp. 159–180). London: The Falmer Press.

Denzin, N. K. (1997). *Interpretive Ethnography*. Thousand Oaks, Sage.

Denzin, N. K. (2002). Performing evaluation. In K. R. Ryan & T. A. Schwandt (eds), *Exploring Evaluator Role and Identity* (pp. 139–166). Greenwich, CT: Information Age Publishing.

Denzin, N. K. (2003) *Performance Ethnography: Critical pedagogy and the politics of culture*. Thousand Oaks: Sage.

Dunne, J. (1993). *Back to the Rough Ground: "Phronesis" and "techne" in modern philosophy and in Aristotle*. Notre Dame, IN: University of Notre Dame Press.

Dunne, J. (1997). *Back to the Rough Ground: Practical judgment and the lure of technique.* Notre Dame, IN: University of Notre Dame Press.

Dunne, J. & Pendlebury, S. (2003). Practical reason. In N. Blake, P. Smeyers, R. Smith, & P. Standish (eds) *The Blackwell Guide to the Philosophy of Education* (pp. 194–211). Oxford: Blackwell.

Emerson, R. E. (ed.) (1983). *Contemporary Field Research.* Prospect Heights, IL: Waveland Press.

Fay, B. (2003). Phenomenology and social inquiry. In S. P. Turner & P. A. Roth (eds) *The Blackwell Guide to the Philosophy of the Social Sciences* (pp. 42–63). Oxford: Blackwell.

Fischer, F. & Forester, J. (eds) (1993). *The Argumentative Turn in Policy Analysis and Planning.* Durham, NC: Duke University Press.

Flick, U. (1998). *An Introduction to Qualitative research: Theory, method, and applications.* London: Sage.

Flyvbjerg, B. (2001). *Making Social Science Matter: Why social inquiry fails and how it can succeed again* (S. Sampson, trans.). Cambridge, England: Cambridge University Press.

Forester, J. (1999). *The Deliberative Practitioner.* Cambridge, MA: MIT Press.

Gadamer, H.-G. (1981). *Reason in the Age of Science* (F. G. Lawrence, trans.). Cambridge, MA: MIT Press.

Geertz, C. (1973). *The Interpretation of Cultures: Selected essays.* New York: Basic Books.

Goodyear, L. K. (2001). Representational form and audience understanding in evaluation: Advancing use and engaging postmodern pluralism. *Dissertation Abstracts International,* 61 (09), 3789A. (UMI No. AAT 9988147)

Greene, J. C. (2002). Telling tales. *Qualitative Social Work,* 1(3), 297–302.

Guba, E. G. & Lincoln, Y. S. (1989). *Fourth Generation Evaluation.* Newbury Park, CA: Sage.

Gubrium, J. F. & Holstein, J. A. (1997). *The New Language of Qualitative Method.* Oxford: Oxford University Press.

Habermas, J. (1971). *Knowledge and Human Interests* (J. J. Shapiro, trans.). Boston: Beacon Press.

Hiley, D. R., Bohman, J. F., & Shusterman, R. (eds) (1991). *The Interpretive Turn: Philosophy, science, culture.* Ithaca, NY: Cornell University Press.

Holstein, J. A. & Gubrium, J. F. (2003). Active interviewing. In J. F. Gubrium & J. A. Holstein (eds) *Postmodern Interviewing* (pp. 67–80). Thousand Oaks, CA: Sage.

Hood, S. (2000). Commentary on deliberative democratic evaluation. In K. Ryan & L. Destefano (eds) *Evaluation as a Democratic Process: Promoting inclusion, dialogue, and deliberation. New Directions for Evaluation,* No. 85 (pp. 77–83). San Francisco: Jossey-Bass.

House, E. R. (1980). *Evaluating with Validity.* Beverly Hills, CA: Sage.

House, E. R. (1991). Evaluation and social justice: Where are we? In M. McLaughlin & D. C. Phillips (eds), *Evaluation in Education: At quarter century. Ninetieth Yearbook of the National Society for the Study of Education, Part II* (pp. 233–247). Chicago: University of Chicago Press.

House, E. R. (1995). Putting things together coherently: Logic and justice. In D. M. Fournier (ed.) *Reasoning in Evaluation: Inferential links and leaps. New Directions for Evaluation,* No. 68 (pp. 33–47). San Francisco: Jossey-Bass.

House, E. R. & Howe, K. R. (1999). *Values in Evaluation and Social Research.* Thousand Oaks, CA: Sage.

Innes, J. E. (1998). Information in communicative planning. *Journal of the American Planning Association,* 64(1), 52–63.

Kemmis, S. (2004). Knowing practice: Searching for saliences. Paper presented at the invitational conference "Participant Knowledge and Knowing Practice," Umeå University, Umeå, Sweden, March.

Kushner, S. (2000). *Personalizing Evaluation.* London: Sage.

Kvale, S. (1996). *InterViews.* Thousand Oaks, CA: Sage.

Lave, J. (1996). Teaching, as learning, in practice. *Mind, Culture and Activity,* 3(3), 149–164.

Lave, J. & Wenger, E. (1991). *Situated Learning: Legitimate peripheral participation.* Cambridge, UK: Cambridge University Press.

McNeill, W. (1999). *The Glance of the Eye: Heidegger, Aristotle, and the ends of theory.* Albany, NY: SUNY Press.

Molander, B. (1992). Tacit knowledge and silenced knowledge: Fundamental problems and controversies. In B. Göranzon & M. Florin (eds) *Skill and Education: Reflection and experience* (pp. 9–31). London: Springer-Verlag.

NSF (2002). *The 2002 User-Friendly Handbook for Project Evaluation.* Arlington, VA: National Science Foundation, Directorate for Education and Human Resources, Division of Research, Evaluation and Communication.

Patton, M. Q. (1997). *Utilization-Focused Evaluation*. Thousand Oaks, CA: Sage.

Patton, M. Q. (2002). *Qualitative Research and Evaluation Methods*, 3rd edition. Thousand Oaks, CA: Sage.

Pendlebury, S. (1990). Practical reasoning and situated appreciation in teaching. *Educational Theory*, 40, 171–179.

Pendlebury, S. (1995). Reason and story in wise practice. In H. McEwan & K. Egan (eds) *Narrative in Teaching, Learning and Research* (pp. 50–65). New York: Teachers College Press.

Polkinghorne, D. (1983). *Methodology for the Human Sciences*. Albany, NY: state University of New York Press.

Prilleltensky, M. (2001). Values-based praxis in community psychology: Moving toward social justices and social action. *American Journal of Community Psychology*, 29(5), 747–778.

Reckwitz, A. (2002). Toward a theory of social practices: A development in culturalist theorizing. *European Journal of Social Theory*, 5(2), 243–263.

Rose, N. (1996). The death of the social: Re-figuring the territory of government. *Economy and Society*, 25(3), 327–356.

Rose, N. (1999). *Powers of Freedom*. Cambridge: Cambridge University Press.

Schatzki, T., Knorr Cetina, K. & von Savigny, E. (eds) (2001). *The Practice Turn in Contemporary Theory*. London: Routledge.

Schön, D. A. (1983). *The Reflective Practitioner*. New York: Basic Books.

Schwandt, T. A. (1989). Recapturing moral discourse in evaluation. *Educational Researcher*, 18(8), 11–16, 35.

Schwandt, T. A. (2001). Responsiveness and everyday life. In J. C. Greene & T. Abma (eds) *Responsive Evaluation. New Directions for Evaluation*, No. 92 (pp. 73–88). San Francisco: Jossey-Bass.

Schwandt, T. A. (2002). *Evaluation Practice Reconsidered*. New York: Peter Lang.

Schwandt, T. A. (2003). "Back to the rough ground!" Beyond theory to practice in evaluation. *Evaluation*, 9(3), 353–364.

Shotter, J. (1996). "Now I can go on:" Wittgenstein and our embodied embeddedness in the "hurly-burly" of life. *Human Studies*, 19, 385–407.

Silverman, D. (ed.) (1997). *Qualitative Research*. London: Sage.

Silverman, D. (2001). *Interpreting qualitative data*, 2nd edition. London: Sage.

Smith, D. (1992). Sociology from women's experience: A reaffirmation. *Sociological Theory*, 10(1), 88–98.

Stake, R. E. (1991). Retrospective on The Countenance of Educational Evaluation. In M. W. McLaughlin & D. C. Phillips (eds) *Evaluation and Education: At quarter century. Ninetieth Yearbook of the National Society for the Study of Education, Part II*. Chicago: University of Chicago Press.

Stake, R. E. (1995). *The Art of Case Study Research*. Thousand Oaks, CA: Sage.

Stake, R. E. (2004). *Standards-Based and Responsive Evaluation*. Thousand Oaks, CA: Sage.

Stern, D. G. (2003). The practical turn. In S. P. Turner & P. A. Roth (eds) *The Blackwell Guide to the Philosophy of the Social Sciences* (pp. 185–206). Oxford: Blackwell.

Stevens, F. I. (2000). Reflections and interviews: Information collected about training minority evaluators of math and science projects. In *The Cultural Context of Educational Evaluation: The role of minority evaluation professionals*. NSF report 01–43. Arlington, VA: National Science Foundation, Directorate for Education and Human Resources.

Strathern, M. (ed.) (2000). *Audit Cultures*. London: Routledge.

Stronach, I. (2001). The changing face of responsive evaluation: A postmodern rejoinder. In J. C. Greene & T. Abma (eds) *Responsive Evaluation. New Directions for Evaluation* No. 92 (pp. 59–72). San Francisco: Jossey-Bass.

Taylor, C. (1985). *Philosophy and the Human Sciences. Philosophical papers*, Vol. 2. Cambridge, England: Cambridge University Press.

Taylor, C. (1995). *Philosophical Arguments*. Cambridge, England: Cambridge University Press.

Thomas, V. G. & Stevens, F. I. (eds) (2004). *Co-constructing a Contextually Responsive Evaluation Framework. New Directions for Evaluation*, No. 101. San Francisco: Jossey-Bass.

Toulmin, S. (1988). The recovery of practical philosophy. *American Scholar*, 57(3), 345–358.

Toulmin, S. (2001). *Return to Reason*. Cambridge, MA: Harvard University Press.

Wagenaar, H. & Cook, S. D. N. (2003). Understanding policy practices: Action, dialectic and deliberation in policy analysis. In M. Hajer & H. Wagenaar (eds) *Deliberative Policy Analysis: Understanding governance in the network society* (pp. 139–171) Cambridge, UK: Cambridge University Press.

Wenger, E. (1998). *Communities of Practice: Learning, meaning and identity.* New York: Cambridge University Press.

Whitmore, E. (1998). Final commentary. In E. Whitmore (ed.) *Understanding and Practicing*

Participatory Evaluation. New Directions for Evaluation, No. 80 (pp. 95–99) San Francisco: Jossey-Bass.

Wiggins, D. (1980). Deliberation and practical reason. In A. O. Rorty (ed.) *Essays on Aristotle's Ethics* (pp. 221–240). Berkeley, CA: University of California Press.

Young, I. M. (2000). *Inclusion and Democracy.* Oxford: Oxford University Press.

EVALUATION, DEMOCRACY, AND SOCIAL CHANGE

Jennifer C. Greene

Educational research [and evaluation] can never be value-free. To the extent it approaches value-freedom in its self-perception, it is to that extent dangerous . . . [and] in fact . . . useless . . . [Moreover] I take it as a given that democratic values are prominent among those that educational research [and evaluation] ought to incorporate, a premise not likely to be challenged in the abstract. (Howe, 2003, pp. 133–134).

From almost the beginning of the contemporary history of program evaluation, there have been theorists and practitioners who anchor their work in an intentional commitment to democratic social justice, equality, or empowerment. These evaluators reject the very possibility of value neutrality in evaluation and instead fully embrace the intertwinement of values with evaluative practice. Moreover, these evaluators go beyond a value-relative stance, which acknowledges and engages the plurality of values that inhabit evaluation contexts, to a value-committed stance, through which evaluation purposefully advances particular values (Schwandt, 1997). The most defensible values to promote, in the reasoning of these evaluators, are those intrinsic to political democratic ideals, namely, social justice, equality, empowerment, and emancipation.

The rationales offered by the theorists in this evaluative tradition for their value-committed stances are complex. They rest on both epistemological arguments regarding the nature and purpose of social knowledge and political arguments regarding the location and purpose of evaluation in society. And they rest on varied conceptualizations of democracy, equality, and justice. Moreover, these arguments are less about particular evaluation designs and methods than they are about evaluative processes and evaluator roles, stances, and commitments. That is, these theories about democratically oriented evaluation do not emphasize prescriptions about the technical aspects of evaluation practice. Rather, these theories focus on (1) the macro positioning of evaluation in society, specifically addressing issues related to which purposes and whose interests evaluation should serve, and (2) the micro character of evaluation practice, in particular the relationships evaluators establish with others in a given context and the processes and interactions that enact these relationships. Clearly, these emphases spill over into more technical issues of establishing priority evaluation questions, criteria for judging quality, utilization, and reporting procedures, as well as evaluation design and methods. But, as will be illustrated throughout this chapter, democratically oriented evaluators' ideas about the technical facets of evaluation practice are most importantly rooted in their understandings of evaluation's location in society and the evaluator's location in the study at hand.

Using this heuristic framework of the macro politics and the micro relationships of evaluation, this chapter first presents the historically influential theories of Barry MacDonald and Ernest House, then important facets of additional theories that have shaped the landscape of democratically oriented evaluation, and finally contemporary developments that continue the tradition. For each theorist or group of theorists, the discussion includes key concepts and rationales – both epistemological and political – as well as key implications for evaluation practice. Examples and critiques of these approaches are interspersed throughout the chapter, with a concluding summary critique. And although the discussion takes place almost exclusively in the public sector, involving evaluations of publicly funded programs, democratically oriented evaluative theory is certainly relevant to the non-profit, civil sectors and even in some cases to private enterprise as well.[1]

Historical Legacies in Democratically Oriented Evaluation

Democratically oriented traditions in evaluation have their genesis in Barry MacDonald's original formulation of "democratic evaluation" for the field of education in England (MacDonald, 1976) and Ernest House's long-standing commitment to social justice for evaluation in the US (House, 1980, 1993; House & Howe, 1999).

Barry MacDonald's "Democratic Evaluation"

MacDonald offered a "political classification of evaluation studies" as a way of helping evaluators choose their "allegiances and priorities," because evaluators inevitably confront "the distribution and exercise of power" in their work (MacDonald, 1976, p. 125). Evaluation is inherently a political activity with potential political influence. "Evaluators not only live in the real world of educational politics; they actually influence its changing power relationships" (MacDonald, 1976, p. 132).

MacDonald's political classification had three types. First, *bureaucratic* evaluation is an unconditional service to government agencies already empowered to allocate educational resources and determine policy directions. The bureaucratic evaluator's role is one of management consultant, and his/her work is neither independent nor available for public scrutiny. Bureaucratic evaluation clients retain control over the products of this work. Second, *autocratic* evaluation is a conditional service to the same governmental agencies. The autocratic evaluator retains independence as an outside expert adviser and thus retains ownership of the evaluation products. His/her work is validated by the scientific research community and thus, when valid, serves to defend existing policy directions.

In contrast, the *democratic* evaluator recognizes value pluralism in service of the public right to know. In democratic evaluation, the methods and results must be presented in ways accessible to multiple non-specialist audiences, in a report that aspires to "best seller" status. Moreover, all participants in the evaluation are guaranteed control over the release and form of the information they provide. In short, the democratic evaluator serves the public interest in education, in addition to the established interests of policy-makers and experts.

Rationale

MacDonald's turn to a democratically oriented approach to evaluation arose from his concerns about "Who controls the pursuit of new knowledge, and who has access to it?" (MacDonald & Walker, 1977, p. 185). He sought primarily to democratize knowledge in evaluation – to broaden the evaluation questions addressed and thus the interests served beyond established decision-makers and experts to include the citizenry at large, and also to disseminate evaluation findings equally broadly so as to engage the public in informed discussion of key policy issues and directions – thus positioning evaluation in service of an informed citizenry.[2] MacDonald also envisioned evaluation as an opportunity for policy critique, rather than an activity constrained by the boundaries of a particular program (which is an enactment of a policy) with the assumptions and values of the policy left unexamined. Evaluation can serve as a "disinterested source of information about the origins, processes, and effects of social action . . . challenging monopolies of various kinds – of problem definition, of issue formulation, of data control, of information utilization. We are not just in the business of helping some people to make educational choices within their present responsibilities and opportunities. We

are also in the business of helping all our peoples to choose between alternative societies" (MacDonald, 1978, p. 12). With this collective and pluralistic vision of evaluation in democratic service for policy-makers, experts, and the public alike, accountability also becomes mutual and collective (Ryan, 2004).

Major Implications for Practice

MacDonald's political turn to democratic values in evaluation was accompanied by a methodological turn to the case study for educational evaluation.[3] Case studies can render portrayals of educational programs "more knowable to the non-research community [and] more accessible to diverse patterns of meaning, significance and worth through which people ordinarily evaluate social life" (MacDonald, 1977, p. 50). Case studies take "the experience of the programme participants as the central focus of investigation [and they] convey images of educational activity which both preserve and illuminate its complexity" (MacDonald, 1977, p. 51). Within MacDonald's democratic evaluation, the case study method focuses on practice and on practitioners' own language and understandings of or theories about the program (Simons, 1987), and further serves to encourage critical self-reflection about the quality of program implementation and its connections to policy intent.

In conjunction with the case study method, MacDonald's democratic evaluation requires that evaluators themselves act democratically, primarily in reference to control over, access to, and release of evaluative information. This is because the personalized information generated in case study evaluations (in contrast to the anonymous information generated in other evaluation approaches) can be importantly consequential for case study participants. Principles of fairness, relevance, and accuracy guide all negotiations between evaluators and study participants regarding the content and dissemination of all evaluation reports.

An Example of MacDonald's Democratic Evaluation

Robin McTaggart, an active member of the CARE–CIRCE network and a renowned proponent of action research, offers a thoughtful critique of the promise and peril of MacDonald's democratic evaluation through reflections on a case example (McTaggart, 1991). The program evaluated was an Australian Language Curriculum Project, which sought to provide specialized instruction for students with identified weaknesses in language skills. The evaluation was self-consciously democratic in the MacDonald tradition, focusing thus on processes related to information control. In fact a written set of *Principles of Procedure* – designed to make "an externally commissioned evaluation as democratic as possible by giving participants considerable control over the interpretation and release of information" (McTaggart, 1991, p. 10) – was shared with all evaluation participants and used to guide the evaluators' actions and decisions regarding information release and especially reporting.[4]

The troublesome incident in this case example involved a male school principal and the female language teacher (hired specifically for the program and thus not on a tenure track) in one of the program sites. When interviewed, the principal offered glowing support for the program but was not aware of any of the program's operational details, encouraging the evaluation team to consult the teacher directly involved. When the language teacher was interviewed, she offered significant criticism of the program primarily with reference to its organization and management. For example, the students who showed up for the program were not the kinds of students the program was intended to serve, nor did they come from the schools designated as participants in the

program. As per the *Principles of Procedure*, both the principal and the teacher reviewed their interview records and agreed that the data, with minor corrections, could be included in the evaluation report. Yet, as the draft report was circulating again for approval and release, the teacher recanted and withdrew much of her interview data from the evaluation, notably the data critical of the language program. When telephoned, the teacher said that the principal had asked her to change her interview data so that the data were not critical of the program's organization and management (because this would reflect badly on the principal). The principal even hinted that the teacher's job could be at stake. This then created a dilemma for MacDonald's democratic evaluation: "Should the public's 'right to know' take precedence over the individuals' rights to 'own the facts about their own lives'" (McTaggart, 1991, p. 15) and to decide for themselves what risks to incur? And, "however democratic the *Principles of Procedure* may have seemed to be, they still gave the evaluators considerable control" (p. 20).

Critique

MacDonald's democratic evaluation supports a *representative* form of democracy in that the power of elected officials and their appointees to make decisions is engaged, but not challenged. (The concluding section of this chapter offers further discussion of different forms of democracy.) Moreover, within the spaces of the evaluation itself, McTaggart's *Principles of Procedure* did actively seek and value the teacher's views about the program, but did not adequately safeguard other rights of the teacher against the established power of the principal. Nor were any evaluation participants actually empowered to speak for themselves, as the evaluator, in the role of "information broker," retained authorship of the final report. MacDonald's approach to democratic evaluation thus serves primarily to "give voice" to and thereby legitimize the perspectives and experiences of multiple stakeholders. It endeavors to provide and protect spaces within evaluation for multiple accounts of program value, but is inherently limited in its ability to guarantee either provision or protection of stakeholder voice, as power remains with the evaluator who is positioned in service to the established representative government.

Ernest House's Deliberative Democratic Evaluation, with Kenneth Howe

For almost as long as Barry MacDonald, Ernest House has championed a democratic approach to evaluation that takes particular American form as it seeks primarily to address inequities of social class and minority culture and to advance "social justice" in the context at hand and in the broader society (House, 1980, 1993; House & Howe, 1999). House attends specifically to the ways in which evaluation not just influences but actually serves to constitute public decision-making institutions and discourses, and thereby policy directions.

> Evaluation always exists within some authority structure, some particular social system. It does not stand alone as simply a logic or a methodology, free of time and space, and it is certainly not free of values or interests. Rather, evaluation practices are firmly embedded in and inextricably tied to particular social and institutional structures and practices. (House & Howe, 2000, p. 3)

Given that evaluation is embedded in the fabric of public decision-making rather than an independent contributor to it, evaluation "should be explicitly democratic" (House & Howe, 2000, p. 4). As such, evaluation can help to constitute a more democratic society.

The character of democracy promoted by House is one of *deliberation in service of social justice*. Historically, House rejected a pluralist model of democracy favored by many liberal social scientists for much of the twentieth

century, because it does not attend seriously to the interests of the least advantaged.[5] In the pluralistic model, "the political system is kept in equilibrium by group elites bargaining for their constituencies and government elites reaching accommodations. There is little need for direct participation by individuals other than to express their demands to their leaders" (House, 1993, p. 118).[6] However, argued House, pluralism often excludes some stakeholders, usually the "powerless and the poor" (House, 1993, p. 121) because there are no special provisions for their inclusion. Further, "many critical issues never arise for discussion, study, or evaluation . . . . [In particular] fundamental issues involving conflicts of interest often do not evolve into public issues because they are not formulated" (House, 1993, pp. 121–122). (This discussion of House's views on democratic theories is continued below under "Rationale.")

In collaboration with philosopher colleague Kenneth Howe, House has most recently presented a *deliberative democratic* model for evaluation (House & Howe, 1999, 2000). This model intentionally insures that the *interests* of all stakeholders, specifically those of the powerless and the poor, are respectfully included.[7] And it prescribes procedures by which stakeholders interests are articulated, shared, and advanced in evaluation, even when, or perhaps especially when, they conflict. These procedures rest on three inter-related principles: *inclusion, dialog,* and *deliberation*. Inclusion means that the interests of all legitimate stakeholders are included in the evaluation. "The most basic tenet of democracy is that all those who have legitimate, relevant interests should be included in decisions that affect those interests" (House & Howe, 2000, p. 5). Dialog (among stakeholders) is offered as the process through which the *real or authentic interests*, as compared to the perceived interests, of diverse stakeholders are identified. And deliberation is the rational, cognitive process by which varying, even conflicting stakeholder claims are negotiated. These may be claims of values, interpretations of evaluation results, or action implications. Deliberation means that all such claims are subject to reasoned discussion, with evidence and argument. In deliberative democratic evaluation thus, the evaluator's role is crucial and challenging, as he/she is charged with insuring these principles of inclusion, dialog, and deliberation through skillful facilitation and diplomatic leadership.

Rationale

The epistemological rationale underlying House's ideas about deliberative democratic evaluation fundamentally involves a rejection of the fact–value dichotomy and thus the possibility of a value-free evaluative science. Instead, "we contend that evaluation incorporates value judgments (even if implicitly) both in the methodological frameworks [see also House, 1993, chapter 8 on "methodology and justice"] and in the concepts employed, concepts such as 'intelligence' or 'community' or 'disadvantaged'" (House & Howe, 1999, p. 5). Also rejecting both extreme relativism (radical constructivism) and post modernism as viable frameworks for a value-engaged evaluation practice, House & Howe (1999) emphasize the importance of legitimizing values as intrinsic to evaluative knowledge claims, but also subjecting them to reasoned deliberation, using appropriate rules of evidence, argument and negotiation.

The question then becomes, what values should evaluation promote? In response, House has argued for fundamental democratic values, namely social justice and equality. The quotation from Howe at the beginning of this chapter attests to the defensibility of democratic value choices. Specifically, House & Howe advance a modified version of political-moral theorist John Rawls' egalitarian formulation of distributive social justice (Rawls, 1971). Rawls' original principles of justice (a) call for

equal liberties for all persons and (b) address social and economic inequalities so that the greatest benefits accrue to the least advantaged, while also attached to opportunities fairly open to all. This conception of justice protects the interests of the least advantaged by allowing unequal distribution of resources under conditions of "fair equality of opportunity." Yet, recognizing that these principles exclude the "least advantaged" from defining their own needs and negotiating for themselves the distribution of societal goods, the revised egalitarian position refocuses equality as a principle of democratic *participation* (rather than only one of distribution, Guttmann, 1987). Equality in this view refers not just to the distribution of goods but also to the status and voice of the participants, in part to enable meaningful participation in the democratic process by all.[8] "Goods, along with needs, policies, and practices, are investigated and negotiated in collaboration, with democratic deliberation functioning as an overarching ideal" (House & Howe, 1999, p. 108; see also Howe, 1997). And so, deliberative democratic evaluation advances "an egalitarian . . . conception of justice that seeks to equalize power in arriving at evaluative conclusions" regarding effective social programs and policies (House & Howe, 1999, p. 134).[9]

Major Implications for Practice, with Illustrations

Deliberative democratic evaluation importantly aims to be "objective," in the sense of being impartial and unbiased, that is, equitably inclusive of all important interests and perspectives. "Objective" in this theory further means to be rational or reasoned through both the methodological canons of the discipline and through the interactive and argumentative processes of dialog and deliberation.

Beyond this, guidelines for deliberative democratic practice emphasize evaluative processes and commitments related to the major tenets of this theory, rather than any particular questions, methods, or procedures. Specifically, 10 questions are offered to guide the deliberative democratic evaluator: (1) Whose interests are represented? (2) Are major stakeholders represented? (3) Are any major stakeholders excluded? (4) Are there serious power imbalanced? (5) Are there procedures to control power imbalances? (6) How do people participate in the evaluation? (7) How authentic is their participation? (8) How involved is their interaction? (9) Is there reflective deliberation? (10) How considered and extensive is the deliberation? (House & Howe, 1999, p. 113).

Instances of deliberative democratic evaluation in practice remain rare, perhaps because it is acknowledged to be an idealized theory (House & Howe, 1999, p. 111), though see Howe & Ashcraft (2005) for one example. At the same time, many evaluators with similar political commitments have both espoused and endeavored to implement particular features of this evaluation theory. Tineke Abma, for example, has conducted a number of evaluations featuring stakeholder dialog (Abma, 2001a). Some of her work suggests that constructing narratives to represent evaluation findings and engaging stakeholders in dialogs about these narratives is a promising approach to meaningful dialog with authentic stakeholder participation (Abma, 2001b).

Ove Karlsson (1996) has also used dialogs in evaluation, particularly to engage stakeholders in developing deeper understandings of program advantages and disadvantages, especially for intended beneficiaries. Karlsson's work indicated that a significant challenge in implementing a meaningful, equitable dialog is that stakeholders come to the table with differential resources for participation (and see Guba & Lincoln, 1989). In this regard, Cheryl MacNeil (2000, 2002) has experimented with the idea of implementing deliberative forums for negotiation of important evaluative findings

and action implications, in conjunction with some advance coaching to prepare for these forums for stakeholders with limited verbal fluency or limited experience in articulating their own ideas, views, and stances.

Deliberative democratic evaluation is a challenging ideal to implement because existing arrangements of power and privilege render equitable, authentic participation by all stakeholders difficult to actualize. But, of course, the very point of this theory is to conduct evaluations that help to rearrange (redistribute) power and privilege in more just and equitable ways.

Critique

House & Howe's deliberative democratic evaluation aspires to help constitute a socially just and equitable society in which all citizens actively and authentically participate in rationale deliberation about their common and conflicting interests toward reasonable agreement about appropriate public decisions and directions. As an important societal institution, evaluation is both constituted by and helps to constitute this just and rational democracy. And the evaluator contributes professional methodological skills but more importantly facilitation in conducting authentic dialogs and meaningful deliberations and strong advocacy for democracy and an egalitarian conception of justice.

This vision is acknowledged by its own authors as idealistic and difficult to implement wholesale in today's democracies, with their special-interest politics and sound-byte media domination. But, to conduct evaluation in the absence of this kind of democratic vision is "to endorse the existing social and power arrangements implicitly and to evade professional responsibility" (House & Howe, 1999, p. 111). So, the ideal can still serve as useful guide and framework for evaluation practice.

More substantively, some critics, even with closely allied evaluation theories (Kushner, 2000; Stake, 2000) do not agree that the promotion of democracy is the main purpose of evaluation and further worry about the imposition of the evaluator's own values in the process of judging quality, which they see as a form of advocacy and activism. And advocacy remains irreconcilable with notions of respectable evaluation in most evaluation communities. [Datta (1999, 2000) has written especially thoughtfully on the intersections of evaluation and advocacy.] Other critics, notably Arens & Schwandt (2000) express concerns that the dialogic and deliberative strands of this theory require further development (along lines of reciprocity, for example) lest they risk "covert domination – a hegemonic process cloaked in pseudo-participation" (p. 333). (Similar concerns are raised about participatory evaluation, as noted below.) And finally, there are those who argue that House & Howe do not go far enough in envisioning an evaluation process with strong potential for meaningful social change. As described in the sections that follow, these arguments include challenges to the expert status and authority of the evaluator and challenges to the assumptive framework within which evaluative knowledge is generated, including the critical and actionable strands of such a framework.

Extending Historical Legacies in Ideologically Based Evaluation: Participation and Social Critique

There are two additional major clusters of conceptual ideas in ideologically based evaluation that have grown up alongside the ideas of MacDonald and House but have drawn their primary inspiration from other traditions in social research. These two clusters, which relate to stakeholder participation and empowerment and structural social critique, respectively, are interconnected and overlapping, but discussed here separately, highlighting both commonalities and differences.

Participatory Evaluation

Originally influenced by trends and developments from outside the evaluation field, notably, participatory research and then participatory action research, especially in contexts of international development in the southern hemisphere (Fals Borda, 1980; Freire, 1970; Hall, 1981), participatory approaches to evaluation directly engage the *micro-politics* of power by involving stakeholders in important decision-making roles within the evaluation process itself. Multiple, diverse stakeholders – most importantly, stakeholders from the least powerful groups – collaborate as co-evaluators in evaluations, often as members of an evaluation team. All collaborators in participatory evaluation share authority and responsibility for decisions about evaluation planning (key evaluation questions, evaluation design and methods), implementation (data collection and analysis), and interpretation and action implications. The primary intention of such participation is individual and group stakeholder agency and empowerment, towards the broader ideal of social change in the distribution of power and privilege.[10] Participatory "evaluation is conceived as a developmental process where, through the involvement of less powerful stakeholders in investigation, reflection, negotiation, decision-making, and knowledge creations, individual participants and power dynamics in the sociocultural milieu are changed" (Cousins & Whitmore, 1998, p. 9).

A leading theorist-practitioner of participatory evaluation is Elizabeth (Bessa) Whitmore, who has used her social work facilitation skills in excellent service of participatory evaluation in varied contexts (Whitmore, 1991, 1994, 1998). Many of the ideas about participatory evaluation advanced in this section come from Whitmore's work. The empowerment evaluation theory of David Fetterman (2001) is also part of this tradition. Fetterman's work extends the concept of empowerment to the ideal of self-determination, so that the primary purpose of evaluation becomes individual and group self-determination through evaluation participation and capacity building. And Egon Guba & Yvonna Lincoln's (1989) fourth-generation evaluation approach is also connected to this tradition (although it more accurately straddles the participatory and critical/emancipatory traditions). While not an explicitly participatory approach, fourth-generation evaluation seeks authentic, localized constructions of program knowledge from multiple and diverse stakeholders through a dialogic process in which the evaluator serves as negotiator. Legitimizing diverse voices and multiple knowledge constructions are core ambitions of fourth-generation evaluation.

Rationale

As noted, participatory evaluation shares significant history with the frameworks and ideologies underlying international development. In the last quarter of the twentieth century, multiple challenges arose to the dominant development paradigms, which were perceived by development workers, advocates, and others as exploitive, fostering dependency, narrowly focused on macro-economics, and divorced from urgent local problems of human suffering due to poverty, lack of education, and disease. Development workers and researchers/evaluators alike found welcome responses to their disillusion with dominant development paradigms in the liberatory ideas of adult educator Paolo Freire (1970), the action-oriented ideas of action researchers like Orlando Fals Borda (1980) and Budd Hall (1981), and the participatory research ideas of Rajesh Tandon (1981) and, in the US, John Gaventa (1980), among others. Collectively, these ideas called for people's own participation in the construction of knowledge regarding their own lives, including the experiences and effects of development interventions on

their lives. Not only are people legitimate authors of their own life stories, but enabling such authorship can itself generate greater efficacy and empowerment among those targeted by development efforts. Moreover, the knowledge to be constructed should be "actionable" knowledge with intrinsic action implications and directions, in contrast to abstract or conceptual knowledge that requires separate application to practice. In these ways, participatory evaluation of development efforts can promote values of respect and equity, serve empowerment aims, and thereby encourage development programs to do the same.

Beyond these specific political and philosophical bases, participatory evaluation shares with critical evaluation (discussed in the next section) justifications in broader radical and emancipatory traditions of philosophy and ideology. These include the theories of Marx, Gramsci, Habermas, and other critical social scientists. From these theories, participatory evaluators understand that "working to achieve emancipation requires more than a textured criticism of oppressive structures. Emancipation demands action and radical change firmly grounded in, but not obfuscated by, theory. Activity gives meaning to the theory, and the melding of both in praxis gives inquiry not only a political but a moral and ethical significance." Further, participatory evaluators "begin, continue, and end with the individuals whose lives are at the center of the evaluation . . . . The ethical starting point is equity in research relationships . . . . [by which individuals can] work collectively toward understanding of one's self, one's place in the world, the societal conditions that permit change" (Brisolera, 1998, pp. 30–31).

So, central to conceptualizations of participatory evaluation is the importance of broadening the bases and control of knowledge production to include the people who are the objects of evaluation, thereby facilitating their empowerment.[11] People are empowered, that is, "through participation in the process of constructing and respecting their own knowledge (based on Freire's notion of 'conscientization') and through their understanding of the connections among knowledge, power, and control" (Cousins & Whitmore, 1998, p. 8). (See Brisolera, 1998, for further discussion of these sociopolitical and philosophical roots of participatory evaluation.)

Implications for Practice, with Illustrations

"It's the process that counts" (Whitmore, 1991). That is, what matters most in participatory evaluation practice is the process and experience of stakeholder participation and its enablement of empowerment. This process is intrinsically valued for its empowerment potential, over and above the evaluative results and reports. Most importantly, "participatory evaluation is a set of principles and a process, not a set of tools or techniques" (Burke, 1998, p. 55).

Given its connections to the vast enterprise of international development, participatory evaluation has a rich practical history, in contrast to other democratically oriented evaluative approaches. Accompanying this history are many thoughtful reflections on the promises and challenges of participatory evaluation in the field, reflections that honor its commitment to principles and process. Samples of these follow, as illustrations of many of the major themes in this literature.

Reflecting on multiple participatory evaluations of local community-based programs (primarily in the fields of education, youth development and child care provision), Greene (1997) asserted that "in its ideal form, participatory evaluation intentionally involves all legitimate stakeholder interests in a collaborative, dialogic inquiry process that enables the construction of contextually meaningful knowledge, that engenders the personal and structural capacity to act on that knowledge, and that seeks action that contributes to

democratizing social change" (p. 174). Greene's attention to the consequentialist character of meaningful stakeholder participation is echoed by many, as action is directly connected to the empowerment agenda of this approach. Burke (1998), for example, asserted that a participatory evaluation process "must . . . be useful to the program's end users . . . [and] rooted in [their] concerns, issues, and problems" (p. 44). And Guba & Lincoln's fourth-generation evaluation approach is oriented around the "concerns, claims, and issues" of participating stakeholders.

More broadly in the domain of participatory evaluation of development assistance, Reiben (1996) offered a set of criteria for distinguishing genuine from more token forms of participation (though see Gregory, 2000 for a critique of these ideas):

1. Stakeholders must have an active role as subjects in the evaluation process, that is, they identify information needs and design the terms of reference, rather than have a merely passive role as objects of mere sources of data.

2. As it is practically impossible to actively include all stakeholders in the evaluation process, at least the representatives of beneficiaries, project field staff, project management, and the donor should participate.

3. Stakeholders should participate in at least three stages of the evaluation process: designing terms of reference, interpreting data, and using evaluation information.

These criteria can be readily mapped onto Cousins & Whitmore's (1998) conceptual emphasis on depth of stakeholder participation, range of stakeholders who participate, and degree of stakeholder versus evaluator control of the evaluation process, respectively, as critical dimensions of participatory evaluation.

Regarding who should actually participate in participatory evaluation, Mathison (1996) has challenged the field to consider forming evaluation teams with varying numbers of stakeholders that correspond to each group's overall size in the context at hand. For example, a participatory evaluation in an educational context would have many more students and parents than teachers or administrators. Mathison also discusses the problematic nature of asking stakeholders to represent the views of their group, absent any formal process for such representation (see also Gregory, 2000). In most contexts, participatory evaluators have come to accept that participating stakeholders can only represent themselves, rather than the views of the group to which they belong.[12]

Concerns about who participates are a common practical challenge in participatory evaluation. Far too often, participatory evaluations are initiated with but one or two token participants from the beneficiary group, even though this is the group directly targeted for empowerment. The reasons for this challenge are complex and contextual and often include issues of access, time, location, familiarity and comfort, language and verbal fluency, and overall understanding. Even when participation is framed in ways more familiar and comfortable to beneficiaries, their participation (and consequent empowerment) are the evaluator's agenda, not theirs. Seigart's (1999) extraordinary but ultimately unsuccessful efforts to recruit beneficiaries (parents) for her participatory evaluation of a school-based health clinic well illustrate these challenges.

Other practical challenges to participatory evaluation include the facilitation skills needed by the evaluator, possible dissonance between the values intrinsic to participatory evaluation and the values embodied in a given program and its context (Coghlan, 1998; VanderPlaat, 1995), the time demands on program staff for participation, and the challenges of conducting an evaluation that requires active staff and beneficiary participation in an organization that lacks an evaluative

culture (Brisolera, 1997) or in a local context with conflicting demands from a national evaluation (Biott & Cook, 2000).

Critique

Participatory evaluation in theory aspires to a participatory form of democracy, in which meaningful participation becomes constitutive of genuine citizenship, both privileges and responsibilities therein (Barber, 1984). There are significant practical challenges to implementing meaningful and effective participatory evaluation, probably because it is more an orientation and commitment to a set of principles than a clearly defined set of procedures. But, even in theory, its reach is limited. Participatory evaluation concentrates on individual empowerment or on changing individuals, primarily within a time-limited evaluation process, with little planned carryover to issues of voice and power outside the evaluation or after it is over, or few concentrated efforts to change institutions and practices of decision-making. Meanings of empowerment also remain unclear and often unrealized or more imposed than authentically enabled.

At the same time, participatory evaluation importantly legitimizes multiple sources of knowledge and multiple and diverse knowledge producers. Participatory evaluation further knits democratic values into the very fabric of evaluative work, positioning evaluation as itself a democratizing practice serving the well-being of those least advantaged in our contemporary societies.

Critical Evaluation

Loosely clustered under the label of "critical evaluation" are several other ideologically oriented evaluation approaches that seek to engage the *macro-politics* of power by focusing evaluation (content *and* process) around societal critique. These evaluation approaches are informed by some form of a critical social science epistemology (Fay, 1987) and endeavor to conduct social analyses that reveal structural injustices and to generate actions that can redress such injustices. Central to all of these approaches are principles of collaboration, critical theorizing and reflection, and political action with a transformative or emancipatory intent. Critical forms share considerable philosophical and ideological ground with participatory evaluation. Among the key differences are that critical evaluation is relatively more oriented toward macro structural issues, compared to the micro emphasis of participatory evaluation; more attentive to the actual substance of the evaluation, compared to participatory evaluation's emphasis on the process; and politically more radical – compare the agendas of empowerment and emancipation.

Critical forms of evaluation fully situate the social and educational practices being evaluated (as well as evaluation itself as a social practice) in their contested socio-cultural-political contexts. Rejecting the atheoretical idea that "practice exists as a commodity on its own that can be separated out for study," critical evaluators see practice as "constructed within legislative, policy, and funding processes and . . . shaped through dimensions of class, gender, race, age, sexuality and disability" (Everitt, 1996, p. 174).

Practice is also "continuously negotiated by all those involved [and] people's interests in practice . . . constitute political interests and [thus] may be conceptualized in terms of who loses and who gains" (Everitt, 1996, p. 178). This perspective disrupts taken-for-granted ways of understanding practice and opens the door to evaluative scrutiny of broader societal, especially political structures and discourses, alongside programmatic practices.

> The program, project, and practices to be evaluated . . . [are] understood as being constructed

through discourses, which in turn need to be understood in terms of power: whose interests do they serve? . . . Evaluation becomes concerned with contributing to the deconstruction of discourses that serve consistently to render some less powerful than others, and some ways of knowing the world more credible than others. (Everitt, 1996, p. 182)

Critical forms of evaluation are multi perspectival, respecting a diversity of stakeholder interests and experiences, but they are not completely relativistic. Rather, evaluative judgments of merit or "goodness" are accomplished through processes of stakeholder engagement, dialog, and critical reflection about the practices being evaluated – intertwined with critical theorizing about how power, opportunity, and privilege are constituted, distributed, and maintained in the context at hand (often by discourses outside the context). The evaluator's role is to facilitate stakeholder engagement, dialog, and reflection and, perhaps most importantly, to contribute the lenses and substance of critical theory. Evaluative judgments in critical evaluation thereby aim to be transformative, deconstructing inequitable distributions of power and reconstructing them more fairly and justly.

Snapshots of four examples of critical approaches to evaluation are offered next, as these abstract ideas gain clarity through specificity.

Examples of Critical Theories of Evaluation

The *critical evaluation theory* of Everitt & Hardiker (1996) offers several principles for critical evaluation practice in service of differentiating judgments of good, poor, and even corrupt practice. These principles, include, for example, "scepticism of rational-technical modes of practice" and "removal of the 'otherness' that may be attributed to those lower in the hierarchy, to users and to those relatively powerless" (Everitt, 1996, pp. 180, 181). In practice, this theory relies primarily on reflective and dialogic methods for generating evidence, accepts that such evidence cannot reveal the one "truth," and thus turns to political considerations as the basis for making evaluative judgments. "If there are no centers of truth . . . then there are only working truths and relative truths. The full participation of those involved in making decisions about what is going on and what should be done is the only way to define non-oppressive, culturally pertinent truths and working, practical judgments" (Howe, 1994, p. 525, cited in Everitt, 1996, p. 186). And so, in this theory, a practice is judged as "good" if it is rooted in development processes and needs identification that themselves are democratic and fair – "having equality as [their] underpinning value and goal" – *and* if the practice serves to bring about equality, "enabling all people, irrespective of their sex, ethnicity, age, economic position, social class and disability, to flourish and enjoy human well-being" (Everitt, 1996, p. 186). A practice is judged "good enough" if it is moving in these directions, "poor" if it makes no attempt to meet criteria of democratic equality, and "corrupt" if it is anti-democratic and unfair.

The *communicative evaluation theory* of Niemi & Kemmis (1999) is rooted in Habermas' theory of communicative action, specifically the character and purpose of public discourse within democracies, and in traditions of participatory action research (PAR) (Kemmis & McTaggart, 2000). Communicative evaluation aspires to help establish and nurture democratic, public conversational spaces in which "citizens can come together to debate and deliberate, creating discourses that may be critical of the state and that have the potential for contributing to the development of new or different public policies or programs" (Ryan, 2004, p. 451). In practice, communicative evaluation establishes a local site for stakeholder conversation and practical deliberation about locally important program issues. In addition, drawing from PAR traditions, communicative evaluation emphasizes joint ownership of the evaluation, collaboration in evaluation implementation, critical analysis and reflection, and an action orientation. The communicative evaluator's role is one of enabling and supporting stakeholder conversation and reflection on action.

Mertens' *inclusive evaluation theory* (Mertens, 1999, 2003) is rooted in a "transformative-emancipatory" paradigm and is especially concerned with discrimination, oppression, and other injustices suffered by people in marginalized groups. Inclusive evaluation intentionally seeks to include such people in the evaluation process and to focus key evaluation questions, and thus designs and methods, around their experiences of injustice. For example, an evaluation of an educational curriculum would probe the ways in which gender, age, class, race, ethnicity, sexual preference, and disability status were portrayed in the curriculum, with an eye to discriminatory portrayals and another eye on possibilities for change. Much like House & Howe's deliberative approach, Mertens' inclusive evaluation strives for objectivity, defined as lack of bias and "achieved by inclusion of all relevant stakeholders in a way that authentic and accurate representations of their viewpoints are considered" (Mertens, 2003, p. 95). Also like House & Howe, the inclusive evaluator retains authority and responsibility for ensuring that "quality evaluation is planned, conducted, and used" (Mertens, 2003, p. 104).

Finally, *feminist perspectives on evaluation* draw their inspiration from feminist theories and feminist politics (Seigart & Brisolera, 2002) and characteristically have two major emphases. First, a feminist lens is centered on the well-being of girls and women, or as expressed in one of Ward's (2002) key principles for conducting feminist evaluation, "Place women and their material realities at the center of evaluation planning and analysis

[and] . . . understand the problem context from a feminist perspective" (pp. 44, 47). This means that whether or not the program being evaluated seeks specifically to benefit females, a feminist evaluation will ask if and how it does so, or not (much like Mertens' concentrated focus on people from marginalized groups). Second, consistent with all ideologically oriented evaluation approaches, feminist evaluation attends seriously to the evaluation process but gives it a particular feminist cast. A feminist evaluation process is self-consciously collaborative and reciprocal, trusting and caring, and ideally conducted with humility and grace, as these are strong feminist values (Beardsley & Miller, 1992; Ward, 1992).

Critique

Critical approaches to evaluation aspire to engender more participatory and deliberative forms of democratic decision-making, through a process of assisting people from oppressed groups to realize, understand, and actively seek to change the historical conditions of their oppression. As such, critical evaluation is subject to critiques similar to those offered for democratic and participatory evaluation approaches, including questions of feasibility and acceptance. Moreover, critical approaches to evaluation, more than the others, impose a particular set of values onto the evaluation context and invite stakeholders to engage with these values – those of structural critique and emancipation. Justification for this imposition remains widely sought. In addition, critical evaluation primarily offers theoretical lenses through which existing ways of setting public policies and designing ameliorative programs for those in need are soundly challenged. Alternatives are not as readily offered in these approaches.

At the same time, the critical voice is an essential one. It guards against satisficing and complacency.

Contemporary Developments

Finally, two ideologically oriented contemporary evaluation theories-in-the-making deserve brief mention. Both attend directly to issues of culture and, relatedly, race and ethnicity, and both seek to supersede historical legacies of enslavement and colonization with theories rooted in once-dominated cultures. The first is primarily relevant to racial and ethnic minorities in the US, and the second to indigenous peoples in North America and the Pacific.

Culturally and Contextually Responsive Evaluation

A group of primarily African–American scholars in the US has been developing an approach to evaluation that is culturally and contextually responsive, meaning, consonant with the ways of knowing and ways of being particular to a given minority community in the US. This group includes Henry Frierson (Frierson, Hood, & Hughes, 2002), Rodney Hopson (2000, 2001), Stafford Hood (1998, 2001), and Veronica Thomas and Gerunda Hughes (Thomas & Stevens, 2004a).[13]

Consistent with other race-conscious theories, culturally and contextually responsive evaluation begins from a standpoint that summarily rejects deficit thinking and embraces starting points that emphasize the "strengths" and "assets" of underserved communities. Further, problem identification and definition must be located within the minority community to be served, as racist and discriminatory habits of mind persist in the larger society, despite considerable legal progress (Madison, 1992). What constitutes a social "problem" from the vantage point of the dominant society (say, "at risk" youth) is likely experienced and understood quite differently from within the communities where such youth live (say, youth without meaningful education, recreation or employment opportunities). For similar reasons, the character and logic (or theory) of an intervention designed to ameliorate an identified problem must be grounded in the culture of the context to be served (Madison, 1992). Just who can be a culturally responsive evaluator is an additional issue; significant shared life experience with those being evaluated is an essential qualification, argue many (Hood, 1998, 2001; Thomas, 2004).

To date, the most comprehensive approach to culturally and contextually responsive evaluation has been developed by the group at Howard University. The approach was developed in tandem with the Talent Development Model of (Urban) School Reform (TD), which is a major project of the Howard University Center for Research on the Education of Students Placed at Risk. The TD program itself is rooted in cultural responsiveness and respect, blending elements from critical pedagogy, school restructuring ideas, and research on the effective education of children of color (Thomas, 2004).

> The TD evaluation approach . . . seeks to be practical, useful, formative, and empowering for the individuals being served by TD evaluations and to give voice to persons whose perspectives are often ignored, minimized, or rejected in urban school settings. . . . [Moreover, the TD] evaluation framework seeks to reposition evaluation in low-income urban contexts as accountable not only for producing accurate and relevant information on the program being evaluated, but also for enabling and contributing to the program's social betterment and social justice intentions. (Thomas & Stevens, 2004b, p. 1)
>
> [Moreover] standards of evidence for evaluations of TD projects encompass both scientific-methodological and political-activist criteria. (Thomas, 2004, p. 6)

The TD evaluation approach rests on five interrelated major principles (from Thomas, 2004):

1. *Key stakeholders*, including students, parents, teachers, and other school personnel,

are authentically *engaged* throughout the evaluation process. "TD evaluators enter the urban school contexts being studied gently, respectfully, and with a willingness to listen and learn in order to plan and implement evaluations better" (p. 8).

2. The substance and process of the evaluation are *co-constructed*. "Co-construction is defined as evaluators' collaborating and forming genuine partnerships with key urban school stakeholder groups . . . and TD project designers and implementers in order to conceptualize, implement, and evaluate school reform efforts in a manner that is responsive to the school's context . . . . Co-construction seeks to democratize the evaluation process by lessening the implicit, and sometimes explicit, power dynamics between evaluators and project stakeholders" (p. 9). Distinctively, as co-construction suggests, the TD evaluator is an engaged member of a larger evaluation team, all of whom are accountable to the aims of the intervention.

3. TD evaluation attends meaningfully to *culture and context*, where context refers to "the combination of factors (including culture) accompanying the implementation and evaluation of a project that might influence its results, including geographical location, timing, political and social climate, [and] economic conditions" (p. 11). In this regard, TD evaluators must be culturally competent, preferably sharing the same cultural background as those being studied. Having a shared cultural life experience affords greater sensitivity to and understanding of relevant contextual issues.

4. "TD evaluations embrace the underlying philosophy of *responsiveness* found in the literature," notably, the importance of "respecting, honoring, attending to, and representing stakeholders' perspectives" (p. 13, emphasis added).

5. Finally, TD evaluators use *triangulation of perspectives* in multiple ways, including

triangulation of investigators, methods and measures, target people, and analyses. Triangulation is valued in this approach primarily for its inclusiveness of perspective.

Evaluation by and for Indigenous Peoples

Linda Tuhiwai Smith's 1999 book entitled *Decolonizing Methodologies: Research and indigenous peoples* is continuing its significant influence well into the twenty-first century. Smith is a Maori educational scholar from New Zealand. "The ways in which scientific research is implicated in the worst excesses of colonialism remains a powerful remembered history for many of the world's colonized peoples" (Smith, 1999, p. 1). In this book, Smith reclaims the meanings of research and knowledge, as well as the right to be a knower, for indigenous peoples. She does so with a relentless critique of Western research on indigenous peoples, followed by an articulation of an indigenous research vision and agenda. This agenda is centered around the goal of indigenous peoples' self-determination and uses processes of decolonization, healing, mobilization, and transformation, processes "which connect, inform, and clarify the tensions between the local, the regional, and the global" (p. 116). Using the metaphor of oceans, there are also three tides in this research agenda – survival (of peoples, languages, spiritual practices, art), recovery (of land, indigenous rights, histories), and development (of communities, economic opportunities, pride) – representing the ebb and flow of conditions and states of movement on the way to self-determination.

Smith further presents Maori approaches to research, called Kaupapa Maori research. "Kaupapa Maori, however, does not mean the same as Maori knowledge and epistemology. The concept of *kaupapa* implies a way of framing and structuring how we think about . . . ideas and practices . . . . Kaupapa Maori is

a 'conceptualization of Maori knowledge'" (p. 188). Kaupapa Maori research is informed and guided by Maori philosophy and worldview. It "takes for granted the validity and legitimacy of Maori [and] the importance of Maori language and culture, [and it] is concerned with the struggle for autonomy over our own colonial well being" (p. 185). Kaupapa Maori researchers disagree whether or not non-Maoris can conduct meaningful Kaupapa Maori research.

Reclamation of native epistemologies as frameworks for social and educational research is happening in other locales around the globe (Cajete, 2000). And evaluators are beginning to use these to develop distinctively indigenous ways of thinking about and conducting evaluation. For example in the US, Joan LaFrance is contributing to efforts to articulate the meanings of culturally competent evaluation "in Indian country," which include "the importance of understanding the implications of sovereignty . . . , the significance of an emerging indigenous framework for evaluation, Indian self-determination in setting the research and evaluation agenda, and . . . particular methodological approaches" (LaFrance, 2004, p. 39). Candidates for elements of an indigenous framework for evaluation include the importance of trust (rather than evidence), community, holistic thinking, and from Cajete (2000), a profound "sense of place" and being part of the web of the natural world. In New Zealand, Fiona Cram and colleagues (Cram, Ormond, & Carter, 2004; Cram et al., 2002) are pursuing conceptual and political questions of research ethics for research and evaluation with Maori people, as well as endeavoring to apply Kaupapa Maori in evaluation studies, "as a basis to explore a political, social and cultural analysis of [for example] domestic violence within the context of [domestic violence] programmes" delivered to Maori people by Maori providers (Cram et al., 2002, p. iii). And across the Pacific, indigenous evaluators from New Zealand and Hawaii met together in 2003–2004 to begin to share common visions and possibilities (http://www.kohalacenter.org/ws_pono0401 16.html and http://www.ksbe.edu/pase/researchproj-evalhui.php).

Reprise

The landscape of democratically oriented approaches to evaluation is richly textured. It is rooted in some very important ideas about knowledge production, legitimacy, and ownership; about the character and role of values in evaluative knowledge generation; and about the connections between evaluation and democratic principles, practices, and institutions. And it is populated today by equally important ideas related to participation and empowerment, dialog and deliberation, public spheres for communication, emancipation and social critique, cultural responsiveness, and self-determination.

Table 5.1 presents a summary of key ideas from each genre of democratically oriented evaluation discussed in this chapter, specifically as related to philosophical framework, views of democracy, and macro and micro positions for evaluation in society. As with any simplified presentation, this table omits important ideas and suggests sharp lines demarcating one genre from another, when actually there are many shared concepts and commitments among them. This table also represents my own sense-making of these complex ideas; others may have differing interpretations. Important sources in the construction of this table were Hanberger (2001) and Ryan (2004).

The meanings of the various kinds of democracy featured in the table are as follows. In a representative democracy, ordinary citizens participate primarily by electing elites, who are empowered to carry out and are responsible for public decision-making. A participatory democracy emphasizes the importance of people's direct participation in activities and decisions that affect their lives. Such participation is viewed as constitutive of democratic citizenship. And a deliberative democracy emphasizes the importance of communication, dialog, deliberation about public issues among free and equal citizens. This democracy features a commitment to reasoned discourse on matters of public policy in spaces free from domination. The different traditions of democratically oriented evaluation variously serve one or more of these different conceptualizations of democracy, though with a shared agenda of making the processes and results of public decision-making more inclusive of multiple stakeholder interests and values, more broadly based on multiple stakeholder knowledge, and thereby more likely to provide an equitable and just distribution of goods and services.

Clearly, there are challenges to the premises of democratically oriented evaluation. Many evaluators and evaluation commissioners, especially in the Anglo-American tradition and especially with today's infatuation with technocratic ideas about public accountability, reject out of hand a value-committed stance for evaluation. Instead, these critics believe that standards of impartial objectivity, attained via excellence of method, are needed to support contemporary accountability concepts like performance indicators, results-based management, and evidence-based decision making, all part of the current "climate of control" (McKee & Stake, 2002). Also problematic are the meanings of such lofty ideals as democracy itself, inclusion, social justice, equity, empowerment, self-determination, along with the meanings of such processes as participation, dialog, deliberation, and cultural responsiveness. These concepts must be specifically and contextually defined if democratic approaches to evaluation are to gain any practically meaningful purchase in the field. They currently offer

Table 5.1   Major elements of democratically oriented evaluation theories

Theory	Philosophical frameworks	Views of democracy	Macro location of evaluation in society	Micro location of evaluator in the evaluation
Democratic evaluation (MacDonald)	Constructivism Interpretivism	Representative democracy	Legitimizes multiple stakeholders' perspectives Serves the public right to know	Brokers information Retains primary authority and responsibility for the evaluation
Deliberative democratic evaluation (House & Howe)	Scientific realism Pragmatism	Deliberative democracy	Democratizes public decision-making (via greater inclusion) Enhances social justice	Facilitates democratic dialog and deliberation Advocates for democratic principles Retains primary authority and responsibility for the evaluation
Participatory evaluation	Constructivism Critical social science	Participatory democracy	Legitimizes multiple sources of knowledge Empowers people from marginalized groups	Facilitates stakeholder participation Shares authority and responsibility for the evaluation
Critical evaluation	Critical social science Feminisms	Participatory democracy Deliberative democracy	Catalyzes action toward emancipatory social change Renders the distribution of power and privilege more equitable	Facilitates critical stakeholder dialog Contributes the perspectives of critical theory Shares/retains authority and responsibility for the evaluation
Culturally and contextually responsive evaluation/ Indigenous evaluation	Constructivism Interpretivism Specific cultural or indigenous worldviews (e.g., Kaupapa Maori)	Multicultural democracy?	Legitimizes culturally specific knowledge and ways of knowing Enables self-determination for once-disempowered or colonized peoples	Facilitates culturally responsive or culturally specific evaluation practices Shares authority and responsibility for the evaluation

Important sources in the construction of this table were Hanberger (2001) and Ryan (2004).

inspiration, much of which remains unrealized in practice.

There are also substantial practical challenges to the implementation of democratically oriented evaluation. These include challenges to the acceptability of ideologically based evaluation among many stakeholders and to the feasibility of its implementation in particular evaluation contexts. Regarding acceptability, persuading evaluation commissioners that it is indeed in their interest to share power more equitably with program staff and especially beneficiaries is a significant practical hurdle in most evaluation contexts. McKee & Stake call this "paying for trouble making" (2002, p. 134). Persuading the disempowered and marginalized people in a given context that it is also in their interest to (a) participate in the evaluation, and (b) share this participatory space with program staff, managers, and others from more powerful groups also poses substantial hurdles in most evaluation contexts. The intensity of the evaluation process in these evaluation approaches presents special challenges of practicability and feasibility. For example, conducting a meaningful participatory or deliberative evaluation within a large-scale, multisite study or within a time-limited study would be difficult at best and likely of limited democratizing value. And even with interested stakeholders and citizens, participation in an evaluation study has to compete with multiple demands and opportunities already present in their lives for professional development, personal commitment, and civic engagement.

Additional practical challenges for implementing democratically oriented evaluation approaches include meaningfully operationalizing lofty democratic ideals and commitments in specific contexts, developing facilitation and dialogic skills in evaluators, creating the time and spaces needed for messy processes like participation and deliberation, and maintaining methodological excellence while advocating for democratic ideals.

Yet, at the end of the day, democratically oriented approaches to evaluation offer considerable promise. They are anchored in a profound acceptance of the intertwinement of values with facts in evaluative knowledge claims and the concomitant understanding that all evaluation is *interested* evaluation, serving some interests but not others. They are also anchored in turn to democratic values

as the most defensible interests to be served in evaluation – democratic values enacted in evaluations designed to serve the public right to know or citizen participation in decisions that affect their lives or reasoned deliberation among diverse stakeholders regarding important policy directions or self-determination among oppressed peoples. These visions position evaluation as itself a democratizing social practice, but not in ways that exclude traditional evaluation audiences like policy-makers and program staff nor reject traditional evaluation roles like gathering credible information useful for program improvement or organizational learning. For democratically oriented evaluation is an inclusive practice, that is distinctive not for its technical methodology, but rather for its societal location in service of democratic ideals and its concomitant evaluator role as a facilitator and advocate of democratic engagement through evaluation.

Notes

1. It should also be acknowledged that many if not most evaluation theorists position their work in service to an open and rational democratic society. These many other theorists characteristically conceptualize evaluation as providing impartial empirical evidence to help public officials make informed and fair decisions about effective policies and programs. As such, they position evaluation on the sidelines of democratic decision-making. What is distinctive about the theorists reviewed in this chapter is their positioning of evaluation as inherently and inevitably entangled with and constitutive of the politics and values of such decision-making.

2. The early roots of Lee Cronbach's vision of an educational role for evaluation are evident here (Cronbach & Associates, 1980).

3. In fact, the turn to the case study preceded MacDonald's articulation of democratic evaluation. The 1972 "Cambridge Manifesto," drawn up by a gathering of evaluators at Cambridge University, sought explicitly to legitimize interpretive methods for evaluation and to anchor evaluative work in a

public service obligation (see McKee & Stake, 2002). MacDonald was joined in this turn to case studies and other qualitative methods for evaluation by a number of prominent evaluation theorists, including in the UK Stephen Kemmis, Helen Simons, David Hamilton and Malcolm Parlett, and in the US Robert Stake, Louis Smith, Elliot Eisner, Egon Guba, Yvonna Lincoln, and Ernest House. During this heady, formative era in evaluation, the Centre for Applied Research in Education (CARE) at the British University of East Anglia and the Center for Instructional Research and Curriculum Evaluation (CIRCE) at the American University of Illinois both served as vital sources of energy and creativity for new developments in evaluation theory. Many of these evaluation scholars gathered a number of times at CARE and CIRCE to share ideas and support, thus catalyzing the rich and highly influential body of work generated during this era.

4. Examples of these principles include: "No participant will have unilateral right or power of veto over the content of the report." "The perspectives of all participants and interested observers have a right to be considered in the evaluation." "The process of negotiation of accounts will, where necessary, be phased to protect participants from the consequences of one-way information flow. Parts of a report may first be negotiated with relevant individuals who could be disadvantaged if the report were negotiated as whole with all participants." (McTaggart, 1991, pp. 10–11).

5. At this time, House maintained that American social scientists had been especially reluctant to "recognize social classes as enduring causal entities that influence life chances in US society" (House, 1993, p. 124), while considerable progress had been made in recognizing gender, race, and ethnicity (and other historical markers of disadvantage and discrimination). House also rejected the libertarian and utilitarian forms of distributive justice within liberal democratic thought.

6. This pluralist model underlay the emergence of stakeholder-based evaluation (Gold, 1983), which explicitly sanctioned the importance of multiple stakeholder perspectives in evaluation, although gave little guidance for the resolution of conflicts among diverse groups (Weiss, 1983).

7. In this theory, "an interest is anything conducive to the achievement of an individual's wants, needs, or purposes, and a need is anything necessary to the survival or well-being of an individual.

To be free is to know one's interest; or to possess the ability and resources, or the power and opportunity, to act toward those interests; and to be disposed to do so" (House, 1993, p. 125).

8. House & Howe's (1999) arguments in favor of a deliberative, participatory vision of democracy also include arguments against views they label technocratic (stripped of values), emotivist (values determined by non-rational means), preferential/ utilitarian (all preferences maximized), hyper-egalitarian (all views count the same), and hyper-pluralist (diversity more desirable than consensus).

9. The meaning of "effectiveness" here is surely consonant with the deliberative, participatory conceptualization of justice that frames this evaluation approach – so that a "good" program is one that advances the well-being of the least advantaged *and* one in which the least advantaged themselves equitably participate in program definitions, decisions, and directions – although this is not explicitly stated.

10. This discussion focuses on "transformative participatory evaluation" and excludes "practical participatory evaluation" (Cousins & Whitmore, 1998). Participation in the latter genre of participatory evaluation is instrumental, designed to enhance evaluation utilization, rather than motivated by ideological agenda. As ideologically oriented evaluation approaches are the focus of this chapter, utilization-oriented participatory evaluation will not be discussed. Similarly, because of its largely instrumental rationale, the early stakeholder model of evaluation (Gold, 1983) is also excluded from this discussion (but see Chapters 3, 12, and 15, this volume, for discussions on stakeholder participation in service of utilization).

11. MacDonald sought to broaden the ownership of and access to the information generated in an evaluation. Participatory evaluation seeks to broaden actual authorship of this information.

12. This challenge of representation is relevant to all democratically oriented evaluation approaches which rest on stakeholder participation or engagement.

References

Abma, T. A. (Guest Editor). (2001a). Special issue: Dialogue in evaluation. *Evaluation*, 7(2).

Abma, T. A. (2001b). Evaluating palliative care: Facilitating reflexive dialogues about an ambiguous concept. *Medicine, Health Care, and Philosophy*, 4, 261–276.

Arens, S. A. & Schwandt, T. A. (2000). Review of *Values in evaluation and social research*, by E. R. House & K. R. Howe. *Evaluation and Program Planning*, 23(3), 331–333.

Barber, B. (1984). *Strong Democracy: Participatory politics for a new age*. Berkeley, CA: University of California Press.

Beardsley, R. M. & Miller, M. H. (1992). Revisioning the process: A case study in feminist program evaluation. In D. Seigart & S. Brisolera (eds) *Feminist Evaluation: Exploration and experiences. New Directions for Evaluation*, No. 96 (pp. 57–70). San Francisco: Jossey-Bass.

Biott, C. & Cook, T. (2000). Local evaluation in a national Early Years Excellence Centres Pilot Programme: Integrating performance management and participatory evaluation. *Evaluation*, 6(4), 399–413.

Brisolera, S. A. (1997). A critical examination of participatory evaluation through the lens of Adelante, a women's microenterprise development organization in Costa Rica. Unpublished doctoral dissertation. Department of Human Service Studies, Cornell University, Ithaca NY.

Brisolera, S. A. (1998). The history of participatory evaluation and current debates in the field. In E. Whitmore (ed.) *Understanding and Practicing Participatory Evaluation. New Directions for Evaluation*, No. 80 (pp. 25–41). San Francisco: Jossey-Bass.

Burke, B. (1998). Evaluating for change: Reflections on a participatory methodology. In E. Whitmore (ed.) *Understanding and Practicing Participatory Evaluation. New Directions for Evaluation* No. 80 (pp. 43–56). San Francisco: Jossey-Bass.

Cajete, G. (2000). *Natural Science: Natural laws of interdependence*. Santa Fe, NM: Clear Light.

Coghlan, A. (1998). Empowerment-oriented evaluation: Incorporating participatory evaluation methods to empower Ugandan communities to prevent HIV/AIDS. Unpublished doctoral dissertation. Department of Human Service Studies, Cornell University, Ithaca, NY.

Cousins, J. B. & Whitmore, E. (1998). Framing participatory evaluation. In E. Whitmore (ed.) *Understanding and Practicing Participatory Evaluation. New Directions for Evaluation*, No. 80 (pp. 5–23). San Francisco: Jossey-Bass.

Cram, F., Ormond, A., & Carter, L. (2004). Researching our relations: Reflections on ethics and marginalization. Paper presented at the Kamehameha Schools 2004 Conference on Hawaiian Well-Being. Hawaii.

Cram, F., Pihama, L., Jenkins, K., & Karehana, M. (2002). *Evaluation of programmes for Maori adult protected persons under the Domestic Violence Act 1995*. Evaluation report prepared for the Ministry of Justice, Wellington, New Zealand.

Cronbach, L. J. & Associates (1980). *Toward Reform of Program Evaluation*. San Francisco: Jossey-Bass.

Datta, L-E. (1999). The ethics of evaluation neutrality and fairness. In J. L. Fitzpatrick & M. Morris (eds) *Current and Emerging Ethical Challenges in Evaluation. New Directions for Evaluation*, No. 82 (pp. 77–88). San Francisco: Jossey-Bass.

Datta, L-E. (2000). Seriously seeking fairness: Strategies for crafting non-partisan evaluation in a partisan world. *American Journal of Evaluation*, 21, 1–14.

Everitt, A. (1996). Developing critical evaluation. *Evaluation*, 2(2), 173–188.

Everitt, A. & Hardiker, P. (1996). *Evaluating for Good Practice*. Basingstoke: Macmillan.

Fals Borda, O. (1980). Science and the common people. Paper presented at the International Forum on Participatory Research, Ljubljana, Yugoslavia.

Fay, B. (1987). *Critical Social Science*. Ithaca NY: Cornell University Press.

Fetterman, D. M. (2001). *Foundations of Empowerment Evaluation*. Thousand Oaks, CA: Sage.

Freire, P. (1970). *Pedagogy of the Oppressed*. New York: Seabury Press.

Frierson, H. T., Hood, S., & Hughes, G. (2002). Strategies that address culturally responsive evaluation. In *The 2002 User-Friendly Handbook for Project Evaluation*. Arlington VA: National Science Foundation.

Gaventa, J. (1980). *Power and Powerlessness: Quiescence and rebellion in an Appalachian valley*. Chicago: University of Chicago Press.

Gold, N. (1983). Stakeholder and program evaluation: Characterizations and reflections. In A. Bryk (ed.) *Stakeholder-Based Evaluation. New Directions for Program Evaluation*, No. 17 (pp. 63–72). San Francisco: Jossey-Bass.

Greene, J. C. (1997). Participatory evaluation. In L. Mabry (ed.) *Evaluation and the Post-Modern*

Dilemma. Advances in Program Evaluation, Volume 3 (pp. 171–190). Greenwich, CT: JAI Press.

Gregory, A. (2000). Problematizing participation: A critical review of approaches to participation in evaluation theory. *Evaluation,* 6(2), 179–199.

Guba, E. G. & Lincoln, Y. S. (1989). *Fourth Generation Evaluation.* Thousand Oaks, CA: Sage.

Guttmann, A. (1987). *Democratic Education.* Princeton, NJ: Princeton University Press.

Hall, B. (1981). Participatory research, popular knowledge and power: A personal reflection. *Convergence,* 14(3), 6–19.

Hanberger, A. (2001). Policy, program evaluation, civil society, and democracy. *American Journal of Evaluation,* 22(2), 211–228.

Hood, S. (1998). Responsive evaluation Amistad style: Perspectives of one African American evaluator. In R. Davis (ed.) *Proceedings of the Stake Symposium on Educational Evaluation.* Urbana IL: University of Illinois.

Hood, S. (2001). Nobody knows my name: In praise of African American evaluators who were responsive. In J. C. Greene & T. A. Abma (eds) *Responsive Evaluation. New Directions for Evaluation,* No. 92 (pp. 31–43). San Francisco: Jossey-Bass.

Hopson, R. K. (ed.) (2000). *How and Why Language Matters in Evaluation. New Directions for Evaluation,* No. 86. San Francisco: Jossey-Bass.

Hopson, R. K. (2001). Global and local conversations on culture, diversity, and social justice in evaluation: Issues to consider in a 9/11 era. *American Journal of Evaluation,* 22(3), 375–380.

House, E. R. (1980). *Evaluating with Validity.* Thousand Oaks, CA: Sage.

House, E. R. (1993). *Professional Evaluation: Social impact and political consequences.* Thousand Oaks, CA: Sage.

House, E. R. & Howe, K. R. (1999). *Values in Evaluation and Social Research.* Thousand Oaks, CA: Sage.

House, E. R. & Howe, K. R. (2000). Deliberative democratic evaluation. In K. E. Ryan and L. DeStefano (eds) *Evaluation as a Democratic Process: Promoting inclusion, dialogue, and deliberation. New Directions for Evaluation,* No. 85 (pp. 3–12). San Francisco: Jossey-Bass.

Howe, K. R. (1997). *Understanding Equal Educational Opportunity: Social justice, democracy, and schooling. Advances in Contemporary Educational Thought,* Volume 20. New York: Teachers College Press.

Howe, K. R. (2003). *Closing Methodological Divides: Toward democratic educational research. Philosophy and Education,* Volume 11. Boston, MA: Kluwer.

Howe, K. R. & Ashcraft, C. (2005). Deliberative democratic evaluation: Successes and limitations of an evaluation of school choice. *Teachers College Record,* 107(10).

Karlsson, O. (1996). A critical dialogue in evaluation: How can interaction between evaluation and politics be tackled? *Evaluation,* 2, 405–416.

Kemmis, S. & McTaggart, R. (2000). Participatory action research. In N. K. Denzin & Y. S. Lincoln (eds) *Handbook of Qualitative Research,* 2nd edition (pp. 567–605). Thousand Oaks CA: Sage.

Kushner, S. (2000). *Personalizing Evaluation.* London: Sage.

LaFrance, J. (2004). Culturally competent evaluation in Indian country. In M. Thompson-Robinson, R. Hopson, & S. SenGupta (eds) *In Search of Cultural Competence in Evaluation. New Directions for Evaluation,* No. 102 (pp. 39–50). San Francisco: Jossey-Bass.

MacDonald, B. (1976). Evaluation and the control of education. In D. Tawney (ed.) *Curriculum Evaluation Today: Trends and implications* (pp. 125–136). London: MacMillan Education.

MacDonald, B. (1977). The portrayal of persons as evaluation data. In N. Nigel (ed.) *Safari: Theory in practice* (pp. 50–67). Norwich: Centre for Applied Research in Education, University of East Anglia.

MacDonald, B. (1978). Evaluation and democracy. Public address at the University of Alberta Faculty of Education, Edmonton, Canada.

MacDonald, B. & Walker, R. (1977). Case-study and the social philosophy of educational research. In D. Hamilton, B. MacDonald, C. King, D. Jenkins, & M. Parlett (eds) *Beyond the Numbers Game: A reader in educational evaluation* (pp. 181–189). Berkeley, CA: McCutchan Publising Company.

MacNeil, C. (2000). Surfacing the Realpolitik: Democratic evaluation in an anti-democratic climate. In K. E. Ryan & L. DeStefano (eds) *Evaluation as a Democratic Process: Promoting inclusion, dialogue, and deliberation. New Directions for Evaluation,* No. 85 (pp. 51–62). San Francisco: Jossey-Bass.

MacNeil, C. (2002). Evaluator as steward of citizen deliberation. *American Journal of Evaluation,* 23, 45–54.

Madison, A. M. (1992). Primary inclusion of culturally diverse minority program participants in the evaluation process. In A. M. Madison (ed.) *Minority Issues in Evaluation. New Directions for Program Evaluation*, No. 53 (pp. 35–43). San Francisco: Jossey-Bass.

Mathison, S. (1996). The role of deliberation in evaluation. Paper presented at the annual meeting of the American Evaluation Association, Atlanta GA, November.

McKee, A. & Stake, R. E. (2002). Making evaluation democratic in a climate of control. In L. Bresler & A. Ardichivili (eds) *International Research in Education: Experience, theory, and practice* (pp. 121–137). New York: Peter Lang.

McTaggart, R. (1991). When democratic evaluation doesn't seem democratic. *Evaluation Practice*, 12(1), 9–21.

Mertens, D. M. (1999). Inclusive evaluation: Implications of transformative theory for evaluation. *American Journal of Evaluation*, 20(1), 1–14.

Mertens, D. M. (2003). The inclusive view of evaluation: Visions for the new millennium. In S. I. Donaldson & M. Scriven (eds) *Evaluating Social Programs and Problems: Visions for the new millennium* (pp. 91–107). Mahwah, NJ: Lawrence Erlbaum Associates.

Niemi, H. & Kemmis, S. (1999). Communicative evaluation. *Lifelong Learning in Europe*, 4, 5–64.

Rawls, J. (1971). *A Theory of Justice*. Cambridge, MA: Belknap.

Rebien, C. (1996). Participatory evaluation of development assistance: Dealing with power and facilitative learning. *Evaluation*, 2(2), 151–172.

Ryan, K. E. (2004). Serving public interests in educational accountability: Alternative approaches to democratic evaluation. *American Journal of Evaluation*, 25(4), 443–460.

Schwandt, T. A. (1997). Reading the "problem of evaluation" in social inquiry. *Qualitative Inquiry*, 3(1), 4–25.

Seigart, D. (1999). Participatory evaluation and community learning: Sharing knowledge about school-based healthcare. Unpublished doctoral dissertation. Department of Human Service Studies, Cornell University, Ithaca NY.

Seigart, D. & Brisolera, S. (eds) (2002). *Feminist Evaluation: Exploration and experiences. New Directions for Evaluation*, No. 96. San Francisco: Jossey-Bass.

Simons, H. (1987). *Getting to Know Schools in a Democracy: The politics and processes of evaluation*. New York: Falmer.

Smith, L. T. (1999). *Decolonizing Methodologies: Research and indigenous peoples*. London: Zed Books.

Stake, R. E. (2000). A modest commitment to the promotion of democracy. In K. E. Ryan & L. DeStefano (eds) *Evaluation as a Democratic Process: Promoting inclusion, dialogue, and deliberation. New Directions for Evaluation*, No. 85 (pp. 97–106). San Francisco: Jossey-Bass.

Tandon, R. (1981). Participatory research in the empowerment of people. *Convergence*, 14(3), 20–29.

Thomas, V. G. (2004). Building a contextually responsive evaluation framework: Lessons from working with urban school interventions. In V. G. Thomas & F. I. Stevens (eds) *Co-constructing a Contextually Responsive Evaluation Framework. New Directions for Evaluation*, No. 101 (pp. 3–23). San Francisco: Jossey-Bass.

Thomas, V. G. & Stevens, F. I. (eds) (2004a). *Co-constructing a Contextually Responsive Evaluation Framework. New Directions for Evaluation*, No. 101. San Francisco: Jossey-Bass.

Thomas, V. G. & Stevens, F. I. (2004b). Editors' notes. In V. G. Thomas & F. I. Stevens (eds) *Co-constructing a Contextually Responsive Evaluation Framework. New Directions for Evaluation*, No. 101 (pp. 1–2). San Francisco: Jossey-Bass.

VanderPlaat, M. (1995). Beyond technique: Evaluating for empowerment. *Evaluation*, 1(1), 81–96.

Ward, K. (2002). Reflections on a job done: Well? In D. Seigart & S. Brisolera (eds) *Feminist Evaluation: Exploration and experiences. New Directions for Evaluation*, No. 96 (pp. 41–56). San Francisco: Jossey-Bass.

Weiss, C. H. (1983). Toward the future of stakeholder approaches in evaluation. In A. Bryk (ed.) *Stakeholder-Based Evaluation. New Directions for Program Evaluation*, No. 17 (pp. 83–96). San Francisco: Jossey-Bass.

Whitmore, E. (1991). Evaluation and empowerment: It's the process that counts. *Empowerment and Family Support Networking Bulletin*, 2(2), 1–7. Ithaca, NY: Cornell University Empowerment Project.

Whitmore, E. (1994). To tell the truth: Working with oppressed groups in participatory approaches to inquiry (pp. 82–98). In P. Reason (ed.) *Participation in Human Inquiry*. London: Sage.

Whitmore, E. (ed.) (1998). *Understanding and Practicing Participatory Evaluation. New Directions for Evaluation*, No. 80. San Francisco: Jossey-Bass.

EVALUATION AFTER DISENCHANTMENT? FIVE ISSUES SHAPING THE ROLE OF EVALUATION IN SOCIETY

Peter Dahler-Larsen

There is no definite destiny for evaluation as a field. Evaluation is a form of "assisted sensemaking" (Mark, Henry, & Julnes, 2000); it is an "artificial" or deliberately "constructed" apparatus by which humans make sense of their world and their initiatives. There is thus no "natural" way of constructing evaluation. Fields of knowledge come and go. Socially constructed knowledge is always relative to time, place, and social institutions (Berger & Luckmann, 1966). With this in mind, it is no surprise that several of the issues mentioned in this chapter will relate to how evaluation becomes linked to particular institutions and socially defined viewpoints, and how it is influenced by its appearance in different social arenas. Assisted sensemaking is thus relative

to particular *relevance structures*. A relevance structure is a socially defined orientation which guides the selection and structuring of knowledge appropriate for particular purposes (Berger & Kellner, 1982). It is equally true, however, that knowledge is not socially predetermined; human beings work actively to construct their knowledge (Popper, 2001). They choose between existing relevance structures and define new ones.

In this chapter, I will discuss five issues and their corresponding relevance structures, which are likely to shape the future of evaluation. Each of the issues illustrates practical and social conditions for what I identify as a central mandate for evaluation: to help society determine its own future through systematic, data-based feedback. I will show that together these issues represent "disenchantment" with the original mandate, and that the mandate needs to be revised, but not abandoned. First, I will place the discussion of the future of evaluation in the context of three observations about evaluation as a field as it is already.

Evaluation as a Field: Diversity, Growth, and Coherence

The first observation is that the field is very diverse. As the reader of the previous chapters of the *Handbook* has noticed already, the field encompasses fundamentally different paradigms and understandings of evaluation. On all important dimensions in evaluation theory, such as what Shadish, Cook, & Leviton (1991) identify as the value component, the use component, and the knowledge component (including paradigm, epistemology, and methodology), different evaluators actually take different positions! Each position implies a view on the role and purpose of evaluation in society, and each one leads to different practices. For this reason, it is difficult to make general and true statements about the whole field which are not at the same time very abstract.

The second observation is that the field continues to grow. The number of journals and books in the field testify to the growing interest in evaluation. Evaluation is becoming a taken-for-granted aspect of policy-making and organizational procedures in international organizations, national governments, local governments, and service-providing institutions. Evaluation is part and parcel of a larger cultural wave consisting also of audit, inspection, and quality assurance, which together constitute "a huge and unavoidable social experiment which is conspicuously cross-sectional and transnational" (Power, 1997, p. xv). Singular studies are being supplemented with evaluation systems which produce online indicators and other streams of evaluative knowledge (Rist & Stame, forthcoming). Although reports of a decline of program evaluation can be found (Shadish, Cook, & Leviton, 1991, p. 27), these are mostly confined to a specific governmental level, sector, or era in a particular country (such as the Reagan era in the US). Most studies report on intense (Hansen, 2003) and increasing evaluation activities (Furubo, Rist, & Sandahl, 2001).

Perhaps the best indicator of the overall growth of evaluation is the increasing number of evaluation societies. An internet search (first presented in Dahler-Larsen, forthcoming) has shown that the number of evaluation societies around the globe has increased ten times since 1984, and it has doubled since 1999.[1] In other words, to say something about evaluation is to talk about a very dynamic phenomenon.

The third observation is, perhaps paradoxically, that despite its diversity and growth, evaluation as a field remains relatively well-defined, distinct, and sufficiently coherent. In practice, the term "evaluation" brings a sufficient number of people together who share enough of the same interests, and who, despite confusions and disagreements about vocabulary, do "evaluation," attend "evaluation" conferences, and take standpoints on "evaluation standards." They read some of the same books and journals, interact considerably across paradigms, topical interests, and national and cultural borders, and position themselves in ways that make sense to others. In addition, although not all evaluators are members, the increasing number of evaluation associations and their increasing number of members build organizational structures which help define the field and the interaction within it. Thus, an increasing number of characteristics in the field of evaluation will outlast individual evaluators.

However, there is no logical reason to expect that the present combination of diversity, growth, and (sufficient) coherence will continue indefinitely.

Following this bird's-eye view of the structure of the field, I will now focus more on the role and mission of evaluation in society. The choice of this theme may have been influenced by my interest in continental sociology (Beck, 1994; Castoriadis, 1997), my upbringing in a universalistic Scandinavian welfare state (Denmark), and other factors. Although my perspective is personal, I will demonstrate that it is not arbitrary.

A Mandate for Evaluation

Modern society is defined by its attempt to replace tradition and prejudice by a belief in rationality and progress. Modern society is one in which the term "society" has been brought into the open as a total, if complex, perspective on social life. "Society" also implies that social forces on the macro level need to be understood for a deliberate shaping of a common future to be possible.

Evaluation emerges at a historical point in time when modern society becomes reflective, as it acknowledges that not all of its attempts to shape its own future are automatically successful, and some have side-effects (Beck, 1994). Yet, society still believes that improvements are within reach based on systematic feedback about interventions to solve common problems. Thus, the mandate for evaluation is to help society shape its own future in a qualified way through systematic, data-based feedback.[2] A society which seeks evaluation is one which prefers rational thought and critical inquiry to tradition, ideology, and prejudice.

In fact, evaluation was born in a period with extremely high hopes about the ability of social science to contribute to the improvement of society, and the reference to Great Society legislation in the 1960s (Patton,

1997, p. 10) in this context is more than just a play on words.

Various schools of thought have embodied the link between evaluation and societal progress. One of them is the experimenting society, in which evaluation has a key role to play in determining which of the alternative strategies – based on experimental or quasi-experimental data – solve social problems most effectively (Campbell, 1988). This and other ideas related to how evaluation could make society better were conceived within a cleverly elaborated division of labor between political decision-making and evaluation, which was designed to transform rational knowledge directly into rational collective decision-making.

The overall ideological framework around the idea of societal progress through evaluation was soon criticized for its emphasis on social engineering, its almost superstitious belief in the power of scientific methods to produce unequivocal results, and its reduction of political questions to technical questions (Albæk, 1988). Studies of political systems, decision-making, and organizational logics made it obvious that the official political machinery did not actually behave according to the assumed rationalistic model (Albæk, 1988; Weiss, 1983). Early evaluation studies were also criticized for adopting elitist perspectives and producing statistically complex results which were largely irrelevant for people working with concrete programs. The underlying assumptions about the ease of transmission of knowledge into improved practice were apparently too naïve.

Yet, as a norm, hope, vision, and justification, the mandate for evaluation, to help society shape its own future through careful and systematic data-based feedback, is neither obsolete nor irrelevant. Many contributions to the field of evaluation today are reflections of the difficulties which evaluators have encountered with the mandate. Whether they revolt against assumptions in earlier versions of the mandate or constructively revise the mandate, the resonance of the mandate is there.

The five issues in the following all describe the changing social contexts in which evaluation occurs and which influence the possibilities for fulfillment of the mandate over time.[3] By an issue I do not mean a trend to which a majority of evaluators conform, but "a question, point, or concern to be disputed or decided, a main matter of contention; a sticking point or grievance, a belief at variance" (Stake, 2004, p. 89).

I will present each issue's contours and describe its resonance in existing evaluation theory and/or practice at the cost of not always respecting the full complexity of each author to whom I refer. (In fact, many evaluators today ask "stretching questions," which challenge the conventional boundaries of their basic paradigm in order to respond to critique, solve problems, and develop their evaluation practice. The issues they struggle with, and the discussions they do not take, cut across conventional schools of thought.)

For each issue, I will hypothesize somewhat schematically about its impact on the mandate for evaluation. I will return to the connections between the issues before the conclusion.

Issue 1: Popularization?

To popularize evaluation means to bring it to "the people" or "the lay person" otherwise not trained in evaluation nor familiar with it. To make something popular, it is important to present it or shape it in such a way that it becomes relevant and appears attractive for non-elites and non-experts. Evaluation is argued to be valuable, worthwhile, ethical, useful, or democratic to invite the "lay" person to engage in it.

Most popularizers of evaluation like narratives of the following form: "There were a lot of problems. Then came evaluation. In the beginning it was very difficult, but after some time, the results were really great. You, too, can benefit from evaluation. Become an evaluator!"

People's participation or involvement in evaluation may extend far beyond merely answering questions; it involves some degree of influence on one or several important parts of evaluation, such as setting the agenda, organizing the process, interpreting data, and taking responsibility for ongoing use. Taken to its logical extreme, popularization means that everybody does self-evaluation.

Popularizers of evaluation differ with respect to how far they take popularization along a number of dimensions, including how many are involved, how deeply they are involved in various aspects of the evaluation process, which degree of control over the evaluation process they have (Cousins & Earl, 1995), and the broadness or scope of activities under evaluation.

Popularization requires strategies for fighting obstacles to evaluation. Obstacles can and should be overcome, popularizers contend, either quickly or gradually. In a similar vein, popularizers of evaluation also seek to enhance the empowerment and self-reliance of a particular social setting (organization, group, or community), and its capacity to do more evaluation in the future.

This being said, popularization happens for very different reasons.

Perhaps the most frequent argument is that involvement increases the chances that evaluations will be used. After systematic studies in the 1970s revealed that official instrumental use of evaluations was rare (Weiss & Bucuvalas, 1980, p. 10), the aim of utilization has been "the main drive and deeper case of all controversies about selection of appropriate methods, concepts and theories in evaluation" (Hellstern, 1986, p. 281).

In response to this problem, involvement in evaluation, including a degree of responsibility for it, will reduce evaluation anxiety, enhance ownership, and increase the relevance of evaluation, because the focus is kept on what users of evaluation need to know (Patton, 1997) in order to make decisions and/or improve services. If several persons need to act in common, they should all be involved in the evaluation process so as to have a shared vision of the benefits of evaluation, to create and develop a shared knowledge base (Cousins & Earl, 1995, p. 159), and thus enhance organizational learning (Preskill & Torres, 1999). However, the evidence base for the link between involvement and use is more limited than one might expect (Henry & Mark, 2003).

There is another major and more political argument for popularization. Evaluation too often identifies with the views of elites and experts, but it ought to attend to a broader set of stakeholders, especially those representing voices of underprivileged groups (Guba & Lincoln, 1989). Evaluation can also be a tool for self-empowerment (Fetterman, 1994). Anti-elitist and anti-fundamentalist values have also been promoted with reference to various forms of democratic evaluation. "Democratic" in this respect refers to participatory and/or deliberative (House & Howe, 2000) notions of democracy (not representative democracy).

While popularization has thus been supported with arguments anchored in different dimensions of evaluation theory, it has often also been promoted without any of these foundations. There are some consultants, trainers, and authors who promise that practically everybody can learn evaluation quickly, and the "involvement and participation of everybody" are sometimes seen as goals in themselves without further qualification.

Altogether, popularization is probably one of the key factors explaining how and why the field of evaluation has continued to grow for some time. However, the problematic aspects of popularization are often not recognized.

First, there is sometimes a conflict between popularization and competence. Good evaluators have been trained in the methods of the social sciences for several years. On top of that, they have some years of experience in research and/or practical evaluation projects. In contrast, popularization is sometimes followed by an expectation that lay persons will become good evaluators based on a short introduction and rudimentary training in methodology. Experienced participatory evaluators find workable divisions of labor so that the overall evaluation process remains a shared responsibility while more technical aspects of, say, data analysis are delegated to the involved specialist (Cousins & Earl, 1995). However, many forms of self-evaluation or internal evaluation do not allow for this option. Other strategies for bridging the competence gap are to make the best of the situation, "get a process going," do some "capacity building," and hope, sometimes desperately without much justification, that the evaluation will be even "better next time."

Second, popularization may imply "overselling" the benefits of evaluation. It may also imply a systematic underestimation of the costs of evaluation, not only financial costs (Hansen, 2003), but political, organizational, cultural (Schwandt & Dahler-Larsen, 2003), and emotional costs as well.

For evaluators engaged in a particular collaborative activity, training project, or capacity-building project, it is often difficult to communicate a fair, balanced, and honest judgment about the benefits and cost of evaluation. The success of such a project often hinges on the support it receives by key stakeholders. This support often depends on the energy, beliefs, commitment, and sometimes salesmanship of the evaluator. In other words, the evaluator has to be an optimist, because belief in evaluation must be promoted for the project to be promoted. Popularization of evaluation sometimes takes the form of self-concealed messianism.

For a counterexample including a careful, modest, and balanced view of some pros and cons of participatory approaches, written by some of its advocates, see Cousins & Earl (1995), and for a sober analysis of the tensions between utilization-oriented and transformative approaches to participatory evaluation, see Greene (1997).

Third, popularization is often followed by an opening of evaluation towards different views, interests, and agendas as legitimate partners in evaluation (Albæk, 1998). This tendency is problematic if evaluation lends itself to a variety of fragmented views without a justification of how and why evaluation attends to a given set of stakeholders. For example, unless they are carefully justified within a new larger normative framework (Dahlberg & Vedung, 2001), the views of clients and customers of public services constitute a normatively fragmented and democratically insufficient framework for evaluation (Fountain, 2001). An interesting counterpoint is developed by House & Howe (2000), who advocate a politically transformative agenda based on dialog with stakeholders, but who anchor their approach normatively, not in any particular group, but in a set of general principles for good democratic deliberation.

Finally, popularization of evaluation may lead to a distortion of the uses of evaluation. For example, a summative use of evaluation is often impeded if the roles of evaluating a good are not strictly separated from producing the good and making recommendations about its improvement (Scriven, 1991, p. 54). Following this logic, it makes no sense to even try to popularize evaluation among those who are responsible for goods and services under evaluation. Although this view is probably too formalistic, it is true that popularizers of evaluation often lack respect for the differences in roles between producing something practically and evaluating it systematically.

Without doubt, popularization has helped expand the field, attract new members, and cultivate new land. On the other hand, if popularization goes hand in hand with overselling evaluation and underestimating its costs, there may be reactions, such as evaluation fatigue. If popularization leads to a permissive view on methodological quality, the reputation of evaluation may be undermined, and the borders between evaluation and other activities (not based on data and systematic inquiry) may break down. Some variants of popularization, such as Guba & Lincoln's (1989) constructivism, which claims that the evaluators' constructions are just one set of constructions among many, in fact make it difficult to explain how and why evaluation is different from any other social process where various views are exchanged and discussed.

Popularization of evaluation may be self-detrimental.

Issue 2: Evaluation Shaped by Organizational Structures and Processes

Evaluation is becoming integrated in organizational structures, cultures, and processes which regulate how organizations function, work, survive, learn, govern themselves, legitimize themselves, and develop. As an alternative to singular external evaluation as a sometimes ineffective stand-alone activity, the integration of evaluation into organizational routines and procedures seeks to secure an ongoing process of reflection and learning as a collaborative effort, and to bring this process much closer to work processes and practices in daily life in an organization. Evaluation should thus be "mainstreamed," that is, moved to "the forefront of organizational thinking and behavior" (Sanders, 2001).

In recent years, a number of initiatives, recipes, and buzzwords represent attempts to fuse evaluation with the way modern organizations function. Regimes for public governance such as New Public Management, which has had a strong impact in many Western countries (Furubo et al., 2001), assume that if organizations are held externally accountable for their scores on certain performance indicators, they will behave as good organizations and optimize their structures, processes, and outputs. An agenda has evolved around how organizations themselves can develop an organizational capacity for evaluation (Compton, Baizerman, & Stockdill, 2002). The interest in supporting organizational learning processes through evaluative inquiry (Preskill & Torres, 1999) and enforcing an "evaluation culture" have also led to concrete organizational recipes for evaluation.

Although evaluation theory has often treated internal evaluation as a "special case," data suggest that at least in some social settings, evaluations internal to organizations constitute more than 60% of all evaluations (Dahler-Larsen, 2000).

This tendency, like popularization, is an important vehicle for the diffusion of evaluation to many sectors and areas of activity in society. It is unique, however, in its fusion of evaluation with a specifically *organizational* relevance structure. This relevance structure transforms evaluation in subtle and controversial ways which are often not recognized.

When evaluation is becoming integrated into organizational structures and procedures, the difference between an evaluation of a program and a management information system within the program may break down (Shadish et al., 1991, p. 56). Because the loyalty of internal evaluators towards evaluation may be under pressure from professional, departmental, and organizational values, and especially because internal evaluators are often expected to demonstrate the immediate usefulness of evaluation (Mathison, 1999,

p. 28), evaluation may focus exclusively on minor issues of practical and/or managerial relevance, while drawing attention away from larger policy issues (Henry, 2000, p. 91). Evaluations in organizations often embody particular organicentric views. For instance, organizationally defined performance indicators may take on a particular reified quality as if they were goals in themselves. The macroquality of evaluands may be lost from focus.

Fashionable organizational recipes emphasize the generic organizational qualities of public activities rather than their specific content (Røvik, 1998). Evaluation from an organizational perspective is often followed by standardization of criteria and methodology, regardless of whether such approaches actually fit with the type of work in specific areas of activity (Abma & Noordegraaf, 2003). The organizational control over evaluation may thus be one of the institutionalized mechanisms which remove evaluation from the concrete and complex practice of professionals, a process described in depth by Schwandt (2002).

The image of an organizational capacity and willingness to carry out evaluation has itself become a symbol of proper modern organization, and a key to legitimacy, status, recognition, and sometimes funding (Dahler-Larsen, 2004). As organizations bring this mechanism with them into their relations with other organizations, evaluation may then become an important part of a constructed interorganizational reality which lives its own life. Maybe this explains why organizations which evaluate organizations often focus on structures, procedures, and control systems (Power, 1997), rather than on more direct measures of their contribution to societal problem-solving. Although rhetorically phrased as "outcomes," performance indicators often focus on managerially defined aspects of quality other than actual client outcomes (Tilbury, 2004).

In the context of modern bureaucratic and technological organization, there is an unprecedented distance between organizational decisions and their impact on the lives of concrete human beings. According to the sociologist Zygmunt Bauman (1995), the result is adiaphorization – meaning that we come to see organizational life as exempt from moral evaluation, as morally dead territory. Perhaps the subsuming of evaluation under organizations as a modern form of rationalized social life has contributed to the anonymity and lack of personal responsibility which, according to Greene (1999), characterize evaluation regimes such as performance indicators.

No organization can question its assumptions and practices constantly. Evaluation is difficult enough as an extraordinary activity, and the ideal is now to turn it into an organizational routine. Many organizations respond to this paradoxical quest by promising reforms (Meyer & Rowan, 1977), corrupting performance-oriented steering models (Modell, 2004), trivializing evaluation, displacing goals, focusing on organicentric issues, maintaining an image of proper management, and obscuring responsibility.

Issue 3: Evaluation as Shaped by the Market

Evaluation is a professional activity which often takes the form of a business (Stake, 2004, p. 270). Evaluation nourishes an industry of conferences, courses, and consultants. Among a sample of consultants, a large majority (12 to 1) reported on growing rather than declining markets (Leeuw, Toulemonde, & Brouwers, 1999). How the business aspect of evaluation influences the shape, role, and function of evaluation is rarely considered, and it is not the favorite official topic among evaluators. Yet, markets tend to shape everything in the form of commodities.

First, as a commodity, evaluation will tend to take place where money flows rather than where there is a societal need for evaluation. Of course, public money earmarked for evaluation is sometimes allocated to policy or program areas which are prioritized as important. In addition, non-governmental organizations (NGOs) and special interests groups sometimes finance special evaluations which influence the public attention to issues and needs in various policy areas. There is no guarantee, however, that important areas of life in society which need evaluation are actually evaluated. (Neither is there a guarantee that those who pay for evaluation will get what they want.) Second, evaluations thriving on the market are not necessarily evaluations which are good in all respects. Many commissioners ask for politically comfortable evaluations, but wealthy commissioners are in position to back up their demands. Third, as a result of evaluation being a business, some evaluators engage in a form of salesmanship which leads to an exaggeration of the benefits of evaluation.

Another set of hypotheses concerns the specific ways that the marketization of evaluation is implemented. EU regulations, for instance, and some national legislation require that all evaluations exceeding a particular financial amount should be offered through public tendering. The official motive for procuring evaluation through tendering is to guarantee impartial evaluation, avoid nepotism, secure an impartial assessment of bids, and get the best possible evaluation at a given cost (Segerholm, 2002).

In practice, however, tendering has a number of drawbacks and side-effects which make the accomplishment of these ideals less credible. Official tendering removes any dialog between the commissioner and the evaluator from the early phases of the evaluation process, and subsequent dialog cannot change the conditions defined in the tender. What can commissioners do if they lack the necessary knowledge to specify the conditions of the tender? They can hire additional expertise (at a cost), or break the rules, or make premature choices on methodology. Next, because the evaluator cannot ask questions about the complexities and "hot potatoes" hidden in the evaluand, it is more difficult to design the evaluation optimally.

Perhaps more disturbing is Segerholm's (2002) observation that sometimes commissioners use the procurement process to introduce barriers against any critical reflection about evaluands. Larsen (2001) describes how all traces were covered and public discussion prevented by a commissioner who cleverly and indirectly controlled all materials produced, not only in the evaluation itself, but also in the procurement of the evaluation. All in all, tender processes may not always lead to the impartiality, efficiency, and optimality suggested by the exposed market-oriented ideology.

A final aspect of the marketization of evaluation has to do with the structure of the industry. According to Leeuw et al., (1999) evaluation is an "infant industry" characterized by many small companies entering a promising market, over-ambitious terms of reference, and unstable standards. More mature markets would be dominated by a few large international companies, much more like the audit industry. Standardization would follow. Whether or not this prediction is correct, the impact of the commodification of evaluation is often not given enough attention.

Issue 4: Evaluation as Shaped by the Media

The form, function, and use of evaluations are influenced by the fact that evaluations appear in the media. When the media mention an

evaluation, this may have an impact which outweighs all the other efforts an evaluator has made to produce a good, respectable, and useful evaluation.

In a conventional form of media influence on evaluation, findings are reported in mass media as news or as background in articles. While the origin of the information is still clearly to be found in an evaluation report, the data, conclusions, and recommendations do not always translate into conventional media genres in uncontroversial ways. Barbier (forthcoming) describes a case in which evaluation results reported in headlines were practically the opposite of what was conveyed in the evaluation report.

In a more contemporary and more radical version, the appearance of evaluative data in the media is not an epiphenomenon of an evaluation process carried out elsewhere, which is represented more or less accurately; rather, the media reports constitute the very form in which data are meant to be provided. Evaluation is sometimes carried out with the deliberate intention of influencing the public attention or attitude to the evaluand. Another example is the publication of systematic and comparable data on the internet such as data on schools, in order to help parents make informed choices about which school to choose for their children. Again, the appearance of evaluation in the media in such cases is not a by-product of an evaluation report, but a facilitator of use of evaluation in its own right.

The field is gradually developing concepts which catch up with the new situation, beginning with the "enlightenment" function described by Weiss and recently followed by both a broadened view of evaluation influence (Kirkhart, 2000) and more specific hypotheses about the influence mechanisms (Mark & Henry, 2004).

Mass media do not only carry evaluative information across time and place to multiple and anonymous audiences with various agendas (Breul, Boyle & Dahler-Larsen, forthcoming), thus making it more difficult for an evaluator to predict the interpretation and use of evaluation data. Moreover, the media edit messages. A specific format for data, redesign of data, or an interpretation of data are often dictated or facilitated by particular media. For example, certain filtering rules are applied when evaluative information is transformed into news. News exaggerates success or failure. News reports are more often negative than positive. They suggest blame or scandal, they emphasize or create conflict, and they have a short life.

In new electronic media, the form and rules of the media influence the content of what is communicated. For example, a web-based feature lets each user custom-tailor his or her own excerpt from a database depending on purpose and perspective. Manovich (2001) identifies this "variability" as a key aspect of the new electronic media. Again, the media imply a reduction of an evaluator's centrality regarding the design, interpretation, and use of the evaluation results.

In trying to understand the interplay between the media, democracy, and evaluation, inspiration may be found in three different very broad views held by those who have already studied the impact of the media (without a specific reference to evaluation).

According to one paradigm, the media connote commercialism and ideological hegemony over public life. Within this paradigm, there is an emphasis on how the large-scale media are organized structurally and economically, on one-way communication, on deceptive political language, and on the general apathy of consumer-oriented audiences. This paradigm predicts political capturing of evaluation and a reduction of its messages to political spin and designed news (for an example, see Barbier, forthcoming). In a slightly different version of this paradigm, public imagery dominates political forces rather than the other way around, and politicians are under pressure to act swiftly and simplistically in response to public issues raised in the media. In any case, it is the reductionist nature of public images and the lack of genuine democratic debate which define this paradigm.

Another paradigm holds an optimistic view of the role of the new media for a revitalization of democracy. The new media facilitate easy and affordable communication across time and space. The new media open new communication lines and create new forums for democratic deliberation and participation, including new ways of involving citizens in evaluation and facilitating its use.

According to a third view, there is no determinism and inherent finality in the media. Instead, the media can both facilitate and undermine intended messages (Thompson, 2001). As a part of the knowledge society, they enhance complexity, uncertainty, and unpredictability (Stehr, 2001). The media (with space/time distance, anonymity, the impact of the media on the message, and perhaps variability) thus reduce the predictability of the use of evaluations. Evaluations, or more precisely streams of evaluative information, may themselves be competitive or contradictory, which adds to the uncertainty of their implications.

In a situation in which most relations between producers, mediators, and users of evaluation data are anonymous, it becomes increasingly clear that decisions about evaluation are not made by one central rational mind in society. Furthermore, conventional approaches which focus on contract and consensus based on personal relationships to intended users (Patton, 1997) are too restricted. Evaluators who want to qualify the use of evaluative information in the public arena may instead want to consider, for example, public hearings, where lay persons can participate in a discussion about the meaning of public evaluative data, education of journalists with respect to understanding evaluative data, evaluative information as a part of civic education, and a role for public information ombudspersons.

Such initiatives may sound utopian, but so did political parties, free elections, and civil rights while modern democracy was founded. The current transformation of the public sphere in information societies may be of similar significance. Today, there is an important challenge in learning how to develop institutions and norms to strengthen a democratic civility in the public handling of evaluative information. Otherwise, the reduction of evaluation to simplistic images and of the public to passive consumers of information may continue to be major obstacles to a better realization of the mandate for evaluation in society.

Issue 5: Evaluation in Relation to Scientific Research

Evaluation is a form of assisted, not natural, sense-making (Mark et al., 2000, p. 5). The type of assisted sense-making that is characteristic of evaluation is careful (Vedung, 1997, p. 3) and systematic. It is based on assumptions about the creation of valid knowledge on ontological, epistemological, and methodological levels similar to those of scientific work. I include within "scientific work" not only the natural sciences, as I understand is a common connotation of "science" in English, but everything called *Wissenschaft* in German, that is, philosophy and all of the humanities as well. Principles in scientific work relate to conceptual clarity, critical thinking, abstraction, generalization, logical consistency, appropriate methodology, transparency of procedures, and so on.

Evaluators who violate the principles of systematic knowledge production can be criticized. Evaluators can also be positively inspired by paradigms, concepts, methods, and ways of critical thinking known from scientific research. The term "evaluation research" and "evaluation" can sometimes be used almost interchangeably, as does Weiss (1998). The difference between evaluation and research may be one of scale, scope, context, and utility. Evaluation and scientific work are not in principle separated by the quality of the conceptual approach or the rigor of the method.

The scientific element in evaluation is thus always present in principle. Evidently, however, there exists considerable variation in how much emphasis is put on this element over time and across various approaches to evaluation.

The alliance with science was strong as evaluation was born in the midst of an unprecedented optimism about the use of social science for the improvement of policies, and ultimately, a better society. Campbell (1988), for instance, an early evaluator who developed what Shadish et al., (1991) call a "stage one theory," sought to prepare the ground for more rational ways to identify and test effective policies through experiments. Thus, scientific experimental method should reign over evaluation.

A self-assured ideology which sought to combine this version of scientific evaluation with rationalistic decision-making soon became criticized as a technocratic evaluation practice which was more or less irrelevant to actual people in concrete program settings and inattentive to the needs and concerns of underprivileged groups. This critique prepared the ground for a development of participatory models of evaluation and the popularization of evaluation (described above). Hence occurred Guba & Lincoln's (1989) version of constructivist evaluation, Fetterman's (1994) empowerment evaluation, Patton's (1997) utilization-focused evaluation, and various forms of participatory evaluation. Although all of these helped renew the field of evaluation, none of them found their strongest and most decisive basis in the affinity between evaluation and scientific thinking, and their contributions do not lie in that area.

A revitalization of the link between evaluation and scientific thinking began to emerge already in the mid-1980s (Caracelli, 2000). This time the affinity between evaluation and research was not primarily methodological, but theoretical. Chen (1990) helped advance theory-based evaluation, where an evaluand is a test case of a more general theory, and the evaluation is the test. Evaluation thus provides information about the validity of the program theory, that is, the assumptions underlying the program under evaluation. This broad idea is further elaborated, contextualized, and operationalized in "realistic evaluation" (Pawson & Tilley, 1997; Mark et al., 2000). This school of thought maintains the idea of causal effect as a central interest in evaluation, but causal effects in program mechanisms are now multiple, complex, and context-dependent.

One of the reasons why theory-based evaluation has attracted a considerable amount of interest in recent years (Rogers, 2000) is probably that it has helped revitalize the scientific element in evaluation. It offers a demarcation of evaluation based on scientific work from other processes found in the context of evaluands, such as discussions, negotiations, and development processes. It inspires critical thinking and reality-testing of assumptions. One of the specific strengths of theory-based evaluation is that it combines a conceptual interest in social processes and program mechanisms with an understanding of outcome measures. One of its practical implications is therefore to suggest how the selection of performance indicators (which are not always carefully done) can be improved based on relevant program theory. Theory-based evaluation has also demonstrated the mutual benefits between evaluation and social science in evaluating program theories across sites, contexts, and policy areas (Pawson, 2002).

At its present stage of development, theory-based evaluation is struggling with a number of interesting problems which have not been fully solved, such as how to bridge the gap between conventions for relatively simple representations of causal models, on the one hand, and complex reality on the other (Pawson, 2002). How to handle the impact of changing social contexts on the truth value of program theories and how to attend to political overtones of treating some phenomena as "variables" and other phenomena as "fixed" in program theory models should also be better understood (Dahler-Larsen, 2001). Another interesting development in theory-based evaluation is the breakdown of a simple distinction between practitioners' everyday assumptions and formal theory. Multiple stakeholders hold diverse assumptions about the nature of an evaluand (Gargani, 2002). Although each of these views may also have systematic blind spots (Friedman, 2001), different ways of bringing the views of stakeholders to the surface as well as different ways of guiding the process by the evaluator will result in different representations of program theories which may be fruitful in various ways depending on the purpose of the evaluation.

All in all, scientific thinking has thus over time contributed much to evaluation in terms of both methodology and theory.[4] Characteristically, in both of these realms, scientific thinking offers more than one prescription. While the experiment was praised in the early days as *the* best method, more methods are accepted today, and several methods in combination may create rich and diverse pictures of evaluands (Greene, Benjamin, & Goodyear, 2001). As suggested above, theory is also in the plural today.

Another productive form of cooperation between scientific work and evaluation, suggested by Mark (in press) and others, is of course applying scientific study to the practice of evaluation itself. So far, there has been a discrepancy between the strict methodological requirements which evaluators ideally make before accepting claims about the worth and effectiveness of programs on the one hand, and on the other, the relatively loose evidence on which claims about the worth and effectiveness of evaluations have been based (Leviton, 2003). The call for more research on evaluation and its effects is clearly justified.

Not all scientific studies of evaluation need to be data-based. For an interesting philosophical reflection about evaluation as a modern, instrumental phenomenon and its often reductionist depiction of professional practices under evaluation, see Schwandt (2002). Scientific studies of evaluation may demonstrate that various unconventional literature bases and theoretical perspectives outside the field of evaluation may be useful in order to better understand evaluation as a political, cultural, sociological, and psychological undertaking.

Scientific self-reflection in evaluation also means taking seriously insights gained from the scientific study of science. Both the philosophy of science and its empirical counterpart, the sociology of knowledge, have made it increasingly clear that all knowledge is contextual, contingent, often contested (Beck, 1994), and itself a source of uncertainty (Stehr, 2001). Through a scientific study of itself, evaluation may go through a similar process in revision of its self-concept.

However, if the relevance structure of doing impartial research on evaluation is adhered to, results may follow which do not easily translate into sales points for evaluation. Compared to its documented merits, evaluation may turn out to be oversold and its costs underestimated.

Yet, the scientific study of evaluation may lead to more reflexivity within the field, to more modest and better grounded claims. It may further help to substantiate and demarcate evaluation as a respectable field producing knowledge which is clearly distinguishable from opinions, hopes, and political statements.

Scientifically inspired evaluation is not morally superior or politically privileged. Science has itself become disenchanted. It is not unequivocal, but comprises many perspectives defined by multiple theories and methodologies. In a similar vein, evaluation knowledge can be based on multiple perspectives. Meta-evaluation, being of the same nature, offers no salvation.

However, scientific knowledge is disciplined and qualified as long as it is produced under guidance of its particular relevance structure, which is embodied in specially trained people, institutional devices, and rules such as those connected to open discussion and peer review. Many of these mechanisms can be applied to protect the integrity of an evaluation process, too. Perhaps paradoxically, evaluators make their best contribution to society if they maintain a certain intellectual autonomy and are not completely subordinated to the interests of one or a few stakeholders. This contribution has not only to do with the quality of methodology, but also with making theory, challenging assumptions, asking critical questions, developing new models and approaches, and keeping the self-critical examination of evaluation intact.

Here lie important foundations of an up-to-date version of the mandate for evaluation in society.

Implications for the Role and Mission of Evaluation in Society

While each of the five issues has a role to play in relation to the role and mission of evaluation in society, they also act together. For example, popularization of evaluation, as well as commercialization and the promotion of evaluation through organizational procedures and management systems, may all contribute to *codification* of evaluation, that is, to a reduction of evaluation to a standardized and thus predictable set of algorithms. Codification means that the sequencing and form of the elements of an evaluation process conform to a given recipe.

Codification is sometimes seen as a help to novices in evaluation. Checklists are often used in introductions to evaluation in order to make life easier for beginners. Many manuals, cookbooks, and courses subscribe to the same idea.

Some commissioners in the evaluation market are among the strongest advocates for codification. Codification is seen as insurance against bad evaluations and as a strategy to improve their quality. Several evaluation associations have themselves adopted a set of standards or guidelines prescribing good evaluation practice. Very often, however, such adopted standards operate on a relatively high level of abstraction, and there is often resistance to further codification.

While codification and standardization of evaluation are powerful vehicles for the social diffusion of evaluation, they also, if taken to extremes, have drawbacks similar to the effects of McDonaldization on the art of cooking.

Experienced evaluators often find the sources of quality in evaluation in their skills, methodological judgment, experience, creativity, *Fingerspitzgefühl*, sensitivity to values in social contexts, and last but not least, their ability to question underlying assumptions. These competencies are all valuable for evaluating with integrity and thus for the fulfillment of the mandate for evaluation in society. They are also ignored or reduced by codification. Therefore, among the advocates of standards are many who see them, at best, as aids to a competent judgment in evaluation, not substitutions for it.

If these reservations are not taken seriously, codification may in fact undermine rather than enhance quality in evaluation. Codified evaluation sometimes teams up with commercially oversold evaluation, or with popular organizational recipes, which, much like snake oil or other panaceas, promise quality, efficiency, learning, and user satisfaction in an instant. This trivialization of evaluation may enhance *evaluation fatigue*.

Evaluation as a large-scale social phenomenon managed by organizations, markets, and the media (and sometimes scientific institutions) is often removed from the practical relevance structures of professionals such as social workers and teachers. The effects on their norms, values, and commitments are sometimes negative, leading to frustration and demotivation. The importance of pride, commitment, and motivation for quality work among service producers are not always appreciated in large-scale evaluation regimes which focus on strict, quantitative performance measurement. Therefore, an emphasis on accountability may sometimes undermine the conditions on which its promises about quality improvements rest. The connection between evaluation fatigue and demotivation may be one of the factors which explain the so-called "performance paradox" (van Thiel & Leeuw, 2002), that is, more performance measurement leading to everything else but better performance. The performance paradox is a major threat to an optimistic belief in the societal mandate for evaluation.

Several advocates of the popularization of evaluation have argued that evaluation can regain credibility and utility if based on an attention to local context and to trust and dialog with all relevant stakeholders. Variations of this idea surface in responsive, utilization-focused, participatory, and constructivist evaluation. While several of these approaches deserve much praise for their renewal of the field, their strongest contribution does not lie in rethinking and explaining the link between evaluation and society. Many of them *defocus from society as the referent for evaluation.*

In responsive evaluation, for instance, the level of analysis is more often than not confined to a specific local case. The case study method is recommended as the best methodological approach to grasp the *uniqueness* of the case. Although readers of a responsive evaluation may see some general relevance in the case with reference to their own experiences, this part of the theory of responsive evaluation is not the most elaborate and explicit. Although responsive case-based evaluation may in fact provide an interesting counterpoint to prevailing ideological understandings of the relevance and impact of large-scale policies on, say, local schools, advocates of responsive evaluation do not make this point very clear. Instead, for responsive evaluators, an interest in policy-making on the societal arena seems to disturb the desired local focus.

Some participatory, constructivist, and utilization-focused forms of evaluation work within the context of a given set of involved stakeholders (with various emphasis on intended users or on disenfranchised groups, etc). More often than not, politicians are either too "remote" to be involved or are only involved in the capacity of just one group of stakeholders among many. The representative democratic dimension among "stakeholders" is thus neutralized (Pollitt, 2004). Philosophically, however, the mere sum of stakeholders does not constitute a society. This does not worry many evaluators who find it irrelevant, impossible, unethical, or meaningless to represent the viewpoint of society in general in any form in their evaluative framework. Their views reflect the weakening of the idea of society in the West in recent years (Bauman, 1995).

Truly, some participatory evaluators view participatory evaluation as a microcosm for a larger dialog in society. For example, House & Howe (2000) delineate generally applicable principles for a deliberative democratic form of evaluation. More often than not, however, there is no theory or well-argued framework about how an evaluation based on stakeholder agendas and a local dialog fits into a larger societal framework in a philosophically convincing way. Instead, many celebrate locality and particularity as such. In this respect, some of the contributions in responsive, participatory, and empowerment approaches normatively justify the dismantling of society as the overall referent in evaluation.

However, the same tendency to defocus from society can be also found in very different orientations to evaluation, such as accountability-oriented and goal-oriented approaches. Within these, an important trend is a change of emphasis from in-depth policy evaluations to ongoing monitoring of organizational performance indicators. The ideal in the performance indicator movement is to pinpoint in quantitative terms how well an organization performs in all key activity areas. A "performance" represented by say, test results, is thus attributed to, say, a school.

Sociologically, an indicator such as a test score is a complicated social construction (Vulliamy & Webb, 2001). The prevailing interpretation, however, is that the school "has" the score. Admittedly, the score does not determine subsequent social actions. Promising initiatives to improve learning in schools can be based on collaborative efforts involving children, parents, teachers, principals, politicians, and other schools. The responsibility for poor-performing institutions can also be lifted upwards in the political-administrative hierarchy. More often than not, however, performance indicator systems attribute results to individual institutions. Through statistical control for other factors, and through ranking, each school is isolated statistically and socially, and thus rendered accountable for "its" own performance. At the same time, larger issues in national school policies may escape evaluation.

Thus, in various approaches to evaluation, society as a primary context and referent for evaluation has become more unclear since the early days of evaluation – in fact not so many years ago. This is not only due to each of the five issues presented above. The thinking and self-understanding of a number of approaches to evaluation pull in the same direction.

Perhaps the term *Entzauberung* (or "disenchantment") summarizes the changes in the belief in the societal role and mission of evaluation. Max Weber used the term *Entzauberung* to denote the effect of modern society with respect to the dismantling of superstition, magic, and mythical world order of traditional society. Today it has become increasingly clear that some of the typically modern, optimistic, and rationalistic beliefs in the role of evaluation for a better society also rested on mythical beliefs in a "magic bullet." The mandate for evaluation today appears "disenchanted," as unequivocal and uncontested evaluation data are rarely produced, and as the social contexts in which evaluation works clearly do not facilitate a seamless transformation of knowledge into societal improvements. Some evaluators respond to this situation by dismantling an optimistic belief in unilinear progress, but they maintain and cultivate the idea that evaluation can contribute to social betterment through "sense-making about what makes up the common good and about how successful a particular course of action is in getting there" (Mark et al., 2000, pp. 20–21).

Entzauberung does not only imply disappointment, but also a sober mind. One of the best allies in this respect may be scientific work, itself becoming "disenchanted" through

critique and self-scrutiny. The mandate for evaluation is thus under revision. It has not become irrelevant. The need for knowledge about activities to solve societal problems is absolutely not diminishing, and knowledge is, despite its limitations, a crucial productive force and organizing principle in society (Stehr, 2001).

The Future of the Field

Given my selective focus on a subset of the factors that influence the field of evaluation, my claims about the future are necessarily tentative and incomplete. In this chapter, not enough attention has been paid to the role of international organizations in shaping evaluation, the ongoing battles over secrecy versus freedom of information in public institutions, career patterns and other motivations of evaluators, competition from other fields, and a large number of other factors.

Nevertheless, in terms of the issues dealt with in this chapter, important tensions in the field can be identified. Perhaps the major tension is between evaluation as a scientific activity, on the one hand, and, on the other, popularization (with its parallel forces in organizations, markets, and the media). This tension does not necessarily split the field. Although more and less scientifically oriented evaluations are in different segments of the field, there are also ways in which the segments are connected, at least loosely, through books, education, training courses, and conferences. The segments also to some extent need each other for reasons of legitimacy. It is often beneficial to popular evaluators to appear scientifically informed, and fruitful for science to be in demand as socially useful.

In a similar vein, other tensions may be handled through segmentation within the field of evaluation. For example, an increasing amount of evaluators specialize in organizational processes. Others may follow up on the link between evaluation and societal decision-making on the policy level. It would in fact create a better balance in the field if a larger and more visible segment of evaluators defined this link as a crucial and central concern in their own work. Evaluation may prove useful not only in classical policy areas such as education, health, social work, and foreign aid, but perhaps also in pressing societal issues related to foreign policy, international cooperation, human rights, and security. A new vitality to the mandate for evaluation in society might follow.

In the end, the growing field of evaluation may not be kept together by a common understanding of the role and purpose of evaluation; without doubt, for many years the field has included conflicting perspectives, interests, and areas of work and will continue to do so. In this light, the ongoing building of social and communicative structures in the field in terms of evaluation associations, conferences, books, journals, working groups, and discussions of good practice may be important factors, not so much due to their specific content, but to their facilitation of interconnections between members of the evaluation field with different views.

The diversity of the field may be evaluation's biggest asset. The struggles within the field have not led to a decomposition of the field or to termination of evaluation, but to ongoing discussions and to a constantly creative and productive search for new approaches to both old and new issues. The discovery of problems in evaluation has generally led to more evaluation in varied forms.

However, as the field is likely to continue to exist, grow, and comprise diversity, perhaps it should take more seriously how the forms and amounts of evaluation sometimes relate to evaluation fatigue. Evaluators should also remember to maintain, protect, and develop what is specific to evaluation. Finally, the field

of evaluation should remind itself of how it keeps alive and renews the mandate for evaluation in society.

Conclusion

The practical possibilities of the realization of this mandate depend on the social contexts in which evaluation is carried out. Each of the five issues presented has a role to play in this regard. For example, the popularization of evaluation may lead to a deterioration of methodological quality and to normative fragmentation. In a similar vein, the integration of evaluation into organizational procedures and management systems may remove the focus of evaluation from policy questions, to more narrow organicentric matters. Market mechanisms may shape evaluation as a commodity and render it more determined by money streams than by societal concerns. The media sometimes reduce evaluations to simplistic images, although they also connect many audiences with information and open new arenas for participation. Taken together, several forces tend to codify and sometimes trivialize evaluation. And evaluation fatigue, which was not foreseen in the early days of evaluation, should be taken seriously.

Scientific research continues to be a necessary partner in evaluation, and a countervailing force to some of the threats described above. However, it is no savior. Its theories and methodologies do not support only one representation of reality. Science has lost some of its aura.

Yet, the disenchantment of evaluation has not made its societal role and mission of evaluation obsolete. Knowledge is more important for the shaping of society than ever before (Stehr, 2001). After disenchantment, more complex, reflective, and sober views on fundamental terms such as "society," "data-based feedback," and "future" may follow.

Notes

1. An internet search in November, 2004, identified 83 such associations, societies, or networks plus three "under construction." All of them included the term "evaluation" in either English, German, Spanish, French, Italian, or Scandinavian languages, and all of them were geographically defined, and not sector-specific. International, national, and regional organizations, and chapters of national associations were recorded. Organizations with nothing else than a reference to one person's e-mail address were not included. The method used was to start with well-known international associations and from there exploit all links to other organizations until dead-ends and repetitions occurred. Obviously, this method is linguistically biased, ignores organizations not linked to other organizations or not on the internet, and overrates web-based organizations with no members and no activities. Of all the organizations found, 45 reported which year they were founded. Most of the strong growth in recent years has taken place in Europe and Africa.

2. Truly, this delineation of a mandate for evaluation highlights some aspects more than others, for instance common and public evaluands (Vedung, 1997) rather than private ones.

3. Classical issues in evaluation theory around values, knowledge claims, purposes and use of evaluation, and methodologies (such as the quantitative/qualitative debate), will not be repeated, as they have been dealt with competently elsewhere (Mark et al., 2000; Shadish et al., 1991; Vedung, 1997; Weiss, 1998).

4. In addition, substantial parts of the new ideas, new books, and work power in evaluation associations are contributed by persons with an academic interest in evaluation. This also suggests that the vitality of the field cannot afford a weakening of the link to scientific milieus.

References

Abma, T. & Noordegraaf, M. (2003). Public managers amidst ambiguity: towards a typology of evaluative practices in public management. *Evaluation*, 9(3), 285–306.

Albæk, E. (1988). *Fra Sandhed til Information*. Copenhagen: Akademisk Forlag.

Albæk, E. (1998). Knowledge interests and the many meanings of evaluation: a developmental perspective. *Scandinavian Journal of Social Welfare*, 7(2), 94–98.

Barbier, J.C. (forthcoming). Evaluation and political communication in the French Public Employment Service. In J. Breul, R. Boyle & P. Dahler-Larsen (eds) *Evaluation in the Public Arena*. New Brunswick: Transaction.

Bauman, Z. (1995). *Life in Fragments. Essays in Postmodern Morality*. Oxford: Blackwell.

Beck, U. (1994). The reinvention of politics: towards a theory of reflexive modernization. In U. Beck, A. Giddens & S. Lash (eds) *Reflexive Modernization* (pp. 1–55). Stanford: Stanford University Press.

Berger, P. & Kellner, H (1982). *Nytolkning af Sociologien. [Sociology Reinterpreted]*. Copenhagen: Lindhardt og Ringhof.

Berger, P. & Luckmann, T. (1966). *The Social Construction of Reality*. New York: Doubleday.

Breul, J., Boyle, R., & Dahler-Larsen, P. (eds) (forthcoming). *Evaluation in the Public Arena*. New Brunswick: Transaction.

Campbell, D. T. (1988). *Methodology and Epistemology for the Social Science: Selected papers*. E. S. Overman (ed.). Chicago: University of Chicago Press.

Caracelli, V. J. (2000). Evaluation use at the threshold of the twenty-first century. *New Directions for Evaluation*, (88), 99–111.

Castoriadis, C. (1997). *World in Fragments. Writings on politics, society, psychoanalysis, and the imagination*. Stanford: Stanford University Press.

Chen, H. (1990). *Theory-Driven Evaluation*. Beverly Hills: Sage.

Compton, D. W., Baizerman, M., & Stockdill, S. H. (eds) (2002). The art, craft, and science of evaluation capacity building. *New Directions for Evaluation*, (93).

Cousins, B. & Earl, L. (1995). Participatory evaluation in education: What do we know? Where do we Go? In B. Cousins & L. Earl (eds) *Participatory Evaluation in Education* (pp. 159–180). London: RoutledgeFalmer.

Dahlberg, M. & Vedung, E. (2001). *Demokrati och brukarutvärdering*. Lund: Studentlitteratur.

Dahler-Larsen, P. (2000). Surviving the routinization of evaluation: the administrative use of evaluation in danish municipalities. *Administration and Society*, 32(1), 70–92.

Dahler-Larsen, P. (2001). From programme theory to constructivism: on tragic, magic and competing programmes. *Evaluation,* 7(3), 331–349.

Dahler-Larsen, P. (2004). *Den Rituelle Reflektion – om evaluering i organisationer.* Odense: Syddansk Universitetsforlag.

Dahler-Larsen, P. (forthcoming). Evaluation and public management. In E. Ferlie, L. Lynn Jr., & C. Pollitt (eds) *Oxford Handbook of Public Management.* Oxford: Oxford University Press.

Fetterman, D. (1994). Empowerment evaluation. *Evaluation Practice,* (15), 1–16.

Fountain, J. (2001). Paradoxes of public sector customer service. *Governance,* 14(1), 55–73.

Friedman, V. J. (2001). Designed blindness: an actions science perspective on program theory evaluation. *American Journal of Evaluation,* 22(2), 161–182.

Furubo, J.-E., Rist, R. C., & Sandahl, R. (eds) (2001). *International Atlas of Evaluation.* New Brunswick: Transaction Publishers.

Gargani, J. (2002). The challenge of evaluating theory-based evaluation. Paper presented at the Annual Meeting of the American Evaluation Association. St. Louis, MO. November 7, 2002.

Greene, J. (1997). Participatory evaluation. In L. Mabry (volume ed.) *Evaluation and the Postmodern Dilemma.* In R. Stake (series ed.) *Advances in Program Evaluation,* 3, 41–59. London: JAI Press.

Greene, J. (1999). The Inequality of Performance Measurements. *Evaluation,* 5(2), 160–172.

Greene, J., Benjamin, L., & Goodyear, L. (2001). The merits of mixing methods in evaluation. *Evaluation,* 7(1), 25–44.

Guba, E. & Lincoln, Y. (1989). *Fourth Generation Evaluation.* Newbury Park: Sage.

Hansen, H. F. (2003). *Evaluering i Staten.* Copenhagen: Samfundslitteratur.

Hellstern, G.-M. (1986). Assessing evaluation research. In F. X. Kaufmann, G. Majone & V. Ostrom (eds) *Guidance, Control and Evaluation in the Public Sector* (pp. 279–313). Berlin: de Gruyter.

Henry, G. (2000). Why not use? *New Directions for Evaluation,* (88), 85–98.

Henry, G. T., & Mark, M. M. (2003). Beyond use: understanding evaluation's influence on attitudes and actions. *American Journal of Evaluation,* 24(3), 293–314.

House, E. & Howe, K. R. (2000). Deliberative democratic evaluation. In K. Ryan & L. DeStefano (eds) *New Directions for Evaluation,* (85), 3–12.

Kirkhart, K. E. (2000). Reconceptualizing evaluation use: an integrated theory of influence. *New Directions for Evaluation,* (88), 5–23.

Larsen, F. (2001). Evalueringers faktiske anvendelse – arbejdsmarkedspolitikken som case. In P. Dahler-Larsen & H. K. Krogstrup (eds) *Tendenser i Evaluering.* Syddansk Universitetsforlag.

Leeuw, F., Toulemonde, J., & Brouwers, A. (1999). Evaluation activities in Europe: a quick scan of the market. *Evaluation,* 5(4), 487–496.

Leviton, L. C. (2003). Evaluation use: advances, challenges and applications. *American Journal of Evaluation,* 24(4), 525–535.

Manovich, L. (2001). *The Language of New Media.* Cambridge, MS: The MIT Press.

Mathison, S. (1999). Rights, Responsibilities, and duties: a comparison of ethics for internal and external evaluators. *New Directions for Evaluation,* (82), 25–34.

Mark, M. M. (in press). Building a better evidence-base for evaluation theory. In P. R. Brandon & N. L. Smith (eds) *Fundamental Issues in Evaluation.* New York: Guilford.

Mark, M. M. & Henry, G. T. (2004). The mechanisms and outcomes of evaluation influence. *Evaluation,* 10(Jan), 35–57.

Mark, M. M., Henry, G. T. & Julnes, G. (2000). *Evaluation. An integrated framework for understanding, guiding, and improving public and nonprofit policies and programs.* San Francisco: Jossey-Bass.

Meyer, J. & Rowan, B. (1977). Formal structure as myth and ceremony. *American Journal of Sociology,* (83), 340–363.

Modell, S. (2004). Performance measurement myths in the public sector. *Financial Accountability and Management,* 20(1), 39–55.

Patton, M. Q. (1997). *Utilization-Focused Evaluation,* 3rd edition. Thousand Oaks: Sage.

Pawson, R. (2002). Evidence-based policy: the promise of "realist synthesis." *Evaluation,* 8(3), 340–358.

Pawson, R. & Tilley, N. (1997). *Realistic Evaluation.* London: Sage.

Pollitt, C. (2004). Performance information for democracy – the missing link? Paper presented at the European Evaluation Society conference in Berlin, September 30 – October 2.

Popper, K. (2001). *Det Åbne Samfund og dets fjender.* [The Open Society and Its Enemies]. Copenhagen: Spektrum.

Power, M. (1997). *The Audit Society. Rituals of verification.* Oxford: Oxford University Press.

Preskill, H. & Torres, R. T. (1999). *Evaluative Inquiry for Learning in Organizations*. Thousand Oaks: Sage.

Rist, R. C. & Stame, N. (eds) (forthcoming). *From Studies to Streams*. New Brunswick: Transaction Publishers.

Rogers, P. (2000). Program theory evaluation: practice, promise and problems. *New Directions for Evaluation* (87), 5–15.

Røvik, K. A. (1998). Moderne Organisasjoner. Trender i organisationstenkingen ved tusenårsskiftet. Bergen-Sandviken: Fagbokforlaget.

Sanders, J. (2001). Presidential address at the American Evaluation Association conference, St. Louis, MO.

Schwandt, T. (2002). *Evaluation Practice Reconsidered*. New York: Peter Lang.

Schwandt, T. & Dahler-Larsen, P. (2003). Evaluation and Community. Paper presented at the American Evaluation Association annual meeting in Reno, Nevada.

Scriven, M. (1991). Beyond formative and summative evaluation. In M. W. McLaughlin & D. C. Philips (eds) *Evaluation and Education: At quarter century* (pp. 18–64). Chicago: Chicago University Press.

Segerholm, C. (2002). The perils of procurement in evaluation. Paper presented at the Nordic Political Scientists Association conference in Aalborg, August 15–17, 2002.

Shadish, W. R., Cook, T. D. & Leviton, L. C. (1991). *Foundations of Program Evaluation*. Newbury Park: Sage.

Stake, R. E. (2004). *Standards-based and Responsive Evaluation*. Thousand Oaks: Sage.

Stehr, N. (2001). *The Fragility of Modern Societies. Knowledge and risk in the information age*. London: Sage.

Thompson, J. B. (2001). *Medierne og Moderniteten: en samfundsteori om medierne*. [The Media and Modernity. A Social Theory of the Media]. Copenhagen: Hans Reitzels Forlag.

Tilbury, C. (2004). The influence of performance measurement on child welfare policy and practice. *British Journal of Social Work* 34(2), 225–241.

van Thiel, S. & Leeuw, F. (2002). The performance paradox in the public sector. *Public Performance and Management Review*, 25(3), 267–281.

Vedung, E. (1997). *Public Policy and Program Evaluation*, 2nd edition. New Brunswick: Transaction.

Vulliamy, G. & Webb, R. (2001). The social construction of school exclusion rates: implications for evaluation methodology. *Educational Studies*, 27(1), 357–370.

Weiss, C. H. & Bucuvalas, M. J. (1980). *Social Science Research and Decision-Making*. New York: Columbia University Press.

Weiss, C. (1983). Evaluation Research in the Political Context. In E. Struering, & M. Brewer (eds) *Handbook of Evaluation Research* (pp. 31–45). Beverly Hills: Sage.

Weiss, C. (1998). *Evaluation*, 2nd edition. Upper Saddle River: Prentice Hall.

PART TWO

EVALUATION AS
A SOCIAL PRACTICE

7

GOVERNMENT AS STRUCTURAL CONTEXT FOR EVALUATION

Philip Davies, Kathryn Newcomer, and Haluk Soydan

Background

This chapter is about government as a structural environment for evaluation. This focus might sound too ambitious given the complexity and diversity of governmental structures around the world. However, we are limiting the scope of the chapter to two specific elements of government. The first element involves governments' use of evaluation as a means of governing, that is, *managing by evaluation*. The second element is government as a locus of evaluation of its own governance, *managing evaluation* (Rist, 1990). Although these two meanings of evaluation are not always accepted as appropriate by all stakeholders, some groups do champion this dual role.

In democratic societies the basis of government is the electorate of the country. The electorate elects its representatives who, for a given mandated period, govern the country through legislative and administrative bodies of the political system. Governments operate to pursue policy goals and to ensure they can continue to stay in power. In this sense, the government is an actor who wants to promote or prevent social change. In essence, the government wants to promote social change to the benefit of its citizenry, and prevent social change that is disadvantageous. For example, the government might wish to change smoking behavior patterns in the population because tobacco smoking is harmful to the public health. By the same token, the government might want to stimulate people to consume more vegetables and less fat to promote public health.

Governments in modern welfare states, as well as in developing countries, use public policy instruments such as regulations, tax credits, or other tools to generate or prevent social change for the betterment of the citizenry. The idea of human betterment has a long history in the development of western societies. It was first formulated by Marie Jean de Condorcet (Soydan, 1999, pp. 19–20) in its most explicit form, and then elaborated by authors such as Saint Simon at the aftermath of the French Revolution (Soydan, 1999, p. 58). Later, the idea of human betterment was strongly integrated with the Positivistic Paradigm and became the leading force of social engineering.

Public policy instruments are designed, implemented, and then assessed to see if they yield expected outcomes or effects. These three stages together constitute a strategy for promoting or preventing social change. Analysis and evaluation of data about policy and program implementation, and about changes in targeted behavior, is expected to inform government on the effectiveness of the policy instrument. This is the rationale of governing *by* evaluation. Before further elaborating on this issue in more detail, we would like to dwell on policy instruments as means for government to bring about social change.

Traditionally a variety of approaches to systematize public policy instruments have been developed. Here we will rely on a typology developed by Evert Vedung (1998). Vedung's typology assumes that government has made strategic decisions and that some kind of interventions are necessary. The question is then what kind of policy instruments can be used to substantiate, implement, and effect change. Vedung differentiates between regulations, economic means, and information as generic clusters of public policy instruments (1998). Policy instruments of the typology are named as Sticks, Carrots, and Sermons, referring to regulations, economic means, and information, respectively.

Regulations include rules, norms, standards, and directives, and are defined as "a state-imposed limitation on the discretion that may be exercised by individuals or organizations, which is supported by the threat of sanctions" (Vedung, 1998, p. 31). Regulations may be designed to bring about positive or negative sanctions. However, it should be noted that this limited definition of regulations as policy instruments is different than other definitions where regulation refers to government intervention in general, and all forms of political control.

Economic policy instruments aim to effect change by giving or withdrawing material resources in cash or in kind. Provision of free education (at the point of delivery) in the public schools, free transportation on the state-owned highways, as well as government spending to stimulate establishment of business in remote regions of a country, all serve as economic instruments. Economic policy instruments do not necessarily prohibit or prescribe measures, but make them less expensive. Program beneficiaries of this type of instrument can make their own decisions as to how to respond to the measures available.

Information as a public policy instrument aims to influence citizenry by persuasion. Such information may consist of objective knowledge about phenomena and circumstances, or a government's judgment of what is good and bad for the citizens. Information can be transferred in many ways, including printed material, mass media, and personal media campaigns, personal visits, training programs, education programs, and demonstration programs.

During the last two decades, governments across the world have developed novel, and typically complex, means of implementing all of the various public policy instruments (Salamon, 2002). Outsourcing or privatizing are two of the terms typically used to describe governments' use of alternative service providers, and multiple providers are involved in policy implementation. This includes multiple governmental units (at different levels in federal systems), nonprofit agencies, and even private sector firms. The new governance systems involve numerous non-governmental employees, termed by Paul Light as the "shadow government" (Light, 1999). These complex systems, with multiple stakeholders involved in implementing public policy instruments, present interesting challenges to governments use of evaluation to manage public policy (Mohan, Bernstein, & Whitsett, 2002).

This chapter describes *why and how governments use evaluation processes to inform management of public programs,* as well as *the variety of evaluation processes and structures that are employed by governments to evaluate public programs.* The descriptions are based on the experiences of the authors, who over the years have been involved closely with evaluation in and for the governments of three western countries. What is presented here provides different examples of government as a structural environment for evaluation. Thus, the frame of reference in this chapter is limited to western European and American government. Although historical and developmental background of the cases described here are rooted in the Western traditions of governing nation-states, we believe it is sensible to expect that governments in other parts of the world would profit from, and eventually move towards, a mode of governing by evaluation as those governments become more transparent and more caring about their citizenry.

The sections that follow will address the following questions about government as structural context for evaluation:

- What do governments typically want from evaluation?
- How do governments traditionally manage by evaluation?
- How is evaluation used to inform budgetary allocations?
- How does government manage evaluation?
- What are some of the pitfalls facing governments' management of evaluation?

- What is the impact of interest in "evidence-based policy" on the use of evaluation processes by and for governments?

What Do Governments Want from Evaluation?

One of the general purposes of evaluation is to promote accountability. From the government's perspective, this means collecting data to inform the public, decision-makers, taxpayers, service users, and other stakeholders about the worth of government policies, programs, interventions, and any other measures taken to impact the state of affairs in the society. Although the public pressure on governments to provide accountability in a general sense goes back to the historical foundations of modern governance, it has increasingly become explicit and stronger during the last three decades. Factors pushing for accountability include the public's concern about better, more efficient and cost-effective services (Behn, 2001; Forsythe, 2001). In some countries, including the US, politicians have enacted legislation calling for the evaluation of public programs to inform oversight bodies so that they may act to reduce waste and corruption, and to facilitate honesty and transparency in public management (Kearns, 1996; Light, 1997). Evaluation, then, is a central feature of evidence-based policy and practice.

Improving governmental management is certainly another reason evaluation is employed by governments. The performance of government has become a target of interest for politicians and the citizenry in countries across the world. The notion of evaluating the performance of policies, programs, and projects as part of good public management underlies many recent reforms in western democracies. Terms such as "managing for results," "results-based management," "performance management," "performance-based management," and "performance-based budgeting," have all been used as tools of new public management.

How Do Governments Traditionally Manage by Evaluation?

Governments typically require evaluation of programs and policies after they have been implemented, in order to provide feedback to program staff or bodies such as legislatures. Increasingly, such as is currently the case in Italy and the UK, the bulk of evaluation efforts are conducted before programs are implemented (ex ante) through cost-benefit analyses and multicriteria analyses to select effective programs for implementation (Marra, 2004; Cabinet Office 2003a). Ex ante approaches are more geared toward assessing the net present value expected to result from public investments, rather than measuring actual implementation or results of programs after they are implemented. The use of policy pilots and demonstrations that can identify effective interventions before national roll out is also increasingly common in many countries (Cabinet Office, 2003b).

Legislative Mandates to Evaluate

Requirements that programs be evaluated are typically made by legislative bodies or executive arms of government. Legislatures may establish requirements that evaluations of specific programs be undertaken in the legislation establishing the programs, such as happened first in the US in a number of laws passed during the so-called "War on Poverty" during the 1960s. More frequently, they may establish agencies that provide on-going support for legislative oversight processes. For example, many governments have national audit organizations (or "courts")

that provide expertise available to the legislatures to analyze programs. In many cases these agencies, such as the US General Accounting Office (GAO – now called the Government Accountability Office) – were originally established to conduct financial audits to ensure that the public monies were spent appropriately.

For example, the US Congress created the GAO as a body independent of the President that would "investigate, at the seat of government or elsewhere, all matters relating to the receipt, disbursement, and application of public funds . . ." (P.L. 67–13, 42 Stat. 20). In creating the GAO, Congress sought to control public expenditures. Congress created the GAO to exercise financial compliance accountability, but the word "accounting" enabled the GAO (starting in the 1970s) to broaden the scope of its activities to include evaluation of non-financial aspects of public programs. In a similar move during the last two decades, the National Audit Office in the UK set up a value-for-money auditing branch to broaden its scope beyond financial auditing to examine programmatic performance.

The US Congress has statutorily established other oversight bodies that evaluate federal programs to monitor management (or mismanagement). In response to perceptions of waste and mismanagement in government, the Congress passed the Inspector General Act of 1978 to institutionalize independent government officers whose job is to detect, prevent, and deal with fraud, waste, and abuse in federal programs (P.L. 95–452, 1, 92 Stat. 1101; October 12, 1978). The act requires the appointment of and provides a uniform set of authorities and responsibilities for Inspectors General (IGs) in each federal department and agency. The IGs in the major departments and some independent agencies are appointed by the President and approved by the Senate; the others are appointed by the agency heads or governing boards. In both cases, the law provides that the IGs act independently, reporting to both the Congress and the agency head on the abuses they find and the actions needed to address them. The IG offices in the US government provide technical expertise to agencies to conduct evaluation work that goes beyond inquiry into alleged wrongdoing. In many cases, agency heads ask the IG offices to provide assistance to evaluate programs and management systems in order to improve internal management.

Executive Mandates to Evaluate

Government executives typically require evaluation by establishing procedures or policies connected with budgetary processes to exert control over agencies. For example, in the US, the Office of Management and Budget (OMB) is a part of the executive branch of the federal government that has established requirements that agencies submit evidence of evaluations along with performance data. The OMB has released rules or "circulars" that require all agencies to assess program effectiveness (more on recent OMB initiatives along this line appears later in this chapter).

Governmental agencies frequently establish and fund their own evaluation units, or fund evaluation work that is conducted by outside contractors. In these cases the evaluators answer to the agency heads rather than the legislative bodies. The work performed by internal evaluation offices or evaluators contracted by the agencies is typically viewed as "internal" evaluation, as opposed to the work undertaken by the oversight bodies such as audit offices, which is viewed as "independent" of the program management. Relatedly, European Commission-funded projects are required to be evaluated by external "independent" evaluators who report to the funders, rather than to the program managers (Marra, 2004).

Evaluation by Commission System

A specific case of managing by evaluation has been exercised through ad hoc commissions. For instance, the commission system has been used in Sweden since the seventeenth century, but more intensively during the whole twentieth century. During the 1960s and 1970s there were periods when more than 300 commissions were working annually (Ahlenius, 1997). Consequently, many policy issues were assessed by these commissions prior to legislative or government decisions. Typically a commission is constituted by membership representing diverse political stakeholders of the country. At the early onset a commission contracts with a researcher, or more often, a group of researchers and other experts to evaluate the state of the art in the specific area of activities the commission is examining. Evaluation of accessible empirical material is used to understand effects of earlier policy or program initiatives measures to better structure future reform interventions in social welfare, education, health promotion, etc.

Furubo (1994) empirically investigated the content and structure of 65 commission reports that were published in 1945. These reports contained comprehensive empirical data, such as statistics associated with the issue, as well as an account of previous experiences and the state of the art. Interestingly, a number of these reports exposed empirical material to demonstrate a causal relation between government interventions and their possible effects. Examples of evaluation studies within the 1945 commission system included:

- A study of the effectiveness of post-institutional care for juvenile delinquents who had been in care of specially tailored institutions. Parliament's 1936 and 1937 reforms of the corrective homes were studied to see effects on the duration of the care given, the education of the youth involved, and their subsequent working careers.

- A commission from 1940 on education made an overview of accumulated effects of school rating system. One aspect studied was, for example, the value of academic grades as a forecasting instrument of professional achievement. The empirical material was collected in three primary schools for students matriculated between 1872 and 1892.
- The 1941 population commission published a report on the significance of social policy on income distribution.

Thus, the ad hoc commission system in Sweden played an important role historically and constitutes a strong background to our contemporary understanding of evaluation research within the government system. Although the commission system still works smoothly, in some areas (such as social services, education, and correctional services), more permanent evaluation units have emerged during the 1990s.

How Is Evaluation Used to Inform Budgetary Allocations?

Evaluation is sometimes used by governments to exert control over programs and to link the allocation of resources to the performance of departments, agencies, and service delivery units through required performance measurement. Performance measurement is the label given to routine measurement of program inputs, outputs, and/or outcomes of services delivered by agencies within government to meet demands for documentation of program performance (Hatry, 1999; Poister, 2003; Wholey & Hatry, 1992; Wholey, Hatry, & Newcomer, 2004). Routine reporting of program performance has been required by politicians at all levels of government in countries across the world to address the demands of citizens and their elected officials for more transparent, entrepreneurial, and efficient government (Amons,

1995; Benowitz & Schein, 1996; Forsythe, 2001; Osborne & Gaebler, 1992).

Starting in the early 1990s in the US Federal Government, there have been executive initiatives pushing agencies to measure and report on programmatic performance, primarily from the Office of Management and Budget in the Executive Office of the President, and also from legislative mandates requiring agencies to provide performance data (Joyce, 2004). The most important legislative initiative in this arena was the Government Performance and Results Act of 1993 (GPRA). GPRA requires all federal agencies to submit strategic plans to Congress (starting in FY 1997), set performance goals (starting in FY 1999) and report on actual performance (beginning with FY 2000) (Kravchuk & Schack, 1996; U.S. GAO, 2004). This legislative mandate for performance measurement and reporting covers all federal programs, but there have also been over fifty more laws passed since 1993 that require the federal agencies to report on the performance of specific policy initiatives. The George W. Bush administration has introduced a new tool to "hold agencies accountable for accomplishing results" that focuses on assessing program effectiveness (see www.whitehouse.gov/omb/budget/FY2004/ performance). The Program Assessment Rating Tool (PART) is a questionnaire consisting of approximately 30 questions (the number varies slightly depending on the type of program being evaluated) that federal managers are required to answer. PART includes questions about program purpose and design, strategic planning, program management, and program results. OMB has used the PART tool to assess 20 per cent of the federal government's programs in each of the last two budget rounds. OMB has promised to assess all federal programs in five years. Once a program has been initially assessed, it is then reassessed, albeit with less intensive scrutiny, in each subsequent year as well.

A notable aspect of the PART tool is its explicit focus on program results. A set of questions addressing program results is to be answered with "Yes," "Large Extent," "Small Extent," or "No." These questions are:

- Has the program demonstrated adequate progress in achieving its long-term outcome goals?
- Does the program (including program partners) achieve its annual performance goals?
- Does the program demonstrate improved efficiencies and cost effectiveness in achieving program goals each year?
- Does the performance of this program compare favorably to other programs with similar purpose and goals?
- Do independent and quality evaluations of this program indicate that the program is effective and achieving results?

OMB budget examiners assign programs' scores based on the answers the program managers in the agencies give to the PART questionnaire. Unlike the reporting requirements under the GPRA, the performance of specific programs is scored. The unit of analysis for the PART is a program, not an agency, so there may be a disconnection between the performance goals set for agencies in GPRA performance reports and the goals for specific programs. In fact, defining exactly what constitutes a program for the purpose of the PART process has sometimes been contentious. Through the use of the PART process, OMB has highlighted the issue of evaluating program effectiveness as a means of focusing upon accountability for program results.

Thus, in the US, managers administering federal programs – wherever they reside – routinely measure and report on the performance of their programs in response to both legislative and executive mandates. The politicians who created this new system of information exchange clearly assumed that performance measurement and reporting would result in improved program performance. And the performance data are to be integrated into budgetary requests to inform allocation decisions both within the executive branch and in the US Congress.

The United Kingdom Government has used performance management since May 1997, when the Labour Government of Tony Blair was elected into office. Performance targets are negotiated with HM Treasury and are evaluated regularly. Successful delivery of effective and efficient programs or services (e.g., those that meet or exceed their targets) are rewarded with financial and other resources in future spending rounds. Services and programs that do not meet their targets are either discontinued (e.g., resources are no longer allocated to them), or they are evaluated further to identify *why* the targets have not been met. This approach has to be seen within the context of the UK Government's strategy for public spending and taxation. The UK public spending and fiscal frameworks seek to improve the quality and cost-effectiveness of public services while ensuring sound public finances. There are four principles underlying the public spending framework, which are to: first, provide a long-term and transparent regime for managing the public finances; second, measure success in terms of policy *outcomes* rather than resource inputs; third, provide strong incentives for government departments and service delivery units to plan over several years (up to five years or more), and to plan together where necessary; and fourth, properly cost and manage capital assets so as to provide the right incentives for public investment (HM Treasury, 2003).

Alongside this public spending framework is a fiscal framework that has two policy objectives. In the medium term, the fiscal objective is to ensure sound public finances and that spending and taxation impact fairly within and between generations. In the short term, fiscal policy supports monetary policy and allows routine policy responses that are designed to limit economic fluctuations to help smooth the path of the economy. These two objectives are implemented through two fiscal rules: the golden rule and the sustainable development rule. The former requires that over the economic cycle the Government will borrow only to invest and not to fund current spending. The latter requires that public sector net debt as a proportion of GDP will be held over the economic cycle at a stable and "prudent" level (i.e., below 40 percent of GDP).

In order to meet these public spending and fiscal objectives, the UK Government has set up a performance management system around Public Service Agreements (PSAs) and Service Delivery Agreements (SDAs). PSAs set out the Government's key priorities and provide the public with a clear indication of what it can expect the Government to deliver with the resources that are available. Each large Government Department has a PSA that sets out an aim, a number of objectives, and up to ten performance targets that are linked to the PSA objectives and are outcome focused. In addition, each PSA has a value-for-money (VfM) target that establishes the cost-effectiveness of policy initiatives and the services that are delivered. PSAs also include a statement of who is responsible for the delivery of the targets (usually the Minister responsible for the department or policy area). In addition to departmental PSAs there are cross-cutting PSAs where responsibility for delivery is shared between two or more Ministers. Currently, there are four cross-cutting PSAs covering childcare and early years, crime and justice, action against illegal drugs, and local government.

Service Delivery Agreements (SDAs) set out key programs or actions that government departments will undertake in order to deliver their high level PSA targets. For smaller departments that do not have PSA targets, the SDA usually sets out the organization's key targets and objectives. Like PSAs, SDAs are agreed upon with the UK Treasury, along with measures to monitor and evaluate their progress. Every two years, as part of the Spending Review process, departments are required to establish baseline information on their work programs and on how they propose to spend their financial allocations. Evidence must be provided to support these plans. Departments must also provide proposals for improving efficiency, as well as details of their administration budgets, investment plans, and capital expenditure. The biennial Spending Reviews assess whether these baseline plans have been met and whether the PSA and SDA targets have been achieved. Public spending by the Government is set and allocated according to success or failure of these plans and targets, and by the evidence that is provided by departments. This evidence comes from national statistics, academic research economic theory, pilots, evaluations of past policies, commissioned research and systematic interviews with delivery agents.

The monitoring and evaluation of PSA targets on a more regular basis than biennially is undertaken by the Prime Minister's Delivery Unit (PMDU), which is part of the UK Cabinet Office. This unit works in close partnership with the Treasury (indeed it is housed at Treasury). The principal objective of the PMDU is to "improve public services by working with departments to help them meet their PSA targets, consistently with the fiscal rules" (PMDU, 2003). It does this by conducting priority reviews, stocktakes of progress towards achieving targets, and challenge meetings with departments and delivery agents. Departments are required to produce trajectories (Figure 7.1) showing the anticipated progress towards a target or long-term strategic goal, against which actual progress can be

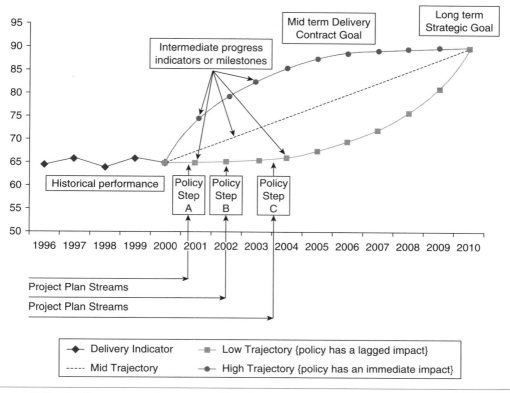

Figure 7.1   Performance trajectories in U.K. Government (PMDU, 2003).

mapped. These trajectories have to be based on historical performance. Good quality, timely data have to be collected by departments to track progress against trajectories. Regular monitoring and reviews of these trajectories allow for prompt diagnosis and problem-solving of failures in progress towards delivery targets. Continual problems with progress require more detailed analysis and plans for remedial action.

The performance management system employed by the UK Government uses a range of evaluation methods. In terms of *impact* evaluation, the target setting and target monitoring that is so central to the performance management process is essentially what evaluation specialists call goals-based evaluation,

or "legislative monitoring" (Patton, 1998). The value-for-money part of the performance management system uses cost-effectiveness analysis and other tools of economic evaluation. These impact assessments are backed up by evaluations of the effectiveness of interventions that have used experimental and quasi-experimental methods as well as systematic reviews and meta-analyses of existing evidence. Statistical and econometric modeling are also used to evaluate the likely and actual impacts of policies under different assumptions and tests of sensitivity.

In terms of *formative*, or *process*, evaluation, the UK performance management system uses in-depth interviews with key stakeholders in the delivery process, including strategic planners, policy-makers, delivery agents, and front-line service staff. It also uses documentary analysis, observational analysis (site visits), and analysis of administrative and survey data.

Performance management provides a relatively clear, transparent, and outcomes-focused approach to evaluation for government. Its shortcomings include a reductionist mentality, goal or policy displacement, perverse incentives, failure to identify unanticipated outcomes, and potential insensitivity to the problems of delivery and the underlying causes of delivery failure. Target-setting can become an end in itself and reduce the complexity of policy development and delivery to a few arbitrary achievements. This can result in goal or policy displacement whereby the pursuit of a given goal or target leads to resources and concentration of effort being withdrawn from other laudable goals in order to meet the targets that are being measured. This, in turn, can lead to unanticipated consequences such as harming the delivery to, and outcomes of, people with these other conditions, needs, and wants. Moreover, if the targets that are set are insensitive to the needs, values and demands of the users of public services, they can result in the charge that the government has "hit the target but missed the point."

The UK Government is aware of these shortcomings of performance management, and has taken steps to avoid some of them. Treasury guidance on the setting of PSA targets, for instance, suggests that they should be SMART (Specific, Measurable, Achievable, Relevant, and Timed), and that they should "not be open to distortion" (HM Treasury, 2003). In terms of the latter, this means that PSAs:

> should not create perverse incentives or encourage staff to massage or misrepresent performance data; encourage staff to focus on easy-win cases above more problematic and important cases; or lead people to compromise quality in order to achieve a measured target. (*op. cit.*)

Nonetheless, the UK National Audit Office (2001) found that "departments faced challenges in devising measures which are shared or influenced by other departments, which capture the essence of their objectives and which can be implemented in ways which avoid promoting perverse behaviours." The same report also noted, however, that "some changes have already taken place" and that "by refining the application of outcome-focussed targets, drawing on the emerging good practices identified in this report and elsewhere, there is the prospect of more firmly evidenced improvement in performance in future" (*op. cit., p.* 9).

How Does Government Manage Evaluation?

Traditionally, auditing agencies, internal evaluation units of governments, and contract evaluators hired by governments have been providers of evaluations pertinent to government interventions. Other independent institutions such as universities and other private and public agencies have also contributed to evaluation of government policies. For understandable reasons, none of these institutions has been able respond to broad and specific needs of evaluation of governments' involvement in social change. Auditing agencies usually have a general mandate and operate on a random and/or selective basis, with the apparent risk of not being able to audit all activities in a systematic and continuous fashion. The inability of independent institutions of evaluation to focus on issues of importance for government interventions has typically reflected the privilege and discretion of those institutions to choose and prioritize objects of evaluation studies.

With this general background, governments around the world increasingly establish specific units of evaluation, thus bringing evaluation into the very cradle of the government structure. The primary reason to establish specific government-based or affiliated, politically autonomous, semi-autonomous or government steered, units of evaluation is to secure production of evaluation studies in specific policy areas.

A few examples may illustrate the recent development of national evaluation structures. In Sweden the case of evaluating the worth of social services is a good example. When, in 1977, social work was established as an academic and research discipline, one of the intentions of the reform was the expectation that the new research discipline would produce research findings pertinent to social work practice and the profession. The purpose was to stimulate practice-relevant knowledge to the betterment of social work practice and consequently to provide effective social services. Unfortunately, the major stakeholders in this context, the university-based schools of social work, have chosen to focus on other types of evaluative studies, thus making them unable to substantially contribute to practice-relevant knowledge. To compensate this imbalance, the Government chose to establish a specific unit, the Center for Evaluation of Social Services at the National Board of Health and Welfare, in 1993. As this effort proved to be useful, this Center was reorganized in 2004 with a more distinct mission to provide systematic research reviews and to develop effect studies of social interventions.

What Are Some of the Pitfalls Facing Governments' Management of Evaluation?

There are many different ways in which governments' management of evaluation might be critiqued. The perspective taken here is that of a citizenry assessing how government may be constrained in overseeing its evaluation agents. The primary points of controversy identified here concern: legitimacy, differential power relationships, transparency, independence, and potentially incompatible objectives for evaluation.

Legitimacy?

How legitimate does it appear to citizens when government agents evaluate the performance of other governmental units? It depends. Certainly there are a variety of circumstances that can affect both perceptions and the reality of the relationships between the evaluators and the evaluands. If the evaluators are funded from the same agency budget as the evaluated programs, there may be some questions raised. The credibility of evaluation work and findings may be weakened whenever the legitimacy of the evaluators to serve as truly objective fact-finders is questionable.

And how does partisan politics affect the evaluation process? For example, in a world where there is never sufficient funding to evaluate all public programs, does what gets evaluated reflect the political priorities of the incumbent political party? Probably. For example, Datta & Grasso (1998) noted that programs for the poor and young are commonly evaluated (in the US), but not instruments such as tax privileges that benefit the well-off (e.g., home mortgage deductions). Might political considerations lead the government in power to publicize only evaluation studies that are supportive of their favored programs? Will performance data suggesting weak or even non-existent results or failure to meet performance targets drive budgetary decisions, rather than political support for favored programs? If not, to what extent is the credibility of the assessment process undermined in both the eyes of those within government and of the public?

Differential Power Relationships?

How does the relative power or authority of different stakeholders in public programs affect evaluation processes? For example, evaluations of programs typically involve multiple stakeholders, including program beneficiaries, program staff, technical experts, and the taxpayers – but are all stakeholders equal in terms of their input into evaluation processes? And with programs that are implemented by groups of governmental, non-profit, and private sector agents, sometimes at different levels of government in federal systems, do all of the stakeholders get an equal say in what gets evaluated, as well as how and when?

Within government, how does the perception of the relative power wielded by an oversight body, such as an audit office or audit court, affect how responsive program staff are to the auditors? And might the power a budget office wields over programs affect program staff decisions on what to measure or where to set targets when performance measures are used to inform budget decisions?

Transparency?

Questions about the effectiveness of programs are always of interest to citizens. However, effectiveness is a very subjective yardstick; it only takes on meaning when criteria are set to measure achievement of program objectives. But who selects the criteria? And how public are the criteria, as well as the deliberations that are involved in determining the appropriate criteria to employ in assessing effectiveness? If criteria are publicized, will program staff work the system to concentrate effort on what is measured, and devote less attention to other valuable tasks or services that are not measured? Teachers are sometimes accused of teaching to the test, but as performance is evaluated in other service areas, the concern with unintended negative consequences is similar.

Independence?

The appearance of independence for evaluators is critical in many arenas. But what ensures independence? In establishing governmental audit or evaluation offices that are intended to be immune to being influenced by partisan politics or by those who are evaluated, there are usually several common precautions taken to protect the office. For example, there is usually an open, non-partisan means for appointing the office head, a long length of tenure protected from arbitrary firing, no leverage for those whose programs are evaluated to affect the budgets of the office, and protection from interference in the reporting process.

Outside contractors who conduct evaluation work for government agencies are assumed to be independent from government influence, but they are funded by government. In addition, in many cases the same contractors work over time for specific agencies, and there may be perceptions that "captive" evaluators may make subtle trade-offs in objectivity for the prospect of continued contracts.

Incompatible Objectives?

As noted above, governments may use evaluation to hold managers accountable, to inform managers so they improve their programs, and to facilitate learning about when, how, and why programs work (or fail). So are these objectives about control or about learning? It is certainly possible that there may be some tensions involved in employing evaluation, whether it is ongoing performance measurement or a one-shot quasi-experimental study, if it is unclear to all stakeholders whether the exercise is undertaken to facilitate control or learning. If evaluation is undertaken allegedly to facilitate learning, but then is used to exert control and punish poor performance, future prospects for evaluation may well be diminished.

Can evaluation efforts be designed to facilitate both control and learning simultaneously? It depends on a variety of factors, including the specific programmatic context and the level of trust between evaluators and those whose programs are being evaluated, but generally speaking it is a challenge. Well-informed decisions on what, how, and when to measure and compare are needed to ensure credible, valid, and useful evaluation data, and the decisions need to be made in good faith, supported by clear expectations about evaluation objectives held by all program stakeholders. Typically, however, program stakeholders will not be in agreement about program or evaluation objectives; thus, a challenge is to bring them into agreement about expectations.

Governments endeavors to manage evaluation are based on the assumption that management by evaluation is a rational process. However, as the pitfalls facing governments management of evaluation show, governments operate in contexts that are to some degree irrational. In the real world, evaluation results and the scientific evidence make only one of several elements involved in decision-making processes. Other elements in decision-making processes include political choices of diverse stakeholders, traditions, values, economic prerequisites and ethical considerations. Governments management of evaluation would be better off if the role of evidence can be strengthened at the expense of political choices and value judgments in managing by evaluation. We are aware that it is not always feasible and even not desirable to eliminate *all* politics or values from government decisions. In addition, the quality of evaluation evidence would not always suffice to make sound decisions. A stronger role for evidence, relative to

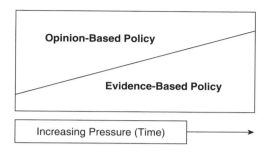

Figure 7.2   The dynamics of evidence-based policy (adapted from Gray, 1997).

the current state of affairs seems, however, desirable.

Evidence-Based Policy – a Renaissance for Government Based and Monitored Evaluation?

Evidence-based policy has been defined as an approach that "helps people make well informed decisions about policies, programs and projects by putting the best available evidence from research at the heart of policy development and implementation" (Davies, 1999). This approach stands in contrast to opinion-based policy, which relies heavily on either the selective use of evidence (e.g., on single studies irrespective of quality) or on the untested views of individuals or groups, often inspired by ideological standpoints, prejudices, or speculative conjecture. Gray (1997) has suggested that there is a new dynamic to decision making in health care and other areas of public policy, whereby the speculation of opinion-based policy is being replaced by a more rigorous approach that gathers, critically appraises, and uses high-quality research evidence to inform policy-making and professional practice. A graphical representation of this new dynamic is presented in Figure 7.2.

This movement towards a more evidence-based approach to policy and practice has resulted in something of a revolution for policy evaluation and government social research more generally. A wide variety of types of evidence and evaluation are used to support evidence-based government.

Systematic Reviews and Meta-Analysis

Systematic reviews and meta-analyses of existing evidence offer a great deal to evidence-based government because they can overcome the shortcomings of single studies (Boruch & Petrosino, 2004; Cooper & Hedges, 1994; Davies, 2003). Single studies may provide an unbalanced and unrepresentative view of the total available evidence on a topic or policy issue. This is because they are almost always sample-specific, time-specific, and context-specific. Also, single studies vary in methodological rigor. Such studies should not be included in the evidence base for policy-making or practice without an assessment of their methodology and quality.

Systematic reviews, by contrast, use explicit and transparent quality criteria, and rigorous standards for searching and critical appraisal, in order to establish "the consistencies and account for the variability of similar appearing studies" (Cooper & Hedges, 1994, p. 4). By only accumulating evidence that is relevant, and by identifying studies that are sample, time, or context specific, systematic reviews are able to provide generalizations, as well as assess the limits of these generalizations, amongst existing research evidence. Details of how systematic reviews and meta-analysis are undertaken, and of their advantages and limitations, are available elsewhere (Cabinet Office, 2003a; Cooper & Hedges, 1994).

Rapid Evidence Assessments

Rapid evidence assessments and interim evidence assessments are being developed by UK Government social researchers and the Swedish Council on Technology Assessment in Health Care to provide real-time research synthesis as a way of helping policy-makers use existing research evidence. These types of research synthesis use systematic review methods but report of provisional findings at interim stages in the searching and critical appraisal stages (e.g., the electronic, papers-based and "gray" literature stages). These methods of harnessing existing evidence are used with caution and with the proviso that the fully developed systematic review may change the balance of available evidence and the implications for policy and practice.

Much of the evidence that is used in policy-making, however, is gathered and appraised less systematically than by research synthesis methods. Policy-makers and other users of evidence may need to be made aware of what systematic reviews offer, and what they should be asking of them. This is sometimes referred to as developing the "intelligent customer" role in policy-making and policy implementation. There is a parallel need for producers of systematic reviews to better understand the evidence needs of policy customers and to produce reviews and other types of evidence that meet these needs. This might be referred to as the "intelligent provider" role.

Single Studies

Single studies are more commonly used than systematic reviews to support government policy and practice. Indeed, the vast majority of the research undertaken by, or on behalf of governments consists of single studies, often without any accumulation of existing evidence using systematic review methodology. If undertaken to the highest possible standards, single studies can provide valuable and focused evidence for particular policies, programs and projects in specific contexts. Unlike systematic reviews, however, single studies are less able to say much about the variability of populations, contexts, and conditions under which policies might work or not work.

Pilot Studies and Case Studies

Pilot studies and case studies are other sources of evaluation and evidence for policy-making and policy implementation. A recent review of pilots by the UK Cabinet Office (2003b) identified impact pilots, process pilots, and phased implementation projects, each using a combination of experimental, quasi-experimental, and qualitative methods, as well as case studies, to help guide policy-makers and policy-making. The Cabinet Office report recommended that "the full-scale introduction of new policies and delivery mechanisms should, wherever possible, be preceded by closely monitored pilots" (Cabinet Office, 2003b, p. 5).

It is sometimes argued that the tight timetables and schedules of the policy-making process make it impossible for systematic reviews, single empirical studies, pilots, or case studies to be undertaken before rolling out a policy, program, or project. This reasoning is often deployed to justify the use of whatever evidence is readily available, regardless of its scientific quality or source. Such urgency and rapidity of action may be understandable, especially in the absence of a well-established evidence base for many areas of public policy, but it is short-sighted and possibly counterproductive. Evidence that is selective, and not subjected to careful critical appraisal and risk assessment, can often lead to inappropriate courses of action which cause more harm than they are intended to prevent. In the UK, the Dangerous Dogs Act is a case in point as is the imprecise use of evidence in the case of the BSE outbreak (Phillips Inquiry, 2001) and the foot-and-mouth crisis (Royal Society, 2002).

Where pilots are used to test policies, it is important that they are completed and that lessons are learned before more widespread

implementation. The Cabinet Office Review of Pilots recommended that:

> Once embarked upon, a pilot must be allowed to run its course. Notwithstanding the familiar pressures of government timetables, the full benefits of a policy pilot will not be realised if the policy is rolled out before the results of the pilot have been absorbed and acted upon. Early results may give a misleading picture. (Cabinet Office, 2003b, p. 5, Recommendation 6)

Experts' Evidence

Expert opinion is also commonly used to support government policy and practice, either in the form of expert advisory groups or special advisers. Using experts as a basis for policy making and practice, however, again raises the problems of selectivity of knowledge and expertise, as well as problems in ensuring that the expertise being provided is up to date and well grounded in the most recent research evidence. In the case of the BSE outbreak, for instance, the Phillips Inquiry subsequently identified the incorrect understanding by experts of the nature, cause, and transmissibility of the disease. This led to an imprecise estimation of the likelihood of BSE being transmitted to humans and the subsequent inappropriate reassurance of the public by Ministers (Phillips Inquiry, 2001). The foot-and-mouth crisis of 2001 was hindered by experts' competing views about the nature and spread of the disease, and about the best ways of dealing with it. The Royal Society Inquiry (2002) into the foot-and-mouth outbreak identified the need for a better evidence base using sound, real-time data based on field epidemiology, mathematical modeling, and valid diagnostic tests and techniques.

Huw Davies (Davies, Nutley, & Smith, 2000) has characterized many experts' panels with the acronym GOBSATT – good old boys sitting around talking turkey. The UK Office of Science and Technology (2001) has published guidelines for the selection and running of UK Government Advisory Groups to ensure that no such characterization can be made of experts' committees in UK Government. Ensuring that government experts are up to date with existing evidence, and with the existing *uncertainty* of scientific knowledge, is one feature of these guidelines.

Internet Evidence

The internet age has brought a revolution in the availability of information and knowledge. Most, though not all, government departments in the UK have desktop access to the internet and, since April 2005, access to social science and political science databases.

Not all of the information available via the internet, however, is of equal value or quality. Many sites provide "evidence" that is either scientifically or politically biased, or both. The uncertain scientific and political basis of much of the information and knowledge on the internet makes it difficult to be assured that it meets the required quality to be counted as sound, valid, and reliable evidence. This makes it all the more important for government analysts and the wider academic community to ensure that such information is critically appraised and scientifically assured before it is used as evidence for policy-making purposes.

Different Types of Evaluation and Research Evidence

There are many types of evaluation and research evidence that can and should be used for evidence-based policy and practice. Privileging any one type of research evidence, or research methodology, is generally inappropriate for evidence-based government. The guiding principle for the types of evidence that are appropriate for policy-making and implementation is: "What is the question?" (Greene, Benjamin, & Goodyear, 2001).

Impact Evidence

The Campbell Collaboration is leading the way in "preparing, maintaining, and disseminating systematic reviews of *the effectiveness of interventions* in education, crime and justice, and social welfare" (Boruch & Petrosino, 2004; Boruch et al., 2004; Davies & Boruch, 2001). Such reviews are mainly (though not exclusively) concerned with the *impact* of policy on outcomes, and are generally best served by studies that use experimental and quasi-experimental research designs with good estimates of the counterfactual. Governments use a wide range of experimental and quasi-experimental methods to evaluate policy and practice interventions, including randomized controlled trials, regression discontinuity designs, matched comparisons (including propensity score matching), single group before and after studies and interrupted time series studies. Systematic reviews, meta-analyses, and rapid evidence assessments (see above) are also increasingly used by governments to identify the likely impact of policies and programs based on the balance of the existing social science evidence.

Implementation Evidence

Governments, however, are not just interested in the effectiveness of interventions in terms of their *outcomes*; they are equally interested in the effectiveness of *the implementation and delivery* of policies, programs, and projects. These two types of effectiveness are indeed closely linked to each other. For example, the importance of effective implementation and delivery has been highlighted in the UK since the General Election of 2001, when the reform and delivery of public services became the defining theme of the second Blair administration.

Experimental and quasi-experimental research designs can greatly help implementation and delivery issues by bringing a degree of comparative rigor to different modes of practice. Effective implementation and delivery, however, also requires high-quality qualitative data using in-depth interviews, focus groups, other consultative methods (such as the Delphi and Nominal Group methods), observational methods, participant-observation methods, and social surveys. The UK Cabinet Office's *Quality in Qualitative Evaluation* framework (Spencer et al, 2003) is one contribution to ensuring that qualitative research is undertaken to agreed high-quality standards. This and other developments, such as work on meta-ethnography (Britten et al., 2003; Campbell et al., 2003) and on including qualitative data in systematic reviews (Dixon-Woods, Fitzpatrick, & Roberts, 2001; Harden et al., 2003), will enhance the synthesis of evidence from qualitative studies.

A recent review of the evidence on effective implementation, however, has described the field as "imperfect" and often inconclusive (Grimshaw et al., 2003). There is a very strong need for more and better implementation studies that can identify the particular conditions under which successful implementation and delivery takes place, or fails to take place, as well as those conditions that are more generalizable.

Descriptive Analytical Evidence

Another important type of evaluation and research evidence for government comes from descriptive surveys and administrative data about the nature, size and dynamics of a problem, a population, subgroups, or social activities. Cross-sectional, time-series, and comparative data on a wide range of variables are regularly collected and used by governments using sophisticated descriptive and analytical methods. In the UK, government work on strategic audit and on benchmarking countries' performance and social changes over time (e.g., Cabinet Office, 2004) use

descriptive analytical evidence extensively. Such data are also used for process and outcome measures in experimental and quasi-experimental studies, as well as for comparative descriptive purposes.

Public Attitudes and Understanding

Research evidence on the attitudes, values, and understanding of ordinary citizens is very important for effective government. This is much more than government by opinion poll, and goes to the point that policies that are too far removed from the grain of public values simply will not work. In the UK, the Poll Tax and the approach of the Child Support Agency are cases in point. By contrast, the Department of Social Security's (now Department of Work and Pensions) program of research on "Attitudes to Welfare Reform" (Williams, Hill, & Davies, 1999) was highly instrumental in framing the design and delivery of welfare-to-work policies. Citizens' perceptions, experiences, and understanding of policy are generally best addressed using qualitative research designs and social survey methods.

Statistical Modeling

Statistical modeling also plays a very important part in the evidence base for government. Such modeling uses linear and logistic regression methods, and assumptions about policy scenarios that need to be manipulated. The more that these assumptions, and the variables used in statistical modeling, are based on sound empirical evidence, the greater will be the precision and external validity of such analysis.

Economic Evidence and Performance Management

Other types of evidence that are routinely used by governments concern the cost,

cost-benefit and cost-effectiveness of policies. Such evidence uses economic appraisal and evaluation methods, including econometric analysis and modeling, and is a central part of most governments' evidence base. Economic appraisal and evaluation is increasingly linked to the implementation and delivery agenda of governments (such as the biennial Spending Reviews of the UK Government), so that cost-effective and cost-beneficial interventions are rewarded with government funding, and cost-ineffective or non-beneficial programs are not.

Performance management in government (see discussion earlier in this chapter) means that target setting and chasing are increasingly being used as a way of establishing whether governments' goals are being met. Much of the criticism of targets concerns their internal and, especially, external validity, and the top-down ways in which they are often determined and imposed upon front-line staff. The need for more sensitive and appropriate targets in many areas of government is compelling, and this requires both summative and formative evidence using experimental and non-experimental research methods.

Ethical Evidence

Governments also make daily decisions that involve trade-offs between one policy and another, or one group and another. This can mean withdrawing a program or service from one group of people in order to provide a more cost-beneficial program for another group. Such action requires evidence of relative effectiveness, relative costs, people's perceptions and experiences, and of the social justice and ethics of doing so. Decisions about the latter often require evidence from social ethics, such as Rawls' (1972) *Theory of Justice*, and public consultation.

In summary, evidence-based policy and practice uses a range of evaluation methods and research evidence, and is usually guided

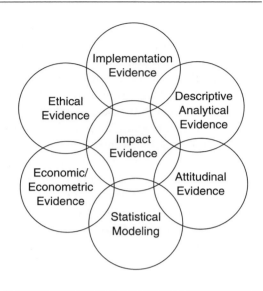

Figure 7.3   Types of research evidence used to support government.

by the questions being posed rather than by any one methodological approach. A graphical representation of the different types of research evidence used in government is presented in Figure 7.3.

Conclusions

Governments use evaluation to provide all sorts of evidence about the implementation and results of policies and programs, to inform decision-making undertaken by politicians and career public servants. The evidence produced may be used to facilitate deliberations concerning accountability for the use of public monies, efforts to improve program delivery, and/or systematic learning regarding how and when programs work.

Evaluation is typically required by both legislative and executive governmental bodies, and established in law or through regulations. Where and how evaluation of programs and policies is undertaken varies across governments and across time within governments. Innovative public management practices can affect the manner in which evaluation efforts are expended, as the current emphasis upon using ongoing performance measurement processes to inform budgetary allocations in many countries demonstrates.

The need to secure useful, credible evidence about governmental policies and programs has driven governments to manage evaluation within public agencies, as well as to purchase evaluation expertise from a variety of private sector and non-profit providers. Political priorities, emergent crises, and funding streams drive evaluation agendas; thus, the focus of and need for evaluation is in constant flux. Perceptions among politicians or the public that evaluation efforts are not totally legitimate or worth the money may result when evaluation is perceived to be "too politically motivated," or are not fairly informed by the multiple stakeholders.

Yet there appears to be renewed support in the need to use evaluation to support evidence-based policy. There are certainly a large number of evaluation strategies and data collection and modeling tools available to generate analyses and evidence of value to governments. And publicized interest in marshalling evidence about when, how, and why government policy instruments work has heightened both public interest as well as more transparency in the use of evaluation by and for governments. The increased demand for evidence as well as for transparency about evaluation processes should only improve the prospects for governments' involvement as user and producer of evaluation.

References

Ahlenius, I. B. (1997). Auditing and evaluation in Sweden. In E. Chelimsky & W. R. Shadish (eds) *Evaluation for the 21st Century. A handbook.* Thousand Oaks, CA: Sage.

Amons, D. N. (1995). *Accountability for Performance: Measurement and monitoring in local government.* Washington, D.C.: International City/County Management Association.

Behn, R. D. (2001). *Rethinking Democratic Accountability.* Washington, D.C.: Brookings Institution Press.

Benowitz, P. S. & Schein, R. (1996). Performance measurement in local government. In *Government Finance Officers Association, Municipal Year Book 1996* (pp. 19–23). Chicago, IL: Government Finance Officers Association.

Britten, N., Campbell, R., Pope, C., Donovan, J., Morgan, M., & Pill, R., (2003). Synthesis of qualitative research: a worked example using meta ethnography, *Journal of Health Services Research and Policy*, 56(4), 671–684.

Cabinet Office (2003a). *The Magenta Book: Guidance notes on policy evaluation*, London, Government Social Research Unit, Cabinet Office. Available at http://www.policyhub.gov.uk/evalpolicy/magenta/guidance-notes.asp.

Cabinet Office. (2003b). *Trying It Out: The role of "pilots" in policy making.* Government Social Research Unit, Cabinet Office. Available at http://www.policyhub.gov.uk/evalpolicy/01_intro.asp.

Cabinet Office (2004). *Strategy Survival Guide.* London: Cabinet Office, Prime Minister's Strategy Unit.

Campbell, R., Pound P., Pope, C., Britten, N., Pill, R., Morgan, M., Donovan, J., (2003) Evaluating meta-ethnography: a synthesis of qualitative research on lay experiences of diabetes and diabetes care. *Social Science and Medicine*, 56(4), 671–684.

Cooper, H. & Hedges, L. V. (eds) (1994). *The Handbook of Research Synthesis.* New York: Russell Sage Foundation.

Datta, L.-E. & Grasso, P. (1998). *Evaluating Tax Expenditures: Tools and techniques for assessing outcomes.* New Directions for Evaluation, No. 79, San Francisco, CA: Jossey-Bass.

Davies, H. T. O., Nutley, S. M., & Smith, P. C. (2000) *What Works?: evidence-based policy and practice in public services.* Bristol: The Policy Press.

Davies, P. T. (1999). What is evidence-based education? *British Journal of Educational Studies*, 47(2), 108–121.

Davies, P. T. (2003). Systematic reviews: how are they different from what we already do? In L. Anderson & N. Bennett (eds) *Developing*

Educational Leadership for Policy and Practice. London: Sage.

Davies P. T. & Boruch, R. (2001). The Campbell collaboration. *British Medical Journal,* 323, 294–295.

Dixon-Woods, M., Fitzpatrick, R., & Roberts, K., (2001) Including qualitative research in systematic reviews: Problems and opportunities. *Journal of Evaluation in Clinical Practice,* 7, 125–133.

Forsythe, D. W. (2001). *Quicker, Better, Cheaper: Managing performance in American government.* Albany, New York: Rockefeller Institute Press.

Furubo, J.-E. (1994). Learning from evaluations: The Swedish example. In F. Leeuw, R. C. Rist & R. C. Sonnichsen (eds), *Can Governments Learn? Comparative perspectives on evaluation and organizational learning.* New Brunswick: Transaction Publishers.

Gray, J. A. M. (1997). *Evidence-Based Healthcare: How to make health policy and management decisions.* New York, Edinburgh, London: Churchill Livingstone.

Greene, J. C., Benjamin, L., & Goodyear, L. 2001. The merits of mixed methods in evaluation. *Evaluation,* 7(1), 25–44.

Grimshaw, J. M., Thomas, R. E., MacLennan, G., Fraser, C., & Ramsay, C. R. (2003). Effectiveness and efficiency of guideline dissemination and implementation strategies. Final Report, Aberdeen, Health Services Research Unit.

Harden, A., Oliver, S., Rees, R., Shepherd, J., Brunton, G., Garcia, J., & Oakley, A. (2003). An emerging framework for synthesising the findings of different types of research in systematic reviews for public policy. Paper presented at the 3rd Annual Campbell Colloquium, Stockholm, Sweden (available at http://campbellcollaboration.org).

Hatry, H. (1999). *Performance Measurement: Getting results.* Washington, DC: The Urban Institute.

HM Treasury (2003). *Public Spending Guidance.* London: HM Treasury (www.hm-treasury.gov.uk).

Joyce, P. (2004). Linking performance and budgeting: Opportunities in the federal budget Process. *Managing for Performance and Results Series.* Washington, DC: IBM Center for the Business of Government.

Kearns, K. (1996). *Managing for Accountability: Preserving the public trust in public an nonprofit organizations.* San Francisco, CA: Jossey-Bass.

Kravchuk, R. S. & Schack, R. (1996). Designing effective performance-measurement systems under the Government Performance and Results Act of 1993. *Public Administration Review,* July, 348–358.

Light, P. (1997). *The Tides of Reform: Making government work, 1945–1995.* New Haven, CT: Yale University Press.

Light, P. (1999). *The True Size of Government.* Washington, DC: Brookings Institution Press.

Marra, M. (2004). Alcuni aspetti e problemi della valutazione nella Pubblica Amministrazione. *Rassegna Italiana di Valutazione (RIV),* 29, 41–114.

Mohan, R., Bernstein, D., & Whitsett, M. (2002). *Responding to Sponsors and Stakeholders in Complex Evaluation Environments. New Directions for Evaluation,* No. 95. San Francisco, CA: Jossey-Bass.

National Audit Office, (2001). *Measuring the Performance of Government Departments,* Report by the Comptroller and Auditor General, HC301, Session 2000–2001, 22 March. London: National Audit Office.

Office of Science and Technology (2001). *A Code of Practice for Scientific Advisory Committees.* London: Office of Science and Technology, Department of Trade and Industry.

Osborne, D. & Gaebler, T. (1992). *Reinventing Government: How the entrepreneurial spirit is transforming the public sector.* Reading, MA: Addison-Wesley.

Patton, M. Q. (1998). Discovering process use. *Evaluation,* 4(2), 225–233.

Phillips Inquiry (2001). *The BSE Inquiry: The Inquiry Into BSE and Variant CJD in the United Kingdom.* London: Ministry of Agriculture, Fisheries and Food (MAFF). Available at www.bseinquiry.gov.uk.

P.L. 95–452, 1, 92 Stat. 1101.

P.L. 67–13, 42 Stat. 20.

PMDU (2003). *Monitoring, Analysis, Evaluation & Reporting.* PMDU Toolbox. London: Prime Minister's Delivery Unit.

Poister, T. (2003). *Measuring Performance in Public and Nonprofit Organizations.* San Francisco: Jossey-Bass.

Rawls, J. (1972). *Theory of Justice.* Oxford: Clarendon Press.

Rist, R. C. (1990). Managing of evaluations or managing by evaluations: Choices and consequences. In Ray C. Rist (ed.) *Program Evaluation of Government. Patterns and prospects across eight nations.* New Brunswick: Transaction Publishers.

Royal Society (2002). *Foot and Mouth Disease 2001: Lessons to be learned inquiry.* London: Royal Society. Available at www.royalsoc.ac.uk/inquiry.

Salamon, L. (2002). *The Tools of Government: A guide to the new governance.* New York: Oxford University Press.

Soydan, H. (1999). *The History of Ideas in Social Work.* Birmingham: Venture Press.

Spencer, L., Ritchie, J., Lewis, J., & Dillon, L. (2003). *Quality in Qualitative Evaluation: A framework for assessing research evidence.* Government Chief Social Researcher's Office, London, Cabinet Office.

US Government Accountability Office (GAO-04-38) (2004). Results oriented government: GPRA has established a solid foundation for achieving greater results. March.

Vedung, E. (1998). Policy instruments: Typologies and theories. In M.-L. Bemelmans-Videc, R. C. Rist & E. Vedung (eds) *Carrots, Sticks and Sermons. Policy instruments and their evaluations.* New Brunswick: Transaction Publishers.

Wholey, J. S. & Hatry, H. (1992). The case for performance monitoring. *Public Administration Review,* 52(6), 604–610.

Wholey, J. S., Hatry, H., & Newcomer, K. (2004). *The Handbook of Practical Program Evaluation.* San Francisco, CA: Jossey-Bass.

Williams, T., Hill, M., & Davies, R. (1999). *Attitudes to the Welfare State and the Response to Reform,* Research Report No. 88. London: Department for Work and Pensions.

THE SOCIAL RELATIONS OF EVALUATION

Tineke A. Abma

In what ways do we attend to the social relations among participants in a program being evaluated? How and why do we relate to program participants and other stakeholders in the evaluation setting? These are the questions I will discuss in this chapter on the relational dimensions of evaluation. With respect to the social relations among program people and other stakeholders in the evaluation setting, I will draw on evaluative traditions and histories, which assume that social interactions are important because they are integral to and partly constitutive of the quality and effectiveness of the program being evaluated. With respect to the social relations between the evaluator and various stakeholders, these are most importantly influenced by evaluation approach and evaluator stance. These latter relationships are important because they are partly constitutive of the evaluative knowledge generated and also because relationships communicate particular values and norms. Which values and norms are promoted is a matter of evaluator choice. Several

positions will be distinguished to identify different kinds of relationships between the evaluator and others in the evaluation setting, ranging from approaches in which social relations are considered irrelevant to or sources of error in evaluative work, to approaches that aim to manage or change relations, to approaches in which social relations are intrinsically valued. The vignettes that follow will provide illustrations for the arguments to be made.

Alexandre Dumas is an elementary school located in the south side of Chicago. An evaluator visits the school to see how they teach the arts at Dumas. The evaluation is part of a larger study of arts education in Chicago's elementary schools. With a single step into the foyer, the evaluator realizes that Dumas doesn't fit the stereotyped descriptions of a school in a poor neighborhood – the school is not run down, dispirited, or chaotic. It doesn't fit the expectations she has not tried to preconceive – Dumas Elementary School is a vital place of energy and activity, of discipline and respect. Ushered into a sea of attentive black faces the evaluator suddenly realizes she is white. And after talking to many teachers and observing several classroom lessons, she concludes that at Dumas the arts are seen as a way to acknowledge and celebrate being African American, as well as an entrée into mainstream culture, an opportunity to experience the good things in life. With no exception everyone attributes Dumas's success to the charisma and dedication of the principal, Ms Sylvia Peters. Her leadership makes Dumas a dream amidst the nightmare of many forsaken and forgotten elementary schools serving African American children in Chicago. The evaluator presents a rich portrayal in order to show us who Sylvia Peters is and how she did it. She made the arts fun, she made them accessible, and she made them important. (Source: Mabry, 1991)

Caroline is an executive manager in a psychiatric hospital – young, ambitious, optimistic, full of ideas. She has just initiated planning for a vocational rehabilitation program for her psychiatric patients, designed to train them to find jobs and meaningful day activities. Caroline wants to start on a small, experimental scale in the Garden and Greenhouse. Instead of planning everything ahead, she prefers to "learn by doing." A multidisciplinary project group is formed to develop the new service. Caroline emphasizes she wants to acknowledge and use the expertise of the staff and to share control with them. Quite soon, however, it becomes apparent that the staff feel ambivalent about the whole project. The staff are less optimistic than Caroline about the possibilities of finding jobs for patients and expect employers will respond negatively. They also are skeptical about Caroline's participatory style of management. In their eyes "involvement" in the project turns out to be a "delegation" of work. They further wonder why they do not have an influence on the decisions with regard to the timeframe of the project, given Caroline's public pronouncements about staff involvement. Staff believe that one year is too short. Behind the scenes, staff members criticize Caroline. They consider her to be hypocritical and complain that she doesn't listen to their concerns. A conflict is

born, but remains hidden. And the staff start to invest more energy and time in criticizing their manager, than in actually carrying out the project. (Source: Abma, 2000)

They might become psychotic! the therapists warn the evaluators when they propose to include psychiatric patients in their evaluation of the rehabilitation program. The evaluators, however, insist on the importance – for political and moral reasons – of taking the experiential knowledge and perspectives of patients into account. Their major concern is how to approach the patients in such a way that they feel respected and accepted. They consider it not appropriate to start with interviews. For isn't the question-answer method – even if the tone is nice – always feeding separation and dualism? Instead the evaluators choose to join in the garden activities of a group of patients for three days. Initially the evaluators feel like voyeurs, but soon they get caught up in the work and develop a relationship with the people and their facilitator. They learn about their lives, the capriciousness of their illness, their struggles, dreams and emerging sense of pride. "*Patients*," the gardener says, "*are much more spontaneous in their reactions when they are actually doing something.*" The evaluators recognize this themselves; sitting or kneeling near someone's body with your hands in the mud is less threatening than a face-to-face situation where one is interviewing the other. Kneeling in the mud with the patients helps to establish respectful and equitable relationships. (Source: Abma, 1998)

Why "Social Relations" Matter in Evaluation

These vignettes illustrate what is meant by social relations in an evaluation setting and why they are important. Social relations in evaluation have at least three facets, each with its own import. First, the social relations among program people and other stakeholders in the evaluation setting are an integral part of the program being evaluated and thus directly involved in assessments of program quality. Second, the relations between the evaluator and program participants and others in the setting influence the possibilities and constraints of the evaluative practice in that context. Third, evaluations are always disruptive of the existing human, social, and political relationships in the contexts they inhabit. An overview of each of these facets is presented next.

Social Relations Among Program People and Other Stakeholders

The first two vignettes highlight the social relations among program people and other stakeholders in the evaluation setting. The evaluation of the arts at Alexandre Dumas Elementary School shows that the school's unusually successful arts program is not a matter of the program itself, but rather rooted in the leadership of the principal. She is the one who motivates the teachers, makes art infectious, raises funds, arranges artists and programs to come to school, and makes the arts important. It is not unusual to find social programs blossoming because of the charisma and dedication of a leader; nor is it unusual to find that the same programs wither when the leader leaves. The second vignette illustrates how an internal staff conflict results in tensions that may themselves hinder the effectiveness of a program. The staff in the psychiatric hospital feel powerless to raise their voice and to share their concerns with the manager. Instead of working on the project the staff invest most of their passion, energy, and time in criticizing their manager, but all behind the scenes. The organizational climate gets worse, people feel worn out, and the program's quality and effectiveness are negatively affected by the emotional burden of the unresolved conflict.

The social relations among people in the setting being evaluated are important because they are integral to the quality and effectiveness of the program being evaluated. Leadership

and charisma, caring and respect, reciprocity and collaboration, safety and structure, opportunities to learn and grow, but also hierarchy, conflict, envy, suspicion, and mistrust – and many more – are all aspects of stakeholders' relationships with one another that become interwoven in the fabric of the program being evaluated and thereby are integral to program quality and effectiveness. The factors that matter in this regard, as will be elaborated later in this chapter, include (a) power and conflict; (b) leadership and decision-making; (c) uncertainty and communication; (d) stability and change; and (e) the wider socio-political context. The social relationships in troubled contexts – those with strife, very limited resources, or marginalization of beneficiaries, as in many mental health facilities – are especially important, as these contexts present particular challenges to envisioning and implementing a program likely to be effective.

This broader conceptualization of evaluation that includes the social and interpersonal dimensions of the program can be traced back to Lee Cronbach's plea for the evaluator as a "social anthropologist" (Stake, 1991), Malcolm Parlett & Donald Hamilton's (1972) *Illuminative Evaluation*, Stake's (1975) *Responsive evaluation*, and Egon Guba & Yvonna Lincoln's (1981) *Naturalistic Evaluation*. Acknowledgment of the social dimensions can also be recognized in evaluators' attempts to use "theories of change" and institutional theories to understand the complexity and dynamics of public policies and programs (Abma & Noordegraaf, 2003; Barnes et al., 2003; Perrin, 2002; Sanderson, 2000; Sullivan, Barnes, & Matka, 2002; Weiss, 2000). I will elaborate on these historical and intellectual legacies more extensively later on in this chapter.

Relations Between the Evaluator and Various Stakeholders

The social relations between the evaluator and various stakeholders are most importantly the kinds of relationships the evaluator establishes in the field and the "roles" and "identities" he or she takes on (Ryan & Schwandt, 2002). These are important in evaluation because they (1) are partly constitutive of the character and contours of the evaluative *knowledge* that is generated, and (2) communicate particular *values and norms*. To elaborate on these points:

1. Evaluative knowledge (like all knowledge) is partly socially constructed, rather than only "discovered" through our methodological tools. So, the relational location of an evaluator in a setting matters to what knowledge is generated. This might be considered mostly an instrumental or an educational/conceptual aspect of the importance of social relationships in evaluation.

2. All evaluations communicate certain norms and values (Greene, 2002; Schwandt, 2002). Evaluation theories and practices inevitably reflect and promote a particular "moral-political ideal of how human beings ought to live" (Schwandt, 2002, p. 200). How evaluators act and relate "inevitably entails normative choices about how the evaluator wishes to 'be' in the social world" (ibid., p. 202). Even an evaluator who intentionally eschews relationships with stakeholders and concentrates on methods and techniques will have a (distant) position in relation to others. In other words, all evaluations are located somewhere in terms of the politics and norms of the context. (Evaluations are not located "nowhere"). The kinds of relationships evaluators establish with stakeholders are a key way in which such norms, values, and political commitments are communicated. So, beyond the instrumental and educational/conceptual importance of evaluators' social relationships, there are moral and political dimensions to these relationships that also matter, inherently, intrinsically, inevitably.

This means that how an evaluator relates to and interacts with people in a setting can be enormously important. The third vignette shows that patients (or more broadly, those participating in a program) should be counted as relevant stakeholders for moral and political reasons. More importantly, the kneeling in the mud story illustrates that it matters what particular kinds of relationships the evaluator establishes with patients/program beneficiaries (and, of course, with other program stakeholders like staff and administrators). The kind of relationships matter because – as articulated in the vignette – (1) these relationships help to shape the evaluative knowledge that is generated in an evaluation and (2) these relationships importantly convey what particular norms and values are being advanced in the evaluation. So, it matters in the third vignette that evaluators kneel in the mud alongside psychiatric patients because relationships thus formed are respectful, equitable, and accepting. The traditional role of the docile patient is deconstructed and a new range of opportunities for relating is explored. The evaluators communicate the values of respect, attentiveness, and engagement.

This kind of relational work supports the kinds of values and knowledge that *I* believe are important. The broader point is that in all evaluations relationships will play a parallel role – helping to shape the content and form of evaluative knowledge and communicating important values.

Evaluations Are Disruptive of the Human, Social, and Political Context

There is still one other reason why evaluators should pay attention to social relations. This relates to the fact that evaluations are always disruptive of the existing human, social, and political character of the contexts at hand (Guba, 1977; Guba & Lincoln, 1981).

Whether they like it or not, evaluators encounter human beings and groups, and very human responses to an evaluation study. In the past works have been written about the political environment of and political consequences of evaluation (Chelimsky, 1997; House, 1980, 1993; Palumbo, 1987). In the recent evaluation literature more attention is paid to the phenomenon of "resistance" to evaluation and possible socio-psychological explanations and strategies (Donaldson et al., 2002; Geva-May & Thorngate, 2003; Taut & Brauns, 2003). Negative attitudes toward evaluation often stem from previous negative experiences and anticipation of negative repercussions, for example, loss of approval of valued tasks. Think of the second vignette in which the staff are afraid the results of the evaluation study will not match the expectations of the manager and repercussions might affect staff responsibilities and tasks. Evaluation can also influence the existing power structure in a context. For example, in the third vignette therapists may have a comfortable patronizing relationship with their patients and are leery of risking their power via more symmetrical relationships. Perceived loss of control or freedom of choice may also engender a negative attitude towards the evaluation. For example, higher management in an organization may unilaterally commission an evaluation, which is then experienced by others as threatening. To maintain current control, stability, and predictability stakeholders in this organization may resist the evaluation or respond with mistrust. People can also find evaluative feedback on their work frustrating, affecting their self-esteem and self-image. It has been argued that continuous communication and involvement of program staff leads to higher acceptance of evaluation.

Attending to social relations in the evaluation setting is important for various reasons, summarized below:

■ Social relations among program participants and other stakeholders are integral to and partly constitutive of the quality and effectiveness of the evaluated program.

■ The relationships are partly constitutive of the character and contours of the evaluative *knowledge* that is generated.
■ The kinds of relationships the evaluator establishes with people in the evaluation setting communicate particular *values and norms.*
■ Evaluation studies are always disruptive of the existing human, social and political character of a context, and, in turn, facets of the social, political, and organizational context may complicate the evaluation.

Yet a full chapter on the social relations of evaluation is still quite unique, especially in a handbook on evaluation. The relational dimensions of evaluation are often not explicitly or well addressed in the standing works on evaluation. In the long subject index of, for example, William Shadish, Thomas Cook, & Laura Leviton's *Foundations of Program Evaluation* (1991) you will find entries for "social engineering" and "social problem solving," but there is no entry for "social relations." The same is true for *Evaluation for the 21st Century, A Handbook* (Chelimsky & Shadish, 1997). The index list in this book includes entries for "social programs" and "social science methods," but no reference is made to "social relations." There are many other examples, all indicative of the scant attention that has been paid to social relations in the field of evaluation. Evaluation, these handbooks suggest, is about *methods*; evaluation is, first and foremost, a scientific and technical affair in order to "solve" and "engineer" the social world (Mark, 2001). Social relations and politics, it is claimed, are not part of evaluation; they only make up the "environment" of evaluation.

In the remainder of this chapter, I will first describe in more detail the way evaluators have been studying and portraying the relationships among program people and other stakeholders. I will relate this work to ideas on evaluation as a kind of "social anthropology."

Second, I elaborate four positions on the relationship between the evaluator and others in the setting. Finally, I will reflect on how attention to the social relations of evaluation can both enhance and undermine evaluation, and I will project my vision for the future of evaluation as a social practice.

Social Relations Among Program People and Other Stakeholders

The growing attention and interest of evaluators in social relations among program participants dates back to the 1970s. At that time Cronbach proposed that the evaluation field needed good social anthropologists, a call that inspired many evaluators (Stake, 1991; personal communication, summer 1994).

Historical Legacies

In the UK, Parlett & Hamilton (1972) further elaborated the metaphor of the evaluator as social anthropologist. The authors proposed an approach to evaluation that is adaptive to situations. The aim was to describe and to interpret. Central features of the so-called "illuminative evaluation" approach were that the evaluator familiarize him/herself "thoroughly with the day to day reality" in order to *"unravel the complexity"* of the program in its context. Being present and conducting observations were the predominant activities. The evaluator should record discussions with and between participants, and keep track of the language, jargon, and metaphors in order to gain insight in the implicit pre-assumptions and interpersonal relations.

In the USA, Stake was also thinking about a broader conceptualization of evaluation that included the social. In his so-called "countenance paper" Stake (1967) captured the collective state in the field and argued for a broader scope of evaluation than the usual focus on intended and observed outcomes. The

countenance paper featured a comprehensive matrix: six cells for judgment, six cells for description, and one for the rationale of the program. Stake (1991) saw it as a plea for broadening the array of data – from only outcomes to antecedents and processes as well. Although he initially only argued for the collection of additional data, later Stake realized a change of methods was also necessary (Abma & Stake, 2001). In addition to quasi-experimental designs and correlational surveys, evaluators needed to consider the use of various qualitative methods in order to be able to attend to different stakeholder issues, argued Stake. His "responsive" approach to evaluation is based on an acknowledgment of the plurality of interests and values of various stakeholders (Stake, 1975). Methodologically, this implies the use of an emergent design. Stake also emphasizes the importance of informal oral communication and feedback as everyday evaluation activities that help the evaluator to stay in contact with as many stakeholders as possible. Guba & Lincoln (1981) refer explicitly to Stake's work in their work on a "naturalistic" approach to evaluation, which can be seen as an attempt to legitimate responsive evaluation by given it an epistemological foundation in social constructivist and hermeneutic perspectives.

To summarize, evaluators of various traditions have been arguing that social interactions influence the evaluated program. This stance has given rise to a debate in which new questions were raised, such as are additional data enough, and should evaluators also change their aims and their methods, from explanation and prediction to understanding, from quantitative to qualitative.

How Social Relations Can Influence Program Quality and Effectiveness

The underlying assumption of the above approaches to evaluation is that the social relations in a program context are at least partly constitutive of program quality and effectiveness. It is not just the inputs and activities in a program theory or logic model that matter for program quality and effectiveness (Blalock, 1999; Davies, 1999), but also the relational quality of the interactions that take place as the program is implemented in context. Specific social dimensions of importance are discussed next.

Power and Conflict

Every social relationship involves power. Power refers to the possibility to let someone do something he or she would not do otherwise. Power is thus relational, and parties in a power relationship are tied to each other by mutual dependency. Power differences may result in conflict. Conflicts do not have to be destructive if handled well. Conflict can stimulate creativity and lead to innovations. However, if conflicts are not managed functionally, they may lead to damaged relationships and the emotional burden can have a negative impact on the job satisfaction and productivity. The second vignette at the beginning of this chapter illustrates how a vertical power relationship between staff and administrator led to an internal conflict and impasse (Abma, 2000).

Leadership and Decision-Making

Leadership is crucial to understanding organizations. Leadership is authority that is attributed to people by their followers and as such it differs from functional power. A leader influences what people think and do, inspires and motivates, reduces ambiguity and uncertainty, and resolves conflicts. The first vignette shows that the principal Sylvia Peters was considered as the person who made the arts program successful because of her authenticity, enjoyment, and vision (Mabry, 1991). If leaders lack credibility, as the second vignette shows, their impact on the program can be negative.

Leadership is especially important in times of crisis and change, but major changes are never the conduct of one person, or hero. Decision-making also plays a role in program effectiveness. In the second vignette the staff did not participate in the decision about the timeframe for the project. As a result they were less willing to accept the decision. Participation improves the acceptance of decisions, as it gives people a sense of ownership.

Uncertainty and Communication

Communication is required to be able to adjust one's actions to the needs and concerns of others and to collaborate. Communication is especially important in situations with a high degree of uncertainty and ambiguity (Abma & Noordegraaf, 2003; Forss & Samset, 1999). Communication is always complex, because it is affected by perceptions and interpretations which are influenced by needs, values, and interests. Misunderstandings easily occur given the fact that words can always have multiple interpretations. Besides distortion, there can be a lack or overload of communication, which can also affect program quality and effectiveness. In either case, people will be working at cross purposes, uninformed about the expectations and concerns of other stakeholders and therefore unable to adjust their actions and responses to others (Widdershoven & Sohl, 1999).

Stability and Change

The implementation of a new program implies a process of change. The staff are, for example, expected to serve a new target group or to approach the same target group differently. Quite often this means that taken-for-granted routines no longer work. It is commonly known that human beings do not like to change their behavior (Kotter & Cohen, 2002). So, whether or not expected changes will succeed depends substantially on the human responses to change. Emotions may range from misplaced pride, panic, and fear to anger and uncertainty. Among others, Weiss (2000) has argued that social scientific theories are helpful to explain the "mechanisms of social change" and program participants' behavior. Recently, more attention has been paid to institutional arrangements – with relatively fixed interactions, norms, and rules – which prevent changes and innovations (Barnes et al., 2003; Perrin, 2002; Sanderson, 2000; Sullivan et al., 2002).

Wider Context

The quality and effectiveness of programs are partly determined by the wider socio-political and cultural context. This context is often marked by complexity, and this implies the need for a non-linear systems model to understand the workings of programs (Barnes et al., 2003; Perrin, 2002; Sanderson, 2000; Stake & Mabry, 1995). The social relationships in especially complex or troubled contexts can be particularly relevant to program quality, as these contexts present notable challenges for envisioning and implementing a program likely to be effective. Think of the second and third vignettes where the staff worried about the willingness of employers to offer training opportunities for psychiatric patients and/or to hire them as employees. Negative stereotypes in the societal context surrounding the psychiatric hospital were hard to fight and ultimately affected the effectiveness of the program.

Having discussed how social relations among people can impact or influence program quality and effectiveness, I end this part of the chapter with several other good examples of detailed evaluation studies and portrayals of interpersonal relationships and social interactions. In the field of health care there is Guy Widdershoven & Carlo Sohl's (1999) portrayal of a supported employment program in the Netherlands. Marian Barnes and her colleagues (2003) have described the

complexity of community initiatives in the Health Action Zones in the UK. In the field of teaching I want to record Karen Malone & Rob Walker's (1999) story of the Laverton Park School and Australian community in crisis. Saville Kushner (2000) has portrayed social relations and interactions among teachers and students in a conservatoire in London, the symphony orchestra in Birmingham and the Royal Opera House in London. These case examples can offer instructive further reading.

Social Relations Between the Evaluator and Others in the Setting

I now turn to the relationship between the evaluator and others in the setting. My main concern is to show how different positions concerning the place of social relations in evaluation depend on particular philosophical epistemologies and theoretical frameworks.

The Argument

The various evaluation traditions treat the role or identity of the evaluator differently, depending on what is most highly valued in evaluation (see Table 8.1). First, some traditions value above all the evaluator's ability to be neutral and objective or impartial. The evaluator's main job in these traditions is to get as close to the "truth" as possible. Relationships are a source of bias or contamination in the evaluation process. Second, in utilization-oriented evaluation, social relations are important to utilization. Relations need to be "managed" since they are critical to utilization and organizational learning. Third, in more ideologically oriented evaluation traditions, a primary intent of the evaluation is some version of social change, and the evaluator's relationships with stakeholders are viewed as one important element in this change process. And fourth, in more recent hermeneutic and

EXEMPLAR 8.1 Social relations between evaluator and participants in major contemporary evaluation traditions

Philosophy	Values	Social relations . . .	Kind of relationships forged
Postpositivism	Good methodology	Are irrelevant or sources of error	Distanced
Utilitarian pragmatism	Utilization	Have to be managed	Functional
Critical, participatory theory	Social change	Have to be changed	Empowering
Interpretivism	Dialog	Are the main point	Educative, hermeneutic

constructivist conceptualizations of evaluation, social relations are the main point. Engaging in meaningful dialog with stakeholders and facilitating their dialog with one another is the main point of this genre evaluation, which is thereby highly relational in its very orientation.

In the rest of this section I will discuss these positions in greater detail considering the following as an outline of what is to be discussed, though not necessarily in this order:

- Relevant evaluative traditions
- What is most highly valued in these traditions, and why
- Relevant philosophical assumptions
- Other relevant assumptions (political, normative)
- Evaluator role or identity
- Implications for the role of social relations in the evaluation, and how this particular role reinforces the above
- Implications for the kind of social relations forged, and how these particular relationships reinforce the above

- Examples
- Critique

Social Relations Are Irrelevant to or Sources of Error in Evaluative Work

In the first stance the main idea is that social relations are irrelevant to or a source of error in evaluative work. They interfere with the desire for impartiality, neutrality, and objectivity. This idea is probably most germane to policy-oriented theories of evaluation (Cook, 1985) and to Scriven's (1997) particular concerns about bias arising from getting too close to the evaluation context. This idea is also connected to current evaluation ideologies that emphasize performance and accountability.

What matters most in this stance is good methodology. The underlying philosophical assumptions include the ontological notion that the world is given (versus socially constructed) and determined by law-like structures that can be explained and captured by causal models and theories. Furthermore, it is assumed that object and subject should and can stay disentangled. The evaluator is disengaged and stands back from the context and the people in it.

In these traditions the "world of politics" appears as the opposite of the "world of science"; politics have to be ignored to prevent a negative influence on the evaluation and its findings. This implies that in this kind of literature politics is associated with power, or more precisely the wrong kind of power – power in the form of guile, imposition, partisanship, threat, authority, and command. Evaluators should make all efforts possible to avoid polluting the evaluation process with the wrong kind of power politics.

The evaluator acts as a social scientist, expert, judge, or technician, and these roles imply a distanced relationship between the evaluator and others. Methods, especially quantitative methods, enable evaluators to gather data while minimizing contact and interactions with people in the evaluated program (Scriven, 1997). Solutions offered against co-optation in local evaluation settings include organizational and administrative arrangements granting independent funding, administrative independence, and emotional distance from an agency.

Ideally in this stance, human interaction between the evaluator and others in the setting should be completely avoided. Yet, evaluators do not work in a social and political vacuum. Given the human responses of "resistance" and related problems that undermine the quality of the evaluators' work, such as lack of information access and cooperation problems, false reporting and bias, and validity and utilization problems, evaluators need to attend to psychological issues even as they strive to minimize relational interference (Donaldson et al., 2002).

Benefits of the focus on good methodology (other than social relations) include the fact that the evaluator does not need to be skilled in interpersonal communication and negotiation (although some knowledge and skills are desired). Furthermore, enacting the evaluator role as one of expert and technician will in many contexts match the expectations of the people in the evaluation setting. On the other hand, the claimed authority of the evaluator may also be experienced as inappropriate in a context where democracy and participation are highly valued. A more fundamental critique relates to the question of whether or not it is possible to avoid or seriously minimize relationships with program stakeholders, and whether this is in fact desirable.

Social Relations Should Be "Managed"

Patton (1990, 1997) and other utilization-oriented evaluators would consider social relations as instrumentally important to use and learning (Barbier, 1999; Forss, Rebien, & Carlsson, 2002; Preskill & Torres, 1999; Valovirta, 2002; Van der Meer, 1999). For these authors relationships between the evaluator and stakeholders are critical to utilization, and so are central to their theory. In this sense social relations should be "managed."

Utilization is the main concern in this stance and utilization of findings is affected positively when there is a frequent contact, communication, and ongoing interaction between the evaluator and "potential users" of the evaluation (Greene, 1988). Contact with potential users enables the evaluator to understand the expectations about the "potential use" of the findings, to balance these expectations (Barbier, 1999) and to tie the evaluation to the culture of the users (Hyatt & Simons, 1999; Van der Meer, 1999).

Interaction and communication among program people are also important to process use and learning. Forss et al., (2002) state: "It would seem that the usefulness of evaluation hinges directly upon the quality of communication in evaluation exercises" (p. 35). They consider it to be crucial that the evaluator creates an evaluation setting in which it is possible for people to contact each other, to interact and to learn from and with each other in professional networks. Individual and organizational learning require social forums, and evaluators should create social learning infrastructures (Preskill & Torres, 1999).

The underlying philosophy of this stance can be characterized as utilitarian and pragmatic. The traditional experimental methodology and required objectivity may be compromised if they interfere with the acceptance and instrumental use of findings. The tension between technical quality and user involvement is understood as a trade-off between truth and utility, and the evaluator must deal with this tension in the light of the evaluation context (Patton, 2002).

The evaluator is in this genre not a judge or expert, but acts like a consultant or broker who is skilled in interpersonal communication and negotiation. These skills include intangible qualities such as cultural sensitivity (Hyatt & Simons, 1999) and *Fingerspitzengefül* (Forss et al., 2002). The developed social relationships are mostly functional (versus personal). In sum, social relations matter in this approach for pragmatic reasons. The kinds of relationships are to a significant extent instrumental, and the evaluator requires good communication and interpersonal skills to aid utilization.

Social Relations Should Be Changed

Relevant evaluative traditions that engage the idea that social relations should be changed include feminist approaches to evaluation (Mertens, 2002), empowerment evaluation (Fetterman, 1994), democratic evaluation (MacDonald, 1974; Murray, 2002), participatory evaluation (Greene, 1997; Themessl-Huber & Grutsch, 2003), critical evaluation (Segerholm, 2001), and evaluative traditions that promote social justice (House, 1980, 1993). The evaluator establishes particular

relationships in her/his evaluation as a way of challenging extant relationships – especially of power – in the context outside the evaluation.

The evaluative purpose is the establishment of equal and just relations in society and the empowerment of marginalized groups in society, and therefore engagement with others is valued. The main point is that in order to help effect the kinds of changes desired, the evaluator purposefully uses the relational dimensions of evaluation. He/she purposefully establishes certain kinds of relationships (e.g., ones that are accepting, respectful, reciprocal) in order to help promote the overall social changes desired.

Philosophically, this position is grounded in a critical or transformative epistemology. Donna Mertens (2002) describes the relationship between object and subject, knower and known as follows: "interactive, sensitive to those with the least power, and empowering to those involved in the process" (p. 106). Other advocates of this position point out that relations between evaluator and program people can be more democratic in terms of sharing power and authority, as the locus of control shifts from the evaluator as an expert to program people and other stakeholders who come to have a say in the process (MacDonald, 1977; Murray, 2002; Themessl-Huber & Grutsch, 2003).

Evaluators working in these traditions understand evaluation as a politicized practice; it has unequal consequences for various stakeholders in the evaluation. They ask themselves *whose* interests they want to serve (Schwandt, 1997; Segerholm, 2001). Social relations and societal structures are not taken for granted, but critically examined with the intent to transform them. The evaluator criticizes power imbalances and the status quo, often from the perspective of critical theories. He or she acts as a social critic, arguing against domination, oppression, exploitation, cruelty, and violence (Mertens, 2002; Segerholm, 2001), and as an advocate of a particular, silenced and marginalized group (Lincoln,

1993). The intention to address to social relations is driven by emancipatory and democratic ideals. There is an engagement to empower people, to enlarge people's abilities to govern their own lives. On an individual level, empowerment refers to the ability to take action in a more self-conscious way in the domain on which the evaluation focuses, but also in other domains of life. On the collective level, empowerment refers to obtaining more power in organizations and, eventually in the processes of decision-making in organizations and institutions.

Given this kind of evaluative purpose, methods such as surveys and experiments are often not very appropriate to reach those who are marginalized (Mertens, 2001). Evaluators should consider other methods to gain access to authentic and accurate experiences, for example, focus groups or public meetings. Deliberative forums can be explicitly used to give voice to program participants in ways they don't usually have voice (House & Howe, 1999). This experience hopefully can affect participants' political power outside the evaluation context. Christina Segerholm (2001) notes, however, that inclusion of stakeholders in a dialog does not guarantee that values like equity and social justice will be prominent. There is always the risk of pseudo-participation. Evaluators should therefore always ask who will profit from an inclusive dialog and deliberation.

Adopting this stance raises critical responses from those who hold on to objectivist ideals; one may be marginalized for being biased, political, and value-laden (Ryan et al., 1998). Another critique is related to the fact that while the evaluator is taking an engaged evaluative stance, role, and identity, relationships still are, at least partly if not mostly, a means to another end.

Social Relations Are the Point

The final stance is rooted in the historical legacies of Parlett & Hamilton, Stake and Guba & Lincoln,

reviewed earlier on in the chapter. But, this stance takes these legacies an additional step forward and focuses primary attention on evaluative social relations. In this stance, social relations are not important primarily to realize a particular goal (utilization, democracy, justice), but rather are intrinsically valuable.

The main concern from this perspective is the relational quality among people in the evaluation setting, including the evaluator. How people relate and should relate is framed in a moral–ethical framework of caring, and as such is *normative* (Schwandt, 2002). The fundamental questions in this kind of work are: Whom do we care about? What kind of community do we wish to have together? The underlying moral assumption is that good care requires a balance in normative expectations among participants in an ongoing relationship (Walker, 1998).

The underlying ontological notion is that human beings are fundamentally relational. Our social world is a product of social interactions and relations. Understanding of our socially constructed world can only be generated in relationship and dialog with and between the inhabitants of this world. Epistemologically, these traditions are grounded in the notion that object and subject mutually influence each other. There is a dialogical relationship: instead of two independent entities standing in front of each other, knower and known are now engaged in a conversation. In this conversation participants may change. Instead of being objective and impartial or acting as an advocate, evaluators working in these traditions show a "multiple partiality"; they identify with each of the people involved and this enables them to act as teachers who can explain the various experiences to the included groups.

The roles of the evaluator include those of facilitator, teacher, and Socratic guide, and indicate a horizontal, friendly, and intimate relationship. They show their engagement with the people in the setting (Kushner, 2000). The evaluator has a "relational responsibility" and will pay deliberate attention to the "social relations of inquiry" (Abma, 2000; Greene, 2002). This means that the evaluator will try to create a "safe space" for participants and stakeholders "to learn how to relate and communicate equally and justly, a space that is unfettered by outside status and role differentials and animated by norms of reciprocity, parity, and respect" (Greene, 1997, p. 176; Greene, 2001). This evaluator is sensitive to subtle mechanisms of exclusion.

The politics in these evaluation approaches relate to inevitable constraints on the engagement and inclusion of various groups of people and on the intention to foster a genuine dialog. Dialog requires a certain power balance to give everyone a fair place in the process (Abma et al., 2001). Constraints on dialog include asymmetrical relationships among groups of people and the sensitivity of issues to be discussed. In general one should take these conditions into account by investing a lot of time developing conditions of trust and safety. If a face-to-face encounter is impossible, one may organize a virtual meeting to stimulate a learning process between participants (Widdershoven, 2001). Or a climate of open discussion and dialog may be fostered by presenting topics through stories (Abma, 1998, 2000, 2001). Active engagement of as many participants as possible as well as deliberation among them minimizes the chance of bias and domination of one party. Afterwards, the dialogical process should be examined to determine whether it was really open, inclusive, and educative.

In these evaluation traditions relationships are no longer a means to another end (Abma, 2006). It is the relationships themselves that matter in this evaluative tradition. And thus what matters is dialog, practice, understanding,

and acceptance (Schwandt, 2003). This is relational evaluation in some important sense. Critique of this stance centers around the required interpersonal and negotiation skills and needed tolerance for ambiguity.

Epilogue

This chapter is an attempt to fill in what has until recently been a blank space in the evaluation literature; heretofore, no explicit attention has been given to social relations in evaluation. The chapter provides an overview of the concept of social relation, along with its various connotations, dimensions, and perspectives.

The very existence of this chapter in a handbook on evaluation is significant. It announces that social relations matter in evaluation – to the quality of the program, both as experienced and as judged. The ideas on broadening the scope of evaluation to include the social, first offered in the 1970s, are now finding wider acceptance. Signaling broader attention to the human dimension of evaluation, there is also increasing attention paid to evaluator roles and to the concept of "identity" as a way of better understanding who the evaluator is in relation with others in the setting. And, there is attention to the notion of "resistance" to evaluation and to the social–psychological factors that help explain this resistance and thus offer avenues for addressing it effectively. Yet, social relations are still predominantly treated instrumentally in evaluative thinking, and this will have consequences in terms of the quality of knowledge generated as well as the values and norms communicated.

My vision for the future of evaluation as a social practice would include a wider acknowledgment that evaluation is not only a technique but also a social practice, a wider acknowledgment that evaluation processes inevitably reflect and establish certain moral values, and a wider acceptance of evaluators' "relational responsibilities." Also I hope more attention will be paid to the intrinsic value of the social relations between the evaluator and others in the evaluation setting. An acknowledgment of the educational/conceptual as well as normative dimensions of the evaluator–stakeholder relationship creates a reflexive space for the communication of a new array of values and norms.

Acknowledgment

The conversations with Jennifer Greene were very helpful to fill in substantially what has been a very blank space in evaluation discourse until recently – that of social relations of evaluation.

References

Abma, T. A. (1998). Storytelling as inquiry in a mental hospital. *Qualitative Health Research*, 8(6), 821–838.

Abma, T. A. (2000). Stakeholder conflict: a case study. *Evaluation and Program Planning*, 23, 199–210.

Abma, T. A. (2001). Evaluating palliative care: Facilitating reflexive dialogues about an ambiguous concept. *Medicine Health Care and Philosophy*, 4(3), 261–276.

Abma, T. A. (2006). The practice and politics of responsive evaluation. *The American Journal of Evaluation*, March.

Abma, T. A. & Noordegraaf, M. (2003). Public managers amidst ambiguity: Towards a typology for evaluative practices in public management. *Evaluation*, 9(3), 285–306.

Abma, T. A. & Stake, R. (2001). Stake's responsive evaluation: Core ideas and evolution. *New Directions for Evaluation*, no. 92(pp. 7–22). San Francisco: Jossey-Bass.

Abma, T. A., Greene, J., Karlsson, O., Ryan, K., Schwandt, T. S., & Widdershoven, G. (2001). Dialogue on dialogue. *Evaluation*, 7(2), 164–180.

Barbier, J. C. (1999). Inter-governmental evaluation: Balancing stakeholders' expectations with enlightenment objectives. *Evaluation*, 5(4), 373–386.

Barnes, M., Matka, E., & Sullivan, H. (2003). Evidence, understanding and complexity: evaluation in non-linear systems. *Evaluation*, 9(3), 265–284.

Blalock, A. B. (1999). Evaluation research and the performance measurement movement: From estrangement to useful integration? *Evaluation*, 5(2), 117–149.

Chelimsky, E. (1997). The political environment of evaluation and what it means for the development of the field. In E. Chelimsky & W. R. Shadish (eds) *Evaluation for the 21st Century, a Handbook* (pp. 53–68). Thousand Oaks: Sage.

Chelimsky, E. & Shadish, W. R. (1997). *Evaluation for the 21st Century*. Thousand Oaks, CA: Sage.

Cook, T. D. (1985). Postpositivist critical multiplicism. In L. Shotland & M. M. Mark (eds) *Social Science and Social Policy* (pp. 21–62). Beverly Hills, CA: Sage.

Davies, I. C. (1999). Evaluation and performance management in government. *Evaluation*, 5(2), 150–159.

Donaldson, S. I., Gooler, L. E., & Scriven, M. (2002). Strategies for managing evaluation anxiety: Toward a psychology of program evaluation. *American Journal of Evaluation*, 23(3), 261–274.

Fetterman, D. (1994). Empowerment evaluation. *Evaluation Practice*, 15, 1–6.

Forss, K. & Samset, K. (1999). Square pegs and round holes, evaluation, uncertainty and risk management. *Evaluation*, 5(4), 407–421.

Forss, K., Rebien, C. C., & Carlsson, J. (2002). Process use of evaluations. *Evaluation*, 8(1), 29–45.

Geva-May, I. & Thorngate, W. (2003). Reducing anxiety and resistance in policy and programme evaluations, A Socio-psychological analysis. *Evaluation*, 9(2), 205–227.

Greene, J. C. (1988). Stakeholder participation and utilization program evaluation. *Evaluation Review*, 12(2), 91–116.

Greene, J. C. (1997). Participatory evaluation, In L. Mabry (ed.) *Evaluation and the Post-modern Dilemma. Advances in Program Evaluation*, vol. 3 (pp. 171–189). Greenwich: JAI Press.

Greene, J. (2001). Dialogue in evaluation. A relational perspective. *Evaluation*, 7(2), 181–203.

Greene, J. C. (2002). Evaluation as education. Paper presented at the European Evaluation Society, October 2002, Seville.

Guba, E. G. (1977). Overcoming resistance to evaluation. Paper presented at the Second Annual Conference of the North Dakota Study Group on Evaluation, North Dakota, USA.

Guba, E. G. & Lincoln, Y. S. (1981). *Effective Evaluation*. San Francisco: Jossey-Bass.

House, E. R. (1980). *Evaluating with Validity*. Berverly Hills: Sage.

House, E. R. (1993). *Professional Evaluation*. Thousand Oaks: Sage.

House, E. R. & Howe, K. R. (1999). *Values in Evaluation and Social Research*. Thousand Oaks: Sage.

Hyatt, J. & Simons, H. (1999). Cultural codes – who holds the key. *Evaluation*, 5(1), 23–41.

Kotter. J. P. & D. S. Cohen (2002). *The Heart of Change. Real-life stories of how people change their organizations*. Boston, MA: Harvard Business School Press.

Kushner, S. (2000). *Personalizing Evaluation*. London: Sage.

Lincoln, Y. S. (1993). I and thou: method, voice, and roles in research with the silenced. In D. McLaughlin & W. Tierney (eds) *Naming Silenced Lives*, (pp. 29–47). New York: Routledge.

Mabry, L. (1991). Alexandre Dumas Elementary School Chicago, Illinois. (pp. 137–176). In R. Stake, L. Bresler & L. Mabry (eds) *Custom and Cherishing: The arts in Elementary schools*. Urbana, IL: National Art Education Research Center.

MacDonald, B. (1997). Evaluation and the control of education, In B. MacDonald & R. Walker (eds) *SAFARI 1: Innovation, evaluation, research and the problem of control* (pp. 9–22). Norwich: Centre for Applied Research in Education, University of East Anglia.

MacDonald, B. (1977). A political classification of evaluation studies, In: D. Hamilton, D. Jenkins, C. King, B. MacDonald & M. Parlett *Beyond the Numbers Game*, (pp. 224–227). London: MacMillan.

Malone, K. & Walker, R. (1999). Crafting counter-narratives in collaboration: An impressionist tale about a school in conflict. In T. A. Abma (ed.) *Telling Tales. On Narrative and Evaluation, Advances in Program Evaluation*, Vol. 6. (pp. 919–214). Greenwich, CT: JAI Press.

Mark, M. M. (2002). Toward a better understanding of alternative evaluator roles. In K. E. Ryan, &

T. S. Schwandt (eds) *Exploring Evaluator Role and Identity* (pp. 17–36). Greenwich, CT: IAP.

Mertens, D. (2002). The evaluator's role in the transformative context. In K. E. Ryan & T. S. Schwandt (eds) *Exploring Evaluator Role and Identity* (pp. 103–118). Greenwich, CT: IAP.

Murray, R. (2002). Citizens' control of evaluations, formulating and assessing alternatives. *Evaluation*, 8(1), 81–100.

Palumbo, D. J. (ed.) (1987). *The Politics of Program Evaluation*. Newbury Park: Sage.

Parlett, M. & Hamilton, D. (1972). Evaluation as illumination: A new approach to the study of innovatory programs, In G. Glass (ed.) *Evaluation Review Studies Annual 1* (pp. 140–157). Beverly Hills, CA: Sage.

Patton, M. Q. (1990). *Qualitative Evaluation and Research Methods*, 2nd edition. Newbury Park, CA: Sage.

Patton, M. Q. (1997). *Utilization-focused evaluation: New century edition*. Thousand Oaks, CA: Sage.

Patton, M. Q. (2002). A vision of evaluation that strengthens democracy. *Evaluation*, 8(1), 125–139.

Perrin, B. (2002). How to–and how not to–evaluate innovation. *Evaluation*, 8(1), 13–28.

Preskill, H. & Torres, R. T. (1999). Building capacity for organizational learning through evaluative inquiry. *Evaluation*, 5(1), 42–60.

Ryan, K. E. & Schwandt, T. S. (eds) (2002). *Exploring Evaluator Role and Identity*.Greenwich, CT: IAP.

Ryan, K., Greene, J., Lincoln, Y., Mathison, S., & Mertens, D. M. (1998). Advantages and challenges of using inclusive evaluation approaches in evaluation practive. *American Journal of Evaluation*, 19(1), 101–122.

Sanderson, I. (2000). Evaluation in complex policy systems. *Evaluation*, 6(4), 433–454.

Schwandt, T. S. (1997). Whose interests are being served? Program evaluation as conceptual practice of power. In L. Mabry (ed.) *Evaluation and the Post-modern Dilemma. Advances in Program Evaluation*, Greenwich, CT: Vol. 3 (pp. 89–104). JAI Press.

Schwandt, T. S. (2002). Traversing the terrain of role, identity and self. In K. E. Ryan & T. S. Schwandt (eds) *Exploring Evaluator Role and Identity* (pp. 193–207). Greenwich, CT: IAP.

Schwandt, T. S. (2003). "Back to the rough ground!" Beyond evaluation theory to practice in evaluation. *Evaluation*, 9(3), 353–364.

Scriven, M. (1997) Truth and objectivity in evaluation In E. Chelimsky & W. R. Shadish (eds) E*valuatrion for the 21st Century, a Handbook* (pp. 477–500). Thousand Oaks: Sage.

Segerholm, C. (2001). Evaluation as responsibility, consience, and conviction. In K. E. Ryan & T. S. Schwandt (eds) *Exploring Evaluator Role and Identity* (pp. 87–102). Greenwich, CT: IAP.

Shadish, W. R., Cook, T. D., & Leviton, L. C. (1991). *Foundations of Program Evaluation, Theories of Practice*. Newbury Park: Sage.

Stake, R. E. (1967). The countenance of evaluation. *Teachers College Record*, 68, 523–540.

Stake, R. E. (1975). To Evaluate an arts program. In R. E. Stake, *Evaluating the Arts in Education: A responsive approach* (pp. 13–31). Colombus OH: Merill.

Stake, R. E. (1991). Retrospective on The countenance of educational evaluation. In M. W. McLaughlin & D. C. Phillips (eds) *Evaluation and Education: At quarter century. Ninetieth Yearbook of the National Society for the Study of Education* (pp. 67–88). Chicago: University of Chicago Press.

Stake, R. E. & Mabry, L. (1995). Case study for a deep understanding of teaching. In A. C. Omstein (ed.) *Teaching: Theory into practice* (pp. 292–304). Boston: Allyn and Bacon.

Sullivan, H., Barnes, M., & Matka, E. (2002). Building collaborative capacity through "theories of change": Early lessons from the evaluation of health action zones in England. *Evaluation*, 8(2), 205–226.

Taut, S. & Brauns, D. (2003). Resistance to evaluation: A psychological prespective. *Evaluation*, 9(3), 247–264.

Themessl-Huber, M. T. & Grutsch, M. A. (2003). The shifting locus of control in participatory evaluations. *Evaluation*, 9(1), 92–111.

Valovirta, V. (2002). Evaluation utilization as argumentation. *Evaluation*, 8(1), 60–80.

Van der Meer, F. B. (1999). Evaluation and the social construction of impacts. *Evaluation*, 5(4), 387–406.

Weiss, C. H. (2000). Which links and which theories shall we evaluate? In P. J. Rogers, T. A. Hasci, A. Petrosino & T. A. Huebner (eds) *Program Theory in Evaluation: Challenges and Opportunities. New Directions for Evaluation*, No. 87 (pp. 35–46). San Francisco: Jossey-Bass.

Widdershoven, G. A. M. (2001). Dialogue in evaluation A hermeneutic perspective. *Evaluation*, 7(2), 253–263.

Widdershoven G. A. M. & Sohl, C. (1999). Interpretation, action and communication: Four stories about a supported employment program. In T. A. Abma (ed.) *Telling Tales*: *On narrative and evaluation. Advances in Program Evaluation*, Vol. 6 (pp. 109–130). Greenwich, CT: JAI Press.

9

INTELLECTUAL CONTEXTS

John Stevenson and David Thomas

Introduction: Purpose and Scope

Evaluation is a relatively young profession, and its origins are diverse. This is particularly true when the development of the field is placed in an international context. The concepts, terminology, methods, and indeed the underlying questions of interest and content domains for practice, have all been shaped by those origins. As Shadish, Cook, & Leviton (1991) pointed out in their book on the foundations of evaluation theory, evaluation practitioners and scholars initially borrowed concepts and methods from other fields, most often the academic disciplines in which they were trained. Rossi, Lipsey, & Freeman (2004, p. 394) elaborated in their widely used evaluation text, noting that "All the social science disciplines – economics, psychology, sociology, political science, and anthropology – have contributed to the field of evaluation" and adding methodological contributions from human service professional fields (e.g., medicine, public health, social welfare, urban planning, public administration, education) as well as the applied mathematics fields (statistics, biometrics, econometrics, and psychometrics).

This has not been a one-way street. As Rossi et al., went on to point out, evaluation

has often served as a ground for "cross-disciplinary borrowing" in which methods from more than one primary discipline (e.g. economics, sociology, psychology) are intertwined in a single project. Furthermore, the ongoing interaction between evaluation and other disciplines creates a reciprocal influence process as all of the fields evolve.

We will examine the diverse influences on the field of evaluation by focusing on a few influential figures in the field to provide illustrations, then go on to note the role of early evaluation texts and journals as well as interdisciplinary training opportunities, concluding with several examples from practice. While acknowledging that much of the English language evaluation literature originates in the United States, we also note some international influences on evaluation traditions and contexts, especially those from other English language sources, such as Canada, parts of Europe, and Australasia.

We view the field of evaluation as an evolving product of the origin-disciplines from which its practitioners have come, interacting with each other and with the specific evaluation contexts into which those

> **EXEMPLAR 9.1   Major categories of evaluation theory (Shadish et al., 1991)**
>
> | Theory component | Theory content | Examples of origin fields |
> |---|---|---|
> | Social programming | Source of ideas for design and implementation of programs being evaluated | Education, public health, mental health, criminal justice |
> | Knowledge | Source of methods knowledge used for the evaluation research design | Psychology, sociology, anthropology, economics, educational measurement |
> | Value | The assessment of the value of the program or its components by the evaluator | Philosophy |
> | Use | The context and procedures which lead to the use of the evaluation findings | Political science, organizational psychology, sociology, public administration, social policy studies |
> | Evaluation practice | The craft and knowledge context drawn on by evaluators | Constructed within the emerging field of evaluation |

practitioners migrated. At this point there are well-developed content domains within the field of evaluation, reflecting those interactions. Shadish et al., (1991) provided five "components" of a comprehensive theory of evaluation, which are shown in Table 9.1. The intellectual contexts for evaluation have provided much of the content and many of the arguments that may be found in these five focal problem domains. Other than the fifth category, which is derivative from direct evaluation experience, the categories reflect research and theory traditions that come from differing background disciplines. This takes us some way toward an understanding of intellectual contexts that have influenced evaluation, and it is clear that each of the categories embodies a set of debates that originate within a discipline, as well as between disciplines contributing to understandings in that category.

Historical Context: Sources of Methods and Ideas

Major Figures in the Field

Evaluation is a human enterprise, and in an important sense the intellectual contexts from which evaluation has emerged are embodied in individual theorist-practitioners. Thus, early figures in the field brought their own intellectual traditions with them as they engaged in research, writing, and teaching that constructed evaluation as a field. For our purposes here, the focus of attention is on the intellectual contexts that influenced these figures. We will trace three dominant traditions in this influence process: an *experimental* cause-establishing social science perspective; a *case/context tradition* which incorporated multivariate, contextualized perspectives in education moving toward qualitative case studies; and an administrative *policy-influence* perspective drawing on political science, sociology, and economics.

Although it might seem a straightforward thing to identify influential background traditions, there are four important caveats that also deserve attention. First, most of these early figures were mavericks and polymaths; they rebelled against narrow disciplinary traditions, sought ideas from many sources, and attempted to link disparate aspects of the disciplines in which they were trained. Second, the "traditional" disciplines themselves (psychology, economics, education, sociology, political science, statistics, and so on) are not, and have never been, monolithic – they are fraught with internal arguments and have also changed over time in ways that reverberate with changes in evaluation and in the broader cultural–historical context. Third, early leaders in the development of evaluation as a profession were altered by their ongoing experiences, both with evaluation practice and with other opportunities for interdisciplinary collaboration. Fourth, government priorities (of nations, subnational units, and international authorities) have interacted with discipline-based influences to play a central role in shaping the field of evaluation through legislation, funding, and evolving intra-governmental perceptions of high status approaches to evaluation.

Nevertheless, let us start with the linear notion that the disciplines in which major figures in evaluation were originally trained have, through them, exerted a tremendous influence on the nature of action and discourse in the field – from philosophical underpinnings, to problem definitions, to theoretical assumptions and value predilections, to research methods and measurement approaches, to characteristic ways of interacting with other stakeholders, to data analysis, to intended consequences of evaluation and means for achieving them.[1]

The Experimental Tradition

Some of the most influential figures were trained as psychologists, and Donald Campbell's profound contributions can easily be linked to his social psychology background. The desire to have control, as in the laboratory, and to construct problems as linear cause–effect questions for which experiments would ideally provide the strongest, most defensible internal validity evidence, is one dominant theme in his work. His leap to "reforms as experiments" (Campbell, 1969) and the careful delineation of quasi-experimental designs (Campbell & Stanley, 1963) for practical application beyond the laboratory may be traced in part to his exposure in graduate school to the action research perspective of Kurt Lewin, an intellectual forebear with the mission of linking applied experimental research to positive social change (Campbell, 1974; Rosenwein & Campbell, 1992; Shadish & Luellen, 2004). It is less clear where Campbell's fascination with philosophy-of-science issues came from, shaking the foundations of logical positivism at a time when it was still the comfortable old philosophical shoe of research psychologists (e.g., Campbell, 1974). Edward Suchman's (1967) classic text, *Evaluative Research*, drew heavily on Campbell for a chapter on research design, using the Campbell & Stanley notation, and it was that book – not his interest in epistemological challenges to an unreflective positivism – that propelled Campbell into the evaluation arena (Shadish & Luellen, 2004). Although Suchman was a sociologist, he was quick to see the merits of an experimental approach for the kinds of policy evaluation questions in public health and education that the Johnson-era Great Society programs were posing in the US.

As Peter Rossi (2004) described his own evolution, his late 1940s training in sociology was highly quantitative and policy-oriented (focused on use of survey data for public policy studies). When he was exposed to the methods and design logic advocated by Campbell & Stanley he, like Suchman, quickly perceived their value for addressing program effectiveness. Schooler (2003), a "sociological social psychologist," noted the interplay of methodological advances between sociology and psychology through the 1960s in the US. As he saw it, psychologists had the advantage in the early 1960s, with strength in "experimentally oriented" analysis of variance methods, affecting the kinds of questions they asked; by the end of the 1960s, as US sociology adopted sophisticated multivariate methods, beginning with path analysis and moving on to structural equation modeling, it was psychology that had the catching up to do. The relevance of this for our examination of intellectual contexts is to the complex interplay of sociology and psychology and their influence on experiment-based quantitative methods in evaluation through such figures as Campbell, Suchman, and Rossi. As Schooler's account implies, the high-status approaches in both fields were quantitative in the US during this era. Qualitative methods in sociology (Atkinson, Delamont, & Hammersley, 1988; Silverman, 1997), consistently influential in Britain and the rest of Europe, as well as in US anthropology, were not dominant in the US as evaluation methods were developing there.

The Case/Context Tradition

Much earlier, another giant figure in the history of evaluation was trying to combine measurement with the practical question of how classroom curricula could work to achieve meaningful learning objectives. Ralph Tyler's 1927 dissertation was already headed down this road, and by the close of the 1930s he was a well-known expert on the measurement of learning objectives (Madaus, 2004). In the history of evaluation as a field, its development in education holds a special place. Campbell & Stanley's landmark treatise was originally published with the longer title *Experimental and Quasi-experimental Designs for Research on Teaching*, and their introduction traced their ideas back to an earlier

book by McCall (1923), *How to Experiment in Education*. Scriven (2003) asserted that "to put it bluntly, educational research was several decades ahead of the rest of social science in the search for useful models of evaluation, and still is, to judge by most of the evaluation texts of the new millennium" (p. 18). Kellaghan, Stufflebeam, & Wingate (2003) more circumspectly suggested that educational evaluation is distinct from other types of evaluation in some important ways, including (1) its roots in testing, student assessment, and curriculum evaluation (which were generally not considered "research" in the classic experimental tradition, but were strongly associated with measurement and psychometric development); (2) the special nature of the educational enterprise as a pervasive social service that affects everyone and is present in some form in all societies; and (3) the role of teachers as powerful stakeholders who conduct studies as well as undergo them. As one of Tyler's students, Lee Cronbach drew on an intellectual heritage that combined measurement theory with a deep appreciation for the need to educate (i.e., inform practice and policy with thoughtfully gathered data) and the importance of context for generalizability (Greene, 2004). The abstract purity of the laboratory was less influential in that heritage; the messy multivariate world of hypothetical constructs without clear criteria; multilevel, time-dependent interactions influencing outcomes; and implementation of "programs" with questionable consistency across settings, was more familiar. Stake (2004), for whom Cronbach was a senior colleague and mentor, quoted him as saying that their curriculum evaluations really called for a social anthropologist. The ideal of nomothetic theory was replaced by the recognition of virtually infinite variety in which theory serves a heuristic purpose, becoming a tool for organizing observations rather than an assertion of immutable laws (Cronbach, 1975). Like

Campbell, Cronbach went far beyond his heritage in creative contributions to psychology and evaluation, contextualizing evaluation itself in the policy-making process (Cronbach et al., 1980) and advocating more attention to local program contexts and other limits on generalizing conclusions (Cronbach, 1982).

Robert Stake is another pioneer in educational evaluation, and he has described the influences on his evolving views in thoughtful, case-study, detail (Stake, 2004). Initially he was drawn by the potential power of good measurement to influence and validate good teaching, and his graduate studies emphasized applied measurement and psychometric theory, with a strong dose of statistics. Tyler's influence was conveyed through Stake's early collaboration with Cronbach at the University of Illinois (in the early 1960s), when they worked with several others in the development of a federally funded "laboratory" (the Center for Instructional Research and Curriculum Evaluation, or CIRCE) devoted to studies linking curriculum development to evaluation. Frustrated by the failure of experimental designs to produce clear-cut findings to guide curriculum development, Stake "gradually learned that educational evaluation can"t be done . . . it's an impossible dream" (Stake, 2004, p. 206). His own ideas, referred to as "responsive evaluation," (Stake, 1974) feature rich observation of curriculum/program practice in a case-study design, with multiple stakeholder perspectives and attention to the history and social context of the program. This approach is clearly qualitative in its emphasis on observation of activities in context, experiential accounts, and triangulation by means of multiple subjective perspectives ("pluralism"). Yet, as Shadish et al., (1991) pointed out, there is little mention of the epistemological issues or reference to traditional proponents of those methods. Similarly, Shaw (1999) noted that mainstream ethnographers

have been critical of the naivete in his work. One acknowledged source of influence was the work of Hamilton et al., (1977) originating at the Centre for Applied Research in Education at the University of East Anglia, in the UK, where the dominance of the quantitative, experimental tradition was less ensconced, and qualitative exploration of the "learning milieu" was advocated (Shaw, 1999).

The intellectual tradition we perceive in Stake's ideas is one that stays rooted in practice – real students and teachers, in real classrooms, in real schools, struggling to make learning happen. Although Stake's work pioneered qualitative, case-study methods in evaluation, others who picked up those methods (notably Guba & Lincoln, e.g., 1981, 2004; Lincoln & Guba, 1985) added the epistemological frame, drawing in relevant philosophical references and fostering debate at a more formal level (Cook & Reichardt, 1979; see also Shadish et al., 1991). As Cronbach and Tyler did, Stake sought answers that educate, credible with those who live in the studied environments, reflective of the non-linear complexity readily apparent when parsimonious models and restrictive controls are forgone for intensive naturalistic observation. A love of mathematical elegance and precision is trumped by the experience-based belief that staying grounded will yield a more informative result.

The qualitative approach of Hamilton et al., (1977) illustrates the wider-ranging interest in explicitly epistemologically grounded methods that prevails in European evaluation. Another influential tradition originating in the UK has been the writing of Ray Pawson and Nick Tilley on what they described as "realistic evaluation" (Julnes, Mark, & Henry, 1998; Pawson & Tilley, 1997). These authors take a self-conscious position on epistemological issues with emphasis on the importance of programme contexts and underlying mechanisms that lead to observed outcomes. Also in the UK, Saville Kushner has been an advocate for democratic and case-study methodologies in program evaluation (Kushner, 2002). He has conducted case studies in fields as diverse as schooling, the performing arts, research funding, police training, and health services. In his book *Personalizing Evaluation*, Kushner (2000) takes a highly contextual approach, maintaining that evaluation should document individual and group experience and use this as a lens through which to read social programs and to measure their significance in people's lives.

The Policy Influence Tradition

A third powerful thread of influence on evaluation is linked to the growth of a social science presence within the government policy establishment (House, 1993). Although House (1993) contrasted the developing role of evaluation in the US, Canada, and Britain, he saw these advanced, highly technological, capitalist societies as the logical context for the growth of specialized evaluation in service to the government. Suchman's (1967) book reflects the recognition that in the US, the rapid expansion of national programs (in health, education, housing, etc.) in the 1960s had already influenced the evolution of social sciences like psychology, sociology, and economics. The new demand for scientific expertise to justify the vast new programs was accompanied by a dramatic upsurge in funding for evaluative research. The work of Carol Weiss drew heavily on her background in political science and sociology but evolved as she became an insider, continuously engaged with government policy-driven evaluation research at the federal level over a long period. The earliest paper cited by Shadish et al., (1991), in their analysis of her theoretical perspective, was one she presented in 1966 at the American Sociological Association meeting, in which she addressed the comparative study of evaluation utilization, and her influential early text (Weiss, 1972b) reflects that emphasis. In her own description of the influences on her ideas (Weiss, 2004), she mentioned influential people (notably ones whose work was on public management in democracies and organizational decision-making, as well as Cronbach and Campbell), but she was emphatic about her need to teach herself, finding ways to take on the challenge of evaluating programs such as a domestic Peace Corps program and reviewing a federally sponsored nation-wide set of juvenile delinquency programs. We believe the large-scale policy-informing studies on which Weiss worked put a special premium on utilization by powerful stakeholders beyond the academic realm and an understanding of the role of evaluation in the policy-making process. The intellectual roots for addressing those priorities lie outside methodological and context-specific domains, drawing on her background in political science, evidenced by her mention of March (e.g., Cyert & March, 1963, March & Simon, 1958) and Lindblom (e.g., 1968) as influential figures in her work. Joseph Wholey was also influenced by long connection with government policy-making. As in the case of Weiss, his "focus is on evaluation utilization" (Wholey, 2004, p. 267). Illustrating the role of the government policy-making context, Wholey (2004) cited work with economists at the US Department of Health, Education, and Welfare in the 1960s Johnson era as influential in directing his interests toward policy analysis, systems analysis, cost-effectiveness analysis, and cost-benefit analysis. His aim was to "help meet the need for program evaluation studies that would support federal decision making" (p. 269). Rather than following Campbell and Suchman to press for rigorous experimental designs, he responded to the needs of policy-makers for cost-effective data, termed by him "sequential purchase of information" (Wholey, 1979). Famous for his advocacy of "evaluability assessment," making use of relatively low-cost initial investigations of program plan and clarity of objectives for both the program and its evaluation, Wholey explicitly intended to save the cost of large-scale experimental or quasi-experimental designs when these were not justified (Wholey, 1987, 1994) Here is a policy-maker's economic perspective applied to the evaluation enterprise itself.

Standing on his own mountain, Michael Scriven is the philosopher king of evaluation (Shadish et al., 1991, p. 340). He was the first theorist of evaluation treated in Shadish et al.,'s (1991) book, termed a "first stage" theorist for his early dominance in defining a truth-seeking mission for evaluation. In Alkin & Christie's (2004) theory tree framework Scriven is the first theorist on the "valuing" branch, consistent with his careful attention to this issue (though not with his own view of his work). Although it is difficult to see Scriven as anything but *sui generis*, his own account (Scriven, 2004) clarified many influences that shaped his thinking. Majoring in mathematics as an undergraduate, he moved on to philosophy of science in graduate school (Oxford). He described his foray into evaluation as for 20 years a "hobby [. . .] while I was a full-time member of philosophy departments" (p. 190). As a philosophy professor he advocated the teaching of critical thinking and became involved with the evaluation of curriculum reform in elementary and secondary education, leading to a 1967 publication on curriculum evaluation with Tyler. If those who have created the field of evaluation can be thought of as mavericks and polymaths, Scriven is the ultimate iconoclast. Delighting in the application of elegant and rigorous logic where others were soft and inconsistent, he has challenged what he viewed as weakly reasoned positions such as goal-oriented evaluation, advocating goal-free evaluation as

an alternative. In his modus operandi method (Scriven, 1974), he drew explicitly on a historian's approach to causal inference. Virtually unique in evaluation, he trusts the logic of his own approach to judgment of objective program value and is indomitable in arguing its merits. He has done much to create the intellectual context for evaluation, often by challenging sacred beliefs.

Influences that Transcend Disciplines

One theme only hinted at thus far in our presentation is the development of participatory, emancipatory, and empowerment concerns, whose proponents in the US may well have been influenced at least in part by the political ferment of the late 1960s, with its resurgence of feminism, and greater attention to racism, sexism, classism, colonialism, and other forms of disempowerment. These same consciousness-raising forces were at work in other industrialized democracies as well. Each of the social sciences found ways to at least partially accommodate these critical perspectives in theory and method; thus shifts in the cultural zeitgeist interacted formatively in the evolution of evaluation practice, where opportunities for discovering, documenting, and confronting power disparities were frequent. Patton, for example, attributed an influential role to his Peace Corps work during that era and saw his utilization-focused approach to evaluation as an outgrowth of those formative community development experiences in Africa. Later, in the mid-1970s, with a strong quantitative background in sociology, Patton undertook educational evaluations with a mentor who favored qualitative case studies (Patton, 2004). By the late 1970s the developing world had drawn some social scientists into a radical, action-oriented break with their academic traditions (Fals Borda, 2001).

It is easy to find protagonists holding very different points of view on how to do evaluation but having the same system-change rationale for their work (Steinitz & Mishler, 2001 versus Wilmoth, 2001; Greene & Henry, 2003). Reflecting on an earlier era, the 1930s, Rossi (2004) reported that he was socialized to care about the poor and powerless and found quantitative social science methods to be a powerful force for social change, and this was certainly true in the European context for Lewin, who influenced Campbell and many others. The Society for the Psychological Study of Social Issues (SPSSI), infused with the ideas of Lewin, has struggled from its inception in 1936 with the tension between the use of expert power to influence government policies (sometimes characterized as an "honest broker" role) and the repudiation of the neutral scientist role as implicitly aligned with the power structure in government (Finison, 1986; Harris, 1986; Unger, 1986). In her 1972 presidential address to SPSSI, Guttentag (1972), who was instrumental in the later founding of the Evaluation Research Society, raised the related issue of "elitist" experts conducting policy-driven social experiments contrasted with "egalitarian" power struggles leading to spontaneous experiments. The field of evaluation has drawn those who are critics, rebels, and challengers of the status quo much more than it has appealed to "pure" scientists or "bean counters," but the approaches they have championed for exerting influence for change have sometimes seemed mutually exclusive, unyielding in their perceived incompatibility. Differing perceptions of power and how best to exercise it appear to undergird these intransigencies even more than epistemological issues.

Two of our initial caveats about linear influence deserve additional comment. First, the social science disciplines on which the field of evaluation has drawn so heavily are not internally unified, nor are they standing still. Qualitative and quantitative traditions in sociology and anthropology coexist, but not always on friendly terms; in psychology the case-study tradition struggles for renewed attention in the work of people like McAdams (1988) and Singer (1997), while the long-standing debate between experimental and correlational traditions (Cronbach, 1957, 1975), though still exerting influence on evaluation, seems to be resolving into the general linear model, with mediation and moderation effects now standard aspects of analysis.

Second, influential figures in the field of evaluation have been profoundly affected by their direct experiences with evaluation and with the many interdisciplinary contexts generated by evaluation activities. Boruch (2004), for example, mentioned a number of commissions and boards on which he served as being influential by exposing him and his ideas to the give-and-take with experts from very different backgrounds, all in the context of serving evaluation and policy needs. Conferences, centers, and commissions continue to play an active role in nurturing evaluation ideas, even as the third and fourth generations of evaluation scholars and practitioners join the discussion. Although observers have pointed out that there are still distinct professional groupings who do not always interact (Rossi, 2004; Shadish & Reichardt, 1987; Shadish et al., 1991), the leading figures in evaluation have sought out connections across disciplines and paradigms – puzzle-lovers happy to cross borders (Leviton, 2003).

Scriven (1993, 2001) declared that evaluation is a "transdiscipline" like measurement, logic, and statistics, claiming that it spreads over many applications across many domains and disciplines, and that it is focused on a specialized set of multidisciplinary tools that can be applied across that wide range.

Thus Scriven proposed a reversal in the direction of influence in asserting that it is evaluation which must be taught in all of the other disciplines where it is essential but badly understood. It is probably most useful to see the interplay between evaluation and more traditional disciplines as transactional. As Cottrell (1967) pointed out in his introduction to Suchman's book, it is important not to overlook the "potentially productive interplay between well-designed and executed evaluative research and the theoretical and methodological developments of the scientific disciplines themselves" (p. viii). For example, the effort to define taxonomies of cognitive and affective objectives for school curricula has in turn shaped the development of curricula and methods of instruction. Importation of ethnographic methods into evaluation has generated more attention to reliability and validity issues for those methods. The concern for how to define and measure utilization of evaluation has influenced the broader study of diffusion of scientific knowledge. In cases such as these the influence process continues to reverberate.

Early Texts and Journals

Another source of evidence about the nature of the intellectual contexts that have influenced evaluation is in the publications in the field. We have mentioned early texts by Campbell & Stanley (1963), Suchman (1967), and Weiss (1972b), all of which are often seen as seminal. Weiss's (1972a) book of reprinted articles, her "tree full of [wise old] owls," is also a seminal source, with almost all of the figures discussed above represented among the contributors. In educational evaluation, important early texts include Stufflebeam et al. (1971) and Worthen & Sanders (1973). By the mid-1970s the US had a lively conversation about evaluation going on in journals, texts, and conferences.

Struening & Guttentag's (1975) *Handbook of Evaluation Research* was a useful resource but also a symbol of the coming-of-age of the nascent profession of evaluation beyond the education context. Based on the chapter content, it would seem that psychology as a discipline, experimental design and psychometric measurement as methods, and mental health as an evaluation context, were dominant. A different view of the field emerges from an examination of the first year's issues of the *Evaluation Quarterly* in 1977. By 1977, the field of evaluation had its own topics (e.g., utilization, training, considerations for design choices), and these account for 19 percent of the articles, with another 22 percent focused primarily on technical methodological issues (necessitating equations in the text). The most prevalent content domain was criminal justice (26 percent), followed by health (16 percent). One interesting aspect of the authorship pattern was the frequency of co-authors representing different disciplines – for example, law and statistics, developmental psychology and pediatrics, criminal justice and sociology. Also represented were combinations between academic departments and non-academic settings (e.g., sociology and a national non-profit social service organization, social ecology and a public policy research organization). For another look at the broad array of disciplines represented in the evaluation literature, see Shadish & Reichardt's (1987) review of the first ten volumes of the *Evaluation Studies Review Annual*. As their review makes clear, by the 1980s evaluation journals had taken their place but not replaced discipline-linked outlets, allowing a continuation of the reverberation effects between evaluation and the social sciences.

Developmental Themes and Crises

The beginnings of program evaluation have been traced variously to personnel evaluation in 2200 BCE China (Shadish et al., 1991),

William Petty's "political arithmetic" for assessing social conditions with numbers rather than words in the 1600s (Cronbach et al., 1980), nineteenth-century reform commissions in Great Britain and the US (Madaus et al., 1983), the mid-nineteenth-century directive to the Federal Bureau of Education to "show the condition of progress of education in the several states" (Rosenthal, 1973), Rice's 1897 quasi-experimental examination of the effects of drilling on spelling outcomes (Guba & Lincoln, 1989), the beginnings of systematic research on the effects of US public health and education programs in the early 1900s (Rossi et al., 2004), and the "Great Society" legislation in the mid-1960s (Patton, 1997). Historical reviews like these illustrate the effects of differing intellectual traditions on perceptions of the narrative history of the field, but they also converge on critical junctures when ideas from particular sources entered the fray to deal with the challenges of the day. There are at least two relatively different perspectives on the history of the field, one from the educational evaluation tradition (e.g., Guba & Lincoln, 1989; Anderson et al., 1973; Madaus et al., 1983), and one from the government policy evaluation tradition (e.g., Rossi et al., 2004; Shadish et al., 1991), with some presentations achieving more balance (e.g., Cronbach et al., 1980). All of these historical accounts are from a predominantly US perspective.

In the 1930s, Tyler's education-based ideas for evaluation-by-objectives were consistent with the rapidly increasing influence of behavioral psychology in the social sciences. His Eight-Year Study (1932–1940), evaluating the benefits of progressive curricula as an alternative to the traditional college-preparatory structure, was a major milestone in educational evaluation when it was published in 1942. For Madaus et al., (1983), this was a moment when progressive educational ideas and behaviorism were joined with measurement methods and Tyler's interest in using local objectives as the standard for comparison. They reported with approval the benefits of moving away from the more comparative, experimental approach pioneered by Rice to the less costly and disruptive use of internal comparisons – a perspective later echoed by Cronbach. At the same time, Lewin's ideas on use of experimentation in the form of action research as a practical means for social change were being formed. Note that both developments were seen as progressive by their proponents, yet they were in contradictory methodological directions.

Following World War Two, there was a boom in the US in many ways, including the growth of programs in housing, preventive health, urban development, and occupational training. At the same time international programs for family planning, health and nutrition, and rural development were also being mounted. Sociologists like Lazarsfeld (Rossi's mentor) were using large survey data sets to examine policy effects. There were technical advances in standardized testing, statistical principles for experimental design, and methods for conducting and analyzing large surveys. However, it was the end of the 1950s when things began to move rapidly for evaluation in the US. The Soviet Sputnik success in 1957 galvanized educational action, with national attention on new curricula in science and mathematics reflected in the National Defense Education Act. In educational evaluation, disillusionment with methods for evaluating curricula in a useful way began to surface by the early 1960s, while the more policy-oriented efforts to justify the vast outlays on Great Society programs were just taking off. By the end of the 1960s, many books on educational evaluation had come out with a new range of ideas responding to the perceived limitations of older approaches and coming largely from the experience of evaluators themselves (Scriven, Provus, Eisner, Stufflebeam, and Stake are examples). Suchman's (1967) promotion of Campbell's experimental approach was very influential in this period for large-scale policy evaluation, but by the early 1970s disillusion was setting in for these evaluators as well. House (1993) suggests that similar processes were unfolding in Canada and Britain, though with greater transfer of responsibility for policy-focused research to the government bureaucracies themselves.

Thus far we have portrayed a developmental process for the field of evaluation in which historical events and issues (like nineteenth-century reformism, early twentieth-century industrial capitalism, and the progressive education movement) have interacted with theoretical and methodological aspects of the developing social sciences (such as survey methods, experimental behaviorism applied to studies of incentives for workers, and refinement of psychometric methods). House (1993) added national ideological influences that shaped methodological and epistemological perspectives within the social sciences (leading to what he viewed as "scientism" throughout the social sciences with the exception of anthropology), and was careful to distinguish these ideological influences from those operating in other countries. Differing sources of funding are an important force in the story as well: the local classroom and curriculum research context funded by school districts was (until the 1930s) the setting for learning about educational evaluation, while the large, policy-oriented data sets of sociologists and public health professionals and the experimental designs of psychologists in the laboratory and workplace provided very different contexts. This difference became more pronounced in the 1960s when curriculum evaluations mushroomed with federal

requirements, but the funding was all channeled through local contracts, while other "Great Society" programs that were part of Johnson's War on Poverty contracted for evaluation at the federal level or were conducted within the government itself. For those working with local contracts (such as Stake), the press for a more qualitative, rich, and responsive approach was powerful, and British use of such methods became influential. For those working at the broader policy level, the press was for ways to justify the vast expenditures, find something meaningful, and channel the findings effectively into the policy-making process. Ideas from psychology were brought in to increase the causal conviction of findings; ideas from the study of organizational decision-making, political science, and policy studies were eagerly adapted to account for difficulties in converting evaluation findings to rational policy-making (shifting from the "sharply articulated" normative structure of economists to the "squishy" understandings of political scientists, as Cronbach et al., (1980) put it); systems-focused analysis was contrasted with goal-focused analysis (drawing on sociologist Etzioni, 1960); ethnographic methods from anthropology were introduced to add methodological gravitas to the informal development of qualitative case approaches (Knapp, 1979); and cost-benefit analysis was mainstreamed for many applications (Levin, 1975). In this way the 1970s were a coming-of-age for evaluation as a discipline, crystallizing the problems central to the field and the major alternatives for approaching answers out of the various contributing intellectual traditions and the "winnowing process" described by Shadish & Reichardt (1987).

It was in the 1980s, with a greater awareness of international applications of evaluation methods and a more multicultural vision within the US and the social sciences themselves, that real "paradigm wars" came to the surface. Social constructivism and critical theory were not so much about observational methods as they were about underlying purposes and power structures shaping evaluation itself. The importation of ideas during this period came from philosophy (House (e.g., House, 2004; House & Howe, 1999) using Rawls's notion of justice; Guba & Lincoln (e.g., 1981) detailing ontological and epistemological contrasts) and the wider world of social change movements, reflected particularly in the newer, international version of participatory action research (Fals Borda, 2001). Methodological sophistication was increased dramatically as computational resources made both quantitative (multivariate) analyses and, somewhat more recently, qualitative analyses feasible on a much larger scale. It was also in the 1980s that the resources for evaluation in the US and UK shifted and shrunk, as the political conservatism of the Reagan and Thatcher administrations altered the questions and the funding mechanisms. Perhaps the paradigm wars would have been less intense if everyone had stayed busier with continuing development of productive evaluation programs. By the time of the writing of this chapter, the refinement of the questions has continued, the sophistication of the dialog has matured, and the underlying controversies have themselves become part of the defining properties of the field.

The maturity of the field is also reflected in newer waves of cross-disciplinary influence. As evaluation has evolved as a transdiscipline and acquired its own conceptual bases (Cook & Shadish, 1986; Shadish et al., 1991), the reciprocity of intellectual influence has become more explicit. For example, the relatively well explored terrain of evaluation utilization can be connected to the logic modeling approach developed in evaluation, and the resulting schematic model can be used to draw on prior theory and research in a variety of social sciences dealing with influence and persuasion processes, including psychology, political science, and the sociology of organizational behavior (Henry & Mark, 2003; Mark & Henry, in press). This can improve evaluation practice and also generate new research on these processes. In addition to perennial controversies, the field draws strength from its enduring interaction with other disciplines, a reciprocal exchange likely to continue unless the field isolates itself in an academic niche of its own.

Examples from Practice

We have examined disciplinary and historical influences on the development and practice of evaluation, and now we turn to examples drawn from the literature: one from the US, the evaluation of Head Start, and two from the developing world, dealing with community health.

Intellectual Contexts for Head Start

Still contested, the role and effectiveness of one major US program in compensatory early childhood education, Head Start, illustrate the interplay of evaluation ideas and methods drawn from different sources. Table 9.2 summarizes the original evaluation. In the text we examine the colloquy of alternative perspectives drawn into the fray over time.

In reaction to the initial negative evaluation report, various critiques and defenses of the original findings erupted. These came from quantitatively sophisticated critics, program designers arguing over the choice of sample and outcome measures, and angry parents and local staff along with their academic sympathizers. Williams & Evans (1969), government staff with social science backgrounds who had designed the RFP, opined that the

EXEMPLAR 9.2   Evaluation of Head Start in the US

Background	Head Start emerged in 1965 as a major component of President Johnson's War on Poverty. Several fields contributed ideas to the design of the program, including public health, developmental psychology, and early childhood education, with a dominant theme of empowerment for poor children via improved life chances
Program features	Planned as a comprehensive education, health, and parent involvement program for qualifying poor children ages 4–5. Parents could hold jobs within the program itself, and could exercise some control over the program by serving on boards at the myriad local sites
Impetus for evaluation	The rapid mounting of the program and flow of federal funds to support it led to urgent calls for evaluation at the national level. A Request for Proposals (RFP) was developed and promulgated in 1968 to provide a very quick but comprehensive look at the effectiveness of Head Start
Plan for evaluation design	A post hoc design was mandated in which Head-Start-exposed children currently in first through third grade would be compared with demographically matched control children. The designated outcomes included cognitive and attitudinal effects, and the measures used in the study included three drawn from those with psychometric credibility for assessing cognitive aspects of academic readiness as well as three others designed by the investigators to assess the "attitude" effects, including teacher-rated achievement motivation in the classroom; self-esteem; and broader attitudes toward peers, school, home, and society
Influences on the design	The design grew out of the mix of social science expertise functioning to guide policy-oriented research at that time: quasi-experimental design approaches as put forward by Campbell & Stanley (1963) and promoted by Suchman (1967) along with the burgeoning use of sophisticated multivariate methods, particularly by economists (Campbell & Boruch, 1975), to statistically control unwanted sources of variance in natural policy experiments. The emphasis on cognitive effects was attributable to the central role of psychologists in selecting the outcome measures (Zigler & Muenchow, 1992)
Results	The results as reported showed no effects on the newly created attitude variables and a "weak" effect on one of the three cognitive outcomes for those in the longer-exposure version of the program. The executive summary concluded that these results were not impressive given the amount of tax dollars poured into the program
Policy impact	In 1968 the presidency in the US shifted from Johnson (a Democrat) to Nixon (a Republican), and social programs like Head Start were at risk. Preliminary findings from the evaluation were used by Nixon to cast doubt on the effectiveness of the program. Controversy ensued, reflecting and influencing various intellectual traditions associated with evaluation

basic problem was the tension between the intellectual context for the *development* of such programs (political pressures to please many constituencies) and the intellectual context for their *analysis*, i.e., evaluation (drawing on a management model developed for the Defense Department, emphasizing costs and measurable outcomes). Smith & Bissell (1970), educational researchers, challenged the methods and conclusions in the report and reanalyzed the data in a way that selected only the most promising parts of the sample and measures to produce somewhat stronger positive results. One of their major criticisms was of the sampling of sites and children, which began as a totally random, unstratified sample of all of the local programs but suffered many forms of attrition, making it impossible to generalize the findings. These critics also complained that the true spirit of the parent-empowering, capacity-building program was ignored in the evaluation. Another widely shared criticism was that the heterogeneity of the local programs was not conducive to a simple, universal impact study, and lent itself much more readily to a comparative design to identify the most effective strategies. Smith went on to conduct just such a study, with results seen as quite informative by Zigler & Muenchow (1992) but criticized by experimentalists Gilbert, Light, & Mosteller (1975) for being as untrustworthy as the original evaluation.

By far the most famous critique was initially put forward by Campbell & Erlebacher (1970) and elaborated by Campbell & Boruch (1975). Campbell & his co-authors patiently detailed the ways in which regression artifacts would inevitably distort the findings in studies not making use of random assignment, particularly risky because the comparison group would almost certainly be drawn from an initially higher-performing population than the intervention group, guaranteeing a negative distortion of the relative outcome for the intervention group. This critique has withstood the test of time, and is one of the major reverberating effects of the Head Start evaluation, influencing statistical methods as well as research design; when the stakes are high, the choice of a non-random comparison group strategy rather than a true experiment (or one of several other quasi-experimental methods less vulnerable to regression effects) will foreordain untrustworthy results, with potentially tragic consequences for the policy-making process. Campbell & Erlebacher (1970) lamented that although academics are prone to attribute bad policy decisions to the political process, "in this instance, the failure came from the inadequacies of the social science methodological community (including education, psychology, economics, and sociology) which as a population was not ready for this task" (p. 204). Reflecting on the history that led to the Head Start design, Campbell & Boruch (1975) mused that "It may be that Campbell and Stanley should feel guilty for having contributed to giving quasi-experimental designs a good name" (p. 202). Quite ecumenically, Campbell & Boruch (1975) also acknowledged the value of Scriven's modus operandi method in *ex post facto* situations; in their view it was clearly superior to the elegant quantitative strategy with its illusory scientific precision. For those who supported the value of Head Start at the local level, and their allies within academe, the entire episode fueled the distrust of quantitative scientific evaluation and added a bitter edge to the perception of a link between all applications claiming the mantle of science and an arrogant, insensitive, patriarchal "objectivity" leaving out the perspectives of those most affected by the program.

The reverberations from this history continue. In response to the Head Start fiasco, a Consortium for Longitudinal Studies was set up to track outcomes for children in 11 other preschool intervention programs for disadvantaged youth. Drawing on sophisticated multivariate methods, the results from these longitudinal investigations have proved substantially more supportive of the value of structured academic preparation (Spodek & Brown, 1993; Henry, 2002). Arguing for enhancement of the "rigor of education research," Whitehurst (2003), the Director of the Institute of Education Sciences at the US Department of Education, asserted that qualitative research should not be used to support causal conclusions and advocated for "randomized trials and experimental methods." (p. 25). On the other hand, warnings about policies driving the mis-measurement of cognitive outcomes for young children continue (e.g., Meisels, Steele, & Quinn-Leering, 1993), and Datta (2003a, 2003b) sounded an alarm for "unwarranted death by evaluation," using Head Start as a major example of this risk. From her standpoint the decision to use a randomized trial design for a newly commissioned study of Head Start was a terrible mistake because the randomly assigned control group would be contaminated by other daycare experiences. Influenced by a qualitative sociological perspective, Ellsworth & Ames (1998) and the authors of other chapters in their edited volume blamed entrenched views of the poor and culturally inappropriate research methods for undermining the evidence for the value of Head Start in the lives of poor women and children. In this they echoed the earlier warnings of Guttentag (1972) against a science by and for the elite.

In the United Kingdom a policy of positive discrimination for low income communities, referred to as Educational Priority Areas (EPAs), was implemented following the Plowden Report in 1967 (see Plowden, 1987). The EPA program, which had similarities to Head Start in the US, initially received widespread support. However, by the end of the 1970s the EPA program had virtually disappeared. One of the central reasons was the failure to generate strong research evidence for effectiveness (Smith, 1987). Concurrently the British government also funded a network of Community Development Projects in deprived communities, and these became seedbeds for radical, sometimes Marxist, critiques of such government programs.

The rationale for Head Start and similar educational interventions is contested, both academically and politically, and the intellectual contexts influencing those alternative visions also shape the debate about methods and measures for evaluation. Ideological conflicts run across the traditional disciplines, producing intra- as well as interdisciplinary contrasts. The urgency of the policy questions has produced a long train of conversation and debate, with effects on evaluation as well as on the disciplines contributing the contrasting ideas. Much of the interplay resulted from a confluence of events and forces that could not have been planned (Zigler & Muenchow, 1992), but the themes seem to have a cyclic resiliency.

Community Health in the Developing World

Next we turn to illustrations of evaluation traditions based outside North America, in developing countries. This is not a comprehensive review, as in Chapter 25; rather, we will use these examples to probe for alternative intellectual influences that may explain particular emphases in evaluations conducted outside highly industrialized contexts. In this review the concept of "decentering" is helpful, leading us beyond dominant, mainstream perspectives to identify emerging, innovative, and alternative perspectives that may be overlooked or under-represented in mainstream research literature. One proviso to this alternative starting point is that we have only reviewed evaluation reports in English that have been published in refereed journals. Another is that the very concept of modern evaluation evolved in the West and its adoption in the developing world is rooted in the history of colonial control and post-colonial emulation of Western traditions (Bhola, 2003).

For our examples we have defined developing countries as those that have low per capita income, low nutrition levels, and less developed health and welfare services. "Developing communities" also include indigenous and other minority ethnic groups in developed countries whose health and well-being profiles are similar to those in developing countries. These include, for example, Aboriginal communities in Australia, Maori people in New Zealand and First nation peoples in Canada. Health evaluations in developing countries and communities are usually focused on health topics or problems that have high salience for local or regional communities, such as prevention of HIV/AIDS through changes in sexual behavior, changing nutritional patterns, and developing village health care services.

Table 9.3 describes an exemplar of a health intervention evaluation with distinctive emphases derived from particular intellectual influences. The role of evaluation in a setting where local groups may resist implementation of health programs from outsiders, and challenge common underlying assumptions about the delivery of health programs, was described in an evaluation of a program to reduce coronary heart disease among residents in Australian coalfields, the "Community Health Heartbeat" (CHHB) program (Higginbotham et al., 1999).

Importance of Local Contexts and Cultures

The focus on understanding the local community and soliciting community involvement was a key component of this evaluation. "Public health interventions will fail to flourish in communities such as the Coalfields unless their strategies and messages somehow connect and resonate with cherished ideas and compelling local identities" (Higginbotham et al., 1999, p. 691). A powerful intellectual influence on this evaluation tradition is the work of Freire on "conscientization." For example, in a review of factors influencing sustainability in village health care programs in rural Cameroon (Freire-influenced), Eliason (1999) noted several key factors: community management of programs, financial self-reliance, village integrity in money management (no embezzlement of program funds), annual continuing education of health workers and continuing support from program staff. As with the example in Table 9.3, the Cameroon work highlights the emphasis on respect for local culture and context, linked to a participatory approach to program development and evaluation. An implication of this point is that external evaluators cannot design effective evaluations without incorporating "local knowledge."

Emphasis on Participatory Evaluations

More commonly than in the developed world, evaluators rely on and respect the contributions of the indigenous population to the evaluation. A recent review (Nichols, 2002) highlighted key aspects of participatory program planning, delivery and evaluation. Such approaches help empower participants by inclusion in decision-making processes, communication strategies, and program operations. Through ongoing involvement, participants develop a greater understanding of the purposes of the program, its structure, the stresses experienced by program administrators and staff, and diverse views among stakeholders, as well as enhanced knowledge and

EXEMPLAR 9.3 Evaluating community action for heart health in Australia

Background	The intervention program (Community Health Heartbeat) and its evaluation were based on a philosophy of "community activation" which was related to the concepts of "empowerment, participatory democracy and self-sustainment" (Higginbotham et al., 1999, p. 684)
Aims and objectives	The aim of the CHHB program was to reduce the prevalence of behavioral risk factors (e.g., dietary fat intake, cigarette smoking, low levels of exercise) which, in the long run, would lead to improved heart health and reduced mortality
Program features	The mechanism for bringing about the health behavior changes was the development of a self-sustaining community action group responsible for heart health
Evaluation strategy used	The evaluators drew substantially on earlier anthropological research. They used an ethnographic account of Australian mining communities (Metcalfe, 1988) to provide contextual information for their evaluation. In designing the evaluation, salient features of the community context included ". . . historical patterns of outsiders criticising the lifestyle of miners, an orientation toward communal rather than individual responsibility for health (i.e. community 'owned' emergency services and hospitals) and anger about risks from environmental hazards imposed by industrialists" (Higginbotham et al., 1999, p. 683)
	The initial data gathering for program implementation used a mail-administered community needs survey covering degree of worry about 17 issues (e.g., crime, drugs, money, having a heart attack) and a health ideology questionnaire. The outcome measures used were suspected coronary events registered in all local hospitals and scrutiny of death certificates. The evaluation aimed to document the nature and sustainability of heart health activities undertaken, as well as trends in risk factor levels and rates of coronary events in the Coalfields, in comparison with nearby regions
Results	Outcome data showed a significant reduction in case fatality for Coalfields men while changes in risk factors levels were comparable with surrounding areas. Positive responses to the program by schools, heart attack survivors, and women interested in body maintenance were related to the meaning these subgroups found in health promotion discourses based on their embodied experiences. The researchers developed an understanding of local cultural and contextual information that led to effective involvement of the local communities in planning the intervention and evaluation activities

EXEMPLAR 9.4   Evaluating AIDS risk reduction in the Phillipines

Background	Both the program and the evaluation design were intended to empower the community participants "through the realization of their own capabilities to be researchers and to induce desired changes in their communities" (Morisky et al., 2004, p. 70)
Aims and objectives	The intervention was intended to reduce AIDS-risk associated with commercial sex
Program features	The primary participants were the male clients of commercial sex workers, including such groups as the military, police and firemen, industrial workers, and pedicab drivers. Peer counselors were selected from each of the groups and trained to deliver the HIV/AIDS program to their peers. They also helped to develop the intervention resources (posters, stickers, and photonovella – picture story presentations of common situations and events)
Evaluation strategy used	The study used a creative mixed-method evaluation, involving both participatory action research and a crossover experimental design. The trained peer counselors participated in collection of baseline data, reviewed frequencies, and requested cross-tabulations (attitudes to condoms, condom use)
Results	The outcomes indicated a significant increase in condom use and knowledge of HIV/AIDS. The counselors themselves showed the greatest improvements in safe sex behaviors, supporting the effectiveness of their participation in the intervention and its evaluation (Morisky et al., 2004)

skills relevant to the program's goals (Nichols, 2002, p. 2).

Table 9.4 presents another evaluation reflecting emphases that are common in health program evaluation in the developing world. The example in Table 9.4 illustrates how participants can become involved in the program planning and delivery as well as collection of information for assessing the program impacts. Other projects have reported similar participatory programs and evaluations, such as one targeting perinatal health in Turkey (Turan et al., 2003). Of course, a participatory approach is also widely advocated in the US (e.g., Cousins & Whitmore, 1998; Greene, 1988), but the influences of both historical realities and academic traditions in the developing world have made this theme a more dominant one there.

Focus on Cost-Effectiveness and Systems Change

In most developing countries, resources for service provision and evaluations are scarce. It is essential to have policy analysis and cost effectiveness factors on the agenda when designing interventions. As in developed countries, those making decisions about health services funding may often prefer to provide facilities and equipment, rather than investing in health promotion activities that may not have high visibility or the associated status and impressive visual evidence for politicians and funding agencies. Given the devastating effects of diseases such as HIV/AIDS in many regions, and the cost-effectiveness of using primary prevention strategies, it is not surprising that there are a considerable number of evaluations on these topics to justify and validate a high priority for a primary prevention approach. Examples include evaluations of programs to address HIV/AIDS in Africa (Patel et al., 2002), sex education in Chile (Silva & Ross, 2003), and workplace health promotion programs in countries such as Costa Rica and Spain (Peltomäki et al., 2003). Evaluations of health promotion programs and policies are of necessity tied to the mechanisms available in developing countries for large-scale influence on health behaviors. Typically they focus on promoting change through groups, organizations, and networks rather than through individual behavior change, as in Eliason's (1999) identification of community management of health programs and financial self-reliance as predictors of sustainability in village health care programs in rural Cameroon.

Influences on Community Health Evaluations in the Developing World

Beyond the range of publication outlets for evaluation in the US and the rest of the developed world, researchers conducting evaluations in developing countries use and contribute to an extensive and diverse set of published resources. We discerned two common patterns among the authors of studies reviewed for this section. Many of the research groups who authored the evaluation reports had academic affiliations across multiple institutions, including both authors from "western" academic institutions and those from "local" academic institutions in the country where the evaluation was conducted. One might surmise that this combination allowed the integration of local needs, contexts, and intervention styles with evaluation design traditions common in western institutions. This point reflects the importance of decentering, referred to earlier. The second point is the relatively high proportion of authors working for international aid agencies. We have observed that the experience of working across several countries seems likely to foster the development of a pragmatic, culture-sensitized approach to evaluation traditions that is consistent with ensuring positive outcomes from interventions. Largely absent from this literature is debate about paradigms, which, as we have noted, is relatively common among evaluation specialists in the larger western countries. While it is likely that many evaluators working in academic or applied settings in developing countries learned their evaluation strategies in western academic settings, what they have used clearly reflects pragmatic eclecticism and synthetic activism in response to local needs.

None of the themes described in this section is unfamiliar to evaluators in the developed world, but the implication of the studies cited is that these themes are more central in places where there is pervasive recognition of culture–power tensions underlying mechanisms associated with causes and solutions for public health problems. Comfort with a full range of qualitative and quantitative methods is essential in order to be responsive to the demands of the circumstances, and the narrow traditions of the social sciences have been less restrictive as distance from ivy-covered walls has increased. Ethnography explores the cultural context that informs stakeholder concerns and program fit, interviews and documents may indicate the ways in which community capacity for self-reliance has been enhanced, and epidemiology tracks the broad health impacts of community-wide preventive interventions.

Lessons from Case Examples

Disciplinary traditions are often quite companionable, for example the psychometric emphasis on high-quality measurement, the experimental design emphasis on internal validity for causal inferences, and the multivariate econometric emphasis on controlling statistically for extraneous variance. On the other hand, ideological differences within a single field can yield intractable oppositions rather than engaging dialectics. In the developing world the underlying issues seem quite similar but the emphases have been altered by the differing role of culture, the profound force of colonial history, the urgent needs of the populace, and the influence of all three on the development of social science traditions. Because our case examples draw on large bodies of published evidence they do not reflect so well the role of intellectual context influences on small, every-day evaluations of the sort done in mental health centers, curriculum research organizations, local social service agencies, and other environments where modest means are used to produce small-scale evaluation reports for local consumption. Cumulative patterns in these settings may show that particular "spheres of influence" (e.g., psychology for mental health, education for curriculum evaluation) are dominant in those contexts and less subject to interdisciplinary enrichment in the short run.

Conclusions

This chapter has highlighted the ways in which pre-existing disciplines, historical and cultural circumstances, and their interplay, have provided "intellectual contexts" in which evaluation ideas and methods have developed and to which they have in turn contributed. We have provided a number of illustrations, in the lives of individuals, in the written sources reflecting the evolution of evaluation as a field, and in examples of evaluation practice, of the role of reciprocal influence, the value of interdisciplinary exchange, and the unique contributions of those who have transcended (and in some cases rebelled against) their disciplinary bases while still preserving essential perspectives drawn from those backgrounds. No simple linear model can capture the ways in which intellectual contexts of origin have played a role shaping the field, and indeed those origin contexts have histories of internal conflict and evolution themselves.

It should be clear that the academic sources on which evaluation has drawn have certainly not been limited to the social sciences. As we have suggested, many other disciplines have also played a role (statistics, logic, history, philosophical explorations of justice, professional fields like education, public administration, and the law, e.g.), and ideas have come from elsewhere as well (e.g., the connoisseurship model of Eisner (see Alkin, 2004; Shaw, 1999), drawn from traditions of criticism in the arts). In the US, forums like EVALTALK (a widely subscribed list server for evaluators operated under the auspices of the American Evaluation Association) have promoted interchanges far beyond those available in traditional journal contexts. For example, the international contributions to the conversation, particularly from Australasia, have been prominent, presaging the growing role of global cross-fertilization in the field. For another example, the application of curriculum evaluation methods to an innovative high-school physics curriculum has brought

US physicists into the conversation. After a plenary address by an anthropologist at a 2002 conference, there was a lengthy discussion on the list of the varying roles anthropological traditions have played in evaluation, including acknowledgment that there is a non-academic, activist strain in anthropology (though less visible in Britain) that may have particular relevance for evaluation in the developing countries. The examples are endless.

At present, the problems and controversies that define the field have become relatively stable, although history suggests that major changes in economic incentives can powerfully alter where the conceptual and methodological lenses are focused. Receptive interaction with other disciplines, rather than a one-way course of influence or relative isolation, seems to characterize the current process of change, with alternative ideological perspectives on science's connection to power persistent in their friction.

Here are some important lessons we distill from our review:

1. Intellectual traditions are pervasive in their influence; the definition of problems, links to prior work and ideas, search for methods, interactions with others involved, activities in the process of evaluation, concluding steps to make the work useful, and philosophical assumptions undergirding all of this, come from somewhere. At this point in the evolution of the field of evaluation, the "somewheres" are often within evaluation itself, but they have historically been elsewhere and there continue to be a variety of dialogs between intellectual traditions within and outside the domain loosely defined as "evaluation as a field."

2. Although historically certain disciplines have been linked to certain evaluation contexts, each of these traditions brings strong and useful perspectives to the engagement with any given evaluation situation. There is no single dimension along which these traditions may be arrayed, nor is there an easy way to say when a particular perspective is the best. It is exciting to juxtapose them because they do bring such varied points of leverage to the task of evaluation.

3. In many cases it is possible to imagine useful combinations of the traditions in a single project, but there are inherent contradictions at a fundamental level, incorporating generations of intellectual and practical experience that cannot easily leap the roadbeds dictated by hard-won wisdom. Like all traditions, these cultures of praxis are proudly maintained; complementary perspectives are welcomed as adjuncts when not rejected outright. Evidence for the advantages of a particular approach is readily generated within the epistemological context of that approach.

4. Despite this, most traditions do lend themselves to combinations in compatible groupings. In much of evaluation practice, a complex interweaving of compatible subsets of intellectual contexts is the rule, with evaluation- specific theory (both espoused and in-use) guiding practice.

5. Frequently influence reverberates and topics studied within a related discipline (e.g., psychology, education, sociology, statistics) are seen differently as a result of evaluation work (and the team effort that connects multiple perspectives to that work).

On the basis of these observations it would be foolhardy to say that in the future evaluation will be problem-driven, or discipline-driven, or economically driven, or culturally driven – all have interacted and will continue to do so. Assimilation and accommodation are likely to continue into the future as evaluation draws its practitioners and theorists from a variety of backgrounds, enlarging its own now-substantial knowledge base with creative adaptations of methods and theories emanating from many sources. Training for that future calls for emphasis on evolving discipline-based strengths, knowledge and skills from the evaluation trans-discipline, and a flexibility of perspective and skills to engage in a dynamic team approach to problem-solving. A bit of the iconoclast and the puzzle-lover might help too.

Note

1. For more extensive treatment of these figures and many more, see Alkin (2004) and Shadish et al., (1991). For a qualitatively informed perspective on many of the same figures, see Shaw (1999). We are greatly indebted to these sources.

References

Alkin, M. C. (ed.) (2004). *Evaluation Roots*. Thousand Oaks, CA: Sage.

Alkin, M. C. & Christie, C. A. (2004). An evaluation theory tree. In M. C. Alkin (ed.) *Evaluation Roots* (pp. 12–65). Thousand Oaks, CA: Sage.

Atkinson, P., Delamont, S., & Hammersley, M. (1988). Qualitative research traditions: A British response to Jacob. *Review of Educational Research*, 58(2), 231–250.

Bhola, H. S. (2003). Social and cultural contexts of educational evaluation: A global perspective. In T. Kellaghan & D. L. Stufflebeam (eds) *International Handbook of Educational Evaluation* (pp. 397–415). Dordrecht: Kluwer.

Boruch, R. F. (2004). A trialist's notes on evaluation theory and roots. In M. C. Alkin (ed.) *Evaluation Roots* (pp. 114–121). Thousand Oaks, CA: Sage.

Campbell, D. T. (1969). Reforms as experiments. *American Psychologist*, 24, 409–429.

Campbell, D. T. (1974). Qualitative knowing in action research. Kurt Lewin Memorial Award Address, Society for the Psychological Study of Social Issues, presented at the 82nd annual meeting of the American Psychological Association, New Orleans, September.

Campbell, D. T. & Boruch, R. F. (1975). Making the case for randomized assignment to treatments by considering the alternatives: Six ways in which quasi-experimental evaluations in compensatory education tend to underestimate effects. In C. A. Bennett & L. A. Lumsdaine (eds)

Evaluation and Experiment: Some critical issues in assessing social programs (pp. 195–296). New York: Academic Press.

Campbell, D. T. & Erlebacher, A. (1970). How regression artifacts in quasi-experimental evaluations can mistakenly make compensatory education look harmful. In J. Hellmuth (ed.) *Disadvantaged Child, Volume 3: Compensatory Education, a National Debate* (pp. 185–210). NY: Brunner/Mazel.

Campbell, D. T. & Stanley, J. T. (1963) *Experimental and Quasi-experimental Designs for Research*. Chicago: Rand McNally.

Cook, T. D. & Reichardt, C. S. (eds) (1979). *Qualitative and Quantitative Methods in Evaluation Research*. Beverly Hills, CA: Sage.

Cook, T. D. & Shadish, W. R. (1986). Program evaluation: the worldly science. *Annual Review of Psychology*, 37, 193–232.

Cottrell, L. S. Jr., (1967). Foreword. In E. A. Suchman (ed.), *Evaluative Research* (pp. vii–viii). New York: Russell Sage Foundation.

Cousins, J. B. & Whitmore, E. (1998). Framing participatory evaluation. *New Directions in Evaluation*, 80, 5–23.

Cronbach, L. J. (1957). The two disciplines of scientific psychology. *American Psychologist*, 64, 671–684.

Cronbach, L. J. (1975). Beyond the two disciplines of scientific psychology. *American Psychologist*, 30, 116–127.

Cronbach, L. J. (1982). *Designing Evaluations of Educational and Social Programs*. San Francisco: Jossey-Bass.

Cronbach, L. J., Ambron, S. R., Dornbusch, S. M., Hess, R. D., Hornik, R. C., Phillips, D. C., Walker, D. F., & Weiner, S. S. (1980). *Toward Reform of Program Evaluation*. San Francisco: Jossey-Bass.

Cyert, R. M. & March, J. G. (1963). *Behavioral Theory of the Firm*. Englewood Cliffs, NJ: Prentice-Hall.

Datta, L. (2003a). The evaluation profession and the government. In T. Kellaghan, D. L. Stufflebeam & L. A. Wingate (eds) *International Handbook of Educational Evaluation* (pp. 345–359). Boston: Kluwer.

Datta, L. (2003b). Avoiding unwarranted death by evaluation. *The Evaluation Exchange*, IX(2), 5.

Eliason, R. N. (1999). Toward sustainability in village health care in rural Cameroon. *Health Promotion International*, 14(4), 301–306.

Ellsworth, J. & Ames, L. J. (eds) (1998). *Critical Perspectives on Project Head Start: Revisioning the hope and challenge*. Albany, NY: SUNY Press.

Etzioni, A. (1960). Two approaches to organizational analysis: A critique and a suggestion. *Administrative Science Quarterly*, V(2), 257–278.

Fals Borda, O. (2001). Participatory (Action) Research in social theory: Origins and challenges. In P. Reason & H. Bradbury (eds) *Handbook of Action research* (pp. 27–37). London: Sage.

Finison, L. J. (1986). The psychological insurgency, 1936–1945. *Journal of Social Issues*, 42(1), 21–23.

Gilbert, J. P., Light, R. J., & Mosteller, F. (1975). Assessing social innovations: An empirical base for policy. In C. A. Bennett & L. A. Lumsdaine (eds). *Evaluation and Experiment: Some critical issues in assessing social programs* (pp. 39–193). New York: Academic Press.

Greene, J. C. (2004). The educative evaluator: An interpretation of Lee J. Cronbach's vision of evaluation. In M. C. Alkin (ed.) *Evaluation Roots* (pp. 169–180). Thousand Oaks, CA: Sage.

Greene, J. C. & Henry, G. (2003). The dialectic of quantitative-qualitative distinctions in evaluation theory and practice. Debate chaired by G. Julnes at the Annual Meeting of the American Evaluation Association, Reno, NV, November 5.

Greene, J. C. (1998). Stakeholder participation and utilization in program evaluation. *Evaluation Review*, 12(3), 91–116.

Guba, E. G. & Lincoln, Y. S. (1981). *Effective Evaluation*. San Francisco: Jossey-Bass.

Guba, E. G. & Lincoln, Y. S. (2004). Competing paradigms in qualitative research: Theories and issues. In S. N. Hesse-Biber & P. Leavy (eds) *Approaches to Qualitative Research: A Reader on theory and practice* (pp. 17–38). New York: Oxford University Press.

Guttentag, M. (1972). Children in Harlem's community-controlled schools. *Journal of Social Issues*, 28(4), 1–20.

Hamilton, D., Jenkins, D., King, C., MacDonald, B., & Parlett, M. (eds) (1977). *Beyond the Numbers Game*. London: Macmillan.

Harris, B. (1986). Reviewing 50 years of the psychology of social issues. *Journal of Social Issues*, 42(1), 1–20.

Henry, G. T. (2002). Review of "Transparency, stakeholder involvement, and explanation in contemporary evaluation: A review essay stimulated by Success in Early Intervention: The Chicago Child-Parent Centers edited by Arthur J. Reynolds. *American Journal of Evaluation*, 23(2), 235–244.

Henry, G. T. & Mark, M. M. (2003). Beyond use: Understanding evaluation's influence on attitudes and actions. *American Journal of Evaluation*, 24(3), 293–314.

Higginbotham, N., Heading, G., McElduff, P., Dobson, A., & Heller, R. (1999). Reducing coronary heart disease in the Australian Coalfields: evaluation of a 10-year community intervention. *Social Science & Medicine*, 48, 683–692.

House, E. R. (1993). *Professional Evaluation: Social impact and political consequences*. Newbury Park, CA: Sage.

House, E. R. (2004). Intellectual history in evaluation. In M. C. Alkin (ed.) *Evaluation Roots* (pp. 218–224). Thousand Oaks, CA: Sage.

House, E. R. & Howe, K. R. (1999) *Values in Evaluation and Social Research*. Thousand Oaks, CA: Sage.

Julnes, G., Mark, M. M., & Henry, G. T. (1998). Promoting realism in evaluation. *Evaluation*, 4, 483–504.

Kellaghan, T., Stufflebeam, D. L., & Wingate, L. A. (2003). Introduction. In T. Kellaghan & D. L. Stufflebeam (eds) *International Handbook of Educational Evaluation* (pp. 1–6). Dordrecht: Kluwer.

Knapp, M. S. (1979) Ethnographic contributions to evaluation research. In T. D. Cook & C. S. Reichardt (eds) *Qualitative and Quantitative Methods in Evaluation Research* (pp. 118–139). Beverly Hills, CA: Sage.

Kushner, S. (2000) *Personalizing Evaluation*. Thousand Oaks, CA: Sage.

Kushner, S. (2002). I'll take mine neat: Multiple methods but a single methodology. *Evaluation*, 8(2), 249–258.

Levin, H. M. (1975). Cost-effectiveness evaluation in evaluation research. In M. Guttentag & E. L. Struening (eds) *Handbook of Evaluation Research*, Vol. 2 (pp. 89–122). Beverly Hills, CA: Sage.

Leviton, L. C. (2003). Scholarship, policy, and personal development at Northwestern. *The American Journal of Evaluation*, 24(2), 277–280.

Lincoln, Y. S. & Guba, E. G. (1985). *Naturalistic Inquiry*. Beverly Hills: Sage.

Lindblom, C. E. (1968). *The Policy-Making Process*. Englewood Cliffs, NJ.

Madaus, G. F. (2004) Ralph W. Tyler's contribution to program evaluation. In M. C. Alkin (ed.) *Evaluation Roots* (pp. 69–79). Thousand Oaks, CA: Sage.

Madaus, G. F., Stufflebeam, D. L., & Scriven, M. S. (1983). Program evaluation: A historical overview. In G. F. Madaus, M. S. Scriven & Stufflebeam, D. L. (eds) *Evaluation Models: Viewpoints on educational and human services evaluation* (pp. 3–22). Boston: Kluwer-Nijhoff.

March, J. G. & Simon, H. W. (1958). *Organizations.* New York: Wiley.

Mark, M. M. & Henry, G. T. (in press). The mechanisms and outcomes of evaluation influence. *Evaluation.*

McAdams, D. P. (1988). *Power, Intimacy, and the Life Story.* New York: The Guilford Press

McCall, W. A. (1923). *How to Experiment in Education.* New York: McMillan.

Meisels, S. J., Steele, D. M., & Quinn-Leering, K. (1993). Testing, tracking, and retaining young children: An analysis of research and social policy. In B. Spodek (ed.) *Handbook of Research on the Education of Young Children* (pp. 279–292). New York: Macmillan.

Metcalfe, A. (1988). *For Freedom and Dignity: Historical agency and class in the coalfields of NSW.* Sydney: Allen and Unwin.

Morisky, D. E., Ang, A., Coly, A., & Tiglao, R. V. (2004). A model HIV/AIDS risk reduction program in the Philippines: a comprehensive community-based approach through participatory action research. *Health Promotion International,* 19(1), 69–76.

Nichols, L. (2002). Participatory program evaluation: including program participants and evaluators. *Evaluation and Program Planning,* 25, 1–14.

Patel, M., Allen, K. B., Keatley, R., & Jonsson, U. (2002). Introduction. *Evaluation and Program Planning,* 25, 317–327.

Patton, M. Q. (1997). *Utilization-Focused Evaluation.* Thousand Oaks, CA: Sage.

Patton, M. Q. (2004). The roots of utilization-focused evaluation. In M. C. Alkin (ed.) *Evaluation Roots* (pp. 276–292). Thousand Oaks, CA: Sage.

Pawson, R. & Tilley, N. (1997). *Realistic Evaluation.* Thousand Oaks, CA: Sage.

Peltomäki, P., Johansson, M., Ahrens, W., Sala, M., Wesseling, C., Brenes, F., et al. (2003). Social context for workplace health promotion: feasibility considerations in Costa Rica, Finland, Germany, Spain and Sweden. *Health Promotion International,* 18(2), 115–126.

Plowden, B. (1987). "Plowden" twenty years on. *Oxford Review of Education,* 13(1), 119–124.

Rosenthal, E. J. (1973). Evaluation history. In S. B. Anderson, S. Ball, R. T. Murphy, et al. (eds) *Encyclopedia of Educational Evaluation* (pp. 140–146). San Francisco: Jossey-Bass.

Rosenwein, R. E. & Campbell, D. T. (1992). Mobilization to achieve collective action and democratic majority/plurality amplification. *Journal of Social Issues,* 48(2), 125–138.

Rossi, P. H. (2004). My views of evaluation and their origins. In M. C. Alkin (ed.) *Evaluation Roots* (pp. 122–131). Thousand Oaks, CA: Sage.

Rossi, P. H., Lipsey, M. W., & Freeman, H. E. (2004). *Evaluation: A systematic approach.* Thousand Oaks, CA: Sage.

Schooler, C. (2003) Reflections of a sociological social psychologist. *APS Observer,* 16(2), 17–19.

Scriven, M. (1974). Maximizing the power of causal investigations: The modus operandi method. In W. J. Popham (ed.) *Evaluation in Education: Current applications* (pp. 68–84) Berkley, CA: McCutchan.

Scriven, M. (1993). The nature of evaluation. *New Directions for Program Evaluation,* 58, 5–48.

Scriven, M. (2001). Evaluation: Future tense. *American Journal of Evaluation,* 22(3), 301–307.

Scriven, M. (2003). Evaluation theory and metatheory. In T. Kellaghan & D. L. Stufflebeam (eds) *International Handbook of Educational Evaluation* (pp. 15–30). Dordrecht: Kluwer.

Scriven, M. (2004). Reflections. In M. C. Alkin (ed.) *Evaluation Roots* (pp. 183–195). Thousand Oaks, CA: Sage.

Shadish, W. R. & Luellen, J. K. (2004). Donald Campbell: The accidental evaluator. In M. C. Alkin (ed.) *Evaluation Roots* (pp. 80–87). Thousand Oaks, CA: Sage.

Shadish, W. R. & Reichardt, C. S. (1987) The intellectual foundations of social program evaluation: The development of evaluation theory. In W. R. Shadish & C. S. Reichardt (eds) *Evaluation Studies Review Annual,* Vol. 12 (pp. 13–30). Newbury Park, CA: Sage.

Shadish, W. R., Cook, T. D., & Leviton, L. C. (1991). *Foundations of Program Evaluation: Theories of practice.* Newbury Park, CA: Sage.

Shaw, I. F. (1999). *Qualitative Evaluation.* London: Sage.

Silva, M. & Ross, I. (2003). Evaluation of a school-based sex education program for low income male high school students in Chile. *Evaluation and Program Planning,* 26, 1–9.

Silverman, D. (ed.) (1997). *Qualitative Research: Theory, method, and practice.* London: Sage.

Singer, J. A. (1997). *Message in a Bottle.* New York: The Free Press.

Smith, G. (1987). Whatever happened to educational priority areas? *Oxford Review of Education,* 13(1), 23–38.

Smith, M. S. & Bissell, J. S. (1970). Report analysis: The impact of Head Start. *Harvard Educational Review,* 40(1), 51–104.

Spodek, B. & Brown, P. C. (1993) Curriculum alternatives in early childhood education: A historical perspective. In B. Spodek (ed.) *Handbook of Research on the Education of Young Children* (pp. 91–104). New York: Macmillan.

Stake, R. E. (1974) Program evaluation, particularly responsive evaluation. Reproduced in W. B. Dockrell & D. Hamilton (eds) *Rethinking Educational Research* (1980). London: Hodder and Stoughton.

Stake, R. (2004). Stake and responsive evaluation. In M. C. Alkin (ed.) *Evaluation Roots* (pp. 203–217). Thousand Oaks, CA: Sage.

Steinitz, V. & Mishler, E. G. (2001) Reclaiming SPSSI's radical promise: A critical look at JSI's "Impact of Welfare Reform" issue. *Analyses of Social Issues and Public Policy,* 1(1), 163–173.

Struening, E. L. & Guttentag, M. (1975). *Handbook of Evaluation Research,* Vol 1. Beverly Hills: Sage.

Stufflebeam, D. L., Foley, W. J., Gephart, W. J., Guba, E. G., Hammond, R. L., Merriman, H. O. & Provus, M. M. (1971). *Educational Evaluation and Decision-Making.* Itasca, IL: Peacock.

Suchman, E. A. (1967). *Evaluative Research: Principles and practice in public service and social action programs.* New York: Russell Sage Foundation.

Turan, J. M., Say, L., Güngör, A. K., Demarco. R. & Azgan, S. Y. (2003). Community participation for perinatal health in Istanbul. *Health Promotion International,* 18(1), 25–32.

Unger, R. K. (1986). Looking toward the future by looking at the past: Social activism and social history. *Journal of Social Issues,* 42(1), 215–227.

Weiss, C. H. (ed.) (1972a). *Evaluating Action Programs: Readings in social action and education.* Boston: Allyn & Bacon.

Weiss, C. H. (1972b). *Evaluation Research: Methods of assessing program effectiveness.* Englewood Cliffs, NJ: Prentice-Hall.

Weiss, C. H. (2004). Rooting for evaluation: A Cliff Notes version of my work. In M. C. Alkin (ed.) *Evaluation Roots* (pp. 153–168). Thousand Oaks, CA: Sage.

Whitehurst, G. J. (2003). Rigor, relevance, and utilization. *APS Observer,* 16(12), 1, 25–26.

Wholey, J. S. (1979). *Evaluation: Promise and performance.* Washington, DC: Urban Institute.

Wholey, J. S. (1987). Evaluability assessment: Developing program theory. *New Directions for Program Evaluation,* 33, 77–92.

Wholey, J. S. (1994). Assessing the usefulness of evaluation. In J. S. Wholey, H. P. Hatry & K. E. Newcomer (eds) *Handbook of Practical Program Evaluation* (pp. 15–39). San Francisco: Jossey-Bass.

Wholey, J. S. (2004). Using evaluation to improve performance and support policy decision making. In M. C. Alkin (ed.) *Evaluation Roots* (pp. 267–275). Thousand Oaks, CA: Sage.

Williams, W. & Evans, J. W. (1969). The politics of evaluation: The case of Head Start. *The Annals of the American Academy of Political and Social Science,* 385, 118–132.

Wilmoth, G. H. (2001) The "honest broker" role and evaluation research affirmed. *Analyses of Social Issues and Public Policy,* 1(1), 195–205.

Worthen, B. R. & Sanders, J. R. (1973). *Educational Evaluation: Theory and practice.* Worthington, OH: Charles A. Jones.

Zigler, E. & Muenchow, S. (1992). *Head Start: The inside story of America's most successful educational experiment.* New York: Basic Books.

10

THE RELATIONSHIP BETWEEN EVALUATION AND POLITICS

Ove Karlsson Vestman and Ross F. Conner

Evaluation is a young discipline that, according to Pawson & Tilly (1997), has passed its adolescence. If evaluation is now in its adulthood, it is reasonable to consider whom evaluation should have as its "life partner" or "partners." The evaluation family traditionally has included good researchers with their ideal of neutral, objective research as the prototype for evaluation and these partners in the evaluation enterprise have been recognized with awards and high status. Evaluation work, however, is always couched within a political context, and this reality brings different kinds of partners into the relationship. These partners, including politicians and policy-makers, often make the evaluation family uneasy. There has been a basic conception that evaluation (and similarly research) becomes adulterated when it mixes with politics. Generally the discussion is permeated by a negative view of politics. Politics conjures up images of trouble, disruption, and even violence, on the one hand, and deceit, manipulation and lies, on the other. It is less common to see a positive or at least neutral view of politics as an important and inevitable part of human life and interaction.

If politics and evaluation are destined to be "life partners" in the adulthood of evaluation, then what forms could the relationship take – marriage, cohabitation or living apart? This chapter will consider some of these possibilities.

Definitions of Evaluation and Politics

"Evaluation" refers to the process of determining the merit, worth, or value of something (Scriven, 1991). The evaluation process involves identifying relevant values or standards that apply to what is being evaluated, performing empirical investigation using techniques from the social sciences, and then integrating conclusions with the standards into an overall evaluation or set of evaluations. The first step in the process, the identification of relevant standards and values to apply to what is being evaluated, has to do with what partners involved in the evaluation see as relevant in the particular case. Should the priority be, for example, on economical, educational, social, ethnic, or democratic standards and values? Making these choices is an exercise of power that connects evaluation to politics. That is an interpretation in line with Hammersley (1995), who says that politics has to do with the use of power and that it also concerns making value judgments and taking actions on the basis of them.

According to Caro (1977), evaluation must fulfill two purposes – information and judgment. The former fits well with the research community's traditional epistemological perspective, whereas making judgments does not. Social research's aim, traditionally and in a narrow sense, is limited exclusively to producing knowledge but not to producing value judgments or evaluative conclusions. There has also been considerable debate about which models should be adopted for making judgments. One strategy is to treat judgments as technical measurements, in order to avoid involving values with their attendant political implications. It is precisely at this juncture, however, where evaluation and politics are related. Both are concerned with values, value judgments, and value conflicts in public life. The reality is that evaluation, in order to fulfill its second purpose of making judgments, cannot avoid the issue of politics.

Politics – a Contested Concept

Politics has been defined in many ways. One could say that politics is regarded as an "essentially contested" concept (Gallie, 1956), in that there are controversies about the term so deep that no neutral or settled definition can ever be developed. In effect, a single term (like "politics," or "evaluation," for that matter) can represent a number of rival concepts, none of which can be accepted as its "true" meaning. For example, it is equally legitimate to define politics as what concerns the state, as the conduct of public life, as debate and conciliation, and as the distribution of power and resources. On the basis of Lasswell (1936), politics is about who gets what, when, and how. The "when" and "how" aspect of politics is put forward by Heywood (2002), who sees politics in its broadest sense as "the activity through which people make, preserve and amend the general rules under which they live" (p. 4). The activities are formed into institutions in Dahl's (1984) definition of politics as "any persistent pattern of human relationships that involves, to a significant extent, control, influence, power or authority" (pp. 9–10). Politics, however, is not just activities (decisions on allocation of recourses, organization of institutions, etc.). Easton (1968) argues that politics is the authoritative allocation of values for a society, and that politics essentially is making moral decisions about what is good and what is bad. This definition places politics close to that definition of evaluation which emphasizes evaluation as the production of information together with the production of judgment.

From a Narrow to a Broad Definition

Heywood (2002) presents some illustrative views of politics that can be taken as a point of departure for elaborating the picture of politics. In the narrowest sense, politics can be treated as the equivalent of party politics. Here, politics is restricted to those state actors who are consciously motivated by ideological beliefs and who seek to advance these beliefs through membership in a formal organization such as a political party. This view can be expanded to see politics as the art of government. Here, politics is what takes place within a system of social organization centered upon the machinery of government. More broadly, politics can be associated with formal or authoritative decisions that establish a plan of action for the community. This means that most people, most institutions, and most social activities can be regarded as being "outside" politics and the policy cycle through which politics and governance takes its form. The politicians are described as "political," whereas civil servants are seen as "non-political," as long as they act in a neutral and professional fashion. Similarly, evaluators are taken to be "non-political" figures when they interpret and value the evaluand (a program or a policy, e.g.) impartially and in accordance with the collected information. From this perspective, evaluators may be accused of being political, however, if personal preferences or some other form of bias influences their judgments.

According to Heywood, this definition can be broadened by taking politics beyond the narrow realm of government and viewing politics as public affairs. From this viewpoint, politics is understood as an ethical activity concerned with creating a "just society." Even if one regards institutions such as businesses, community groups, clubs, trade unions, and also evaluation, as "public," this broader perspective still remains a restricted view of politics in that it does not, and should not, infringe upon personal affairs and institutions. This view is illustrated, for example, by the tendency of politicians to draw a clear distinction between their professional conduct and their personal or domestic behavior. By classifying, say, cheating on their partners or treating their children badly as personal matters, they are able to deny the political significance of such behavior on the grounds that it does not touch on their conduct of public affairs.

Critical thinkers, in particular feminists, have pointed out that this implies that politics still stops at the front door, that it does not take place in the family, in domestic life, or in personal relationships – a view these and other critical thinkers disagree with. This kind of critique takes us to the broadest view on politics, which is also the most radical. Rather than confining politics to a particular sphere (the government, the state or the "public" realm), this view sees politics at work in all social activities and in every corner of human existence. Politics takes place at every level of social interaction; it can be found within families and among small groups of friends just as much as among nations and on the global stage. What makes politics a distinctive activity, distinguishable from any other form of social behavior, is that politics at its broadest concerns the production, distribution, and use of resources in the course of social existence. Politics is power: the ability to achieve a desired outcome, through whatever means. The essential ingredient is the existence of scarcity: the simple fact that, while human needs and desires are infinite, the resources available to satisfy them are always limited. From this perspective, politics is seen as a struggle over scarce resources, and power as the means through which this struggle is conducted, says Heywood.

Conflict and Consensus

From the discussion thus far, it is clear that politics is inextricably linked to the phenomena of conflict and consensus. On the one hand, the existence of rival opinions, different wants, competing needs and opposing interests guarantees disagreement about the rules under which people live. On the other hand, people recognize that, in order to influence these rules or ensure the rules are upheld, they must work with others. Hauge, Harrop, and Breslin (1992), for example, point out that politics does not always involve conflict. They argue that one reason for studying politics is to search out the conditions under which groups can achieve their goals peacefully and effectively. From this view, politics is a constructive and practical subject and one can emphasize its compromising and consensual aspects. Politics relates not so much to the arena within which politics is conducted as to the way in which decisions are made. Politics is more seen as a particular means of resolving conflict, that is, by compromise, conciliation and negotiation, rather than through force and naked power. This is why Crick (1962) portrayed politics as that solution to the problem of order that chooses conciliation before violence and coercion. Crick, who is one of the leading exponents of this view, argues that when social groups and interests possess power, they must be conciliated; they cannot merely be crushed. This view on politics is also based on resolute faith in the efficacy of debate and dialog. In other words, the disagreements that exist can be resolved without resort to intimidation and violence. Politics is no utopian solution (compromise means that concessions are made by all sides, leaving no one perfectly satisfied), but it is undoubtedly preferable to the alternatives: bloodshed and brutality. In this sense, politics can be seen as a civilized and civilizing force. People should be encouraged to respect politics as an activity, and should be prepared to engage in the political life of their own community.

Evaluation Researchers' Views on the Evaluation and Politics Links

In the light of these definitions of evaluation and politics, evaluation can be part of the big political process (that is, evaluation in politics) and politics can be an aspect of the relationship between the actors involved in the evaluation process (that is, politics in evaluation). Even though evaluation in politics and politics in evaluation are not the most widely discussed issues in the evaluation literature (compared with, e.g., models, methods, and utilization), several evaluation researchers have dealt with the subject. The discussion below provides some notable examples that are illustrative rather than exhaustive of past discussion.

In the early years, Cronbach and his colleagues (1980) viewed evaluation as essentially a political activity through its influence on political decisions and policy formulation. More recently, one who extensively has discussed the matter is Weiss (1973, 1991). She points out at least three ways in which evaluation and politics are linked. First, the policies and programs with which evaluation deals are themselves the products of political decisions. Second, because evaluation is undertaken in order to feed into decision-making, its reports enter the political arena, where evaluation provides information. Third, evaluation itself has a political stance. Evaluation, by its very nature, makes implicit political statements, such as those challenging the legitimacy of certain program goals or implementation strategies. In this case, evaluation serves as critical inquiry.

The different kinds of information needs in the policy cycle are links that Chelimsky (1987, 1989) underlines in discussing the relationship between politics and evaluation. She argues that evaluators must recognize and accept that politics is involved in evaluation and try to understand the dynamics of the policy cycle and the political process into which the evaluation is fed. The policy cycle consists of agenda setting, problem definition, policy design, program implementation, policy or program impact, and termination. At all stages, there is an information need where program evaluation can serve general audiences and individual public decision-makers.

They may need information from evaluation for three very broad kinds of purposes.

- for policy formation—for example, to assess and/or justify the need for a new program;
- for policy execution—for example, to ensure that a program is implemented in the most cost/effective way; and
- for accountability in public decision-making—for example, to determine the effectiveness of an operation program and the need for its continuation, modification, or termination. (Chelimsky, 1989, p. 75)

Palumbo (1989) also notes that politics play an important role in evaluation design, process, and utilization of results. He comments on the claims that evaluators should not simply be advocates or collaborators of the program managers but of the program and policy itself, as well as of the clients and consumers of the program.

> . . . evaluators may be the only way that the poor, students, offenders, welfare recipients, or mentally ill can influence the policy. These "stakeholders" often are not included in the formulation and implementation of the evaluation. It is in this way that evaluators can represent the public interest rather than specific power holder interest. (p. 38)

Being an advocate for, or at least having an ambition to give unprivileged stakeholders a voice in the evaluation is one way that evaluators incorporate politics into their works.

Micro- and Macro-Levels

Greene (2003) shows how evaluation and politics are interwoven from micro- and macro-levels. She starts with the question of what the war in Iraq in the spring of 2003 had to do with evaluation. Her answer is that, in a discussion of evaluation and politics, world events such as war and peace, weapons and diplomacy, oppression and freedom are of central importance. Then she describes how macro politics and micro politics are combined when she meets people in her evaluation work who express concern for relatives in the war; this reality then has effects on the evaluation activities and even how the evaluators' questions (unrelated to the war) are answered. In this way, macro events like the war in Iraq affect the micro work the evaluator does both in conducting the evaluation and reporting the results. This example shows that the evaluator must consider what occurs at both the macro-political and micro-political levels.

House (2003) provides one more example of this perspective, illustrating how the micro-level view of the role of evaluation in politics has implications on the micro-level choice of an evaluator. He frames a future scenario in which evaluation is a tool at the disposal of the powers in force. House describes how evaluators who stand for a perspective that is critical of society will have greater difficulty winning government contracts. Instead, the evaluators who are willing to tow the party line will be hired. Thus, in a sophisticated way, politically correct evaluators are selected by a process of reverse discrimination whereby one does not blacklist people (which would risk a public debate) but instead "white lists" those one knows are favorable in terms of competence and appropriateness.

How Does Evaluation Influence Politics?

The focus so far has been on evaluation writers' perspectives on politics' influence on evaluation. How can evaluation influence politics? This question can be answered from several perspectives. First, from a positivist, rational, or social engineer's perspective, evaluation fulfills a rational feedback function within the political system and a steering control function. Evaluation provides the "rational" and "unbiased" data that the system needs to determine whether it is on course. Second, from a cultural perspective, evaluation can be understood as one answer to the fundamental need to be able to associate an organization with meaning and rationality. Evaluations can also fulfill a symbolic or ritual function and can be an answer to the trust that has declined in society today. Those in power and public organizations can use evaluations to recreate legitimacy for a program or operation, according to Hanberger (2003). He mentions that an evaluation can fulfill an enlightening (Weiss, 1977), a conceptual (Peltz, 1978), or a learning function (Preskill & Torres, 2000). In addition, evaluations can be used in media debate or in direct meetings with interested parties where the results from the evaluation and possible lines of action are discussed. Such an evaluation function can be described as stimulating public debate.

Stern (2005) distinguishes the following five purposes for evaluation, providing a view of how evaluation can have an impact on political decisions for planning, learning, developing, and termination of a program.

- Planning/efficiency – ensuring that there is a justification for a policy/program and that resources are efficiently developed.
- Accountability – demonstrating how far a program has achieved its objectives and how well it has used its resources.
- Implementation – improving the performance of programs and the effectiveness of how they are delivered and managed.
- Knowledge production – increasing our understanding of what works in what circumstances and how different measures and interventions can be made more effective.
- Institutional and community strengthening – improving and developing capacity among program participants and their networks and institutions. (Stern, 2005, p. xxvii)

In summary, some evaluation writers have noted that evaluation and politics can be interpreted from a narrow perspective, as the art of government where evaluation is seen first and foremost as a technical instrument to get information and basic data to the decision-making process. Other commentators take a broader perspective that expands the concept of politics to the public arena and thereby to different social institutions, including evaluation. Political- and value-laden aspects are therefore part of evaluation. Finally, in the broadest interpretation of politics, some evaluation writers argue that all aspects of social life, in both the public and private spheres, are inherently political. From this perspective, not only is evaluation as an institution and undertaking political, but the individual evaluator's values, background, gender, and the like also become part of the explicit and implicit operation of politics in evaluation.

Three Positions on How Evaluation and Politics are Related

The examples above suggest that more and more evaluators are accepting the reality of connections between evaluation and politics. What remains unclear is the inherent nature of these connections and, based on this, the range of possibilities for and the limitations of the evaluation–politics relationship. In this section, we propose and describe a framework to help clarify the nature of the connections between evaluation and politics. We also explore the implications of the three different positions that comprise the framework, both for the conduct of evaluation and for the evaluation profession.

The connection between evaluation and politics can be framed in three different ways (see Table 10.1). These ways, which can be characterized as "positions" or "perspectives,"

> ## EXEMPLAR 10.1   Three positions on the inherent connections between evaluation and politics
>
> | Three positions | Possible to separate evaluation and politics? | Desirable to separate evaluation and politics? |
> |---|---|---|
> | First position | Yes | Yes |
> | Second position | Yes, in providing information; Not entirely when providing judgments | Yes, in providing information |
> | Third position | No | No |

differ along two dimensions: whether it is possible operationally to separate evaluation and politics, and whether it is desirable conceptually to separate evaluation and politics. In this framework, we have adopted the conception that the two main components of evaluation are providing information (the epistemological component) and providing judgment (the value component).

The first position holds that it is both possible and desirable, operationally and conceptually, to separate evaluation and politics. The second position maintains that it is possible and desirable to separate evaluation and politics operationally when providing information but not entirely possible to do so when providing judgments, nor it is conceptually desirable. The third position is that it is neither possible nor desirable, operationally or conceptually, to separate politics and evaluation.[1]

It is important to acknowledge that the three positions are general characterizations and that individual evaluators do not neatly fit into only one position, especially if we consider those with long histories of evaluation work of many sorts and in different contexts. We have made the boundaries appear more distinct than they are in the complex, pragmatic undertaking that is evaluation. We have done this to highlight the primary differences, across the three positions, in the view of the relationship between evaluation and politics.

First Position – the Value-Neutral Evaluator

The viewpoint from the first position is that politics and evaluation can and should be kept operationally and conceptually apart. The evaluator works independently to provide an objective, neutral assessment of the program, project, or policy; the politician then receives this assessment and does with it what he or she decides. This view suits the definition of politics as the art of rational government, where the evaluator is an objective, impartial civil servant. The information function of evaluation should be under the control of the evaluator and be his/her primary activity. The judgment function, based on the information, should be under the control of others, including politicians, program planners and implementers, and the electorate. In this view, evaluation is "social research."

According to Schwandt (2003), some of those who hold this type of position look at politics as something incomplete and faulty which needs to be held in check to prevent it from poisoning the good relations between people. The cure for these faults is objective, impartial, rational, and professional officials who are above the temptation to promote their own or selected others interests, who maintain the public's interests, and who assert general principles of justice that treats everybody equally. As House & Howe (1999) have noted, this relationship between politics and evaluation neatly fits the representative liberal model of democratic theory (Ferree et al., 2002) in which disinterested, apolitical experts inform public decision-making in a detached (i.e., emotion- and value-free) manner, thereby enhancing both the rationality as well as the civility of the debate about a suitable course of action in the free marketplace of ideas.

Against this picture of how politics can become a threat to objectivity, impartiality and rationality, the question to ask is how the evaluator can protect him or herself from political influences. One way to separate evaluation from politics is to emphasize its autonomy in relation to political institutions and to powerful interests in society. Closely connected to this is the idea that power is a source of corruption which evaluation must be insulated against if it is to be conducted effectively.

How can these political influences be minimized? In his winning response to the 1988 AEA President's Problem (Patton, 1988) around the question of evaluation and politics, Robin Turpin (1989) focuses on ways to minimize the political influences in evaluation. Specifically, politics can influence (p. 55):

- the selection of the evaluator or evaluation team
- chances of funding
- the selectivity of information given to the evaluator
- the general approach or scope of the evaluation project
- the methods used
- the subject or subject pool selection
- the instruments used or developed
- data analyses
- the interpretation of data

- final recommendations
- information that is disseminated

To "produce good, solid, objective research" (p. 55) Turpin suggests that the evaluator should take the following precautions to avoid or minimize political influences (which we have rewritten in minor ways):

1. Uncover who wants the evaluation and the motivation behind it

2. Uncover all sides of the story by talking to the people involved (not just those officially involved)

3. Develop peer review procedures (even for internal, non-funded or routine evaluations)

4. Make use of expert panels and/or outside consultants in the whole evaluation process

5. Use established scales and instruments whenever possible

6. Include in the report a "limitations" section that discusses possible political influences and details critical decisions

Although Turpin also notes that politics can have positive effects on evaluation by opening doors to cooperation and information, even these positive effects can extract a cost, often in the form of subtle pressure on the evaluator. "Politics has a nasty habit of sneaking into all aspects of evaluation," Turpin comments.

The recurring idea that is emphasized is the evaluator as a conscious actor, on guard against undesirable influence and attempts to hinder the evaluation from its task of critical evaluation. The idea is a professional, politically disconnected actor, who completes his or her assignment without regard to the more-or-less explicit desires of the powers that be.

Second Position – the Value-Sensitive Evaluator

In the second position on the connection of evaluation and politics, it is accepted that evaluation takes place in a political environment and that evaluation and politics therefore cannot entirely be separated, specifically in the judging component of evaluation. In the operational, information-finding aspects, however, the evaluator can and should stay separate from the political component, according to this perspective. For example, Chelimsky (1987) points out the need for evaluators to place themselves in the political context that constitutes the program evaluation; she further suggests that evaluators must understand the political system in which evaluation operates and the information needs of those policy actors who utilize evaluations. She says that evaluators must devote much time to negotiating, discussing, briefing, accuracy-checking, prioritizing, and presenting. At the same time, the evaluator takes a professional role for the conduct of the evaluator that is non-political in the narrow definition of politics.

This second position emphasizes the evaluator's role as a professional expert, but it includes two distinctively different ideas on how politics and expertise can be conceptualized. The first idea has a market perspective and reduces the evaluation–politics relation to a technical task, where the profession is defined by the measurement of quality and efficiency. This is in line with the narrow definition of politics as governance that was presented above. The other idea represents a value-committed perspective on the relation that concerns a professional role that makes the evaluation more democratic. This is more in line with the definition of politics as a public sphere.

Evaluation and Politics as a Market

From a market perspective, politics is reformulated to be primarily a matter of practical problem-solving (Amy, 1984). This technocratic view of politics has come to prominence as part of the worldwide spread of neo-liberal discourse. Politics is replaced by rational consumer choice. Here, evaluation becomes a means for quality assurance that measures the performance (efficiency) of practices against indicators of success in achieving the targets. The profession of evaluation is reduced to technical expertise to measure quality and performances through prefabricated schemas and formula. The current emphasis in some counties in the education and health arenas for indicators-based performance management also fits within this characterization.

The movement is known as New Public Management (NPM) and represents a solution to problems in the public sector based on the introduction of management ideas from the private sector. Power (1997) describes what is characteristic of the movement:

> Broadly speaking the NPM consists of a cluster of ideas from the conceptual framework of private sector administrative practice. It emphasizes cost control, financial transparency, the autonomization of organisational sub-units, the decentralization or management authority, the creation of market or quasi-market mechanism separating purchasing and providing functions and their linkage via contracts, and the enhancement of accountability to customers for quality of service via the creation of performance indicators. (p. 43)

The citizens are transformed to consumers who make choices on a market of health care, education, social welfare, etc. Evaluation is seen as a practice that can guide consumer's choice. The view is that institutional structures for control and "accountability" should be strengthened and that evaluation in the first instance should be defined as a steering instrument for management. Through performance management and measurement and the control of quality, politicians are in a position to demonstrate "value for money" to tax-payers. Furthermore, NPM provides a rationale for reducing public sector spending through its support for private solutions rather than politically controlled activities.

*Politics and the Democratization
of Evaluation*

The other variant of the second position clearly admits that evaluation and politics are not entirely possible to separate, especially when talking of politics in a broad definition that places it in the public sphere. Evaluation is an activity necessarily couched in a political context, and the evaluator must take responsibility for how the evaluation is done, not only in regard to the technical aspects but also with attention to ethical aspects and democratic values. This does not mean that evaluation is totally integrated in politics because the evaluator has a distinctive role separated from politics, in the narrower sense of that term, as the provider of relevant, meaningful information.

From this perspective, there is a responsibility for evaluators to make their own professional perspectives on the evaluation visible. The answer to how this could and should take place is given in different forms. Some forms include the evaluator being a facilitator, a critical friend, a dialog partner, or an educator. In general, the evaluator is expected to support active involvement from stakeholders in the evaluation (Conner, 2005). Special attention is often directed to those who lack power to get their problems and questions observed in the evaluation. Here, evaluation is not reduced only to a technical matter, but also includes attention to the democratization of the evaluation process, thereby potentially contributing to a larger democratization of the program and its context.

The democratization occurs in the central components in the evaluation process. These components include deciding on the aims for the evaluation (control, development, enlightenment, learning, etc.), determining the resources for the evaluation (economic, social, and political), and selecting the evaluation questions and methods. Politics, values, and power are also apparent in decisions about access to information and where in the organization the evaluation is centered, as well as whether an internal or external evaluation is undertaken.

Some evaluation models can be connected to this view on evaluation and politics. One of the first researchers to formulate a demand for democratic evaluation was MacDonald (1973, 1977). In his version of democratic evaluation, the starting point is the assumption that power is distributed among interest groups and that the evaluator ought to serve the public's right to know. One of the recent contributions to the field of democratic evaluation is House & Howe's (2000) deliberative democratic approach. In their view, evaluation process must be based on the full and fair inclusion of all relevant stakeholders and represent the views of socially disadvantaged groups. Therefore, House & Howe are keen to emphasize that the evaluator has a special responsibility to those stakeholders who might not normally be "heard" (because they are relatively powerless, invisible, unorganized, or for some other reason not likely to be included). To serve the interests of socially disadvantaged groups, the evaluator has to give them a voice in the evaluation.

At the same time, House & Howe reserve the right of the evaluator to make the final pronouncement of the merit, worth, or value of the program under consideration. The idea of procedural justice – central to a theory of deliberative democracy – demands that all voices have had a fair hearing and are involved in deliberation. However, this does not mean that the evaluator necessarily takes the side of these less powerful voices. Advocating for the inclusion of those less heard from is not the same as endorsing their interests or points of view. Others, who also urge the evaluator to involve interest groups in an evaluation, designate the evaluator's role as that of consultant for these interest groups (Fetterman, 1994; Patton, 1994, 1996). In this situation, the evaluator becomes a "facilitator" and throughout the evaluation adopts a neutral position with respect to the interests of different groups as they strive to empower themselves as individuals and as a group.

There are several other models of participatory and collaborative evaluations that have strong emphasis on the aim to democratize not only the program context but also society as a whole. Cousins & Whitmore (1998) distinguish between practical and transformative evaluations. Practical participatory evaluation focuses on participation in evaluation. The evaluator assumes responsibility for carrying out technical evaluation tasks, and stakeholders are involved predominantly in the definition of the evaluation problem, scope-setting activities, and, later, the interpretation of data emerging from the study. In transformative participatory evaluation, the aim has expanded. Here, one strives for more extensive engagement of stakeholders, for radical social change, and for clarifying values that inevitably shape evaluations.

Third Position – the Value-Critical Evaluator

In comparison with the first and second positions on evaluation and politics, the third position does not see politics stopping at the private sphere but instead views politics as something integrated in our everyday life. Because of this, there can be no separation between evaluation and politics and therefore no neutral value or operational position taken by the evaluator. The position is associated with a perspective which claims not only that human values are inseparable from descriptions of facts but also that science will benefit from admitting this. With reference to Taylor (1985), Geir (2004, p. 197) says that:

> . . . values are an intrinsic part of the interpretive process in two ways, individual and common. The interpreter chooses a theoretical framework or conceptual structure in which she understands the phenomenon in question.

> These frameworks are pre-models of understanding, initially opening some possible connection and closing others. (p. 197)

In this view, it is important for evaluators to formulate a theoretical framework for a broader understanding of the program or subject that is evaluated. Evaluation approaches that could be connected with this kind of ideas are characterized to be:

> intentionally and directly engage[d] with the politics and values of an evaluation context, in order to explicitly advance particular political interests and values, and often also, to effect some kind of socio-political change in the evaluation context itself. Examples of value-engaged evaluative stances include feminist, empowerment, and democratizing approaches to evaluation. Proponents of these approaches are characteristically informed by ideologically-oriented methodological traditions such as feminism and critical theory. (Greene, 2003)

It is important to note that the borderline between this third position and the "democratic and participatory" variant of the second position is by no means clear-cut. Among those who argue for the desirability of separating some parts of evaluation and politics, as those in the second position do, are evaluators who also embrace the value-laden quality of human action and thus also of knowledge about human action. What differs between the second and third positions is the relative importance given to the values of social change and transformation.

A Broad View on Politics and Evaluation

From the third position, politics is not viewed as something negative. It is conceptualized in considerably broader terms than only a question of asserting one's own interests and exercising power. Politics is defined as an activity through which we live together and regulate or adapt our goals and efforts. It is also conceptualized as critical reflections on the public good. The basic idea is that it is via citizenship – through people deciding together how they will act and then following through with it – that an individual can achieve his or her full potential. Politics is concerned with taking a stance, being touched and engaged by something, defining right and wrong, good and evil, and acting on one's convictions. With these viewpoints politics is inherently human, with roots in morals and values (Schuman, 1977).

With morals and values brought into the picture, a number of new critical questions arise concerning who conducts evaluation and for whom, which evaluative questions will be raised, and what judgment criteria will be employed. The stand the evaluator takes on these questions determines the judgment he or she presents. This kind of idea plays a central role in the understanding of how the relations between evaluation and politics are conceptualized. Politics like citizen activity requires both an intellectual and physical arena, a public forum in which people can come together and plan for action. The space provided in voting halls is insufficient; politics requires involvement between elections. One alternative is to go to the streets and demonstrate; others are public enterprises where people meet, for example in pre-schools, schools, and in associations where one has an active interest. Another example of an arena for citizen involvement is evaluation conducted openly with the participation of various interested parties.

Dahler-Larsen (2003) is an evaluation researcher who places the question of evaluation politics on this broader societal level or "res publica." He views evaluation as a creative force in our understanding of society. He looks at evaluation as a cooperative and structuring force in our understanding of society. Evaluation is defined as a practice that describes other practices and that forms our impressions of these by naming the efforts, goals, criteria, standards, and the like. In this way, evaluation gives prior interpretation of the public efforts and the values that comprise them. Based on Beck's (1994) term, Dahler-Larson notes that we live in a "reflexive modernity" where confidence in progress decreases in concert with the increasing time spent grappling with the problems that these create. According to Beck, the security that has until now been associated with the modern projects progress has been weakened in the new "reflexive modernity." Instead, "reflexivity" reigns in a double sense. First, the reflexivity is a throwing-back of side-effects onto society itself (environmental problems, highway congestion, coordination problems, iatrogenic illnesses, etc.). Second, the reflexivity is an increased moral, ethical, and political concern for the handling of these side effects. One such "side-effect" is reactions to public policies from users and other stakeholders.

These changes in how one looks at the ontological and epistemological foundations for evaluation, and on society in the perspective of new reflexive modernity, have also changed the political framework for evaluation. Society is not the only thing that has become more complex. Evaluations have been given many different functions as well. These functions include some traditional ones, such as the use of evaluation as an instrument for national and local governments to exercise control and as an instrument for society and citizens to receive information and knowledge. A newer function for evaluation includes its use as an instrument for interested parties and organizations to observe and influence.

Evaluation, however, does not simply disseminate results; it also provides a deeper, better understanding of the evaluated object.

Through linguistic designations of "the evaluand," "the points of measurement," "criteria," "standards", evaluation discourse draws attention to certain phenomena and orientations. Hereby evaluation is an interpretation of what the public effort is altogether and in wherein its value consists. (Dahler-Larsen, 2003)

From this point of view, evaluation informs about the merits and value of a program but also has a broader perspective. This type of evaluation informs about a larger framework, with reference to roles and relations. Evaluations become a meta-communication about the character of people and their relations, which in turn are an arrangement of politics in its deep meaning. This does not mean that evaluations always have this impact on our conceptions of the world and ourselves. How strong the impact is depends on a number of contextual factors such as organization, culture, and structure.

Summary

In our discussion of the subject of evaluation and politics, we have assumed that evaluation is not an isolated island but instead an enterprise in a political context. This context means that there are multiple actors and institutions with power and interests to influence the evaluation, from the choices of criteria, standards, and methods, to the choice of an evaluator.

We have described three views on the relationship between evaluation and politics. The first position sees politics as driven to protect its own interests and as harmful to evaluation. In this view, politics is at best a fickle partner, driven by many influences other than information, and at worst an unsavory one. Evaluation can and should be kept apart from it. If an evaluator has to deal with politics, the evaluator must be careful not to be too engaged and not to scrutinize the political influences to decide how to behave. Instead, the evaluator uses professional standards and guidelines to produce objective information, so that if and

when the possibility to use it arises, the information is available.

In the second view, in one interpretation, politics is replaced by the idea of the market with rational consumers making choice based on evidence. Here, the political is paradoxically transformed into an outwardly apolitical phenomenon – a style of formalized accountability that becomes the new ethical and political principle of governance (Power, 1997). The role of evaluation in this view is to provide professional technical help to measure quality and to produce quality-assurance. A different interpretation of the second position is to acknowledge the inseparable connections between evaluation and politics in the area of value- or judgment-making and therefore to democratize the evaluation process at critical stages (for example, deciding on the evaluation questions), with special attention to those whose voice may not be easily heard in the public arena. At the same time, however, evaluation is kept separate from politics in the implementation of the evaluation, to avoid biases in the information produced.

The third position views evaluation and politics as inseparable, both in the conceptual as operational aspects. Here, the evaluator accepts that evaluation and politics are connected in many intricate ways and acts accordingly. The evaluator acknowledges and states his or her own ethical and moral standpoints so that these are transparent during the evaluation process. Actions such as these suggest a more prominent role for evaluation and evaluators in shaping society and its politics.

Discussion and Implications

Each of the three positions (and sub-positions) can be criticized on different aspects. One could question the claims held in the first position that evaluation can be independent from external power. Those who criticize the idea of evaluation's autonomy from external power believe that evaluation easily can become a part of, and work for, the ideological state apparatus in society. Another criticism of the first position focuses on the idea that evaluation is a value-free practice of objective research. Social science has prided itself on being value-free for many decades. However, Scriven (2003/04) notes that this view of social science research is changing as social science becomes more involved with serious social problems, interventions, and issues. To be successful in this new arena, social science will have to incorporate evaluation or evaluative elements, he says. A final criticism of the first position is that it is difficult to separate the judgment-making component of evaluation from politics, both on an individual level and on a societal level. Hammersley (1995) presents several arguments why values cannot be insulated from research. According to one of his arguments, because information and knowledge is always produced within a perspective or framework, the knowledge that one prioritizes is also dependent on circumstances in the socio-political context. Another of his arguments focuses on how the researcher's or evaluator's own personal and positional realities (ethnic, gender, economic, and the like) play an important role in shaping priorities and interests that can affect an evaluation.

Criticism could also be directed at the second position, with evaluation and politics related conceptually in judgment-making but separated in information-making. The market-oriented variant of this position expects that central values will be based on the needs of the market and expressed by the multiple actors representing different interests. However, only a subset of actors are effectively involved, and the particular subset will shape the normative content of an evaluation, determining the boundaries of the "knowledge base, the scope,

and potentially the outcomes of evaluation" (Dabinett & Richardson, 1999, p. 233). The indicators-based performance management focus that is central in the market-oriented perspective also carries risks. Four of these risks are that indicators may not measure what they are intended to; that unwarranted attributions of causality for outcomes may be made to indicators; that performance information may be used for purposes for which it was not intended; and that goal displacement may occur if incentives divert effort from attaining program objectives to meeting the requirements of measuring and reporting (Davies, 1999). Performance measurement systems also decouple accountability from ownership and responsibility, thus assigning to accountability a role in regulation and control and inhibiting shared responsibility among stakeholder-citizens. They "also let the evaluator off the hook, by heavily obscuring their authorship and thereby muting their responsibility" (Greene, 1999, p. 170).

Some criticize the other variant of the second position, focused on democratic approaches to evaluation, because it tends to be connected to the macro politics of society, in that evaluation is expressly positioned as an instrument of democracy and as an advocate for democratic ideals and for change. The explicit ideological stance and political positioning are democratic and the express point of evaluation in these approaches is to render an assessment and judgment of evaluation quality that inherently incorporates democratic standards of judgment and thus serves to advance democratic ideals and values. Above, we mentioned several evaluation researchers that represent these ideas. One more example on this is Mark, Henry, & Julnes (2000) who clearly put evaluation in a political discourse of democratic decision-making and also reject the fact-value dichotomy. At the same time, Greene & Walker (2001) notes that these authors have:

. . . positioned evaluators and the knowledge they generate apart form the politicized fray of democratic decision-making. From this position, evaluators can use a mix of methods within selected inquiry modes to impartially make sense of the quality of, and the diverse values that accompany, a given social program or policy and then offer that assisted sense-making to those in democratic institutions for their deliberations. (p. 371)

Against this position, Greene & Walker argue for an alternative view that:

does not separate the practice of evaluation from socio-political practices and institutions to which it is designed to contribute or in which it is embedded . . . . Evaluators should not be absolved from the moral and ethical responsibility for the practice choices we make and the knowledge claims we generate. If we wish to claim that a particular social program or policy can indeed contribute to social betterment, we must be responsible for that claim-both as a warranted representation of human experience and as a defensible valuing of what is "good" and "right" about that experience, (Greene & Walker, 2001, p. 371)

What Greene & Walker criticize is the idea of a detached "professional" evaluator that is central in the concept of evaluation and politics held by those working in the democratic variant of the second position. Those working from this perspective also need to address and resolve the problem of identifying and securing comprehensive, representative stakeholder involvement. Furthermore, one could ask how the representatives of groups, sectors, or interests are to be chosen, and how the differences in power among stakeholder groups influence their roles in the evaluation. These questions highlight the dilemma facing the evaluator when he/she tries to strengthen powerless stakeholders. One could also ask about the value position that motivates such a decision, and about the influence such an

"empower-the-powerless" standpoint is likely to have on confidence in the evaluation among other more traditional, empowered groups (Karlsson, 1996, 2001).

Finally, the third position, that evaluation and politics are inseparable in all ways, has some limitations and raises some questions, as is the case with the other two positions. The ethical and moral standpoint that demands a better world, a more equal society and a fight against any discrimination leaves no private zone where less-than-enthusiastic support for these ideas can be hidden. Here, the evaluator cannot, so to say, hide behind a professional role if one chooses not to take a stand on these issues. One could ask if this broad and expanded role for evaluation makes the evaluator more of an intellectual discussant on general political, ethical, and moral issues, and less of a professional narrowly examining a program in accordance with more specific goals and chosen criteria. Are evaluators trained and skilled to play such a broad, prominent role in societal discussions, and, even if they are, can they reasonably and responsibly fulfill such a broad role? In this more prominent role, what assurances are there that the reasons for the evaluator's value stance are transparent? How can we know, for example, the extent to which an evaluator's views are motivated by his/her general personal values rather than by specific factors related to the evaluation? Also, are there safeguards in place that will allow the evaluator to share his/her viewpoints without silencing the views of others who could participate, including those who are often voiceless in the political process? Rather than being the spokesperson for others views, maybe the evaluator should work to let them speak for themselves.

An interpretation of evaluation from this broad moral perspective could be that all who work with people in different situations, especially when one has power over others lives, health, education, or security, have the responsibility to reflect actively and systematically about one's own behavior and to be self-critical. Here, we can talk about an "evaluator role" that is integrated in every responsible profession, including physicians, teachers, social workers, lawyers, and others. This view raises the question of whether there is space for a profession that exclusively deals with evaluation, not as an alternative but as a complement to all other professionals and to their own evaluations and critical reflections on what they are doing.

Implications

One of the things we can learn from our review of the relationship between evaluation and politics is how the relationship between the two is much more complex and difficult to grasp than thought in earlier decades (the 1970s, 80s and 90s). Today, we must take a more nuanced view of the evaluator, not simply considering him or her to be a neutral, independent, objective methodologist who presents facts. That older, traditional image can be contrasted with an image from the other extreme that places evaluators (and evaluations) in a political powder keg where various interests and values meet and clash. The better image, we believe, is probably one in the middle of this spectrum: a professional, skilled, well-trained evaluator working in a context with explicit or implicit political, cultural, and personal implications, all of which can potentially exert some influence in the decisions about evaluation questions, methods, and results. It is clear that, for better or worse, evaluation and politics are partners. The decisions an evaluator makes are affected not only by issues of science but also by politics and ethics.

What can evaluators do to maximize the benefits of the link between evaluation and politics and minimize its risks? One piece of advice is for the evaluator to watch for the diverse supports and unexpected opportunities that exist in a large, complex context. Another suggestion is that the evaluator be clear about the special skills and perspectives or "added value" that he or she brings to the situation, in relation to the other participants. These are the anchors around which the evaluator should build. Another suggestion is to have a supportive base in the evaluation profession, an evaluation network or some other professional group. This provides another type of anchor and perspective, when pressures build that the evaluator is not fully in control of. Although these suggestions mostly focus on the individual evaluator, we also think that there is a need to scrutinize more critically what purpose evaluations can serve. In the wake of increasing uncertainty about how public enterprises can be steered, controlled, and developed through democratic decisions, expectations increase about evaluations ability to solve these steering problems. This has led to evaluation enterprises being viewed as a self-evident requirement at all levels of society. Management and personnel are expected to spend more time finding out about how their efforts are perceived by users and other people who are affected. As a consequence of these increased evaluation efforts, there has been an expansion of administrative systems to handle the information that comes in, which in turn requires more resources. We would argue for an alternative to this expansion of evaluation into a large bureaucratic system, in favor of a shift toward more reflective, critical-focused evaluation as part of every practitioner's work toward a democratic, humanistic ideal that gives marginalized groups a voice.

Note

1. From a logical standpoint, there is a fourth position: that it is not possible to separate evaluation and politics (either the information or the judgment aspects), but that it would be desirable to do so (in both aspects). Because this is not a realistic possibility to guide evaluation work, we have not considered it here. There are some, however, who might argue that serious consideration should be given to this position, because, if it can be shown to be highly desirable, the evaluation community might begin to set in place policies and procedures to bring about the separation. The latter assumes, of course, that the "evaluation community" could and would speak with one voice on this matter. As the three positions described here show, this is unlikely to occur.

References

Amy, D. J. (1984). Why policy analysis and ethics are incompatible. *Journal of Policy Analysis and Management*, 3(4), 573–591.

Beck, U. (1994). The reinvention of politics: towards a theory of reflexive modernization. In U. Beck, A. Giddens & S. Lash (eds) *Reflexive Modernization* (pp. 1–55). Stanford: Stanford University Press.

Caro, F. G. (1977). *Readings in Evaluation Research*, second edition. New York: Sage.

Chelimsky, E. (1987). The politics of program evaluation. In D. S. Cordray, H. S. Bloom & R. J. Light (eds) *Evaluation Practice in Review. New Directions for Program Evaluation*, No. 34, (pp. 5–21). San Francisco: Jossey-Bass.

Chelimsky, E. (1989). Linking program evaluation to user needs. In J. D. Palumbo (ed.) *The Politics of Program Evaluation* (pp. 72–99). London: Sage Publications.

Conner, R. F. (2005). The Colorado Healthy Communities Initiative. *American Journal of Evaluation*, 26, 363–368.

Cousins, J. B. & Whitmore, E. (1998). Framing participatory evaluation. *New Directions for Evaluation*, No 80 (pp. 5–23). San Francisco: Jossey-Bass.

Crick, B. (1962). *In Defence of Politics*. London: Weidenfeld and Nicolson.

Cronbach, L. J., Ambron, S. R., Dornbusch, S. M., Hess, D. C., Hornik, R. C., Phillips, D. C., Walker, D. F. & Weiner, S. S. (1981). *Toward Reform of Program Evaluation: Aims, methods, and institutional arrangements*. San Francisco: Jossey-Bass.

Dabinett, G. & Richardson, T. (1999). The European spatial approach. The role of power and knowledge in strategic planning and policy evaluation. *Evaluation*, 5, 220–236.

Dahl, R. (1984). *Modern Political Analysis*. Englewood Cliffs, NJ: Prentice-Hall.

Dahler-Larsen, P. (2003). The political in evaluation. *E-journal Studies in Educational Policy and Educational Philosophy*, 2003, 1. http://www.upi.artisan.se.

Davies, I. C. (1999). Evaluation and performance management in government. *Evaluation*, 5, 150–159.

Easton, D. (1968). *The Political System: an inquiry into the state of political science*, 2nd edition. New York: Knopf.

Ferree, M. M., Gamson, W. A., Gerhards, J., & Rucht, D. (2002). Four models of the public sphere in modern democracies. *Theory and Society*, 31, 289–324.

Fetterman, D. (1994). Empowerment evaluation. *Evaluation Practice*, 15, 1–15.

Gallie, W. B. (1956). Essentially Contested Concepts. *Proceedings of the Aristotelian Society*, 56, 167–220.

Geir, A. (2004). Facts, values and moral education. *Nordisk Pedagogik*, 24(3), 195–211.

Greene, J. C. (1999). The inequality of performance measurements. *Evaluation*, 5, 160–172.

Greene, J. C. (2003). War and peace . . . and evaluation. *E-journal Studies in Educational Policy and Educational Philosophy*, 2003, 1. http:\\www.upi.artisan.se

Greene, J. C. & Walker, K. (2001). Book review *Evaluation and Program Planning*, 24, 368–371. of Mark, M. M., Henry, G. T. & Julnes, G. (2000). *Evaluation: An integrated framework for understanding, guiding, and improving policies and programs*. San Francisco: Jossey-Bass.

Hammersley, M. (1995). *The Politics of Social research*. London: Sage.

Hanberger, A. (2003). Evaluation's hidden politics. *E-journal Studies in Educational Policy and Educational Philosophy*, 2003, 1. http://www.upi.artisan.se.

Hauge, R., Harrop, M., & Breslin, S. (1992). *Comparative Government and Politics. An Introduction*, 3rd edition. London: McMillan Press.

Heywood, A. (2002). *Politics*, 2nd edition. London: MacMillan Press.

House, E. R. (2003). Bush´s neo-fundamentalism and the new politics of evaluation. *E-journal Studies in Educational Policy and Educational Philosophy*, 2003, 1. http://www.upi.artisan.se.

House, E. R. & Howe, K. R. (1999). *Values in Evaluation and Social Research*. Thousand Oaks, CA: Sage.

House, E. R. & Howe, K. R. (2000). Deliberative democratic evaluation. In K. E. Ryan & L. DeStefano (eds) *Evaluation as a Democratic Process: Promoting inclusion, dialogue, and deliberation. New Directions for Evaluation*, No. 85 (pp. 3–12). San Francisco: Jossey-Bass.

Karlsson, O. (1996). A critical dialogue in evaluation. How can the interaction between evaluation and politics be tackled? *Evaluation, 2*, 405–416.

Karlsson, O. (2001). Critical dialogue: Its value and meaning. *Evaluation, 7*, 211–227.

Lasswell, H. D. (1936). *Politics: Who gets what, when, how*. New York: McGraw-Hill.

MacDonald, B. (1973). Briefing decision makers. In E. R. House (ed.) *School Evaluation: The politics and process*. Berkeley, CA: McCutchan Publishing Corp.

MacDonald, B. (1977). A political classification of evaluation studies. In D. Hamilton, D. Jenkins, C. Kong, B. MacDonald & M. Parlett, *Beyond the Numbers Game*. London: Macmillan.

Mark, M. M., Henry, G. T., & Julnes, G. (2000). *Evaluation: An integrated framework for understanding, guiding, and improving policies and programs*. San Francisco: Jossey-Bass.

Palumbo, J. D. (ed.) (1989). *The Politics of Program Evaluation*. London: Sage Publications.

Patton, M. Q. (1988). Politics and *evaluation. Evaluation Practice, 9*, 89–94.

Patton, M. Q. (1994). Developmental evaluation. *Evaluation Practice, 15*, 311–319.

Patton, M. Q. (1996). *Utilization-Focused Evaluation*. London: Sage.

Pawson, R. & Tilley, N. (1997). *Realistic Evaluation*. London: Sage.

Peltz, D. C. (1978). Some expanded perspectives on use of social science in public policy. In J. M. Yinger & S. J. Cutler (eds) *Major Social Issues: A multidisciplinary view*. New York: Free Press.

Power, M. (1997). *The Audit Society: Rituals of verification*. Oxford: Oxford University Press.

Preskill, H. & Torres, R. T. (2000) The learning dimension of evaluation use. In V. Caracelli & H. Preskill (eds) *The Expanding Scope of Evaluation Use. New Directions for evaluation*, No. 88 (pp. 25–38). San Francisco: Jossey-Bass.

Schuman, D. (1977). *A Preface to Politics*. Toronto: D. C. Heath & Company.

Schwandt, T. (2003). In search of political morality of evaluation practice. *E-journal Studies in Educational Policy and Educational Philosophy*, 2003,1. http://www.upi.artisan.se.

Scriven, M. (1991). *Evaluation Thesaurus*, 4th edition. London: Sage Publications.

Scriven, M. (2003/04). Michael Scriven on the differences between evaluation and social science research. *The Evaluation Exchange*, 7.

Stern, E. (2005). Editor's Introduction. In E. Stern (ed.) *Evaluation Research Methods*. Vol. I (pp. xxi–xliii) London: Sage.

Taylor, C. (1985). *Philosophy and the Human Sciences. Philosophical Papers 2*. Cambridge: Cambridge University Press.

Turpin, R. (1989). Winner of 1988 President's problem. *Evaluation Practice*, 10(1), 53–57.

Weiss, C. H. (1973). Where politics and evaluation research meet. *Evaluation, 1*, 37–45.

Weiss, C. H. (1977). *Using Social Research in Public Policy Making*. Lexington, MA: Lexington Books.

Weiss, C. H. (1991). Evaluation research in the political context: Sixteen years and four administrations later. In M. W. McLaughlin & D. C. Phillips (eds) *Evaluation and Education: At quarter century* (pp. 210–231). Chicago: The University Press.

ETHICS IN EVALUATION

Helen Simons

Some of the most intractable ethical problems arise from conflicts among principles and the necessity of trading one off against the other. The balancing of such principles in concrete situations is the ultimate ethical act. (House, 1993, p. 168)

Ethics is a branch of politics. That is to say, it is the duty of the statesman to create for the citizen the best possible opportunity of living the good life. It will seen that the effect of this injunction is not to degrade morality but to moralise politics. (Thomson, 1953, p. 26, commentary on The Ethics of Aristotle)

Introduction

The two quotations above underscore much that will be explored in this chapter as evaluators go about their business of evaluating programmes and policies in the socio-political contexts in which they are commissioned, enacted and disseminated. Drawing attention to the interdependence of politics and ethics and conflicts among principles, highlights the unique nature of the evaluation task and the key responsibilities of the evaluation role. Evaluation involves at least four levels of social–political interaction – with government and other agency policy makers who commission evaluation; with participants in the programmes, policies and institutions evaluated; with the evaluation profession; and with the wider audiences to whom evaluators in a democratic society have a responsibility to report. Evaluation has to operate in this multilayered context of different interests, providing information to inform decisions while remaining independent of the policies and programmes themselves. In such a context it is not surprising that ethical dilemmas arise as to which is the best course of action to take.

Most evaluation and research texts where ethics are mentioned start with a reminder that there is no context-free abstract set of principles that can be applied to guide ethical decision-making in evaluation. What we encounter in the practice of evaluation are ethical dilemmas, where we have to make a complex judgment, a choice between alternative courses of action, taking into account a myriad of factors – social, personal, political, cultural – that are pertinent in the particular context (House, 1980; Lincoln, 1990; Mabry, 1999; Pring, 2000; Simons & Usher, 2000).

Take, for example, the following dilemma. A powerful institution, sponsor of a multi-country evaluation study, threatens to hold back payment to colleagues employed by them on projects which have been completed and independently evaluated, until the director of the evaluation agrees to the changes the institution wants made to the final evaluation report. The participants in the projects are dependent on release of the evaluation report for payment and for their livelihood. The institution wants the evaluation to blame certain people in the report. The evaluator argues for the fairness and balance of the report, as he sees it, to be maintained. How should the evaluator respond? Give in to the institution's wishes so that the participants are paid, though it will compromise the integrity and impartiality of the evaluation? Or continue to negotiate for a reasonable outcome that will maintain fairness to individuals and how they are represented and ensure credibility to external audiences and international sponsor, though it will delay payment to participants and have consequences for them and their families? These are not the only options available in resolving the dilemma. They are merely illustrative of how the argument could run.

Or take the dilemma Morris (2004a, p. 236) raises as to whether or not it is appropriate to have a client representative on the steering committee of an implementation evaluation of an agency providing community-based residential services to the chronically mentally ill. The evaluator, who has experience working with community-based programmes for the mentally ill, thinks it is appropriate to have such a client representative. The director of the agency does not, believing that the psychiatric disabilities of the agency's clients would make it extremely difficult for them to be productive and that it might end up doing more harm than good.

Resolving dilemmas such as these is rarely a choice between right and wrong. This would be relatively easy to resolve. More often than not, it is a choice between mutually conflicting principles, what Russell (1993) has called a "clash between right and right" or House (1993) "trading one off against the other." In such situations, principles are needed to guide action but they do not determine what is the "right" action to take. How then can the evaluator be assisted to conduct evaluations that are ethically defensible?

Evaluation textbooks on the whole offer little guidance on this issue. Newman & Brown (1996) surveyed 21 evaluation texts from 1972 to 1994 and found that 80 percent did not mention ethics at all and those that did averaged about four pages per book. A survey ten years on may reveal more attention to ethics, although the contemporary context for evaluation has led to procedures and mechanisms that frequently have more to do with control and surveillance than principles for ethical behaviour. In the last ten years we have witnessed an intensification of accountability and managerialism in institutions, an increase in governance and quality assurance of programmes, and a preoccupation with audit, monitoring, regulation, and control.

The rise of evaluation standard setting by evaluation associations and the intensification of ethical committees and institutional review boards (IRBs) within institutions may be one response to this external pressure for regulation by government and other agencies. However, it is important to distinguish institutional mechanisms for oversight of evaluation which have a regulatory function from the trend in the evaluation profession for setting ethical guidelines, principles, or standards. The latter are properly part of the self-regulation and self-accountability demanded of a profession with responsibility to its members, those they evaluate and the public. It is a separate question, however, to what extent ethics is a central feature of such guidelines or a subset of more general standards.

Ethics is about how we behave or should behave as individuals and as part of the society in which we live in interaction with others. It is, at one level, a personal morality, to do with the rights and wrongs of our actions, pervading our everyday life. Guiding precepts are honesty, sincerity, kindness, respect for persons, being honourable. "Do unto others as you would have them do unto you" is a golden rule, a categorical imperative that often guides our action and enables us to "know" we have done the right thing.

As members of a liberal democratic society we are also likely to share certain principles about how we should behave and how we should treat people in the conduct of our private and public lives. Such principles would include respect for persons, respect for "truth", equality, justice, freedom and autonomy.

However, as evaluators and as a profession we also share principles about how we should conduct and disseminate evaluation. This is not just a question of our personal predilection or moral stance. It is a question of community – promoting and underpinning what it means to act ethically and promote "right" practice in the professional field of evaluation. This will incorporate public criteria, such as those noted above, and in practice involve recourse to the sources of our personal morality. But there is a professional ethic or ways of thinking ethically concerned with the work that evaluators do. It is this that is the main focus of this chapter.

Characteristics of the Field of Evaluation

As much of the literature on ethics is applicable to all social research, I first outline some

identifying features of the field of evaluation to provide a context for discussing ethical evaluation. I am aware that not all evaluators may subscribe to these characteristics. Perspectives on the nature and function of evaluation and the role of evaluation in society are contested and differ according to different world views, preferred methodologies, and in different cultural contexts. The characteristics below represent for me a coherent set of statements for the conduct and dissemination of evaluation in a liberal democratic society.

First, the role of the evaluator is to elicit and make public the essential values and merits of programmes so that individuals and groups can contribute to informed policy-making and debate. In this sense "evaluation is a public decision procedure" (House, 1980), and the role of the evaluator that of the "public scientist" (Cronbach et al., 1980), providing an evidence base for informed judgment and public dialogue.

Secondly, evaluation is about judgment, ascertaining the merit or worth of a programme, distinguishing good from bad. Different methodological approaches consider the role of judgment in different ways but at a fundamental level, the task is to discern quality. In the last four decades in which evaluation has emerged as a separate field of inquiry, the roles evaluators can adopt and the methodologies they can employ have proliferated enormously. The choice of evaluation roles is a moral choice for society. And the choices evaluators (and sponsors) make about the methodologies they value have political implications.

Thirdly, evaluation is inherently political, concerned with the distribution of power and the allocation of resources and opportunities in society. That is its purpose, to assist choices between different courses of action by collecting and presenting evidence relevant to these choices. Evaluation has consequences for who gets what, whose interests are served in an evaluation, who stands to gain or lose by the findings of an evaluation and so on. Evaluation cannot be value free, nor can it safely be left to the personal values of the evaluator nor confined to the interests of those who have the power to commission it.

Fourthly, evaluation needs to be independent – conducted "without fear or favour" to any one group. He who pays the piper should not call the tune. Evaluation cannot be bought. It should be sponsored as an impartial service to all stakeholders in the matters under review. It should envision accountability as a two-way process that includes reporting to the public about government-sponsored policies and programmes that are conducted in the public interest. In this context "respect for truth", "fairness", "justice", "equality" are all generic ethical principles to underpin an independent evaluation process.

Finally, where evaluation is funded by public money, ethical issues arise not only in relation to contractual obligations but also the nature of the topic being investigated. Are there some evaluation contracts one would refuse to take on ethical grounds, such as when certain groups might be put at risk or disadvantaged?

In the following sections I indicate the various routes and stances evaluators can take in deciding how to conduct evaluation that is ethically defensible. First, I examine the different ways in which ethics has been conceived professionally, including the generation of standards, principles, codes and guidelines, as well as ethical committees and institutional review boards. Second, I briefly outline different ethical theories and offer some examples of how they might provide justification for ethical decision-making. Third, I draw attention to the interrelationship of politics and ethics indicating, through a brief account of democratic approaches to evaluation, how ethics may be procedurally managed in specific

socio-political contexts. Finally, I re-examine certain procedural ethical conventions, focusing on those aspects that present particular ethical issues in evaluation.

Professional Ethics

Evolution of Ethical Standards/Codes/Principles in Professional Societies

Most professional associations in disciplines from which evaluators stem and evaluation societies now have written ethical guidelines/principles/standards/codes to facilitate ethical practice. Such guidelines traditionally embody a normative ethics – concerned with how people ought to behave, in this case in conducting and disseminating evaluation. However, there is little consistency in how these terms are used. According to Newman & Brown (1996, pp. 21–22) the terms – rules, codes, standards, principles, theories – are distinguished by degree of specificity and purpose. Their summary may be useful.

> Ethical rules are specific statements about ethical behaviour; ethical codes are compilations of ethical rules. Ethical standards can be synonymous with ethical rules and codes but may go beyond that definition to suggest model behaviour. Ethical principles are broader than rules serving as the foundation for codes. Principles stand as models of behaviour and practice, providing and encompassing not only situational rules but also serving as guides for unspecified practice. Ethical theories provide a justification for how we make ethical decisions and aid us in resolving conflicts among principles or rules. (ibid., p. 22)

In practice some evaluation societies have set standards to judge the quality of the evaluation and product (e.g., Joint Committee

Standards). Others prefer more general statements of principle for the conduct of evaluation (e.g., Australasian Evaluation Society, Canadian Evaluation Society), accompanied in some cases by guidelines for interpreting the principles in practice. Yet others are couched in terms of more regulative rules or codes which promote and protect the profession and the public and to which members of a society must subscribe.[1] In this chapter I shall use the term guidelines to cover all these attempts to set norms for the profession (see also Bustelo, 2004) but make the distinction between *standards and codes* that are quite specific, often prescriptive, and reflect model behaviour (Newman & Brown, 1996, pp. 21–22) and *principles* that are more general, often normative, and, most importantly, aspire to good practice.

The evolution of ethical guidelines in evaluation societies and in other professional associations (see e.g., Goldner, 1967; Simons, 1995) has been gradual and for the most part has only occurred in the last ten to fifteen years.[2] The exceptions are the Joint Committee Standards in the US (1981, revised in 1994) and the standards of the Evaluation Research Society (ERS, 1982), which merged with the Evaluation Network to become the American Evaluation Association (AEA) in 1986. The AEA chose not to adopt the old ERS standards but rather to develop its own guiding principles (Fitzpatrick, 1999, p. 6), drawing attention perhaps to the distinction between standards and principles referred to above. In setting up a Task Force for this purpose in 1992, the AEA Board "specifically instructed the Task Force to develop general guiding principles rather than specific standards of practice" (AEA, 2004, p. 6). The AEA has not formally adopted the Joint Committee Standards, though it does support the Joint Committee's work and has a representative on its committee (http://www.eval.org/Publications/publications.html).

The resulting AEA's Guiding Principles for Evaluators were adopted by the association in 1994 (http://www.eval.org/Guiding%20Principles.htm) and address both behavioural (as in the importance of "systematic inquiry") and normative (as in the importance of "respect for people") strands of evaluation practice. The most extensive of the current published guidelines remains the Joint Committee on Standards for Educational Evaluation (1994), which also address both standards of practice (e.g., "accuracy" and "feasibility") and principles of practice (e.g., "propriety"). These standards have been adopted and/or adapted by several evaluation societies (including the Swiss Evaluation Society, and the German Evaluation Society).

The difference between *standards/codes* and *principles* may perhaps best be exemplified in the evolution of ethical guidelines within the Australasian Evaluation Society (AES). The AES started with an interim code of ethics but, failing to gain endorsement on standards of behaviour for society members, developed a set of "Guidelines for the Ethical Conduct of Evaluation" framed around general principles and procedures for the conduct of evaluation. These were endorsed by the AES Board in 1997, accompanied by a statement which indicated that they complemented the Joint Committee Standards. A Code of Ethics incorporating the former Guidelines was eventually endorsed in 2000, reflecting the need to protect the public and the profession in a changing context (http://www.aes.asn.au/about/ethics.htm). The development of specific AES quality standards has been on the agenda since the late 1980s but has not yet reached resolution.[3] Fraser (2005) suggests that this is partly due to the growth of quality standards and frameworks in several state government departments and the emerging concern of indigenous communities to develop culturally relevant quality standards (Fraser, 2005, p. 78).

There are a number of reasons why professional associations took time to develop or adopt a code of ethics for their members. First, the field of evaluation practice is complex and any code cannot anticipate all contingencies nor offer guidance for mediating conflicts that may arise. Second, codifying behaviour implies that sanctions might be imposed on those who do not comply. While peer group evaluation is acceptable in some situations – for example, anonymous refereeing of proposals – pronouncements on unethical behaviour that would lead to sanctioning the right to be evaluators is likely to be perceived by colleagues as a step too far, indicating lack of trust in one's personal ethics and competence. It is also the wrong end of the process. The aspiration in such codes, many would argue, should not be to sanction bad practice or ensure that evaluators do nothing wrong through "commission or omission" (Newman & Brown (1996, p. 3), but rather to promote good practice.

Third is the difficulty of actually enforcing a code of ethics and who would do so. Fourth, it may have simply been too soon, not a priority for an association establishing itself within a still-developing professional field, and where there may have been little consensus over what constituted appropriate behaviour or practice (Fitzpatrick, 1999, p. 12; Fraser, 2005).

The increase in published ethical guidelines by evaluation societies in the past decade may be a reflection of the rapid growth and/or "hallmark of maturity for a profession" (Newman & Brown, 1996, p. 19). Professional associations may have become more confident about the issues which united their members and realised it was time to assert a collective intent to serve the public interest in governance of and access to quality research and evaluation. Institutional norms, as Bustelo (2004, p. 6) points out, also help to create an evaluation culture, share language and terminology, define the field and provide a means of professional socialisation and training.

However, there are also political and economic factors. In the UK, contractual arrangements for funding evaluation became more prescriptive, restricting reporting (written or spoken) stipulating methodologies, and prescribing ownership and copyright of data (Simons, 1995, pp. 438–440). Guidelines were required to protect the role of evaluation in producing impartial evidence to inform public programmes and policies. Increasingly it was possible to cite evidence of evaluation reports being censored by non-publication, delayed until the issue was no longer relevant, or edited by the sponsor. This resonates with Morris & Cohn's (1993, p. 18) US research on ethical problems identified by evaluators, the most frequent and serious of which was presentation of evaluation findings.

A further factor in the US relates to economic and structural change in the field. Many evaluations are conducted by private research firms that hire evaluators who often have no specific training in evaluation and spend only a few years in the field before moving on. This high turnover of evaluators makes ethical problems possibly more salient and the corresponding need for guidelines on quality more imperative. The more evaluation is privatized the more guidelines are needed to generate trust in the process and quality of the products of evaluations. Fraser (2005, pp. 68–69) also makes the point that evaluation rises and falls in periodic economy drives in government, resulting both in the loss of skilled practitioners and producing a "radical loss of collective memory".

In recent years, the number of national evaluation societies that have introduced "standards" for their profession has increased and there have been efforts to examine their universality (Picciotto, 2005; Russon & Russon, 2005). Given that many build on the

Joint Committee Standards, it is not surprising to find similarities among them. However, Russon (2005) concludes, in an examination of the development towards international standards, that the utility of standards is more likely to be enhanced when they maintain a connection with the culture in which people live and work. Similarly the European Evaluation Society has chosen not to advocate common standards preferring national societies, at this stage, to be responsive in their development of standards and guidelines to their different cultural contexts (Stame, 2004, p. 506; http://www.europeanevaluation.org/docs/standardspolicy v2 18022004.pdf).

Content and Purpose

A major purpose of ethical codes in professional associations is "to socialize and educate the practitioner about common standards", a process more likely to be successful through development of "'inner controls' than the 'external management of conduct'" (Plant, 1998, p. 165, quoted by Fitzpatrick, 1999, p. 12). This distinction of the locus of control for ensuring ethical practice – and whether codes are educative or regulatory – is often not clear in published guidelines. The choice of the word "principle" or "guideline" rather than "standard" may be a reflection of educative self-regulatory intent. Standards or codes are often assumed to have more of an institutional regulatory function. However, in practice, since few professional societies have instituted enforcement of standards (Fitzpatrick, 1999, p. 12), their use has been educative by default, if not by intent. This may be because the preferred route is development of "inner controls", though the more likely reason for the absence of enforcement mechanisms in the AEA Guiding Principles Fitzpatrick suggests may be "the need to reach consensus on the meaning and application of the principles, the

continuing tensions among the diverse paradigms used in evaluation, and the relative newness of the evaluation profession" (Fitzpatrick, 1999, p. 12).

Whichever terminology is used, ethical guidelines vary on a number of dimensions. These include how they distinguish between ethical–moral issues and scientific–methodological issues (the degree to which methodological competence is regarded as an ethical issue, for instance); whether they address ethical issues for all stakeholders or solely those of professional evaluators[4] and whether and how they acknowledge difference.

Common to many ethical guidelines are the principles of mutual respect, non-coercion and non-manipulation, justice, equality, and beneficence (see, e.g., Clark, 1997; Fitzpatrick, 1999; House, 1993; National Commission for the Protection of Human Subjects in Biomedical and Behavioral Research, 1979). House (1993) also includes support for democratic values and institutions. The AEA guidelines have five principles – Systematic Inquiry, Competence, Integrity/ Honesty, Respect for People and Responsibilities for General and Public Welfare. The AES guidelines also have five statements of principle covering fully informed consent; opportunity to weigh up and reduce anticipated risks; respect for the rights, privacy, dignity and entitlements of those affected by and contributing to the evaluation; judgments based on comprehensive, sound information; and fair and balanced reporting.

These principles on the whole stem from a Western view of the world and, while they embrace respect for diversity and the norms of different cultures and subcultures, few explicitly address the inherent nature of different cultures in their statements of ethical guidelines. The exception is the evolving ethical guidelines stemming from indigenous communities (see, e.g., AIATSIS, 2000; Burchill,

2004; Mataria, 2003; Nga Ara Tohutohu Rangahau, 2004; NHMRC, 2003). These guidelines challenge evaluation practice, as Smith (1997) has argued in relation to a Kaupapa Maori research framework, to move beyond western epistemological understanding. Ethical guidelines from these indigenous groups emphasize the familiar values of respect for persons, equality, non-coercion and non-manipulation. However, they go beyond the individual and his/her rights to privacy, dignity and justice to place greater emphasis on recognizing and respecting indigenous knowledge systems and processes, uniqueness of peoples, social cohesion, cultural property rights and reciprocity, both in the process of evaluation and in the distribution of benefits from research and evaluation.

For example, included in the NHMRC (2003) guidelines are reciprocity, survival and protection, spirit and integrity. It is not just cultural sensitivity evaluators need to be attuned to here. The guidelines that accompany these principles emphasize – beyond the need to become familiar with cultural customs, property rights and ethical norms of the society – the very manner in which relationships are built and the culture of a people is sustained. In some indigenous cultures, the making of decisions is a collective process involving substantial deliberation among elders and leaders. In such cases time becomes an important ethical consideration in accessing cultural wisdom and, in some instances, determining which methodologies can be used. Take, for example, the Kaupapa Maori framework prescribed by Smith (1997). The second precept *Kanohi kitea* ("the seen face"; a requirement to present yourself "face to face") or the third, *Titiro,whakarongo* ("look. listen . . . then speak") (cited in Mataria, 2003, p. 6), suggest that only certain methodologies are appropriate when evaluating programmes in this culture.

Limitations of Ethical Codes

Antagonists of ethical codes point to their self-serving nature designed to protect the interests of the profession rather than the researched, their inherent conservatism when built on consensus, and the regulation that may accompany their use. Some authors go further (see, for instance, Punch, 1986) and suggest that such codes threaten to restrict research, create barriers where none exist, and inadvertently protect the powerful rather than the weak.

As a guide for ethical practice in the field, published guidelines have three further difficulties. The first is that ethics do not feature as largely as codes/standards on other dimensions of practice. In the informal analyses of codes conducted by Russon & Russon (2005), standards related to ethics were far fewer than other dimensions such as methodology, quality, utility, and contractual relationships between sponsors and evaluators (see also Fraser, 2005, p. 77, in the same volume). And Newman & Brown observe that in the Joint Committee Standards, "the use of the word ethics is assiduously avoided" (Newman & Brown, 1996, p. 21), though embedded within them, in the section on propriety for instance, are standards that might be considered ethical in nature.

Secondly, in focusing on what to do in order to avoid harm, guidelines frequently do not offer positive guidance to promote "good", and so an opportunity is lost to advance ethical practice in evaluation. Where guidelines are generated from actual case examples and where the intent is educative rather than regulatory, this is less of a problem. As noted above, however, the intent of a given set of guidelines is not always clear.

Thirdly, there is the obvious nature of codes themselves. Codes cannot capture, nor could they hope to, the "messy" reality of the field, the unanticipated effects, conflicting political priorities and all the personal factors – fears, anxieties and differences involved in the social/political engagements of evaluation on the ground (Mabry, 2004; Worthen & Sanders, 1987).

Ethical Committees/Institutional Review Boards

Ethical Committees or Institutional Review Boards (IRBs) have long been established in the field of medicine to protect participants from harm in the conduct of medical research, especially in clinical settings. Increasingly, they are being set up in the social sciences and other professional fields. While set up by institutions, not professional associations, they are another element in the armoury of activities designed to improve ethical practice.

Ethical committees or IRBs exist to ensure that any research or evaluation proposal has considered the ethical issues that are likely to arise in an evaluation or research study and has developed protocols to protect participants. With the best intent, they contribute along with other practices to a growing sophistication of sound ethical research practice.

However, many of the issues that worry people in relation to codes of evaluation practice also apply to ethical committees. In their formulation and enactment – usually as a lengthy set of questions – and the time they take to process, IRB forms can often seem unduly restrictive and regulatory, offering power to the gatekeeper to control the evaluation even though their overarching intent is to govern good practice.

Five particular concerns have been raised over such committees or IRBs. The first is that this vigilance is at the front end of the research or evaluation. It is not possible either to anticipate all the risks that might arise nor develop protocols to manage all the interpersonal relationships and situations that may affect ethical decision-making. Secondly, as Nelson (2004, p. 210) has pointed out, one of the most consistently cited principles adopted by these committees, "respect for persons", cannot entail respect for every human action, but the critical point, he says, is that IRBs are "ill equipped to negotiate the difference".

Thirdly, and partly because ethical committees have their origin in the field of medicine, to protect participants from harm in the conduct of medical research, such committees are frequently more familiar with quantitative methods and randomized controlled trial designs. Qualitative researchers and evaluators often have to explicate their methodologies and respond to questions that do not easily transfer to qualitative evaluation (Ritchie & Lewis, 2003, p. 63).

Fourthly, increasingly such committees also act as the guardians of research design and of what is to count as research methodology. Lincoln & Tierney (2004) point out that in the US as a result of pressure from the political right to discredit certain methodologies and a heightened sense of legal issues surrounding medical protection, "the stances of IRBs have shifted from assuring that human subjects' rights are protected towards monitoring and censoring, and outright disapproval of projects that use qualitative research, phenomenological approaches and other alternative frameworks for knowing and knowledge" (Lincoln & Tierney, 2004, p. 220). This inhibits freedom to research, especially topics that may be sensitive and, in curtailing access to certain kinds of knowledge, is anti-democratic.

Fifthly, some have claimed (Furedi, 2002) that ethical committees are in practice not merely concerned with moral dilemmas, but are acting as gatekeepers, defenders of reputations, and to prevent litigation. Some IRBs are quite open about acknowledging that their main concern is to protect the institution from damage. This is a fundamental shift, Lincoln & Tierney (2004, p. 220) state, from the original purposes of such committees to ascertain risks and assure that informed consent was adequate to prepare human subjects for associated risks. Christians (2000, p. 141) has also noted that while IRBs ostensibly exist to protect the subjects who fall under approved protocols, in reality they protect their own institutions. Where such gatekeeping is the norm, the function of such committees has become one of research regulation, part of the culture of audit and managerialism, and is not necessarily concerned with ethics at all.

As evaluators and supervisors of evaluations, we have a role to play in trying to ensure that ethical committees and IRBs act with integrity in relation to their original purpose and do not disadvantage methodologies and forms of knowing that are not currently privileged by government dictate or custom. Not only should we continue to articulate and argue for methodological inclusion, but we should also advocate for consumer representation on such committees. The former will further understanding of different methodologies, the latter demonstrate an ethical commitment to representation of different voices. Both can counter a prevailing dominance of a specific methodology and the self-interest of such committees in safeguarding their institutions.

Role of Ethical Theories in Ethical Decision-Making

It may not be obvious which ethical theory guides our judgment in the field, as theories tend to come into play at a distance. In practice there are several levels at which our ethical behaviour is influenced. Firstly, we are guided by those moral and professional dispositions – qualities of character and virtues (Schwandt, 2001) – which have been cultivated

over time and which we have internalized in concepts such as integrity, trust and reliability. Secondly, there are the broad principles we accept as guiding behaviour, some of which have been built into the ethical codes mentioned previously and which we adopt before entering the field. Thirdly, there are the particular decisions we actually make in the field taking into account the exigencies of the case guided by principles and by ultimate recourse to preferred ethical theories. In exploring possible choices of ethical theories to justify decision-making in evaluation, I broadly follow the categories of ethical theories cited by Newman & Brown (1996, p. 24). These categories are based on key criteria for deciding whether the behaviour is right or wrong – consequences, duty, rights, social justice, and the ethics of care, which has also been called relational ethics (Mabry, 2004).

Different Ethical Theories and Examples

The ethics of consequences stress utility and outcomes. The decision is right based upon a consideration of its consequences, although one has to ask consequences for whom and in whose interests. Utilitarian ethics – stressing the greatest good for the greatest number – can help to address this question in giving equal consideration to all. However, in certain situations the end could come to justify the means, for instance, where advancement of knowledge is the rationale for deception to gain access. A utilitarian response to the ethical dilemma posed by Morris (2004b, p. 383), in which the new evaluator recruit uncovers deficiencies in the design of the evaluation being conducted by her agency, might take the view that it is better to protect the integrity of the evaluation profession or a larger number of stakeholders than protect those in the immediate programme team from embarrassment through exposure.

A relational ethics justification would lead to a different outcome, one that would focus on care for the immediate information sharers and preserve working relationships with colleagues rather than insist on methodological rigour for the overall reputation of the profession (Mabry, 2004, p. 386).

Another ethical theory is rooted in duties and obligations. For example, a duty to tell the truth may be revoked by a higher duty to do no harm, although the issue of how to prioritize is difficult in the absence of standards for doing so (Clark, 1997, p. 158). What constitutes harm may also vary in different contexts. A theory of duties and obligations will also not necessarily focus on the consequences. If deficiencies are encountered in the process or in a policy itself, the "right" thing to do may be to expose this inadequacy, irrespective of the consequences.

Evaluators who adopt rights theories to justify their actions believe that every person must be treated with dignity and respect and that there may be cases where rights to privacy take precedence over advancement of knowledge, programme objectives or the evaluator's theory of the programme. The ethical guidelines on privacy of the Canadian Social Sciences and Humanities Research Council, for example, advocate this precept in the statement "the question of invasion of privacy should be looked at from the point of view of those being studied rather than from that of the researcher" (1981, p. 5). In other words if there is ever any doubt that harm may be done to individuals through the generation of knowledge, then respect for the individual should take precedence over search for knowledge.

Those who advocate social justice in evaluation take this rights-based philosophy to a group and society level. One of the main advocates of a social justice approach to evaluation is House (1980, 1993) who argues, following Rawls (1971), for a principle of fairness in evaluation in which all persons have an equal right to basic liberties. To realise such a principle it may be necessary in certain cases to redress inequalities by giving precedence, or at least equal weight, to the voice of the least advantaged groups in society who may not be represented, or powerfully enough represented, in primary stake holding groups in an evaluation. Evaluators working from this ethical base would also not take on an evaluation that violated a participant's rights to fairness and justice, where, for example, participants were involved in an experiment that suppressed their autonomy or which might render them worse off than before.

If we return to the first dilemma in the introduction, where participants in a programme evaluation were denied payment that affected their livelihood, while the evaluation report was being negotiated with the managers of the programme, a decision to aspire to maintain the integrity of the evaluation could be justified by an appeal to fairness and justice to those beyond the case and the evaluation profession. A decision to compromise might be justified by an appeal to relational ethics – a consideration of how it would affect the livelihood of those who remained unpaid. But these are not the only choices. A further choice – to bypass the institution and release the report to the overall sponsor (beyond the managers) could be justified by an appeal to utilitarian ethics – the participants get paid, all the stakeholders get the report, the evaluation maintains its methodological integrity and the wider audience gets to debate the findings.

In the last ten to fifteen years the ethics of care (Gilligan, 1982; Noddings, 1984) has expanded our choices of ethical theories to justify our actions. This emphasizes greater attention to the primacy of relationships in the programme (Christians, 2000, p. 143), rather than individual human rights and rules, and to specific contexts, not universal laws or principles (Newman & Brown, 1996, p. 33). Rational thinking is not rejected in this approach but rather must serve something higher – caring for others (Noddings, 1984). Into the frame of ethical thinking here is a concern for how an individual's personal life circumstances affects the decision and how he/she would be affected by the available alternative choices. Often the preferred choice in feminist ethics (Denzin, 1997; Usher, P., 2000), the ethics of care also has much in common with participatory and democratic forms of evaluation (House & Howe, 1999; MacDonald, 1976) and with the ethical theory of feminist communitarism proposed by Denzin (1997).

Take, for example, the scenario where a local administration, ten months into the life of a project that is providing bilingual education to young children to help raise their selfesteem and adjust to schooling, realise that they have appointed the wrong director to the project. The administration wish to persuade the director to leave and, when this is resisted, seek to sack him. The project director seeks union advice. These relationships constitute data that partly explain the slow development of the project. The ethical dilemma the evaluator faces is whether to record the history of the project and its negative effects on the development and outcomes for the children concerned, or to protect the director's anxiety about his future career, as requested by him, by omitting certain details and transactions. An evaluator adopting an ethics of care position might opt for protecting the privacy and future career prospects of the director; one operating from an ethics of consequence might be more concerned about getting the programme on track so positive outcomes for the children would have a better chance of being realised.

"The Ultimate Ethical Act"

I have briefly outlined key differences in ethical theories with some illustrations to indicate how a theory or combination of theories may ultimately guide our ethical decision-making. However, as the first introductory quotation to this chapter suggests, actual ethical decision-making is balancing mutually conflicting principles in concrete socio-political situations. This is "the ultimate ethical act" to which House (1993, p. 168) refers. For further examples of ethical dilemmas and indications of how they might be resolved see the Ethical Challenges section in the *American Journal of Evaluation* and for examples of actual concrete ethical decisions in action see Lee-Treweek & Linkogle (2000) and Simons & Usher (2000).

In reaching a decision evaluators have a number of resources to draw upon to inform ethical thinking. Soltis (1999) suggests that the issue/situation be considered from three different perspectives: of the person (the evaluator in this case), the profession, and the public, noting the different dilemmas that occur for each. Newman & Brown (1996) offer a framework that includes intuition, rules and codes, principles, theory, personal value and beliefs and action. While this may appear overly rationalistic, given the uncertainty, complexity and finely tuned professional judgment we have to make in the "ethical moment" (Usher, R., 2000), it draws our attention to a range of sources that we may need to integrate to inform the ethical decisions we make.

Furthermore, as several authors have pointed out (House, 1993; Mabry, 2004; Simons, 2000; Thomas, 2000), we need to keep in mind that interpersonal and political factors also impact on decisions we take in the field. Many of the responses offered to the ethical challenges outlined by Morris (2000, 2001, 2004a, 2004b) are as much common-sense, relational and political as ethical, as Thomas (2000, p. 269) points out in his commentary on "The Case of the Sensitive Survey". This brings our attention back to the broader political space within which evaluation is located, where politics is often intertwined with ethics and methodology and where findings often result in the allocation and reallocation of resources (Thomas, 2000, p. 269).

Inter-relationship of Politics and Ethics

The second quotation with which this chapter began highlighted this interdependence of politics and ethics. This section explores how these inter-relationships may be procedurally managed in an evaluation given the political values and interests of the different actors – commissioners, sponsors, participants, managers and evaluators – with specific reference to two democratic practices. During the past thirty years, as the field of evaluation acknowledged its inherent political dimension (Apple, 1974; House, 1972; MacDonald, 1976), various approaches to evaluation have developed which attempt to address the democratic obligation to conduct defensible, just and fair evaluation in political contexts where the values and interests of different stakeholders often conflict. These approaches include stakeholder evaluation (Greene, 1988), democratic evaluation (MacDonald, 1976), deliberative democratic evaluation (House & Howe, 1999; Ryan & DeStefano, 2000), and various forms of participatory evaluation (Cousins & Earl, 1992).

In their different ways these practices evolved to honour the different values and interests represented in projects and programmes and offered procedures to mediate conflicts of values and interests. They all acknowledge the role the evaluator plays in generating knowledge in society and that creating and maintaining relationships in an evaluation is central to the generation and dissemination of evaluation knowledge to maximize its utility.

This emphasis on politics and relationships in the process of evaluation subsequently came to be embedded in ethical codes and standards. Fitzpatrick (1999) points out that a comparison of ethical codes produced in the early 1980s with those in the early 1990s reveals a major move to focus on non-methodological issues. This is apparent both in the AEA guiding principles which "are more concerned with qualities or principles that permeate the evaluation process" and changes in evaluation training where there is "a greater examination of the many political factors and personal judgements entailed in conducting evaluations" (Fitzpatrick, 1999, p. 6). (See also Greene, 1994.)

The essence of what it means to evaluate ethically within a democratic approach may be demonstrated briefly through two approaches, the first from the UK, and the second from the US. Stemming from liberal democratic theory, democratic evaluation (MacDonald, 1976), aspires to find an appropriate balance in the conduct of evaluation between the rights of privacy of individuals and the public's right to know. In a particular case, this may mean that the public's right to know has to give way to an individual's right to retain some information in confidence and not allow public release. Alternatively, a person's "right to privacy" may need to be balanced in the public interest and, in certain instances, to be breached as, for example, where an illegal act is revealed in the course of the evaluation.

This central aspiration was translated into a set of ethical principles and procedures for the conduct of evaluation that accords equal treatment to people and ideas; that allows a flow of information which is independent of powerful, hierarchical interests; that does not allow any one person or group to veto what has already been cleared by others as public knowledge. These ethical procedures (for examples in practice see Simons, 1987, 1989;

Bridges, 1989) are based upon principles of equality, justice, fairness, and respect for persons and for public knowledge. They are embodied in a contract or agreement that is endorsed by all parties to the evaluation at the outset and to which reference can be made in the event of disagreement.

In the US, House (1980) has long been an advocate of democratising evaluation and of justice in evaluation. He also draws from liberal democratic theory in advocating a concept of liberal democratic evaluation to aid in making choices about public programmes and policies (House, 1980, p. 141). Essential concepts in this approach are respect for the interests of all relevant stakeholders, equality of choice and the "public interest". However, House accords more weight to distributive principles, like equality, justice and fairness, in judging the procedures by which decisions are made (ibid., p. 151), not the decisions themselves. Drawing on the work of Barry (1965) and Care (1978), who advanced the concept of "procedural moral acceptability", House (1980) proposes that evaluators draw up a fair evaluation agreement to guide their evaluation practice based on twelve conditions under which policy agreements among persons are morally acceptable. (For further explication of these conditions see House, 1980, pp. 162–170.)

In more recent work, House & Howe (1999, p. 94) have advocated deliberative democratic evaluation, which has the three general criteria of *inclusiveness* – to represent all interest and values, *dialogue* with relevant groups – so the views are properly and authentically represented, and *deliberation* – to arrive at proper findings. While the authors do not specifically mention ethical procedures in their account of this approach, it is clear that respect and autonomy for persons, beneficence, openness and transparency of process are key ethical concerns.

Ethical Conventions/Procedures in Evaluation Studies

When it comes to the actual conduct of evaluation, evaluation shares with other forms of social research many of the usual conventions for the protection of participants, such as informed consent, privacy and confidentiality and pre-publication access. However, evaluation has specific demands and dilemmas given its function and inherent political nature. These include, for example, how we arrive at evaluation questions; how we determine which values to promote (given legitimate concerns among stakeholders); how we determine which evaluation theory or principles to follow; how we design and implement evaluations, including choices of methodology; how we determine costs and benefits; and how we report to legitimate stakeholders in different cultural contexts. In this section I draw attention to the ways in which some of these issues are manifest in evaluation, starting with a comment on differences in methodology and then exploring how certain common ethical precepts may be reinterpreted in conducting and reporting evaluations.

Some Differences in Methodology

Several authors (see, e.g., Lincoln, 1990) have made the point that the ethical issues facing evaluators adopting qualitative methods are different from those encountered when using quantitative methods. However, they are not type-specific (Lincoln, 1990, p. 278). Differences relate to broader issues in ethical decision-making including ethical theories about the right to know, the right to privacy, respect for persons, honesty, justice, respect for knowledge and how it is generated and disseminated and to whom. But whichever methodology is chosen, it has consequences for participants and beneficiaries, directly or indirectly.

There are certain ethical principles that apply whatever the methodology chosen – one should not lie to respondents, one should not deliberately deceive in order to gain access and one should not falsify results of an evaluation. However, the choice of methodology and the procedures adopted in using that methodology reflect a particular ethical and political stance which will affect how the evaluator resolves dilemmas such as the following: Is deception ever warranted? Are some interventions inherently unethical whichever methods are adopted? What counts as doing no harm? How do you protect the rights of children or cultural minorities affected by misuse of evaluation results? Do contractual obligations have ethical implications or simply legal responsibilities? Who decides who tells the truth?

It is sometimes inferred that ethical issues are not so present when using quantitative methods, as people are not so directly involved and it is easier to anonymize respondents and institutions. Conversely, it is often assumed that ethical dilemmas are faced more acutely when qualitative methods involving direct interpersonal interaction are adopted. Neither is the case. Ethical issues may be more hidden in the use of quantitative measures but they are not absent (see, e.g., Jones, 2000; Lincoln, 1990; Sammons, 1989).

However, there is little, if any reference to ethical issues in popular texts on statistics in the social sciences (Jones, 2000, p. 48). This is either an oversight, Jones suggests, or a significant omission given the harm that can ensue, for example, for students' life chances from the bias that may be built into psychometric tests, or from the manipulation of statistical data. The manipulation of some of the international comparative data on mathematics teaching, for example, could be harming the educational chances of the very students it seeks to benefit. (Jones, 2000, p. 147). Randomized controlled design studies also raise serious ethical issues for groups who are not given treatments that are demonstrated to have positive effects. The question of ownership of data is also less easy to attribute. For example, who owns the test results of a test that is taken by a child in school hours – the child, the school (in locus parentis), or the local education authority/district?

By contrast, reference is made to ethics in many qualitative inquiry texts, especially those which emphasize naturalistic, phenomenological, and narrative inquiry, where much of the data are gathered by direct observation and interviewing of people. One cannot conduct a personal narrative or study a person's life without seeking personal informed consent and clearance of interpretation or observe a child who is severely disabled without seeking parent's consent. The above differences in applied ethics and methodology refer to research in general. In the next section I re-examine common ethical procedures in the context of evaluation.

Reframing Ethical Procedures in Evaluation

Designing and Planning the Evaluation

Design. In discussing a cost–benefit approach to weighing the risks and benefits of an evaluation, Mark, Eyssell & Campbell (1999) indicate that the debate on whether there is an ethical dimension to the quality of a design has a further complexity in evaluation, given the importance of the criterion of use. They outline a range of positions an evaluator could take, drawing on authors discussing psychological research, namely Pomerantz (1994) who argues that design quality and use are not ethical issues and Rosenthal (1994) who argues that bad evaluation design is actually unethical. In studies of low risk, Mark et al., (1999, p. 50) conclude that design issues "should not be viewed primarily from the lens of ethicality. . . . When risks for participants are high, a utilization focus (Patton, 1997) becomes an ethical mandate, necessary to justify the high risk" (ibid., p. 51). Once again we have a judgment to make in a specific case, in this instance, whether the quality of design is a technical or ethical issue.

Quality of design for Mark et al., (1999, p. 52) includes a whole range of questions related to whether evaluation methods are adequate to achieve the evaluation's purpose and whether the evidence provides a reasonable warrant for the claims and conclusions made. Take the example of a participatory evaluation design of a community project, which aims to provide services to multi-ethnic groups, and where people have chosen to participate in deciding what questions should be asked in order to inform community action. A trade-off might be that partial feedback is more useful to the community to engage their participation than a more comprehensive design of pre–post surveys and in-depth interviews of all potential recipients of the services.

Planning. In planning an evaluation the ethical issues proposed by Perloff & Perloff (1980) also help set ethical limits and formulate specific procedures for action. While the four these authors mention can all be said to stem from "respect for persons", each focuses on a different aspect of this principle. The first is withholding the nature of evaluation research from participants or involving them without their knowledge. The imperative here is clearly not to withhold information, though there are some who claim some practices would not be evaluated unless covert access was gained. How would one evaluate a corrupt police force, for instance, or a sect that was manipulating adolescents? The second is exposing participants to physical stress, anxiety

[potentially the case in physical education or medical evaluations],[4] or acts that would diminish their self-respect. The third is invading the privacy of participants, an issue that is embedded in relationships as much as in procedures (see later section on privacy) and the fourth, withholding benefits, is clearly not something evaluators should do. These are all aspects that need to be considered prior to seeking informed consent.

Informed Consent. In gaining informed consent there are four particular issues beyond those just mentioned that have ethical implications for evaluation. The first relates to the uncertain political nature of the enterprise. Gaining informed consent is an ethical imperative in any research study and signing an informed consent form is a familiar formal procedure in many contexts. Yet for many this is not consent at all, as it is never possible to know what will transpire as the programme unfolds in a precise socio-political context. Whatever forms are signed, "free and fully informed consent" needs to be realized through the additional different procedure of "rolling consent"– renegotiating consent with each person and/or site once a greater awareness of the context and structure of the study is known, or what Ramcharan & Cutcliffe (2001) have called process consent – renegotiating consent at different stages in the process of the evaluation. Such "rolling consent" is a particularly important procedure to maintain in evaluation studies that have emergent designs, stakeholder involvement, and a democratic or participatory intent.

The second informed consent issue concerns children. Morris (1999, p. 20) draws attention to the ethical dilemma that has been raised over active versus passive consent by parents, querying whether it is ethically appropriate to rely on passive consent from parents knowing that active consent generally produces lower participation rates (Morris,

1999, p. 20). A further issue, not often addressed, is active consent from children themselves. At what age and in what contexts can children be considered to give active consent? Even quite small children have ways of demonstrating their agreement to be involved in an evaluation study and to continue to participate.

The third concerns payment – whether it is ethically appropriate to offer payment as part of informed consent procedures. In some contexts, where respondents are poor, for example, or the cultural context necessitates, it may not be possible to evaluate the programme without offering payment. The AIATSIS (2000) principles, for instance, expressly state that researchers and evaluators should "Recognise that certain cultural information is owned and may need to be paid for" (Principle 7, point 5, p. 12). In other contexts payment may be seen as coercion to participate.

The fourth issue is trust. Where indigenous communities mistrust the language and intention of government and those evaluating government initiatives, guidelines on reciprocal benefits, collective rights of ownership, and recognition of cultural understanding need to be thoroughly negotiated at the outset, maintained throughout and renegotiated if necessary in the light of the findings.

Conducting the Evaluation and Safeguarding Privacy and Confidentiality

Mark et al., (1999, p. 48) succinctly summarize the usual guidelines on ethics in data collection and analysis as minimizing risk; only conducting evaluation when benefits outweigh the risks; obtaining fully informed consent; upholding principles of non-coercion, respect for participants' privacy and decency, preservation of confidentiality to the fullest extent where data cannot be collected anonymously, avoidance of fraud; and following technical requirements. Yet they also recognize

that "the devil is in the details" (ibid., p. 48). Decisions still need to be made in specific contexts as to when cash payments for completing questionnaires, for example, can cross into coercion (Mariner, 1990) or where particular trade-offs need to be made.

The traditional means of protecting individuals' privacy and confidentiality in evaluation studies is to anonymize participants. This is relatively easy to guarantee in evaluations that use quantitative methods, more difficult in those which adopt qualitative methods and participatory approaches that have educative or emancipatory intent. Numerous procedures have developed to acknowledge this difficulty. These include offering participants control over what they say and how they are represented, seeking clearance of comments in contexts when it is possible to identify individuals, even when anonymized, and engaging participants at every stage of the evaluation so that even if they are identified they have come to trust the process and accept the findings.

However, even if it is possible to anonymize, this does not mean that privacy is protected or confidentiality respected. Confidentiality is easily offered but difficult to assure, and Morris (1999, p. 19) reports that promising confidentiality when it cannot be guaranteed is one of the most serious ethical violations in evaluation. Respecting privacy or non-intrusiveness is partly methodological – what questions get asked and how as well as what is reported. However, important protection and respect for privacy also lie in the relationships established in the conduct of the evaluation.

Torres & Preskill (1999, p. 64), in considering ethical dimensions of stakeholder participation and evaluation, note that relationships (and the credibility, trust, rapport and mutual understanding they create) are central to successful evaluations but question whether the pragmatic agenda of evaluation will compromise its relational dimensions. In considering this issue they appeal to Schwandt's concept of "knowing *through* relationships 'as a possible solution to the question Are *we* doing the right thing, and are *we* doing it well?"' (p. 11, italics in original, quoted by Torres & Preskill, 1999, p. 65).

Similarly, respecting confidentiality is more than mere anonymization. Anonymization is a technical procedure which may offer some protection for an individual from public gaze, but the ethical promise in confidentiality is met in how one negotiates the use of the data. It actually means in certain cases not reporting information that a person has given in confidence.

Furthermore, there are situations where anonymization is not the most appropriate procedure to employ. Clearly this is the case where public figures are concerned, where there is only one lead figure in an organization or where there is a need to acknowledge the participation and contribution to knowledge of those involved in the evaluation. It may also be important not to anonymize where the aspiration is to build a collaborative reflexivity about the process of evaluation; discussing moral dilemmas and how to resolve them collectively will generate further trust. Finally, there may be situations where there is a need in the public interest to reveal dubious or corrupt practices or those which potentially may harm.

Reporting the Evaluation Fairly

One of the most frequently encountered problems in evaluation, which was also deemed the most serious by evaluators in a study by Morris & Cohn (1993), involved the presentation of findings. The most specific problem was pressure to slant the findings to suit the interest of a particular stakeholder, usually the main client.

The ethical procedures to ensure fairness and justice rooted in a democratic ethic help to avoid such partiality in reporting. Yet the politics of evaluation practice in a customer-contracting culture often mean that the

dominant stakeholder threatens this ethical stance. This can be avoided to some extent by ongoing engagement of stakeholders in the process of the evaluation, involving them in identification of issues, checking with them whether their perspectives and actions have been interpreted and/or represented accurately and fairly and, perhaps most importantly, making interim results public. In this way knowledge is shared by a range of stakeholders in the evaluation throughout the process making it more difficult to modify or censor findings at the final report stage.

Further respect for participants in forms of participatory evaluation can be achieved by acknowledging them as co-authors of reports and, in certain cases, where it is unquestionably *their* story which is told, offering them a share of the profits if the report is sold. See McKeever (2000) for an example of this principle in action. The issue of profits for participants introduces an arguably problematic notion into evaluation studies, but in certain contexts it may facilitate the educational aim of evaluation and the development of community. In the case of indigenous communities, reporting will need to take account of the reciprocal obligations agreed at the outset, the different culture, language and ways of understanding and forms of reporting (which may include oral reporting) that acknowledge cultural difference. In early negotiations, it is important to establish what financial remuneration and intellectual property rights or portion of them will be accorded to the community (AIATSIS, 2000, principle 6, point 4, 5, principle 9, point 7, 10).

Summary and Conclusion

As the field of evaluation has developed over the past four decades, ethics has come to assume more visibility. Many of the alternative evaluation approaches that evolved feature people's experiences, perspectives, and values, giving rise to the need to establish procedures to protect individuals' privacy. Recognition of the inherent political nature of evaluation led to the emergence of principles, agreements, and contracts that aspire to treat stakeholders equally and fairly in the evaluation process and ensure that findings contribute to public discourse and debate. Evaluation has also intensified at the professional level with the rise of professional standards and at the institutional level in the setting up of ethical committees or Institutional Review Boards (IRBs). While the latter developments are often linked to discussion on ethics, it is noteworthy that these practices in some situations are more concerned with defending institutions and controlling what evaluation gets done and which methodologies are appropriate.

In such a changing context evaluators need to be vigilant on a number of fronts. First, we need to distinguish those practices that facilitate and those that inhibit ethical evaluation and challenge the latter. Controlling which methodologies receive funding, for example, is not beneficial for programme participants, evaluators or clients and is certainly not conducive to informed public debate or social justice. Sanctioning evaluation practice according to universal standards that are not sensitive to different cultural contexts and practices is similarly unlikely to lead to better ethical practice.

Secondly, it is clear that ethical committees and IRBs, while potentially useful to consider what requires ethical consideration in proposed evaluations, cannot control or determine that the evaluation subsequently conducted will be ethical. IRBs are only one element in a number of processes that are needed to ensure ethical practice (Mark et al., 1999). Some would argue, furthermore, that ethical practice can only be achieved through relationships in the field (Schwandt, 1998;

Torres & Preskill, 1999). Too much attention to pre-procedures in such committees may be a distraction from the ethics of evaluation, as evaluators assume that procedures endorsed by these committees can simply be carried out as methodological dictate or moral rules.

Thirdly, it is clear that some changes to field procedures for ensuring ethical practice in the conduct and reporting of evaluation are required. Anonymization, for instance, needs to be decoupled from concerns with confidentiality and privacy. Not only are there methodologies where anonymization is inappropriate, it does not guarantee confidentiality or protection of privacy. Ensuring privacy in certain qualitative methodologies is an intimate, responsive, field decision linked to, for example, asking non-intrusive questions and making strategic political decisions that would not harm a person's career or position in an organization if information were released. Furthermore if democratic evaluation approaches gain greater credibility, it may not be possible and/or it may be counterproductive to anonymize a range of individuals with whom one has had extensive deliberations during the conduct of evaluations and the findings.

Fourthly, it will be important to document specific ethical dilemmas we encounter in our practice and how these were resolved so that increasingly we can demonstrate which principles and ethical theories influenced our decision-making in the "ethical moment" (Morris, 1999; Usher, 2000). In this way a strong evidential base for ethical decision-making in situ can be developed, which offers integrated examples of principles in practice.

Fifthly, many evaluators (see Fitzpatrick & Morris, 1999) stress two further points. One, that we still have a long way to go in finding the best ways to resolve ethical issues (Morris, 1999, p. 16); and two, that dialogue between evaluators and with evaluators, clients, sponsors and participants may be the most effective way to resolve them (Mabry, 2004; Torres & Preskill, 1999). Similarly, Mark et al., (1999, p. 54) conclude that "it is perhaps better not to dance with the devil alone" in advocating engaging in many forms of deliberation (e.g., review panels, advisory panels, evaluator networks and discussions) to advance ethical practice.

Finally, we need to remember that whatever procedures are set in place, it is only in the field – the political ethical space (Kushner, 2000, pp. 151–152) – in which we negotiate relationships and meanings in full cognizance of all the relevant factors in a specific sociopolitical context, and the ethical theories and principles which have informed our actions, that we can know if we have acted ethically in an evaluation. This is the complex integrity Glen (2000) speaks of – the constant reflexive re-examination of values (ours and others) in relationship with those we evaluate.

Acknowledgements

I am grateful to the editors of the Handbook and to David Bridges, Ernest House, Robert Picciotto, and Patricia Rogers for their critical, generous, and helpful comments.

Notes

1. This is distinct from the broad purpose of principles which may be used to promote ethical practice for evaluation in general and which is not tied to society membership.

2. In the US the American Educational Research Association (AERA) and the American Psychological Association (APA) published guidelines in 1992; the revised Joint Committee Standards were published in 1994; the American Evaluation Association (AEA) principles in 1995; the Canadian Evaluation Society (CES) Guidelines in 1996; the Australasian Evaluation Society (AES) Guidelines in 1997, the United Kingdom Evaluation Society Guidelines in 2003.

3. Standards in the AES have had a more protracted history. While the issue has been on the association's agenda since the late 1980s exploring a possible adaptation of the Joint Committee Standards, 'there is a lack of resolution on quality standards' (Fraser, 2001a, 2001b). No set of Australasian standards has yet been endorsed (Fraser 2005:76), though an *ethical code*, which may be seen as a subset of standards, was endorsed in 2000.

4. For the most part codes are drawn up by evaluators for the profession. The exception is the AES who include commissioners within their broad frame of reference and the UKES who cite separate guidelines for commissioners.

References

AIATSIS (The Australian Institute of Aboriginal and Torres Strait Islander Studies) (2000). Guidelines for ethical research in indigenous studies. Available at http://www.Aiatsis.gov.au/corp/docs/EthicsGuide.

American Educational Research Association (1992). Ethical standards of the American Educational Research Association. *Educational Researcher*, 21(7), 23–26.

American Evaluation Association (2004). Guiding principles for evaluators. http://www.eval.org/Guiding%20Principles.htm. Accessed 30/3/05, first published 1995.

American Psychological Association (1992) Ethical principles of psychologists and code of conduct. *American Psychologist*, 47, 1597–1611.

Apple, M. W. (1974). The process and ideology of valuing in educational settings. In M. Apple, M. G. Subkoviak, & H. S. Lufler (eds) *Educational Evaluation: Analysis and Responsibility* (pp. 3–34). Berkeley, CA: McCutchan.

Australasian Evaluation Society (2002). Guidelines for the ethical conduct of evaluations. www.aes.asn.auorhttp://www.aes.asn.au/about/guidelines for the ethical conduct of evaluations.

Barry, B. (1965). *Political Argument*. London: Routledge & Kegan Paul.

Bridges, D. (1989). Ethics and the law: Conducting case studies of policing. In R. G. Burgess (ed.) The *Ethics of Educational Research* (pp. 141–159). London: The Falmer Press.

Burchill, M. (2004). Enough talking – more walking – achieving deadly outcomes. In

Stronger Families Learning Exchange Bulletin, 6 (Spring/Summer), 6–9. http://www.aifs.giv. au/sf/pubs/ bull6/enough.html.

Bustelo, M. (2004). The potential role of standards and guidelines in the development of an evaluation culture: The case of Spain. Paper presented to the 6th European Evaluation Society Biennial Conference, Governance, Democracy and Evaluation, Berlin, 30 September–2 October, 2004.

Care, N. S. (1978). Participation and policy. *Ethics,* 88(July), 316–337.

Christians, C. G. (2000). Ethics and politics in qualitative research. In N. K. Denzin & Y. S. Lincoln (eds) *The Handbook of Qualitative Research* (pp. 133–155). London & Thousand Oaks, CA: Sage Publications.

Clark, J. (1997). *Educational Research: Philosophy, Politics and Ethics.* Massey, NZ: ERDC Press, Massey University, Palmerston North, New Zealand.

Cousins, J. B. & Earl, L. M. (1992). The case for participatory evaluation. *Educational Evaluation and Policy Analysis,* 14, 397–418.

Cronbach, L. J., Ambron, S. M., Dornbusch, S. M., Hess, R. D., Hornik, R. C., Phillips, D., Walker D. F., & Weiner, S. S. (1980). *Toward Reform of Program Evaluation: Aims, methods and institutional arrangements.* San Francisco, CA: Jossey-Bass.

Denzin, N. K. (1997). *Interpretative Ethnography: Ethnographic practices for the 21st century.* Thousand Oaks, CA: Sage.

Fitzpatrick, J. L. (1999). Ethics in disciplines and professions related to evaluation. In J. L. Fitzpatrick & M. Morris (eds) *Current and Emerging Ethical Challenges in Evaluation. New Directions For Evaluation,* 82 (pp. 5–14). San Francisco: Jossey-Bass.

Fitzpatrick, J.L. & Morris, M. (eds) (1999). *Current and Emerging Ethical Challenges in Evaluation. New Directions for Evaluation,* 82 (pp. 15–24), San Francisco: Jossey-Bass.

Fraser, D. (2001a). Beyond ethics: Why we need evaluation standards. *Evaluation Journal of Australasia,* I(1), 53–58.

Fraser, D. (2001b). Development of AES Standards. *Evaluation Journal of Australasia,* I(1), 59.

Fraser, D. (2005). National evaluation standards for Australia and New Zealand: Many questions but few answers. In C. Russon & G. Russon (eds) *International Perspectives on Evaluation Standards. New Directions for Evaluation,* 104 (pp. 67–78). San Francisco: Jossey-Bass.

Furedi, F. (2002). Don't rock the research boat. *Times Higher Educational Supplement,* 11, 01, 20.

Gilligan, C. (1982). *In a Different Voice.* Cambridge, MA: Harvard University Press.

Glen, S. (2000). The dark side of purity or the virtues of double-mindedness. In H. Simons & R. Usher (eds) *Situated Ethics in Educational Research* (pp. 12–21). London & New York: Routledge/Falmer.

Goldner, F. H. (1967). Role emergence and the ethics of ambiguity. In G. Sjoberg (ed.) *Ethics, Politics and Social Research* (pp. 245–266). London: Routledge & Kegan Paul.

Greene, J. C. (1988). Stakeholder participation and utilization in program evaluation. *Evaluation Review,* 12, 91–116.

Greene, J. C. (1994). Qualitative program evaluation: Practice and promise. In N. K. Denzin & Y. S. Lincoln (eds) *The Handbook of Qualitative Research.* London: Sage.

House, E. R. (1972). The conscience of educational evaluation. *Teachers College Record,* 73(3), 405–414.

House, E. R. (1980). *Evaluating with Validity.* London: Sage.

House, E. R. & (1993). *Professional Evaluation: Social impact and political consequences.* Newbury Park, CA: Sage.

House, E. R. & Howe, K. (1999). *Values in Evaluation and Social Research.* London: Sage.

Joint Committee on Standards for Educational Evaluation (1981). *Standards for Evaluation of Educational Programs, Projects and Materials.* New York: McGraw-Hill.

Joint Committee on Standards for Educational Evaluation (1994). *The Program Evaluation Standards,* second edition. Thousand Oaks, CA: Sage.

Jones, K. (2000). A regrettable oversight or a significant omission? Ethical considerations in quantitative research in education. In H. Simons & R. Usher (eds) *Situated Ethics in Educational Research* (pp. 147–161). London & New York: Routledge/Falmer.

Kushner, S. (2000). *Personalizing Evaluation.* London: Sage.

Lee-Treweek, G. & Linkogle, S. (eds) (2000). *Danger in the Field: Risks and ethics in social research.* London & New York: Routledge.

Lincoln, Y. S. (1990). Towards a categorical imperative for qualitative research. In E.W. Eisner & A. Peshkin (eds) *Qualitative Inquiry in Education:*

The continuing debate (pp. 277–295). New York: Teachers College Columbia University.

Lincoln, Y. S. & Tierney, W. G. (2004). Qualitative research and institutional review boards. *Qualitative Inquiry*, 10(2), 219–234.

Mabry, L. (1999). Circumstantial ethics. *American Journal of Evaluation*, 20, 199–212.

Mabry, L. (2004). Commentary "Gray skies are gonna clear up". *American Journal of Evaluation*, 25(3), 385–390.

MacDonald, B. (1976). Evaluation and of the control of education. In D. Tawney (ed.) *Curriculum Evaluation Today: Trends and implications*. Schools Council Research Studies (pp. 125–136). London: Macmillan.

Mariner, W. K. (1990). The ethical conduct of clinical trials of HIV vaccines. *Evaluation Review*, 14(5), 538–564.

Mark, M. M., Eyssell, K. M., & Campbell, B. (1999). The ethics of data collection and analysis. In J. L. Fitzpatrick & M. Morris (eds) *Current and Emerging Ethical Challenges in Evaluation. New Directions For Evaluation*, 82 (pp. 47–56). San Francisco: Jossey-Bass.

Mataria, P. (2003). Maori evaluation research, theory and practice: Lessons for native Hawaiian evaluation studies. Paper presented at June 2003 meeting of the Evaluation Hui, Kamehameha Schools, Honolulu, HI. Available at www.ksbe.edu/pase/pdf/EvaluationHui/Maitaira.pdf.

McKeever, M. (2000). Snakes and ladders: Ethical issues in conducting educational research in a postcolonial context. In H. Simons & R. Usher (eds) *Situated Ethics in Educational Research* (pp. 101–115). London & New York: Routledge/Falmer.

Morris, M. (1999). Research on evaluation ethics: What have we learned and why is it important? In J. L. Fitzpatrick & M. Morris (eds) *Current and Emerging Ethical Challenges in Evaluation. New Directions For Evaluation*, 82 (pp. 15–24). San Francisco: Jossey-Bass.

Morris, M. (2000). The case of the sensitive survey. *American Journal of Evaluation*, 21(2), 261– 274.

Morris, M. (2004a). The steering committee. *American Journal of Evaluation*, 25(1), 123–126.

Morris, M. (2004b). Put on a happy face. *American Journal of Evaluation*, 25(3), 381–391.

Morris, M. & Cohn, R. (1993). Program evaluators and ethical challenges: A national survey. *Evaluation Review*, 17, 621–642.

National Commission for the Protection of Human Subjects in Biomedical and Behavioral Research, (1979). *The Belmont Report: Ethical principles and guidelines for the protection of human subjects of research*. Washington, DC: US Department of Health, Education and Welfare.

Nelson, C. (2004). The brave new world of research surveillance. *Qualitative Inquiry*, 10(2), 207–218.

Newman. D. L. & Brown, R. D. (1996). *Applied ethics for program evaluation*. London & Thousand Oaks, CA: Sage.

Nga Ara Tohutohu Rangahau Maori (2004). Guidelines for Research and Evaluation with Maori. Centre for Social Research and Evaluation Te Pokapu Rangahau Arotake Hapori, Ministry of Social Development, Te Manatu Whakahiato Ora, Wellington: New Zealand. Available at http://www.msd.govt.nz/documents/publications/csre/guidelines-research-evaluation-maori.pdf.

NHMRC (2003). Values and Ethics: Guidelines for Ethical Conduct in Aboriginal and Torres Strait Islander Health Research.

Noddings, N. (1984). *Caring: A feminine approach to ethics and moral education*. Berkeley: University of California Press.

Patton, M. Q. (1997). *Utilization-Focussed Evaluation: The new century text*, third edition. Thousand Oaks, CA: Sage.

Perloff, R. & Perloff, E. (1980). Ethics in practice. In R. Perloff & E. Perloff (eds) Values, Ethics and *Standards in Evaluation. New Directions in Program Evaluation*, 7, (pp. 77–83). San Francisco: Jossey-Bass.

Picciotto, R. (2005). The value of evaluation standards: A comparative assessment. In *JMDE Journal of MultiDisciplinary Evaluation*, 3 October, 2005. ISSN 1556-8180. Available at http://www.wmich.edu/evalctr/jmde.

Plant, J. F. (1998). Using codes of ethics in teaching Public Administration. In J. Bowman & D. Menzel (eds) *Teaching Ethics and Values in Public Administration Programs*. Albany, NY: State University of New York Press.

Pomerantz, J. R. (1994). On criteria for ethics in science: Commentary on Rosenthal. *Psychological Science*, 5(3), 135–136.

Pring, R. (2000). *Philosophy of Educational Research*. London & New York: Continuum.

Punch, M. (1986). *The Politics and Ethics of Fieldwork*. London: Sage.

Ramcharan, P. & Cutcliffe, J. (2001). Judging the ethics of qualitative research: Considering the "ethics as process" model. *Social Care in the Community*, 9(6), 358–366.

Rawls, J. (1971). *A Theory of Justice*. Cambridge, MA: Harvard University Press.

Ritchie, J. & Lewis, J. (eds) (2003). Qualitative Research Practice: A Guide for Social Science Students and Researchers. London & Thousand Oaks: Sage Publications.

Rosenthal, R. (1994). Science and ethics in conducting, analyzing and reporting psychological research. *Psychological Science*, 5(3), 127–134.

Russell, C. (1993). *Academic Freedom*. London: Routledge.

Russon, C. & Russon. G. (eds) (2005). *International Perspectives on Evaluation Standards. New Directions for Evaluation*, no. 104, a publication of Jossey-Bass and the American Evaluation Association, San Francisco: Wiley Periodicals.

Ryan, K. E. & DeStefano, L. (eds) (2000). *Evaluation as a Democratic Process: Promoting Inclusion, Dialogue and Deliberation. New Directions for Evaluation*, no. 85. San Francisco: Jossey-Bass.

Sammons, P. (1989). Ethical issues and statistical work. In R. G. Burgess (ed.) *The Ethics of Educational Research* (pp. 31–59). London: The Falmer Press.

Schwandt, T. A. (1998). How we think about morality: Implications for evaluation practice. Paper presented at the annual meeting of the American Evaluation Association Conference, Chicago, November.

Schwandt, T. A. (2001). Ethics of qualitative inquiry. *Dictionary of Qualitative Inquiry*, second edition (pp. 73–77). London & Thousand Oaks, CA: Sage Publications.

Simons, H. (1987). *Getting to Know Schools in a Democracy: The politics and process of evaluation*. Lewes: The Falmer Press.

Simons, H. (1989). Ethics of case study in educational research and evaluation. In R. G. Burgess (ed.) *The Ethics of Educational Research* (pp. 114–140). London: The Falmer Press.

Simons, H. (1995). The Politics and Ethics of Educational Research in England: *Contemporary Issues, British Educational Research Journal*, 21(4), 435–449.

Simons, H. (2000). Damned if you do, damned if you don't: Ethical and political dilemmas in evaluation. In H. Simons & R. Usher (eds) *Situated Ethics in Educational Research* (pp. 39–55). London & New York: Routledge/Falmer.

Simons, H. & Usher, R (eds) (2000). *Situated Ethics in Educational Research*. London: Routledge/Falmer.

Smith, G. H. (1997). *The Development of Kaupapa Maori: theory and praxis*. Auckland, New Zealand: University of Auckland.

Social Sciences and Humanities Research Council of Canada (1981) Ethical Guidelines for the Institutional Review Committees for Research with Human Subjects.

Soltis, J. F. (1999). The ethics of qualitative research. In E. W. Eisner & A. Peshkin (eds) *Qualitative Inquiry in Education: The continuing debate* (pp. 247–257). New York: Teachers College Columbia University.

Stame, N. (2004). The Sixth European Evaluation Society Conference on "Governance, Democracy and Evaluation". *Evaluation*, 10(4), 503–507.

Thomas, C. L. (2000). The case of the sensitive survey. *American Journal of Evaluation*, 21(2), 261–274.

Thomson, J. A. K. (1953). *Ethics of Aristotle*. Harmondsworth: Penguin.

Torres, R. T. & Preskill, H. (1999). Ethical dimensions of stakeholder participation and evaluation use. In J. L. Fitzpatrick & M. Morris (eds) *Current and Emerging Ethical Challenges in Evaluation. New Directions For Evaluation*, 82, (pp. 57–66). San Francisco: Jossey-Bass.

United Kingdom Evaluation Society (2003). *Guidelines for Good Practice in Evaluation*. London: Professional Briefings, 37 Star Street, Ware, Hertfordshire SG12 7AA. Email: eiscc@profbriefings.co.uk.

Usher, P. (2000). Feminist approaches to a situated ethics. In H. Simons & R.Usher (eds) *Situated Ethics in Educational Research* (pp. 22–38). London & New York: Routledge/Falmer.

Usher, R. (2000). Deconstructive happening, ethical moment. In H. Simons & R. Usher (eds) *Situated Ethics in Educational Research* (pp. 162–185). London & New York: Routledge/Falmer.

Worthen, B. R. & Sanders, J. R. (1987). *Educational Evaluation: Alternative approaches and practical guidelines*. New York: Longman.

A COMPARATIVE ANALYSIS OF EVALUATION UTILIZATION AND ITS COGNATE FIELDS OF INQUIRY: CURRENT ISSUES AND TRENDS[1]

J. Bradley Cousins and Lyn M. Shulha

Some time ago Huberman provided a challenge to researchers interested in evaluation utilization by noting that "the communities of research utilization and evaluation utilization have evolved an overlapping corpus of work to guide future research applications, with little concern for the meaningful distinctions between the two fields" (1994, p. 7). Needed is serious inquiry to explore how these cognate fields overlap and in what ways they part company. Over a decade later, we observe that some important progress has been made in this regard, but considerable gaps remain. Hofstetter & Alkin (2003) contributed in a very direct way to

our understanding of evaluation and knowledge use relationships by providing an excellent historical overview. They reviewed studies of knowledge utilization to inform social sciences and policy and made links to evaluation utilization as a domain of inquiry. Their conclusion was that "many of the bourgeoning ideas related to knowledge utilization and evaluation utilization research overlapped, some even occurred simultaneously in both areas, in part due to the goals, process and use found in research and evaluation studies" (2003, p. 204). But more importantly, we think, they helped to clarify the distinctions between evaluation utilization and its cognate field social sciences research utilization. In particular, they reminded us that, despite remarkable overlap in methods with social science research, evaluation by definition is context-bound; knowledge is produced for a particular purpose for a particular set of users in a specific context. While social science research can have significant uses and influences in the community of practice, its use is not context bound in the way that evaluation knowledge is. For this reason, the "*applied* versus *basic* research dichotomy . . . does not adequately capture the evaluation-research distinction" (Alkin & Taut, 2003, p. 3, emphasis in original). (See also distinctions between evaluation and social sciences research made by Levin-Rozalis, 2004, and Scriven, 2003/2004.)

Our present purpose is to take up Huberman's challenge, to further examine interconnections between evaluation use and related domains of inquiry. We add to the contribution made by Hofstetter & Alkin (2003) in two principal ways. First, Hofstetter & Alkin's focus was primarily historical; they identified several points of overlap with regard to the conceptualization of the utilization construct and factors related to the pattern and extent of observed use. In many ways, their analysis captures the historical evolution of inter-relationships among cognate fields. Our focus, on the other hand, is on current developments in research, and knowledge use and the extent to which those relate to developments in evaluation use. Our inquiry is thus more future-oriented regarding utilization theory, research, and practice. Second, our inquiry provides a more thorough and comprehensive look at the inter-relationships between evaluation and knowledge use. As will be detailed below, our conceptualization of knowledge use is more broadly encompassing and extends beyond the use of social sciences research to the diffusion of innovation and planned change literatures. We are persuaded that these literatures are highly

relevant as cognate fields of inquiry to evaluation use and for that reason their inclusion would provide for a more complete analysis.

In our 1997 paper (Shulha & Cousins, 1997) we identified a number of themes emerging from research and theory on evaluation utilization during the period 1986–1996. We noted how, at that time, many in the evaluation community felt constrained when thinking about evaluation use in one of three conventional, ways: instrumental, conceptual or symbolic (see Leviton & Hughes, 1981, for a complete discussion on the origins of these dimensions). While newer notions of evaluation use have in many ways changed the face of practice, these three foundational dimensions remain relevant. A look at some contemporary evaluation examples tells us why.

In describing an evaluation commissioned by a high school's administration in order to assess the strengths and weakness of the current curriculum, McNamee (2003) provided a practical example of appreciative inquiry (Preskill & Coghlan, 2003). She gives a thorough and engaging explanation of the process and how it led to a four-step action plan for program improvement. While her discussion centers primarily on the strengths of the appreciative process and how it acted as a catalyst for collective understanding, it is clear that the evaluation was able to generate information that was used to support subsequent program decisions and directions (instrumental use).

For Shulha (2000) a school-university professional learning partnership offered a rich context for expanding the scope of evaluation use. The needs assessment she described sheds light on the complexity of reaching out across organizational boundaries and on the negotiation of authority for decision-making. Embedded in this discussion, however, is how evaluative inquiry served a significant educative function for both the participants and the evaluators, enabling them to learn about each other and the state of teaching and learning in the school (conceptual use).

Program evaluators must remain cognizant of the fact that their work can be conscripted for politically persuasive purposes or as a rationale for calculated action (symbolic use). Kleit's (2004) evaluation of an experimental public housing self-sufficiency program is an example of the kind of evaluation that runs this risk. Implicit in the program he evaluated are controversial values and beliefs about the responsibility of government in aiding low-income workers. The evaluation findings also appear to have significant social policy and resource implications. Kleit, perhaps in anticipation of the contexts in which his findings could be used, protects the integrity of his work by presenting a thoroughly grounded and defensible mixed-method design and displays his data and findings in ways that discourage simplistic interpretation.

Each of these exemplars demonstrates how conventional notions of evaluation utilization still serve. They also exhibit the very quality that we observed burgeoning in 1997, namely the expanding conceptions of use, especially "process use" or effects that are independent of evaluation findings. Other developments in evaluation utilization as a domain of inquiry that we identified at the time included the influence of context (political considerations, diversity, support for learning); emergent practices and role implications (collaborative, participatory, and empowerment evaluation); and considerations of misuse (understanding misuse, link to standards of practice).

Since the turn of the millennium there have been additional important developments and trends in research, theory and practice on evaluation use. In this chapter our goal is to situate current trends in the study of evaluation use within the broader intellectual landscape of research and knowledge utilization.

We begin by providing some conceptual background on knowledge utilization as a domain of inquiry in order to help shape the intellectual landscape into which evaluation use will be situated. We then proceed to summarize a series of emergent and ongoing themes related to contemporary developments and issues for utilization inquiry. We do this by sequentially considering particular developments in the broader cognate fields and then related developments in evaluation use. Finally, we comment on points of divergence and convergence and conclude with some broad-stroke impressions about contemporary utilization inquiry and implications for future research and practice.

Conceptual Framework for Knowledge Utilization

Knowledge utilization as a field of inquiry has expanded rapidly in a relatively short period of time and has taken on many facets (Davies, Nutley, & Walter, 2005; Nutley, Walter, & Davies, 2003). We are guided by Zhang's (1989) framework on knowledge use because we find it to be most parsimonious relative to others that exist (e.g., Backer, 1991).[2] In his first of five categories of major theoretical perspectives, Zhang collapses technology transfer and the innovation diffusion perspective on the assumption that knowledge is relatively well defined and utilization is equated with a decision to adopt the innovation. Rogers (e.g., 1995) has guided scholars, policy-makers, and change agents for over four decades with his continuous examination of this field. Second, Zhang categorized the program implementation or planned change perspective as a major focus for the study of organizational innovations embodied in programmed actions. This practical problem-solving approach was championed by scholars such as Havelock, Zaltman, and others. Third, evaluation for decision-making is suggested by Zhang to be an extension of the planned change perspective

EXEMPLAR 12.1   Comparison of contemporary issues in knowledge and evaluation use domains of inquiry

Thematic category	Knowledge and research use	Evaluation use
Epistemological challenges	✓	✓
Emphasis on context for use	✓	✓
Focus on user characteristics	✓	✓
Linking knowledge production and use	✓	✓
Utilization as process	✓	✓
Methodological challenges	✓	✓
Considerations of misuse	na	✓
Influence versus use	na	✓

where knowledge is equated with findings arising from the systematic investigation of practical problems. Essentially, this category is the domain of evaluation utilization; Alkin, Patton, and Davis are named as proponents. Fourth, on a somewhat broader plane are those subscribing to the study of knowledge for policy-making, who construe knowledge as being predominantly that arising from social science research (e.g., Dunn, Knorr-Cetina, Lindblom, Rich, Weiss). Social science research may be differentiated from evaluation on contextual (Hofstetter & Alkin, 2003; Zhang, 1989) or valuing dimensions (Levin-Rozalis, 2003; Scriven, 2003/ 2004). Zhang's final category is broader yet and is considered a knowledge system-utilization perspective, a macro approach concerned with the impact of knowledge on society. Dunn and Holtzner are the scholars credited with pioneering work in this domain.

And so we can see that the breadth and scope of knowledge utilization inquiry is enormous. We believe that the cognate domains of most relevance to the study of evaluation utilization are the diffusion or transfer of innovation (including technology) orientation, the program implementation/ planned change perspective, and the research for policy-making perspective. The impact of knowledge on society, in our view, is sufficiently abstract as to diminish its relevance to evaluation use.

Contemporary Issues and Trends in Utilization Inquiry

As shown in Table 12.1, our review of contemporary issues in knowledge and research utilization has resulted in the identification of six principal themes of interest. These are (1) epistemological challenges, (2) emphasis on context for use, (3) focus on user characteristics, (4) linking knowledge production and use (5) utilization as process, and (6) methodological challenges. For each of these thematic areas, we located developments and contributions in the evaluation utilization domain. Some of these we recognized in our earlier paper (Shulha & Cousins, 1997), others we explore more thoroughly in this chapter. Table 12.1 also reveals two themes associated with evaluation use that appear to be unique to the domain. We failed to locate serious scholarship about such themes in the broader cognate fields. We now turn to an abbreviated summary of substantive developments and issues within each of these themes and, ultimately, a comparison of fields of inquiry.

Epistemological Challenges

Epistemology in its simplest terms is concerned with the nature of knowledge. When researchers and evaluators ask themselves, "How do I know?" or "How certain am I about what has happened here?" or "Under what conditions might others view my findings inadequate?" they are asking epistemological questions about the attributes, scope, and sources of their knowledge. They are examining the manner in which they have gathered information, constructed and manipulated concepts, and used their thoughts, memories, senses, and emotions to analyze and justify what they are presenting as "knowledge about." Evaluation like social science research is now rooted in a growing diversity of epistemologies. As a consequence, practitioners in both venues are challenged to be more cognizant of how their methods and their dispositions towards "what is most worth knowing" together influence the selecting, combining, and discarding of information, and thus the constructing of knowledge claims.

Knowledge Use

Concurrent with debates in other domains of inquiry, several serious challenges to traditional modes of conceptualizing research-based knowledge have been recently launched. Watkins (1994) provides a well-developed argument for a postmodern, critical theory of research use. He critiques traditional theories as being entrenched in objectivism and alleges that knowledge, once separated from the knower, is no longer valid. This assertion is based on a critique of the assumption that knowledge is value-free, an increasingly untenable position. A strong response to this perspective resides within an interpretivist framework that assumes the existence of multiple realities, no one more valid than the next. But Watkins criticizes the interpretivist

perspective because it does not acknowledge power inequities and value systems. Clearly, from a critical stance, some interpretations (e.g., those of the more powerful and dominant group) are taken as more valid than others. Watkins then advances his critical theory of knowledge use and proceeds to express concern about the domination of the knowledge production process by researchers and to question the need for a research community as opposed to strategies that infuse a culture of systematic inquiry into the community of practice. His view is that knowledge is not disseminated per se, but that it is information that can be transferred and subsequently fed into local knowledge production.

Huberman (1989, 1994) and Louis (1996) both ascribe to some of Watkins' arguments but take exception to his more extreme views. Huberman maintains that constructivists' perspectives on knowledge utilization have provided an impetus for improving linkages between researcher and practitioner communities. He develops a revised traditionalist perspective on knowledge utilization having acknowledged the original knowledge transfer "theory-to-practice" framework as being deficient in its absence of a link between user needs and knowledge production. He suggests as necessary the need to acknowledge the bargained nature of research knowledge and the likelihood that findings will be used strategically. Huberman rejects the postmodernist perspective because its assumptions render dissemination a "dead letter." Louis (1996) shares this view. She acknowledges the integral role of social constructivism and that knowledge from outside must be interpreted from within. Communication happens and knowledge gets used and because this happens within a social frame, this does not imply that knowledge cannot be disseminated. Rather, knowledge will need to be reconstructed in any local use setting (Louis, 1996; see also Breslin, Tupker, & Sdao-Jarvie, 2001).

Yet contemporary theorists continue to elevate social responsibility and cultural sensitivity in considering knowledge use. In a recent essay, Manzini (2003) provides a compelling argument that public accessibility into science and participation in it are matters of equity and basic human rights. In keeping with this thinking, the concept of "civic scientist" is receiving increasing attention of late. Civic scientists articulate and illuminate science content in the context of societal issues and interact with general audiences with goals ranging from passive appreciation of science to enhancing citizen ability to analyze and take action (Chui, Petit, & Riordan, 2001).

Evaluation Use

Similar to virtually all domains of inquiry in the social sciences, the traditional, dominant paradigm for the study of evaluation and indeed the conduct of evaluation has met with significant challenges. These challenges are wide-ranging and include various approaches associated with interpretivist (e.g., Stake, 1983; Guba & Lincoln, 1995) and critical theoretic (e.g., McTaggart, 1991; Sirotnik & Oaks, 1990) perspectives. The central problem with the traditional perspective lies in its extremist modern notions of objectivity, correspondence theories of truth, and the belief that facts and values can be separated. Relativists argued that knowledge is context bound and once removed from the context within which it was created is no longer valid. But, as has been argued elsewhere, the relativist perspective is itself extreme and limited in explaining knowledge production and use (e.g., House, 2001; Howe, 1988; Louis, 1996).

For evaluation, the critical theoretic epistemological perspective is normative in form and function. Of central interest is the use of evaluation to help ameliorate social injustice and inequity. As Greene (1998) observed:

Feminist, neo-Marxist, critical and other theorists in this genre promote "openly ideological" forms of inquiry that seek to illuminate the historical, structural and value bases of social phenomena and in doing so, to catalyze political and social change toward greater justice, equity and democracy. (pp. 377–378)

Epistemological challenges have carried with them significant implications for evaluation use, mostly centered around interconnections among evaluator and program stakeholder communities. House & Howe's (2000, 2003) democratic deliberative approach embraces this principle. They specify three requirements for evaluation that would support democracy: inclusion, dialog, and deliberation. Evaluation from this perspective is less about practical problem-solving and more about learning (Preskill & Torres, 2000; Rossman & Rallis, 2000). The evaluation process itself is used as a social intervention. In essence, evaluation use is construed as action arising from learning from the evaluation, particularly its deliberative processes. "If we view evaluation as learning and see learning as a socially constructed, appreciative process, then evaluation use becomes reconceptualized as continual and collective knowledge generation and application" (Rossman & Rallis, 2000, p. 59). But essential to action are considerations of power differentials. Despite the rhetoric of valuing diversity and different ways of knowing, critical theorists argue that the system is inherently unjust. From a utilization standpoint, evaluators need to be mindful of whose interests are being served. Whose knowledge counts?

Emphasis on Context for Use

The attention social scientists and evaluators pay to the context for knowledge use can differ significantly. For many researchers this context is an enigma. Not usually privy to the intricacies of the political or social cultures for which findings are intended, historically, social scientists often have had little recourse but to assemble their findings either in ways that demonstrate the credibility of their new understandings, or in the case of an innovation, in ways that will have most appeal to potential users. Once this is done, they release them and hope for the best. Evaluators, by the very nature of their work, are often drawn into the context for use, learning about the assumptions that ground the program, the social networks that support program processes and the vested interests that may or may not be served by the inquiry and its findings.

Knowledge Use

Perhaps among the more significant developments, then, and one arising from epistemological debates in research and thinking about knowledge utilization is the heightened emphasis on the context for utilization and the recognition that utilization cannot be understood in the absence of a detailed understanding of context. There is wide agreement that utilization is a social process subject to political influences and that the organizational context in which utilization is expected to take place operates in non-rational ways (Davies et al., 2005; Hutchinson & Huberman, 1994; Rich & Oh, 2000).

A detailed sociological understanding of the context for utilization is important for several reasons. First, as a social process knowledge utilization occurs in the context of social interaction and processing (Cousins & Leithwood, 1993; Louis, 1996) and must be interpreted locally. Second, there exist inside organizations hierarchies of knowledge and power. As Huberman (1994) puts it, "There is, in fact, probably no formulation of an educational problem devoid of partisan interests.

Research findings drop into that field of interests, and the researchers themselves are usually powerless – or indifferent – to affect the ensuing debate" (p. 18).

Some researchers have endeavored to understand non-linear, unpredictable patterns of research use in context-sensitive "forward tracking" approaches. Molas-Gallart et al., (2000) (cited in Davies et al., 2005) employed "user panels," members of which were interviewed several times during the duration of the intervention project. Walter et al., (2004) (cited by Davies et al., 2005) propose three models for research uptake: the evidence-based practitioner model (evidence sought in response to locally generated researchable questions); the embedded model (research is distilled and codified before being incorporated into organizational processes and procedures); and the organizational excellence model (local strategies of continuous improvement that draw on both research and local experimentation). This framework implies different environments for research uptake and a customized approach to impact assessment.

Evaluation Use

A recent American panel on evaluation use that was ultimately published (see special section of the *American Journal of Evaluation* introduced by Sridharan, 2003) underscores the continuing primacy of evaluation context as a utilization consideration. Leviton (2003), who synthesized papers in the panel, reminds us that knowledge of context is essential to enhanced use of evaluation and that context must be understood as both content knowledge of the program as well as the organizational context within which this is to be understood. Leviton supports the conclusion of Ginsburg & Rhett (2003) that evaluation use is about knowledge production and is most likely to occur when a body of evidence (as opposed to individual studies or reports) accrues. But what is more important, she claims, is the extent to which evaluation succeeds in challenging collective assumptions held by the user (in this case policy-making) community. Collective assumptions may be flawed or understanding may not be well-informed (i.e., high uncertainty). In each instance, evaluation can provide the challenge that will help to address these deficiencies, regardless of the extent to which such knowledge is definitive.

As a point of departure from inquiry on knowledge and research use, the clear implication of this perspective for the study of evaluation use and for evaluation practice is the need to know and understand the program *and* the decision or policy context (Leviton, 2003). Understanding the fit of evaluation findings with the users' construction of reality and the extent to which uncertainty exists or collective assumptions may be in error is likely to have potent explanatory value for evaluation use.

In addition to the ongoing interest in program and decision setting context, of late there has been a considerable focus on integrating evaluation into organizational culture and organizational capacity building. We recently completed an integrative review of relevant empirical literature (Cousins et al., 2004) and located several studies on evaluation capacity building (ECB) (e.g., Brandon & Higa, 2004; Compton et al., 2001; Compton et al., 2002; Gilliam et al., 2003; Milstein et al., 2002; King, 2002). Many ECB studies examine the direct contribution to the development of evaluation capacity from interventions involving personnel, training, resources, and conceptual models. Other researchers studied external initiatives that carry with them accountability requirements and found that process use catalyzed the development of

evaluation skills, knowledge and "habits of mind." From these studies we concluded that "the integration of evaluation into the culture of organizations . . . has as much to do with the consequences of evaluation as it does the development of skills and knowledge of evaluation logic and methods." (Cousins et al., 2004, p. 101). Yet developing capacity for use has met with less attention than the capacity to do evaluation.

Focus on User Characteristics

Increasingly, both social scientists and evaluators are learning that attention to the characteristics of knowledge users is a potent way to stimulate the utilization of findings. For social scientists, this attention may be, in part, compensatory given the constraints they can face in developing deep understandings of the contexts for knowledge use. For evaluators, immersion into program contexts, almost by definition, requires learning about the individuals directly affected by the inquiry. There is evidence that evaluators are learning how to shape the activities of data collection and analysis in ways that can help users better integrate and then communicate constructed knowledge. The process of shaping and disseminating knowledge in light of user characteristics appears to take on significant refinements as the distance between the knowledge producer and knowledge user decreases.

Knowledge Use

Often is the case in diffusion research that new ideas enter the system through higher status and more innovative members, usually with the assistance of an external change agent. This process is problematic in diffusion if the functioning interpersonal networks of the system are composed primarily of like-minded individuals. In this context there is minimal "'trickle-down' to non-elites" (Rogers, 1995, p. 288). *"One of the most distinctive problems in the diffusion of innovations is that the participants are usually quite heterophilous"* (Rogers, 1995, p. 19, emphasis in original) meaning that gaps in communication occur among individuals, including the change agent, when they do not share the same space or attributes such as beliefs, education, and social status.

Over time, scholars of knowledge utilization have come to recognize users as being active as opposed to passive recipients of information. Knowledge, especially knowledge in the form of technology, may be difficult to understand and its use is likely to be discarded unless potential adopters are provided with opportunities to experiment with it on a limited basis in a low-risk context (Rogers, 1995). Knowledge entering an organization from outside will not be used unless it successfully passes truth and utility tests (Weiss, 1983). Truth tests determine the extent to which knowledge corresponds to what is already known by the user and speak to the credibility of the knowledge, but it must also be judged by users as being usable. In large part, according to Weiss (1983), this determination will be a function of the user's ideologies and interests as well as attributes of the knowledge to be used. Rogers (1995) confirms the importance of a high degree of compatibility between the innovation and the current values and needs of the potential adopters of innovation. Interests and needs, on the other hand, correspond to people's stake in the policy or practice under study. Weiss alleges that interests are rarely hard-and-fast, single-position commitments. The effect of research knowledge can be to reduce uncertainty and thereby lead to a major re-estimate of where interests lie.

Users of innovation are known to have very pragmatic concerns. Consistent with the inadequacies of the rational actor model (Rich & Oh, 2000) users are more open to potential changes

in thinking and behaving that contribute directly to some economic gain, social prestige, work convenience or sense of satisfaction. At every stage in diffusion the more visible positive evidence there is for these outcomes the more likely adoption is to continue (Rogers, 1995). Finally, in their study of policy-makers, Landry, Lamari, & Amara (2004) found that user acquisition efforts are positively related to their propensity to use university research. In some Canadian policy domains this finding was mediated by level of education.

Evaluation Use

Patton's "personal factor" continues to be an integral force supporting the normative utilization-focused evaluation approach that he advocates (1997, 2003). In his words "To target an evaluation at the information needs of a specific person or a group of identifiable interacting persons is quite different from what has been traditionally recommended as "identifying the audience for an evaluation. . . . People, not organizations, use evaluation information – thus the importance of the *personal factor*" (2003, p. 225, emphasis in original). Leviton (2003) considers user learning characteristics, specifically program practitioner cognitive processes and learning capabilities. She describes techniques and applications for eliciting constructed knowledge by creating mental models; the techniques have been used to understand and communicate risk information and are adaptable to the evaluation context.

> A user's decision context depends on a mental model of the program, including specific practices within a program, the nature of the social problem being addressed, the workings of the policies that control the program, the characteristics and behaviors of both the service providers and recipients. New information from the evaluation would be processed in terms of the user's mental model of the program. (Leviton, 2003, p. 529).

User's learning characteristics are another related focus for inquiry. Preskill & Torres (1999, 2000) lay out evaluator role and practice options (e.g., learning diagnosis, clinical approaches) that would position evaluative inquiry as a force in stimulating learning in users. Learning is essential to the approach addressed by Rossman & Rallis (2000), as well. In their terms, evaluation as a stimulus for learning seeks to raise questions, rather than to solve problems; learning is seen as a platform for action on a cyclic basis.

Linking Knowledge Production and Use

There are now concerted efforts by some social scientists to purposefully bridge the community-of-theory/community-of-practice gap in knowledge production and knowledge use. Letting go of the "two worlds" conception of how knowledge is constructed and disseminated has illuminated the importance of better understanding the intricacies of collaborative inquiry and joint meaning-making. Those concerned with evaluation use have embraced this challenge, examining what it means to expand the goals of evaluative inquiry and distribute authority for decision-making to those who are most affected by its processes and outcomes. The notion of linking knowledge production and use through a partnership appears to be more easily embraced by evaluators than university-based researchers. Yet the study of interventions and interactive processes between production and use communities has emerged as a focus of contemporary inquiry on research use (Davies et al., 2005; Lomas, 2000; Nutley et al., 2003).

Knowledge Use

Perhaps among the more salient developments in the study of knowledge and research utilization has been the heightened interest in and attention to the connectedness of knowledge production, and utilization functions. In traditional knowledge utilization frameworks, knowledge production, dissemination, and utilization were typically considered to be sequential if not cyclical activities. In contrast, contemporary theorists and researchers have adopted a more integrative perspective, one that captures reciprocal influences among these activities in a non-sequential, continuous way (Huberman, 1994; Nutley et al., 2003). Researchers have focused on the consequences for the community of practice of increasing the frequency and intensity of contacts between members of both sides. Huberman dubbed such contact "sustained interactivity" and worked within a research utilization framework of reciprocal influence – researchers using analytic power and practitioners drawing on clinical and pragmatic experience. He casts the experience as a "sense-making and interpretive exercise on both sides" (1994, p. 23). Lavis et al., (2003) further added to understanding of researcher–user interactions. They identified three models of interaction – producer-push, user-pull, and exchange – the final corresponding most completely with Huberman's reciprocal influence conceptualization.

While reciprocal influences of increased linkages are alluring, empirical evidence has largely addressed effects in the user community. In a survey of Canadian school district decision-makers, Cousins & Leithwood (1993), for example, showed the potency for knowledge use of interpersonal networks and other forums for practitioners' "social processing" of knowledge. This finding was replicated by Mycio-Mommers (2002) in a North American survey of educators using a well-developed environmental program innovation. Mycio-Mommers showed that social processing and user engagement led to higher levels of process and conceptual types of use.

Unquestionably, considerable empirical support for strategies designed to increase links and contacts between knowledge user and knowledge production communities is beginning to accumulate (Amara, Ouimet, & Landry, 2004; Castillo, 2000; Cousins & Simon, 1996; Davies et al., 2005; Landry, Amara & Lamari, 2001a, 2001b; Landry et al., 2003; Lomas, 2000). However, little research on knowledge use examines inquiry partnerships between members of these respective communities. An exception is a study by Latowski (2003) which reports on a community-based participatory research project in Massachusetts. Community residents, environmental scientists, and local health agencies collaborated in a study that documented significant health hazards and ultimately led to substantial educational outreach activities.

Evaluation Use

In contrast to inquiry on knowledge utilization, collaborative, participatory, and empowerment forms of evaluation have captured considerable interest among evaluation theorists, researchers, and practitioners in recent years (Cousins, 2003; Fetterman, 2001; Fetterman & Wandersman, 2005; O'Sullivan & D'Agostino, 2002; O'Sullivan, 2004). Such forms of evaluation might be differentiated on the basis of their goals and interests (Cousins & Whitmore, 1998; Weaver & Cousins, 2004). First, there may be justifications for collaborative forms of evaluation on the basis of practical problem-solving pursuits. This approach – "practical participatory evaluation" (Cousins & Whitmore, 1998) – would be openly associated with the use of evaluation for program decision-making and improvement. Second, collaborative forms of evaluation may be guided by normative or political pursuits, such as the amelioration of social inequity. This we called "transformative participatory evaluation." Finally, collaborative evaluation might be motivated by epistemological interests,

associated with deepening meaning and understanding of programs or other social phenomena. Stake's (1983) responsive model may be an exemplar of that justification, although Stake might argue that the approach is hardly collaborative (see Cousins, 2004a)

In a recent review and integration of literature, Cousins (2003) showed that stakeholder involvement in evaluation is potentially powerful in enhancing program practitioners' sense of ownership and understanding of programs and can lead to conceptual and instrumental uses of evaluation data. Even more evident were effects on process use, or effects resulting from evaluative processes independent of results.

It is also possible to differentiate collaborative evaluation approaches in terms of process or form (Cousins & Whitmore, 1998; Weaver & Cousins, 2004). Any given evaluative inquiry might be characterized by (1) the extent to which control of the evaluation rests with the evaluator or program stakeholders, (2) diversity among program stakeholders, (3) power relations among program stakeholders (conflicting or neutral), (4) the manageability of the evaluation, and (5) the extent or depth of participation in the evaluation by program stakeholders. For example, practical participatory evaluations tend to be characterized by balanced control, modest diversity among stakeholder groups, and an absence of conflict among those with access to different levels of power. They are also relatively manageable and involve program stakeholders in significant aspects of the evaluation knowledge production function (Cousins, 2003; Weaver & Cousins, 2004).

More needs to be known about what forms of collaborative evaluation are likely to generate higher levels of use and under what conditions. For example, practical participatory evaluation may be best suited to improvement-oriented evaluation pursuits and not suited to the kinds of policy-oriented evaluation referred to by Henry (2003) and Leviton (2003). Yet the need to understand the decision context at deep levels is essential to use within the policy arena (Leviton, 2003). This need is addressed in collaborative forms of evaluation where knowledge of program logic and the context within which programs are implemented is introduced by virtue of participation in the evaluation by members of the program practice community.

Utilization as Process

Possibly the most significant development of the past decade in both the research and evaluation communities has been a more general acceptance that *how* we work with clients and practitioners can be as meaningful and consequential as *what* we learn from our methods. Evaluators and evaluation researchers, in particular, have been exploring the implications of this phenomenon. Evidence continues to grow on how the act of inquiry, orchestrated in fully engaging ways demonstrates a capacity to support individual and collective knowledge production. What makes this learning unique is that it is both emergent and regulated primarily by the participants themselves. In effect, the researcher/evaluator creates the conditions that allow knowledge to be generated by those who, at least tacitly, know what they most need to learn. It is thus the process itself that facilitates utilization.

Knowledge Use

Increased attention to the investigation of linkages between knowledge production and utilization communities has put the conceptualization of utilization in a new light. To be sure, scholars continue to think of the utilization of research findings or program knowledge in instrumental, conceptual, and symbolic terms (Amara et al., 2004; Huberman, 1994; Mycio-Mommers, 2002) but utilization is now considered to be linked in direct ways to stages of the knowledge production process, stages thought to be interdependent and non-linear. Fundamental to such a perspective is the conception of the user as an active participant in knowledge production. Inasmuch as dissemination will not automatically engage users unless the knowledge being transferred is compatible with users' opinions and beliefs, Huberman (1994) proposes that researchers need to negotiate their continuance and their presence in the user context and that doing so may raise users' awareness of problems and the permeability of unwanted findings.

In addition to the positive influences of sustained interactivity and the intensification of contacts, considerable evidence suggests that direct participation in knowledge production may be, at least as, if not even more potent. Mycio-Mommers (2002), for example, found that educators' participation in implementation of an educational innovation led to benefits that were quite unrelated to the target program. Such benefits included enhanced pedagogical confidence, self-efficacy, and even career considerations. From this perspective, direct participation in the knowledge production loop occurs at the point of local interpretation and adaptation (Dunn & Holtzner, 1988; Rogers, 1995)

In a mixed-method, Canadian nation-wide empirical study, Cousins & Simon (1996) focused on research funding strategies designed to involve members of the community of practice in social sciences research knowledge production. While results were somewhat favorable, several barriers and obstacles to this general strategy emerged. Many of these were directly tied to the establishment of partnerships between researcher and practitioner communities. Impediments to the successful establishment of partnerships were predominantly reflected in differences in culture, but micro-political issues of ownership and control also surfaced. Such concerns have been noted by Weiss (1983) and more recently by Watkins (1994), who highlights the potential for domination by researchers who enjoy a relatively privileged position as compared to that of their practitioner colleagues. Further, Jacobson, Butterill, & Goering (2004) noted several organizational factors that may constrain researchers in connecting with the community of practice, even for the purposes of transmission and dissemination. Incentive systems, competing demands, and unavailability of resources were prominent among these constraints.

Evaluation Use

In evaluation circles, Patton's concept of process use (1997) has come to the fore and has stimulated much interest on several levels. First, the concept has been operationalized and studied empirically. For example, in a large-scale survey, Preskill & Caracelli (1997) observed that evaluators' self-reported user benefits and effects of evaluation were attributable to the process of user participation in or proximity to the evaluation. Russ-Eft, Atwood, & Egherman (2002) carried out an evaluation utilization reflective case study within the American corporate sector. Through satisfaction interviews and surveys they concluded that ultimately the fate of the sales program within a business services organization was determined by forces outside of the evaluation (e.g., rumors of merger). However, despite this apparent non-use of findings, the authors identified several process uses: supporting and reinforcing the program intervention; increasing engagement, self-determination, and ownership; program and organizational development; and enhancing shared understandings. In a more recent exploratory study of

process use within the context of the Collaborative Evaluation Fellows Project of the American Cancer Society, Preskill, Zuckerman, & Matthews (2003) concluded that evaluators should intentionally enable stakeholders to understand learning as part of the evaluation process. In addition to process use the authors also observed other instances of conceptual instrumental use.

Process use has also found its way into theoretical formulations about integrating evaluation into the organizational culture (Cousins, 2003; Cousins et al., 2004; Preskill & Torres, 1999; Shulha, 2000; Torres & Preskill, 2001). Developing the capacity to learn by virtue of proximity to evaluation logic and processes can occur at the individual, group, or organizational level. Evaluation playing a role in developing organizational learning is considered by some to be an instance of process use (e.g., Cousins, 2003; Cousins et al., 2004).

Finally, those advocating expanding thinking beyond use into theories of evaluation influence have identified process uses as important examples of evaluation influence (Kirkhart, 2000; Mark & Henry, 2004). More will be said about this issue below.

Methodological Challenges

Knowledge Use

How does one measure use? For classical diffusion researchers the answer is straightforward—adoption (Rogers, 1995). For others this question has been and continues to be a very slippery one in contemporary work on knowledge and research utilization. Several issues appear to dominate the methodological agenda. First, as has been the case for quite some time, researchers remain interested in capturing the utilization phenomenon as a process thereby supporting the utilization of longitudinal methodologies (Davies et al., 2005; Rich, 1991).

The utilization process has many facets – production, transmission, processing, and application – and in order to more completely understand utilization it will be necessary to measure variables at each of these stages. Although they did not employ a longitudinal methodology, Landry et al., (2001b) took up the challenge of operationalizing use in stages by adapting a scale developed by Knott & Wildavsky (1980). The scale is cumulative and involves six stages of utilization, including transmission, cognition, reference, effort, influence, and application. Landry et al., showed that different factors affect the impact of social sciences research at different stages, prompting them to consider researcher dissemination strategies that might optimize use.

It has been the lack of a longitudinal orientation accompanied by an interest primarily in the transmission and processing elements of use that has led to what Rogers (1995) identifies as the most significant methodological issue in diffusion research – a pro-innovation bias or "the implication in diffusion research that an innovation should be diffused and adopted by all members of a social system, that it should be diffused more rapidly, and that the innovation should be neither re-invented nor rejected" (Rogers, 1995, p. 100). An important force supporting pro-innovation bias is that diffusion research tends to focus on successful diffusions. While understandable, the result is that the field has collected little information on innovation failures. This kind of study would no doubt lead to a more in-depth look at the nature of the innovation, both how it is developed and how it is used in the adopting context and what is the role of aspects of context in determining utilization outcome.

A second concern is more deeply grounded in issues associated with the development of constructivist and other subjectivist theories of knowledge. Some researchers such as Gabbay et al., (2003) have employed ethnographic techniques to understand the complexities of research uptake. Others have been working to develop research methods that embrace and integrate constructivist perspectives with more traditional approaches to research. Cousins & Leithwood (1993) provide a fairly conventional approach to this problem. They content-analyzed written comment data from a survey of educational practitioners and found these data to be comparatively more powerful than quantitative indicators in uncovering the potent influence of interactive processes on conceptual and instrumental knowledge utilization. Hutchinson (1995) developed a grid interview technique that enables the subsequent construction of survey instruments to be directly informed by the perspectives of practitioners. More recently, Shulha & Wilson (2003) constructed an assessment framework for inquiry that allows academic and practice-based researchers together to judge the degree to which their efforts and understandings are anchored in joint meaning-making and thus represent collaborative learning.

A third methodological issue also has substantive attraction. Moving beyond the identification of types of use – symbolic, conceptual, instrumental – some authors have given consideration to relationships among them. Amara et al., (2004) surveyed 833 Canadian government officials and observed that the three types of use of research simultaneously play a significant role. They confirmed that conceptual use is considerably more frequent than instrumental use; that symbolic use is relatively prevalent; and that day-to-day use of university research, though not extensive, is significant considering the array of other sources of knowledge and information available to decision-makers. The authors conclude that more needs to be known about how conceptual, instrumental, and symbolic uses interact in complementary ways.

Much of the research on knowledge utilization focuses on either the knowledge-production or the knowledge-use communities. Given that most of these are self-report studies with inherent potential for bias, needed are studies that compare and contrast knowledge-production and knowledge-use perspectives. Cousins (2001) provided such a study on collaborative forms of evaluation with some quite remarkable differences between evaluators' perspectives and those of members of the community of program practice. In general, evaluators attributed relatively greater impact to the evaluation.

Finally, Davies et al., (2005) acknowledge additional perennial methodological challenges faced by those interested in assessing knowledge use. In particular, *when* to gather data (forward versus backward tracking) and identifying from *whom* data will be gathered are chief concerns. The framework put forward by Walter et al., (2003) (cited by Davies et al., 2005) provides some useful guidance on the latter issue.

Evaluation Use

Several authors have argued that research on evaluation use has diminished significantly over the years or that there is remarkably little empirical study to support many of the claims concerning evaluation use (Henry & Mark, 2003a; Ginsburg & Rhett, 2003; Leviton, 2003). Leviton even suggests that even the body of available evidence suffers from flawed standard of evidence.

> People's self-report about use of information is frequently taken at face value, with no validation of measurement . . . or triangulation of information . . . . A standard of evidence that many of us would never dream of applying to the conduct of evaluations, too often predominates the study of evaluation use. (2003, p. 526)

We are somewhat but not entirely sympathetic to these points of view. First, there is little argument that the amount and nature of research on evaluation use has changed significantly since the "golden age" of the 1970s (Henry & Mark, 2003b; Weiss, 1998). Yet, we would argue, this change is pervasive in evaluation as an applied field and not limited to the study of evaluation use. Others have been lamenting the lack of empiricism in evaluation for quite some time (e.g., Smith, 1993; Worthen,1990). In our own words, "we have more than a niggling feeling that empirical research in the field remains largely undervalued" (Cousins & Earl, 1999, p. 315). Having said that, in a recent integration of empirical work on evaluation capacity building and use, we located a substantial number of studies (36), published within the previous five years (Cousins et al., 2004). Further, Leviton, for one, either fails to recognize or dismisses out of hand that the face of research in the social sciences has changed, due largely to emerging challenges to the dominant epistemological paradigm, as we described above. Valuing epistemological diversity implies that reflective narratives or case analyses are legitimized as ways of knowing. Such choices can provide rich and deep understanding of highly complex phenomena, such as the use of evaluation. We acknowledge such approaches and recognize them as legitimate, but not without qualification. First, most such studies, in our experience (e.g., Cousins, et al., 2004), are written from the point of view of the evaluator and infrequently involve members of the program stakeholder community. They rely heavily on the story-telling capabilities of the evaluator. We believe that more balance is warranted, since reflective narratives do not typically include explication of the basis for narrative development for the purposes of verification. Second, we would suggest that such approaches are best used in conjunction with or complementarily to more conventional approaches to empirical inquiry, ones that do include explicit methodological procedures and strategies that help to establish trustworthiness.

Considerations of Misuse

The study of misuse of knowledge continues to present significant challenges to scholars. We were unable to locate any scholarship explicitly focused on this important topic in the knowledge utilization domain using such search keywords as "misutilization," "misuse" in conjunction with "knowledge," and "social sciences research." While the direct study of the misuse construct does not appear to have made its way into the scholarly literature, there has been a developing trend in contemporary political discourse to embrace, at least at a rhetorical level, research support as essential to political argumentation. Regardless of the social issue or policy up for debate, politicians in Western societies tend to rely on what is known or not known, supported and not supported by research. The call for evidence-based decision-making in virtually all domains of social, health, educational, and human services inquiry and practice is testament to this sensitivity. Under such circumstances and with stakes increasing, it would not be difficult to imagine increased manipulation of research processes and findings, even if such tendencies have not been well documented in the academic knowledge base.

On the side of evaluative inquiry, only a limited amount of published work has addressed directly the phenomenon of misuse. To be sure, much is written about standards of evaluation practice and ethics, typically to do with the development and explication of standards and suggestions for their intended uses (Hood, 2004; Shadish et al., 1995; Stufflebeam, 2003). They tend to focus on what evaluators should do in order to bring about good quality and ethically defensible evaluations. To this point, however, standards of practice have not stimulated a great deal of research on evaluation (Stufflebeam, 2003).

Christie & Alkin (1999) revisited some prior work by others (Alkin & Coyle, 1988; Patton, 1988) to help conceptualize evaluation misutilization. One of us recently reformulated this framework from the perspective of the user and applied it in conjunction with the *AEA Guiding Principles* as a mechanism to analyze and develop a response to an ethical challenge (Cousins, 2004b). The framework, reproduced in Figure 12.1, was helpful for that purpose and may have potential to assist research on misutilization. A paucity of research with this focus continues to exist.

The figure is divided into four quadrants by two orthogonal dichotomous dimensions corresponding to the intended user's choices and actions: (1) Use: evaluation findings are either used or not used and (2) Misuse: evaluation findings are either handled in an appropriate and justified manner or they are not. Evaluation findings may either be used in appropriate ways (quadrant 1), or used inappropriately (quadrant 2) as a result of flawed evidence (misevaluation) or mischievous intent (misuse). Alternatively, the findings might be ignored, suppressed, or buried when they should not be (quadrant 3) or this may occur for justifiable reasons (quadrant 4). Alkin calls the former *abuse* or *blatant non-use* of sound evaluation findings (Alkin & Coyle, 1988; Christie & Alkin, 1999). An interesting question would be what criteria are used to determine when a decision not to use sound evaluation findings is justified and when it is not? Some would argue that blatant non-use of sound evaluation findings is entirely defensible in the political context of program and policy decision-making. This issue reflects the sometimes ambiguous boundaries of misutilization and the political use of evaluation, a

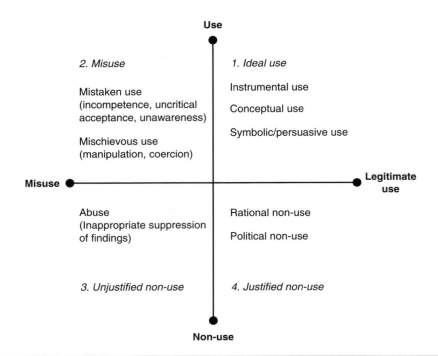

Figure 12.1 Intended user uses and misuses of evaluation findings (from Cousins, 1994b)

concern we have raised elsewhere (Shulha & Cousins, 1997) and one that Henry & Mark (2003b) rightly suggest is problematic.

Influence versus Use

The final theme that we identified corresponds to a contemporary issue concerning evaluation use. Should we move beyond conceptions of utilization to a theory of influence? Kirkhart (2000) critiqued theory and research on evaluation use on a number of fronts. Among her chief concerns are a narrow focus on an inappropriate imagery of instrumental and episodic application and attendant construct underrepresentation. She maintains that models of use imply purposeful, unidirectional influence and that a broadened perspective is required in order to more fully and completely understand evaluation impact.

Kirkhart advocates abandoning conventional thinking about use in favor of a theory of influence. She proposes a conceptual framework of utilization that consists of three fundamental dimensions: source of influence (evaluation process, evaluation results); intention (intentional use, unintentional use); and time (immediate, end-of-cycle, long-term). A theory of influence, according to Kirkhart, would permit: (1) tracking of evolving patterns of influence over time; (2) sorting out conceptual overlap between use and misuse (by expanding conversations about misuse and illuminating beneficial and detrimental consequences of influence); (3) improving the validity of studies of evaluation consequences (by dealing with the problem of construct underrepresentation); (4) tracking the evolution of evaluation theory; (5) comparing evaluation theories; and (6) supporting theory building through empirical tests of evaluation theory.

A theory of influence would have positive implications for evaluation profession as a whole, says Kirkhart. At question is not just a validity issue; the scope of evaluation influence would become increasingly visible and that would be a good thing. "Understanding long term evaluation impact builds credibility for the profession and generates support for evaluation among service delivery professionals" (p. 20).

In two significant papers, Henry and Mark recently extended thinking about a theory of influence in important and complex ways (Henry & Mark, 2003b; Mark & Henry, 2004). They acknowledge and accept many of Kirkhart's arguments and use her initial framework as a platform for further conceptual development and contribution toward a theory of influence. One of their concerns about alleged conceptual constraints inherent in models of use is that research productivity has been hampered. They also question why evaluators would be guided by the goal of maximizing use in the first place. "Use is inadequate as a motivation for evaluation because it fails to provide a moral compass . . . and falls short of recognizing and promoting the ultimate purpose of evaluation as social betterment" (2003b, p. 295). Part of this argument is based on House's (1995) identification of the "fallacy of clientism" in evaluation.

Having elaborated their framework and linked it to prior work on evaluation use, Mark and Henry make several claims germane to ongoing inquiry on evaluation impact. First, they suggest that more research may be stimulated by virtue of the new framework and its links to change theory. Second, they purport that the framework provides the clarity lacking in extant models of evaluation use, and third that greater clarity will make it a better guide to practice. Finally, by thinking in terms of the sorts of mechanisms (processes and

outcomes) that evaluators are likely to influence (i.e., immediate and short-term influences within complex influence pathways) more appropriate expectations about evaluator responsibilities can be developed.

These new developments are exciting and stimulating and add considerable value to the prospect of the study of the effects of evaluation. While many of the claims are supportable, others, we believe, are problematic. First, as we observed earlier, claims about the paucity of recent empirical research on evaluation utilization are somewhat overstated in the face of changes in the nature of research on evaluation, specifically the emergence of the reflective case narrative as a popular mode of inquiry. Second, Henry and Mark proclaim that social betterment is the ultimate goal for evaluation. There are two problems with this proclamation. First, it excludes the many and valued types of evaluation that take place outside of the social policy domain (see, e.g., Russ-Eft et al., 2002). Second, some would argue that evaluation is a service industry and as such, in the social policy world, social betterment is the proper goal of the program providers and sponsors.

A third concern is raised by Alkin & Taut (2003) who point out that a conscious awareness of use-oriented effects, whether intentional (e.g., instrumental support for decision making) or not (e.g., skill development as a consequence of proximity to the evaluation or process use), are important concerns and will continue to be so. In their words, "Influences of evaluation are undoubtedly of importance, but they are unintended and cannot be addressed until after they have occurred. Practicing evaluators have to do their best in actively ensuring and promoting evaluation use, while at the same time noting evaluation influences that might occur but which are outside of their sphere of action" (p. 10).

Despite these concerns, the prospect of moving beyond use to a theory of influence is an intriguing one and is likely to stimulate ongoing debate and inquiry in the field.

Conclusions

Our primary goal in this chapter has been to situate current trends in the study of evaluation use within the broader intellectual landscape of research and knowledge utilization. In doing so, we observe several points of convergence, but many points of divergence, too. This analysis helps to frame evaluation utilization as a unique and interesting domain of inquiry. Our analysis is not without limitations and shortcomings, however. One significant example is associated with our sample of material. While we are relatively confident that we captured all current trends in research and theory on evaluation use, the same cannot be said for the more broadly defined multifaceted landscape of knowledge use. Boundaries in the latter category are more diffuse and ambiguous. Nevertheless, we are satisfied that our sample of scholarship on knowledge use is adequate for the present purpose.

We identified a considerable list of emergent themes in the literature, most common to both spheres of inquiry but two that are unique to evaluation use. While these themes are comprehensive, they did not accommodate all of the current contributions being made. For example, in the study of knowledge use, specific findings about influences were not addressed. A case in point would be the observation by Landry and associates that quantitative studies tend to be more useful to policy-makers than qualitative ones (Amara et al., 2004; Landry et al., 2001a), or the finding of Hijmans, Pleijter, & Wester (2003) that even the most sophisticated media coverage of scientific research tends to avoid reporting complex findings. Regardless, on the whole, the identified themes adequately reflect the current landscape.

Table 12.2 presents a summary of the points of convergence and divergence that we observed in knowledge versus evaluation utilization emergent themes. Both domains of inquiry show developments aligned with emergent epistemological challenges. The discourse is predominantly philosophical in the knowledge-use literature, whereas that associated with evaluation is decidedly normative in tone. True, the concept of civic scientist has recently emerged in the former, but we found a much more thorough treatment in the evaluation literature through the exploration of concepts of diversity, evaluation as a social intervention, and power relations, for example. Both domains of inquiry placed significant emphasis on context for use but differences emerged. In the broader knowledge use domain, we observed a distinct focus on the analysis of sorts of conditions likely to support or engender use. The primacy of context considerations continues to be pervasive in the evaluation literature; here we observed a substantial amount of interventionist work. Studies of evaluation capacity building tend to integrate rather penetrating analyses of context.

Another emergent theme touched upon in both domains is a focus on user characteristics. Discourse on knowledge utilization within this theme centered on users' evaluation of new knowledge against existing cognitive and belief systems. Weiss's concept of truth and utility tests typifies the focus of interest with regard to the use of research. Similarly, from the diffusion literature, innovations are compared against existing belief and value systems. A corollary from the evaluation literature would be the test of the extent to which evaluative knowledge is consistent with pre-existing mental models. However, other user attributes were profiled by authors. The integral nature of the personal factor or the importance of interpersonal relations to the use of evaluation remains prominent. Linked to this is new work conceptualizing

EXEMPLAR 12.2   Points of convergence and divergence between Knowledge-use and evaluation-use domains of inquiry

Theme ('Notes')	Knowledge use	Evaluation use
Epistemological challenges (Convergence)	• Challenges to dominant paradigm • Revised traditionalist perspective • Emergence of civic scientist	• Challenges to dominant paradigm • Valuing diversity • Use of evaluation as social intervention • Power relations; whose knowledge counts?
Emphasis on context for use (Divergence)	• Partisan interests, findings drop in • Analysis of contextual conditions under which use is more likely to occur	• Continued primacy of context • Challenge collective assumptions of user • Evaluation capacity building focus
Focus on user characteristics (Mixed)	• Heterophilous nature of participant group • Active users; truth and utility tests • Compatibility of innovation and values/beliefs	• Pervasiveness of personal factor • Importance of individual mental models • Evaluation role and practice options • Critical inquiry for learning
Linking knowledge production and use (Divergence)	• Reciprocal influence through sustained interactivity (theory versus practice) • Increased contacts	• Direct participation in production of knowledge • Collaborative, participatory, and empowerment approaches • Justification for collaboration • Process variation • Use to what end?
Utilization as process (Divergence)	• Negotiated continuance and presence • Direct participation potency but barriers exist • Privileged members of research community	• Process use; effects independent of findings • Intentionality in promoting process use and learning • Link to organizational learning
Methodological challenges (Mixed)	• Lack of longitudinal research • Operationalization problems • Innovation bias • Constructivist methods • Inter-relationships among types of use • Lack of studies comparing production and use communities • When and from whom to gather data	• Lack of empiricism • Epistemological diversity; dominance of reflective case study

evaluation as a learning system that feeds into individual and organizational learning. Connections between knowledge production and use communities was a fourth theme that emerged. Emerging from research on knowledge use is the concept of sustained interactivity and the potential for reciprocal influences between production and user communities arising from increased contacts. In evaluation, such contacts are much more intimate to the extent that members of the utilization community become integral members of evaluation knowledge production through participation in collaborative, participatory, and empowerment modes of inquiry. Considerable work has been done on understanding the justification for collaborative work, the nature of its process, and ultimately its consequences.

Through negotiated access, researchers or members of the knowledge production community affect change in the user community, an observation associated with the utilization as process theme. To a very limited extent, research on knowledge use has identified positive spin-offs from user participation in research. Yet such processes have been recognized as difficult to enact given a host of barriers and constraints, not the least of which would be the relatively privileged position enjoyed by researchers. On the other hand, participatory and collaborative approaches to evaluation that involve direct or indirect participation in knowledge production by members of the user community have generated considerable insight into the benefits of process use or effects arising from proximity to the evaluation as opposed to an appreciation of evaluation findings. Organizational learning has been conceived to be an instance of process use at the group or organizational level, a conceptual relationship that has generated much interest in research and theory on evaluation use. Finally, a variety of methodological challenges were identified as being associated with

both domains of inquiry. On the knowledge-use side, these have included a lingering paucity of longitudinal research, problems associated with the operationalization of variables and conceptual issues in ferreting out inter-relationships among different types of use. Within the evaluation domain, concern appeared to be focused on a general shortage of original empirical research on evaluation use and an increasing prevalence of narrative inquiry or the reflective case study as a popular mode of inquiry. This observation does not appear to generalize to the knowledge-use domain where relatively more sophisticated approaches to empirical inquiry continue to be published.

Finally, two themes that emerged appeared to be unique to the evaluation literature. The first is the study of misuse. It seems likely that interest in the topic arises from considerations of evaluation as a professionalized body of practice with relatively well-developed standards of practice and codes of behavior. Yet research on the topic beyond reasoned responses to hypothetical ethical challenges has not developed. This may be partly attributable to the technical, ethical, and moral complexities involved in studying such a delicate topic. Regardless, we would look forward to a more concerted systematic effort to understand issues of evaluation misuse, its antecedent causes and its consequences for programs, organizations, and program recipients, alike. The other unique emergent theme concerns a call to move beyond use to a theory of influence. While there are strong arguments both for and against such direction, it strikes us that the debate lies at the heart of the intersection of evaluation and knowledge use more broadly defined. Further inquiry along these lines, particularly that relying on principles of change theory, is likely to assist further in understanding evaluation use situated among its cognate fields. To that end, a theory of influence might help to pursue Huberman's (1994) challenge of meaningfully distinguishing evaluation use from its cognate fields in more direct and penetrating ways.

Notes

1. Sections of this chapter were adapted from a paper presented at the 2002 American Evaluation Association annual meeting, Washington, DC.

2. At the outset it is important to differentiate "information" from "knowledge." We concur with others (e.g., Backer, 1991; Dunn & Holtzner, 1988) that information is essentially raw data, whereas knowledge is interpreted data. But as Weiss (1983, p. 225) observed, ". . . 'knowledge' might be a better label but it often communicates a sense of accuracy, rightness and validity . . . whereas 'information' has a tentative enough aura to contain the partial, biased, or invalid understandings" (Weiss, 1983, p. 225). Regardless of differences over terms, there is some agreement that scientific and professional knowledge is corrigible and may be subjected to non-arbitrary standards of assessment thereby permitting judgments of merit (Dunn & Holtzner, 1988). This proposition, however, is contested, as is described below.

References

Alkin, M. C. & Coyle, K. (1988). Thoughts on evaluation misutilization. *Studies in Educational Evaluation*, 14, 331–340.

Alkin, M. C. & Taut, S. (2003). Unbundling evaluation use. *Studies Educational Evaluation*, 29, 1–12.

Amara, N., Ouimet, M., & Landry, R. (2004). New evidence on instrumental, conceptual and symbolic utilization of university research in government agencies. *Science Communication*, 26, 75–106.

Backer, T. E. (1991). Knowledge utilization: The third wave. *Knowledge: Creation, Diffusion, Utilization*, 12, 225–240.

Brandon, P. R. & Higa, T. A. F. (2004). An empirical study of building the evaluation capacity of K-12 site-managed project personnel. *Canadian Journal of Program Evaluation*, 19(1), 125–142.

Breslin, C., Li, S., Tupker, E., & Sdao-Jarvie, K. (2001). Application of the theory of planned behavior to predict research dissemination. *Science Communication*, 22, 422–437.

Castillo, A. (2000). Communication and utilization of science in developing countries. *Science Communication*, 22, 46–72.

Christie, C. A. & Alkin, M. C. (1999). Further reflections on evaluation misutilization. *Studies in Educational Evaluation*, 25, 1–10.

Chui, G., Petit, C., & Riordan, M. (2001). Cultivating the civic scientist. *Science Communication*, 23, 57–65.

Compton, D., Baiserman, M., Preskill, H., Rieker, P., & Miner, K. (2001). Developing evaluation capacity while improving evlauation training in public health: The American Cancer Society's Collaborative Evaluation Fellow's Project. *Evaluation and Program Planning*, 24, 33–40.

Compton, D., Glover-Kudon, R., Smith, I. E., & Avery, M. E. (2002). Ongoing capacity building in the American Cancer Society (ACS) 1995–2001. In D. W. Compton, M. Baizerman & S. H. Stockdill (eds) *The Art, Craft and Science of Evaluation Capacity Building. New Directions for Evaluation.* No 93 (pp. 47–61). San Francisco: Jossey-Bass.

Cousins, J. B. (2001). Do evaluator and program practitioner perspectives converge in collaborative evaluation? *Canadian Journal of Program Evaluation*, 16(2), 113–133.

Cousins, J. B. (2003). Utilization effects of participatory evaluation. In T. Kellaghan, D. L. Stufflebeam & L. A. Wingate (eds) *International Handbook of Educational Evaluation* (pp. 245–265). Boston: Kluwer.

Cousins, J. B. (2004a). Crossing the bridge: Toward understanding use through empirical inquiry. In M. C. Alkin (ed.) *Evaluation Roots: Tracing theorists' views and influences* (pp. 319–330). Thousand Oaks: Sage.

Cousins, J. B. (2004b). Minimizing evaluation misutilization as principled practice. *American Journal of Evaluation*, 25, 391–397.

Cousins, J. B. & Earl, L. (1999). When the boat gets missed: Response to M.F. Smith. *American Journal of Evaluation*, 20, 309–317.

Cousins, J. B. & Leithwood, K. A. (1993). Enhancing knowledge utilization as a strategy for school improvement. *Knowledge: Creation, Diffusion, Utilization*, 14, 305–333.

Cousins, J. B. & Simon, M. (1996). The nature and impact of policy-induced partnerships between research and practice communities. *Educational Evaluation and Policy Analysis*, 18, 199–218.

Cousins, J. B. & Whitmore, E. (1998). Framing participatory evaluation. In E. Whitmore (ed.) *Understanding and Practicing Participatory Evaluation. New Directions in Evaluation*, No. 80 (pp. 3–23). San Francisco: Jossey-Bass.

Cousins, J. B., Goh, S., Clark, S., & Lee, L. (2004). Integrating evaluative inquiry into the organizational culture: A review and synthesis of the knowledge base. *Canadian Journal of Program Evaluation*, 19(2), 99–141.

Davies, H., Nutley, S., & Walter, I. (2005). Assessing the impact of social sicence reserach: conceptual, methodological and practical issues. Paper presented at the Economics and Social Research Council symposium on assessing non-academic impact of research, London. May.

Dunn, W. N. & Holtzner, B. (1988). Knowledge in society: Anatomy of an emergent field. *Knowledge in Society*, 1, 6–26.

Fetterman, D. (2001). *Foundations of Empowerment Evaluation*. Thousand Oaks: Sage.

Fetterman, D., & Wandersman, A. (2005). *Empowerment Evaluation Principles in Practice*. New York: Guilford.

Gabbay, J., le May, A. C., Jefferson, H., D, W., Lovelock, R., Powell, J., et al. (2003). A case study of knowledge management in multi-agency consumer-informed 'communities of practice': Implications for evidence-based policy development in health and social services. *Health*, 7, 283–310.

Gilliam, A., Barrington, T., Davis, D., Lacson, R., Uhl, G., & Phoenix, U. (2003). Building evaluation capacity for HIV prevention programs. *Evaluation and Program Planning*, 26, 133–142.

Ginsburg, A. & Rhett, N. (2003). Building a better body of evidence: New opportunities to strengthen evaluation utilization. *American Journal of Evaluation*, 24, 489–498.

Greene, J. (1998). Qualitative program evaluation: Promise and practice. In N. K. Denzin & Y. S. Lincoln (eds) *Collecting and Interpreting Qualitative Materials* (pp. 372–399). Thousand Oaks: Sage.

Guba, E. & Lincoln, Y. (1995). *Fourth Generation Evaluation*, 2nd edition.. Newberry Park, CA: Sage.

Henry, G. T. (2003). Influential evaluations. *American Journal of Evaluation*, 24, 515–524.

Henry, G. T. & Mark, M. M. (2003a). Toward an agenda for research on evaluation. In C. A. Christie (ed.). *The Practice-Theory Relationship in Evaluation: New Directions in Evaluation*, No. 97 (pp. 69–80). San Francisco: Jossey-Bass.

Henry, G. T. & Mark, M. M. (2003b). Beyond use: Understanding evaluation's influence on attitudes and actions. *American Journal of Evaluation*, 24, 293–314.

Hijmans, E., Pleijter, A., & Wester, F. (2003). Covering scientific research in Dutch newspapers. *Science Communication*, 25, 153–176.

Hofstetter, C. & Alkin, M. C. (2003). Evaluation use revisited. In T. Kellaghan, D. L. Stufflebeam & L. A. Wingate (eds) *International Handbook of Educational Evaluation* (pp. 189–196). Boston: Kluwer.

Hood, S. (2004). A journey to understand the role of culture in program evaluation: Snapshots and personal reflections of an African-American evaluator. In M. Thompson-Robinson, R. Hopson & S. SenGupta (eds) *In search of cultural competence. New Directions in Evaluation*. No. 102 (pp. 21–37). San Francisco: Jossey-Bass.

House, E. R. (2001). Responsive evaluation (and its influence on deliberative democratic evaluation). In J. C. Greene (ed.), *Responsive Evaluation. New Directions in Evaluation*, No. 92, (pp. 23–30). San Francisco: Jossey-Bass.

House, E. R. (1995). Principled evaluation: A critique of AEA guiding principles. In W. Shadish & M. A. S. D. Newman, C. Wye (eds) *Guiding principles for evaluators. New Directions in Evaluation* Vol. 66 (pp. 27-34). San Francisco: Jossey-Bass.

House, E. R. & Howe, K. R. (2000). Deliberative democratic evaluation. In K. E. Ryan & L. DeStefano (eds) *Evaluation as a Democratic Process: Promoting inclusion, dialogue, and deliberation. New Directions in Evaluation*, No. 85 (pp. 3–12). San Francisco: Jossey-Bass.

House, E. R. & Howe, K. R. (2003). Deliberative democratic evaluation. In T. Kellaghan, D. L. Stufflebeam & L. A. Wingate (eds) *International Handbook of Educational Evaluation* (pp. 79–100). Boston: Kluwer.

Howe, K. R. (1988). Against the quantitative qualitative incompatability thesis or dogmas die hard. *Educational Researcher*, 17(8), 10–16.

Huberman, A. M. (1989). Predicting conceptual effects in research utilization: Looking with both eyes. *Knowledge in Society: The International Journal of Knowledge Transfer,* 2(3), 6–24.

Huberman, A. M. (1994). Research utilization: The state of the art. *Knowledge and Policy,* 7(4), 13–33.

Hutchinson, J. R. (1995). A multimethod analysis of knowledge use in social policy. *Science Communication,* 17, 90–106.

Hutchinson, J. R. & Huberman, A. M. (1994). Knowledge dissemination and use in science and mathematics education: A literature review. *Journal of Science Education and Technology,* 3(1), 27–47.

Jacobson, N., Butterill, D., & Goering, P. (2004). Organizational factors that influence university-based researchers' engagement in knowledge transfer activities. *Science Communication,* 25, 246–259.

King, J. A. (2002). Building the evaluation capacity of a school district. In D. Compton, M. Baiserman & S. H. Stockdill (eds.) *The Art, Craft and Science of Evaluation Capacity Building. New Directions for Evaluation.* No. 93 (pp. 63–80). San Francisco: Jossey-Bass.

Kirkhart, K. (2000). Reconceptualizing evaluation use: An integrated theory of influence. In V. Caracelli (ed.) *The Expanding Scope of Evaluation Use. New Directions in Evaluation,* No. 88 (pp. 5–24). San Francisco, CA: Jossey-Bass.

Kleit, R. G. (2004). Designing and managing public housing self-sufficiency programs: The Youngs Lake Commons program. *Evaluation Review,* 28(5), 363–395.

Knott, J. & Wildavsky, A. (1980). If dissemination is the solution, what is the problem? *Knowledge,* 1, 537–578.

Landry, R., Amara, N., & Lamari, M. (2001a). Utilization of social sciences research knowledge in Canada. *Research Policy,* 30, 333–349.

Landry, R., Amara, N., & Lamari, M. (2001b). Climbing the ladder of research utilization: Evidence from social science research. *Science Communication,* 22, 396–422.

Landry, R., Lamari, M., & Amara, N. (2003). Extant and determinants of utilization of university reserach in public administration. *Public Administration Review,* 63, 191–204.

Latowski, G. (2003). Report: Community-based, participatory research in Lawerence, Massachusetts, flags environmental health hazards and fuels education and action. *Science Communication,* 25, 204–208.

Lavis, J., Ross, S., McLeaod, C., & Gildiner, A. (2003). Measuing the impact of health research. *Journal of Health Services Research and Policy,* 8, 189–203.

Levin-Rozalis, M. (2003). Evaluation and research: Differences and similarities. *Canadian Journal of Program Evaluation,* 18(2), 1–32.

Leviton, L. C. (2003). Evaluation use: Advances, challenges and applications. *American Journal of Evaluation,* 24, 525–535.

Leviton, L. C. & Hughes, E. F. X. (1981). Research on the utilization of evaluations: A review an synthesis. *Evaluation Review,* 5(4), 525–548.

Lomas, J. (2000). Using 'linkage and exchange' to move reserach into policy at a Canadian foundation. *Health Affairs,* 19, 236–240.

Louis, K. S. (1996). Do we need a new theory of dissemination and knowledge utilization? In B. Gundem & K. Z. Ozerk (eds) *Dissemination and Utilization of Research Knowledge* (pp. 58–102). Oslo: University of Oslo, Institute for Educational Research.

Manzini, S. (2003). Effective communication of science in a culturally diverse society. *Science Communication,* 25, 191–197.

Mark, M. M. & Henry, G. T. (2004). The mechanisms and outcomes of evaluation influence. *Evaluation,* 10, 35–57.

McNamee, S. (2003). Appreciative evaluation within a conflicted educational context. In H. Preskill & A. T. Coghlan (eds) *Using Appreciative Inquiry in Evaluation. New Directions for Evaluation,* No. 100, pp. 23–40. San francisco: Jossey-Bass.

McTaggart, R. (1991). When democratic evaluation doesn't seem democratic. *Evaluation Practice,* 12(1), 9–12.

Milstein, B., Chapel, T. J., Wetterhall, S. F., & Cotton, D. A. (2002). Building capacity for program evaluation at the Centers for Disease Control and Prevention. In D. Compton, M. Baiserman & S. H. Stockdill (eds) *The Art, Craft and Science of Evaluation Capacity Building. New Directions for Evaluation,* No 93. (pp. 321–330). San Francisco: Jossey-Bass.

Molas-Gallart, J., Tang, P., Sinclair, T., Morrow, S., & Martin, B. (2000). Assessing research impact on non-academic audiences. Unpublished manuscript, London: Economic and Social Research Council.

Mycio-Mommers, L. (2002). Sustained interactivity as a predictor of use of a well-developed innovation. Paper presented at the annual meeting of the American Evaluation Association, Washington DC, November.

Nutley, S., Walter, I., & Davies, H. T. O. (2003). From knowing to doing. *Evaluation*, 9 (2), 125–148.

O'Sullivan, R. G. (2004). *Practicing Evaluation: A collaborative approach.* Thousand Oaks, CA: Sage.

O'Sullivan, R. G. & D'Agostino, A. (2002). Promoting evaluation through collaboration: Findings from community based programs for young children and their families. *Evaluation*, 8, 372–387.

Patton, M. Q. (1997). *Utilization-Focused Evaluation: A new century text*, 3rd edition. Thousand Oaks, CA: Sage.

Patton, M. Q. (1988). Six honest serving men. *Studies in Educational Evaluation*, 14, 301-330.

Patton, M. Q. (2003). Utilization focused evaluation. In T. Kellaghan, D. L. Stufflebeam & L. A. Wingate (eds) *International Handbook of Educational Evaluation* (pp. 223–244). Boston: Klewer.

Preskill, H. & Caracelli, V. (1997). Current and developing conceptions of use: Evaluation use TIG survey results. *Evaluation Practice*, 18, 209-225.

Preskill, H. & Coghlan A. T. (eds) (2003). *Using Appreciative Inquiry in Evaluation. New Directions for Evaluation*, No. 100. San Francisco, CA: Jossey-Bass Publishers.

Preskill, H. & Torres, R. T. (1999). *Evaluative Inquiry for Learning in Organizations.* Thousand Oaks, CA: Sage.

Preskill, H. & Torres, R. T. (2000). A learning dimension of evaluation use. In V. Carcelli & H. Preskill (eds) *The Expanding Scope of Evaluation Use. New Directions in Evaluation*, No. 88 (pp. 25–37). San Francisco, CA: Jossey-Bass.

Preskill, H., Zuckerman, B., & Matthews, B. (2003). An exploratory study of process use: Findings and implications for future research. *American Journal of Evaluation*, 24, 423–442.

Rich, R. F. (1991). Knowledge creation, diffusion and utilization: Perspectives of the founding editor of Knowledge. *Knowledge: Creation, Diffusion, Utilization*, 12, 319–337.

Rich, R. F. & Oh, C. H. (2000). Rationality and use of information in policy decisions. *Science Communication*, 22, 173–211.

Rogers, E. M. (1995). *Diffusion of Innovations*, 4th edition. New York: The Free Press.

Rossman, G. & Rallis, S. (2000). Critical inquiry and use in action. In V. Carcelli & H. Preskill (eds) *The Expanding Scope of Evaluation Use. New Directions in Evaluation*, No. 88 (pp. 55–69). San Francisco, CA: Jossey-Bass.

Russ-Eft, D., Atwood, R. & Egherman, T. (2002). Use and non use of evaluation results: Case study of environmental influences in the private sector. *American Journal of Evaluation*, 23, 19–32.

Scriven, M. (2003/2004). Michael Scriven on the differences between evaluation and social sciences research. *Evaluation Exchange*, 9 (4), 4.

Shadish, W. R., Newman, D. L., Scheirer, M. A., & Wye C. (eds) (1995). *Guiding Principles for Evaluators. New Directions for Program Evaluations*, No. 66, San Francisco: Jossey-Bass.

Shulha, L. M. (2000). Evaluative inquiry in university/school professional learning partnerships. In V. J. Caracelli & H. Preskill (eds) *The expanding Scope of Evaluation Use. New Directions for Evaluation*, No. 88, 39–54.

Shulha, L. & Cousins, J. B. (1997). Evaluation use: Theory, research and practice since 1986. *Evaluation Practice*, 18, 195–208.

Shulha, L. M. & Wilson, R. J. (2003). Collaborative mixed method research. In A. Tashakkori & C. Teddlie (eds) *Handbook of Mixed Methodology.* (pp. 639–670). Thousand Oaks: Sage.

Sirotnik, K. & Oaks, J. (1990). Evaluation as critical inquiry: School improvement as a case in point. In K. Sirotnik (ed) *Evaluation and social justice: New Directions for Program Evaluation.* No. 45, (pp. 37-59).

Smith, N. L. (1993). Improving evaluation theory through the empirical study of evaluation practice. *Evaluation Practice*, 14, 237–242.

Sridharan, S. (2003). Introduction to special section on "What is useful evaluation?" *American Journal of Evaluation*, 24, 483–487.

Stake, R. (1983). Program evaluation, particularly responsive evaluation. In G. F. Madaus, M. Scriven & D. L. Stufflebeam (eds) *Evaluation Models: Viewpoints on educational and human services evaluation* (pp. 287–310). Norwell MA: Kluwer Nijhoff Publishing.

Stufflebeam, D. L. (2003). Professional standards and principles for evaluation. In T. Kellaghan, D. L. Stufflebeam, & L. A. Wingate (eds) *International Handbook of Educational Evaluation* (pp. 279–302). Boston: Kluwer.

Torres, R. T. & Preskill, H. (2001). Evaluation and organizational learning: Past, present and future. *American Journal of Evaluation, 22,* 387–395.

Walter, I., Nutley, S., Percy-Smith, J., McNeish, D., & Frost, S. (2004). *Improving Use of Research in Social Care.* London: Social Care Institute for Excellence/Policy Press.

Watkins, J. M. (1994). A postmodern critical theory of research use. *Knowledge and Policy, 7*(4), 55–77.

Weaver, L. & Cousins, J. B. (2004). Unpacking the participatory process. *Journal of Multidisciplinary Evaluation, 1,* 19–40.

Weiss, C. H. (1998). Have we learned anything new about evaluation use? *American Educational Research Journal, 19,* 21–33.

Weiss, C. H. (1983). Ideology, interests, and information. In D. Callahan & B. Jennings (eds), *Ethics, the Social Sciences and Policy Analysis* (pp. 231–245). New York: Plenum Press.

Worthen, B. R. (1990). Program evaluation. In H. J. Walberg & G. D. Haertel (eds) *Internional Encyclopedia of Educational Evaluation* (pp. 42–47). Oxford: Pergamon Press.

Zhang, K. (1989). The development of knowledge use studies. Unpublished doctoral dissertation, Graduate School of Public and International Affairs, University of Pittsburgh, Pittsburgh PA.

CONTEXTUAL CHALLENGES FOR EVALUATION PRACTICE

Elliot Stern

Introduction

Evaluation as a practice occurs within a context that is nowadays dynamic, complex, and geographically dispersed. Many acknowledge that evaluation as an identifiable activity has grown dramatically in recent years (Leeuw, Toulemonde, & Brouwers, 1999; Furubo, Rist, & Sandahl, 2002) driven by a host of factors – institutional and occupational, sectoral and disciplinary, national and international. The organizational development of the evaluation community, which has been similarly dramatic, also bears witness to this dynamism. Evaluation societies and associations for evaluators that were once confined to North America, one or two European Countries and Australasia now span the globe – with 12 national or regional societies in Europe, networks that in one form or another cover most of Latin America and Africa (26 countries were represented at the 2004 AfrEA – African evaluation

network – conference), and a similar process of diffusion now appears to be underway in Asia. There is even an initiative to establish an umbrella organization to link national and regional evaluation associations, societies, and networks (see www.ioce.net). Conferences for evaluators now occur throughout the year and throughout the world. Other media – print and electronic – that disseminate evaluation knowledge and facilitate evaluator interaction are pervasive.

This chapter mainly looks forward whilst still relating to many of the topics that appear in this Part – and indeed to some other parts of the Handbook. So I touch on ethical issues, issues of use and utilization and the intellectual context within which evaluators work and research. However, there is no attempt to respond to or integrate the specific arguments of other chapters. The emphasis is to reflect on the dynamics that appear to shape these topics and evaluation practice more generally. The chapter starts from the view that evaluation as practice is an "open system", shaped by many particular societal, institutional and global contexts. Context is used here in the dictionary sense of "ambient conditions" and the surrounds that help "determine meaning" (*New Shorter Oxford*). The aims of this chapter are to unpick the main processes that are shaping the context in which evaluation nowadays happens and in which evaluators work; and to discuss how these contextual processes appear to be shaping evaluation practice. The main argument centres around changes in the contexts of evaluation driven by global shifts in the nature of the State and public policy that are reshaping evaluation practice. Such contextual changes may not support and may even undermine the identity of evaluation as an occupation with professional aspirations. At the same time the nature of globalization is itself challenging evaluation practice.

First some caveats. This is a personal and sometimes speculative reflection by someone who sees himself as inhabiting the world of evaluation practice rather than that of the academy. An attempt is made to stand outside the community and consider evaluator and evaluation claims with a degree of distance and dispassion. It is also the view of someone whose working experience is mainly based in Europe even though with close collegiate relations with evaluators from other parts of the world. This should be borne in mind when this author's own assumptions and generalizations appear to jar with the experience of colleagues and readers based elsewhere! Even though an important part of the thesis being developed is around globalization, there remains as Giddens (1990) suggests, continuing scope for national, cultural and institutional diversity, even within a globalized context.

One point of departure is the self-understandings of the evaluation community with regard to practice, which have featured in the various contributions to this part and to

an extent other parts of the Handbook. We can deduce a great deal about practice contexts from the way evaluators conceive of practice, what is regarded as salient and influencing. This is not to suggest that such self-understandings should be accepted at face value. However, they should be taken as at least one starting point in mapping the contexts of practice, revealing as they do contested terrain and aspirations – and even sometimes denial of unpleasant alternative possibilities.

Conceptions of Practice and Context

First it must be said most evaluators acknowledge that they are engaged in some form of practice, insofar as they undertake as well as study evaluations – even though there is an influential subgroup among evaluators composed of scholars and teachers who spend more of their time studying and advising than doing evaluations. So according to Weiss (1998, p. 5) "Evaluation is a practical craft, designed to help programmes work better and to allocate resources to better programmes". But surrounding this widely shared view are various taken-for-granted assumptions about what constitutes practice that are very different in focus and are not always consistent.

Among these the most common appear to be:

- Evaluation as technical practice
- Evaluation as professional practice
- Evaluation as the practice of judgement
- Evaluation as an engaged practice
- Evaluation as a management practice
- Evaluation as a dialogical/argumentative practice
- Evaluation as a social practice

Before unpicking what appear to be the main assumptions about context that these various expressions of practice suggest, a brief high-lighting of the main assumptions made about "practice" itself.

Evaluation as a Technical Practice. If we look at the various principles, guidelines and competency lists that abound in evaluation journals and list servers as well as many of the textbooks and websites of evaluation societies, they usually emphasize the technical, analytical and method-oriented nature of practice. Donald Schon's critique of "technical rationality" (Schon, 1983) as the assumed basis for many professions and practitioners remains highly relevant to evaluation today. Of course methods are buttressed by concerns for demonstrating standards, ethical behaviour and quality assurance – in the sense of reassuring the wider world of the quality of what they can expect from evaluation and evaluators. However, the emphasis is on strong methods (and sometimes theories). Hence the justification and legitimacy of evaluation is based on the excellence of the evaluator's toolkit, hence "traditional worries regarding reliability and validity" (Shaw, 1999, p. 3) and definitions that emphasize the "use of social research procedures" (Rossi, Freeman & Lipsey, 1999, p. 4) are characteristic of the field.

Evaluation as Professional Practice. The Australasian Evaluation Society website exhorts members to "belong to the premier professional evaluation organization in Australia and New Zealand", whilst the American Evaluation Association describes itself as "an international professional association". This assertion of professional status needs to be confronted with reference to the wider literature on occupational control (Johnson, 1972; Larson, 1977) and is further explored below. Yet at the heart of this identity are assumptions that practice is about skilled, ethical and trusted individuals operating within

codes and standards, delivering a "service" to "clients". And interestingly these assumptions are increasingly diffused internationally as well as nationally: similar assertions of professionality can be found in Africa and Latin America as in North America, Europe or Australasia.

Evaluation as the Practice of Judgement. Whilst many experts and professionals must exercise judgement, evaluators place the act of judgement – applying values and criteria to judge success – at the heart of their work. For Scriven it is about "determining merit and worth", for Weiss comparing "what is with what should be", and even among those who do not buy-in to that framework, disagreements are likely to be about who makes judgements – not whether they should be made (Schwandt, 1997). The word "value" is in the job-title of and definitions of what we do and it remains at the heart of evaluators' claims for distinctive competence.

Evaluation as an Engaged Practice. There is also in the literature considerable advocacy for more interactive, participative and communicative forms of practice. It is suggested that evaluators need to communicate clearly, treat different stakeholders fairly and disseminate findings effectively. There is a mixture here between the instrumental and the ethical motive for managing interactions. In order to access data, in institutions and other settings or systems where evaluation objects are to be found, effective "handling skills" are needed. At the same time evaluators deal with people and have responsibilities to treat them with honesty and respect. Action research and social experiment traditions variously associated with Lewin (1948), Carr & Kemmis (1986) and more recently Fetterman (1996), also combine instrumental and ethical concerns.

Evaluation as a Management Practice. This perspective is concerned with the day-to-day practice of evaluation management. One expression of this can be found in the way Shadish, Cook, & Leviton (1991, p. 58) talk of a theory of evaluation practice which aims to "prioritize the content given the limited time, resources and skills that constrain any given evaluation". In a more operational vein a recent evaluation guide (www.evalsed.info) put out by the European Commission addresses issues of how to manage an evaluation team or project – both from the standpoint of evaluators and commissioners of evaluation. Procurement rules worldwide, including those of international bodies and national bodies operating internationally disseminate these notions of practice.

Evaluation as a Dialogical/Argumentative Practice. There is a strand in the evaluation literature that argues for an argumentative and dialogical relationship with stakeholders and programme beneficiaries. This is partly seen as a way of ensuring the production of more valid knowledge and utilization (Valovirta, 2002; van der Knaap, 1995) It is consistent with contemporary notions of distributed knowledge production which regards knowledge as no longer the preserve of the academy or the expert but necessarily dispersed, being "produced in the context of application" and "under conditions of continuous negotiation" (Gibbons et al., 1994). Dialogue is also seen as a means of putting into practice some of the principles of a democratic society: "through dialogue, the notion of what constitutes 'higher authority' or 'legitimate knowledge' is broadened beyond scientific rationality to legitimize for example, the voices of marginalised stakeholder groups" (Abma, 2001).

Evaluation as a Social Practice. This tends to be critical regarding the social relations of evaluation – how evaluators relate (or should relate) to their paymasters and to their informants, communities, beneficiaries, stakeholders or clients. But there is also a moral and political orientation towards action and the social forces and relationships that evaluation encounters in the world. This stands apart from a more technical or scientific orientation. This latter representation of practice (or praxis) is closer to an Aristotelian or even Marxist understanding – evaluation should/could/might change the world and evaluators are therefore exhorted to be properly committed to social betterment (Mark, Henry, & Julnes, 2000), dialogue (Greene, 2001), democratization (House & Howe, 1999) or empowerment (Fetterman, Kafterian & Wandersman, 1996)

On the other hand, there are some assumptions about practice that sit uneasily alongside each other, for example a service orientation with the more critical stance of praxis; and a methods focus that is mainly data-analytic alongside the skill prerequisites of dialogical, engaged or empowerment orientations. Notions of practice that are different or even contradictory may also tell us something about the contexts that shape evaluation practice. For example the longstanding aversion to evaluators becoming involved in action and implementation that might follow evaluations, appears to be increasingly called into question nowadays just as the assertion of evaluation as a distinctive discipline is often accompanied by a counter tendency that if anything appears to integrate evaluation methods more closely into the broader social (and economic) sciences, crossing disciplinary boundaries. There is also some tension between an individualistic vision of the heroic evaluator embedded in some principles, codes and guidelines (see AEA, 2004) and a more systemic vision that seeks to build common understandings among evaluators, commissioners and other stakeholders in more recent guidelines – for example the guidelines of the

UK Evaluation Society and the Australasian Evaluation Society (1997).

The images of context communicated by these visions of practice include most obviously:

- A *disciplinary context* with claims to expertise around distinctive methods and theories.
- An *institutional context* within which evaluators are characterized by an ability to make judgments, choose methods and disseminate findings.
- An *occupational context* which has standards, autonomy and the semblance of self-regulation.
- An *action context* in which evaluators are seen – sometimes – as actors with agency appropriately managing their relationships with the field or with commissioners whilst also learning through action.
- A *normative context* in which evaluators facing choices have to make judgments, operate ethically and pursue goals that are value-based and informed by an aspiration for a better future.

These "images of context" may be rooted in practice on the one hand, but they are also rooted in broader societal processes and developments. The context of evaluation is quite reasonably itself embedded in this wider context which, however, indirectly also shapes evaluation practice.

Shaping the Context of Evaluation at National and International Levels

I would suggest that we need to look beyond immediate and perceived contexts to broader, *formative contexts* (borrowing from Unger, 1987, and Ciborra & Lanzarra, 1994), characterized by demands and resources which offer new and changing opportunities for action. It is these demands, resources and opportunities that translate abstract notions of context into new work routines and practice.

Attempting to identify formative contexts, *the* drivers that shape the practice of evaluation unless accompanied by a major research effort, must risk being partial if not downright idiosyncratic! However, as noted at the outset, this chapter aims to offer a personal view, albeit one that has been informed by personal experience and more recent scans of evaluation journals, list servers and conference proceedings.

I would argue that the aspects of context that have come to the fore in the last decade centre around linked processes of policy and administrative change at national and international levels (Pollitt & Bouckaert, 1999) This is quite different from the shapers of evaluation context in earlier decades which were often based in the academy or in neighbourhoods or establishments such as schools. In an age of "globalization" we need not be surprised that evaluation is also facing what have become universal challenges. However, I would also argue that evaluation is distinctive because of its location on the front line of these processes.

It is widely acknowledged that globalization is closely intertwined with reductions in capability among nation states to deal with its own often "local" problems. As Daniel Bell suggested, nation states are "too small for the big problems of life and too big for the small problems". The redistribution of capabilities between the local, national, regional and international is also consistent with other debates in political science about the supposed emergence of a new "global paradigm" of public administration (Osborne & Gaebler, 1992). There is a contrast here between North American and European theories and perspectives even though they often address the same phenomena and dynamics. North Americans tend to proclaim the demise of state action or at least "progressive" public management with greater enthusiasm. Europeans tend to favour theories such as neo-functionalism (Haas, 1964) and multilevel governance (Hooghe, 1996; Majone, 1993) which retain a more optimistic view of new if changing roles for the nation state. These are after all the theories that underpin the evolution of the European Union.

The clearest operationalization of these ideas as they affect evaluation is to be found at national levels, even though national innovations are inseparable from international processes. Crises of legitimacy and fears for social cohesion as well as resource scarcity have pressured public administrations worldwide to pursue "reform". Arguments can be had as to the extent to which these pressures derive from "global" factors such as technology change, international trade, international financial systems, international treaties and institutions, from the spread of new dominant ideologies or to what extent they derive from structural changes in modern societies and what their governments attempt to achieve. However, for our purposes the response in terms of reform is less in dispute. Common elements of these "reforms" include:

- Moves towards decentralization.
- Greater concerns for public sector management and efficiency.
- Subcontracting and using markets to deliver services.
- The withdrawal of the state from some traditional policy areas.
- Cutbacks in certain kinds of welfare provision.
- A focus on results and outcomes rather than inputs.
- Attempts to build consensus and partnerships among stakeholders.
- The provision of information to citizens to facilitate "consumer" choice.
- More general attention to transparency and accountability.

How the Reform Context Influences Evaluation Practice

There are many and different ways in which these reforms have and continue to impinge on evaluators. For example, they influence:

- The evaluation agenda that nowadays confronts the evaluation community with new and pressing policy demands – including demands to accommodate civil society;
- The focus of evaluation methods with a renewed emphasis on performance management and improvements in policy delivery;
- The role of the evaluator, nowadays expected to both engage with others in policy-making communities and take cognizance of and relate to intended policy change;
- The institutionalization of evaluation within public sector bureaucracies that has led to a far more managed and regulated working environment for many evaluators.

The Evaluation Agenda

The mix of demands now being made of evaluators has changed dramatically in recent decades, even though there are also elements of continuity. Whilst there have been some shifts into more contemporary policy areas (information and communication technologies, public health with an emphasis on HIV/AIDS, welfare reform, etc.) these vary between countries and regions and changes over time are always to be expected. The more striking changes in the agenda are in *ways* that any particular policy area is approached: *policy-making* is as important as *policy content* in setting the evaluation agenda.

There is, for example, a more consistent expectation that evaluators will know about policy content and less tolerance now among evaluation commissioners for generic evaluation knowledge, unless backed up by understanding of specific policy debates and histories. This is played out for evaluators in a number of ways. Sometimes there is a tussle, in terms of who undertakes an evaluation, between domain experts – those who specialize in policy areas such as criminal justice, healthcare, science and technology – or evaluators whose strengths are generic and methods based? Sometimes there is an expectation for multidisciplinary teams that combine these different kinds of domain and analytical expertise. And sometimes through the creation of specialist evaluation sub-communities working more or less exclusively in a particular policy area – science and technology, community development, social work, criminal justice etc.

Another common trend in policy-making is away from traditional legislation and regulation towards policy instruments that rely on consensus and collective, multistakeholder action. In many of the more intractable policy areas such as public health, urban regeneration and even policies intended to enhance the diffusion of technological innovation, policy-making and delivery relies increasingly on compacts, consortia, collaboratives and partnerships. These attempt to build a consensus across civil society and among institutions and agencies so as to support efficient service delivery, involve users and citizens and even address attitudinal and cultural issues – such as low trust, community divisions and institutional turf wars. Such tendencies are reinforced by resistance in settled democratic societies to what is described as too much regulation and "red-tape".

There are direct implications for evaluation practice. For example:

There is greater value attached to an ability to work in multidisciplinary teams. This is correlated with perceived limitations of the contribution of individual evaluator working in isolation. To some extent this appears to be a reflection of the stage of maturity of evaluation practice in a country or region. In early days evaluators are more likely to be offered small-scale assignments that can be undertaken by individuals. Once evaluation practice becomes established and especially if it is taken seriously by governments, the complexity of assignments tends to pull for a division of labour. It is unlikely that a single evaluation "expert" can cover all the skills and competencies needed. So

it is unsurprising that in many European settings it is generally understood that being able to work in teams is a necessary work-related social skill for evaluators (Treasury Board of Canada, 2002; Stevahn et al., 2005). Evaluators also have a growing need for tools and theories that allow them to work in problem or topic focused rather than disciplinary ways, which may go some way to account for the continued popularity of logical frameworks and variants of "programme theory".

Parts of the evaluation community in many countries are separated off from the mainstream. Indeed the fragmentation of evaluation into sub-communities that specialize in their own favoured methods has become common. This is partly the consequence of the scale of activities in different sectors. The sheer volume of activity and the demands to keep abreast with what is taking place in different policy areas encourages a division of labour. I would argue it can also be part of the control strategies used by evaluation commissioners who often form close links with favoured evaluation contractors with whom they share assumptions and values and a commitment to certain methods.

Evaluators have to learn to work with stakeholders. In order to accommodate multi-stakeholder working evaluators have to adapt their practice in several ways. Most obviously partnerships are often characterized by overlapping, unarticulated and even inconsistent objectives among partners. Evaluators who use objectives as a basis of their work – a still common approach – need to help construct an evaluation agenda that at the very least clarifies stakeholder expectations of an evaluation or more ambitiously attempts to elicit shared assumptions and areas of agreement that may not be self-evident from policy or programme documentation. This need to work with stakeholders is likely to continue throughout the life-cycle of an evaluation: when results come through their use and usefulness also have to be negotiated. Hence the relevance of "engagement" and "argumentation" forms of practice referred to earlier. Especially in a multi-stakeholder environment, evaluators have to become consensus builders, conciliators and negotiators – alongside being analysts of the logic of programmes and of data. When the purposes of evaluation include empowerment then the need for these skills becomes even more vital.

The Focus of Evaluations and Their Methods

I have already noted that a concern with effective policies that deliver credible results for citizens is at the heart of public sector reforms. Evaluation has been increasingly harnessed to this end. Performance management integrates monitoring into the policy process (Wholey, 1981). This is made possible by the way policies are structured, the use of benchmarking, the choice of indicators and linking individual incentives and policy or programme budgeting to such indicators. Yet the relationship between performance management and evaluation can be tenuous and problematic. For some (Davies, 1999) performance management has come to displace evaluation in government circles – evaluation having failed to deliver timely and usable results, a tendency to be overly formative and complex. Davies argues that evaluation still has a contribution to make to performance management – both to its "technical difficulties" such as attribution and causal analysis and to "people issues" that surround change, such as trust and ownership, participation and utilization. Some practitioners regard performance management as indivisible from evaluation, or at the very least assume that the broad church of evaluation can also accommodate performance management under its roof (van der Knaap, 2000; Kusek & Rist, 2004).

Practice implications include:

A renewed emphasis on performance management. For performance management to succeed it needs to find ways to demonstrate that plans lead to anticipated results and that targets are achieved. Evaluators are expected to demonstrate results much further downstream than inputs or even outcomes: "does this really make a difference to the lives of poor people in developing countries?" is a more likely evaluation question now in the UK's Department for International Development than "were programmes well conceived or well-implemented?" But paradoxically, evaluators are also expected to contribute to upstream programme planning and policy design, even though planning and design is in the interests of results: anticipating results by testing the plausibility of the assumptions on which plans are made. The use of impact assessments, ex ante evaluation, evaluability assessments and logic models all fall out from this emphasis on results.

Shifts towards policy as a unit of analysis. A further consequence of public sector reforms has been shifts in the level of analysis that evaluators are expected to address. Policy-makers are asking about policies and strategies rather than about programmes or projects. The view that success has to be judged at the level of the overall policy is associated with a view that piecemeal evaluation of individual programmes are not simply additive; many good programmes do not make a good policy. This has technical and analytical implications. For example: the emergence of various theory-based models and representations of policies (Rogers, 2000); the use of systematic reviews (Gallo, 1978, Popay Rogers & Williams, 1998) to build up a more rounded understanding of what is being learned than is possible from individual evaluations; and evidence-based policy and practice perspectives (Nutley, Walter & Davies, 2003).

EXEMPLAR A: PERFORMANCE MANAGEMENT AND EVALUATION

The Netherlands has recently introduced a policy evaluation system that explicitly links budgets to operations and results. The new regulation "Central government achievement data and evaluation research" came into force in all Dutch government departments in January 2002. This regulation overseen by the Ministry of Finance is the result of an inter-departmental working group which had two aims:

> *to ensure that the evaluation function within central government is sufficiently guaranteed, and; to ensure that the policy information supplied within the framework of the departmental budget and the departmental annual report complies with the quality requirements applying to this information.*

In order to achieve these targets, the regulation contains further conditions regarding:

I.   *the integrated deployment of evaluation instruments;*
II.   *the weighing up that needs to be made when making use of ex ante evaluation research;*
III. *the degree to which policy is covered by periodical evaluation research and its frequency (completeness and periodicity);*
IV.   *the methodological-technical quality of evaluation instruments and the way in which policy information is obtained;*
V.   *the way in which civil servants and top politicians are informed about the results of periodical evaluation research, and;*
VI.   *the responsibilities within a department for proper implementation of the regulation.*

(Policy Evaluation in the Netherlands, van der Knaap, 2000)

Moving the Boundaries of the Evaluator's Role

Implicit in the changes in methods and focus are changes also in the evaluator's role. One way of conceiving the activity of evaluators is in terms of a linear sequence running from planning, priority setting and design through to implementation, utilization and follow-up. We have already noted that evaluators are being pulled upstream towards planning and design work (not of course that the same evaluators will undertake the upstream work). There has been a similar pull downstream towards use, influence and implementation. Reservations about evaluators

becoming directly involved in change (e.g. Scriven, 1991), have given way to a much more positive view about the unavoidable and often desirable input that evaluators bring to change, utilization and even programme management (Torres, 2001; Patton, 1997; Martin & Sanderson, 1999):

- Evaluation should be used and influential, anticipating therefore the context of use.
- Recommendations are an important part of the evaluation process – even though there may be disagreements over how recommendations are put together.
- Evaluators have some contribution to make to programme management.

The above also have implications for practice:

Evaluators are asked to share their special claims to knowledge and expertise. Once the logic of evaluation is applied earlier in the policy and programme design process, as noted above, we can see the spread of evaluation thinking to other specialist groups within agencies. The special knowledge of evaluators is no longer so special! Indeed, some of those who adopt and adapt evaluation concepts and methods use other frameworks, such as performance management, change management and evidence-based policy. This threat to the special claims of evaluators is paradoxically one consequence of the success of evaluation practice. It opens up new opportunities and career paths for those whose entry point into policy-making has been evaluation, thus blurring another boundary with policy analysts and political scientists (Geva-May & Pal, 1999). This tendency is further reinforced by the need for evaluators working in these ways to become familiar with policy-making in general, as well as particular policy domains. However, it can also put evaluators in the strange position of "policing" the way that others, experts and administrators, use "their" ideas.

Evaluators are becoming involved in policy delivery and the management of change. Arguments about independence and for some "objectivity" are central to evaluation discourse. This is often understood as maintaining separation between the responsibilities of evaluation and management. Upstream this distinction has been relatively well maintained, by contractual requirements that those involved in evaluation should have had little involvement with the formulation of that particular policy or programme. However, this has proved more problematic once initiatives are up and running. In the UK there is an expectation in long-term programmes in the field of urban and community regeneration

that "real-time" evaluation will contribute directly to programme management. Indeed, the expectation that evaluation will enhance "steering" during implementation, has led to evaluations being funded out of "programme budgets" rather than traditional research and evaluation budgets. In some cases this can present evaluators with real challenges to their role: avoiding short-term pressures on an evaluation agenda and the temptation to become involved in programme management (Martin & Sanderson, 1999). Some see this less as a matter of role management and more of engagement with change in a developmental, formative or "accompanying" role: the evaluator as change agent, orchestrator of change or action researcher (Finne et al., 1995; Wadsworth, 1993).

Institutionalizing Evaluation

Public sector "reforms" which have had direct implications for the way the machinery of government is managed and organized, also shape the management and organization of evaluation in public and "third" sector agencies. A concern for performance and results of itself increases the demand for evaluation within government and in particular from the executive arms of government (administrative bodies and implementing agencies) rather than legislatures. Most of these assignments are contracted out – itself a tendency that mirrors the outsourcing of services within the wider public sector. The sheer scale and perceived importance of such activities encourages government departments or more frequently their in-house specialists in evaluation to begin to pay attention to the way contracted evaluations are managed. But these do not remain an internal government concern. Once subcontracting becomes the norm, the State passes on its accountability and control concerns to those with whom it contracts

(Power, 1997). Evaluation is built into service delivery contracts (in, for example, education, employment and training, environmental services) thus opening up new markets for evaluators. However, *how* evaluations are conducted – what they measure, describe, seek to explain or improve – inevitably becomes a preoccupation of those who manage the subcontracted State. These preoccupations affect what evaluators are asked to do, well down the supply chain of "third" sector organizations (voluntary, community based etc.) and, often, the private sector as well.

This is not to deny the survival of enclaves of a less regulated evaluative activity, usually to be found in small-scale local settings or where funding comes through research or charitable foundation channels rather than from the executive arm of government. However, for the majority of evaluators in countries or jurisdictions with a large evaluation sector based on public sector contracts, their work-life brings them face-to-face with institutionalized evaluation arrangements on a daily basis.

There is also, if European experience is anything to go by, a life-cycle aspect to the way that institutionalized evaluation evolves. In the early stages of the development of evaluation capacity the concern within public sector commissioners of evaluation is to establish a supply of evaluators within a relatively "protected" and innovative environment. Suppliers have to be enticed into the field of evaluation, from universities or consultancy firms, and there is little competition. They are offered freedom, resources and contracts. Management is relatively informal. Once evaluation becomes well-established it can come to resemble other mature markets for services. Evaluation commissioners begin to develop strategies for market control and regulation – with many consequences for evaluators.

Practice implications of the institutionalization of evaluation include:

Greater regulation of evaluation activity. Terms of reference are nowadays drawn up in ways that seek to shape evaluation content, questions, goals and often methods. Proposals will have to follow a particular format. Contractors are by competitive tender, consistent with more general procurement procedures. Evaluators are also likely to encounter various attempts at "quality control", including quality assessment schema for evaluation reports. There are procedures that steer and control evaluations once underway through steering committees and monthly management reports. There are contractual rules that govern the dissemination and "clearing" of reports and possibly of publications. This level of procedural and administrative regulation has many consequences for practice. First and foremost it narrows down the range of "contractors" who are likely to bid for and therefore "win" evaluation work. Evaluators must be able to navigate their way through contractual and management systems and throughout an assignment need "client-handling" skills. A premium is placed on those who can perform well in contract-getting. Arguably to do their work, evaluators must be able to build sufficient trust and credibility within the contracting/client system to be given the freedom to design and implement evaluations with minimum constraints.

A shift from the operational to strategic evaluation priorities. Policy-makers have different interests from local managers and service providers. Even when evaluation work is directly with front-line agencies and community groups there is pressure on evaluators to give priority to the interests and agendas of those who are ultimately funding the work.

This can be a subtle process. For example, the data requirements of main funding agencies will often be clearly specified and elaborate, whilst the evaluation priorities of front-line managers and workers may at first, be exploratory and ill-defined. It is easy for the former to crowd out the latter. It may also be difficult to combine the evaluation packages that each requires. Combining participative and developmental work with client groups can be hard to combine with the collection of standard indicators on attendance, housing and lifestyle (Biott & Cook, 2000) Similar processes even occur in large government agencies where the policy and accountability priorities of senior officials can crowd out the more operational concerns of front-line public service managers. These pressures both constrain the evaluation agenda and the prioritization of evaluation questions rather than others and more importantly reduce the usefulness of evaluation to those who seek to improve their performance, rather than judge that performance retrospectively.

An ever more competitive market. Public sector managers remain keen to recruit new "providers" as evaluation markets mature, just as at the early stages of the emergence of institutionalized evaluation – but for different reasons. Once evaluation is established as a reasonably large-scale activity markets tend to stratify. Certain evaluators gain experience in particular domains and methods and it becomes difficult for new entrants to compete. In economic terms the costs of market entry become high. The concentration of contracts among a few contractors is reinforced by pressures on evaluation commissioners to reduce their management efforts. Experienced providers who understand the rules of the game are easier to manage than new entrants. Sometimes a relationship of mutual dependence will emerge: the sector leaders (usual

suspects) may assume a dominant position in an evaluation sector because they are seen as safe pairs of hands. Yet "old hands" also tend to be better able to insert their own priorities, challenge the rules and negotiate for greater "professional" freedom. If there are few providers in a market, let alone one or two sector leaders they may also be able to demand a higher price for their services. Evaluation managers working within an institutional setting will have to balance their concerns for quality and minimized management and transaction costs with their wish to retain control and possibly minimize costs. So the continued recruitment of new entrants is often part of the institutional managers' strategy. Beyond the early days of the evolution of an evaluation sector there will also be a tendency to look as widely as possible for new entrants. Evaluators may find themselves competing with general purpose generic project management companies that assemble evaluation teams (as they would for construction or shipbuilding projects) and accountancy firms that also undertake evaluations. They may also compete with sector experts (in housing, international development, criminal justice, social work or education) who know little about evaluation theory or methods but do know the field and even evaluators from other countries. It is common in Europe for evaluators to work across national borders and US evaluators especially from the larger "contract shops" have been encouraged to enter the UK market by UK government departments, because of apparent concerns about national capacity.

Occupational Control in a "Global" Context

Not all the drivers of context and practice change for evaluation can be attributed exclusively to

State and government reform. Evaluators have their own agency; they can act and take initiative. Evaluators also respond to value change, social movement, economic developments and their own occupational interests. It is only possible to explore some of the contextual demands at this level and again these will be a personal selection of what appear to this author to be amongst the most salient of these demands.

The three main contextual demands I would highlight at this level are:

- The professional claims of evaluators.
- Value and cultural shifts and human rights.
- Globalization, standards and free trade in evaluation services.

Professional Claims

Reference has already been made to assertions of professional identity that are common among evaluators. The trappings of professional identity are certainly extensive, including the growth and spread of evaluation societies, a variety of networks, discussions at least of accreditation, the elaboration of codes of ethics, standards and guidelines, a growth in bodies of theory to underpin practice, journals and conferences. As was also noted above, important elements of how evaluators understand practice are intertwined with notions of the professional, including the ethical behaviour, commitment to certain altruistic goals, and a trusted position in society which carries authority. Nonetheless the reality and meaning of professional identities among evaluators bears scrutiny.

There is an extensive literature on occupational control and the sociology of professions which can provide a useful starting point for these reflections. An early advocate of still widespread thinking in this area is Terrence Johnson (1972). He noted, for example, that many long-established models of professionalism

rely heavily on the self-description of the occupational group concerned, usually in fairly explicit comparison with the traits of classic professions such as medicine and law. Johnson put notions of power and markets centre stage in the analysis of occupations. For him professionalism can only arise in specific circumstances:

> where the tensions inherent in the producer-consumer relationship are controlled by means of an institutional framework based upon occupational authority. This form of control occurs only where certain conditions exist . . . . (Johnson, 1972)

These conditions include a large market of diverse consumers with "diverse" interests, "unorganized, dependent and exploitable". Where there is "a single client or a small group of powerful clients" professional strategies of control are less likely to be successful. Johnson notes the rarity of these conditions even some three decades ago. Others have since elaborated theories of occupational control that have, for example, focused on the consequences of specialists working in large bureaucracies where managerialism and deskilling are seen as a serious threat to autonomy and even occupational survival (Larsen, 1977; Haug, 1973; Benoit, 1994); and on the consequence of the demanding consumer who challenges and questions professional authority (Pfadenhauer, 2003). Indeed the very threat to the legitimacy of action in the public sphere that has fuelled public sector reform now reaches far deeper, affecting many experts and occupations as well as the traditionally accepted professions. Similarly, the "reflective practitioner" as understood by Schon reconceptualizes authority as interactive, negotiated and even democratized knowledge, far distant from that of the privileged holder of specialized theoretical knowledge. So paradoxically encouraging professionals to be receptive to the experience, know-how and skills of "clients" in order to become more effective practitioners may reinforce dilution in occupational authority and ultimately deprofessionalization.

Within these frameworks the assertions of professional identity and the creation of institutional arrangements associated with professions can be seen partly as a response to the very real threats that evaluators face that have been discussed in this chapter, which include:

- The employment of many evaluators within large-scale bureaucracies that routinize, fragment and may even threaten to deskill.
- Well-organized and institutionalized evaluation functions that are managing and contracting for evaluation services in ways that reduces evaluators' autonomy.
- The promotion of competitive markets that encourage new entrants and challenge evaluators' knowledge with more client service models of patronage.
- The advocacy of alternative paradigms such as performance management, change management, action research, experimental trials, evidence-based policy and policy analysis.

Investments in professional activities and organizational arrangements by evaluators can be seen in this context as a reasonable defence of occupational autonomy. Reasonable, that is, both as a way of ensuring that there is sufficient space to choose the methods and theories that are appropriate *and* as a defence of the interests of an occupational group under threat.

The use of professionalization strategies to these ends shapes evaluation practice extensively. For example:

- It provides one justification for the considerable investment in theoretical knowledge by evaluators as reflected in the content of published books and articles.

- It helps explain attempts to build shared understandings between commissioners and contractors for evaluation as evinced by the involvement of both parties in conferences, associations and discussions about standards.
- It provides a rationale for the recurrence of demands for the accreditation of evaluators.
- It justifies attempts by evaluators to build bridges between "traditional" evaluative ideas and methods and newer paradigms such as performance management.

Value and Cultural Shifts

Sensitivity to cultural diversity alongside a philosophy of human rights has shaped evaluation practice as it has the practice of most other professions. Indeed together with the ready access to information through electronic media such as the web, these now pervasive values underpin many consumer challenges to the authority of evaluative activity. "Freedom of information" and data protection legislation, concerns for "social inclusion", the rights of ethnic communities and of women are among the most obvious expressions of this diversity. However, it extends wide and deep to include among others, people with disabilities, those with different sexual orientations, those with serious conditions such as HIV/AIDS, and those living in "marginalized" linguistic communities. Similarly, in the international development field where, in post-colonial settings especially, there is nervousness, in particular among "beneficiary" governments about any reassertion of external (neo-colonial) dominance, there is an emphasis on cultural sensitivity and avoiding donor-led perspectives.

This value shift has been mirrored in many aspects of evaluation practice:

Greater respect to the rights of "subjects."
There has been a longstanding acceptance

that evaluators should treat those who inform and cooperate with evaluations with respect. This sensibility combines both instrumental and ethical rationales: ensure valid data and acknowledge the rights of human beings. We now see a far more elaborated understanding. This extends from the importation of notions of "informed consent" from medical research to a more radical assertion of the need to integrate the perspectives of minorities and those who have been oppressed in society (Mertens, 1999).

Evaluation as an emancipatory practice. Newer types of evaluation that combine emancipatory goals with developmental methods also exemplify the way that the context for evaluation practice has evolved. Terms such as "participatory", "empowerment" and "transformative" capture this thinking. Although in their pure form these approaches to evaluation retain their character as particular and sometimes even marginal, the underlying thinking is more widely integrated. Especially in evaluations that focus on disability and other excluded social groups there is a general acceptance that at the very least the process of an evaluation should not reinforce negative experiences or stereotypes. Giving voice to the marginalized is seen as "good practice" in a far broader spectrum of evaluations that focus on "consumers", "clients" and "users" of public services.

A focus on social exclusion rather than problematizing the excluded. Social exclusion, unlike earlier generation of concepts of poverty or anti-discrimination, highlights the process of exclusion and how integration can be achieved. This is a discernable shift in the evaluation agenda informing, for example, welfare to work with its emphasis on removing the barriers to employment and policies to reduce child poverty which emphasize childcare, parenting skills and flexible school regimes.

Self-determination in international development policy and evaluation. International development evaluation has been one of the most dynamic areas of evaluation practice in recent years. A cognate area, that of humanitarian aid and relief, shares many of the same basic assumptions. This has been accompanied by the emergence of a number of major new international associations devoted to evaluation in these domains such as ALNAP and more recently IDEAS (see e.g. Chapter 25 in this Handbook). The core thinking that informs many of the policies in international development has shifted dramatically in the last decade. There has been a shift from donorled to beneficiary-led development processes and a belief that it is the task of donors "to help people to help themselves" (Ellerman, 2005). For evaluators working in these domains there have been parallel tendencies. There has been a discernable shift in focus towards the evaluation of capacity development in developing countries in order to support greater autonomy and self-determination. This has incidentally encouraged a blurring of boundaries between evaluation and organizational and institutional studies.

EXEMPLAR B: RIGHTS-BASED PROGRAMMING AND EVALUATION IN SAVE THE CHILDREN UK

A rights-based approach to development makes use of the standards, principles and approaches of human rights, social activism and of development to tackle the power issues that lie at the root of poverty and exploitation, in order to promote justice, equality and freedom.

Human rights are a set of internationally agreed legal and moral standards. They establish the basic civil, political, economic, social and cultural entitlements of every human being anywhere in the world at all times. Central to the idea of human rights is the relationship between right holder and duty bearer. Duty bearers (governments, institutions and individuals) are obligated to respect, protect and fulfil human rights. Right holders are entitled to demand their own rights from duty bearers, but they also have to respect the rights of others.

Social and political activism mobilises people to demand the redistribution of power. Examples include the redistribution of wealth between rich and poor nations through debt relief or a change in trade rules, women demanding equal pay for equal work, workers demanding fair pay and benefits, or landless peasants demanding the redistribution of farmland.

Development is concerned with the distribution of resources and the access to services, such as health, education, social welfare, poverty alleviation and income generation.

A rights-based approach promotes three main principles: the accountability of duty bearers, the participation of right holders, and equity/non-discrimination. It aims to increase impact and strengthen sustainability by addressing root causes, bringing about policy and practice changes, working together with others towards common goals and by changing power relations. The primary role of a rights-based development organisation is to contribute to the fulfilment of human rights by getting duty bearers to meet their obligations, and by empowering poor and exploited people to claim their entitlements. Directly meeting needs and fulfilling rights helps people, but it does not necessarily strengthen the accountability of duty bearers. It also does not strengthen people's own ability to claim their rights.

Monitoring the extent of the fulfilment and violation of human rights is a fundamental approach to promoting human rights. The collection and dissemination of data about unfulfilled rights and about rights violations puts pressure on duty bearers to meet their obligations to respect, protect and fulfil human rights. Human rights monitoring can help strengthen the compliance of duty bearers with human rights standards. All human rights treaties come with their own mechanisms to monitor government commitment, compliance and progress towards fulfilling rights. Human rights watchdog organisations, such as Amnesty International and Human Rights Watch monitor human rights abuses, such as torture, imprisonment of political opponents, and extra-judicial killings. Some countries have established ombudsman positions and national human rights institutions to monitor human rights abuses.

Detailed international standards have been developed, for example, for the treatment of children in conflict with the law. These standards apply universally and are binding for governmental and non-governmental bodies. They should form the basis for national legislation and should be used by all law enforcement agencies dealing with children in conflict with the law. The application of international juvenile justice standards can be measured and monitored by reviewing relevant legislation and law enforcement practices.

For rights-based development organisations the collection, analysis and dissemination of data are an essential part of the overall approach to work, not just something that is done in addition to the 'real work'. In addition to being used to better understand the situation of communities in a particular context for the purpose of tailoring interventions, data and analysis are crucial to effectively holding to account duty bearers and to raise awreness on rights violations. Data collection and analysis also strengthens an organisation's own credibility, legitimacy and its accountability to the people and communities it works with. For all these reasons monitoring, evaluation and research become more important as development organisations take a rights-based approach.

What should be measured? The ultimate aim of development, human rights and activism is to bring about improvements in people's lives. Measuring changes in people's lives is therefore a key aspect of rights-based monitoring and evaluation. Development targets are generally time-bound, narrowly focused on one indicator and not complete (i.e. not 100% goals). A typical example is the Millennium Development Goal for child mortality: "Reduce by two-thirds the mortality rate among children under 5 by 2015." A rights-based perspective, on the other hand, considers the right to health as a whole rather than just one particular aspect, such as child mortality.

One way to monitor a right would be to select an integrated set of indicators that covers all aspect of this right. However, such an approach poses major methodological and practical challenges. A more practical way is to measure different dimensions related to the realisation of a right. In addition to changes in people's lives, three other dimensions should be measured: changes in accountability, equity, and participation.

Changes in the accountability of duty bearers can be made more concrete by measuring changes in policies, laws and resource allocations, and changes in attitudes, values and practices, although it should always be remembered than changes in laws and policies do not automatically translate into improvements in the lives of poor and exploited people. It is therefore necessary to monitor changes in policies and practices, in equity and non discrimination and in participation, as well changes in people's lives.

Save the Children UK has developed a rights based framework using common dimensions of change to monitor the impact of its work on children's rights. In addition to the 4 dimensions mentioned above, children's participation and active citizenship has been added, reflecting the particular focus of Save the Children programmes.

Common dimensions of change of SC UK work (see the SC UK GIM guidelines for more details)

1. Changes in the lives of children and young people
Which **rights** are being better fulfilled? Which rights are no longer being violated?

2. Changes in policies and practice affecting children and young people's rights
Duty bearers are more **accountable** for the fulfilment, protection and respect of children's and young people's rights. Policies are developed and implemented and the attitudes of duty bearers take into account the best interests and rights of the child.

3. Changes in children's and young people's participation and active citizenship
Children and young people **claim their rights** or are supported to do so. Spaces and opportunities exist which allow participation and the exercise of citizenship by children's groups and others working for the fulfilment of child rights.

4. Changes in equity and non-discrimination of children and young people

In policies, programmes, services and communities, are the most marginalised children reached?

5. Changes in civil society and communities capacity to support children's rights

Do networks, coalitions and/or movements add value to the work of their participants? Do they mobilise greater forces for change in children and young people's lives?

Models of change are developed to translate theories of change into practice, providing a more realistic picture of what a programme can achieve. Models of change are useful for identifying the most relevant and useful data for monitoring and evaluation. They are also important for checking whether assumptions about social change are correct or not. Where the assumptions are incorrect, the direction of the programme can be changed. For example, much of human rights education is based on the assumption that education leads to behaviour change. If an evaluation shows that this assumption is not valid, the programme has to look for other ways to change behaviour.

(From: Rights-based Monitoring and Evaluation. A Discussion Paper, Joachim Theis, Save the Children, April 2003.)

Globalization, Standards and Free Trade in Evaluation Services

The formulation of evaluation standards, guidelines and codes of ethics has become a core activity of evaluation societies and associations worldwide. Standards have also been elaborated by international bodies such as the Development Aid Committee of the OECD and the European Commission. Standards are seen as having several benefits, including reassuring citizens that they will not be harmed by evaluations, reassuring customers that they will receive a quality service and encouraging consistency and good practice within the evaluation community.

The US Program Evaluation Standards first developed by the Joint Committee on Standards for Educational Evaluation in 1981 and revised in 1994 is probably the best known and was accepted as a standard by the American National Standards Institute in 1994. The AEA has also developed its own ethical code, *Guiding Principles for Evaluators*, published in 1995. The Joint Committee Standards have been widely disseminated and with minor modifications adopted by among others the German Evaluation Society (DeGeval) and the African Evaluation network (AfrEA). Other countries and institutions have gone down different paths. They have done so for a number of reasons:

- A view that the cultural and value assumptions embedded in US standards are not universal.
- Concern that the targets for US standards focus mainly on evaluators and do not sufficiently include the commissioners of evaluation and policy-makers.
- Different institutional assumptions, especially with regard to the way evaluations are used by national governments.
- Different taken-for-granted units of analysis, in particular an interest more in policy rather than programme evaluation.

Other standards for evaluation to various degrees address these issues. For example, both the UK and the Australasian standards address potential users from policy communities as well as evaluators.

International and regional societies and networks for evaluators active in the internationalization of evaluation, provide an interesting arena within which to view debates about standards. For some the logic of adopting the Joint Standards is strong. "The model of Joint Committee on Evaluation Standards could be modified to suit the needs of the international evaluation community" (Mertens, 2005). When the European Evaluation Society convened a meeting of national evaluation societies and other bodies with an interest in standards, advocates of the Joint Standards were confronted by well-developed and quite different alternatives from France and the UK, seen by those countries' representatives as more appropriate to their national settings. European Commission standards were internally directed to the organization of evaluation within the Commission and DAC standards were geared specifically to the international development context.

In some ways the debates about the international transferability of evaluation standards parallel other debates about internationalization/globalization. For example, in international management there is a debate about whether corporate cultures are or are not likely to converge (Hofstede, 1991). If there is convergence this has implications for what international managers do and how they are trained. Confidence about the transferability of evaluation standards similarly rests on an assumption about the convergent nature of the international context for evaluation. This also has implications for the international practice of evaluation and the training and education of evaluators. The extent to which the conditions for such convergence exist is open to dispute. On the one hand, I have argued that the diffusion of a public sector reform agenda supported by international

bodies such as the World Bank and OECD has helped shape a remarkably uniform international administrative and institutional context for evaluation. On the other hand, the ideological foundations of this reform model are widely critiqued both by activists (those whose slogan is: "think globally act locally") and by theoreticians. Thus there is a strong argument that globalization itself generates demands for local and regional autonomy:

> The development of globalised social relations probably serves to diminish some aspects of nationalistic feelings linked to nation-states (or some states) but may be causally involved with the intensifying of more localised nationalist sentiments. (Giddens, 1990, p. 65)

Yet there is another dimension to this debate that carries the argument still further into realm of norms, ideology and power. A key driver of globalization is the intention to create an international market in goods and services. At the cutting edge of this intention is the WTO and more particularly the General Agreement on Trade in Services (GATS). Protagonists of the new market opportunities are prone to wax lyrical. Thus the Executive Director of a US-based international education and training body argues:

> The twenty-first century will see the rise of the global professional, an individual qualified to provide professional services in any country worldwide. Inspired by radically shifting assumptions about the global community's past present and future, the movement to redefine the role of the professional is propelled by the many regional and global trade agreements that encourage movement of professional services as well as goods, across national borders. (Lenn & Campos, 1997, p. 1)

She goes on to argue that:

> traditional nationalistic ideas about professionals and the quality of their education will inevitably

give way to global definitions founded on common evaluation criteria – education, experience and ethics . . . Countries that ignore this emerging global reality risk catastrophe . . . these countries will forfeit their labour forces future to those who have read the signs and prepared their professionals for the global marketplace. (p. 1)

Underpinning this lyrical (or nightmarish) future vision are common international standards and codes of ethics, core curricula, accreditation and certification. It is instructive to reframe the debate about standards and indeed the internationalization of evaluation more generally in terms of the impetus to create such an international market also for evaluation services. Nor is this entirely absent from current developments. Take a recent initiative of the International Board of Standards for Training, Performance and Instruction (http://www.ibstpi.org/) whose mission is to "develop, validate and promote implementation of international standards to advance training, instruction, learning and performance improvement for individuals and organizations". This not-for-profit voluntary body has recently launched an initiative:

> to identify the competencies needed by internal staff or external consultants conducting evaluations in the following settings: in for-profit and not-for-profit organizations, in the military, and in government agencies evaluating their own internal programs.

This will clearly not be the last such initiative! But it does bring into focus a looming shift in context that may well come to reshape evaluation practice dramatically in the future. In summary, the implications for evaluation practice of current trends to internationalize evaluation in combination with moves to create an international market in evaluation services include:

- The adoption of international evaluation standards, themselves an essential base for common

curricula and accreditation, can be seen as a vehicle to diffuse evaluation good practice in an institutionally converging world.
- The adoption of such evaluation standards can simultaneously be seen as reinforcing the spread of a particular model of governance and public sector architecture thus restricting the development of locally appropriate models of public administration.
- Alongside the spread of a particular set of standards there may well emerge an international market for evaluation services that privileges those whose standards are adopted and increases the likelihood that the strong players will dominate a globalized market.

In that context, moves to internationalize evaluation through bodies such as IDEAS and IOCE could unintentionally become the vehicle to limit rather than strengthen national and regionally diverse models of evaluation. They could also come to limit the scope for evaluators who might practice such models for obtaining a significant share of this market – even in their own localities, countries and regions. The quid quo pro on offer, however, is that in return for adopting certain standards and practices even evaluators from peripheral sectors and countries could come to share in the promised new global market for evaluation, should that vision be realized.

Conclusions

This chapter has offered a personal reflection of evaluation practice shaped by changes in context that are at the same time institutional – based on a model of public sector reform – and global. Yet the starting point for this discussion has been a multifaceted understanding of what is meant by practice within contemporary evaluation communities. It has also been suggested that some of the most important assumed meanings of practice should themselves be regarded as a response to the kinds of "formative contexts" that are changing and reshaping evaluation. This, for example, appears to be true with regard to technical, professional and managerial assumptions about practice. All make most sense as a response to the kinds of challenges to the legitimacy and credentials of evaluators in a policy environment of "reform" and "globalization". In part these challenges are expressed as new forms of institutional control being exercised by the commissioners of evaluation, cutting back on degrees of autonomy that evaluators have taken for granted in the past. In part they are expressed through the emergence and championing by evaluation commissioners of other paradigms – performance management, change management and action research, experimental trials, evidence-based policy, policy analysis – that appear to discount or by-pass much "traditional" evaluation wisdom. Many of the efforts of the organized evaluation community – associations, societies and networks – to professionalize, develop standards and codes, accredit – can be seen as an attempt to resist these pressures – to resist deskilling. They seek to incorporate new paradigms – not without success; and to build a consensus about independence, technical excellence, needs for theory, and fair contracting. However, these efforts should be thought of within understandings of occupational control – whether through markets, certification or self-regulation. Evaluators are, in that regard, no different from many other groups of knowledge workers confronting managerialism and globalization, and I have raised doubts about whether the conditions for a professional model of occupational control exist. I have also argued that some of the favoured approaches of the organized evaluation community, in particular standard-setting and internationalization, may prove to be two-edged swords. Thus "standards" are not just about legitimacy and quality assurance for clients and those affected by

evaluation. They are also a vehicle for international trading in professional services offering new opportunities to reduce the autonomy of evaluators, especially those from the less dominant parts of the worldwide evaluation community, unless they sign-up to the standards of the already strong.

References

Abma, T. A. (2001). Opening thoughts. *Evaluation*, 7(2), 155–163.

AEA (2004). *Guiding Principles for Evaluators*. American Evaluation Association.

Australasian Evaluation Society (1997). Guidelines on Ethical Conduct of Evaluation [online]. Available from internet www.aes.asn.au/ethics_guidelines-1.pdf.

Benoit, C. (1994). Paradigm conflict in the sociology of service professions: Midwifery as a case study. *Canadian Journal of Sociology*, 19(3), 303–309.

Biott, C. & Cook T. (2000). Local evaluation in a National Early Years Excellence Centres Pilot Programme: Integrating performance management and participatory evaluation. *Evaluation*, 6, 399–413.

Carr, W. & Kemmis, S. (1986). *Becoming Critical. Education, knowledge and action research*, Lewes: Falmer.

Ciborra, C. U. & Lanzarra, G. F. (1994). 'Formative Contexts and Information Technology: Understanding the Dynamics of Innovation in Organizations', *Accounting, Management and Information Technologies*, 4 (2) 1994

Davies, I. (1999). Evaluation and performance management in government. *Evaluation* 5(2), 150–159.

Ellerman, D. (2005). *Helping People Help Themselves: From the World Bank to an alternative philosophy of development assistance*. University of Michigan Press.

Fetterman, D., Kaftarian, S. J., & Wandersman, A. (eds) (1996). *Empowerment Evaluation*. Thousand Oaks, CA: Sage.

Finne, H. Levin, M. & Nilssen T. (1995) Trailing research: A model for useful program evaluation. *Evaluation*, 1, 11–31.

Furubo, J.-Eric, Rist, R., & Sandahl. R. (eds) (2002). *International Atlas of Evaluation*. New Brunswick, NJ: Transaction Publishers.

Gallo, P. S. (1978). Meta-analysis – a mixed metaphor. *American Psychologist*, 33, 515–517.

Geva-May I. & Pal L. (1999). Good fences make good neighbours. Policy Evaluation and policy analysis – exploring the differences. E*valuation*, 5, 259–277.

Gibbons, M. Limoges, C. Nowotny, H. Schwartzman, S. Scott, P. & Trow M. (1994). *The New Production of Knowledge. The dynamics of science and research in contemporary societies.* London: Sage.

Giddens, A. (1990). *The Consequences of Modernity.* Cambridge: Polity Press.

Greene J. (2001). Dialogue in evaluation: A relational perspective. *Evaluation*, 7(2), 181–187.

Haas, E. B. (1964). *Beyond the Nation State: Functionalism and international organisation.* Stanford University Press.

Haug, M. R. (1973). Deprofessionalisation: An alternative hypothesis for the future. In P. Halmos (ed.) *Professionalisation and Social Change.* Sociological Review Monograph No. 20. University of Keele.

Hofstede, G. (1991). *Cultures in Organisations: Intercultural cooperation and its importance for survival.* McGraw-Hill International.

Hooghe, L. (1996). Building a Europe with the regions: the changing role of the Commission. In L. Hooghe (ed.) *Cohesion policy and European Integration: Building multi-level governance* (pp. 89–126). Oxford: Oxford University Press.

House, E. R. & Howe, K. R. (1999) Values in evaluation and social research. Thousand Oaks, CA: Sage.

Johnson, T. J. (1972). *Professions and Power.* London: The Macmillan Press.

Kusek, J. & Rist, R. C. (2004). *Ten Steps to a Results Based Monitoring and Evaluation System.* World Bank Washington.

Larson M. S. (1977). *The Rise of Professionalism: A sociological analysis.* Berkeley, CA: University of California Press.

Leeuw, F. L. Toulemonde, J. & Brouwers A. (1999). Evaluation activities in Europe: A quick scan of the market in 1998. *Evaluation*, 5, 487–496.

Lenn, M. P., & Campos L. (eds) (1997). *Globalisation of the Professions and the Quality Imperative.* Madison, WI: Magna Publications.

Lewin, K. (1948). *Resolving Social Conflicts,* New York: Harper and Brothers.

Majone, G. (1993). The European community between social policy and social regulation. *Journal of Common Market Studies*, 32(2), 153–170.

Mark, M. M. Henry, G. H., & Julnes, G. (2000). *Evaluation: an integrated framework for understanding, guiding and improving policies and programmes.* San Francisco: Jossey-Bass.

Martin, S. J. and Sanderson, I. (1999). Evaluating public policy experiments: measuring outcomes, monitoring processes or managing pilots? *Evaluation*, 5(3), 245–258.

Mertens, D. M. (1999). Inclusive evaluation: Implications of transformative theory for evaluation. *American Journal of Evaluation*, 20(1), 1–14.

Mertens, D. (2005). The inauguration of the International Organization for cooperation in Evaluation. *American Journal of Evaluation*, 26(1), 124–130.

Nutley, S. I. Walter, I. & Davies, H. T. O. (2003). From knowing to doing: A framework for understanding the evidence-into-practice agenda. *Evaluation*, 9, 125–148.

Osborne, D. & T. Gaebler (1992). *Reinventing Government: How the entrepreneurial spirit is transforming the public sector.* Reading, MA: Addison-Wesley.

Patton, M. Q. (1997). *Utilization-Focussed Evaluation: The new century text,* Third edition. Thousand Oaks, CA: Sage.

Pfadenhauer, M. (2003). Crisis or crash? Problems legitimation and loss of trust of modern professionalism. *Proceedings of European Sociological Association Conference Murcia,* Spain.

Pollitt, C. & Bouckaert, G. (1999). *Public Management Reform: A comparative Analysis.* Oxford University Press.

Popay, J., Rogers, A., & Williams, G. (1998). Rationale and standards for the systemic review of qualitative literature in health services research. *Qualitative Health Research,* 8(3), 341–351.

Power, M. (1997). *The Audit Society: Rituals of verification.* Oxford University Press.

Rogers, P. J. (2000). Program theory: Not whether programs work but how they work. In D. L., Stufflebeam, G. F., Madaus, T. Kellaghan, *Evaluation Models Viewpoints on Educational and Human Services Evaluation,* second edition. Boston: Kluwer Academic Publishers.

Rossi, P., Freeman, H. E., & Lipsey, M. W. (1999). *Evaluation: A systematic approach*, 6th edition. Thousand Oaks, CA: Sage.

Schon, D. (1983). *The Reflective Practitioner: How professionals think in action*. Basic Books.

Schwandt, T. (1997). Evaluation as practical hermeneutics. *Evaluation*, 1, 69–83.

Scriven, M. (1991). *Evaluation Thesaurus*, 4th edition. Newbury Park: Sage.

Shadish, W. R., Cook, T. D., & Leviton, L. C. (1991). *Foundations of Program Evaluation: Theories of Practice*. Newbury Park: Sage.

Shaw, I. F. (1999). *Qualitative Evaluation*. Thousand Oaks, CA: Sage.

Stevahn, L., King, J. A., Ghere, G., & Minnema, J. (2005). Establishing essential competencies for program evaluators. *American Journal of Evaluation*, 26(1), 43–59.

Torres, R. T. (2001). Evaluation and organizational learning: Past, present, and future. *American Journal of Evaluation*, 22(3), 387–395.

Treasury Board of Canada (2002). *Internship Program for Entry-Level Evaluators*. Ottawa, Canada.

Unger, R. M. (1987). *Social Theory: Its situation and its task*. Cambridge: Cambridge University Press.

Valovirta, (2002). Evaluation utilization as argumentation. *Evaluation*, 8, 60–80.

van der Knaap, P. (1995). Policy evaluation and learning: Feedback, enlightenment or argumentation. *Evaluation: the International Journal of Theory, Research and Practice*, 1(2), 189–216.

van der Knaap, P. (2000). Performance management and policy evaluation in the Netherlands: towards an integrated approach. *Evaluation*, 6(3), 335–350.

van der Knaap, P. (2000). Policy Evaluation in the Netherlands. In Evaluating Socio Economic Development. http://www.evalsed.info.

Wadsworth, Y. (1993). *Everyday Evaluation on the Run*. Melbourne: Action Research Issues Association.

Weiss, C. (1998). *Evaluation, Methods for Studying Programs and Policies*. Englewood Cliffs, NJ: Prentice-Hall.

Wholey, J. S. (1981). Using Evaluation to improve program performance. In R. A. Levine, M.A. Solomon, G.-M. Hellstern & H. Wollmann, (eds) *Evaluation Research and Practice: Comparative and international perspectives*. Beverly Hills, CA: Sage.

PART THREE

THE PRACTICE OF EVALUATION

14

METHODS FOR POLICY-MAKING AND KNOWLEDGE DEVELOPMENT EVALUATIONS

Melvin M. Mark and Gary T. Henry

Evaluations are done for a number of purposes, as the first part of this Handbook illustrates. Some evaluations are intended primarily to contribute to policy-making. Evaluations for policy-making purposes often involve assessments of merit and worth. These evaluations are meant to assist judgments about policy or program alternatives, by assessing the consequences and costs of alternative solutions to recognized social problems. Other evaluations for policy-making seek to document the existence, prevalence, and import of social problems in ways that may justify and legitimize government intervention (Henry, 2000). For the most part, knowledge development evaluations seek to generate new ideas or test theories about social problems,

their causes, their consequences, and solutions. Evaluations for policy-making purposes can also generate knowledge, as in the evaluation of the effect of a ban on public smoking on restaurant revenues.

Evaluations for policy-making and evaluations for knowledge development are related but distinct types of evaluations that often share common characteristics. One characteristic that distinguishes evaluations serving policy-making *and* knowledge development purposes from evaluations conducted for several other purposes, such as improvement-oriented or oversight evaluations, is that they do not assume that the policy or program in place can work. Many program improvement or oversight evaluations begin with the assumption that the program is a good thing and can yield the desired benefits if it is well run. Improvement and oversight evaluations are likely to give more weight to describing program operations and/or outcomes, to developing program theory as an aid to program management, to assessing actual operations against external standards for operations, or to assessing the extent to which variations in program implementation are related to differences in outcomes. In contrast, both policy-making and knowledge development evaluations tend to focus on questions such as: Does the policy enhance the well-being of the targeted beneficiaries? Which kinds? What are the side-effects or unintended consequences? How large are the effects, if any? Why did the intervention work? How are the effects produced? These types of evaluation questions lead to heavy reliance on causal methods, specifically methods designed to assess the effectiveness of policies or programs, as well as methods that test theories about why an program or policy is (or is not) effective.

Evaluations germane to policy-making and knowledge development seek to influence judgments about the *significance* of a social problem or about the *effectiveness* of a remedy or intervention designed to address the problem. In other words, evaluative evidence can: (1) support or undermine claims about the importance of a social problem; or (2) validate or fail to validate a potential remedy for a problem (Henry, 2000). We highlight causal methods in this chapter, a choice that largely derives from these two potential ways that evaluation evidence can contribute to social betterment.

The Special Role of Causal Methods

Evaluations that address causal questions often are central when the purpose of evaluation involves either policy-making or knowledge development. Why is this so? In the case of policy-making-oriented evaluations, cause–effect statements are inherent in policy-related arguments (Pressman & Wildavsky, 1973). For example, legislators considering adoption of a universal preschool policy might well want to know: Will universal preschool improve children's school readiness? Does universal preschool result in children being more successful in school (e.g., on-time promotions or higher test scores) or later in life (e.g., reductions in crime or poverty)? Does it have unintended effects such as encouraging mothers to go into the workforce earlier than they otherwise would? In the language of Sabatier & Jenkins-Smith (1998), evaluations using causal methods can contribute to policy-oriented learning. When decisions are to be made about whether to adopt, maintain, expand, curtail, or terminate some potential solution(s) to a problem, evaluation methods that estimate the effects of the relevant program, practice, or policy alternatives often have the potential to make noteworthy contributions to policy-making.

Similarly, evaluations that employ causal methods can contribute substantially to the purpose of knowledge development. In some instances, simply testing the effects of a program can be seen as analogous to testing a hypothesis in a traditional scientific experiment. In criminal justice, for example, scholars have in the past hypothesized that labeling effects (whereby young people come to be labeled as criminal offenders by themselves and others) increase crime and delinquency. Consider an evaluation that tests the effects of a juvenile diversion program, which is designed to get youthful offenders out of the formal criminal justice system before labeling effects occur. This evaluation can be viewed as a test of the labeling hypothesis. In this way, evaluations that estimate the effects of programs and policy alternatives can contribute to knowledge development. In the language of Carol Weiss (e.g., 1979), such evaluations can facilitate enlightenment about the causes of problems and their potential solutions.

In recent years, a particular form of causal question has received growing attention for its potential to contribute both to policy-making and to knowledge development. Specifically, the idea is that both of these evaluation purposes can be advanced by evaluations that assess *how* a program has its effects. This general idea has been advocated under different banners, including program theory (Bickman, 1990), theory-driven evaluation (Donaldson, 2003), realist testing of underlying mechanisms (Pawson & Tilley, 1997; Mark, Henry, & Julnes 2000), the theory of change approach to evaluation (Weiss, 1995), and tests of mediation (Mark, 2003). The basic idea is the same: test the *process* through which some program, policy, or practice has its effects. It is one thing to know, say, that a particular juvenile justice program works. It is another thing to know *how* it works. Does the program work because it avoids labeling, or because it enhances adolescents' self-esteem, or because it strengthens their ties to the community, or because it offers attractive activities that reduce opportunities for getting in trouble? Understanding why a program works (or doesn't work) obviously contributes to the knowledge base. Attention to program theories can likewise inform policy-making. For example, theory-driven evaluations can show how to revise an ineffective program, by showing where the program theory failed (Donaldson, 2003). For instance, evaluations of drug-abuse resistance programs showed that they were ineffective because they tended to make the adolescent clients think, essentially, that everybody was using drugs, which increased their own tendency to take drugs (and offset the beneficial effects of increased

resistance skills) (Donaldson, 2003). Moreover, as Cronbach (1982) pointed out decades ago, explanations are an important form of knowledge, in part because they may provide understandings that can transcend the specific evaluation context.

To this point, we have emphasized the use of causal methods for evaluating alternative solutions to a problem for policy-making, and to increase the knowledge base. Less recognized is the possibility that causal methods can also be useful in establishing the significance of a problem. That is, causal methods are not limited to after-the-fact evaluations of policies, programs, and practices. Rather, cause-probing methods can also be used to assess the consequences of ongoing social problems or processes, such as school segregation or lack of health insurance. Although there are limits to the certainty with which causation can be established in investigations of this sort, they may reveal whether (and to what extent) there is need for a social intervention. For example, a study might estimate the health consequences of not having health insurance. More severe consequences would strengthen the case for government action to extend health care coverage. In the case of knowledge development, evaluation studies of this sort can contribute to broader understanding of the role of the relevant social processes (e.g., highlighting the costs that are borne by society because uninsured individuals use emergency rooms for health care rather than standard physician visit, or dispelling the argument that a ban on public smoking reduces revenues in restaurants and bars). In short, using a distinction that has been fruitfully used by policy scholars (Kingdon, 1995), causal methods can be used by evaluators to assess ongoing social problems, as well as to estimate the apparent consequences of a program or other intervention.

Because of the special contribution that causal methods can play for evaluations that have as their purpose contributing either to policy-making or to knowledge development, we emphasize such methods in the present chapter. At the same time, non-causal methods can contribute to knowledge generation and policy-making.

The Role of Non-causal Methods

Although causal methods often are central for policy-making and knowledge development, both purposes can also be well served by other methods. For example, establishing the importance of a social problem often calls for information about its prevalence. For instance, early studies of homelessness in the US often focused on efforts to estimate the number of homeless individuals (Wright, 1998). Decisions about the significance of a problem may also be shaped by information about *who* is affected. For example, information from early evaluations, documenting the number of homeless women and children, appeared to affect policy discussions as well as to change the knowledge base about this social problem (Rog & Fitzpatrick, 1999). As the homelessness examples illustrate, descriptive methods, including surveys, questionnaires, observations, and the like, also have a role to play in contributing to policy-making and knowledge development. In contrast to causal methods, however, it appears that descriptive methods generally will contribute more by helping demonstrate the significance (or lack thereof) of a social problem and by improving the knowledge base about the nature of the problem, rather than by assessing the validity of a potential solution to the problem.

That said, one special form of descriptive method can be useful in policy processes that involve choosing solutions to a problem. Specifically, evaluations can be influential – not only by demonstrating the *consequences* of a program or other intervention, as causal methods can – but also by demonstrating the *feasibility of its implementation*. For example, early studies of welfare reform in the United States were highly influential, not so much because of what they found regarding the effectiveness of alternatives to the then-standard welfare system; rather, these evaluations were influential because they demonstrated it was feasible, in practice, to implement alternative welfare practices (Greenberg, Mandell, & Onstott, 2000).

Yet another family of methods deserves mention here, especially in regard to policy-making: cost–benefit analysis and related forms of cost analyses (e.g., Levin & McEwan, 2000). For example, Barnett (1992) showed that society's returns from an early childhood education program (Perry Preschool) were five to seven times larger than the costs to operate the program. These rates of return have echoed through state legislatures across the US as state after state has adopted prekindergarten policies. One reason cost–benefit and similar methods are attractive to policymakers is because they provide direct comparison of policy alternatives using a common metric (e.g., the magnitude of benefit translated into economic terms, relative to the cost of each alternative).

Although descriptive and cost methods can clearly contribute to policy-making and to knowledge development, our primary focus in the remainder of this chapter is on causal methods. In part, this is because the practice of major descriptive and cost methods is well described elsewhere (e.g., Henry, 1990; Levin & McEwan, 2000). In part, our focus on causal methods is also motivated by the considerable controversy that has surrounded such methods in recent years (e.g., AEA, 2003; Lederman & Flick, 2003). And in part this focus reflects the emergence of a number of methodological developments in recent years that address some of the important problems associated with employing causal methods in evaluations in the past.

Overview of the Remainder of This Chapter

In the next section, we review major methods evaluators use to estimate the causal effects of a policy, program, practice, or social problem. These include randomized experiments, quasi-experiments of various kinds, and (quite briefly) case studies and qualitative methods. We expand on many past treatments of these topics by discussing a formal depiction of causality developed by Donald Rubin and his colleagues, which has been termed Rubin's causal model (RCM). Rubin's approach to causal attribution has helped spawn a variety of methodological innovations, such as propensity score analysis and multiple imputation to deal with missing data; these and related developments can strengthen evaluations that are designed to estimate the effects of a program or other intervention. In a subsequent section, we describe a variety of methodological ancillaries and options that have been developed to improve the quality and informational value of experimental and quasi-experimental studies, including estimation of effect sizes, implementation analysis, study of mediation and moderation, and meta-analysis. In the concluding section, we address the current state and the likely future of evaluations that seek to contribute to knowledge and influence attitudes and actions related to policy-making.

A Recurring, Illustrative Case

In several of the sections that follow, in order to illustrate several of the methods and issues related to cause-probing evaluations for policy-making and knowledge development, we draw on an evaluation of the Chicago Public School's (CPS) Summer Bridge program. The Summer Bridge program was implemented as one component of a policy ending "social promotion" in one of the largest school districts in the US (Roderick, Jacob, & Bryk, 2002). Social promotion refers to the practice of promoting school children to the next grade, whether their performance seems to justify it or not. In ending social promotion, CPS specified that children finishing the 3rd grade, 6th grade, or 8th grade would not move on to the next grade unless they had passing scores on standardized reading and math tests. For those who failed to pass either the reading or math tests in the spring, participation in Summer Bridge, a remedial summer school program, was mandated. The evaluation of Summer Bridge was one component of a larger, comprehensive evaluation of the CPS policy eliminating social promotion.

Causal Methods: Randomized Experiments

In randomized experiments, individuals (or other units, such as classrooms) are assigned to treatment conditions (e.g., treatment versus comparison group) at random. Why is random assignment valuable? Put simply, such assignment helps avoid impediments to confident causal inference that would otherwise arise. Using language from one important tradition of writings about the randomized experiment and its alternatives, stemming from the work of Donald Campbell and his colleagues (e.g., Campbell & Stanley, 1966; Cook & Campbell, 1979; Shadish, Cook & Campbell, 2002), well-conducted randomized experiments render implausible nearly all "internal validity threats." Internal validity threats are generic categories of alternative explanations – alternatives to the claim that the treatment made a causal difference on the outcome variable, within the study itself. Particularly important within the literature on the effectiveness of public policies and programs is that randomized experiments render "selection bias" implausible. Because members of the target population are assigned at random to treatment, it is implausible that the treatment group had systematically selected themselves into treatment (or were assigned by others) and therefore differed from those not participating in the program in terms of motivation, interest, ability, or some other important factor. Without random assignment, in contrast, at best it is difficult to rule out the rival hypothesis that the observed difference between the treatment and comparison groups is the result of initial differences in the two groups.

Donald Rubin and his colleagues have proposed a model of causation which states in more formal language the benefits of randomized experiments.[1] First they define a population, a treatment, and an outcome. For example, if we are interested in the effects of Head Start on children's ability to recognize letters and words, we could let: i index the population of children under consideration from the first to the last child, i ($i = 1, \ldots, N$); Y_{i1} be the score on the Woodcock Johnson Letter-Word assessment for child i *if* the child attends Head Start (with Head Start, the treatment in this example, designated $Z_i = 1$); and Y_{i0} be the value of the hypothetical counterfactual assessment of the same child *not* attending Head Start (the control, designated, $Z_i = 0$). The treatment effect across the population of children indexed by child i is then defined as: $\tau_I|_{z=1} = E(Y_{I1}|Z_I = 1) - E(Y_{I0}|Z_I = 0)$. That is, the treatment effect is the difference in the expected value of the assessment score, conditioned on the children attending Head Start. More simply, the treatment effect is defined here as the score on the Woodcock Johnson,

given that the children attended Head Start, minus the score that those same children would have received if they had not attended Head Start. However, given that any individual child attends Head Start, one can only observe $E(Y_{i1}|Z_i = 1)$ and not $E(Y_{i0}|Z_i = 0)$ which, again, would be the obtained score *if* that child had not attended Head Start.

To determine whether there is an effect (roughly, whether τ_i is unlikely to be equal to 0), random assignment of children to either Head Start or a control group offers an approximation of the desired counterfactual comparison of the same students in both conditions. In technical terms, with random assignment the expected values of the treatment and control, *apart from any treatment effect*, do not differ, $E(Y_{i0}|Z_i = 0) = E(Y_{i0}|Z_i = 1) = E(Y_i|Z_i = 0)$ Rubin (1977) refers to this as ignorable treatment assignment, which means that outcomes and treatment are independent of pre-treatment covariates. Random assignment establishes independence in the assignment to treatment and, when researchers maintain fidelity to randomization and stave off other threats such as attrition, the expected (on average) pre-existing differences in the treatment and control groups is reduced to zero (and to nonsignificance in almost all cases). As a result, the outcomes of the treatment and control groups can be compared directly, without bias. Of course, in practice achieving and maintaining fidelity in a random assignment evaluation is no mean feat (Boruch, 1997). However, great strides have been made in doing so, to which Greenberg & Shroder (2004) attest in their compendium of social experiments.[2]

Although randomized experiments have been rare in some areas, in particular education (Cook, 2001, 2003), the use of experiments appears to be increasing. One important, albeit contentious example is the increased pressures that exist to use randomized experiments in evaluating educational programs and interventions, at least in the US. The federal No Child Left Behind legislation calls for scientifically based evidence, and recent policies of the US Department of Education provide incentives to use randomized experiments (or a select a few high-quality quasi-experimental methods) in one common type of evaluation, the evaluation of the *effectiveness* of programs and interventions. Experiments have also become typical in evaluations of various areas of social or psychological interventions, such as welfare reform and other employment initiatives (e.g., Friedlander, Greenberg, & Robins, 1997; Riccio & Bloom, 2002). A catalog of social experiments, *The Digest of Social Experiments*, is available (Greenberg & Shroder, 2004). Although a rationale for randomized experiments exists, largely in terms of the ability of such studies to avoid serious selection biases, there are harsh critics of randomized experiments – or at least critics of political pressures for the use of randomized experiments (e.g., AEA, 2003; Lederman & Flick, 2003). Even advocates of increasing the use of randomized experiments note their limitations, in terms of questions that can be addressed, cost, and the difficulties of implementing and maintaining random assignment (e.g., Boruch, 1997, Shadish et al., 2002).

As described in a subsequent section, a set of methodological advances have been made in recent years; these can substantially improve the quality and usefulness of experimental evaluations. Nevertheless, even when program effectiveness is a key evaluation question, alternatives to randomized experiments may be needed. We turn to such alternatives next.

Causal Methods: Quasi-experiments

The term "quasi-experiments" refers to approximations of randomized experiments.[3] Like randomized experiments, quasi-experiments involve comparisons across two or more conditions (e.g., program versus no-program), and they may include before-after and/or other comparisons. Unlike randomized experiments, by definition quasi-experiments lack random assignment to conditions. Quasi-experiments are frequently used when evaluations are meant to inform policy-making or knowledge development. One reason for this is that randomized experiments are sometimes infeasible for practical or ethical reasons (e.g., Cook & Campbell, 1979). For instance, random assignment was not feasible in the previously described Summer Bridge evaluation; school district policy mandated that all students who failed the relevant tests were to participate in Summer Bridge. In addition, in some cases the less convincing causal evidence from a quasi-experiment is expected to suffice for the particular decision or research question at hand (Mark et al., 2000). Moreover, given that validity threats are not always plausible, or can sometimes be ruled out in other ways, quasi-experiments, even relatively simple ones, can in certain circumstances give compelling answers to cause-and-effect questions (e.g., Eckert, 2000).

Many quasi-experimental designs and variants exist. Rather than attempting to detail the full array of quasi-experiments, in this chapter we focus on one relatively common quasi-experimental design, as well as on another design that is relatively strong in terms of causal inference and has been used rarely but is showing signs of increasing use. Shadish et al., (2002) provide a comprehensive discussion of quasi-experimental design options.

The so-called *pretest–posttest non-equivalent comparison group design* is among the most common quasi-experimental designs. As the name suggests, this design involves comparing a treatment group and a control/comparison (or alternative treatment) group, when the groups have not been formed by random assignment (hence, "non-equivalent"). A pretest and/or other relevant pre-treatment variables are measured in an effort to control for selection bias. However, selection bias can be difficult to rule out. Participation in the program can be affected by individual characteristics, family resources or motivations, or program implementation decisions, such as who gets selected from a waiting list of "eligibles" or where the program services are offered. To the extent that such differences between groups exist and are associated with differential outcomes, selection bias looms large.

Numerous approaches to the analysis of the non-equivalent groups design have been offered, typically in an effort to provide statistical adjustments that eliminate selection bias. One simple approach is to match treatment group participants with potential comparison group participants, matching on what are thought to be possible sources of bias. Matching strategies rely on the availability, for the entire sample, of data on the factors that are related to selection into program participation. A conceptually similar analysis approach relies not on literal matching, but on analysis of covariance or related regression procedures. Whether matching or some other adjustment procedure is used, the variables controlled for are often called covariates. Multiple covariates may exist that seem likely to represent important sources of differences between the groups. However, matching participants and nonparticipants on numerous covariates at once may be impractical. Fortunately, techniques have been developed that allow evaluators to use the covariates to select cases for the comparison group, and also in the subsequent analysis to control for differences in the outcome, Y_i.

To overcome the constraints that arise from trying to match on numerous covariates, Rosenbaum & Rubin (1983) proposed use of the propensity score, a single-dimensional variable that incorporates all available covariate information. In a first step in the analysis, one uses covariate information to create a statistical model predicting membership in the treatment (versus the comparison) condition. Technically, the propensity score is the conditional probability of treatment conditioned on the covariates. More formally stated, one uses the pre-treatment covariates to estimate treatment condition, for example, the probability that a child attended Head Start, using the propensity score, $p(x)$, such that $p(x) = \Pr\{Z_i = 1 \mid X_i\}$.[4] This model is not interpreted in and of itself; rather, its function is to reduce the large number of covariates to one propensity score and facilitate matching (or analysis as a single covariate).

The idea is that, if one adequately models the forces that led individuals to self-select into the treatment (versus the comparison) group, and then matches or otherwise controls statistically for the propensity score that summarizes these forces, then unbiased estimates of the treatment effect should result. According to the balancing hypothesis of Rosenbaum & Rubin, if $p(x)$ is the propensity score, then the treatment assignment is independent of the covariates conditioned on the propensity score ($Z \perp X \mid p(x)$). That is, individuals with the same propensity score should have the same distribution of pre-treatment covariates independent of treatment assignment. Rosenbaum & Rubin further showed that the assignment to the treatment group is not confounded when conditioned on the propensity score. Specifically, while randomization produces outcomes that are independent of assignment to treatment (Y_{i1}, $Y_{i0} \perp Z_i$) *by design*, Rosenbaum & Rubin demonstrated that independence can also hold if the treatment is conditioned *statistically* on the propensity score (Y_{i1}, $Y_{i0} \perp Z_i \mid p(x)$).

The development of propensity score methods has enabled evaluators and other researchers to form matched comparison groups that appear to have the potential to greatly reduce the bias in observational studies and quasi-experiments. However, analytic work and methodological research continues regarding whether selection bias is reduced to the extent that it can be considered ignorable (e.g., Heckman & Navarro-Lazano, 2004). One approach to the possibility that non-ignorable selection bias remains is to employ "sensitivity analyses." Sensitivity analyses assess whether findings would change substantially under alternative assumptions. When conducting a propensity score analysis, one can assess whether the conclusion that there is a significant program effect would change if there were unmeasured or hidden covariates of a given magnitude. Leow et al. (2004) describe and illustrate this kind of sensitivity analysis.

In addition, important developments have occurred for other methods for the analysis of non-equivalent group designs. For example, differences-in-differences methods, which have been used to look at differences in outcomes for cohorts before and after a change in policy, have been subjected to methodological inquiry and the estimation methods improved as a result (e.g., Bertrand, Duflo, & Mullainathan, 2004). Multilevel models have been developed and popularized (e.g., Bryk & Raudenbush, 1992). These models account for the nested and hierarchical nature of some data, such as in educational evaluations where students reside within classrooms. Without taking such arrangements into account, bias can be introduced (because the independence assumption is violated, with data from within the same classroom likely to be more closely related than data from different classrooms).[5]

In contrast to the non-equivalent groups design, the *regression-discontinuity design* has been implemented infrequently in practice but is among the best quasi-experimental design for causal inference (Shadish et al., 2002). The conditions necessary for this design are quite specific: Assignment to conditions must be based on some quantitative eligibility criterion, with a firm cutoff such that people scoring on one side of the cutoff are assigned to one group (e.g., the treatment), while those on the other side of the cutoff are assigned to the other group (e.g., the control). An example of the regression-discontinuity design comes from the previously mentioned Summer Bridge evaluation, specifically the work of Jacob & Lefgren (2004).[6] The Summer Bridge case generally meets the requirement of the regression-discontinuity design: the end-of-year high-stakes test determines assignment, with those below the cutoff (i.e., the passing score) required to attend Summer Bridge, while those on the other side of the cutoff do not attend.

At first glance, this arrangement might seem to be a way to ensure selection biases – after all, the Summer Bridge and promoted groups by definition differ in terms of their scores on the original high-stakes test. However, the test scores themselves can be used in controlling for selection bias. The reasoning is akin to the logic of propensity scores: You know precisely what led to membership in the treatment and comparison condition, and can control for it. As an additional aid to understand the logic of the regression-discontinuity study, see Figure 14.1, which shows alternative, hypothetical results from the regression-discontinuity design. As in Summer Bridge, the treatment group is to the left of the cutoff, while the comparison group is to the right. If Summer Bridge has no effect, the relationship between scores on the original high-stakes test and the subsequent test should show a nice smooth regression line across the two groups (e.g., the Summer Bridge and promoted students). In contrast, if Summer Bridge is truly effective, the regression line for the Summer Bridge students should be elevated relative to where you would

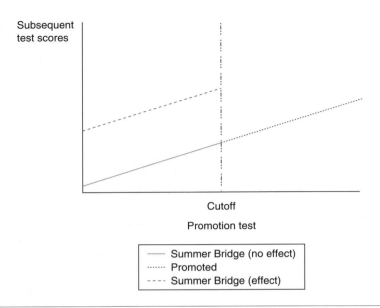

Figure 14.1 Regression discontinuity design, hypothetical findings

expect it to be from looking at the promoted students. One way to think about the regression-discontinuity design is: How likely is it that there would be a jump in scores on the outcome variable precisely at the cutoff, unless there really is a treatment effect?

Another recent example of the regression-discontinuity design comes from Gormley and his colleagues' evaluation of Oklahoma pre-kindergarten programs. These programs use an age cutoff, which requires that children be four years old by September 1st of the year that they attend pre-kindergarten. This provides the quantitative eligibility criterion needed for implementing a regression discontinuity design. Again, the logic of the regression-discontinuity design is premised on the notion that the children just below the cut off and those just above it should be relatively similar, except to the extent that those just above it are exposed to the program. If these two groups differ in terms of outcomes (imagine

Figure 14.1, but with the treatment group on the right side of the cutoff), then the effect can reasonably be attributable to exposure to the program. In the Oklahoma pre-kindergarten evaluation, Gormley et al., (2005) conclude that "children exposed to pre-K experience a gain of seven to eight months in letter-word identification, six to seven months in spelling, and four months in applied problems, above and beyond the gains of aging or maturation."

As already noted, a variety of quasi-experimental designs and options exist. At the simpler end of the continuum, these include relatively simple comparisons of an outcome before and after a program ("the one-group pretest–posttest design"). Simple pre–post comparisons are usually subject to a number of alternative interpretations, such as that change occurred because of events other than the program (history), or that naturally occurring maturation of the participants was responsible for the observed change. More complex designs include the interrupted time series design, in which a string of pretest and posttest observations are collected (this can help assess and thus rule out maturational patterns); when time series data from a comparison group are added, this can help rule out history. Interrupted time series designs with a comparison group can be especially useful in evaluating the effects of policy changes that apply universally across some jurisdictions/ states, but do not occur in others (such as changes in laws about seatbelts, speed limits, and the like). For example, to evaluate the effects of a law requiring the use of passenger restraints for children three years of age and younger, Guerin & MacKinnon (1985) used an interrupted time series with a comparison group.

Case Study and Qualitative Methods for Causal Inference

Experimental and quasi-experimental traditions, along with associated developments in statistical analysis, do not exhaust the kinds of methods that evaluators use to try to assess the consequences of policies, programs, and practices. Some evaluators instead are predisposed to employ more qualitative methods (e.g., Patton, 2003) and/or conduct case studies (e.g., Stake, 1995). It appears, however, that evaluators intending to influence policy-making or generate knowledge are less likely to use qualitative or case study methods, and more likely to conduct experiments or quasi-experiments. Thus, we give relatively less attention to case studies and qualitative methods here, even though these methods can be used effectively to probe the causal consequences of programs and other interventions.

Instead, we wish simply to join others in noting that the logic of causal inference does not discriminate between qualitative and quantitative data (Campbell, 1975; Mark et al., 2000; Maxwell, 2004; Yin, 2002). A key element of the logic of causal inquiry is estimating the counterfactual, that is, what would have happened if the program had not been implemented. Another aspect of estimating program effectiveness involves ensuring that one has ruled out alternative explanations to the conclusion that the program is responsible for observed effects. Viewed in this light, the argument for random assignment can be framed in terms of how well the design itself (if implemented successfully) estimates the counterfactual and rules out threats such as selection. Without such a design, the evaluator would have to try to rule out validity threats by other means – or suffer the resulting ambiguity about causal attribution. For instance, Stake & Davis (1999) describe an evaluation of a program designed to improve the quality of writing in a social service agency for veterans; a key part of the evaluation consisted of a pretest–posttest quasi-experiment which showed that the quality of writing improved. In such an instance, the evaluator might contend it is implausible that other historical events, or maturation, or other validity threats would cause a change in writing quality between the pretest and posttest (Eckert, 2000). Alternatively, one might need to use evidence from observations and interviews to argue that no event other than the program has occurred that could plausibly explain changes in the way agency staff writes to its veteran clients.

Advances in Cause-Probing Methods

Early experimental and quasi-experimental evaluations could be critiqued in terms of their failure to penetrate the "black box" (i.e., to describe what the treatment consisted of and how it had its effects) and their exclusive focus on estimating the statistical significance of net effects. Implicit in such critiques was a call for an expanded range of information from evaluations. This call has been met with numerous methodological innovations, many of which have become standard practice in high-quality evaluations that are aimed at estimating program effects. In particular, the increasing prevalence of program theory and the associated desire to know more about the underlying mechanisms that produce effects has been met by a number of innovations. These include procedures for testing for mediators, including both implementation variation and more theoretically meaningful mechanisms, and for testing moderators, including individual participant and site characteristics. No longer is it sufficient to proffer a plausible but untested explanation for the observed effects (or lack of effects); rather, empirical methods for assessing potential explanations are increasingly being employed in evaluations. In addition, it is increasingly common to go beyond statistical significance as a criterion and instead also to estimate the size of the program's or policy's effect.

In this section, we discuss and illustrate a set of methodological advancements which have become more common in evaluation. In general, these have been used as adjuncts to experimental or quasi-experimental evaluations. When used in this way, these adjuncts can go a long way toward neutralizing criticisms that have been applied to many experiments and quasi-experiments, especially the criticism that these evaluations fail to look within the "black box."

Effect Size Estimates

Early experimental and quasi-experimental evaluations relied heavily on statistical significance as a criterion for concluding that a program or policy had an effect. But simply because the observed difference between treatment and comparison groups was unlikely to have arisen by chance (i.e., is statistically significant), this doesn't mean that the finding is important enough to act on for policy-making.

In some evaluations, statistical significance plus a simple presentation of descriptive statistics such as treatment and comparison group means may suffice. However, this may only be the case when the key outcome measures are in a metric that stakeholders can readily understand. For example, a health promotion program might reduce the average number of cigarettes smoked a day by a group of smokers from 30 to 5. When the outcome measure itself is naturally meaningful, reporting the mean difference is generally advisable.

On the other hand, many evaluations use scales that, while important and valid, may lack everyday meaning for relevant stakeholders. How can the size of effect be conveyed in such cases? In addition, evaluators and others often want to compare across two or more evaluations which used somewhat different measures – making it impossible to compare the two studies directly using their original metrics. For such reasons, and principally because of the desire of researchers to combine the results of multiple studies (i.e., meta-analysis), conventions have developed regarding computing an effect size estimate for experimental and quasi-experimental evaluations.

The most common effect size estimate is the mean difference between groups (e.g., the treatment mean minus the comparison group mean), divided by the pooled standard deviation. A variety of effect size calculations have been developed to meet the needs of different research designs (Cook et al., 1992; Hedges, 1985; Lipsey & Wilson, 2001). Moreover, there have been advances in how to communicate with stakeholders about what a given effect size means (e.g., Cook et al., 1992;

Lipsey & Wilson, 2001). Such developments can help evaluators communicate evaluation findings in ways that might better assist stakeholders make more thoughtful judgments about the implications of evaluation findings for action.

Implementation Assessment

In many early experimental and quasi-experimental evaluations, surprisingly little attention was given to what the program looked like in practice – sometimes with important negative consequences. Without knowing whether the program was implemented, no-effect findings become hard to interpret, for example. Were there no effects because the underlying policy was flawed, or because a potentially sound policy was doomed by poor implementation? In addition, even if evaluation findings are favorable, they can be hard to act on without a reasonable description of what the program consisted of in practice. In particular, it can be quite difficult to consider adoption of a program that has been evaluated elsewhere, unless adequate description is given of what the program actually looked like as implemented. Fortunately, it has become far more common for some form of implementation assessment to occur within an evaluation.

Mark & Mills (in press) have recently described several different approaches to implementation assessment. One, which has variously been called the measurement of *compliance, dosage, treatment exposure,* or *treatment intensity,* simply involves measuring how much of the treatment the participants received (e.g., hours of caseworker services received). For example, one might measure the number of hours of caseworker services received in an evaluation of a social work intervention. In some instances, the evaluator simply reports information about treatment exposure descriptively. In other cases, the

evaluator might want to test whether there are greater effects for clients who received a higher dosage of the treatment. However, a potential selection bias exists; clients who self-select into different amounts of exposure may differ in other important ways. Propensity scores or other forms of statistical adjustment can be used to try to alleviate this bias.

A second, more recent approach to implementation assessment has been used in programs that offer a menu of services from which clients can select. For example, welfare reform programs in the US often allow clients to choose from services such as center-based child care, subsidies for other child care providers, high-school equivalency training, various forms of job training, and job counseling and referral services. In the face of such cafeteria programs, some evaluators have measured *client "uptake,"* that is, the dosage received of each type of service offered (e.g., Yoshikawa, Rosman, & Hsueh, 2001). With uptake data, the researcher can then identify various patterns of service use and see if these patterns are differentially related to client outcomes.

A third approach to implementation examines, not how much treatment was received, but how well the treatment was implemented. In particular, a *fidelity assessment* uses any of a variety of methods to determine the extent to which treatment implementation was faithful to a pre-existing treatment model or curriculum. In what may be considered an important complement or alternative to implementation fidelity assessment, programs can be assessed, not relative to a pre-existing curriculum, but to more general standards of quality (e.g., the Early Childhood Environment Rating Scale, or ECERS, can be used to assess the quality of preschool programs, across curricula; see Henry et al., 2003, for an example).

Fidelity assessment requires a pre-existing curriculum or other clear, a priori specification of what the program is supposed to look like. In some instances, however, a program is implemented without a clear a priori plan. In such cases, a more *inductive or bottom-up implementation assessment* may be undertaken, for example, using qualitative methods to describe the intervention as it was implemented. In some instances, the focus may be to identify distinguishable *subtypes* of the overall program, or otherwise to measure variations in implementation practices across sites.

Finally, it is important to note that various combinations and variants of these general categories of implementation assessment are possible, and also that implementation questions can be specific to the details of a particular evaluation. For example, Henry et al. (2004) address both implementation fidelity and variation in implementation in the evaluation of the Georgia Pre-kindergarten Program.

Case Example of Implementation Assessment and Its Use in Evaluation

In the evaluation of Summer Bridge (previously described), different kinds of data on implementation were used in several ways. First, implementation assessment was used to examine specific claims about possible negative side-effects that had been raised by critics of the new policy. For example, concerns were raised that the need for students to pass a make-up test at the end of the summer would lead teachers to focus on test preparation, rather than on student learning. From direct observations of the instruction in 36 classes, the evaluators estimated that less than 1 percent of the instructional time was spent explicitly teaching test-taking strategies and about 4 percent was spent taking practice tests or quizzes (Roderick et al., 2003, p. 28).

Second, the evaluators compared the foci of questions on the test (e.g., the proportion of items dealing with interpretation of non-literal language) to the foci of the curriculum (e.g. the

amount of class time spent on interpretation of non-literal language). Results showed the two were closely aligned. This is a kind of fidelity assessment, with the results showing that, to the extent that the materials covered on the test represent valid basic skills, the curriculum that was taught covered basic skills.

Third, the evaluators observed classrooms in order to make systematic judgments about the quality of instruction and the efficiency of the use of instructional time. Approximately 52 percent of the reading lessons observed were rated as being of sufficient quality, while 21 percent exceeded the standard for minimal fidelity to high-quality instruction and 28 per cent failed to meet the standard of sufficiency. We return to the use of this implementation measure shortly, in discussing mediational analyses from the Summer Bridge evaluation.

Mediators: Testing an Explanation of Program Effects

A *mediator* is a variable that falls between two other variables in a causal chain, such as between a program and its outcome. Substantively and statistically, the mediator also accounts for or is responsible for the relationship between the intervention and outcome. To take an example, certain kinds of anti-littering campaigns are mediated by what are called injunctive social norms. That is, the campaign announcements make it salient to listeners that people in general disapprove of littering (Cialdini, 2003); this normative approval in turn leads to reduced littering. Mediational analyses are becoming more common in evaluations. For example, a family of behavior change theories often guides mediational analyses of certain kinds of behavioral health interventions. Theory-driven evaluation, a growing approach to program and policy evaluation, includes mediational analyses as a routine methodology (Donaldson, 2003).

Structural equation modeling (SEM) is often used for mediational analysis (e.g., Ullman & Bentler, 2003). SEM and related statistical methods are valuable, but not without limits (e.g., Freedman, 1987; Kenny, Kashy, & Bolger 1998). Simple statistical procedures, including a multistep regression procedure, can also be used for simple mediational models (Baron & Kenny, 1986). Alternatively, more qualitative methods are sometimes used to assess whether the steps in a program's theory of change have unfolded as expected (Weiss, 1995). More detailed discussion of these techniques is beyond the scope of this chapter. Suffice it to say, first, that mediational tests in evaluation can contribute to the knowledge base and, second, that mediational evidence can also strengthen evaluation's value for policy-making. Finding evidence of mediation: (1) allows evaluators to open up the "black box"; (2) provides a more persuasive set of findings, by including an explanation of why the program worked (or didn't); (3) offers a concrete basis for recommendations to modify the program; (4) can help influence adoption of the policy or program elsewhere; and (5) strengthens confidence that the policy or program produced the effect.

Case Example of Testing for Mediation

Returning to the Summer Bridge example, the previously noted implementation measures were used in analyses to assess the extent to which variations in implementation led to differences in reading score gains. Analyses revealed that classes with high-quality instruction averaged approximately one quarter of a full year's gain during the summer *above the average gain*, while those with insufficient instruction achieved below average gains (Roderick et al., 2003, p. 96). Other associations between implementation and outcomes were based on data from teachers' responses

to surveys. For example, students gained the equivalent of about half a month more when the teachers in the school individualized instruction (Roderick et al., 2003, pp. 76–77).

By itself, the mediational evidence from Summer Bridge is not the strongest causal evidence that might be presented. Nevertheless, the mediational findings do to some extent increase confidence that Summer Bridge is responsible for the improvement in achievement. In short, this is because it seems unlikely that alternative explanations for the overall Summer Bridge findings (e.g., maturation) would have predicted that instructional quality would be so strongly related to student outcomes; in contrast, this is precisely what would be predicted according to the program theory underlying Summer Bridge. In addition, the mediational findings can inform future policy-making and program management, in that they highlight the importance of instructional quality. More generally, testing for mediational effects, especially involving more substantive mediators, is a major enhancement that allows evaluations to open up the "black box" and add to our understanding of how effects are produced.

Moderators: Testing for Differences in Effects across Groups

A *moderator*, in contrast to a mediator, is a variable that modifies the strength or direction of the relationship between two other variables. In a program evaluation context, a moderator might be associated with stronger (or weaker) effects of the program on an outcome. For example, if the effect of Summer Bridge was moderated by the skill level of the children in the program, this would mean that the effect of the summer program is different for children who were close to passing the initial high-stakes test that for those who failed the test by a large margin. Using different terminology (from an analysis of variance tradition), one could say that the skill level of students entering into the program interacts with the treatment. In evaluation, tests of moderation are often important in terms of equity considerations, such as whether an educational program reduces or exacerbates achievement gaps across racial, ethnic, gender, or other groupings.

Case Example of Testing for Moderated Effects

In addition to probing for mediation, program evaluators looked to see if Summer Bridge was more effective for certain types of students and in different types of schools. These investigations were motivated by concerns for equity. The Summer Bridge evaluation therefore tested for possible differences across high-risk, moderate-risk, and low-risk students.[7] The findings indicated that students in all risk categories gained, but the patterns of gains were not consistent across grades or subjects. For example, high-risk third graders gained the most in reading but the least in mathematics (Roderick et al., 2003, p. 41). For eighth graders, low-risk students gained more in reading, while the gains in mathematics were about the same across the three risk groups (Roderick et al., 2003, p. 41). Even so, the rate at which these students passed the end of summer exam was about 70–80 percent for low-risk students and about 10–30 percent for high-risk students. Of course, the latter group had much more ground to make up during the summer compared to the low-risk students. These student-level analyses indicate that, overall, Summer Bridge did not unfairly advantage those students closest to the test cutoff. But, unfortunately, the findings also indicate that summer school does not compensate for starting out at higher risk.

In general, testing for moderation requires a pre-treatment measurement of the potential moderator (e.g., high versus low risk in Summer Bridge). However, Hill, Waldfogel, & Brooks-Gunn (2002) have adapted propensity score methods in a way that lets evaluators investigate moderators that are not measured in advance. In their analysis of a randomized experiment that assigned children of ages 1–3 to a high-quality child care program or to a comparison group, different child care arrangements emerged in the comparison group: maternal care, home-based non-maternal care, and center-based care. Hill et al., then used propensity score analysis to construct subgroups, in both the treatment and comparison group, representing a propensity for maternal care, non-maternal home care, or center care. The propensity scores both allowed testing for moderation with a factor that had not been measured before the treatment, and reduced the plausibility of selection bias in these estimates of the differential effects of high-quality child care. Hill and colleagues concluded that the program's effects were largest and most enduring for mothers who would have selected family day care or kept their children at home.

Meta-analysis

Meta-analysis refers to procedures for the quantitative synthesis of primary research. Before meta-analysis became popular, those who wished to summarize a research or evaluation literature typically conducted a "narrative review." Narrative reviews often included simple tallies, for example, of which evaluations showed statistically program benefits, which studies' findings were not significant, and which showed harmful outcomes. Meta-analysis offers numerous advances over the older narrative review. In particular, especially when the original studies in an area have low statistical power (as has often been the case in evaluation; Lipsey, 1989), even meaningful effects may not achieve statistical significance in some evaluations. In addition, although early meta-analyses typically looked at relatively simple questions (especially the size and statistical significance of a treatment effect), recent meta-analyses are more likely to study possible moderators of the treatment effect, and perhaps even to examine mediational questions (see, e.g., Cook et al., 1992).

Well-conducted meta-analyses can summarize the best available answer across multiple studies. The results of a single evaluation can be influenced greatly by arbitrary methodological choices (e.g., the wording of a key survey item); however, meta-analyses are far less dependent upon the idiosyncrasies of any single study. Perhaps most importantly, meta-analyses can provide at least somewhat greater confidence about generalization across persons, settings, and times. Meta-analytic results typically are based on findings from evaluations with at least somewhat different kinds of participants, carried out in varying kinds of settings, and at different points in time. If an intervention's effect is consistent across these multiple forms of heterogeneity, greater confidence may warranted in generalizing to most specific circumstances (see Shadish et al., 2002, on the ways meta-analysis can contribute to generalization). In addition, meta-analytic procedures include tests for assessing whether a group of effect sizes are homogenous; that is, it is possible to see whether the overall findings appear to hold across all the studies included in the meta-analysis (e.g., Hedges, 1985). If the studies do not appear to have arisen from a single overall effect, it may be possible to search for moderators.

Meta-analyses are not without limits. In general, meta-analyses cannot go beyond the shared validity limitations of the original studies. For example, if all of the evaluations of a given program share the same selection bias, then this shared bias will affect the overall meta-analytic finding. On the other hand, if the evaluations in a program area use different designs, then meta-analysis can be used to assess whether, for this particular program, the different designs lead to different outcomes. One can examine, for instance, whether randomized experiments are associated with different effect sizes than quasi-experiments.

Case Example of Using Meta-analysis Findings

The Summer Bridge evaluation was focused on a single program in the Chicago Public Schools, and thus the evaluators did not consider doing a meta-analysis. However, a meta-analysis did figure in their work. Specifically, a meta-analysis by Cooper and his colleagues (Cooper et al., 2000) summarized the available evaluations of the effects of summer school programs. The Summer Bridge evaluators used the results of that meta-analysis as a kind of comparative standard. They were able to show that Summer Bridge students showed a considerably larger gain than did the average participants in the many summer school programs Cooper et al., had synthesized. This added another basis for arguing that Summer Bridge was effective.

Meta-analyses appear to be taking on additional importance for policy-making and for knowledge development. To some extent, this probably reflects the increase in the number of quantitative studies available for synthesis and the increased refinement of the methods for meta-analysis. This increasing importance also may reflect new endeavors to facilitate and disseminate meta-analytic findings, beyond the efforts of individual investigators. For example, the Cochran Collaboration (http://www.cochrane.org/index0.htm) focuses on meta-evaluations in medicine, while the Campbell Collaborative (http://www.campbellcollaboration.org/) is conducting and disseminating meta-analyses in the various areas of social interventions.[8]

Missing Data

Rubin and colleagues' framing of treatment effects has helped stimulate work on another methodological problem in many quantitative evaluations – missing data. Traditional methods for dealing with missing data have potentially severe shortcomings. Dropping cases limits generalizability and reduces statistical power, and can bias estimates of treatment effects if – as seems likely in practice – missing data are related to condition (in the terms of Rubin and his associates, if the data are not missing completely at random, or MCAR). The old option of substituting the mean of a variable for missing data is also problematic. While cases are not lost, bias is again introduced if the data are not MCAR; after all, not every missing case is likely to be well represented by the mean. A more subtle consequence of substituting the mean is that variability is reduced. This in turn can affect hypothesis tests (e.g., by underestimating the amount of error variance).

Work stimulated by Rubin's causal model has suggested "multiple imputation" as a method for dealing with missing data. Multiple imputation uses the covariation across all available variables to estimate a value for those instances where data are missing. That is, missing data are replaced by estimates based on the values for the variables for the case that are not missing; some random error is also added (King et al., 2001). The joint distributions remain unchanged but the missing data bias can be reduced. Multiple imputation methods provide unbiased estimates of the missing data, even in the face of substantial attrition (Graham, Cumsille, & Elek-Fisk, 2003; Schafer, 1997). Standalone software programs, such as NORM (Schafer, 2000), are often used to impute missing values (see also King et al., 2001; Schafer, 1997; Schafer & Graham, 2002), and multipurpose statistical software (e.g., SAS) increasingly offer routines to impute multiple data sets.

Other missing data issues, in particular, selection bias, can be addressed using the RCM framework. For example, Henry & Gordon (2006) sought to assess the effects of competition between publicly subsidized pre-kindergartens on children's third-grade school success five years later. The missing data in this case, the subsequent assessment scores, could not be considered "ignorable." Some were missing because the children had been retained in grade (12.3 percent) and so were not eligible to take the state tests as third graders. Others had moved or their parents had chosen to remove them from the study. Therefore, Henry & Gordon (2006) used propensity scores (estimating the probability that a student would have a test score) to control for the bias that could arise from the missing test score data, that is, the bias from being selected into the tested group, in their evaluation of the effects of educational competition on third-grade test performance.

Summary and Conclusions

This chapter has focused on methods evaluators can and do use in service of policy-making and knowledge development. For both these evaluation purposes, evaluative evidence often is important to the extent it can: (1) support or undermine claims about the importance of a social problem; or (2) validate or fail to validate a potential remedy for a problem. Given these two forms of contributions, both policy-making and knowledge development can be served well by a variety of methods. These include descriptive methods that indicate the prevalence of a social problem, descriptive methods which demonstrate that a new policy or program option can successfully be implemented, and cost–benefit and related methods that attempt to compare policy or program alternatives in a common (perhaps financial) metric.

Despite the potential of these and other methods to contribute to policy-making and to knowledge development as evaluation purposes, this chapter has focused primarily on causal methods. When decisions are to be made about whether to adopt, maintain, expand, curtail, or eliminate some potential solution(s) to a problem, evaluation methods that estimate the effects of the relevant alternatives have a special potential contribution to policy-making. Similarly, evaluations that employ causal methods can contribute substantially to the purpose of knowledge development. Of growing interest are evaluation studies that examine the underlying mechanisms through which programs have their effects.

In reviewing causal methods that evaluators use, we discussed randomized experiments, quasi-experiments (especially the pretest–posttest non-equivalent group design and the regression-discontinuity design), as well as case studies and qualitative methods. Mixed-method designs, multisite designs, interrupted time series, and longitudinal designs are among other approaches that could also have been addressed in this chapter if space allowed. Instead, this chapter has discussed a variety of methodological innovations and enhancements to causal analysis. These include effect size estimation, implementation assessments of various kinds, tests of mediation and moderation, meta-analysis, and techniques for dealing with missing data. The development of several of these innovations is linked directly to the formal model of causal inference developed by Rubin and his colleagues. The methodological advances we have discussed are important not only because they increase the validity of causal inferences. Also, they help dispel the validity of several criticisms previously raised by critics of experiments and quasi-experiments.

While the labels for evaluation designs (e.g., randomized experiments; the pretest–posttest non-equivalent groups design) have remained largely the same, as our discussion of methodological innovations shows, the specific methods employed to carryout high–quality evaluations have changed tremendously in recent years. The changes constitute real improvements in evaluation practice. And the pace of improvement promises to continue in the future. Innovative ways of thinking, new techniques, more sophisticated management of large studies and the data they produce, and attention to human study participants have dramatically altered the craft of evaluation, especially evaluation aimed at improving policies and contributing to knowledge.

Concomitant with the changes in evaluation practice, especially for causal methods, has been an increase in the knowledge and skills required for evaluators who wish to contribute to these studies. At least in the US, many evaluations that inform policy discussions and/or contribute new knowledge have become so technically requiring that they appear increasingly to be conducted by teams in large private or not-for-profit research firms or through sizable university-based research centers. Therefore, generalist evaluators, who do not concentrate in specific substantive fields, and solo practitioners are less likely to be able to conduct such evaluations, perhaps indicating the development of a possible schism that has been noted elsewhere (Mark, 2001). Unless statisticians and methodologists develop comparable procedures that are better suited to smaller scale and smaller budget evaluations, the old qualitative versus quantitative battles may recur based on a division between small-scale local and large-scale national evaluators.

Despite the many advances in methods that have occurred, causal methods – and evaluations for policy-making and knowledge development more generally – continue to face challenges. For example, Mark & Mills (in press) have recently summarized several of the challenges that arise in moving from experimental or quasi-experimental evidence to decision-making. Even when relatively convincing evidence has been obtained that, for example, a program causes improved outcomes, this does not automatically yield a straightforward policy implication. Questions arise about: how big an effect needs to be to suggest a policy change; whether the program was compared against the appropriate alternative (e.g., a no-treatment control group versus the most plausible alternative treatment); how to deal with trade-offs across different outcomes; how well past evaluation findings generalize to current circumstances and to the settings the policy will affect; how to deal with the inherent uncertainties associated with any single finding; and how important evidence is for decision-making, relative to other value-driven and political considerations.

There is little doubt that the sophistication of methodological practices will continue to grow, offering improvements in how to deal with these and other challenges. The stakes are simply too high for policies not to be carefully and rigorously examined. Of course, some of the challenges are political and social, and technological advances presumably have a limited role in addressing these. Regardless, the pace of development is sufficiently rapid and the application of innovations in practice sufficiently widespread, that any attempt to depict the current state-of-the-craft in evaluation method is necessarily a snapshot of a point in time. Efforts continue to improve methods for those evaluations that are intended to offer better information for contributing to knowledge and improved policy-making. One of the many challenges evaluators face is in keeping pace with the developments surrounding them.

Notes

1. We recognize that this presentation of Rubin's causal model may be difficult for some

readers. We ask such readers to try to make it through this material, for the model has had important consequences for causal methods – and we quickly return to more accessible material.

2. Challenges, of course, remain, such as possible difficulties in generalizing from experimental findings to the broader population of interest, including what economists call social equilibrium effects.

3. The term "quasi-experiment" was apparently coined by methodologist Donald Campbell. Many quasi-experiments would be labeled as "observational studies" within another tradition associated more with statisticians such as Rosenbaum (2002).

4. The bias reduced by the use of the propensity score is limited by the quality and quantity of covariates used to generate the propensity score. Only if the possibility of treatment is random among individuals who have the same propensity score can one say that all bias is eliminated.

5. More recently, innovations in the use of application hierarchical linear models (HLM) have allowed evaluators to control for regression to the mean, another threat to validity. For example, in the Summer Bridge evaluation, a student who failed the high-stakes test, and therefore had to go to Summer Bridge, might have been sick and done worse on the test than she should have (i.e., error may have lowered the student's score); if so, some increase should occur in that student's subsequent test score even if Summer Bridge is effective. Roderick et al. (2002) used a clever application HLM to control for this possible bias.

6. We present a slightly simplified description of Jacob & Lefgren's work here.

7. Summer Bridge evaluators also tested for differences among schools that were high, moderate, and low achieving during the regular school year.

8. In a related effort, the US Department of Education's What Works Clearinghouse (http://www.whatworks.ed.gov/) is offering summaries of studies of various educational programs, practices, and products (see, e.g., What Works Clearinghouse, 2005).

References

American Evaluation Association (2003). Response to U.S. Department of Education Notice of proposed priority, *Federal Register* RIN 1890-ZA00,

November 4, 2003 "Scientifically Based Evaluation Methods". Retrieved August 30, 2005 from http://eval.org/doestatement.htm.

Barnett, W. S. (1992). Benefits of compensatory preschool education. *Journal of Human Resources*, 27, 279–312.

Baron, R. M. & Kenny, D. A. (1986). The moderator-mediator variable distinction in social psychological research: Conceptual, strategic, and statistical considerations. *Journal of Personality and Social Psychology*, 51(6), 1173–1182.

Bertrand, M., Duflo, E., & Mullainathan, S. (2004). How much should we trust differences-in-differences estimates. *The Quarterly Journal of Economics* (February), 249–275.

Bickman, L. (ed.) (1990). *Program Theory in Program Evaluation*. San Francisco: Jossey-Bass.

Boruch, R. F. (1997). *Randomized Experiments for Planning and Evaluation: A practical guide*. Thousand Oaks, CA: Sage.

Bryk, A. & Raudenbush, S. W. (1992). *Hierarchical Linear Models for Social and Behavioral Research: Applications and data Analysis Methods*. Newbury Park, CA: Sage.

Campbell, D. T. & Stanley, J. C. (1966). *Experimental and Quasi-Experimental Designs for Research*. Skokie, IL: Rand McNally.

Campbell, D. T. (1975). "Degrees of freedom" and the case study. *Comparative Political Studies*, 8, 178–193.

Cialdini, R. B. (2003). Crafting normative messages to protect the environment. *Current Directions in Psychological Science*, 12, 105–109.

Cook, T. D. (2001). Sciencephobia: Why education researchers reject randomized experiments. *Education Next*, 1, 62–68.

Cook, T. D. (2003). Why have educational evaluators chosen not to do randomized Experiments? *Annals of American Academy of Political and Social Science*, 589, 114–149.

Cook, T. D. & Campbell, D. T. (1979). *Quasi-experimentation: Design and analysis issues for field settings*. Skokie, IL: Rand McNally.

Cook, T. D., Cooper, H., Cordray, D. D., et al., (eds) (1992). *Meta-analysis for Explanation: A casebook*. New York: Russell Sage Foundation.

Cooper, H., Charlton, C., Valentine, J., & Muhlenbruck, L. (2000). Making the most of summer school: A meta-analysis and narrative review. *Monographs of the Society for Research in Child Development* 65, 260. Malden, MA: Blackwell.

Cronbach, L. J. (1982). *Designing Evaluations of Educational and Social Programs*. San Francisco: Jossey-Bass.

Donaldson, S. I. (2003). The theory-driven view of evaluation. In S. I. Donaldson & M. Scriven (eds) *Evaluating Social Programs and Problems: Visions for the new millennium* (pp. 109–141). Hillsdale, NJ: Erlbaum.

Eckert, W. A. (2000). Situational enhancement of design validity: The case of training evaluation at the World Bank Institute. *American Journal of Evaluation*, 21, 185–193.

Freedman, D. A. (1987). As others see us: A case study in path analysis. *Journal of Educational Statistics*, 12, 101–128.

Friedlander, D., Greenberg, D. H., & Robins, P. K. (1997). Evaluating government training programs for the economically disadvantaged. *Journal of Economic Literature*, 25, 1809–1855.

Gormley, W. T., Gayer, T., Phillips, D., & Dawson, B. (2005). The effects of Universal Pre-K on cognitive development. *Developmental Psychology*, 41(6), 872–884.

Graham, J. W., Cumsille, P. E., & Elek-Fisk, E. (2003). Methods for handling missing data. In S. A. Schinka & W. Velicer (eds) *Comprehensive Handbook of Psychology*, Volume 2, (pp. 87–114) New York: Wiley.

Greenberg, D. & Shroder, M. (2004). *The Digest of Social Experiments*. Washington, D.C.: Urban Institute Press.

Greenberg, D., Mandell, M., & Onstott, M. (2000). The dissemination and utilization of welfare-to-work experiments in state policy-making. *Journal of Policy Analysis and Management*, 19(3), 367–382.

Guerin, D. & MacKinnon, D. P. (1985). An assessment of the impact of the California child seat requirement. *American Journal of Public Health*, 75, 142–144.

Heckman, J. & Navarro-Lazano, S. (2004). Using matching, instrumental variables, and control functions to estimate economic choice models. *Review of Economics and Statistics*, 86(1), 30–57.

Hedges, L. V. (1985). *Statistical Methods for Meta-analysis*. New York: Academic Press.

Henry, G. T. (1990). *Practical Sampling*. Thousand Oaks: CA: Sage Publications.

Henry, G. T. (2000). Why not use? In V. Caracelli & H. Preskill (eds) *Evaluation Use. New Directions for Evaluation*, 88, pp. 85–98.

Henry, G. T. & Gordon, C. C. (2006). Competition in the sandbox: A test of the effects of preschool competition on educational outcomes. *Journal of Policy Analysis and Management*, 25, 1.

Henry, G. T., Henderson, L. W., Ponder, B. D., Gordon, C. S., Mashburn, A., & Rickman, D. K. (2003). *Report of the Findings From the Early Childhood Study: 2001–02*. Andrew Young School of Policy Studies, Georgia State University.

Henry, G. T., Ponder, B. D., Rickman, D. K., Mashburn A., Henderson, L. W., & Gordon, C. S. (2004). *An Evaluation of the Implementation of the Georgia Pre-K Program: A Report of the Findings From the Early Childhood Study: 2002–03*. Andrew Young School of Policy Studies, Georgia State University.

Hill, J., Waldfogel, J., & Brooks-Gunn, J. (2002). Differential effects of high-quality child care. *Journal of Policy Analysis and Management*, 21(4), 601–627.

Jacob, B. A. & Lefgren, L. (2004). Remedial education and student achievement: A regression-discontinuity analysis. *The Review of Economics and Statistics*, 86(1), 226–244.

Kenny, D. A., Kashy, D. A., & Bolger, N. (1998). Data analysis in social psychology. In D. T. Gilbert, S. T. Fiske et al., *The Handbook of Social Psychology*, Volume 2, 4th edition (pp. 233–265). Boston: McGraw-Hill.

King, G., Honaker, J., Joseph, A., & Schieve, K. (2001). Analyzing incomplete political science data: An alternative algorithm for multiple imputation. *American Political Science Review*, 95(1), 49–69.

Kingdon, J. W. (1995). *Agendas, Alternatives, and Public Policies*. New York: Harper Collins.

Lederman, N. G. & Flick, L. B. (2003). Never cry wolf. *School Science and Mathematics*, 103, 61–63.

Leow, C., Marcus, S., Zanutto, E., & Boruch, R. (2004). Effects of advanced course-taking on math and science achievement: Addressing selection bias using propensity scores. *American Journal of Evaluation*, 25, 461-478.

Levin, H. M. & McEwan, P. J. (2000). *Cost-Effectiveness Analysis Methods and Applications*, 2nd edition. Thousand Oaks, CA: Sage.

Lipsey, M. W. (1989). *Design Sensitivity: Statistical power for experimental research*. Thousand Oaks, CA: Sage.

Lipsey, M. W. & Wilson, D. B. (2001). *Practical Meta-analysis*. Thousand Oaks, CA: Sage.

Mark, M. M. (2001). Evaluation's future: Furor, futile, or fertile? *American Journal of Evaluation*, 22, 457–479.

Mark, M. M. (2003). Program evaluation. In S. A. Schinka & W. Velicer (eds) *Comprehensive Handbook of Psychology*, Volume 2 (pp. 323–347). New York: Wiley.

Mark, M. M., Henry, G. T., & Julnes, G. (2000) *Evaluation: An integrated framework for understanding, guiding, and improving policies and programs*. San Francisco: Jossey-Bass.

Mark, M. M. & Mills, J. (in press). The use of experiments and quasi-experiments in decision making. In G. Morcöl (ed.) *Handbook of Decision Making*. New York: Marcel Dekker.

Maxwell, J. A. (2004). *Qualitative Research Design*, 2nd edition. Thousand Oaks, CA: Sage.

Patton, M. Q. (2003). *Qualitative Research and Evaluation Methods*, 3rd edition. Thousand Oaks, CA: Sage.

Pawson, R. & Tilley, N. (1997). *Realistic Evaluation*. Thousand Oaks, CA: Sage.

Pressman, J. L. & Wildavsky, A. B. (1973). *Implementation: How great expectations in Washington are dashed in Oakland; Or why it's amazing that federal programs work at all*. Berkeley: University of California Press.

Riccio, J. A. & Bloom, H. S. (2002). Extending the reach of randomized social experiments: New directions in evaluations of American welfare-to-work and employment initiatives. *Journal of the Royal Statistical Society: Series A*, 165, 13–30.

Roderick, M., Jacob, B. A., & Bryk, A. S. (2002). The impact of high-stakes testing in chicago on student achievement in promotional gate grades. *Educational Evaluation and Policy Analysis*, 24(4), 333–357.

Roderick, M., Engel, M., Nagaoka, J., Jacob, B., Degener, S., Orfei, A., Stone, S., & Bacon, J., (2003). *Ending Social Promotion: Results from Summer Bridge*. Chicago: Consortium on Chicago School Research.

Rog, D. J. & Fitzpatrick, J. L. (1999). The evaluation of the Homeless Families Program. Dialogue with Debra J. Rog. *American Journal of Evaluation*, 20, 558–575.

Rosenbaum, P. R. (2002). *Observational Studies*. New York: Springer.

Rosenbaum, P. R. & Rubin, D. B. (1983). The central role of the propensity score in observational studies for causal effects. *Biometrika*, 70(1), 41–55.

Rubin, D. B. (1977). Assignment to treatment group on the basis of a covariate. *Journal of Educational Statistics*, 2, 1–26.

Sabatier, P. A. & Jenkins-Smith, H. C. (1998). The advocacy coalition framework. In P. Sabatier (ed.) *Theories of Policy Change* (pp. 117–166). Boulder, CO: Westview Press.

Schafer, J. L. (1997). *Analysis of Incomplete Multivariate Data*, Volume. 72. London: Chapman & Hall.

Schafer, J. L. (2000). NORM (Version 2.03). University Park, PA.

Schafer, J. L. & Graham, J. W. (2002). Missing data: our view of the state of the art. *Psychological Methods*, 7(2), 147–177.

Shadish, W. R., Cook, T. D., & Campbell, D. T. (2002). *Experimental and Quasi-Experimental Designs for Generalized Causal Inference*. Boston: Houghton Mifflin.

Stake, R. E. (1995). *The Art of Case Study Research*. Thousand Oaks, CA : Sage

Stake, R. & Davis, R. (1999). Summary of evaluation of Reader Focused Writing for the Veterans Benefits Administration. *American Journal of Evaluation*, 20, 323–343.

Ullman, J. B. & Bentler, P. M. (2003). Structural equation modeling. In S. A. Schinka & W. Velicer (eds) *Comprehensive Handbook of Psychology*, Volume 2. New York: Wiley.

Weiss, C. H. (1979). The many meanings of research utilization. *Public Administration Review*, 39, 426–431.

Weiss, C. H. (1995). Nothing as practical as a good theory: Exploring theory-based evaluations for Comprehensive Community Initiatives for children and families. In J. P. Connell, A. C. Kubisch, L. B. Schorr & C. H. Weiss (eds) *New Approaches to Evaluating Community Initiatives, Volume 1: Concepts, methods, and contexts*. Washington, DC: Aspen Institute.

What Works Clearinghouse (2005). Retrieved January 13, 2005 from http://www.whatworks.ed.gov

Wright, J. D. (1998). *Beside the Golden Door: Policy, politics, and the homeless*. Aldine de Gruyter.

Yin, R. K. (2002). *Applications of the Case Study Methodology*, 2nd edition. Thousand Oaks, CA: Sage.

Yoshikawa, H., Rosman, E. A., & Hsueh, J. (2001). Variation in teenage mothers' experiences of child care and other components of welfare reform: Selection processes and developmental consequences. *Child Development*, 72, 299–317.

15

EMBEDDING IMPROVEMENTS, LIVED EXPERIENCE, AND SOCIAL JUSTICE IN EVALUATION PRACTICE

Elizabeth Whitmore, Irene Guijt, Donna M. Mertens, Pamela S. Imm, Matthew Chinman, and Abraham Wandersman

What would an evaluation look like that aims at *program improvement*? How might one implement an evaluation that focuses on *understanding lived experience* as a critical component of improvement? And, how does one conduct an evaluation that foregrounds the promotion of *social justice*? The purpose of this chapter is to explore answers to these challenging questions that are not standard components of evaluation processes and yet are often of concern to evaluation consultants[1] and to stakeholders. To that end, we present examples from three distinct, but related approaches to evaluation that endeavor to achieve the goals of program improvement, understanding lived experience, and social justice, respectively: (1) empowerment evaluation, (2) the monitoring of "most significant changes," and (3) transformative evaluation.

Guiding Principles

While each example is a unique illustration of one or more of the three evaluation purposes that frame this chapter, they share four common underlying principles: participation, learning, negotiation, and flexibility. To articulate these principles, we have drawn from the work of Estrella & Gaventa (1998).

Evaluations for improvement, understanding lived experience, or advancing social justice are fundamentally participatory, involving key stakeholders in critical decisions about the evaluation's agenda, direction and use. Such a principle is rooted epistemologically in the importance of understanding multiple perspectives and experiences in evaluation, and also politically in the importance of democratic inclusion (J. C. Greene, personal communication). A key question is who initiates and who drives the evaluation process, and whose perspectives are particularly emphasized. While some may include a broad range of stakeholders in the process, others may focus more on marginalized groups or "beneficiaries." The focus in all three examples is on lived experience – an evaluation anchored in the experiences of those who have lived through the challenges and opportunities that are being evaluated, as opposed to talking only to top-level managers. Levels of participation will vary, of course, depending on time, availability, interest, and resources. An evaluation may be externally or internally led or some combination.

Evaluations dedicated to the three goals are premised on the idea that participants are, and want to be, engaged in their own process of learning. A key emphasis here is on practical or "action-oriented" learning, rather than satisfying external information needs. It is both an individual and collective process, which creates conditions conducive to change and action (Estrella & Gaventa, 1998, p. 22). It is learning that improves understanding by building on existing participant knowledge of what works or does not work in a given circumstance. The learning process is a means of local capacity building wherein participants may gain skills in planning, problem-solving, and decision-making. At the same time, they may also increase their understanding of various external and internal

factors that affect what they are trying to achieve, thus opening the door to innovative solutions or alternative actions (ibid, p. 23). Creating a learning culture is assumed to lead to enhanced accountability, as participants feel more a part of a collective process and thus more responsible for what occurs.

Negotiating meanings, perspectives, roles, and responsibilities is an essential part of evaluation practice that aims to achieve these goals. The term "negotiation" is understood broadly here to encompass not only the social processes but also different intellectual traditions, sources of evidence and knowledge, and methodologies. Negotiating social processes recognizes the complexity of interrelationships among stakeholders. Issues of power and the political nature of how decisions are made about what should be done, how and by whom, are often unspoken yet strongly present. It is through these processes that participants clarify their own roles and responsibilities, which in turn strengthens collaboration and builds trust among partners (ibid., p. 25). Part of the challenge is balancing respect for local knowledge and what outsiders may think are "effective practices" based on "scientific" evidence. Patton (2002) cautions us about using the language of "best-ness" (as in "best practices"), suggesting that it is much more fruitful to foster "dialogue about and deliberation on multiple interpretations and perspectives" (p. 232). Such negotiations contribute a sense of ownership of the process, which is critical for a sustained impact from the evaluation efforts.

Issues related to differing intellectual traditions are also an integral part of any such negotiations, as participants come to evaluation with varying assumptions about methodology, appropriate sources of knowledge, and what constitutes valid evidence. In any evaluation situation, coming to a shared understanding about these issues is fundamental to being able to work together. Negotiating is thus not only an issue of perspectives, but also involves questions of method and evidence.

The process of working together is flexible and open to experimentation, and it continually evolves and adapts according to project-specific circumstances and needs (Estrella & Gaventa, 1998, p. 26). While the process is often characterized as "cyclical," it has also been described as a "very slow, multi-layered, backward and forward stop-start experience" (Jobes, cited in Estrella & Gaventa, p. 26). This is not an easy way to work, one that takes a particular kind of commitment, style, and tolerance for ambiguity. It is also challenging for evaluators who are used to defining and then sticking to an evaluation plan from the outset.

The three examples illustrate how these principles can guide an evaluation, while at the same time addressing the purposes of the chapter. Pamela Imm, Matthew Chinman, and Abraham Wandersman apply the principles using empowerment evaluation methods to illustrate how evaluation consultants worked with a community coalition in the US around issues of drug-use prevention among schoolchildren. The broader goal here was to foster the capacity to implement programs effectively. Irene Guijt describes the "most significant change" approach as a way of monitoring what was happening in two projects in Brazil. She and her colleagues used it to capture aspects of local work that were elusive for other methods. In gathering stories of peoples' direct experience in the project, this approach illustrates a way to ground the collection and analysis of qualitative data in the "lived experience" of participants. Finally, Donna Mertens shares her work with the United Nations Development Fund for Women in South Africa, in which she engaged in training participants to plan and conduct an evaluation. Using a transformative evaluation approach, she employed a combination of techniques to stimulate critical thinking about key topics and linking

them to social action. The explicit goals of the program involve the advancement of development and human rights, consistent with the promotion of social justice.

Utilizing an Empowerment Evaluation Approach to Enhance Program Improvement and Capacity Building[2]

Empowerment evaluation is defined as "an evaluation approach that aims to increase the probability of achieving program success by (1) providing program stakeholders with tools for assessing the planning, implementation, and self-evaluation of their program, and (2) mainstreaming evaluation as part of the planning/management of the program/organization" (Wandersman et al., 2005, p. 28).

Case examples of empowerment evaluation are the subject of a three-year study that we have been conducting since 2002 with funding from the Centers for Disease Control in the US. This study is a meta-evaluation of how and to what extent two community-based coalitions (in Santa Barbara, California and Columbia, South Carolina) utilize the Getting to Outcomes (GTO) model and realize the model's intended evaluative aims of program improvement and staff capacity building.

The GTO model is an operationalization of empowerment evaluation. It was developed to enhance practitioners' capacities for planning, implementation, and evaluation, as well as the likelihood of achieving positive results. The GTO model is based on a system of 10 accountability questions, which encompass needs assessment and program planning in addition to evaluation:

1. What are the underlying *needs* and conditions that must be addressed?

2. What are the *goals*, target population, and objectives (e.g., desired outcomes)?

3. What science or evidence-based *models* will be useful in helping achieve these goals?

4. How does this intervention(s) *"fit"* with other intervention(s) already being offered?

5. What organizational *capacities* are needed to implement the intervention(s)?

6. What is the *plan* for this intervention(s)?

7. How will the *quality of implementation* be assessed?

8. How do you know the intervention(s) are *working*?

9. What *continuous quality improvement* strategies are needed to improve the intervention(s) over time?

10. If the intervention(s) are successful, how will they be *sustained*?

The Santa Barbara Fighting Back Coalition

The Santa Barbara Fighting Back (SBFB) coalition in California has a small number of paid staff supporting a large volunteer base, which is divided into committees based on different community sectors (criminal justice, youth, health, media). Volunteers include public and private agency representatives and prominent local citizens. This coalition receives core funds from state and federal agencies to diagnose and prioritize their communities' needs regarding substance and tobacco use, implement programs to address those needs, and then evaluate their progress.

The goals of the SBFB are to reduce alcohol and drug use among adolescents aged 12–17, increase treatment access for youth and adults, and reduce excessive alcohol consumption and related problems in the southern region of the county. Santa Barbara County faces high rates

of poverty (15 percent of residents) and alcohol and drug use. Significant numbers of 11th graders in southern Santa Barbara County reported alcohol use (60 percent) and marijuana use (30 percent) during the past six months (Skager & Austin, 2002), and a quarter of 11th graders reported being drunk or high at school in the 2000–2001 (SBFB, 2001).

The SBFB coalition, which began addressing substance abuse among youth in 1991, designated four of its prevention programs to utilize the GTO model, three of which are included in this write-up. First, the Youth Services System is a program that places two individuals in each of Santa Barbara County high and middle schools to provide education regarding alcohol and other drugs, public awareness, prevention, early identification, and referral services. They teach personal and social skills, critical thinking, responsible decision-making, and tools for coping with anxiety. Second, Teen Court is an early intervention for first-time offenders that diverts them out of the traditional juvenile system while still holding them accountable for their actions. All functions of Teen Court are carried out by teens, and sentences include jury duty, community service, counseling, and educational classes. Third, the Mentor Program provides students in grades 4–8 with an adult mentor, who meets with students once a week, for a minimum of one hour, on-site at the child's school campus. Volunteer mentors explore mutual interests and offer support and friendship that helps build self-confidence, resiliency, and social skills in their mentees.

Utilizing GTO: Implementation in Santa Barbara

The key elements of implementing the GTO model include utilization of the GTO manual and related tools, training, and face-to-face and telephone technical assistance.

GTO materials

The current manual explains GTO and provides tools to assist with many planning implementation, evaluation, and sustaining tasks. These tools, mostly text documents, are contained on a CD-ROM that accompanies each manual so that they can be tailored for each user (www.rand.org/publications/TR/TR101).

Training

All SBFB program staff and coalition volunteers (approximately 80 people, including prevention practitioners and supervisors, and community volunteers) received a one-day training course in the GTO model at the beginning of their implementation of the GTO model. This interactive training provided concrete examples of how each of the 10 questions in the model can be addressed using GTO tools. Participants were also given the opportunity to complete several GTO tools for a simulated case example and then for their own individual programs.

Technical assistance

Technical assistance is critical for ensuring that the GTO model is being utilized with quality (Altman, 1995; Backer, 1991, 2001; Wandersman & Florin, 2003). Ongoing technical assistance is provided weekly to the Santa Barbara site for about two hours a week. Additional information about the GTO model is provided, and staff receive specific assistance on how to use each step to guide the implementation of their programs. Examples of the technical assistance provided in Santa Barbara include:

- developing realistic goals and objectives (Question #2)

- ensuring that programs/strategies fit the school and community context (Question #4)
- consideration of the resources necessary for high-quality implementation (Question #5)
- planning the key activities of the program/strategy (Question #6)
- identifying methods for process and outcome evaluations (Questions #7 & #8)
- using evaluation data to improve current and future programs/strategies (Question #9)
- developing strategies to sustain the efforts within the setting (Question #10)

Reflections on GTO Implementation and Effectiveness

The GTO model is intended to support quality program development and implementation as well as attainment of important program outcomes, while also building the capacity of program staff so that they can utilize the model independently and so that this process becomes a "way of doing business" for that program, and ultimately the larger organization (in this case, the coalition). The meta-evaluation has identified certain variables associated with achieving these goals, as well as challenges to implementing the GTO model. Specifically, successful implementation of this model requires organizations with a certain amount of *general organizational capacity*. For example, conducting evaluation often requires computers and statistical and database management software, and some organizations may not be able to secure these resources. Another example of organizational capacity is the resources needed to pay for technical assistance, which in this case was provided by highly skilled researchers.

In addition to *having* sufficient resources, organizations also need to have a *commitment to expending* those resources when beginning a program improvement process such as GTO and endeavoring to sustain it. This commitment includes a reconceptualization of what is involved in doing community-based prevention. In GTO, "doing prevention," means all the tasks outlined in the ten steps. For some staff, this may represent an addition of tasks to an already busy schedule (for example, adding new evaluation activities) or a requirement that new skills be learned. Commitment further means that leadership and program staff have to be willing to make difficult choices that might involve eliminating popular, yet poorly performing programs (Livet & Wandersman, 2005). The challenge of organizational commitment is ongoing. We found that it can take nearly two years of training and technical assistance in order to achieve improvements in capacity.

In the meta-evaluation conducted, to what extent did GTO build the coalitions' capacity to conduct their own planning, implementation, and evaluation activities? Our survey data from members of both coalitions prior to and following two years of GTO implementation show that GTO participation was associated with improvements in knowledge, attitudes (e.g., importance of evaluation) and skills (e.g., frequency of doing evaluation) across all of the prevention capacities targeted by GTO. Moreover, all the programs in the coalitions either started new ongoing program evaluations where before there were none, or significantly improved the rigor of their current designs. These survey data were supported by data from qualitative interviews.

Assessing Lived Experience by Monitoring the "Most Significant Change"[3]

Indicators are a common language in evaluative processes through which people translate diversity of observations into manageable information "bits." Yet indicators only provide information about the incidence of anticipated phenomena of change. As indicators are identified in relation to the goals that are meant to be achieved, they are couched in terms of what is *expected* to happen. This significantly reduces a person's or project's ability to learn from surprise[4] and the unexpected that inevitably occurs.

A method that goes some way towards breaking the "knowing the known" feature of indicator-based monitoring is the Most Significant Change (MSC) method. In the mid-1990s, the Christian Commission for Development in Bangladesh (CCDB) worked with Rick Davies to develop a monitoring system that deliberately abandoned the use of predetermined indicators in their micro-enterprise development project (Davies, 1998). Although earlier attempts at comprehensive and rigorous use of indicators to track success had not been sustained, the MSC method is still going strong in Bangladesh.

At the heart of MSC lies the sharing stories of lived experiences, and systematically selecting those most representative of the type of change being sought to share with others. In so doing, the method allows for an open-ended and rich discussion on a range of aspects of change, rather than snippets of reality that are defined through outsiders in the form of indicators. As a vehicle for learning, MSC has similarities with critical incident analysis but differs in several important ways, notably its explicit use for systematic monitoring of change, rather than as a research tool.

How the MSC Method Works[5]

The method has two core parts, the first of which is identifying the stories of change. A group of people who share common goals share stories of change related to these goals, and subsequently identify which of the stories best reflect the goals towards which they are aspiring. The composition of the group will depend on the organizational/project purpose and key stakeholder groups. This part consists of several clear steps. (Davies, 1998).

1. *Identify who is to be involved and how.* Who will be asked to share stories (where is the lived experience that others need to hear about)? Who will help to identify the domain(s) of change? To whom will information be communicated?

2. *Identify the domains of change to be discussed.* These are often related to key goals of the project/organization/initiative.

3. *Clarify the frequency* with which stories will be shared and the most significant one selected.

4. *Share stories* using a simple question for each type of change: "During the last month, in your opinion, what do you think was the most significant change that took place in . . . [for example, the lives of the people participating in the project]?"

5. *Select the most significant one* from among the stories (per type of change).

6. *Document the answer.* The answer has two parts: descriptive – describing what happened in sufficient detail such that an independent person could verify that the event took place, and explanatory – explaining why the group members thought the change was the most significant out of all the changes that took place over that time period.

The second part of the MSC method involves communicating the *most* significant story for each domain of change. How the communication pathway is constructed will depend on the reason for which the method is being used and on the organizational structure. In CCDB in Bangladesh, the prime motivation was for different levels of management to learn about what was happening. So, the communication pathways involved flows to the top, while building in feedback loops back to each level

below on the nature of the "most significant change" story that had been fed up the system. If the purpose of the method is, as in the Brazil case discussed in more detail below, mutual understanding of different partners in a collaborative venture, then sharing need happen only between partners. Other purposes will dictate what is communicated to whom.

Central to the method is the opportunity provided by the story-sharing process for the individual values and concerns of respondents to be made explicit, debated, and compared. The answers are not predetermined, but are lived experiences voiced as significant change events. They thus provide a flexible approach to monitoring impact. For example, the selected MSC in year 1 of the Bangladesh project might be that the poorest member of a micro-credit group repaid the loan on time. As the group matures, the micro-credit group might indicate some event that represents a very high return on investment. Later yet, they might identify a group member's capacity to gain the title to her own land as the MSC. These change events are milestones for the group, continually changing as the group's achievements grow.

A key strength of the MSC method is that it allows participants to make explicit the criteria for success that they value. This occurs as a result of the built-in reflection, not just stating the most significant change but making clear why this was collectively selected as the most significant one. By allowing diverse stakeholder experiences and perspectives to meet and share, the emergent criteria for success provide important insights about what is valued about the initiative being monitored.

Using the MSC Method in Brazilian Rural Development

In Brazil, the method was introduced in a three-year action research process aimed at developing a participatory monitoring system to track the efforts by local non-government organizations working with poor farmers. Our research process took place in two sites, one in the state of Paraíba and one in the state of Minas Gerais, where long-term local efforts are creating more sustainable rural development alternatives. In each site, diverse groups were involved, and representatives from each of the parties were active at all stages of designing and implementing the monitoring process. For example, in Paraíba, this involved two rural trade unions and a local non-governmental organization (NGO). in Minas Gerais, university researchers participated, as did farmer groups working together on specific issues.

The Gap that the MSC Method Was Supposed to Fill

Before I introduced the idea of the MSC method, the first two years of the work had focused on developing sets of indicators to monitor the effectiveness of existing development activities. In the second year, we reviewed the work in both sites and agreed that the indicator focus would not provide insights about broader institutional issues, partnership, methodological innovation, and policy objectives. Besides tracking the micro-world of activities, the groups now needed to tackle the monitoring of less tangible aspects of their rural endeavours. The lack of enthusiasm for an indicator focus arose partly out of a concern with the time involved but also due to the intangible nature of changes related to these themes. I offered them the MSC method as an alternative. A trial run during plenary workshops in both sites left participants keen to try it in the field. The method was deemed simple and initially seemed effective at provoking the sought after reflection and sharing on complex topics.

The application of the MSC method in the two sites was slightly different. The intention of the Paraíba partners was to share views on change among themselves on four domains: influencing policies for more sustainable agriculture, strengthening and broadening partnerships, improving (communication) methodologies, and constructing a new vision for the farmer union. Thus exchanging the full lists of changes and their selected "most significant change" event was to take place every four months. They expected that during their annual review meetings they could use the outputs from the three analyses to generate an overall assessment of the impacts achieved and problems encountered that year. In Minas Gerais, on the other hand, participants decided to try it in the farmer union executive committee meetings and to complement the indicator-based monitoring of five thematic groups: beekeeping, livestock management, herbal medicine, agroforestry, and maize trials. They did not define domains per group but referred to the overall work. The outputs from the farmer groups would be shared with the union executive committee, and outputs from the farmer groups and the union would be shared with the local NGO. The NGO helped facilitate the initial use of the method by the groups but did not use the method itself.

Initial Assessment by Users

The initial assessment of the MSC method in both sites was very positive (AS-PTA & IIED, 1998, Guijt, 1998). The method was considered feasible, good at provoking essential debates about the farmer trade union's strategy and providing information that would otherwise have been lost. For example, the homeopathy group in Minas Gerais applied it several times and found it gave them a sense of overall achievement, helping to highlight the problems they need to resolve if they were going to make a significant local impact and gain the municipal council's support.

Interestingly, despite the positive assessment, none of the groups continued with this method. In Minas Gerais, the demise of three of the five farmer group activities, meant that group meetings stopped and with it application of the MSC method. In Paraíba, after the change of presidency following trade union elections in one of the unions, there was little interest in using this method because it was associated with their ousted opponents. The sharing between the two unions and the NGO quickly fell by the wayside. Furthermore, the participants were extremely busy with their everyday farming tasks, besides their union- and NGO-related volunteer activities. Any extra task was viewed with skepticism. As union members said during our evaluation of the Minas Gerais process, "Monitoring, even with this relatively simple method without indicators, is still perceived as one more task."

Critical Discussion of the MSC Method

The solid, long-term, systematic and structured application of the Bangladeshi experience contrasts in an interesting manner with that of Brazil. This offers various methodological insights for those considering whether or not to experiment with this evaluative approach that prioritizes lived experiences. Davies & Dart (2005) discuss many other interesting features, strengths, and limitations of the method. Here I will focus on four observations.

Positive and/or Negative Stories

Davies' (1998) original method does not stipulate whether stories should be positive or negative. He reports that about 90–95 percent of all the changes documented were positive changes, while Dart et al., report that only 10% had "some element of bad news." The tendency towards positive stories may reflect project staff worries about how their own performance will be seen if negative changes are shared. In Brazil, we explicitly sought positive and negative stories as both sides were considered critical to give a balanced view. This did make the method considerably more cumbersome – two discussions instead of one for each of the domains and then comparing them. But it also allowed for a more balanced analysis.

Stories, Yes, but What About Learning?

In the original methodology, the stories are not explicitly linked to action. They simply provide information on impact. Kolb's (1984) "experiential learning" definition *includes* improved next actions. Thus learning from the experience of implementing a program, project, or initiative involves the generation of knowledge or lessons learned, and then using these lessons to improve ongoing implementation.

To ensure that MSC stories actually improve practice in an organization, a third part of the method is needed beyond the two identified by Davies – story identification and story communication. To learn what needs to change, a mechanism or opportunity needs to be identified that allows discussion of "so what does this say about our work?" and "now what are we going to do differently?"

Who Defines Domains

In Bangladesh, the domains for the stories were identified by higher-level management. In Brazil, those who were going to share the stories chose whether or not to have domains, and if so, what these would be. The purpose of the MSC method should determine who specifies the domains and how this is undertaken.

The Context of Application and Sustained Use

The Bangladeshi context was one with a clear organizational hierarchy, where the MSC method was adopted by higher-level management and required of lower-level staff. In the Brazilian context, we were dealing with a loose civil society partnership without hierarchy or staff obligations in which relationships were continually being reshaped due to events such as trade union elections. No matter how simple and effective the method appears in an externally facilitated forum, when it comes to continual use, these groups had their own systems and discussion cultures within which MSC was perceived as an extra task. Their pre-existing reflection processes prevailed. In the absence of collective sustained interest in using MSC as a focused and systematic opportunity for reflection on lived experiences and insufficient insight into the particularities of local organizational cultures, local adaptations were inadequate and the MSC did not prove to be a long-term methodological option.

MSC, as a relative newcomer to the field of evaluation methodology, is in full development (see Davies & Dart, 2005). While the focus on selected stories means the method does not lend itself well to assessing the full breadth of impact or generalizing from it, the method does allow for new insights about impact to emerge that would otherwise not have been noted. Thus the MSC stories are a valuable complement to conventional methods and provide a launching pad for a more systematic assessment of what works for whom under what conditions. When subjected to mass analyses or meta-analyses, further reviews of the stories can help identify key features of context and program experience that matter.

Transformative Evaluation and Social Justice: A Case Study from Africa[6]

African women have a saying, "You strike woman, you strike rock and you will be crushed." This saying captures the experiences of African women in a number of ways. It intimates the oppression that they live with, as

well as the resilience with which they respond to that oppression. African women face enormous challenges in terms of economics, government, health, and safety (United Nations Development Fund for Women, 2003). The HIV/AIDS pandemic impacts women in many ways. In sub-Saharan Africa, 15 million women are infected with HIV/AIDS, representing 58 percent of the people infected on the continent, with the greatest increases in infection occurring in young women. Many women, even those infected, are taking care of sick family members and orphan children, thus limiting their ability to generate sufficient funds to support themselves and their families. Gender-based violence continues to be pervasive in Africa, exacerbated by conflict and the precarious economic situation. Trafficking in young girls and women is increasing. Despite improvements in some countries (for example, women represent more than 30 percent of parliamentarians in Mozambique and South Africa), generally women are grossly under-represented in governance.

In 1976, the United Nations established the Development Fund for Women (UNIFEM) to provide financial and technical assistance to innovative programs and strategies that promote women's human rights, political participation, and economic security (United Nations Development Fund for Women, 2003). Based on an explicit agenda to advance their human rights agenda, UNIFEM is guided by the women's bill of rights: The Convention on the Elimination of All Forms of Discrimination against Women (United Nations, 1979) which delineates specific fundamental rights to vote and stand for election, as well as education, health, and employment. In 2003, UNIFEM Africa adopted the following objectives as part of its 2004–2007 strategic framework:

- Reduce feminized poverty and exclusion
- End violence against women
- Halt and reverse the spread of HIV/AIDS amongst women and girls

EXEMPLAR 15.1 **Philosophical assumptions of the transformative paradigm (Mertens, 2005)**

Basic beliefs	Transformative assumptions
Ontology: assumptions about the natureof reality	Multiple realities shaped by social, political, cultural, economic, ethnic, gender, and disability values
Epistemology: assumptions about the nature of the relationship between the evaluator and the stakeholders	Interactive link between evaluator and stakeholders; knowledge is socially and historically situated; developing a trusting relationship is critical
Methodology: assumptions about appropriate methods of systematic inquiry	Inclusion of qualitative (dialogic), but quantitative and mixed methods can be used; contextual and historical factors are described, especially as they relate to oppression

- Achieve gender equality in democratic governance in times of peace and in recovery from war.

UNIFEM Africa sought ways of monitoring and evaluating the multiyear programs that were developed to address these objectives from a rights-based and participatory approach. It allied with the African Evaluators Association to form the African Gender and Development Evaluators Network as a means to strengthen the effectiveness and gender responsiveness of development programs and projects in Africa. UNIFEM then sponsored a training workshop in Pretoria, South Africa in November 2003 that included major stakeholders, members of the Network of Gender and Development Evaluators, and UNIFEM staff from regional and national offices across Africa. The UNIFEM directors organized the training based on the assumptions that indigenous evaluators should conduct the evaluation (rather than bringing in non-Africans), and evaluation training should be provided that focused on the cultural complexity surrounding their priorities for women in Africa.

To this end, they invited Thelma Awori, Independent Consultant Training Specialist from Africa, as the workshop facilitator and me as an expert presenter on transformative evaluation theory and practice. In the eyes of the training organizers, the underlying philosophical assumptions of the transformative paradigm aligned with the desired approach to evaluation that they envisioned for the UNIFEM initiative (see Table 15.1).

Overview of the Training Workshop

Each decision about the training was based on the assumptions of the transformative paradigm. For example, the choice of topics for inclusion in the training was determined by a collaborative process and reflected an emphasis on human rights, cultural complexity and competence, and gender issues and their implications for evaluation practice. My training topics included:

- Rights and participatory issues in monitoring and evaluation within the context of ethical treatment of human beings in an evaluation
- The link between participation and social justice in terms of conducting transformative participatory work as an evaluator

- Viewpoints on the meaning of cultural competency, with special emphasis on the African context
- Principles of gender-responsive evaluations through the lens of feminist theory, principles, and practice of evaluation
- Dimensions of diversity and their implications for decisions about sampling issues
- Issues of methodological choice in terms of diversity and the use of mixed methods, along with implications of theoretical paradigms and criteria to judge rigor

I began my portion of the training by acknowledging my position as a Western, White, hearing, able-bodied woman from the United States of America who teaches and writes about transformative research methods. As such, I indicated that I came to South Africa with the firm belief that we needed to work together as a community of concerned human beings if we are to solve the pressing problems of women in Africa. I acknowledged that my experience with African literature and ways was limited. However, I was prepared to share with them what I know and then allow them to discuss and decide what was worthwhile for them in their particular context. Consequently, I designed the training to adhere to the principles of the transformative paradigm by presenting information on each topic in a brief plenary session, and following this with either large or small group discussions in which participants were encouraged to critically analyze the information in terms of its implications for the conduct of evaluation in their particular context. The next sections focus on three illustrative topics in the training: philosophical assumptions, cultural competency, and gender-responsive evaluation principles and practices.

Philosophical Assumptions

The goals of the training session on philosophical assumptions of the transformative paradigm were to clarify the meaning of the assumptions, as well as to stimulate ideas about the implications of these beliefs for evaluation practice. After a brief presentation using the information in Table 15.1. I used a series of slides that integrated cartoons to stimulate discussion along with text about the paradigm. For example, I introduced the concept of multiple realities by asking participants to recall the children's story "Little Red Riding Hood." To insure that the African participants understood this American cultural tale, I asked if everyone was familiar with this story before engaging in further discussion. Although all participants indicated familiarity, I asked one participant to briefly explain what happened in the traditional tale as a safeguard. I then used this as a basis to consider possible reactions to the final words of the story: "And they all lived happily ever after." The participants acknowledged that the accepted reality of that statement might be challenged by some of the characters in the story, especially by the wolf.

The inference for evaluation practice that they associated with the cartoon was the importance of critically examining the willingness to accept depictions of reality that align with "things we heard at our mother's knee." How many people's parents read them that story? How many people questioned the ending? How many people analyzed it from the wolf's point of view? Upon reflection, the participants suggested that a variety of factors may have influenced the wolf to eat the grandmother, such as hunger or poverty. They raised the possibility that the natural prey of the wolf might have been eliminated by clear cutting or other unsound environmental practices. Thus, the wolf was adapting to oppressive and unjust actions on the part of others that left him starving and unable to survive without breaking the norms of society.

Extensions of the methodological implications include: How can evaluators be sure they are getting the full picture of reality, and not the picture that is easiest to get or the most comfortable in terms of our past experiences and norms? If there is a voice that has not been traditionally included, how can the evaluator build a relationship of trust with that stakeholder group? How can an evaluator avoid reaching a conclusion that leaves unexamined variables that may reveal oppressive behaviors and practices that lead people to break social norms in order to survive? Participants discussed how they, as evaluators or program managers, needed to be aware of the social construction of concepts and their implications for the continuation or interruption of discrimination and oppression against women in Africa.

Cultural Competency in Evaluation

The assumptions of the transformative paradigm emphasize the importance of evaluators working with a high appreciation for cultural context. I set the context for the topic by reminding participants that the concept of culture includes shared behaviors, values, beliefs, attitudes, and languages, and is broadly construed to be multi-dimensional in nature. The participants reviewed several examples of definitions of cultural competency within an evaluation context, such as the American Psychological Association's (2002) statement that defines a culturally competent psychologist as an agent of prosocial change who "carries the responsibility of combating the damaging effects of racism, prejudice, bias, and oppression in all their forms, including all of the methods we use to understand the populations we serve . . . . A consistent theme . . . relates to the interpretation and dissemination of research findings that are meaningful and relevant to each of the four populations[7] and that reflect an inherent understanding of the racial, cultural,

and sociopolitical context within which they exist" (p. 1). Sue & Sue's (2003) definition added several dimensions to what it means to be a culturally competent evaluator.

As part of the opportunity for critical reflection and sharing their own experiences and resources, the participants discussed the following questions in small groups:

- In your world of experience, how would you define cultural competence in an evaluation context?
- What do the presented definitions of cultural competence mean to you?
- Reflect on the cultural context in which you work. How would you modify your original thinking regarding the meaning of the concept, or how would you modify the definitions presented to capture a more particular meaning in your context?
- What is the importance of considering such a concept in the context in which you do evaluations?
- How can improved understandings be linked to the furtherance of social justice?

The participants expanded the given definitions of cultural competence by adding concepts such as understanding the political context in which you are working, the importance of self-awareness and your influence in the situation, and acknowledgment of what you do not know. They offered several implications for the practice of evaluation, including strategies for learning about a cultural group, understanding the dimensions of diversity that are important in that context, and building trust with stakeholders. They noted a potential conflict with the principles associated with cultural competency and the constraints commonly associated with their evaluation work. They are typically asked to conduct evaluations by visiting a setting for a week or so. In such situations, they do not have sufficient time or resources to become immersed in the culture and build trusting relationships. This creates a tension between the goal of conducting a culturally competent evaluation and the realities they face in their work.

Gender-Responsive Evaluation

I included a session on feminist evaluation because UNIFEM addresses the priorities of women in Africa, and the transformative paradigm is partially based on the work of feminist scholars who address theoretical and methodological issues related to discrimination and oppression on the basis of gender. I presented the following set of principles associated with feminist evaluations as they are derived from Western literature in a plenary session (Sielbeck-Bowen et al., 2002):

■ The central focus is on gender inequities that lead to social injustice. Every evaluation should be conducted with an eye toward reversing gender inequities.
■ Discrimination or inequality based on gender is systemic and structural.
■ Evaluation is a political activity; the contexts in which evaluation operates are politicized; and the personal experiences, perspectives, and characteristics evaluators bring to evaluations lead to a particular political stance.
■ The evaluation process can lead to significant negative or positive effects on the people involved in the evaluation.
■ The evaluator must recognize and explore the unique conditions and characteristics of the issue under study; critical self-reflection is necessary.
■ There are multiple ways of knowing; some ways are privileged over others. Transformative knowledge is sought that emanates from an experiential base.

The participants reviewed the principles, after which they considered the following questions: What are the basic principles of feminist evaluation that can shed light on how to do

better evaluation for women? What are the points of resistance associated with feminist principles in evaluation? What are the implications for evaluation practice that can be inferred from feminist principles?

The principles of transformative evaluation are illustrated by the nature of the discussion that occurred in this training session. The participants' discussion of the term "feminist" challenged the appropriateness of its use in the African evaluation context. In their experience, feminism is subject to many different interpretations amongst women's rights advocates. In developing countries, the term feminist may be associated with white women to the neglect of concerns of women of color, or with women who are lesbians. To counteract this more exclusionary interpretation of the term, many of the participants indicated that they were more comfortable with the term "gender-responsive" evaluation rather than feminist evaluation.

Authentic participation by stakeholders in the process of developing implications for evaluation practice is an important principle underlying the transformative paradigm. This principle is illustrated by the contribution by one participant of a method for conducting gender analysis following the United Nations model grounded in a human rights framework (March, Smyth, & Mukhopadhyay, 1999). Such a framework offers a methodology to examine the extent to which women and men have the opportunity to participate in various social, economic, and political activities. A gender analysis begins with diagnostic activities to identify the causes of gender inequality focusing on differential socioeconomic and political status of men and women with regard to the division of labor, access to resources and benefits, and decision-making power. The analysis then proceeds to the identification of the causes of gender gaps using an analytical framework that examines legal and policy frameworks, stakeholder and institutional analyses, and stereotypes associated with decision-making. Finally, plans for interventions are developed to address the causes and gaps. Thus, the workshop participants themselves were able to bring their own resources, expertise, and knowledge into the understanding of doing evaluation within a transformative paradigm.

Reflections

The transformative approach to evaluation is not a defined step by step process. Rather it is a way of thinking about issues of cultural complexity and social transformation within the evaluation context. Consequently, participants who engage in this type of training may feel discomfort because of the lack of specific procedures to conduct a transformative evaluation. However, the provision of opportunities for group processing can be used to support those participants with less tolerance for ambiguity as they work through the application of the principles to their evaluation context. Another challenge associated with this example of training indigenous evaluators using the transformative approach is that the trainers went home and the participants were expected to conduct the evaluation themselves. The UNIFEM staff recognized this challenge and provided additional opportunities for training and support for the group who participated in the South African training.

Weaving the Threads Together

The three examples illustrate differing ways of operationalizing the principles of participation, learning, negotiation, and flexibility. Here we analyze some of the strengths, dilemmas, and challenges encountered in these processes, using meanings of participation, timeframe and resources, audience and purpose, and role and capacities of the evaluation consultant as points of reference.

Participation

Engaging in evaluations such as these is a complex and unpredictable undertaking. While stakeholder participation is generally accepted among evaluators,[8] not everyone agrees with this principle. Therefore how participation is actually implemented will depend on the preferences of the stakeholders, on who is conducting the evaluation, and under what conditions. Our examples illustrate the diversity of interpretation of the term "participation." In empowerment evaluation, "participation" is seen as a means – a practical way to engage stakeholders actively in the process of acquiring and using knowledge for the purposes of program improvement, organizational learning, and achieving outcomes, ownership, and accountability. The MSC approach is driven by the importance of participation in the collaborative process, of the need to share experiences among groups as a grounded way to identify what changes are actually occurring in a project. It fits smoothly with the highly participatory nature of development activities themselves. Transformative evaluation moves to a philosophical and ethical imperative of inclusiveness. "Participation" is understood as essential for the evaluation process to reflect the diversity of stakeholder groups and thus of the perspectives being honored and represented in evaluation findings.

Our challenge is to critically examine not only how participation is operationalized, but also what this really means. It is helpful to draw on the literature from other fields, notably international development, where issues around participation have been actively debated for some time (Absalom, 1995; Cornwall & Pratt, 2003; Mosse, 1994; PLA Notes, 2004; Welbourn, 1991). Cooke & Kothari (2001), for example, raise critical questions about the common assumption that participation is automatically a "good" thing.

They argue that those pushing the "participation" agenda often engage inadequately with issues of power and politics, and that professionals too often treat participation as a technical matter, thereby depoliticizing what is an inherently political process. The authors also raise questions that are salient for evaluators whose goals include empowerment of more marginalized populations. What is the evidence, they ask, that empowerment actually takes place? How do we know what "ownership" is, when it occurs and who has it? Do participants have genuine decision-making authority and if so, which participants, and what accountability mechanisms or processes are there in relation to that authority? They warn against juxtaposing top-down and bottom-up approaches as value-laden and far too simplistic. The mainstreaming and scaling-up of participatory approaches has blurred such divisions and broadens the agenda to encompass issues of governance, policy, and practice.

While these authors are rooted in the field of international development, their critique has direct relevance for evaluators interested in participatory methods. Hickey & Mohan (2004) respond to these critiques and, though they are more optimistic about the potential of participatory approaches to effect genuine transformation, they underline the enormous complexity of engaging in this kind of work. They conclude that we need more conceptual clarity about what participation is and what claims it can (and cannot) make.

The debates about challenges to rigor arising from stakeholder participation are also relevant here, but it is not a matter of either/or, but both/and. The methods outlined in this chapter can usefully complement more traditional approaches, bringing in a learning dimension to an evaluation focused more on judgment or outcomes.

In the empowerment approach, the roles (rights and responsibilities) of funder, community,

and evaluator for each of the 10 principles have been described elsewhere (Fetterman, 2005). Rigor for the MSC method is derived from six mechanisms (Davies & Dart, 2005): thick description via the stories, systematic process of selection by stakeholders, transparency through documentation and sharing, the option of verification through detailed documentation of events and participants, equal expression of views through stories and thus encompassing diverse experiences, and finally checking of the accuracy of the story by the person who "lived the experience." In transformative evaluation, the conscious involvement of diverse stakeholders improves the rigor of the process and the findings in that bias based on an elite perspective alone is avoided.

Timeframe and Resources

The timeframe for participatory evaluation approaches tends to be longer than that for non-participatory approaches. All three approaches regard evaluation as a continuous activity during the life of a project. In practice, this must often be reconciled with the predominance of the parachute-in model, especially in international development evaluation, in which external consultants are hired for their supposed "objectivity" and expertise. Sometimes short term work is all one can do.

In Brazil, the MSC method was explicitly built around creating a continuous flow of information between groups or layers in a project. Thus timeframe here has two connotations – how long is sustained use of the method required and how much time is needed per application of the method. The time needed to apply the method is not long – it is simply a focused discussion that can be incorporated in any other regular meeting that participants might be attending. As for sustained use, this requires more attention to the organizational embedding of the method, as mentioned above and pursued below.

In addition to the time factor, important evaluative resources in these types of evaluation include specific competencies and an active presence. In the short run, the time investment needed to establish interest, build basic understanding of evaluation, negotiate roles, and co-design the process is a drain on resources. These elements, however, are critical for building relationships of mutual trust and respect, and ending up with a feasible, acceptable, and appropriate evaluation process. In the long term, one could argue that the resources needed may be reduced if stakeholder capacity for self-evaluation is successfully built. Major challenges to these long-term aspirations include the commitment needed by staff and staff turnover. Much work can be undone if/when key players leave, which is likely to be inevitable in some settings (organizational), perhaps less so in others (community). "Strong convictions in the value of community involvement will be essential to overcome the inevitable obstacles" (Guijt, 2000, p. 216). Often forgotten are the transaction costs of non-staff participants, such as neglect of other activities, cash contributions, or social position (Guijt, forthcoming) These costs must be recognized, made explicit and any compensation options agreed to; otherwise the process may be jeopardized in the long term.

With the MSC example, a specific competency required was organizational savvy. In Brazil, local and inter-organizational politics played a major role in stopping the process, however, once the players changed. What endures are people's "own systems and discussion cultures" and the challenge is to build collective sustained interest in reflecting on these in a critical way, and foster an openness to different ways of doing things. Thus, while sharing personal and organizational stories creates an opportunity for people to feel heard and to find the common threads that allow

them to move from the particular to broader understanding, if these people are not in positions of relative power in their organizations or other information needs dominate, then the MSC method will be difficult to embed.

Transformative evaluation requires being in the field, engaging actively with participants. This involves personal engagement, most particularly a willingness and interest in learning about other cultures and recognizing the challenges of being an outsider. The demands for cultural competence are personally and professionally complex, requiring the evaluation consultant to engage in an examination of his/her own assumptions, location, and privilege.

As with the other examples, empowerment evaluation sets out to create an atmosphere of honest, self-critical, and mutual support. It also rewards continuous quality improvement. Only in this situation, the authors argue, will participants be willing to share the failures and dilemmas that foster personal and organizational learning. Imm, Chinman, and Wandersman note the importance of an internal dedicated champion, a conclusion supported by others (Gaventa, Creed & Morrissey, 1998). The inevitability of stakeholder turnover, and thus ongoing commitment to maintaining a critically reflective culture, remains a challenge for the sustainability of this work.

Audience and Purpose

Who are the appropriate audiences and purposes for these evaluations? Imm, Chinman, and Wandersman propose that empowerment evaluation can be used in almost any program or policy setting where key stakeholders want to be effective and achieve results. The approach is oriented around the empowerment of program participants and the capacity building of program staff.

The MSC method has gained a wide following over the past decade,[9] and it is being used in large-scale globally operating organizations as well as local projects. Each application of the method is unique and depends on the prime purpose – is it about gauging experiences of managers, of dairy farmers, of peasants in Brazil or of teachers in South Africa? However, what is *not* negotiable is that the source of the stories of change are the people who have lived the experiences. In that sense, inclusion of the lived perspective is inherent in the method – and not an option. From this array of experiences, Davies & Dart (2005) summarize the core purposes and characteristics of MSC:

- identifies unexpected changes
- surfaces the values prevalent in an organization
- does not require specific monitoring or evaluation skills
- encourages analysis as well as data collection thus building capacities
- helps paint a rich picture of diverse changes
- enables the monitoring of initiatives that do not lend themselves easily to evaluation via predefined outcomes

Transformative evaluation consciously tries to represent all stakeholders, especially those not traditionally included. It works especially well when there are power differences among project administrators, staff, and participants. An open and frank discussion of the need to be inclusive, the criteria for the inclusion of participants, and issues of power differentials are part of the transformative evaluation process. Thus, the evaluation consultant can play the role of provocateur, challenging those with power to invite and supporting those with less power in the program context.

Rethinking the Role and Capacities of the Evaluation Consultant

The methodology in each example implies a particular role and set of skills on the part of the evaluation consultant. In all three cases,

the authors acted as methodology guides and process facilitators rather than as classical evaluators who designed, implemented, judged and documented. The importance of being flexible, prepared to "work in the moment," within a broad framework and set of principles, cannot be overemphasized. Recognizing the tacit knowledge that participants bring to the process moves the evaluation consultant to help make this understanding more explicit. Thus, we become facilitators who can help put sometimes sensitive issues onto the table. In doing so, we may choose to share some of our own experience – personal as well as professional – as a way of building trust and rapport. In this way, the evaluation consultant also becomes a participant. This does not mean that we cease to be experts, and outsiders, but that we enact that role in a way that attempts to balance these functions.

The evaluation consultants worked in teams in each of these approaches. They recognized the complexity and value of ongoing interaction with others as a collective process, not only for those with whom they worked, but for themselves as well.

This chapter has aimed to illustrate, in some detail, how one might go about doing an evaluation for the particular purposes mentioned – practice improvement, assessing lived experience, and social justice. Our examples capture the complexity of diversity – of ideas, culture, interpretation, and experience. They offer a range of ways to think about evaluation and a rich array of techniques to consider when conducting evaluations under differing circumstances.

The examples are clearly far more than technical tasks. They require that the evaluation consultant is politically astute about the challenges of participatory processes, has the organizational savvy to understand where adaptations are needed, and is most patient during implementation. The consultant's flexibility is a strength, with the resulting complexity comprising the challenge. The key to effectiveness is an integrative and adaptive use of methodology, as each context and purpose and mix of stakeholders will demand new configurations. It calls for creativity and reflexivity, without compromising the groundedness in the core principles of participation, learning, negotiation, and flexibility.

Notes

1. We use the term "evaluation consultant" rather than "evaluator" here, because it more accurately describes what we do. Evaluation consultants work with groups of people to develop, deliver, and/or improve their programs, while evaluators focus on judging the merit and worth of a program.

2. This case example is authored by Pamela S. Imm, Matthew Chinman, and Abraham Wandersman.

3. This case example was authored by Irene Guijt.

4. A surprise signals that that the person is experiencing incongruity between his/her assumptions of what *should* be happening and what *is* happening. Thus it provides an opportunity for revising assumptions.

5. This section draws on Davies (1998) and Davies and Dart (2005).

6. This case example was authored by Donna M. Mertens.

7. The APA developed guidelines for four specific groups: Asian American/Pacific Islander populations, persons of African descent, Hispanics, and American–Indian participants.

8. At least in the US. They are included in both the Joint Committee's Standards and in the Guiding Principles, for example. See www.eval.org, for details.

9. See http://groups.vahoo.com/group/Most SignificantChanges/.

References

Absalom, E. et al. (1995). Sharing our concerns and looking to the future. *PLA Notes*, 22, 5–10.

Altman, D. G. (1995). Sustaining interventions in community systems: On the relationship between researchers and communities. *Health Psychology*, 14, 526–536.

American Psychological Association (2002). Guidelines on multicultural education, training, research, practice, and organizational change for psychologists. Washington, DC.

AS-PTA & IIED (1998). Monitoramento Participativo da Agricultura Sustentável: O Quinto Passo em Paraíba. AS-PTA, Esperança and IIED, London. Workshop Report, 33 p.

Backer, T. (1991). *Drug Abuse Technology Transfer.* DHHS Publication [ADM] 91–1764. Rockville, MD: National Institute on Drug Abuse.

Backer, T. (2001). Finding the Balance: Program Fidelity and Adaptation in Substance Abuse Prevention. CSAP.

Cooke, W. & Kothari, U. (2001). *Participation: The new tyranny?* London: Zed.

Cornwall, A. & Pratt, G. (eds) (2003). *Pathways to Participation: Reflections on PRA.* London: Intermediate Technology Publications.

Dart, J. J., Drysdale, G., Cole, D., & Saddington, M. (2000). 'The most significant change approach for monitoring an Australian Extension project', In *PLA Notes*, 38, 47–53. London: International Institute for Environment and Development.

Davies, Rick (1998). An evolutionary approach to organisational learning: an experiment by an NGO in Bangladesh. *Impact Assessment and Project Appraisal*, 16(3), 243–250. See also http://www.swan.ac.uk/cds/rd/ccdb.htm.

Davies, Rick and J. Dart. (2005). *The 'Most Significant Change' (MSC) Technique: A Guide to its Use.* Available online at http://www.mande.co.uk/docs/MSCGuide.htm. Funded by nine donors in UK, Denmark, Australia, New Zealand and the USA.

Estrella, M. & Gaventa, J. (1998). Who counts reality? Participatory monitoring and evaluation: A literature review. *IDS Working Paper No. 70.* Brighton: IDS.

Fetterman, D. (2005). A window into the heart and soul of empowerment evaluation. In D. Fetterman & A. Wandersman (eds) *Empowerment Evaluation Principles in Practice.* New York: Guildford Press.

Gaventa, J., Creed, V., & Morrissey, J., (1998). Scaling up: Participatory monitoring and evaluation of a federal empowerment program. In E. Whitmore (ed.) *Understanding and Practicing Participatory Evaluation, New Directions for Evaluation*, No. 80. San Francisco: Jossey-Bass.

Guijt, I. (1998). Tracking agricultural change together: participatory monitoring of sustainable agriculture initiatives in Brazil. Paper submitted to the AFSR-E Conference. Pretoria, South Africa.

Guijt, I. (2000). Methodological issues in participatory monitoring and evaluation. In M. Estrella (ed.) *Learning from Change: Issues and experiences in participatory monitoring and evaluation.* London: Intermediate Technology Publications; Ottawa: International Development Research Centre.

Guijt, I. (2005). Strengthening a critical link in adaptive collaborative management: The potential of monitoring. In I. Guijt (ed.) '*Triggering Adaptation in ACM: Learning through collaborative monitoring.* CIFOR.

Hall, G. E. & Hord, S. M. (2001). *Implementing Change.* Boston: Allyn and Bacon.

Hickey, S. & Mohan, G. (eds) (2004). *Participation – from Tyranny to Transformation? Exploring new approaches to participation in development.* London: Zed.

Kolb, D. 1984. *Experiential Learning: Experience as the source of learning and development.* Englewood Cliffs, NI Prentice-Hall.

Livet, M. & Wandersman, A. (2005). Organizational functioning: Facilitating effective interventions and increasing the odds of programming success. In D. M. Fetterman & A. Wandersman (eds) *Empowerment Evaluation Principles in Practice* (pp. 123–154). New York: Guilford.

March, C., Smyth, I., & Mukhopadhyay, M. (1999). *A Guide to Gender-Analysis Frameworks.* New York: United Nations.

Mertens, D. M. (2005). *Research and Evaluation Methods in Education and Psychology: Integrating diversity with quantitative, qualitative, and mixed methods*, 2nd edition. Thousand Oaks, CA: Sage Publications.

Mosse, D. (1994). Authority, gender and knowledge: theoretical reflections on the practice of Participatory Rural Appraisal. *Development and Change*, 25(3), 497–525.

Participatory Learning & Action (2004). Special issue on critical reflections, future directions, October. IIED.

Patton, M. Q. (2002). *Qualitative research and evaluation methods* (second edition). Newbury Park: Sage.

Santa Barbara Fighting Back (SBFB) (2001). *Measuring up: Facing the challenges of substance abuse.* Santa Barbara: SBFB.

Sielbeck-Bowen, K. A., Brisolara, S., Seigart, D., Tishler, C., & Whitmore, E. (2002). Exploring feminist evaluation: the ground from which we rise. In D. Seigart & S. Brisolara (eds) *Feminist Evaluation: Explorations and experiences. New Directions for Evaluation*, N. 96. San Francisco: Jossey-Bass.

Skager, R. & Austin, G. (2002). Eigth biennial statewide survey of drug and alcohol use among California students in grades 7, 9, and 11, Winter 1999–2000. Sacramento, CA: Office of the Attorney General.

Sue, D. W. & Sue, D. (2003). *Counseling the Culturally Diverse: Theory and practice*, 4th edition. (pp. 17–18). John Wiley & Sons.

United Nations Development Fund for Women (2003). *UNIFEM Annual Report 2002–2003.* New York: United Nations.

United Nations, Office of the High Commissioner for Human Rights (1979). Convention on the Elimination of All Forms of Discrimination against Women. General Assembly resolution 34/180 of 18 December 1979. http://www.unhchr.ch/html/menu3/b/e1cedaw.htm. Accessed February 12, 2004.

Wandersman, A. & Florin, P. (2003). Community interventions and effective prevention: Bringing researchers/evaluators, funders and practitioners together for accountability. *American Psychologist*, 58, 441–448.

Wandersman, A., Snell-Johns, J., Lentz, B. E., Fetterman, D. M., Keener, D. C., Livet, M., Imm, P., & Flaspohler, P. (2005). The principles of empowerment evaluation. In D. M. Fetterman & A. Wandersman (eds) *Empowerment Evaluation Principles in Practice* (pp. 27–41). New York: Guilford.

Welbourn, A. (1991). RRA and the analysis of difference. *RRA Notes*, 14, 14-23. IIED. Sustainable Agriculture Program. http://blds.ids.ac.uk/cgi-bin2/dbtcgi.exe

16

MANAGING EVALUATIONS

Robert Walker and Michael Wiseman

Assumptions and Approach

It is assumed that the policy community has accepted that public policies should be evaluated[1] and this chapter is therefore about getting evaluations done rather than ensuring that evaluation occurs.

Within this brief, the focus is on evaluations that operate in real time and concern policy processes that are not, at the time the evaluation begins, finished. In such circumstances the evaluator has no control over the timetable or schedule, and this has important implications for evaluation management. This kind of evaluation is often termed prospective or *programme evaluation* and addresses questions such as "Will this policy work?", "What policy would work?" and "Can we make this policy work and how?", Evaluation thus defined is a practical tool of policy-making designed to inform current or near-future decisions rather than an academic exercise intended primarily to shape longer-term policy concerns and understandings. Space is the only reason for limiting coverage in this way, and many of the issues raised are equally relevant for other kinds of evaluation discussed elsewhere in this volume.

Managing an evaluation is similar to managing any project. However, since libraries are already stacked ceiling high with books on project management of both the "how to do it" and "principles of" varieties, a different approach is taken that focuses on context and on the management of relationships. The chapter is structured with reference to a relational model of evaluation comprising four communities: policy-makers and shakers; service-users who constitute the target of policy; evaluators and the wider research community; and the media (Figure 16.1). Different degrees of power and dependency are implicit in the relationships among these four sets of policy actors that often, through design or happenstance, become apparent during the management of evaluations.

Certain of the relationships depicted in Figure 16.1 exist by definition. Others are a requirement for effective management, others are desirable, and yet others are possible and may have either beneficial or deleterious consequences that have to be managed.

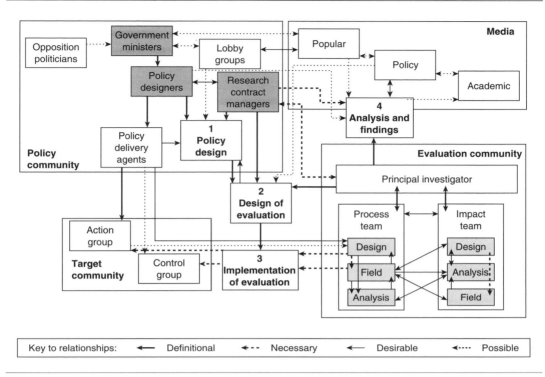

Figure 16.1   Relational model of the management of policy evaluations

Successful management entails fully exploiting definitional, necessary, and desirable relationships while being appropriately responsive to possible relationships when they occur.

The model focuses on four elements in the policy evaluation process: policy design, design of the evaluation, implementation, and analysis and dissemination. Each element is usually conceptualized as a sequential stage in the evaluative process that occurs in a fixed order. In reality, however, evaluation is often recursive rather than linear, with each element shaped by reference to the other three.

The four elements are considered in turn while making clear the connections with the rest. Each element is viewed from the varying perspectives of actors in the four relevant communities, drawing attention to their differing views and interests and to the fact

that the management of policy evaluation is seldom exclusively technical or susceptible to Fordist or bureaucratic strategies and procedures. As already noted, the management of evaluation is primarily about managing these different perspectives and is easiest when consensus exists or is attainable among the policy actors. However, reality is often less about eliciting consensus and more about reconciling diversity and difference among, and sometimes within, the four relevant communities.

Neither the model nor this chapter does full justice to diversity within the various communities. The needs, resources, constraints and understanding of evaluation vary dramatically between central, state and local governments. Likewise, there are important differences within the evaluation community among, for example: commercial consultants; specialist policy evaluation firms, some being for profit and others not; research centres, both university based and independent; and academics acting as contractors and reviewers. Similarly, the perspectives and responses of service-users are likely to differ from those of taxpayers. These within-community differences have purchase on all aspects of the management of evaluation but for economy are referred to only where unavoidable.

To the extent that any one perspective is prioritized in this chapter, it is that of the evaluator and the evaluative community, the perspective of those most likely to use this *Handbook*. On most occasions it will be the evaluator who is held responsible should an evaluation fail to deliver valid results, even though they will seldom have had the lion's share of influence or authority. It is therefore greatly in their interests to seek to manage the relationships in ways that promote effective evaluation. Hopefully, experience drawn together in this chapter will aid readers to achieve this goal; it derives largely from the authors' involvement in evaluations of statutory employment and welfare policies in the USA and Britain. However, readers need to be aware of bias introduced by this emphasis, since institutional context matters and preferred modes of evaluation vary among jurisdictions (Nolan & Wong, 2004). The USA is sometimes considered to be the market leader in policy evaluation, especially in social experimentation, while the British government has, since 1997, sought to implement a model of evidence-based policy-making (Smith, 2004; Walker, 2004).

Managing Policy Design

Only a minority of government policies have ever been formally evaluated and very few have been evaluated prior to implementation. The reason is partly historical: many policies were first implemented before the existence of an evaluative infrastructure comprising methodology, technical expertise, political interest and administrative structures for commissioning and receiving evaluations. It was only in the 1970s that the technical feasibility of prospective evaluation was demonstrated with the execution of the negative income tax experiments in the US (Watts & Rees, 1977), and in Britain it was not until the 1990s that political support for evaluation emerged with the concern over excessive public expenditure and the adoption of private sector audit and managerial techniques (the so-called New Public Sector Management). In 1997 the UK Labour Government committed itself to piloting policies prior to full implementation (Walker, 2001).

Although an over-simplification, Figure 16.1 assigns government ministers and their staffs to pole position in the design of policy. While subject to influence from pressure groups, media and the electorate, politicians in government are also often ideologically committed to particular policies that they may have been mandated to implement. As such, they are generally keen to implement policy at the earliest opportunity (and/or when politically opportune) and are not likely to be much enamoured by the prospect that evaluation might prove their ideas to be wrong (Blunkett, 2000; Walker, 2004). In this regard, it is significant that the commitment to evaluation has generally not come from policy ministers but those with a strategic overview. In Britain, evaluation was first promoted by HM Treasury, the agency responsible for adjudicating competing expenditure claims from departments within the same government, while the widespread piloting of new welfare policies by US states resulted, under the so-called waiver system, from an obligation imposed on states by federal government to demonstrate the cost effectiveness of any departure from federal guidelines (Gueron, 2003).

Politicians frequently have to respond quickly to crises and unanticipated events that leave inadequate time for effective evaluation. Officials tasked with designing the details of policy and its implementation have to accommodate both the bidding of their political bosses and practical realities that are often well-articulated by staff and organizations charged with implementation and delivery. This typically results in complex policies with multiple, often imprecisely defined objectives that are variously tailored to different subgroups. Similarly, implementation is often intricately varied as the product of myriad compromises. Such policies are very difficult to evaluate and constrain the use of experimental and quasi-experimental designs (Table 16.1).

Government research staff are likely to have sight of a policy only late in its development when the principal design features and implementation timetables are already fixed. Their task, either in isolation or with the evaluation community, is limited to determining how best to evaluate the policy in question.[2] With limited status or "firepower" within the bureaucratic hierarchy, they are severely constrained in their ability to meet the aspirations of the wider evaluation community, namely: simple policies with clear, preferably measurable, objectives; adequate planning horizons and resources; and stability in both the policy environment and implementation.

If the typical model is that of policy-driven evaluation, the more successful one (from an evaluation perspective) has been evaluation-led policy in which a policy experiment is designed to test a nascent policy concept or strategy. This approach is strongly represented in the USA (Exemplar 16.1) but by only one fully worked evaluation in Britain (Table 16.1).[3] Evaluation-led policy increases the chances of obtaining precise estimates of impact by explicitly designing the policy and its implementation to be amenable to effective evaluation. Evaluators are typically involved from the beginning of policy development (or closely thereafter) and often have a quasi-management role to ensure that day-to-day implementation of the policy does not corrupt any aspect of the evaluative design. (The latter role is generally performed by technical advisers who may be recruited from the policy implementation agency but are employed by and report to the evaluation team.) Policies tested in this way are necessarily simple, and subtle changes to fit local circumstance or unanticipated developments are rarely possible. From the perspective of policy-makers, this may be a disadvantage, but the real aim of such experiments is to evaluate an idealized policy model or policy principle rather than a specific implementation.[4]

Wisconsin New Hope Project, 1994–98

Aim: To demonstrate the administrative feasibility and to measure the effects of a programme of earnings supplements and other work supports intended to guarantee that families with an adult employed full time (at least 30 hours per week) would gain income in excess of poverty, health insurance, and necessary child care. The programme was voluntary and targeted on families with incomes at or below 150% of the US poverty standard. "Community Service Jobs" were provided for participants unable to find other employment.

(Continued)

(Continued)

Management: New Hope was designed and fielded by a private, community-based organization and funded with a combination of private and public funds. The evaluation was similarly funded. Lead contractor: MDRC, New York.

Design: Classical random assignment in two sites in Milwaukee, Wisconsin with a total 678 participants assigned to the programme group and 679 to a control with impact assessed as the difference in mean wage income, use of alternative benefits (Aid to Families with Dependent Children), and various family–child-related outcomes between the two groups over two- and five-year horizons. The evaluation includes cost-benefit analysis from participant and social perspectives as well as studies of process based on survey and interview data collected from participants and project staff.

Selected management issues

1. *Recruitment*: Since New Hope was a voluntary (not a mandatory) programme, it was necessary to recruit participants. The New Hope "offer", which combined an out-of-poverty guarantee with random assignment, proved difficult to communicate and generated some community hostility. Ultimately, most persons attending New Hope orientations applied for the programme, and random assignment was successfully implemented.
2. *Explanation of benefits*: The New Hope earnings supplement, health insurance, and child care benefit were all provided on a sliding scale, and the relationship between own income and benefits proved puzzling to participants, especially those accustomed to the stable monthly payments characteristic of traditional welfare.
3. *Chaotic counterfactual*: The New Hope offer lasted three years, with some benefits being paid through 1998. During this period Wisconsin introduced substantial changes in its social assistance system that raised barriers to access and work requirements for both applicants and recipients. Since families in the control group with children were subject to these changes should they have needed support, interpretation of the experimental/control differences in outcomes is complicated.
4. *Political peril*: National welfare reform in 1996 substantially altered the fiscal relationship between the federal government and the state of Wisconsin. The change increased the authority of state government over project financing and threatened early termination. A political compromise, involving federal support for another demonstration viewed as important by the state's political administration, allowed New Hope completion.

Sources: Brock et al., (1997), Bos et al., (1999).

While there is limited scope for individual evaluators to influence the design of policy ahead of evaluation, collectively they may be able to help shape the culture of policy-making. Placing social scientists in influential policy positions can be important. In Britain,

EXEMPLAR 16.1   Selected UK Policy Evaluations, 1997–2006

Initiative name	Policy content
NDYP: New Deal for Young People	Compulsory job search and activation policies organized through a caseworker (called a personal advisor)
NDLP: New Deal for Lone Parents	Voluntary employment orientated advice and support provided by personal advisors
NDDP: New Deal for Disabled People	Voluntary access to advice and rehabilitation services provided by a person advisor
EMA: Educational Maintenance Allowance	Means-tested financial assistance to young people to stay on in school
ERA: Employment Retention and Advancement	Mixed voluntary and mandatory financial incentives and services to increase employment and retention

Characteristics of the initiative	NDYP	NDLP	NDDP	EMA	ERA
Multiple policy models being tested	✔	✔		✔	✔
No clear policy model			✔		
Multiple policy objectives	✔	✔	✔	✔	✔
Macroeconomic objectives	✔	✔	✔		
Behavioural objectives	✔	✔	✔	✔	✔
Different modes of implementation	✔	✔	✔	✔	
Macroeconomic counter-indicators foreseen	✔		✔		
Impact small to modest	✔	✔	✔	?	?

Policy environments	NDYP	NDLP	NDDP	EMA	ERA
Policy implementation ahead of evaluation results	✔	✔	✔	✔	
High political profile	✔✔	✔	✔	✔	
Joint policy responsibility	✔	✔	✔		
Implementation by intermediate agency	✔	✔	✔	✔	
Substantial exogenous change occurs during evaluation	✔	✔	✔	✔	?
Multiplicity of adjacent policy changes	✔	✔	✔	✔	✔

(Continued)

EXEMPLAR 16.1   (Continued)

Evaluation process	NDYP	NDLP	NDDP	EMA	ERA
Location of pilot areas determined ahead of tendering	✔	✔	✔	✔	✔
Evaluative design devised ahead of tendering	✔	✔	✔	✔	✔
Evaluation period short in relation to policy objectives	✔	✔	✔	✔	
Contract let by competitive tender	✔	✔	✔	✔	✔
Design phase 4–5 weeks	✔	✔	✔	✔	✔
Evaluation undertaken by consortium					
Number of organizations	7	3	5	4	6

Evaluation strategy	NDYP	NDLP	NDDP	EMA	ERA
External consultation on design					✔
Quasi-experimental:	✔	✔	✔	✔	
Matched areas		✔		✔	
National control			✔		
Longitudinal control	✔				
Individual matching		✔			
Natural random assignment component		✔	✔		
Random assignment		✔[a]		✔[b]	✔
Summative evaluation	✔	✔	✔	✔	✔
Formative (process) evaluation	✔	✔	✔	✔	✔
Multimethod:	✔	✔	✔	✔	✔
Interview surveys	✔	✔	✔	✔	✔
Individuals (approximate sample size)	6,000	4,300	4,400	19,000	
Follow-up interviews	✔	✔	✔	✔	✔
Employers	✔	✔			
Analysis of administrative data	✔	✔	✔[c]	✔	✔
Depth interviews	✔	✔	✔	✔	✔
Focus groups	?	✔	✔		
Ethnography	✔	?	✔	✔	
Local labour market studies	✔	✔	✔		
Event history analysis	?	✔	✔		
Econometric modelling	✔	✔		✔	✔
Cost–benefit analysis	✔	✔	✔[c]		✔

[a]Initially proposed, not implemented.
[b]Included as an option in the invitation to tender, not implemented.
[c]Undertaken internally, separate from the evaluation contract.

attempts have been made to increase the influence of government research staff, creating a post of Chief Research Officer with a cross-departmental remit and locating research staff alongside policy-makers rather than in separate professional divisions. Despite a predilection for generalist rather than specialist skills, it is now accepted that all officials in HM Treasury should have economics training, and since 1997 a series of handbooks have been issued to British civil servants emphasizing the importance of evaluation in policy design (Cabinet Office, 1999, 2000, 2004).

It is probably not coincidental that the principle of evaluation-led policy is better established in the USA where the practice is for incoming administrations to replace the top tiers of federal officials with people of a similar ideological persuasion, many drawn from universities. However, the professionalization of policy-making in the US has also been important with the development of masters and doctoral programmes in public administration and public policy providing prospective officials with the skills for rational, positivist policy-making that prioritizes the need for evidence and information. Similar orientations have shaped the competition for influence on federal and local governance among think tanks, interest groups, for-profit companies and not-for-profit agencies, some of whom are able to promote their claims by reference to evaluated implementations of their policy ideas. The success in delivering robust findings of interest to the policy community has generated goodwill, further commissions and the accumulation of expertise with people skilled at working at the interface between social science and policy development.

It is important, though, not to exaggerate the influence of the evaluation community in the US nor to over-emphasize evaluation-led policy. Most evaluation remains post-hoc— which is probably no longer true for new policies in Britain – and the more politically important the policy, arguably the less it is shaped by evaluation.[5]

Managing the Design of Policy Evaluation

Good design lies at the heart of effective management; without it, the chances of a successful outcome are low even with exemplary project management. Yet the competing interests of the relevant communities often generate circumstances that inhibit good design with the result that the evaluator is often left negotiating for the least bad methodological solution.

Most policy evaluations of any scale are commissioned by government departments (or their agencies) and let through competitive tender in both the USA and Britain. The time allowed for tendering is generally between four and six calendar weeks, which favours organizations with the capacity to fit the design activity around existing work. Typically the process entails advertising a competition and/or mailing an invitation to tender (Request for Proposals – RFPs – in the US) to potential contenders, an oral briefing for those expressing intent to tender, preparation and submission of tenders, interviews with short listed contenders, post-tender negotiations with the successful contenders and (as good practice) feedback to the vanquished. Often the process is constrained by procurement requirements that tend to lead to formulaic documentation and procedures. Personnel drafting an invitation to tender may not be fully cognizant with the political context of the evaluation or fail to appreciate its significance either for the evaluation design or the evaluator. Hence the invitation to tender invariably warrants multiple very careful readings by all parties that will typically yield a list of issues for clarification.

Sometimes evaluation contracts may be negotiated with a single contractor chosen for their particular expertise, typically though not always from a pool of potential contractors that have all passed an entry competition. (Both the US Department of Health and Human Services, Office of the Assistant Secretary for Policy Evaluation and Design [ASPE] and the UK Department of Work and Pensions operate a preferred contractor model, the latter commissioning virtually all its research and evaluation from around 60 organizations and individuals included in a "Framework Agreement".) Occasionally, evaluators are themselves proactive and take on responsibility for soliciting funding for both the implementation of a policy and its evaluation; this is more common with evaluation-led policy-making.

Major constraints on good design typically comprise irreconcilable evaluation goals, tight time horizons, restricted resources and the rules of procurement process. The art of managing design is to shape the evaluation tightly to fit the conceptual space defined by the constraints and, if possible, to expand the space by negotiating a relaxation in the constraints.

Multiple Objectives and Requirements

Whereas the evaluator might wish to optimize a design with respect to a single objective, the contracting agency may have mixed motives and varying demands. Beyond (hopefully) wanting to know whether a policy works or is working (impact assessment), the contracting agency may wish to understand how a policy works or fails to work, formative (or process) evaluation that is typically more reliant on qualitative research. Whereas results from impact analyses, if positive, are useful in defending policies from criticism, knowledge from formative studies is often more important during the scaling-up of policy experiments to full implementation, when fine-tuning existing implementation, and in policy learning when other jurisdictions seek to emulate the policies evaluated (Greenberg, Mandell, & Onstott, 2000).

Politicians and officials may be unclear or confused about what they want from evaluation. They may hope to demonstrate that a policy works rather than determine whether or not it does. They may be keener to learn how to fine-tune and implement a policy rather than wait to determine whether it has the desired effect. They may be eager to cherry-pick components of a policy or implementation without paying much attention to the context that allows the cherries to appear ripe for picking. They may wish to do all these things, despite some being mutually exclusive, or be uncertain how evaluation can assist at all, following the letter of the policy-making guidelines rather than appreciating their intent. Quite often aspirations and expectations will change with events and personnel with sometimes disastrous consequences for evaluation (Exemplar 16.2).

New Deal for Disabled People (NDDP) Personal Advisor Pilots, 1998–2001

Aim: Initially "to test how disabled people can be helped into work" with 15 specific objectives grouped into three sets concerned respectively with: the specification of implementation models; their impact on employment and well-being; and lessons for national implementation.

Management: Commissioned and funded by the UK Department for Social Security; Lead contractor: Centre for Research in Social Policy, Loughborough University with four partners.

Design: Quasi-experiment with implementations in 12 areas matched against a national sample of disabled people clustered according to criteria used to select the implementation sites; a two-wave interview survey with two cohorts of programme participants (4,790 respondents) and non-participants (620) in the programme areas and single interviews with the national sample (4,390); a natural experiment in which persons randomly invited to join the programme were to be compared with those not yet invited; a survey of employers; and process evaluation comprising qualitative interviews with participants, non-participants, staff and employers.

Selected management issues

1. *Budget surprise*: Tendered competitively, the contract budget was reduced by 58% during post-tender negotiations. The survey with employers was abandoned and remaining surveys halved in size, preventing evaluation of the separate implementation models. Greater emphasis was given to process evaluation.
2. *Lagging take-up*: Recruitment in response to letters of invitation was very slow and, combined with a fixed research period, led to the abandonment of the two-stage cohort design. A single two-wave survey was undertaken instead with date of application treated as an independent variable.
3. *Contamination*: A significant number of participants learned about NDDP by word of mouth rather than from the letter of invitation, which, combined with low uptake, destroyed the natural experiment. Greater reliance had to be based on the national comparison survey.
4. *Shifting objectives*: Change of ministers (politicians) resulted in a shift of emphasis away from discovering how best to help people into employment towards getting as many as possible into work. The early months of survey samples were abandoned and the sampling ratios in subsequent months increased.
5. *Rush to implement*: Within a year of commencing the research, policy ministers had determined the basic design of the national scheme to supersede the pilots and the impact evaluation became largely irrelevant. The national comparison sample was used as a baseline survey for the national implementation, the detailed design of which was informed by the early process evaluation.

Sources: Sainsbury (2004); Walker (2000a); Loumidis et al., (2001).

Frequently, politicians commissioning evaluations will demand results quickly and may even prioritize timely results over robust ones if evidence is needed to support a political argument. Similarly, they will probably be keen to see preliminary and/or provisional results that may sometimes be offered by the evaluator as a bargaining counter to secure additional time for the full evaluation. Politicians and officials will typically insist on measures of intermediate outcomes, namely changes in the type, volume and quality of services, as well as final outcomes appertaining to the overt, and sometimes the covert, objectives of the policy. They will often also be interested in the effect of the intervention on subgroups of the target population.

Government agencies are likely to be risk-averse and to reject methodologies considered to be untested. They are also likely to wish to avoid controversy in the execution of research. In Britain, for example, the ethics of random assignment are still a matter of some contention and several such evaluations have been dropped on Ministerial dictate.[6] Government agencies will also be sensitive to concerns of staff and non-governmental organizations (NGOs) engaged in the delivery of policy. These are likely to focus on the need to avoid the evaluation contributing significantly to the workload of staff, to ensure confidentiality for staff and customers, to avoid direct criticism of work practices and to make certain that the customer base is not alienated.

The evaluator needs to be aware how all the above considerations apply to a particular evaluation, and what priority is attached to each by the various policy actors. This may require specific investigative inquiry as well as general intelligence best acquired by active, long-term exposure to the policy environment in question.

Cost and Quality

From the perspective of managing design, timing and cost are the most important considerations after clarifying objectives. Timing is almost invariably included in the invitation to tender, although often without much precision and with a focus on the timing of outputs rather than inputs. Often the cost, depending on competition law and acquired practice, is not.

Arguments as to whether an invitation to tender should include a guideline price or some other indication of the funding available are complex and differ from the perspectives of the commissioners and potential contractors. The former will wish to obtain the evaluation at the lowest possible cost consistent with some quality threshold; by not indicating a price, they can capitalize on the joint expertise in the tender field to make judgments on resource requirements and quality thresholds. However, because quality choices are matters of judgment, the range of possible solutions is enormous. While there are conventions relating to the precision of estimates that may be used to fix sample sizes, there is more debate about acceptable rates of survey response and sample attrition and disagreement about the role and scale of formative evaluation.

Not surprisingly, contractors generally prefer to be given some indication of the price or scale of the evaluation (SRA, 2002). They respond to concerns that all contractors will bid just short of the guideline price, thereby increasing the cost of the evaluation, by arguing that value for money is the most appropriate selection criterion and that a guideline price reinforces good practice in procurement. Walker (2000a) provides an example of the perils of tendering blind on price. The winning consortium in a competition to evaluate a UK welfare to work initiative for disabled persons were informed that their successful bid overshot the budget by 72 percent. Paring down the design by halving sample sizes reduced the precision of the estimates to the point at which an alternative design could have been a better option.

Determining the Design

While textbooks insist that good design results from careful matching of methods to objectives, subject to immutable constraints, the design of evaluations is often prespecified in the invitation to tender, especially when commissioned by government agencies. Moreover, many of the constraints are exogenous to the research problem and imposed by political considerations, bureaucratic regulation and happenstance.

Circumstances permitting, the prescribed design for the evaluation of a welfare policy is likely in the USA to be randomized controlled trial (RCT or RFT, randomized field trial), whereas in Britain it will be some form of quasi-experiment often entailing control areas.[7] Designs in contracts let by not-for-profit organizations and other NGOs may be less well specified, not least because they may have less access to social science expertise and less experience of commissioning evaluations. In such cases, expectations can sometimes wildly exceed what is achievable both in methodological terms and with respect to cost. Contenders may well have to spend considerable time in dialogue with the commissioning organization to ascertain their needs and to develop an appropriate response even when the contract value is low (which may deter contenders from competing). Indeed, some evaluative models that are well suited to the evaluation of small-scale initiatives without the prospect of a control group (for example, theory of change [Rogers et al., 2000] and action research [Lewin, 1946; Winter, 1996]) build this initial consultation or consultancy period into the main contract.

The choice of an RCT design has profound implications for the management of an evaluation (see below). Whereas other methods entail an essentially passive and benign relationship with members of a control group who may not even be aware of the policy experiment, with random assignment controls have first to be actively recruited into the experiment and then denied access to the policy provisions being allocated (cf. Exemplar 16.1,

The Wisconsin New Hope Project).[8] Extra resources and systems are required in order to explain the principles to staff, participants in the experiment and to other relevant policy communities, to implement random assignment and to manage and monitor its efficacy. Contenders have to convince the commissioning agency that they have the ability to manage the politics and practice of random assignment, typically by reference to past experience.

Potential contractors face a harsh dilemma when confronted by a detailed design in the invitation to tender that they consider to be suboptimal. The presumption must be that the commissioning body has given considerable thought to the design and is committed to it.[9] Rather than risk ruling themselves out of the competition, the time-honoured strategy is for contenders to cost the specified design but also to argue cogently that an alternative design is to be preferred. This entails additional work and runs the risk that the alternative design will be rejected with the contract being awarded to a competitor or, perhaps worse, that the contender will win the contract (since they demonstrated creativity) but be asked to implement the original design (when the choice that they confront is between principle and pecuniary reward). Pre-specifying the design in detail prior to tendering constrains the expertise that is brought to bear on the problem and reduces the dimensions upon which contenders can be differentiated, in effect transforming the tendering process into an exercise in pricing.

In sum, design is born from three sets of constraints: those that circumscribe the evaluation; those that derive from the competitive procurement process; and those that limit the creativity of the contender (of which, lack of time attracts most comment). Restated positively, design is limited only by the imagination of evaluators to make the most of what is possible.

Pricing and Costing

Logically, costs follow from the design, although in reality they, and the price charged, are the result of an iterative process of trade-offs made by contenders. These trade-offs take account of the objectives of the evaluation (as understood), the volume and quality of resources required to meet them, the desire to win the contract, the nature of the competition (often presumed) and the size (often only estimated) of the budget available. The trade-offs made by contenders are therefore between more-or-less educated guesses in conditions of considerable uncertainty. For those commissioning the research, some of the factors (the budget and objectives) are known but there is more uncertainty about the others. The game of poker comes to mind.

For contenders, the starting point is usually the estimated budget (even when this is not specified in the invitation to tender) and, hence, the maximum charge (or price). This stems not only from the desire of contenders to maximize income but also from the need to determine the scale of the design, since there is typically no logical upper limit to the resources that could be used in improving an evaluation. Contenders will then decide how much they wish to win the contract, whether they can compete on cost (usually not viable in the long term, since the trade-off would normally have to be with quality) and in what other ways they might be able to establish a competitive advantage. From these deliberations they will fix a target cost, the monetary value of the maximum resources to be devoted to the evaluation, and a target price, the sum to be charged for undertaking the evaluation. Sometimes the target cost will exceed the price, in which case the potential contender will withdraw from the competition unless continued participation can be justified on other grounds, such as the prestige gained from being successful, future funding possibilities opened up or the need to generate cash flows. If the perceived budget and price exceed cost, the contender stands to make above average profit (average profit being included in the basic costing formulae) but risks being undercut by the competition. In situations where post-tender negotiations are permitted and the commissioning agent is intent on negotiating the tender price down, the element of above average profit could be offered up without undermining the financial viability of the contract.

Most of the costs incurred in evaluations are time costs, and there is no satisfactory alternative to identifying each task and estimating how long it will take. While each task is unique, the art is to seek comparable tasks for which evidence is available and to factor in the consequences of any differences. For each task it is also necessary to consider the kind and level of expertise required to perform it and whether someone with the required experience will be available. If expertise is absent, suitably qualified personnel may have to be bought in (probably at additional cost), trained up (a cost in itself) and estimated durations increased to take account of inexperience. Alternatively, the decision may be taken to muddle through (a gamble) or not to pursue the contract (a frustration). Asking experienced people individually to estimate task durations and then collectively to reach a consensus can produce robust estimates while analysis of time sheets from previous projects is also a vital tool in this regard. The cost of non-task items such as travel, interview strike rates, transcription costs, dissemination expenses etc. are sensibly derived from expenditure on past projects.

Two other cost elements warrant mention: management and overheads. Management costs are sometimes forgotten (perhaps more often by commissioning agencies than by contenders). These appertain to the project per se and include the time spent managing relationships within the research team or consortium, and those with external organizations, including the commissioning body. Apportionment of overhead or fixed costs, the cost of maintaining and developing the physical and intellectual infrastructure of the contending organization, can be contentious. In Britain, for example, charitable organizations refuse to meet overheads for university research (arguing that state funding already covers them) while the government is insisting that universities move to full economic pricing (which means including, for example, student welfare costs in research contracts). Overheads are frequently included in the daily rate charged for staff working on an evaluation project. Major American philanthropies follow no-overhead policies similar to those in Britain.

The Tender Documentation

The tender document, or proposal for evaluation research, encapsulates the outcome of all the considerations discussed above and serves as a management blueprint and as the basis of a potential contract. But first, and foremost, it is a piece of persuasive writing designed to market the evaluation strategy, the contender, and the contender's ability effectively to deliver the proffered strategy on time, within budget and with minimum hassle.

The golden rule for RFP response is: begin by interrogating the invitation to tender (or competition rules) listing everything required to be included in the tender documentation, the form in which it is to be presented, the number of copies to be supplied, and the date and time when they are to be delivered. Once checked, this list becomes the template to be followed and the quality standard against which the final tender documents are assessed before submission.

Within this template, the contender engages in a one-way virtual dialogue with representatives of the commissioning agency charged to evaluate the tenders. The better the contender knows the representatives, the more persuasive the argument can be, speaking to each of their concerns and demonstrating, without conceit, that the contender understands the evaluation brief as well as, if not better, than the commissioning agency and is also able to deliver the evaluation to the letter and beyond, better and more cost-effectively than any other contractor. Sensitivity, succinctness, relevance, and completeness underpin this dialogue.

A good tender is therefore a work of art; a successful one is also the materialization of good luck.

Managing the Implementation Process

While the adrenalin pumps during a tender competition, for the successful contender this is only the prelude to the real work.[10] After any post-tender negotiations, the focus of attention shifts from the relationship with the commissioning body towards that with delivery agencies and service-users. The key management task is to ensure that the evaluation proceeds as much according to plan as possible and that damage inflicted by accommodation to the needs of other policy actors or change in the policy environment is kept to a minimum. A key defence is effective monitoring of the environment within and without the evaluation consortia so as to provide early warning and to maximize the time in which to take evasive action.

Post-tender Negotiations

Much can happen between winning a tender competition and signing the contract. Negotiations over price are common, as are revisions to the design. The latter may sometimes be limited to decisions over the options offered by the contractor, but can involve major accommodations to budgetary constraints and the integration of design ideas offered by unsuccessful contenders (intellectual property rights are generally sacrificed in a tender exercise). In the US it is quite rare for expenditure to be committed by the contractor ahead of the signing of the contract, but in Britain delays in the government bureaucracy are such that contractors have little choice but to commence work on the basis of a letter of intent or even a handshake.

The contractor's hand is strengthened in post-tender negotiations by the knowledge that they were preferred over all other contenders. Consequently, it may be possible to ensure that marginal costs will be fully recovered and any deficit in unit costs is reduced or removed. However, given that evaluators may be tempted to prioritize good design over more mundane considerations of cost, it may be wise for contractors to separate responsibility for the design and implementation of evaluations from that for finance control.

Negotiating Delivery

Programme evaluation differs from post-hoc evaluation and policy research in that the policy is implemented for the purpose of evaluation. Staff involved in the delivery of policy are therefore not just objects of investigation but active contributors to the evaluation process, especially when random assignment is involved.

To oversimplify, staff delivering services aspire to minimize inconvenience and maximize benefits for their service-user clients and for themselves. They are also typically concerned by the prospect of their own work being appraised for fear that it might negatively affect their employment and promotion prospects. Moreover, for the most part they have limited understanding of the niceties of evaluation research. However, oversimplification can be misleading. Frequently, such views

are nuanced by locality, experience and grade. For example, senior management may understand research but emphasize legal and formulaic constraints, while junior staff may seek enthusiastically to please researchers and service-users at the expense of concern for robust design or research ethics.[11]

Most evaluation involves delivery staff in extra monitoring and collating of data about service-users or administrative procedures. Formative evaluation may additionally entail probing interviews with, and observation of, staff. This involvement may be required by employment or service contracts. In Britain, contracts with suppliers of pilot services to government departments now usually include clauses on evaluation because, previously there were difficulties in securing full compliance. Nevertheless, the goodwill of staff always needs to be secured as often does the informed consent of the individuals involved. Both entail tiers of explanation and negotiation with management, trade unions and individual members of staff. Transparency is of utmost importance. Staff need to appreciate the importance of the evaluation and of rigour; to be convinced that confidentiality will be respected and that neither they nor their clients will be put unduly at risk; to believe that their voice will be heard; to know what is expected of them and finally, to know from whom to seek advice and who to tell if things go wrong. Providing staff with written explanations, access to explanatory websites and selected feedback on interim results are desirable adjuncts to, but no substitute for, repeated contact with members of the evaluation team.

Ironically, of course, this degree of contact with agency staff may cause them to perform their duties more efficiently, or at least differently, simply as a result of being involved in a policy evaluation: double-blind trials are very difficult to construct in policy evaluation.

Moreover, there is evidence that policy evaluations attract more ambitious and less risk-averse staff and that implementations chosen for post-hoc evaluation on the grounds that they are unusual or pioneering are frequently found to have exceptional staff and/or leadership (Orr, 1999; Greenberg & Shroder, 2004). It is not easy to control for these eventualities in impact analyses, especially in a single site, but process studies can supply circumstantial evidence as to their importance.

Some modes of evaluation seek to exploit rather than to control such staff and institutional enthusiasm. In theory of change evaluations, for example, when the policy model may be weak and an empirical counterfactual missing, managers and other staff in the delivery organization will be actively engaged in discussions about the models of causality that drive the intervention and their actions, and in devising methods for partially testing their ideas. Similarly, in action research, evaluators involve staff in an iterative process of developing, implementing, reviewing and revising working practices and strategies. In these and other circumstances self-evaluation by staff may be explicitly encouraged in the expectation that it will result in changed behaviour and, potentially, in improvements in delivery.

Many random assignment evaluations involve agency staff recruiting service-users into the experiment and allocating them either to programme or control groups. Agency staff are often concerned that random assignment is unethical, with service-users being denied access to beneficial services, and unfair in that some "undeserving" service-users will receive assistance whereas other "deserving" ones will not (Stafford, Greenberg & Davis, 2002). The temptation, therefore, is for staff to manipulate the allocation of service-users to programme and control groups (thereby violating the assumption of equivalence) or to allow members of the control group to access programme services (thereby introducing contamination). While explaining the principles of random assignment to staff is important, it is generally best to distance staff from the control of random assignment and carefully to monitor service-users' use of programme services. Nowadays distancing is usually achieved by providing staff web access to random assignment software that both allocates cases and automatically records the allocation.

The success or failure of an evaluation is also dependent on management and staff delivering the policy intervention in the way intended. Sometimes, particularly in evaluation-led policy, agency staff design the services that are to be evaluated, but more frequently, agencies are expected to implement an externally prescribed policy intervention. It is an important duty of agency management, but arguably also of technical advisers and others attached to the evaluation team, to ensure that the programme implemented is as close as possible to the model ostensibly being evaluated, and for the process evaluation to establish and account for any departures from the ideal. However, there are trade-offs here to be negotiated. While it is essential to know what policy is being implemented and evaluated, policy is always transformed during implementation. Therefore the ability to generalize from the experiment to a larger rollout of the policy may be lessened if evaluators impose an artificial straightjacket on the experimental implementation.

Engaging Service-Users

In programme evaluation, service-users are consumers of policy, objects of evaluation and actors in the policy domain. They are also deliberately subjected to an element of risk – to receive or not to receive the policy intervention – for the benefit of the common good (knowing whether the policy works). As such, there is an onus on evaluators to ensure that the evaluation is designed to maximize the chances of obtaining an interpretable result and on the commissioning body to give due credence to the results in the policy-making process to justify the risk imposed on service-users (Walker, 2004).

As already noted, it often falls to frontline staff to recruit service-users into random assignment experiments and to supply them with sufficient information to allow them to express informed consent. Randomization is not an altogether simple concept to convey to lay people. Moreover, staff working to recruitment targets may be tempted to be too economical with the truth: it is all too easy to imply, as it is when seeking permission to observe service-users or to interview them at the point of service, that access to all services is conditional on participation in an evaluation. In quasi-experimental evaluations with saturation provision in one geographic area and reliance on area-based controls, consent is generally not sought at all for the passive participation in the experiment itself, only for participation in research interviews and observation.

There is a duty on evaluators to ensure that agency staff, and of course research staff, rigorously abide by professional codes of ethics when recruiting service-users. This responsibility of care also extends to avoiding unnecessary intrusion, over-lengthy research instruments and breach of confidentiality. It also entails paying careful attention to the needs of service-user diversity. A failure to do so is not only a violation of research ethics but invites negative press comment: A "good" story on "service-user abuse" by evaluators fuels the appetite of the prurient reader while allowing the media to lay claim to the moral high ground.

Service-users involved in a policy experiment may, like staff, behave unnaturally.

Merely alerting service-users to the existence of new service interventions may cause them to seek them out irrespective of whether or not they are assigned to the programme group. Service-users disappointed by not being included in the programme group might do this with exaggerated intent and perhaps seek the collusion of staff in their endeavours; others may adopt a strategy of non-compliance. Even if behaviour is unaffected, selection effects that mean that less risk-averse or more fearful service-users differentially refuse to participate could bias the evaluation. While none of these possibilities is easy to prevent, and only some can be detected by effective monitoring and direct questioning, it is important to try.

Managing Change

Despite the hopes and best intentions of the evaluator, disruptive change is almost unavoidable in policy evaluations that run for more than a few months. It is in coping with such change that evaluators are perhaps most reliant on the traditional tools of project management (Nokes et al., 2003). Without good project management software, it is very difficult to estimate the impact of even small delays or staff changes on the profiling of resource requirements and the timing of activities.

The specification of project tasks and their duration undertaken for the initial costing lies at the heart of the project management process. Typically the dependencies between tasks, illustrated by the fact that one or more tasks might have to have been completed before another began, would also have been specified at this stage, as would the staff and other resources required to complete each task. Software is often used to display dependencies as a Gantt chart that plots tasks, durations and relationships on a calendar, and further analysis allows critical paths or chains of tasks to be identified that affect the timing of, and resources available for, other tasks and progress of the project as a whole.

It is good practice to revise the project management database after post-tender negotiations and to keep it updated throughout the lifetime of the evaluation. The software can then be used to examine the impact of delays or alterations to the project and to make appropriate amendments. Perhaps as importantly, it can be used to inform risk assessment and management by exploring the consequences of possible contingences before they occur, so that action can be taken to prevent them occurring or to lessen their consequences.

External Changes

Changes in the economic and policy environment can have very destructive effects on policy evaluations. Much depends on the robustness of the evaluative design. Randomized designs can, in theory, withstand major changes in, for example, the economic environment because they ensure that external changes apply equally to the programme and control group. In contrast, "before and after" designs, that use the period before a policy is introduced as the sole counterfactual, are vulnerable to exogenous change coinciding with the policy experiment (Smith et al., 2000).

Changes in governments, or even in elected or career officials, can be more disruptive leading to for example, the cancellation of policies or the "hijacking" of existing evaluations to test out new policy variants (Walker, 2001). At a minimum, this may mean the evaluator being forced to accept a step change in the design with separate analyses conducted before and after the policy change with probably reduced sample sizes and less precision (recall Exemplar 16.2). Political enthusiasm can sometimes prove equally problematic when policies are rolled out ahead of time or, as in Britain, pilots of new policies are introduced in the same localities as existing ones (Cabinet Office, 2004).

Changes of political administration tend to have a greater impact on policy in Britain than in the USA (reflecting the more adversarial political culture and a voting system that generates large majorities). This partly explains why British policy evaluations tend to run for shorter periods than in the US.

Internal Policy Changes

Evaluators often need to accommodate developments in the policy under evaluation that are sometimes the product of early findings from the evaluation and which range from delays to wholesale redesign. It typically takes time for systems to stabilize, for information to be disseminated, for service-user populations to be recruited, for staff to gain experience, and for administrative procedures to bed down. Delays are often ubiquitous and, while the policy community should foresee developments of these kinds, blinkers imposed by political and administrative enthusiasm and funding opportunities often mean that they do not. For the evaluation, delays may mean shorter evaluation windows, less time for the policy to stabilize and hence less reliable results plus, if reporting deadlines cannot be renegotiated, rushed analysis and reporting.

Pressures to respond to interim findings may prove irresistible since it is irrational to proceed with a scheme that is demonstrably ineffective.[12] However, changing policy can significantly weaken the power of impact evaluation or increase its cost since, if the design is unaltered, the true impact of any policy change that improves effectiveness will generally be understated while the possibility that a change has had no effect cannot be formally detected. It may well be necessary to extend the evaluation window and increase sample sizes to permit outcomes before and after the modification to be compared but, since this is costly, conventional thresholds of statistical significance may be relaxed and greater reliance placed on formative analysis that can at least offer informed speculation about the likely impact of policy modifications (Loumidis et al., 2001).

The time required to establish a project management database and, especially to collect and collate the information required to keep it current is considerable. Nevertheless, attempting to accommodate change without it turns the fairground-like thrills usually associated with managing a sizeable evaluation into a nightmare.

Managing the Consortium

Complex evaluations often demand a range of expertise rarely found within one organisation. Consortia established in these circumstances tend to work best if founded on a high level of trust that often derives from prior experience of successfully working together. However, consortia are frequently formed during the short tendering period and may even by created artificially at the request of the commissioning body during post-tender negotiations. In such circumstances, the learning and appreciation curves have to be very steep and underpinned by especially intensive management.

The comparatively flat management structure of knowledge-based organizations tends to be replicated in consortia engaged in policy evaluation. Power is therefore widely dispersed within the consortium because each member's skills are rare, highly valued, difficult to replace, and essential for the successful completion of the evaluation. Moreover, while consortium members are mutually interdependent, each could, theoretically at least, readily find alternative, equally remunerative, work. Even so, leadership and management are crucial to the effective working of the consortium. Where there is a single contract, this is usually vested in the contract holder, but typically authority cannot be enforced

and has to be earned through competence, intellect and force of personality. Moreover, members often have diverse styles of working that reflect, in part, the nature of their expertise and contribution and these typically have to be accommodated within the consortium.

Consortia are often bound together by a shared interest in the topic and a common commitment to a final product of which they can be proud. Task allocation and definition are usually arrived at through discussion and delivery ensured by the inherent mutual dependency and associated peer pressure. Similarly, quality control is typically established through peer critique and joint working with honesty and transparency encouraged through mutual feedback. Conflicts of ideas, values, personalities and interests have to be resolved through discussion and informal, peer-led arbitration.

Much time is necessarily spent in discussion and on, planning, monitoring of progress and troubleshooting. Generally overseen by a project management team comprising senior staff from the various constituent members, these activities are often supported by task-based working groups that may be disbanded or reconfigured many times during the evaluation. There is a premium on members keeping in touch with progress on component parts of an evaluation and being aware of emergent findings that can influence the form and content of other elements (see below). Sharing project management information, holding internal research seminars, circulating newsletters, and sharing research instruments and draft reports widely within the consortium help to facilitate this.

Indeed the key to effective evaluation is successfully to exploit these knowledge dependencies – for example, those between the impact and process evaluations and between design, fieldwork, and data collection (Figure 16.1). But the obstacles to achieving high levels of integration are legion. Practical matters of timing together with a lack of cross-method competence and even ongoing ontological and epistemological disputes all help to explain why process and impact evaluations are often undertaken in parallel with separate reports, and why triangulation, if attempted at all, is deferred until late in the analysis process (Walker, 2001). Similarly, the aspiration that the design of research instrumentation should be driven by the needs of analysis and not vice-versa is often frustrated by the fact that design and analysis require different skills and are often undertaken by different people employed in different organizations. Equally, analysts are often forced to undertake analysis without adequate feedback from field staff concerning the quality and nature of the data available.

In effective consortia, the dependencies between process and impact work are recognized in project planning and, where possible, placed on the critical path with adequate time allocated for transmission and interpretation of information. Likewise, it is the managed norm for process and impact teams, instrument designers and analysts to be engaged in mutual dialogue as relevant points throughout the research process. Even so, such doctrines of perfection are often sacrificed when circumstances mean a rescheduling of tasks puts at risk even the minimalist performance criterion of "good enough". It is, of course, the goal of management to anticipate such circumstances and to prevent them having such dramatic consequences.

Managing Analysis and Impact

The purpose of the evaluation discussed is this chapter is to inform and possibly to influence policy decisions. To achieve this, the right information has to be available at the appropriate time to people who are in positions to make or shape decisions and are willing to do so. The evaluator has most control over the nature and quality of the information

available and, subject to the timely commissioning of the evaluation, the timing of its availability. Negotiating access and making results accessible to decision-makers, opinion leaders and others in relevant communities is also part of the management task but whether recipients of the findings will act upon them may not be within the gift of the evaluator.

Since much has been written on the role of evidence in policy-making (Wilensky, 1997; Davies et al., 2000), the focus here is limited to the contribution that evaluators can reasonably make. Within the policy community the key players are the clients of the evaluation: policy officials, researchers and, certainly in Britain, ministers. They will all want timely, clear-cut results with as many interim findings as possible. Whereas ministers will want the big picture, typically filleted to a few paragraphs of "executive summary", their officials will demand detail. Researchers are likely to be interested in effect sizes; administrators information on cost effectiveness and what works best; and practitioners information on best practice. All will typically be more amenable to "positive results", those consistent with their prior expectations, than negative ones that may be more robustly challenged, often on methodological grounds. The receptivity of policy clients may be increased by preparing the ground by means of ongoing contact with officials, alerting them early to unwelcome findings to avoid them being caught off-guard and informing them of developments that affect the quality of the results. Reflecting, too, on the diverse information needs may enable reporting to be differentiated and targeted to particular groups perhaps using different media as appropriate. For example, if it is known that the research report is to be synthesized for key personnel, providing the synthesis may enable the evaluator to retain control over the interpretation of the findings.

Good reporting needs obviously to be underpinned by thorough analysis, although this can be lacking for several reasons, some linked to the initial tendering process. Costs and timetables are often driven by fieldwork, and the temptation is to assume that analysis can be fitted into whatever time remains between the end of fieldwork and the exogenously determined reporting date. For similar reasons the specification of analysis in tender documents may also be perfunctory and formulaic. This may also reflect the failure to integrate analysis and data collection explained above and fear that description of sophisticated analysis may deter rather than impress numerically challenged policy customers. As a result, analysis is not infrequently rushed, partial, and focused on descriptions of impacts rather than explanation. There may also be a failure adequately to integrate qualitative and quantitative findings and fully to explore sufficient analytic avenues. One consequence of this has been a growth in the secondary analysis of evaluation-based data (Greenberg et al., 2005) although this has yet to happen on the same scale in Britain as in the USA. The problem of shallow analysis is difficult to resolve since the policy community, especially in Britain, has become accustomed to rapid turnaround. However, making analysis and the management of analysis more visible in tenders and Gantt charts is an essential first step.

Clients for policy evaluations are liable to want to control both the content and the timing of dissemination often for narrow political reasons. There is scepticism in academic circles about how successfully these pressures have been resisted by evaluators, and distinctions are commonly drawn in the evaluation community between research, where publication is the norm, and consultancy, where this is sometimes not the case. Certainly, disclaimers in publications to the effect that the views expressed are not necessarily those of the commissioning agency are suspect, since published reports invariably incorporate comments on earlier drafts. However, it may be tone rather than substantive content that is changed in this process, since evaluators are likely to be more sensitive to loss of professional integrity than to threats of lost contracts.

There is also a growing acceptance that publication is desirable and institutional developments that encourage it. In the US, major contractors, such as MDRC and Mathematica, publish research reports in-house and on-line, while in Britain, government departments now typically have their own report series, frequently available on the web. There has also been a growth in academic journals devoted to policy evaluation and analysis and, thereby, increased peer review. Control of the timing of publication is key and is usually actively retained by the evaluation client since it allows them judiciously to promote coverage of positive evaluation findings while "burying" negative ones. This emphasis on control reflects the inherently adversarial nature of policy debate and the ease with which opposition politicians and interest groups can selectively cite evaluation reports. Both "sides" may want to court the popular media that is keen to find stories, which fuel controversy and sales, and that can be presented in the form of simple messages, often devoid of analytic nuance but not necessarily of ideological slant. Rather than simply being caught up in this presentational merry-go-round, it is wise for evaluators to think strategically and to manage their involvement in ways consistent with their own goals. Becoming linked to a particular ideological position may undermine the credibility of both the evaluator and evaluation.

Conclusion

In providing an overview of the process of managing evaluations, attention has been drawn to the varied perspectives of the often-diverse groups or communities that are necessarily involved in, or affected by, an evaluation. The different communities will be more or less clear as to their objectives and interests and vary in their relative ability to influence the form, direction, quality and outcome of an evaluation. Nevertheless each community contributes to the success or otherwise of the evaluation, sometimes deliberately and at other times unconsciously. Moreover, the communities may differ in their definition of a successful evaluation.

It follows that the management of evaluation must be about managing relationships usually through various forms of negotiation. The perspective that has been forefronted is that of evaluators commissioned to undertake a programme evaluation, but this not to suggest that their concerns are either unique or the most important. The viewpoint of other policy actors, or of evaluators engaged in other forms of policy evaluation, could equally have been presented in which case certain other issues and priorities might have been emphasized. Prescription has generally been avoided. Instead, evaluators have been encouraged to think of ways in which they might be able to improve evaluation through effective management of relationships while being aware of the limits to their autonomy.

Finally, returning to ethics, prospective evaluation deliberately subjects groups of service-users to a degree of risk and necessarily throws a critical spotlight on staff involved in delivery. Ensuring that both groups receive appropriate feedback and support is an item that should be underlined in the evaluators' code of ethics.

Notes

1. It is not yet the case that all policy communities have accepted that policies should be systematically and robustly evaluated or that, in principle at least, the results of policy evaluations should inform the policy-making process. Equally, it is a problem that has been discussed elsewhere and is being addressed in a number of countries and at supranational level (OECD, 2004).

2. Some kinds of policy are very difficult empirically to evaluate prospectively: the decision to alter national tax rates or to declare war are obvious examples. Micro-simulation models can be, and are, used to investigate tax changes but are highly sensitive to theoretical assumptions, while dynamic behavioural models that can predict second order effects are still in their infancy. War games can have heuristic intent but the dynamic imposed by real casualties and the fractal-like complexity of real war severely curtail the predictive power of gaming. Moreover, in neither case is it possible to define a real-time counterfactual, the situation and outcomes that would have occurred in the absence of policy.

3. This difference is probably attributable to the localized nature of policy development in the USA compared with the highly hierarchical and centralized system in Britain (Walker, 1997).

4. Unfortunately, of course, unless the same policy is evaluated in multiple sites, it is very difficult analytically to separate the policy from its implementation. Pooling the results of evaluations of several implementations, meta-evaluation, can aid disentangling design from implementation (Ashworth et al., 2004; Greenberg, Robins & Walker, 2005).

5. Witness the decline in the level of prospective evaluation undertaken prior to and following passage of the Personal Responsibility and Work Opportunity Reconciliation Act in 1996. Evaluation-led policy is also lacking in relation to tax and social security reform and developments in homeland security.

6. As one example, random assignment was dropped from the evaluation of the national extension to New Deal for Disabled People (an activation programme targeted on recipients of Incapacity Benefit) after the evaluation contract had been let in 2001. No official reason for the decision was given which was apparently opposed by other senior ministers although supported by the disability lobby which had campaigned against the evaluative method but not generally against the policy nor the principle of evaluating it (Stafford et al., 2002).

7. This difference reflects the influence of the respective evaluation communities. The strength of positivist social science in the USA stimulated an

early emphasis on experimentation that in 1988 received legislative backing in the Family Support Act, which included a facility for states to vary welfare provision subject to an evaluation using random assignment. In Britain, on the other hand, there was a marked reaction against positivism in sociology and the policy sciences (economics excluded) from the 1970s onwards, a greater focus on institutional analyses, more concern about the systemic effects of policy (difficult to investigate with a RCT design) and greater doubts about the ethics of random assignment. Given the highly centralized nature of British governance with uniform national policies there has also been a greater reliance on post-implementation and pluralistic designs (Walker, 2000b). Preferred evaluation designs also vary by policy area (Davies, Nutley & Smith, 2000).

8. The difference may be less marked when a mandatory programme is to be evaluated by RCT and random assignment into the programme and control group is itself mandatory.

9. While experience suggests that it is rare for radically different designs to be accepted, it does happen. In 1993, the UK Department of Social Security tendered a contract for qualitative research to explore what prevented people from moving off benefit into employment. The successful contender demonstrated that sufficient qualitative research had already been undertaken and that by exploiting a newly available administrative database it would be possible to draw a dynamic sample of the claimant population and not only to identify the barriers but also to establish their prevalence and longer-term consequences. The budget was substantially increased to accommodate the alternative design (Shaw et al., 1996).

10. For unsuccessful contenders, a post-mortem should follow closely on the initial sense of despair aided by detailed feedback from the responsible commissioning body.

11. Note, though, that it is Ian Shaw's experience (personal communication) that "junior staff are often more sensitive (or at least vocal) about ethics than senior ones".

12. Interim results are not necessarily reliable, especially if they relate to the period before the policy and administrative systems stabilize.

References

Ashworth, K., Cebulla, A., Greenberg, D., & Walker, R. (2004). Meta-Evaluation: Discovering what works best in welfare provision. *Evaluation.* 10, 2, 193–216.

Blunkett, D. (2000). *Influence or Irrelevance: Can social science improve government?* London: ESRC Lecture, 2 February.

Bos, H., Huston, A., Granger, R., Duncan, G., Brock, T., McLoyd, V. with Crosby, D., Gibson, C., Fellerath, V., Magnuson, K., Mistry, R., Poglinco, S., Romich, J., & Ventura, A. (1999). *New Hope for People with Low Incomes: Two-year results of a program to reduce poverty and reform welfare.* New York: MDRC.

Brock, T., Doolittle, F., Fellerath, V., Greenberg, D., & Wiseman, M. (1997). *Creating New Hope: Implementation of a program to reduce poverty and reform welfare.* New York: MDRC .

Cabinet Office (1999). *Professional Policy Making for the Twenty First Century.* London: Cabinet Office, Strategic Policy Making Team.

Cabinet Office (2000). *Adding It Up: Improving analysis and modeling in central government.* London: Cabinet Office, Performance and Innovation Unit.

Cabinet Office (2004). *Trying It Out: Review of the effectiveness of government pilots.* London: Cabinet Office.

Davies, H., Nutley, S., & Smith, P. (eds) (2000). *Evidence and Public Policy.* Bristol: Policy Press.

Greenberg, D. & Shroder, M. (2004). *The Digest of Social Experiments*, third Edition. Washington, DC: Urban Institute Press.

Greenberg, D., Mandell, M., & Onstott, M. (2000). The dissemination and utilization of welfare-to-work experiments in state policymaking. *Journal of Policy Analysis and Management*, 19, 367–382.

Greenberg, D., Robins, P., & Walker, R. (2005). Conducting meta-analyses of evaluations of government-funded training programs. *Review of Policy Research*, 22(3), 345–367.

Gueron, J. (2003). Fostering research excellence and impacting policy and practice: the welfare reform story. *Journal of Policy Analysis and Management*, 22(2), 163–174.

Lewin, K. (1946). Action research and minority problems. *Journal of Social Issues*, 2, 34–46.

Loumidis, J., Stafford, B., Youngs, R., Green, A., Arthur, S., Legard, R., Lessof, C., Lewis, J., Walker, R., Corden, A., Thornton, P., & Sainsbury, R. (2001). *Evaluation of the New Deal for Disabled People Personal Adviser Pilots.* London: Department of Social Security, Research Report, 144.

Nokes, S., Major, I., Greenwood, A., Allen, D., & Goodman, M. (2003). *The Definitive Guide to Project Management.* London: Prentice Hall/Financial Times.

Nolan, A. & Wong, G. (2004). Evaluating local economic and employment development: an overview with policy recommendations. In *Evaluating Policies for Local Economic and Employment Development.* (pp. 63–111). Paris: OECD.

OECD (2004). *Evaluating Policies for Local Economic and Employment Development.* Paris: OECD.

Orr, L. L. (1999). *Social Experiments: Evaluating public programs with experimental methods.* Thousand Oaks, CA: Sage.

Rogers, P. J., Hacsi, T. A., Petrosino, A., & Huebner, T. A. (2000). *Program Theory in Evaluation: Challenges and opportunities. New Directions for Evaluation,* No. 87. San Francisco: Jossey-Bass.

Sainsbury, R. (2004). Policy ignoring research: the case of housing benefit appeals and a new deal. In S. Becker & A. Bryman (eds) *Understanding Research for Social Policy and Practice.* (pp. 26–28). Bristol: Policy Press.

Shaw, A., Walker, R., Ashworth, K., Jenkins, S., & Middleton, S. (1996). *Moving off Income Support: Barriers and bridges.* Department of Social Security Research Report No. 53. London: HMSO.

Smith, J. (2004). Evaluating local economic development policies: theory and practice. *Evaluating Policies for Local Economic and Employment Development.* (pp. 287–332). Paris: OECD.

Smith, A., Youngs, R., Ashworth, K., McKay, S., & Walker, R. (2000). *Understanding the Impact of Jobseeker's Allowance.* Department of Social Security, Research Report no. 111. London: HMSO.

SRA (2002). *Commissioning Social Research: A good practice guide.* London: Social Research Association.

Stafford, B., Greenberg, D., & Davis, A. (2002). *A Literature Review of the Use of Random Assignment Methodology in Evaluations of US Social Policy Programmes,* DWP In-house Report No. 94, London: DWP.

Walker, R. (1997). Public policy evaluation in a centralised state. *Evaluation,* 3(5), 261–279.

Walker, R. (2000a). Learning if policy will work: the case of new deal for disabled people. *policy studies,* 21(4), 313–345.

Walker, R. (2000b). Welfare policy: tendering for evidence. In H. Davies, S. Nutley & P. Smith (eds) *Evidence and Public Policy* (pp. 141–166). Bristol: Policy Press.

Walker, R. (2001). Great expectations: Can social science evaluate New Labour's policies? *Evaluation,* 7(3), 305–330.

Walker, R. (2004). Evaluation: Evidence for public policy. *Evaluating Policies for Local Economic and Employment Development* (pp. 63–111). Paris: OECD.

Watts, H. W. & Rees, A. (eds) (1977). *The New Jersey Income Maintenance Experiment,* New York: Academic Press.

Wilensky, H. (1997). Social science and the public agenda: reflections on the relationship of knowledge to policy in the United States and abroad. *Journal of Health Politics, Policy and Law,* 22(5), 1241–1265.

Winter, R. (1996). Some principles and procedures for the conduct of action research. In O. Zuber-Skerritt (ed.) *New Directions in Action Research.* London: Falmer Press.

17

COMMUNICATING EVALUATION

Marvin C. Alkin, Christina A. Christie and Mike Rose

Introduction

Communication is a part of all program evaluation activities. Indeed, it is probably not an exaggeration to say that evaluation without communication would not be possible. The nature of evaluation has as an ultimate purpose: the improvement of the entity being evaluated. Reporting or communication of evaluation results helps to assure that evaluation will lead to this improvement. Unlike research, which may be conducted for its own sake, evaluation implies the necessity for communicating to stakeholders and other audiences.

The very conduct of an evaluation is, itself, communication. The particular evaluation perspectives (or "theories") employed (see Alkin, 2004) will have different implications for the nature of communication. For example, in many evaluation-research approaches, communication may be more formal in character, relying primarily on a final written report. Other approaches advocate substantial, and continuing, involvement with stakeholders and users. (These and other differences related to theoretic approaches will be summarized later in the chapter.) But in all cases and from all perspectives the act of evaluation communicates.

Consider some of the various aspects of focusing an evaluation. Evaluators engage stakeholders – they communicate – when they try to understand the entity to be evaluated, identify stakeholders and their information needs, and prepare a proposal. They communicate when they seek to reach agreement on evaluation design, procedures, and measures. Evaluators also communicate when they negotiate joint responsibilities and report expectations. That is, evaluators communicate about the evaluation process – about the doing of the evaluation.

The evaluator also engages in various communication activities when collecting and analyzing evaluation data, and the impact of these activities on the evaluation process can also be considered communication. In this instance, what is communicated is an understanding about a program and evaluation's role in program change. Stakeholders learn from observing and/or participating in these activities. The literature on evaluation recognizes this impact and refers to it as "process use" (Patton, 1997).

Evaluation writers have considered process use and its role in improving the organizations being evaluated (e.g., King, 2002; Greene, 1990; Preskill, Zuckerman, & Matthews, 2003). These writers recognize the need for evaluators to be particularly attentive to the way in which stakeholders' involvement in the evaluative process enhances their knowledge and understanding. When those involved in the evaluation learn from the evaluation process, it seems reasonable to suggest that engagement in evaluation, in and of itself, becomes a particular type of communication. While there is this broader role of communication in evaluation, this chapter has as its primary focus communicating about findings.

Communication of Findings

A major task of evaluators is communicating the results of their evaluation efforts. Findings are communicated on an interim basis (throughout the course of the evaluation) as well as at the end of the evaluation (final findings). First, however, it is important to understand the main actors in the evaluation communication act. Who are the evaluators? Who is the audience? Each of these, and the way they are identified and function, are critical in differentiating the type of evaluation communication that will take place. Also, before communication takes place, the evaluator must structure the communication process to ensure that there is full

agreement by all parties and to avoid subsequent misunderstandings.

Let us first consider issues related to the evaluator and audience. Then we will discuss some ways of providing structure to the communication process and, finally, consider issues related to the communication of findings – both interim and end of evaluation.

Roles in Evaluation Communication

There are several sets of main "actors" in evaluation communication. The evaluator (or evaluators) fashion the evaluation message in various ways and formats. A second set of participants in the communication act are usually referred to as "audience," although, as we will see, the term itself carries varied meanings from different theoretical perspectives.

Evaluators

Evaluators orchestrate and perform numerous activities during an evaluation and play a critical role in communicating their findings. How one views his or her role as an evaluator will, in part, influence how one facilitates and participates in the communication process. For example, if one believes that the evaluator should encourage use of the evaluation and its findings, he or she is likely to also believe that the evaluator should stimulate and facilitate dialog amongst stakeholders, not simply provide a written report. Because the role of the evaluator varies according to what one perceives to be the primary purpose of evaluation (e.g., to provide information for decision-making; to judge the merit or worth of a program), it is critical that the evaluator communicates his or her beliefs about the role of evaluation.

Furthermore, in addition to views about how to conduct evaluations (the "model" or approach employed), evaluators have personal beliefs and value systems. In truth, these values and beliefs are strongly related to the approach that the evaluator takes. Nonetheless, evaluators should be open and explicit about their own *values and biases*. Klein (in Alkin, 1990) notes, "As with any arena of disciplined inquiry, it is important for evaluators to share their biases, criteria, standards, and methods publicly so that the user will be able to take these into account" (p. 235). With respect to evaluation communication, this sharing is particularly important for reports that may be controversial. These views concur with suggestions made in the Program Evaluation Standards (Joint Committee, 1994) that the basis for value judgments be made clear and that evaluators must pay heed to and avoid possible "distortion caused by personal feelings and biases of any party to the evaluation" (p. 181).

Should evaluators be creating impartial evaluation reports and offering recommendations to the best of their abilities or, instead, because evaluation "inherently involves advocacy," as some believe (e.g., Greene, 1995; Lincoln, 1990), should evaluators be advocating for a particular goal (e.g., social justice) through their study and reporting? Though these value positions are quite distinct, Datta (1999) astutely recognizes that, in each case, it is possible to obtain appropriate evaluation reporting by being open and explicit in one's beliefs and purposes, using as a guide fairness to stakeholders and respect for their dignity.

Audience

As previously stated, the term "audience" can have multiple meanings. In large-scale evaluations and/or evaluations adhering to theoretical approaches that are more methodologically inclined, the identification of audience might be more fixed and less specific (e.g., not directed at specific individuals). Alternatively, for evaluations that have greater stakeholder participation, the notion of audience is more personal, individual, and likely modifiable. In such approaches, also, communication may well be viewed as more interactive – rather than simply the delivery of a message.

But whatever the theoretical approach, evaluators must be attentive to who will be the recipients of evaluation communication. Generally, evaluators want to know which clients, stakeholders, and others will, and ought to be, recipients of evaluation communications. Communication is further facilitated by developing as complete an understanding as possible of what these audiences want to know, why they want to know it, and what use they intend to make of it.

Structuring the Communication Plan

It is important that the evaluator clarify all aspects of communication expectations. Some theorists (e.g., Stufflebeam, 2000) strongly recommend that all issues related to communication be negotiated up front and be included as part of the evaluation contract. And others (e.g., Torres, Preskill & Piontek 1996; Morris, Fitz-Gibbon & Freeman, 1987) go beyond this position and suggest the development of a formal communication reporting plan. We are not sure that such formality is compulsory; however, we recognize the necessity of reaching agreements on the general structure of what is to be communicated: when, to whom, and at what dollar cost. Further, when unplanned evaluation reporting is required, as it may, it is often a good idea to formally document the terms of such reporting as a revision to the original agreement.

In structuring the communication plan, the first concern is identifying the participants in this structuring. It is important to recognize that those with whom the evaluator communicates during planning and structuring are privileged parties relative to others. Thus, an essential part of the evaluation structuring activity is determining which audiences will participate in the process of structuring the communication plan. To the degree that the participating group is not broadly representative, the evaluator has a special responsibility to raise the issue of potential relevant audiences for the evaluation communication. Again, the extent to which the evaluator would feel obliged to advocate for broader inclusion is related to the evaluator's personal theoretic position.

In many instances the dissemination of findings (both interim and final) beyond the organization is the responsibility not of the evaluator but of those who commissioned the evaluation. The evaluator benefits by avoiding any unforeseen legal responsibility related to the misuse or erroneous dissemination of findings. Alternatively, some evaluators who view external reporting as part of their civic responsibility would resent users/stakeholders' restrictions on communication activities. These differences in views serve to reinforce the importance of reaching agreement on acceptable communication.

When evaluators are sanctioned to communicate broadly, they should proceed with the utmost caution and adhere to the contractual guidelines agreed upon. Further, it is important that evaluators are careful in presenting reports that might be easily misinterpreted. This is particularly true with respect to the media. Morris et al., (1987) caution about the danger of misquoting by reporters and the evaluator's responsibility for carefully constructing communication to the media within the bounds of what the public needs to know (p. 42).

Other matters to be clarified in structuring the communication include issues such as the type of evaluation report, frequency and timing, format and style, and deadlines. Information preferences may differ not only for the issues of concern, but also for types of acceptable information, for format and for level of readability. Remember: reporting need not be written; alternative and innovative forms of reporting might better serve the needs of the various stakeholders/audiences.

Interim Evaluation Findings

Interim findings are communicated both formally and informally. Formal communication of interim findings includes written reports, which might be in a form similar to a final written report, or these findings may be presented a bit less formally. Formal interim report quality is subject to guidelines similar to that of the final formal report (discussed in the following section). But given the immediacy (and perhaps frequency) of interim reporting, there are a number of additional issues that should be considered. Evaluators obviously want to keep stakeholders as well informed as possible during the course of the evaluation. By doing this, they lessen the possibility of major surprises when the final report is presented. However, evaluators should be cautious about submitting to stakeholder pressures to provide extensive information prematurely, and must understand that such reporting has its hazards. Evaluators should be certain that appropriate cross-checking has taken place and, more generally, that enough data have been collected to form an accurate picture.

Aside from the more formal written reporting of interim findings, there are forms of reporting which are thought to be more casual. The evaluator may chose e-mail as a way to communicate interim findings regularly, and this would be an excellent way to keep communication lines alive and open. For example, in an evaluation of a pilot transitional living program for formerly homeless adults being conducted by one of the authors, aggregate client interview summaries are e-mailed to the program director almost immediately upon completion so that program modifications can be implemented with little delay. E-mail correspondence may often seem to be a more casual means of communication; however, given that these exchanges are a form of written communication, similar to letters or memos, which can be referred back to and archived, they should be subject to the same care that would be taken with any written report.

Of course, interim findings are also communicated orally. This can take place over the telephone or more officially in the form of a presentation. While formal oral communication can take the place of a written report, informal oral communication relates to the ongoing and regular activities of the program. Oral communication often promotes a natural dialog about findings, which can lead to more immediate use.

The most prominent form of oral communication is to be found in evaluators' day-to-day interaction with staff, stakeholders, and others. These conversations might be thought of lightly but must be considered a communication mode and, as such, warrant at least some reflection. Evaluators should think carefully about what is being said during more casual, less formal conversations with stakeholders and other participants and how it may be interpreted. Stakeholders will pick and choose what they hear (or wanted to hear) and will certainly modify what was said based on other comments or personal beliefs. Remember, as Torres et al., (1996) write: "the contents of personal communications are

frequently based on selective recall" (p. 152). As evidence of this, consider the children's game of "telephone," where an original message or phrase is communicated orally from person to person, usually resulting in a final message quite different from what was initially said.

On the other hand, formal oral presentations – while providing a forum for dialog about findings – are thought to decrease the likelihood of information being misconstrued. To enhance the use of such reporting, we recommend videotaping formal oral presentations in order to allow others not present to hear and see the evaluation report and to provide documentation for the further consideration of results. Because of the dialog that can follow, a formal oral presentation is also a useful tool for the evaluator when looking for stakeholder assistance with the interpretation of findings. In fact, oral communication, both formal and informal, is often necessary when the evaluator is trying to better understand data or results. Thus, oral communication is of benefit to the evaluator as well as to program stakeholders.

Providing more than a few basic hints on oral communication presentation skills is beyond the scope of this chapter. Indeed, books have been written on oral communication (e.g., McGlone & Fausti, 1972; Ramsey, 2002). In essence, this literature shows, and the authors concur, that the major skills involved include being a good listener, showing genuine concern, considering the implications of what you are saying, and being tactful.

Reporting Final Results

There are a variety of formats for the presentation of final results or end-of-evaluation findings. While most end-of-evaluation findings involve a written report, that is not always the case. Some authors have questioned the necessity of a final written report, offering the possibility of alternative modes of representing evaluation results. Nonetheless, written reports are the most common form of reporting.

When written reports are presented, there is much that evaluators can do to make the communication more readable, meaningful, and useful. We provide some suggestions that would lead to improvement in the writing of formal reports, and we comment on appropriate report format and structure. Finally, we suggest some alternative reporting formats for final results. These topics will be discussed in the following sections.

Focus on Written Report – the Writing

In all report writing it is important that the writer has a sense of the reader, and an evaluator's most important readers are potential users. Though this chapter is clearly not the place to provide detailed guidance on writing style and form, let us offer a few suggestions and references. All of them can be subsumed under the broad recognition that writing is a public, communicative act, and thus the writer must keep in mind the question: Am I writing in a way that can be read and understood, and am I being considerate of my reader as I do so?

Writing for the Audience

In all writing it is important that you write for those who will be the readers of the evaluation report. Who are they? What do they need/ expect? Why do they need the information? Be sure that what you communicate is on target with what your audiences want to know. To the extent that the evaluation has a readily visualized audience, the evaluator's ability to communicate is enhanced. This is perhaps easier on smaller project evaluations. In writing reports, we have found that communication can be enhanced by imagining that we are talking with a moderately informed (but not fully knowledgeable) stakeholder. Picture this potential reader, and as you write the report ask yourself whether that individual will understand what you are saying.

While close knowledge of the stakeholders enhances communication, such knowledge is not always possible. On some large-scale evaluations, the report is written to inform broad policy communities – perhaps a legislature, a Senate committee, or a nationwide audience of policy shapers for similar programs. Close knowledge (and interaction) is nearly impossible. If communication is to be effective in helping to make change, evaluators may want to contemplate the nature of the policy communities that are to be potential recipients of evaluation reporting and their potential information needs. Moreover, communication style is important. Cabatoff (2000) notes that each policy community "has its own language, traditions, and professional culture" (p. 46). Thus, evaluators need to become aware of the language of various policy communities and be attentive to framing reports in accord with their language.

Accessible Style

The evaluation literature (see, e.g., Morris et al., 1987; Torres et al., 1996) addresses the importance of writing in a clear, accessible style, a style that is direct, relatively free of jargon, and not convoluted with an abundance of complex syntactic and passive voice constructions. Since most academic training does not explicitly educate us to write this way – and given the abundance of bad models in academic writing, such advice is not easy to follow. Several textbooks that we have found useful (along with the ubiquitous *Elements of Style* by Strunk & White, 1959) are Richard Lanham's

Revising Prose (2000) and Joseph Williams's *Style: Ten Lessons in Clarity and Grace* (2002). These books, though each has its own approach, agree on general principles such as the aforementioned warnings about jargon, complex syntax, passive constructions, and obtuse word choice. As well, they provide technique and illustration as to how to vary the length of sentences to avoid monotony; how to trim verbal fat (Lanham calls it the "lard factor") from sentences; and how to choose sentence patterns, words, and punctuation that heighten clarity and impact.

In a study of reports submitted to the US Department of Education, Lynch (1986) found that writing quality was a major factor in the reports' acceptance or rejection. Because writing well is such a critical facility for the evaluator – as much a part of one's repertoire of skills as statistical, survey, or qualitative methodology – it is recommended that evaluators pursue instruction in writing while still in one's training or as part of professional development (Rose & McClafferty, 2001). Such instruction would have immense payoff in one's career.

Voice

A related stylistic issue is the issue of voice, or those characteristics of style that mark one's writing as distinctive, as having its own . . . well, *style*. The issue of voice is a complex one and might spark debate within the field of evaluation. Among other issues, there is the potential tension between dispassionate, objective reporting of the facts and the vocabulary one chooses to render those facts. (Style manuals like those just recommended advocate, for example, the use of strong verbs, but might not the use of such verbs move one away from neutrality? The same could be said, perhaps with even greater concern, about the use of vivid adjectives.) One's theory of evaluation and the methods one advocates play into this issue.

Pleasing Verbal Quality

First, writing can be true to the facts, and still be crafted with care and a pleasing verbal quality. In fact, to truly capture certain aspects of the evaluation – for example, the feelings participants have about a program – an evaluator might have to rely on evocative verbs and adjectives. Second, an evaluation report has to be readable and convincing, and a writing style that is flat, mechanical, or worse, plodding, works against those aims. Third, it is an illusion to think that writing can be without style, broadly defined. There are commonplace beliefs in our culture – and we will say more about this in the concluding section – that language, particularly professional and technical language, serves as a neutral vehicle to carry information from a writer to a reader. But the way one writes influences the effectiveness of that communication and the degree to which information is comprehended and retained. So the question is not whether style is important, but what style you have as a writer, how able you are to handle written language effectively, what kinds of linguistic resources you have developed. Thus, we see value in honing this aspect of your professional skills, and in taking the time to craft the evaluation report in ways that enhance its effectiveness.

Avoidance of Jargon

It is best to avoid the specialized, professional language of evaluation and its related fields when writing the report. There may be times, however, when some jargon is necessary (perhaps, for example, when reporting the techniques used in framing or interpreting a survey). In such cases, the writer should use specialized language sparingly and define it in context.

Patton (2000) notes that "it is incumbent on every evaluator to be clear about what he or she means by key terms used in specific contexts . . . and to work with stakeholders to develop shared definitions and meanings for each specific evaluation process" (p. 8). Use of the jargon, acronyms, and abbreviations of the program being evaluated might well be unavoidable. But, again, use them judiciously and define them, particularly the first time you use them. In our experience, reports can become cluttered with specialized terms and abbreviations, and it is important to remember that some of the readers of the report might not be intimately familiar with all the specifics of a program's structure and function.

Illustration and Metaphor

Communication can be enhanced – and one's writing made more powerful – through the strategic use of illustration and metaphor. Few devices make writing more effective and compelling than the carefully chosen illustration: the striking statistic, or telling example, or memorable quotation. Likewise, there is the value of metaphor, the vivid comparison that can help a reader understand a complex process or vexing situation. Kaminsky (2000) suggests "while language represents how people think and act, metaphor frames these processes. Metaphors can provide insight into the assumptions and values that frame language" (p. 70). However, the writer needs to be careful that the illustration is representative of a broader state of affairs and that the metaphor is as accurate as it is artful in the way it represents a given situation.

Focus on Written Report – Format and Structure

Aside from the quality of the writing in the written report, there are various format and structure issues to be considered. These include such things as enhancing the readability of the report by the use of tables, charts, and photographs. Also to be addressed:

a strategy for guiding the reader through the report; dealing with findings; the status and nature of recommendations; constructing an executive summary; and the issue of notes and attachments.

Tables, Charts, and Graphics

A number of writers have dealt with specifics of the use and formatting of tables, charts and graphs (e.g., Henry, 1995, 1997; Hathaway, 1982; Tufte, 1983). These graphic devices can be valuable aids to a reader's understanding, but the writer must make sure that their use adds to, rather than detracts from, the report, that they are well-crafted, and that their purpose is clear. They should be presented simply and be well-labeled. We have found it valuable to guide the reader through them, explaining each briefly and clearly in the text that precedes them, indicating how to read them and what to look for. The use of color in graphics often enhances the reader's understanding; however, we urge evaluators to remember that the colors red and green should be avoided because they may be indistinct to those who are color-blind.

Guiding Paragraphs and Sentences

While executive summaries provide an overview of the report, there are other ways of structuring the report to enhance communication. It can be very helpful to provide the reader with periodic guiding paragraphs and sentences throughout the document. These alert the reader to the issues or findings that will follow; they provide a "road map" to the way a section is structured and supply the reader with occasional reminders as to why particular findings or recommendations are important to the overall themes of the report. Obviously, there is a danger in overdoing such guiding; too much could make the report repetitious and patronizing. But in our experience, writers do not do enough of this kind of guiding and directing – and its inclusion can make a report more accessible and reader-friendly.

Findings

No program is perfect. Therefore, to make informed and fair decisions, it is the responsibility of the evaluator to present a comprehensive picture of the program, including positive, unfavorable, and ambiguous findings. Evaluators rarely question how to present positive findings. Usually the evaluator is pleased to communicate favorable findings, and audiences are happy to receive them. On the other hand, evaluators regularly consider how to most judiciously communicate unfavorable or ambiguous findings. Receptiveness to receiving unfavorable or ambiguous findings often depends upon the relationships established by the evaluator and, thus, the extent to which potential audiences and users come to view these findings as suggestions for improvement. Some evaluation theoretic positions place a premium on establishing close, non-threatening relationships with potential evaluation users. Thus, the ability of the evaluator to portray his or her role as a helper concerned with bettering the program could set the tone for constructively viewing potential areas of improvement. The issue becomes not one of positive or negative findings but, rather, identifying areas of strength and areas for potential revision. However, establishing such relationships may not be feasible within some evaluation approaches or in large national evaluations with legislative or other policy-making audiences.

No matter what the approach, it is inevitable that there will be unhappiness, if not pain, associated with unfavorable findings. This pain may get translated into particular demands from clients/stakeholders. The evaluator must be sensitive in dealing with situations related to the presentation of unfavorable data, and to potential attempts at inappropriate modifications.

At the conclusion of an evaluation study, it also is not uncommon for there to be some ambiguous findings; definitive answers to all evaluation questions may not have been obtained. Such uncertainty can present a particular challenge when communicating results. The evaluator must communicate carefully and effectively the extent of the uncertainty that remains about evaluation findings without discrediting the evaluation and, thus, inadvertently jeopardizing its findings during the client's decision-making process.

One example of ambiguity or a possibly misleading result can be found in those evaluations that include quantitative studies, specifically ambiguities in interpretation that can arise because of validity threats or confounds. However, even when validity threats are accounted for and adequately discussed, the nature of statistical findings often creates a challenge for communicating about uncertainty. In particular, the reporting of statistical significance is common in quantitative evaluation studies, but significance alone is often inadequate and potentially misleading as a criterion because it is so dependent on sample size (e.g., a small effect with a large sample can be significant; a larger effect with a small sample may be non-significant). Moreover, statistical significance is not a measure of the size of an effect, rather it is a measure of how unlikely the data are under the assumption that the null hypothesis is true. Thus, while significance tests are typically used to generalize from the sample studied to a broader population in program evaluation, we are often not concerned with generalization. Therefore, reporting effect sizes in addition, or as an alternative, to statistical significance is advocated by many social scientists and evaluators in order to reduce some of the ambiguity that can accompany interpreting the impact of a program on different groups (i.e., intervention or experimental group and comparison or control group).

The issue of communicating uncertainty is not simply a technical one or one that applies only to treatment effect estimates and statistical relationships. Ambiguity is found when analyzing qualitative data as well, and such uncertainty should also be taken seriously. Uncertainty in data can, in some instances, have a positive outcome in that ambiguities often identify areas in need of greater understanding as well as provide the impetus for further study of a particular program.

There would seem to be no simple answer to the question of how to deal with ambiguity other than to be very careful in clarifying what was found and in stating the implications of the finding. Most important, however, is that the evaluator be clear about when findings are ambiguous, and, indeed, keep in mind that in some instances stakeholders might be able to help clarify some of the ambiguity found in the evaluation study.

Related to clarity (and ambiguity) is the issue of limitations. While statements of limitations are a part of every evaluation study, this is particularly necessary when findings are ambiguous. In these and all studies, evaluators must make explicit in their communications the particular limitations that affect the findings, including their own particular values and biases.

Recommendations

Consider now the question of recommendations. Hendricks & Papagiannis (1982) note that "recommendations are one of the most critical products of an evaluation" (p. 121). Indeed, they are the most carefully examined part of any report. The general theme of this chapter certainly applies here as well: know your audience. The unique social, political,

and organizational characteristics that define the entity being evaluated should be considered in framing recommendations.

Of the various issues related to recommendations, the first is whether or not to have them. The authors of this chapter are at variance with much of the evaluation community on the issue of recommendations. Alkin (2004) believes that the evaluator should not insert his/her own value system into the process by making judgments about findings. Instead, he advocates working with intended primary users at the onset of the evaluation to establish a future "framework for judging results," (2004, p. 300). Alkin proposes the use of scenarios to help in developing these frameworks:

> On quantitative measures, I would ask users to consider what would be satisfactory results and I would present possible findings and ask what the implications for action would be. A variety of outcome scenarios are posed in order to delimit the judging framework. ("Suppose I found x outcome, what would it mean in terms of possible changes in your program?") With descriptive or qualitative information to be gathered, I inquire as to what they think we will find – what they think the program will look like descriptively or qualitatively – in order to use these initial descriptions and conceptions as a basis for subsequent comparison. (p. 300)

Alkin writes that even when it is not feasible to establish a framework for judging results, he tries to report descriptive data that can be assessed and judged by the various stakeholders.

Even in instances where the evaluator is required or prefers to include recommendations, Alkin's framework for judging results can be helpful. At the outset, the evaluator could think jointly with the primary stakeholders about possible recommendations under different sets of findings. More generally, whether or not evaluators are involved in collaborative deliberation, they should not wait until the end of evaluation to begin contemplating recommendations. Further, as findings begin to emerge, informal reporting can begin to presage possible recommendations – and, thus, facilitate likely use. Again, as in many aspects of communication, this approach is highly dependent on both the evaluators' theoretic approach as well as the program context. Jointly developed judgment frameworks are more likely to be employed by those who advocate participatory/collaborative evaluation approaches as opposed to those theorists who are more research-oriented in their approach. Likewise, programs that are more large scale and complex offer less possibility for defining specific stakeholders who could engage in such deliberative discussions.

If evaluators believe that their recommendations are sound (and most do), they want to see them have influence on decisions and policy-formation. How, then, can useful recommendations be framed? In considering the format of recommendations, one important issue is this: How specific should they be? Possibilities range from highly specific recommendations that dictate a particular action or choice to more general recommendations framed as alternatives to consider. The worry that we have with highly specific recommendations concerns the extent to which the evaluator goes beyond areas of evaluation expertise and ventures into a consultant role requiring specific program expertise. In such instances programs acting under such advice might not improve but could worsen. In any case, when specific recommendations follow from the evaluative data, they should be bounded by the constraints of the findings and the specific implications derived from them.

Hendricks & Papagiannis (1982) offer suggestions for making recommendations easy for potential users/stakeholders to understand. Among their list of suggestions are the following: don't offer a long undifferentiated list of recommendations; draw a clear, physical boundary between recommendations and findings or conclusions; test the clarity of recommendations by presenting them to "cold readers" (those not involved with the program); and, finally, decide carefully where in the text to place them (p. 124).

Summaries

There is also the issue of summaries. Morris et al., (1987) note that "when asked what evaluators could do to make evaluation information more useful to State Assembly members, a legislative assistant once commented, 'Just write down the conclusions of your report in one sentence, in large type, in the middle of a sheet of paper.' Influential reports are short and to the point" (p. 10). While not going so far as to advocate a single sentence centered on a page, we note the importance of brief summaries as useful communication.

One such strongly advocated summary is popularly referred to as the executive summary. The time and patience of potential recipients of evaluation reports is frequently limited. When confronted with a massive and sometimes imposing report, there may be a tendency to avoid it. Evaluators can help ease the load by guiding potential readers through the report via the executive summary. It is suggested in the *Evaluation Standards* (Joint Committee, 1994) that the executive summary should contain condensed versions of all of the sections of the full report.

While summarizing all sections of the report is certainly a possibility, our experience suggests a variation of this approach. Evaluators should think of the executive summary as a one-page or two-page guidebook for learning about the most important things that stakeholders and other readers might want to know. Thus, the executive summary should focus primarily on the evaluation results and recommendations (if any). In terms of format, our suggestion is that the ordering in the executive summary should be presented in a way that corresponds with the priority of potential readers' interests (but so, too, should the final report).

Executive summaries should not be written as direct narratives but should employ descriptive phrases only long enough to convey the essential idea. The use of "bullets," stars, or other highlighting devices is encouraged, along with indentations and differences in typeface and size. Macy (1982) suggests the use of a question-and-answer format. All of these suggestions should be carried out in moderation, so as to not create an unduly complicated or confusing appearance.

The executive summary also serves as a reference for further study – a guide to the report. To serve this purpose, our experience in producing executive summaries suggests the need for referencing summary ideas to specific pages in the body of the report so that those who are interested can easily access a more thorough discussion of the summary item.

Notes or Attachments

In order to keep a report within a reasonable length and to enhance its readability, material will often be located outside the main text, in notes or attachments. Of course, different projects will have different requirements as to the amount of such material that is required. That said, let us offer a few rules of thumb. When deciding what to put in the body of the text versus in a note or attachment, ask yourself how important it is in clarifying or supporting the point you are making. If it is critical, then it should be in the text rather than in a note; if

it is material of some length (documents or tables of data), then be sure to summarize it clearly and crisply in the text itself, and explain exactly why it is important to the point you're making. Also, think about attachments strategically; that is, don't simply append everything you collect to the end of the report. Some material may not be necessary, and whatever you do attach should have some clear purpose.

Multiple Reports

There are various situations that demand multiple reports. One of these is when the technical material to be presented is so extensive that a simple attachment is not complete enough and the full material would overwhelm the body of the evaluation report. For many complex evaluations there is a relatively commonplace practice of providing both an evaluation report and a detailed technical appendix, sometimes extending to multiple volumes.

Another situation which often requires multiple reports occurs when there is a multiplicity of potential audiences, including many groups that have a strong stake in the evaluand. The unique focus and interests of each group sometimes requires "tailored" reports to best satisfy various interests and needs. Such reporting might be accomplished in several ways. Multiple reports can be produced or, alternatively, combination reports prepared consisting of common and customized sections. That is, a comprehensive, more lengthy report could be written and given to the stakeholder group that commissioned the evaluation, and from this larger document, shorter, more specific reports could be derived to meet the particular needs of other relevant stakeholder groups. Alternatively, the same comprehensive report given to the group that commissioned the evaluation could be disseminated to all interested stakeholder groups with customized executive summaries. These summaries would include only the findings that are most relevant to a particular group, and would direct readers to the specific sections of the document that are most pertinent to them.

Alternative Final Reporting Forms

While written reports are the most common reporting format, there are many other means of communicating, which some believe have more impact than the written report. For example, Smith (1982) asserts, "If evaluators are to improve their communication of evaluative information, they need not only to deepen their understanding of the ways in which representation influences our understanding of reality, but they also need clear procedural alternatives for use in their daily work" (p. 177). Thus, evaluators are urged to consider multiple presentation formats that engage stakeholders and other potential users. Indeed, Patton (1997) notes that he does not feel bound to write a report in all instances. Oral presentations, discussed previously as a way of communicating interim evaluation findings, are one frequently used procedure for communicating end-of-evaluation results. Beyond the oral presentation there have been numerous suggestions for other alternative modes of communicating evaluation findings. These include: conferences, debates, videotapes of program activities, role-plays, and photographs; narratives, poems, and performance drama.

As with all communication of evaluation findings, when considering alternative communication modes it is critical for evaluators to understand their audience. Often there is more than one evaluation audience, and each audience might benefit from a different mode of communication. If the evaluator believes that alternative communication forms will increase the impact of the evaluation findings, they should be considered. Patton, in a book entitled *Creative Evaluation* (1981), indicates that the evaluator should be innovative in devising evaluation procedures that fit each particular situation. So, too, alternative communication forms cannot be prepackaged; evaluators may conceive of many different ways of communication. The authors strongly encourage exploring such options, and perhaps generating creative alternatives appropriate for a given study, program, context, and audience. In the next few paragraphs, we will examine some alternative communication modes proposed in the literature. These should be considered as but a starting point.

Weiss (1998) describes using alternative forums for communicating interim findings, such as a conference that serves as a mechanism both to disseminate existing findings about crucial observations and to obtain comments on (and reactions to) possible approaches to addressing areas of needed improvement. In this forum, not only would the evaluator be communicating findings formally through short written summaries and visual presentations (e.g., Power Point), but would also have the opportunity to engage in more informal communication with stakeholders.

Another procedure that evaluators might employ is an interactive approach in which evaluators present data to stakeholders, and they jointly engage in the analysis of the data. Evaluators can use these interactive sessions as the initial step in framing an evaluation report – or the session, in and of itself, can constitute the evaluation reporting.

Morris et al., (1987) recommend that evaluators "do something different" (p. 36); that is, do something that will surprise the audience. They maintain that such an approach will keep the audience alert, involved, and interested. Often it is recommended that a role-play technique be used (e.g., Morris et al., 1987; Smith, 1982). For example, when presenting findings, the evaluators can involve the audience in an advocacy–adversary (or debate) process (e.g., Morris et al., 1987; Levine, 1982). This involves dividing the audience into three groups, advocates, adversaries, and neutrals. Each group reviews the report and engages in a lively and balanced debate over the data and results. As another form of role-play, skits or plays can be performed. Here, evaluators might participate in a skit in order to communicate a finding that is better understood with a real-life example. Or, stakeholders and evaluators may develop a short play to illustrate a challenging evaluation situation or result. No matter what the method, when using role-play to communicate evaluation results, it is critical that the presentation be well-practiced and engaging (e.g., Rallis & Rossman, 1998; Morris et al., 1987).

When communicating findings to policymakers, Haensly, Lupkowski, & McNamara (1987) suggest creating what they call a *chart essay* as a written alternative to the traditional final report. Chart essays are "brief policy-oriented reports that have two objectives: (a) to link the specific research questions addressed to real policy decisions; and (b) to arrange each answer in a chart that highlights the actual research data gathered in the field" (p. 72). Chart essays are intended to promote decision-making based on a sound study efficiently presented. They are designed explicitly for a briefing, and as such are organized by the key stakeholder questions, in order of priority or importance. For each of the key questions a single chart is prepared that succinctly presents an answer derived from the evaluation data. Thus, each chart is designed to stand alone, though they might collectively address a common problem.

It is also important to mention the use of photography and video. Templin (1982) was the first to call attention to photography's role in portraying the results of evaluation, either alone or to enliven written reports. Understanding that photos present a single instant in time, evaluators should be careful in their selection to assure that depictions are truly representative. Advances in digital technology have increased the ease with which photos can be prepared and shared in a variety of ways with stakeholders. Torres et al., (1996) provide some excellent specific suggestions for the use of photography in evaluation reporting.

Finally, there is the World Wide Web, which expands the evaluator's opportunity to disseminate reports, as well as the ease with which reports can be accessed by stakeholders and other relevant groups. Additionally, it facilitates the inclusion into reports of digital media such as videos, photos, sound, and music. The web can be used simply as a medium to post written evaluation reports, or used in more complex ways such as an interactive forum for stakeholders to discuss findings. Particular means by which evaluators utilize the web for reporting include: links to incorporate (download) video and audio clips to illustrate findings in a written report, links to references (and other websites) cited in documents, the posting of multimedia presentations, and the hosting of a website for evaluation information and materials. Privacy and security concerns should be discussed with stakeholders when contemplating the use of the web for reporting; however, advances in these areas such as the development of password-protected sites have made using the web for evaluation reporting more feasible.

Beyond the Report

Finally, when does the evaluator's communication responsibility start and when does it end? The authors have previously discussed the communication role of the evaluator prior to the start of the evaluation itself. A dialog between evaluators and stakeholders about what an evaluation might look like is, in fact, communication directed at clarifying the nature of the program and its information needs. Beyond communicating the results of the evaluation, many evaluators believe that the evaluator has a role in helping to assure that evaluation findings have impact. Thus, the evaluator's communication role may extend beyond the report and include a consideration of the implications of the report, helping users to facilitate possible next steps.

We provide several examples from a series of case studies conducted by noted evaluators who examined factors influencing evaluation use (Alkin, Stecher, & Geiger, 1982). The study identified the important communication role of teaching stakeholders about how results might be better used. Larry Braskamp (one of the case study authors) noted the effort of the evaluators to produce a communication network, which ensured that evaluation results were passed to all decision levels, reacted to, and fed back through the system. Jean King reported on an evaluator whose enhanced communication activities included providing specific information and then encouraging participation on a related task such as "suggesting changes on the program, planning next year's workshop, developing a dissemination plan, (or) creating a meaningful attendance policy" (Alkin et al., 1982, p. 92).

Relationship to Theoretical Approaches

Evaluation approaches, often referred to as evaluation theories or models, are intended to be prescriptions or guides for practice. Theories address the focus and role of the evaluation, the specific evaluation questions to be studied, the evaluation design and implementation, and the use of evaluation results (Christie & Alkin, 2003). They emphasize, prioritize, and combine a range of evaluation techniques. Categorizing evaluation approaches by major emphasis or other important dimensions can be a helpful way to understand and compare the varying characteristics of approaches to evaluation. In order to describe the evaluation communication issues discussed in this chapter in relationship to evaluation approaches, we present in Table 17.1 a modified version of an evaluation theory classification scheme developed by Fitzpatrick, Sanders, & Worthen (2004). In this table we describe how the approaches differ along a number of criteria related to communication. (For a complete discussion of the criteria, please see Fitzpatrick et al., 2004.)

Evaluation as Research

Evaluation as research includes those approaches that promote the use of experimental methods for studying programs. This includes the use of experimental and control or comparison groups and, when possible, random assignment of participants. Evaluations conducted using an evaluation-as-research approach resemble what are thought to be more traditional social science research intervention studies. Often, the desire to contribute to a greater understanding of a given social phenomena – that is, reporting to a more academic or public policy community – shapes the evaluation communication. An evaluation communication reporting plan is not necessarily developed by evaluators using a research approach. In the case when one is developed, however, it is likely to be done so with program funders and developers. Reporting formats are more formal and tend to focus on final results rather than interim findings.

Objectives-Oriented Evaluation

Objectives-oriented evaluation refers to a class of evaluation approaches that center on the

EXEMPLAR 17.1 Communication

Communication formats		Theory type				
	Evaluation as research[a]	Objectives-oriented	Management-oriented	Expertise-oriented	Participant-oriented
Purpose of evaluation	Providing scientific evidence – hypothesis testing	Determining, the extent to which objectives are achieved	Providing information to aid managements' decision-making	Providing professional judgments of quality, accreditation	Understanding and portraying the complexities of programmatic activity, responding to an audience's requirements for information
Reporting audiences	Program developers, leaders, and academic community	Program developers, leaders, general public	Program leaders	Program developers, leaders, general public	Program developers, leaders, staff, and participants
Generally	Focus on formal, final reporting	Focus on formal, final reporting	Formal, interim, and final reporting	Formal and informal, final reporting	Informal and formal, interim and final reporting
Structuring the evaluation communication plan	With a select audience or stakeholder group (i.e., program developers)	With a select audience or stakeholder group (i.e., program developers)	With a select audience or stakeholder group (i.e., primarily program leaders)	With a select audience or stakeholder group (i.e., program developers and leaders)	With a larger audience or stakeholder group (i.e., program developers, leaders, staff, participants)
Informal oral communication	Infrequent	Occasionally	Occasionally	Occasionally	Usually
Use of alternative reporting formats	Limited	Limited	Limited	Limited	Moderate
Provide an interim report	Occasionally	Occasionally	Frequently	Occasionally	Usually
Provide a final report	Usually	Usually	Usually	Usually	Frequently

[a]This category is not included in the Fitzpatrick. Sanders, & Worthen (2004) classification system and was added by the authors of this chapter. This category replaces the "Consumer-Oriented" category included by Fitzpatrick et al., (2004).

specification of objectives and the measurement of outcomes. Specifically, objectives-oriented approaches focus on generating information for accountability and decision-making by developing and measuring the appropriate objectives for these purposes. Objectives-oriented evaluation approaches require very specific, detailed, precise objectives and the development of valid measures for each objective. Most often, emphasis is on the measure of objectives, i.e., outcomes. As a result, the audience for an objectives-oriented evaluation is often program developers or leaders, or in the case of educational evaluation (where this approach is most commonly utilized), teachers are sometimes included. It is the evaluation audience that helps to develop an evaluation communication plan. Because the focus is on measurement of outcomes, communication is typically formal and is most likely to occur at the conclusion of a program (or curriculum), rather than on an interim basis.

Management-Oriented Evaluation

Management-oriented evaluation approaches are concerned with providing useful information for decision-making to program leaders or managers. It is the program managers' information needs that shape the evaluation purpose and questions. The evaluator takes the lead in developing the evaluation design, choosing methods and data collection, but typically will consult with program leaders with respect to the appropriateness and feasibility of his/her choices. Since the goal of management-oriented evaluation approaches is to provide information for decision-making, recurrent communication is common. Thus, the communication plan, which is developed with program leaders, can be an important guide for the overall evaluation structure. Generally, because of the nature of the evaluation audience, communication is more formal.

It is a common expectation that communication be in both oral and written formats, and that it be tailored to meet the information needs of program leaders, and not a more general audience.

Expertise-Oriented Evaluation

The expertise-oriented evaluation approach is concerned with making value judgments about the quality of a situation based on the evaluator's knowledge and experience. While expertise-oriented evaluation is concerned with outcomes, there is also a focus on what creates or contributes to outcomes so that they can be enhanced. Methods often incorporate observation of the program, including site visits and interviews. It is most commonly used for self-study, examination by committee, or accreditation. As a result, generalizations are often restricted to the context, and so communication is usually focused on the program community. However, when used for accreditation purposes, information must also be communicated to a more general audience. It is uncommon for an evaluation communication plan to be developed when using this approach because information is not usually communicated at multiple times throughout the evaluation. Rather, expertise judgment is typically rendered at the conclusion of the evaluation.

Participant-Oriented Evaluation

The purpose of participant-oriented evaluation is to respond to a specific audience's requirements for information, with the goal of having the information influence program decisions. It is thought that involving program participants (e.g., program developers, leaders, staff, and those affected by the program) in all aspects of the evaluation process increases the likelihood that information yielded from the evaluation will be used for its intended purpose. There is a focus on description, concern for context, and openness to an evolving evaluation plan. The evaluation communication plan is developed with those stakeholders who are involved in the evaluation process, and in some approaches serves as a central element in the conduct of the evaluation. Communication is both formal and informal, and occurs as a result of participating in the evaluation process, as well as on an interim basis. Alternative communication formats are often desirable when conducting participant-oriented evaluations. Some participant-oriented evaluators believe that a formal final evaluation report is not necessary because communication has transpired throughout the evaluation process. Often, however, there are external audiences who are concerned with the evaluation findings, and in that case a formal final report would be prepared.

Summary: Moving in New Directions

As we survey the literature on communication and evaluation, we find that it consists primarily of discussions of communication as it relates to reporting, both interim and final, formal and informal. It also offers discussion of alternative modes of communicating results – for example, on modes drawn from the arts as well as from the traditional social sciences. Included in this literature are issues of scope and breadth of audience and accessibility – topics we have addressed.

We believe that there is another, frequently neglected, element to this account of communication. To make our point, we will draw on a classic article in communication theory by Michael Reddy (1979), in which he suggests that so much common talk about communication relies on what he refers to as a "conduit metaphor." This metaphor suggests that communication is simply a function of a speaker/writer capturing ideas and words and then sending them – as if through a conduit – to a receiver on the other end of the communication system. The receiver then unpacks the ideas and communication is complete. Reddy argues, however, that communication is much more complex than that, involving a good deal of what today we would refer to as interpretation and construction, imbued with a good deal of subjective response and uncertainty.

Evaluators are keenly aware of the fact that the context in which a program operates has a profound impact on the evaluation process and on its potential use and outcomes. However, the evaluator may not be aware of the degree to which this complexity holds true for the act of communication itself. Even evaluators who are sensitive to these issues of context and the complexity of utilization may still operate with a notion of communication that would, in essence, suggest that the evaluator's job as communicator is done once a report is produced. But theoretical work like Reddy's reminds us that, in fact, there are multiple "internal, human systems responsible for nine-tenths of the work in communicating" (p. 310).

As the literature on use and utilization has sensitized evaluators to the complexity of the conditions under which programmatic change can occur, we believe that the more nuanced sense of communication that we offer here enhances the thought and care that go into the presentation of evaluation findings. Ideas are not simply little bundles of cognition that are then neatly unpacked by those that receive them. Rather, the evaluator needs to draw on all the resources available to him or her to consider the context of the program, to encourage processes that will animate reporting (that is, that make results come alive), and to consider alternative forms of communication, appreciating the fact that multiple forms of presentation may increase the likelihood that a larger audience will be reached, realizing that what clicks with one stakeholder may not click with another.

Evaluation communications are part of a larger communication network, and there are continual interactions between the parts of the network. We are surrounded by language. We believe that a heightened awareness of language makes us better communicators and better evaluators because it helps us to reflect on evaluation itself. Taking care to be precise and thoughtful in our communication is a discipline that affects not only our speaking and writing, but all the practices we use for evaluation, the very way that we do our work.

References

Alkin, M. (ed.) (2004). *Evaluation Roots.* Thousand Oaks, CA: Sage.

Alkin, M. (1990). *Debates on Evaluation.* Newbury Park, CA: Sage.

Alkin, M., Stecher, B., & Geiger, F. (1982). *Title I Evaluation: utility and factors influencing use.* Northridge, CA: Educational Evaluation Associates.

Cabatoff, K. (2000). Translating evaluation findings into "policy language." In R. Hopson (ed.) *How and Why Language Matters in Evaluation. New Directions for Evaluation,* No. 86, (pp. 43–54). San Francisco; Jossey-Bass

Christie, C. & Alkin, M. (2003). The user-orientated evaluator's role in formulating a program theory: Using a theory-driven approach. *American Journal of Evaluation* 24(3), 373–385.

Datta, L. (1999). The ethics of evaluation neutrality and advocacy. In J. Fitzpatrick & M. Morris (eds) *Current and Emerging Challenges in Evaluation. New Directions for Evaluation,* No. 82, (pp. 77–88). San Francisco: Jossey-Bass.

Fitzpatrick, J. L., Sanders, J. R., & Worthen, B. R. (2004). *Program evaluation: Alternative approaches and practical guidelines* (3rd ed). Boston: Allyn & Bacon.

Greene (1990). Three views on the nature and role of knowledge in social science. In E. G. Guba (ed.) *Paradigm Dialogue.* Thousand Oaks, CA: Sage.

Greene, J. (1995). Evaluation as advocacy. *Evaluation Practice,* 18, 25–36.

Haensly, P., Lupkowski, A., & McNamara, J. (1987). The chart essay: A strategy for communicating research findings to policymakers and practitioners. *Educational Evaluation and Policy Analysis,* 9(1), 63–75.

Hathaway, W. (1982). Graphic display procedures. In Smith, N. (ed.) *Communication Strategies in Evaluation.* Beverly Hills, CA: Sage. (pp. 191–207).

Hendricks, M. & Papagiannis, M. (1982). Oral policy briefings. In N. Smith (ed.) *Communication Strategies in Evaluation* (pp. 249–258). Beverly Hills, CA: Sage.

Henry, G. (1995). *Graphing Data: Techniques for display and analysis.* Thousand Oaks, CA: Sage.

Henry, G. (ed.) (1997). *Creating Effective Graphs! Solutions for a variety of evaluation data. New Directions for Evaluation,* No. 73. San Francisco, CA: Jossey-Bass.

Joint Committee on Standards for Educational Evaluation (1994). *The Program Evaluation Standards,* 2nd edition. *How to Assess Evaluations of Educational Programs.* Thousand Oaks, CA: Sage.

Kaminsky, A. (2000). Beyond the literal: metaphors and why they matter. In R. Hopson, (ed.) *How and Why Language Matters in Evaluation. New Directions for Evaluation,* No. 86, (pp. 69–80). San Francisco, CA: Jossey-Bass.

King, J. (2002). Building the evaluation capacity of a school district. In D. Compton, M. Baizerman, & S. Stackdill (eds) *The Art, Craft and Science of Evaluation Capacity Building. New Directions for Evaluation,* No. 93, (pp. 63–80). San Francisco, CA: Jossey-Bass.

Lanham, R. (2000). *Revising Prose.* New York: Longman.

Levine, M. (1982). Adversary hearings. In N. Smith, (ed.) *Communication Strategies in Evaluation* (pp. 269–278). Beverly Hills, CA: Sage.

Lincoln, Y. (1990). The making of a constructivist: A remembrance of transformations past. In E. Guba (ed.) *The Paradigm Dialog.* Thousand Oaks, CA: Sage.

Lynch, K. (1986). Style versus substance in evaluation reports. *Evaluation Practice,* 7(4), 75–76.

Macy, D. (1982). Research briefs. In N. Smith (ed.) *Communication Strategies in Evaluation* (pp. 179–189). Beverly Hills, CA: Sage.

McGlone, E. & Fausti, R. (1972). *Introductory Readings in Oral Communication: Theories, opinions, examples*. Menlo Park, CA: Cummings.

Morris, L., Fitz-Gibbon, C., & Freeman, M. (1987*). How to Communicate Evaluation Findings*. Newbury Park, CA: Sage.

Patton, M. (1981). *Creative Evaluation*. Beverly Hills, CA: Sage.

Patton, M. (1997). *Utilization-Focused Evaluation: The new century text*, 3rd edition. Thousand Oaks, CA: Sage.

Patton, M. (2000). Overview: language matters. In R. Hopson, (ed.) *How and Why Language Matters in Evaluation. New Directions for Evaluation*, No. 86, (pp. 5–16). San Francisco, CA: Jossey-Bass.

Preskill, H., Zuckerman, B., & Matthews, B. (2003). An exploratory study of process use: Findings and implications for future research. *American Journal of Evaluation*, 24(4), 423–442.

Rallis, S. & Rossman, G. (1998). *Learning in the Field: an introduction to qualitative research*. Thousand Oaks, CA: Sage.

Ramsey, R. (2002). *How to Say the Right Thing Every Time: Communicating well with students, staff, parents, and the public*. Thousand Oaks, CA: Corwin Press.

Reddy, M. (1979). The conduit metaphor – A case of frame conflict in our language about language. In A. Ortony, (ed.) *Metaphor and Thought* (pp. 284–324). Cambridge: Cambridge University Press.

Rose, M. & McClafferty, K. (2001). A call for the teaching of writing in graduate education. *Educational Researcher*, 30(2), 27–33.

Smith, N. (ed.) (1982*). Communication Strategies in Evaluation: New Perspectives in Evaluation*, 3, Beverly Hills, CA: Sage.

Stufflebeam, D. (2000). Lessons in contracting for evaluations. *American Journal of Evaluation*, 21(3), 293–314.

Strunk, W. & White, E. (1959). *The Elements of Style*. New York: Macmillan.

Templin, P. (1982). Still photography in evaluation. In N. L. Smith (ed.) *Communication Strategies in Evaluation* (pp. 121–175). Beverly Hills, CA: Sage.

Torres, R., Preskill, H., & Piontek, M. (1996). *Evaluation Strategies for Communicating and Reporting: Enhancing learning in organizations*. Thousand Oaks, CA: Sage.

Tufte, E. (1983). *The Visual Display of Quantitative Information*. Chesire, CT: Graphics Press.

Weiss, C. (1998). *Evaluation* (2nd edition). Upper Saddle River, NJ: Prentice Hall.

Williams, J. (2002). *Style: Ten lessons in clarity and grace*. New York: Longman.

ON DISCERNING QUALITY IN EVALUATION

Robert E. Stake and Thomas A. Schwandt

Evaluation studies are fundamentally a search for and claim about quality. This is so whether we are concerned with evaluating projects, programs, or policies, or evaluations per se (i.e., meta-evaluation). Quality is a broad term that encompasses notions of merit, worth, and significance. This chapter addresses matters of the recognition and representation of quality in professional and lay evaluation. It begins with an exploration of the concept of quality and then considers two views of quality in light of evaluands that can be personally embraced and those that cannot. The chapter then examines technical viewpoints on how quality is to be discerned in evaluation as well as viewpoints on the evaluator's responsibility to represent quality.

Defining and Understanding Quality

The evaluation of programs and projects is premised on the common idea that quality is discernible and capable of representation. To distinguish quality one must be able to discriminate – to tell the difference between the absence and presence of quality. Discerning quality is always a matter of expectation and comparison. Notions of quality (and merit, value, worth, and significance) have no meaning absent notions of inferiority, insignificance, worthlessness, and unimportance. One rarely deals with a situation in which the judgment of quality is clear-cut and straightforward. Judgments of quality usually leave room for doubt.

Evaluators of different persuasions share the expectation that judging variations (whether subtle or stark) of quality are central to evaluation. Evaluators speak differently about what quality is, how quality is discernible, and how judgments of quality are to be represented. Quite a few evaluators routinely use goal fulfillment, effectiveness, productivity, or popularity to represent quality. Quite a few move directly to the raising of staff or organization ability to attain quality. Regardless of how it is conceived and perceived, quality, as an anchor to program understanding, is a widely shared expectation.

Some methodologists emphasize gauging the quality of an evaluand against particular external standards. Others emphasize gathering judgments of participants and stakeholders. Some argue that quality is best represented in carefully articulated evaluative statements arising from procedures or rules for decision-making. Still others claim that quality is represented best by description of insightful practice using evidence, intuition, and lived experience.

The word "quality" [Latin *qualitas*] is used in ways that both describe and appraise. It is commonplace to speak of "quality" as if we are referring to the aspects or properties that constitute or characterize something. For example, one identifies the "qualities" (read "features") of an educational program as being composed of staff qualifications, pedagogy, materials used, students served, institutional support, and so on. A particular piece of music can be described as lyrical, sonorous, earthy, or conventional. To speak of the qualities of management, we often use terms such as creative, decentralized, and public-minded. But the *quality* of an educational program is often spoken of in terms of its meeting its objectives, enhancing student outcomes, and so forth. It is also common to speak of "quality" in such a way that it signifies an appraisal or judgment of excellence, merit, or worth. Whether one is describing or appraising when stating terms that denote quality depends, in part, on the context in which the terms are used (House & Howe, 1999).

Evaluators are concerned with making judgments or appraisals of quality. To appraise is to offer an informed opinion about the quality of the matter at hand by means of comparing it to some decisive experience, factor, principle, norm, or condition. Evaluators appraise the quality of both procedures and outcomes. They seek to discern what makes for both good provision and good performance.

An evaluation of the quality of a program or project is incomplete if it attends only to integrity or only to impact. The default position and ordinary aim of much evaluation is to discern the quality of what has been provided, the input and process. The quality of outcomes, of course, matters as well. However, too strict a devotion to measuring outcomes may mean that the evaluator moves too quickly past appropriate appraisal of the integrity of the evaluand. The quality of the provision may affect subsequent offerings more than the measured quality of outcomes.

Process assessment is a search for quality in the provision of services, the routine operation and coping with problems. Almost every program stakeholder cares about the quality of the arrangements, materials, and staffing as well as the quality of the transactions, safety, and provision of opportunity. It is not enough to know that the results meet or exceed standards. It is usually important to obtain the best provision possible, given costs and other constraints, always expecting that even better outcomes or side-effects can be attained with better input.

Many evaluators subscribe to the belief that the quality of an evaluand is best represented by superiority of performance, particularly as performed by a beneficiary group such as welfare mothers or military recruits. Quality of outcomes usually requires indicators of performance, and the general view is that a single indicator of performance is better than no indicator at all. Of course, this can be a dodgy assumption: Enemy body count and villages occupied by US armed forces in Vietnam are examples of performance indicators that failed to reflect failure.

Quality is multifaceted, contested, and never fully representable. Procedures for identification, specification, and measurement support the judging of quality, yet judgment-making is always practical rather than instrumental in character. We construct, fashion, craft, and hammer out an argument, or make a case aimed to persuade particular stakeholders in a given place and time. The argument or case for quality is presumptive – it is what we think most likely or reasonable given the features of the evaluand at hand, the context, circumstances, audience, evidence, and so on.[1] At least in such human endeavors as social and educational programs, we never establish quality once and for all. These are defining characteristics of all human endeavors to evaluate. The contingent, interpretive character of our judgment is something we must live with rather than regard as fixed and eliminable.

The perception and appraisal of quality is influenced by the values of the perceiver, including the evaluator. For example, we might expect that an evaluator committed to making the social system more rational would recognize quality in the rational management of a program and see less quality in an administration responsive to political pressures. Shadish, Cook, & Leviton (1991) made the "valuing component" one of five theoretical dimensions of evaluation theory, and raised the question of how theorists handle the question of "What makes a program a good program?" In other words, "What is its quality?" But within the valuing component they also raised the question, "What value commitments are implicit in the theory?" This is a different question, yet related to the first. What one perceives as quality is often influenced by the kinds of social and behavioral theories of society one brings, explicitly or implicitly, into an evaluation.

In the best of circumstances, the activities that constitute judgment of the quality of projects, programs, even entire evaluations – e.g., the discernment of needs, the explication of criteria, the appeal to evidence, the significance

of personal experience – are "political" in the sense that the judgment is "a function of a commonality that can be exercised only by citizens interacting with one another in the context of mutual deliberation and decision" (Barber, 1988, p. 200). Judgment of this kind is "we-judgment" or public judgment that assumes a view of mutually engaged citizens. This way of thinking resonates with Ernest House & Ken Howe's view (1999) of how judging program quality should look in a deliberative democracy.

The view of quality as the outcome of judgment that is deliberative, political, public, and interpretive is currently threatened by a technocratic view of politics evident in theories of neo-liberal governmentality. In these theories, the "political" is paradoxically transformed into an outwardly *apolitical* phenomenon – a style of formalized accountability that becomes the new ethical and political principle of governance (Power, 1997). What is particularly troublesome here is the explicit equation of quality solely with *performativity* – the measurement of performance against *indicators* of target achievement. The movement towards an exclusive focus on performativity is subtle and surreptitious: subtle because the language of quality is actually retained (we talk about "quality assurance") and made to appear so relevant and cleverly targeted that it needs no defense; surreptitious because, although an apparent concern for quality is maintained and even made more prominent, it is neutered and emptied of meaning. Quality is rendered *adiaphoric* – it is neither good nor bad, but depicted as indifferent and simply measurable against technical indicators (Bauman, 1993). This is worrisome because the idea of "evaluating program quality" is rendered moot or so carefully finessed that the substitution of performance for quality goes unnoticed.

Conceptualizing Quality-as-Measured

Sometimes the experiences, factors, principles, norms, and conditions used in the appraisal of quality are clearly articulated and treated as explicit standards or criteria. In these circumstances, quality is regarded as measurable, and judging quality takes on the characteristic of thinking criterially – explicit comparison of the object in question to a set of standards for it. This familiar way of judging quality is represented in Michael Scriven's (1991) view of the logic of evaluation – (1) establish criteria of merit, (2) construct standards, (3) measure performance and compare to standards, (4) synthesize and integrate results into a judgment of merit, worth, or significance. Carol Weiss (1998) echoes this view in her claim that "evaluation is the systematic assessment of the operation and/or the outcomes of a program or policy, compared to a set of explicit or implicit standards, as a means of contributing to the improvement of the program or policy" (p. 4).

Criterial thinking in evaluation is widespread. It underlies the kinds of comparisons of educational achievement in different countries undertaken in OECD's program for International Student Assessment, UNESCO's "Education for All" initiative, the Research Assessment Exercises that take place in higher education in the United Kingdom, New Zealand, Hong Kong, and elsewhere, and the International Review of Curriculum and Assessment Frameworks managed by the National Foundation for Educational Research. The judgment of quality as a criterial undertaking is also evident in the work of the member organizations of the international Campbell Collaboration who aim to apply explicit criteria to judge the quality of scientific studies of social interventions. Quality assurance models and performance auditing that stress conformance to requirements are other examples of criterial thinking (Schwartz & Mayne, 2005).

Judging quality criterially is more or less an "experience-distant" undertaking, to borrow a notion from the anthropologist Clifford Geertz. In other words, quality is perceived and rendered in the concepts and language of the social scientist or evaluator. The meaning of quality is structured in evaluation theory and practice by a set of constructs. These can be fixed and powerful concepts, often anticipating quantitative relationships among what a program provides, its effects, and its quality. Among the most common measurement constructs associated with judging the quality of the provision and performance of programs and policies are values, goal attainment, effectiveness, efficiency, productivity, functions, treatments, needs, performance outcomes, units, context, input, process, product, dependent and independent variables, side-effects, program theory, program logic, and so forth. In common practice, the evaluand is identified and described by means of these constructs, one or more attributes associated with each key construct are studied, and the results are arranged so that quality can be made apparent. These constructs and their measurements are weighted in terms of their importance. Most evaluators agree that performance of the evaluand should be measured in more ways than one and more than once. A composite score or judgment can be obtained. Some kind of comparison is made, against an earlier performance, against another group's performance, or against a hypothetical performance.

Constructs vary from theory to theory and from practice to practice, but each reflects an ordinary notion operationalized in a particular way by the community of professional evaluators and social scientists. The quality of the evaluation design is dependent on the ingenuity of the evaluator to represent these constructs with validity and parsimony (Cronbach, 1982; Scriven, 1986; Elliott, 2002).

Various problems with quality-as-measured are well known. The evaluand is usually more complex and its functions insufficiently correlated to be fully represented by a few indicators. Michael Scriven (1994) urged selection of criteria so compelling that any substantial improvement in performance will be prima facie evidence of quality. But such criteria are rare. Setting cut scores as standards of program success is problematic as well. Seldom can they be derived scientifically or obtained from an authoritative bureau or connoisseur or agreed upon by stakeholders. Setting weights and creating standards has traditionally been a matter of evaluator judgment. Nonetheless, a standards-and-measurement-based conceptualization of discerning quality is widely considered ideal (Stake, 2004). It has been the most trusted way of carrying out evaluations of large, unembraceable evaluands (see below).

Conceptualizing Quality-as-Experienced

Judging quality criterially, thinking of quality-as-measurable (and measured), is met by the view that quality is a phenomenon that we personally experience and only later make technical, if need be. This view emphasizes grasping quality in experience-near understandings, that is, in the language and embodied action of those who actually are undergoing the experiencing of a program or policy. Criterial thinking is important, but it is rooted in interpretation of personal experience (Schwandt, 1994).

The notion of quality-as-experienced draws attention to both the subjective and intersubjective meanings we attach to events, personal encounters, and places. It emphasizes our practical knowledge and sensitivities to virtue and trauma, and all the happenings and fixtures of life. It holds that this practical embodied knowledge – that is at once both cognitive and emotional – is a source both of our ability to discern quality and our efforts to ascribe meaning to the quality we see in an evaluand.

In social phenomenology, the notion of practical knowledge refers to what an actor knows in relation to her or his own actions and social situation, but cannot necessarily state ("Practical knowledge or practical consciousness," *Collins Dictionary of Sociology* (2000); retrieved August 11, 2004 from http://www.xreferplus.com/entry/1417477). This knowledge is often more tacit or "silent" than expressed in propositions (Molander, 1992). It is neither necessarily consciously reflective (i.e., we do not routinely stand back from our involvement with the world and say to ourselves, "see, this is why I am acting the way I am"), nor is it fully capable of articulation in a direct, conceptual, and propositional manner, yet it constitutes a distinctive kind of competence in acting in both general and specific ways (Van Maanen, 1995).

Practical knowledge of various kinds belongs to our everyday, shared worlds of social interactions such as shopping, banking, meeting friends and strangers, and so forth. In everyday life we are often unaware of this practical knowledge, and only recognize it when something happens to startle us or confuse our habituated and confident practices of being with one another. (This is the point of the "breaching experiments" conducted in ethnomethodological studies.) There are other kinds of practical knowledge. Every professional practice – like teaching, nursing, managing, and so on – has its own unique kind of practical knowledge that comprises the tact, dispositions, and considered character of decision-making in that practice.

Practical knowledge (or, more broadly, the practical knowledge tradition) can be further characterized by the following features (Molander, 2002, p. 370):

- In contrast to knowledge regarded as "in the head" of an individual, knowledge is based on participation and dialog with other people, as well as living with materials, tools, and the physical circumstances of a situation.
- Knowledge and application form a unity; in other words, knowing and doing are not two separate steps in a process.
- Knowledge is knowing-in-action, living knowledge *in* the world. That is, practical knowledge does not depict or represent reality, but instead leads rather seamlessly from question to answer and from task to execution within various human activities.

Van Maanen (1999) adds that practical knowledge is a form of non-cognitive knowing inhering in a person; it is "agentive" knowing and it resides in several forms:

- In action as lived, e.g., as confidence in acting, style, and practical tact, as habituations and routine practices.
- In the body, e.g., as an immediate corporeal sense of things, as gestures and demeanor.
- In the world, e.g., as being with the things of our world, as situations of "being at home" with something or "dwelling" in it.
- In relations, e.g., as encounters with others, as relations of trust, intimacy, and recognition.

The lived, active, or better said, the "enacted," character of this kind of knowledge cannot be overemphasized. Practical knowledge is located "not primarily in the intellect or the head but rather in the existential situation in which [a] person finds himself or herself . . . . [T]he practical active knowledge that animates [a given practice like teaching, evaluating, nursing, etc.] is something that belongs phenomenologically more closely to the whole embodied being of the person as well as to the social and physical world in which this person lives" (Van Maanen, 1995, p. 12).

This practical or experiential knowledge is a source of our discernment of quality. It is not some mysterious intuition but a genuine form of understanding as personal awareness and confidence in action rather than as instrumental command. When we speak of knowing in this way, we are not speaking of explanation or justification. It is knowledge from personal experience that shapes appraisals of quality. The audiences hear, the readers read, and sometimes, through their knowledge, simple or sophisticated, they feel drawn by their understandings of quality. The task of the evaluators in this way of thinking is not to bypass this kind of knowledge as a source for understanding quality, but to describe and respect it for its discriminative and operational power.

The evidence of quality in this view of quality-as-experienced is not of the same species as the evidence of quality in an approach that views quality-as-measured (Stake, 2004). In the latter way of thinking, evidence is a matter of observable and measurable indicators of performance against articulated criteria or standards. In the former, evidence is a matter of the narrative account that reflects the perception of quality. More on this distinction is provided below.

The problem with the quality-as-experienced approach is that too much rests on the acuity and credibility of the observer. We do not have good enough standards for recognizing an evaluator's practical knowledge that arises from a combination of observational skill, breadth of view, and control of bias. In a confrontational situation, few people are willing to accept personal perceptions of quality from opponents. And yet, as with connoisseurs and the best blue ribbon panels, some of the best examples of synthesizing values across diverse criteria are those that rely on the personal, practical judgment of fair and informed individuals.

Embracing Quality

The relative suitability of quality-as-experienced and quality-as-measured depends, in part, on whether or not the evaluand can be intellectually and practically embraced by a single evaluator (or a small evaluation team). When evaluating a small agency or an organization's staff or a workshop, given reasonable time and access, an evaluator can become personally knowledgeable about the activities and spaces, the strengths and shortcomings of the evaluand. Possibly with help from a few others, he or she can become experientially acquainted with the evaluand. It then is an embraceable evaluand and through observation, enumeration, and talk, the evaluator can personally come to perceive the quality of the activity. When the evaluator can see and inquire about the evaluand personally, with or without scales and rubrics, the evaluator can come to know its quality in the most expected and respected ways.

But when the evaluator finds the evaluand obscured, extended into far regions, or beyond his or her comprehension, and thus beyond personal encounter, the evaluator conceptualizes the evaluand differently. The evaluand becomes abstracted into a combination of criteria. For data, the evaluator is obligated to depersonalize the assignment, to rely heavily on instruments and protocols and to obtain abbreviated and indirect reporting from people too distant for sharing personal experience. Some personal contact with the evaluand usually occurs still but it is a weak sample. This is an evaluand beyond personal embrace. One view of the relationship between embraceability and sources of quality is shown in Figure 18.1. Almost every evaluation will use records of experience and measurement data. The data most useful will depend on (1) whether the evaluand is "embraceable," capable of being known by one or a few persons, or (2) whether the evaluand

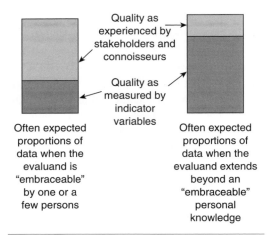

Figure 18.1 Ratings of perceptions of the quality of an evaluand as a function of embraceable

extends beyond personal knowledge, thus greatly requiring aggregate of measurements.

The shift from embraceable to beyond embrace is partly a shift from objective (i.e., warrantable, supportable) assessment grounded in first-hand experience to that grounded in proxies for such experience. Procedures for bias control, substantiation of claims, triangulation, and so on are necessary regardless of the kind of grasp one has of the evaluand. These procedures are necessary, but not sufficient. We also regularly need a certain kind of personal sizing up, an awareness of subtle commitment, sensitivity to unreplicated events, all with reliance on practical knowledge. This lived experience must be recognized for what it is and appreciated for what it reveals as a way of knowing and understanding. The data set for any evaluation should be a combination of "hard" evidence and personal experience. Such a blending is not just the expectation of senior evaluation directors but of clients and community members alike. Across the political and corporate landscape, there is consistent call for hard data, yet almost every policy-maker and opinion leader wants also to hear the best judgment and personal conviction of evaluators.

For all evaluands, embraceable and beyond embrace, evaluators will gather measurement and experiential data. If the assessment of an embraceable evaluand rests heavily on measurement data, the work will often be seen as too mechanistic. If the assessment of an evaluand beyond embrace rests heavily on personal experience, the work will often be seen as too subjective.

Discerning Quality

However conceptualized, quality will be viewed in more than a single way. As indicated earlier, one view of quality is defined in advance, as expectation, often in terms of criteria and formal standards. Another view of quality is formed in the encounter, in ongoing personal embrace of the evaluand. And another view is retrospective, formed from record and recollection. If allowed to, all these views operate in a single evaluation. It is in the nature of human experience to discern several different manifestations of quality.

In 1940, Coca Cola was sold at the soda fountain. The soda jerk squirted one ounce of chilled syrup into a six-ounce coke glass, added ice, filled the glass to the brim with cold carbonated water and stirred. Having a reputation for quality control, as well as for recipe-secrecy, advertising and globalization, the Coca Cola Company sent an evaluator to visit fountains across the country. Sitting at the bar, his identity undisclosed, he would order a coke and observe the process. When served, he would slip a thermometer into the glass, check the temperature, and sip. In addition to temperature, his checklist included these questions:[2]

- Is this Coca Cola or a substitute?
- Were glass and spoon clean?

- Was the ratio of syrup to water to ice accurate?
- Was the pump set to one ounce; was it squirted more than once?
- Was the water sufficiently carbonated?
- Did foam and water overflow the glass?
- Was it spilled in delivery?

Not long after, the mixing was taken over by shiny red dispensers hovering over the counter, and later by pre-mix tanks. Itinerant evaluators today go to bottling plants. But the 1940 version was a brew master, using instruments and eyes, tongue, and fingers to assess the quality of the product, viewing and tasting ingredients and judging the service, a multiplicity of manifestations of quality.

Discerning quality is a human behavior. It may rely on all the instrumentation of space exploration, but there is no recognition of quality or mishap until a mind acknowledges it. Something is not recognizable as being of quality – or its inverse – without experience, including the mensuration of conditions and perception of action against a background of experience. Experience is not a guarantee of correct interpretation but inexperience is almost a guarantee of misinterpretation.

The profession of evaluation, as all professions, is obligated to assure that its practitioners have the experience needed to combine measurement and perception to make valid judgment. The experience of any single evaluator is enhanced by training and diversity of practice, by the solicited experience of other specialists and non-specialists, by histories and documentaries. Training in theory and methodology is not enough.

Just how evaluators ought to combine information to synthesize quality is a matter of dispute. Michael Scriven (1994, p. 385) wrote of a rational weight-and-sum approach to synthesis and Stake and his students (1997) disagreed. Whatever the means of synthesis, it can get better with reflective repetition and it cannot get better without it. However, the lack of a master plan for values synthesis is not a mark of the immaturity or impotency of mathematical rubrics for evaluation practice, but recognition that perceptions of quality are arbitrary, contested, cultural, and temporal – modified in each encounter with the evaluand. Even in the least mathematical of syntheses, comparison is an essential part of discerning quality.

Comparison

Yes, fundamental to discerning quality is comparison. It may be a comparison to formal standards, to silent expectations, to randomly selected control groups, or to the way things used to be. The fundamental idea of conceptualizing quality is through comparison, direct or even vaporously indirect. The comparison can be casual, interpretive, or formalistic. It can be a simple act resulting in a simple declaration. It can be an act so complex that only a comprehensive and equivocal write-up can do the job.

Clients, stakeholders, and fellow evaluators have an appetite for clear winners, but seldom is the winning clear. People may suppose that faintly appearing results are not real differences but merely obscurities. But faint differences may be the truth. When the comparisons are acknowledged to come from tentative and evolving views of the evaluand and when the multiple realities of participating stakeholders are taken into account, then the misuse of comparison is diminished.

Choice of Criteria

Clients, staff members, and stakeholders may have strong preferences for using certain criteria as a basis of quality; however, the evaluator should have the knowledge and responsibility to broaden, narrow, or redirect the inquiry. Even if no criteria are established in advance, the evaluator should help put

forth the reasons for and against the alternatives. As noted earlier, comparisons may be made against criteria or, against archetypes, such as model arrangements or bel canto performances.

Concerns mount when inauthentic parties set criteria or when the views of authentic parties are omitted. Some people will doubt that any party is authentic or that any definition is sufficient, but less when constructs are consensual. Most people are troubled by specious terms and promotional rhetoric about the quality of public services. The stalwart are put off by sacrifice of principle for the sake of compromise. When evaluators become aware that neither word nor measure stands well for the complexity of experience, they wisely back away from "indicators." We hope there will be more objection to the argument that first approximations are at least a step in the right direction. Rough approximations can be a step toward the neglect of subtle concerns, a step away from better understanding.

Majority opinion should not be considered sufficient. When challenged to back up their criteria, evaluators should show more than the acquiescence of passersby. Standards of quality generated by representative groups and quotations from learned papers are but starting points. They often lack consensual power and critical acuity. The poll needs to be rooted in action observed. Evaluators need the patience to gather subtle and indirect objection to the constructs (Stufflebeam, 1983). It takes a special discipline to seek flaws in one's own choice of criteria. If after carefully seeking them, objection is small and if the standard stands up to challenge, one may claim consensus.

The Pace of Discerning Quality

In human affairs such as personnel training, social work and public administration, quality sometimes is discerned quickly, sometimes slowly. The experience can be brief but the impression can remain long. The experience may be insubstantial, yet memorable. It can be brief not only because the moment passes quickly, but also because what we first take to be good, on pondering and hearing others, makes it less good or more good, or good in different ways. The experience of quality is seldom rooted in fully explicated ground, having meaning we can thoroughly explain, with standards we are sure of. We are of two minds, of many minds. We change. What we mean by "merit and worth" eludes the rigor of our methods, no matter how technologically sophisticated. Our personal discernment of quality may last a lifetime or only a few minutes. Even so, it is real and indispensable.

Take teaching. What is good teaching? There are lots of criteria for teaching. We will not all agree but each of us smiles upon good teaching when we see it. As evaluators, we try to capture it in criteria such as evoking learning and nurturing, stability, sensitivity, and scholarship. Yet, the meaning and weight of such criteria change with the situation. Likewise, our discernment of merit changes as we increasingly realize the obstacles and the complexity of circumstance.

Take evaluation. What is good evaluation? We try to capture it in criteria: technically competent, useful, informative, ethical, educative, empowering, and so on. Yet these general concepts are only filled with particular meaning in a given circumstance or situation. Perceptions of quality vary from the perspective of the evaluator, the stakeholder, and the reader. The evaluator worries about low technical sophistication in the evaluation; the client, meanwhile, is satisfied with the final report. Quality is often seen differently depending on the observer's closeness to the action. Assessments of quality vary temporally – what one earlier presumed to be embraceable, durable, there to be measured,

observed, and scaled as meritorious, often becomes insubstantial in the light of new knowledge and experience. Increasingly, we realize that quality belongs to us in our present circumstance rather than enduringly to the object evaluated.

The pace and temporal character of discerning quality are seldom mitigated by the choice of methodological strategies. Professional evaluators have long taken into consideration the necessity of understanding different cultural expectations, the importance of rival hypotheses, the validity of approximations, the significance of multi-trait multiple measures, and the triangulation of witnessing. Methodology is rooted in assumptions about the fallibility of knowledge and the necessity for cautious interpretation. But neither choice of, nor agreement on, methods forces us to pursue the search for quality, that is, to ask the right questions.

Representing Quality

A common view, aligned with the notion of quality-as-measured, is that to represent quality, we need an explicit standard for comparison: A scale running from lower quality to higher quality or a comparison made to an existing representation of quality, such as a norm group, a previous performance, or an icon.

Everyone knows that a "C" on schoolwork indicates lower quality than a "B." The grading scale is an ordinal scale, showing ranks but not amounts of quality. A grade may be poorly given or poorly received, but the scale itself is widely accepted. We have no public scale even this good for representing program quality. In product evaluation, one item can be compared to a number of others, and categories such as Good, Better, Best represent a scale. In experiments, we compare performance of treatment and control groups (Cook & Campbell, 1979). Psychometric scaling procedures can be employed to give more than ranked categories of quality, but scales would seldom endure and the work to create and validate them would cost more than the evaluations themselves.

The quality of products is frequently determined by the degree to which they conform to design specifications, or by comparing the performance of similar products on a shared set of features (e.g., durability, ease of use, etc.). This creates the impression that there is something like a technical solution to the problem of determining quality. "Technical" here means formulaic, computable, calculable, absent the need for interpretive judgment. However, programs and projects are not products. The only way to represent program quality is for people to analyze the information available and interpret it in the prose of merit and worth. This synthesis can be improved by many technical efforts, such as training observers and panels, validating instruments, and holding independent meta-evaluations, but the final representations of quality will be judgments made by evaluators and others.

Even in what is regarded as the description of the evaluand, the evaluation report is filled with representations of quality. For example, at least at one time, the evaluation report to close every World Bank overseas development project explicitly had to state whether or not the work of the Bank there was satisfactory or unsatisfactory. The report briefly described what project was undertaken – e.g., irrigation, training, entrepreneur support. It included a discussion of objectives, actions taken, and impediments to full implementation – all representations. It was important for the World Bank evaluator – and for the rest of us – to represent the nature of the evaluand. A full description provides some of the representation of quality.

It is the nature of a representation to be incomplete. Some representations will be misrepresentations only because they are incomplete. We sometimes seek symbolic representation that can be quickly comprehended – names, acronyms, categories, and indicators. At other times, we seek representations that portray something of the complexity and the several contexts of the evaluand.

Some evaluators value parsimony, unification, and synthesis in the representation of quality and favor the reduction of representation to the fewest indices. Other evaluators, more committed to the perspectival, the conditional, and the comprehensive, urge representing quality in more generous and intricate experiential accounts, narratives, and stories that convey the sense of the quality as a multifaceted, lived phenomenon. Neither of these schools of thought about representation is completely satisfactory. Every effort to represent is always in some sense a misrepresentation, for representation is always an act of selection. Representations oversimplify, leave out some aspects of quality in order to signify others, displace the complex with the simple, and so forth. Yet, incompleteness is less a worry than obfuscation. Some representations are just plain confusing.

Evaluation as Interpretation

Representation requires interpretation. Measurement is easy. Interpreting measurement is difficult. Evaluators are challenged to give meaning to events, relationships, needs, and aspirations far more complex than the reporting can convey. Representations created by an evaluator seldom adequately mirror the things observed. All languages fall short, but some more than others. Analytic specification and operationalization are sometimes useful, less because they get closer to truth but more because they can be grasped and rather straightforwardly communicated.

The evaluator composes representations of the evaluand and of its quality. Drawing from all the languages of art and science, the evaluator describes program activity, staffing, contexts, coping, and accomplishment, sometimes hoping to provide a vicarious experience, sometimes hoping to create descriptors well beyond personal experience.

As noted above, within the descriptions are clues to quality. A good description cannot but tell of quality. But the evaluator goes further, summarizing the conclusions of merit, grounds for the conclusions, and implications of the findings of merit. Evaluators struggle to relate quality to the issues, to the complexities, to the implications for action. There are no formulae for this task. Michael Scriven has argued that:

> the value of programs, the merit of teachers, the quality of products are simply theoretical constructs that can be indefinitely unpacked into factual implications, tied into the net of our concepts and needs and environment, and used like any other constructs in the practical or intellectual world. (Quoted in Shadish et al., 1991, p. 41)

These constructs (e.g., "goal attainment," "effectiveness," "usability," "meeting needs," "conforming to standards") provide essential intellectual structure for disciplined inquiry into quality. They help us define, understand, evaluate, and report on the evaluand. Investigations of such constructs are intimately tied to data-gathering procedures such as surveys and fieldwork. Because these constructs are powerful legitimating devices, they often are reified, leaving investigation of the sense of quality underdeveloped. Thus, the constructs themselves must be amplified and redefined during the course of the study. For example, we may have a statement of goals specified by the program staff, but we know that some of their aspirations and most of their aversions remain unstated, that some priorities remain unexplored, and that goals change during

the course of a program, particularly under challenge or in response to opportunity. Even in a carefully planned and fixed contract, definition of the constructs will be problematic. In the assessment of student achievement, for example, criterion instrument construction is both voraciously consuming of resources and pathologically under-inclusive about educational aims attained.

How well does program quality get presented? Often the evaluator cannot find time to go beyond vague and promotional descriptions. Complexities of program activities and criteria press us to define only a small number; the rest seldom get more than passing reference. Much of science in general works at finding relationships among a few targeted variables, with others held constant, and evaluation sometimes follows that model. In program evaluation, intervention and holding constant (two ingredients of "science-based" evaluation) make matters artificial. Many of the common constructs described earlier too often are considered unessential to a particular evaluation and are taken as needing no attention by evaluators, sponsors, participants and other stakeholders. Against a sunny sky, few doubts are raised as to the several meanings of goals, needs, standards, and so on. As technical terms, they help evaluation to be a manageable, politically respectable process. Without careful investigation of these constructs themselves it still may be possible to provide an impression of quality, but it will be incomplete and under explicated.

Explicating Quality

Criterial thinking, i.e., seeing the world in terms of qualities or criteria, probably helps reduce the number of views of what quality is. Experiential thinking, on the other hand, probably helps increase the number. Regularly, evaluators strive for agreement on criteria and standards, even a consensus. But it is not clear that agreement on a particular definition of quality leads to better evaluation than lack of agreement. Agreement leads to agreement, not necessarily to the most valid meanings. Agreement can mean that personal or partisan conditions are insufficiently considered. Lack of agreement can mean that community and ideological positions are insufficiently considered. A situational definition of quality is not necessarily preferable but it can be derived from common, perhaps universal, experience and should not be avoided.

Evaluators will not always find it useful to speak with precision about the quality being sought. We should be wary of explicating a single or even just a few criteria. At least at the outset we should want to become acquainted with a large number of qualities of the program, some beyond immediate explication. Explicit criteria help us communicate but often circumscribe the communication. A client once said, "I am reluctant to limit perception of the evaluand to the caliber of my evaluator's mind."[3] The difference in number of criteria is one of the big differences between qualitative and quantitative methods of research.

Assurance of Quality

Evaluators will continue to be entangled in the advocacies of programs, in the imagery of the marketplace, and in the compulsion of the accountability movement (Stufflebeam, 1971). In order to demonstrate good work, almost every modern department and agency is caught up in demonstration of performance. They are required to represent quality of impact by identifying aims, strategies, and outcomes. Here and elsewhere, a media-saturated demand for clear and unequivocal representation of quality far outruns our ability to represent.

For quantitative and qualitative interpretation alike, we need a qualitative "confidence interval," that counterpart to the standard error of measurement. We have no indicator but we do have "critical meta-evaluation," the periodic and concluding review of process and product. We can be more confident in the messages of evaluation when such reviews raise challenges to our representations. Like other ways of assessing quality, meta-evaluations too draw on conceptions of quality-as-measured (e.g., checklists and scales, audits of procedures, and data) as well as quality-as-experienced (e.g., the judgment, grounded in practical experience, of peer evaluators and stakeholders). Procedures for such meta-evaluations are hardly systematized or standardized in most cases, but they already are part of the best evaluation studies.

Final Thought

Making judgments of quality constitutes a core professional responsibility of evaluators (just as making judgments of health and illness constitute a core imperative of doctors, and making judgments of guilt or innocence is a core imperative of judges). Evaluators shoulder the responsibility of judging quality – a responsibility of getting it right (or of at least making a significant contribution to discussions of getting it right) in the face of the lived reality of the ambiguity of quality and the absence of hard and fast, steady and universal standards for quality. In other words, discerning and representing quality that serves a social purpose is a professional imperative of the practice – it is what makes the practice itself of social worth. Despite profound disagreements in method and means, evaluation practices focused on the discernment of quality admit in a general and profound way that:

1. The flourishing of human experiences of teaching, providing health care, social

services, and the like depend on discernments of quality; however,

2. The determination of quality is endemically ambivalent, and

3. Quality is never fully redeemable once and for all in any discursive way; therefore,

4. Evaluation practice is forever trying to establish the lines between what is of value and what is not, what is meaningful and what is meaningless, what is useful and what is without worth.

Notes

1. Presumptive arguments are contrasted with formal, logical (in a classical sense) arguments. In the latter, the premises of the argument guarantee the truth and certainty of the conclusion, so to speak. A presumptive argument does not claim such certainty, but is, instead, more of a prime facie case for a conclusion (Scriven, 1994) that, nonetheless, is considered "good enough to bet the farm on" (Scriven, 1995, p. 67).

2. Having witnessed a lone gray-suited man slipping a thermometer into a 1930s coke, we made most of this story up.

3. The client, in personal conversation with Stake, was Myron Atkin, then an elementary science curriculum developer.

References

Barber, B. (1988). *The Conquest of Politics*. Princeton, NJ: Princeton University Press.

Bauman, Z. (1993). *Postmodern Ethics*. Oxford: Blackwell.

Cook, T. D. & Campbell, D. T. (1979). *Quasi-experimentation: Design and analysis issues for field settings*. Chicago: Rand McNally.

Cronbach, L. J. (1982). *Designing Evaluations of Educational and Social Programs*. San Francisco: Jossey-Bass.

Elliott, J. (2002). The paradox of educational reform in the evaluatory state. *Prospects*, 32(3), 273–287.

House, E. R. & Howe, K. R. (1999). *Values in Education and Social Research*. Thousand Oaks, CA: Sage.

Molander, B. (1992). Tacit knowledge and silenced knowledge: Fundamental problems and controversies. In B. Göranzon & M. Florin (eds) *Skill and Education: Reflection and experience* (pp. 9–31). London: Springer-Verlag.

Molander, B. (2002). Politics for learning or learning for politics? *Studies in Philosophy and Education*, 21, 361–376.

Power, M. (1997). *The Audit Society*. Oxford: Oxford University Press.

Schwandt, T. A. (1994). Constructivist, interpretivist approaches to human inquiry. In N. K. Denzin & Y. S. Lincoln (eds) *Handbook of Qualitative Research*. Thousand Oaks, CA: Sage.

Schwartz, R. & Mayne, J. (2005). Assuring the quality of evaluative information: Theory and practice. *Evaluation and Program Planning*, 28, 1–14.

Scriven, M. S. (1986). New frontiers of evaluation. *Evaluation Practice*, 7, 7–44.

Scriven, M. S. (1991). *Evaluation Thesaurus*, 4th edition. Newbury Park, CA: Sage.

Scriven, M. S. (1994). The final synthesis. *Evaluation Practice*, 15(3), 367–382.

Scriven, M. S. (1995). The logic of evaluation and evaluation practice. In D. M. Fournier & N. L. Smith (eds) *Reasoning in Evaluation. New Directions for Evaluation*, No. 68, 49–70. San Francisco, CA: Jossey-Bass.

Shadish, W. R., Cook, T. D., & Leviton, L. C. (1991). *Foundations of Program Evaluation: Theories of practice*. Newbury Park, CA: Sage.

Stake, R. E. (2004). *Standards-Based and Responsive Evaluation*. Thousand Oaks, CA: Sage.

Stake, R., Migotsky, C., Davis, R., Cisneros, E. DePaul, G., Dunbar, Jr., C., Farmer, R., Feltovich, J., Johnson, E., Williams, B., & Chaves, I. (1997). The evolving syntheses of program value. *Evaluation Practice*, 18(2), 89–103.

Stufflebeam, D. L. (1971). The relevance of the CIPP evaluation model for educational accountability. *Journal of Research and Development in Education*, 5, 19–25.

Stufflebeam, D. L. (1983). The CIPP model for program evaluation. In G. F. Madaus, M. S. Scriven & D. L. Stufflebeam (eds) *Evaluation Models: Viewpoints on educational and human services evaluation* (pp. 117–141). Boston: Kluwer-Nijhoff.

Van Maanen, M. (1995). On the epistemology of reflective practice. *Teachers and Teaching: Theory and practice*, 1, 33–50. Retrieved August 11, 2004 from http://www.phenomenologyonline.com/max/epistpractice.html.

Van Maanen, M. (1999). The practice of practice. In M. Lange, J. Olson, H. Hansen & W. Bÿnder (eds) *Changing Schools/Changing Practices: Perspectives on educational reform and teacher professionalism*. Luvain, Belgium: Garant. Retrieved August 11, 2004 from http://www.phenomenologyonline.com/max/practice.html.

Weiss, C. (1998). *Evaluation*. Upper Saddle River, NJ: Prentice-Hall.

19

THE PRACTICE OF EVALUATION: CHALLENGES AND NEW DIRECTIONS

Lois-ellin Datta

The preceding five chapters present some lessons from the past forty years of evaluation practice, particularly the practice of program evaluation in a public policy context. This summary chapter honors past challenges that have been reasonably well met, examines unfinished business, and considers new directions. These will be mentioned briefly in this overview, and then discussed at greater length.

In this discussion, "we" are people who consider themselves evaluators, spending much of their professional time on evaluation-type tasks. Lacking a systematic survey of what we think about challenges met, unfinished business, and new directions, what we think has been gleaned from the chapters in this section, journal articles in various journals, presentations at professional conferences, and exchanges in Evaltalk.

A distinction is made between ideological and methodological frameworks. "Social justice" refers to an ideological stance that sees this as the primary concern in conducting evaluations. "Quantitative," "qualitative," and "mixed" refer to methodologies for designing, carrying out, and analyzing studies.

With regard to *challenges met*, first is a deep appreciation that evaluation is about dynamics, not statics, in program development. Second, we have learned – or rather, it has been seared into us – that effective evaluation use is dependent on context, the evaluation process, and the methods themselves. Third, we now have a broadened methodological repertoire, including acceptance of qualitative, quantitative, and mixed approaches. These understandings can be expressed as frameworks for evaluation and as practical considerations. They cascade, for example, into professional training and development and into the agreements guiding our services. Fourth, we have made progress in assessing the quality of quantitative evaluation studies and have made strides in judging the quality of mixed methods evaluations.

Finally, we have learned about the importance of communication in all aspects of evaluation and have become good – arguably, very good – at communicating the results of our work.

This said, as the authors in this part indicate, there is unfinished business. Some challenges have been recognized, but not resolved, for many years. New challenges have emerged for technical, historical, and political reasons, including issues of values and evaluator roles in a time of "scientifically based" accountability. From this unfinished business and from the new challenges, come new directions.

Considering the *unfinished business*, four items seem particularly urgent. First, despite the good work of evaluators such as Schwandt (1990), Fetterman (1990), and Greene, Caracelli, & Graham (1989), we need better ways of assessing the quality of practice for qualitative approaches. Second, not enough progress has been made in systematic means for cumulating understandings gained through the qualitative and mixed methodologies and through social justice ideologies. Third, more work – much more work – is needed in evaluating the outcomes of evaluator training. Fourth, we need well-tried solutions to problems such as unequal opportunities to be the participating stakeholder, stakeholder turnover, and unpaid stakeholder time.

New challenges have emerged from the changing social context of evaluation. We are, I fear, making others the victims of our own success in several ways, and we need to deal with this better.

First, "scientific-research-based programs and evaluations," "evidence-based resource allocation," "program logic models," and similar terms of our trade have become widely institutionalized for all manner of programs. The landscape of the resulting evaluations is poorly mapped, but quality is not likely to be uniformly high or benefits commensurate to the costs incurred.

Second, the political misuse of evaluations, particularly large national evaluations with high-stakes decisions, seems to be growing bolder and more devastating. Third, the impacts of evaluations on their settings have made for considerable tossing and turning. Anecdotes abound; systematic study, while available, remains too rare. Such studies, for example, as initial reports on how high-stakes testing requirements are affecting the educational process, suggest the act of evaluation shapes social changes in ways whose benefits, compared to costs, seem unsure. The political tides won't pause while evaluators thrash out the many issues of value, methodology, and relations between our field and the government, including the costs of doing nothing. Our heightened awareness of evaluation in a time of heightened accountability adds urgency to our conversations, both for having them and keeping them civil.

The next sections, drawing on the chapters in this topic area, present these points in more detail.

Past Challenges Reasonably Well Met

Evaluation Dynamics

What is happening, programmatically, doesn't stand still for us evaluators. We have learned that proposed goals, strategies, activities, and even outcomes are only starting points. Initially, divergence from implementation fidelity was seen as program failure. Later, such information was used to sort out when it would be fair to evaluate the program. Then we realized that some changes were adaptations, some were improvements, some were indicators of the incongruence between program assumptions and realities, and only some were failures in the initial sense. Process evaluations, understanding the reasons for change, and capturing the evolving consequences became, and now are often, central to our task. With recognition of the inevitable, often highly complex dynamics of policy space has come a less Promethean stance. Rarely do we seize the divine fire of unqualified conclusions; often, we seek more modestly to reduce uncertainty and increase certainty in more than trivial ways.

More specifically, looking back a bit, early in the practice of evaluation, adaptations of the relatively static audit model were fairly common. In program auditing, one begins by determining the goals or purposes of a program (intended or expected outcomes), then assessing the achieved or observed outcomes. The disparities between intended and achieved outcomes indicate degree of program success. Another model for evaluation, experimentation, assigns program participants at random to treatment or non-treatment conditions, again assumed to be fairly static or mature. Randomization is held to rule out many biases and to permit the most solid attribution of between group differences (relative to within group variation) to the treatment condition (Boruch, 1997). Quasi-experimental designs, such as comparison groups or time-series approaches when randomization is difficult or inappropriate, are used to estimate the probable value-added of the intervention.

These models remain appropriate in many conditions, particularly where the intervention is stable, well-specified, and likely to stay bounded during the evaluation period; where the control or comparison groups are passive, unlikely to seek conditions similar to the treatment; and where the primary interest is estimation of the net value-added of the intervention.

Where these conditions did not hold, two primary limitations became apparent. First, the approach, sometimes referred to as "the black box model," gave meager insight into whether the root cause of disparities was implementation failure or theory failure. Quickly indeed,

evaluation practice expanded to identify the reasons why program developers expected the program would achieve the intended outcomes, laying out the detailed pathways between initial problem statements, the theory or prior experiences that led to selection of the program strategies, and the "if-then" sequences of activities, outputs and outcomes. Evaluators such as Weiss (1972) argued that delineation of program theory and analysis of the extent to which the "if-then" linkages occurred was a primary evaluative task. Chen (1994), Donaldson (Donaldson & Scriven, 2003), Rogers (2000), and others have developed rationales for the program theory and program logic approaches. These rationales in turn have been adapted into practical evaluation handbooks such as those of the Kellogg Foundation, the United Way, and others (see also Mowbray et al., 2003). The approach has become enshrined as perhaps the dominant evaluation model in proposal requirements for program funding. While embellishments surely are possible and will be forthcoming, it seems reasonable to place a "completed" check on this task.

A second limitation in the intended/achieved results approach – and a limitation in the program theory approach, too – is that the initial program proposal often is only a starting point. During the development and operation of the program, problem definition could change; strategies and activities seen as appropriate could be dropped, modified or added, and salient outcomes shifted. This could be seen as a failure of planning, as a deficit in implementation, or as an appropriate response to the real world. The adaptations themselves could actually lead to beneficial changes in the program being evaluated or perhaps serve as reality therapy in program, particularly national program, operation in loosely connected, highly decentralized circumstances (see, e.g., Pressman & Wildavsky, 1974; Sechrest et al., 1979).

A classic example from the US, which stimulated development of implementation studies, was the Follow-Through Planned Variation quasi-experimental test of the relative effectiveness of 21 early childhood education interventions selected as models or as exemplary on the basis of good results from original development sites. Each intervention was tested in several different sites, with communities selecting which model was most appropriate for their circumstances. Stallings and her colleagues at Stanford Research Institute (1975), together with the program developers, prepared protocols for observers in the classrooms. Some models were found much easier (usually the structured behavioral approaches) than others (usually the conceptually based, Bank Street and Montessori type of curricula) to implement with fidelity. Whatever the model, degree of implementation was related to good results.

The study was among the forerunners of the now extensive evaluation work on implementation and program dynamics. It is a rare national evaluation that does not include qualitative and quantitative in-depth, intensive studies of what actually happens in programs. There are now well-developed methodologies for using this information as an integral part of process and outcome analysis (see, e.g., Orwin et al., 1998, 2004).

In summary, with regard to dynamics, evaluation has reached a good destination in an appreciation of the constancy of change, including the more central role that process evaluation now plays in our thoughts, words, and deeds. To many evaluators, the emphasis is appropriately on understanding the meaning of the program to those involved, including "thick," "rich" descriptions of all aspects of the process of program development, implementation, and evolution in the sites studied. Some evaluators, such as Patton (1978), argue that the role of the evaluator is one of facilitator of development, a friendly critic and consultant. The originally intended outcomes, their measurement, and analysis of achieved outcomes (intended and unintended) become secondary or tertiary to participation in the program dynamics. Admittedly, in some hands, the resulting reports read as easily as a good novel; in other hands, the thick, rich description can make for thick, turgid reports hated by policy audiences.

Evaluation Utilization and Stakeholder Involvement

The character and interrelationship of evaluation use and stakeholder participation is a second broad area where our field has reached a good destination, albeit not without considerable angst. In the early days, evaluators completing their often arduous work were dismayed to find that in some instances the reports were door-stops; and in some instances, the evaluators' findings were read but not listened to, whether the results pointed to expansion, modification, or contraction of the program evaluated. In other instances, the evaluations were used selectively and politically.

No one was really happy with these experiences, although there certainly were examples of appropriate and meaningful evaluation utilization (Alkin, Daillak, & White, 1979). Views on the reasons for non-utilization and what our field should do varied from (1) acceptance of a valuable but limited function for evaluation, that of illuminating complexities in situations and being among the many influences on changing a climate of belief (Weiss, 1972, 1977) to (2) adducing instances of when evaluations quite definitely were used and the lessons learned acted upon (Chelimsky, 1997) to (3) quite dramatic new approaches to how evaluation should be done and the role of the evaluator (Torres, Preskill, & Piontek, 1996).

Focusing on the third approach, evaluation utilization has become almost a field in itself in evaluation. Central elements are the importance of engaging all relevant stakeholders (or their representatives) in all aspects of the evaluation; tuning the evaluation method, measures, and process to meet stakeholder needs and interests; and focusing on utilization as part of evaluation planning. Patton's "Utilization-Focused Evaluation" led the way and is probably among the most widely cited references in evaluation. His work was followed shortly by related developments such as empowerment evaluation (Fetterman, Kaftarian, & Wandersman, 1996) and the ideologically oriented evaluation approaches that emphasize social justice. While the roots of empowerment and social justice frameworks include a profound sense that evaluation must serve as a force for achieving better lives and more balanced decisions by, as well as for, the most disenfranchised in our society, other roots of these evaluation models include the awareness of stakeholder involvement as crucial to utilization (Alkin, Christie, & Rose, Chapter 17 this volume).

An indicator of how widely accepted and infused these concerns have become is that texts on evaluation theory and method written from a quantitative perspective now include discussions of stakeholder involvement and utilization (Mosteller & Boruch, 2002; Rossi, Lipsey, & Freeman, 2004). While there is unfinished business in this area (as will be discussed later), a check mark can be made here too, as a topic that has reached the good destination of infusion into evaluation practice.

Appropriate Methodological Choices

One size never really fits all circumstances in evaluation, and our field is hardly of one mind about whether designs such as the randomized control approach should be considered the gold standard for outcome-oriented evaluations. Nonetheless, it is true that one of the past challenges quite outstandingly met is articulation of the concept of the congruence among purposes, situation/context, and methods. Further, we now have a fine array of methodological frameworks for guiding discussions.

The initial frameworks, well and enduringly presented by Campbell and his colleagues (Campbell & Stanley, 1966; Cook & Campbell, 1978), were based on adaptations of experimental methods. Historically, this was a period of social experimentation in the US aimed at reducing poverty and achieving greater social justice: "the Great Society." Since the programs were framed (partly to achieve political acceptability, partly from uncertainty and humility) as experiments, having the evaluation procedures presented as "Experimental and Quasi-Experimental Methods" was philosophically congruent with the political and social period. The benefits of these methods became rapidly clear, in instances such as the DIME/SIME tests of income supports.

So did their methodological limitations, in instances such as the Westinghouse/Ohio evaluation of Project Head Start, to which Campbell & Erlenbacher responded with their classic paper on how regression artifacts mistakenly make compensatory education look like a failure (1970). This work led, in turn, to outstanding advances in quantitative analysis and designs that refined quasi-experimental approaches, such as interrupted time series and hierarchical linear modeling methods (Raudenbush & Bryk, 2002).

These advances are well-described in Chapter 14 by Mark & Henry. As they make clear, quasi-experimental designs now include the internal counterfactual, interrupted time series, large-scale non-experimental studies that create a post hoc counterfactual, and panel studies that test differences based on program variations. These can present reasonably robust evidence permitting more confident attribution, as debates move from assessment of apparent effects to causality and attribution. Mark & Henry's point that the some of the most exciting methodological advances are subsumed under familiar terms is convincingly illustrated in their review of how threats to validity have been addressed with better models of regression to the mean, cluster effects, implementation variation, moderated effects, and selection effects. The discussions are well-anchored in analyses of how these methodological advances have been applied in five significant evaluations.

Campbell's analyses also helped stimulate the ground-breaking development of quantitative evaluation syntheses approaches (see, e.g., Lipsey & Wilson, 2001). Our methodological resources now include both subtractive designs (ruling out alternative explanations, leaving the program as the most plausible explanation of results) and additive designs (incorporating program and other variables to explain as completely and convincingly as possible the path through which results were obtained). While, as Mark & Henry note, the reliability of effect size estimates remains contested, if attribution is important to the evaluation, the past ten years have provided a strong array of alternative designs as well as solutions to common analytic problems.

In addition, however, to this noble line of evaluative research and development, the limitations of quantitative design led to examination of what approaches might be best adapted to what evaluative purposes and real-world circumstances (Alkin, 2004). This equally noble line of evaluation development has given us important developments in realistic evaluation (Mark, Henry, & Julnes, 2000; Pawson & Tilley, 1997), and has stimulated the exceptional and

exceptionally rapid development of case studies (Yin, 2003), methods of qualitative analysis (Miles and Huberman, 1994), and of mixed methods approaches to evaluation (Bamberger, 2000; Greene, Caracelli, & Graham, 1989; Tashakkori & Teddlie, 1998). This work too can be fairly regarded as among the great achievements of the "old directions."

Evaluation Quality

Another area where old directions have reached some significant destinations is awareness of the importance of evaluation quality and development of methods for defining and assessing it. Scriven's Evaluation Checklists arguably should be required reading for all. Stufflebeam and his colleagues at the Center for Evaluation at Western Michigan University have written extensively on evaluation quality. They have seen many of their ideas embodied in the Joint Committee on Standards for Educational Evaluation (American Educational Research Association, 1981) and in the American Evaluation Association's Guiding Principles for Evaluators (Shadish et al., 1995). Assessing the quality of evaluations prior to using them in evaluation synthesis is part of the methodology of the US Government Accounting Office, in meta-analyses such as those of Glass (1976), Glass & Smith, (1981), Lipsey & Wilson (2001), Light & Smith (1971) and Light (1984). In general, quality assessment seems infused, methodologically, into the practice of evaluation (see, e.g., Greene's 1998 meta-evaluation of the effectiveness of bilingual education).

Granted, these checklists and discussions reflect different views of what constitutes quality: truth and objectivity, causal explanatory power, promotion of social justice. Without glossing over the likelihood that applying the different frameworks to the same array of completed evaluations would have some but probably not complete congruence, this area still has come a long way toward practical, well-thought through approaches.

Further, evaluating the evaluations has its own name, meta-evaluation, given by Scriven. Here, an evaluation is assessed in depth, against clearly stated standards of evaluation excellence, and the results reported. This can be a free-standing effort, dedicated to a particularly important evaluation, or it can be, as noted above, part of an evaluation synthesis. In any event, the idea of evaluation quality and evaluating the evaluations has become infused in evaluation practice; the Joint Committee has presented separate standards for such reviews (1994). Some organizations routinely submit draft reports to the evaluand, publishing their uncensored critiques along with the evaluation; others routinely incorporate a meta-evaluation into their procedures through extensive, formal reviews of drafts; others use the guidelines and principles to comment on published work.

Stake & Schwandt, in Chapter 18, have discussed these issues in the larger context of the political process; that is, a world in which the programs and policies are (a) changing, (b) interacting with each other, sometimes benignly and sometimes not, (c) widely bounded or with highly permeable, diffuse boundaries, (d) influenced primarily by decisions made far from the center of evaluative focus, and (e) affected by elected or appointed decision-makers whose concerns may be with larger policy, control, and budget issues.

Of particular value is Stake & Schwandt's emphasis on assessing quality in both relatively straightforward situations, such as evaluating the effectiveness of a distance learning approach, and situations that are considerably more complex, such as evaluating the effectiveness of a community collaboration approach to reducing drug abuse. Their analysis is particularly successful in grounding discussions of quality in the complexities of dynamic, often unpredictable, systems-based contexts and in encouraging evaluator vigilance against the dominance of a single stakeholder group's perspectives, interests, and values. Related points, using different vocabularies but similar in their implications, have been made by Patton, in his comparison of program logic, systems-based, and complex adaptive systems frameworks for evaluation.

Communication

One indicator of destinations reached in communication is that authors such as Alkin, Christie, & Rose (Chapter 17) can provide a useful array of practical guidelines based on experience, particularly with regard to communicating findings. New technologies, such as the internet and new capabilities in embedding graphic, visual, and auditory communications mean that the specifics of excellent books such as Henry's (1995) may need frequent updating. The broad communication principles, however, of avoiding pitfalls and reaching good destinations bring closure to many of our earlier perplexities. This applies primarily to the how-to; knottier socio-political dilemmas, some of which are ethical and legal as well as technical, are part of the dynamics of evaluation itself.

One can surely point to other past challenges that have been met. These include such problems as evaluation readiness, where evaluability assessment has proven useful for program design and theory as well as for assuring that the right evaluation questions are asked at the right time; advances in understanding the ethics of doing evaluation; and higher-quality processes for commissioning evaluations, such as more sensible requests for proposals or terms of reference, better contract management, and more consideration of training as important for those who commission as well as those carrying out evaluations.

The "mission mostly accomplished" areas discussed seem particularly integrated in evaluation practice today.

Unfinished Business and New Directions

Progress has been made, or at least, changes have been made in adding concepts, expanding the vocabulary, and reshaping the debates in evaluation. Much remains incomplete, uncertain, and contentious. This is unfinished business where the concepts and issues were recognized years ago, in quite elegant and well-elaborated theory, but practice remains less thoroughly developed.

Some of these issues may remain durably unresolved, and perhaps healthily so. The paradigm wars of the 1980s between the "quals" and the "quants" may have achieved a truce or even peace through the development of mixed methods approaches and the infusion of such qualitative ideas as stakeholder involvement into more quantitative thinking. The underlying concerns may have re-emerged, however, in a focus on establishing causality, performance assessment, and accountability. At its best, this can be seen as putting more of a floor of rigorous attention to outcomes in a house that can seem constructed of process walls only, and inspiring a more careful examination of what designs, in fact, may be possible to carry out well in practice. The limitations of this emphasis are discussed in the new challenges section.

The primary focus for this section is on a somewhat different kind of unfinished business: work that can feasibly be completed and if so, could make a good difference in the practice of evaluation. This includes assessing the quality of practice grounded in qualitative methodology and in social justice ideologies; establishing systematic means of cumulating knowledge gained through social justice approach evaluations; better articulating the needs, quality, and outcomes of evaluator training in both academic and non-academic settings; and identifying tested, effective solutions to methodological problems such as unequal opportunities to be the participating stakeholder in evaluations.

Assessing the Quality of Qualitative and Social Justice-Based Practice

Considerable progress has been made in assessing evaluation quality for quantitatively based evaluations. As noted earlier, the work of Glass, Lipsey, Light, Scriven, and others has emphasized the need to review the trustworthiness of completed evaluations before their findings are integrated to help answer policy questions. Recently, Stufflebeam has taken these meta-evaluation techniques to the next level, in response to the need for expert testimony in legal cases. Typically, the reviews examine such matters as sample selection, quality of data collection, how missing data are handled, analytic appropriateness, measures of uncertainty or error, whether disaggregated analyses are based on sufficient sample sizes, adequacy of bias control, and similar matters. Many of these criteria are technical, such as greater understanding of the bases for selecting instances for in-depth study and the consequences of these choices for later generalizations.

For approaches grounded in qualitative methodologies or in a social justice framework, however, indicators of quality are just becoming visible. Such indicators are needed if these approaches and frameworks are to enter fully the stream of large national studies.

Some progress has been made in assessing the quality of qualitatively based evaluations. Schwandt, for example, more than a decade ago, proposed the evaluation audit methodology.

This is not fast nor is it cheap, and it requires development of what auditors describe as work papers, which trace every step from original data through various stages of analysis and aggregation. The task is for a wholly independent evaluator, well-trained in the qualitative methods used, to walk the analytic path and determine whether the same conclusions would be reached by another examiner.

A somewhat different but congruent strategy for achieving quality in mixed methods studies has been used by Millsap et al., (2000) who frequently conduct large-scale, multisite, multimethod evaluations of national demonstration programs. Their technique is somewhat like the qualitative equivalent of double-cross validation in test construction. The quantitative researchers work side-by-side every step of the way as full members of the case study team, bringing the analytic rigor of their quantitative frameworks to bear on case study and observation design, data collection, analysis, integration with other methods, and reporting. The qualitative researchers, in turn, are full members of the quantitative team (analysis of administrative data, survey research, and time series assessments), bringing their own rigor to survey designs, data reduction decisions, and interpretations. As a result, assumptions are more rigorously examined, methodological lacunae more clearly (and early) identified, and the team leaders become sufficiently methodologically multilingual that they can discuss both qualitatively and quantitatively based findings with equal confidence.

In addition, checklists and frameworks have been offered for assessing the quality of mixed-method studies and, to a certain extent, for evaluating ex post the reports of qualitative and social-justice-based studies. There is, for example, an exceptionally extensive and rich body of case study reports available through the World Bank, US AID and other international organizations that rely primarily on the case approach to evaluations. Evaluators such as Bamburger and his colleagues have provided detailed, hands-on, practical, wise handbooks on conducting mixed-method studies in developing countries, handbooks that include thorough attention to evaluation quality.

In the areas of formative and outcome evaluations on a small scale and from the "strong," archetypical social justice ideology, these efforts have been limited, however, in several ways.

- There is no parallel, at this point, with the Campbell Collaborative and similar groups, in bringing together completed evaluations based on qualitative methodologies or social justice frameworks.
- Only fairly recently have reports from qualitative and social justice evaluations been publicly available at all. Efforts to seek examples of best practices in completed studies by requesting nominations and copies from outstanding theorists and methodologists have yielded a scant harvest. Stake is a leader in making his qualitative evaluation reports publicly available and in seeking meta-evaluations, as have Kushner et al., (2003). Part of the challenge is that some qualitative evaluators infuse findings with the processes of program implementation so a written "final report" is believed superfluous. Others work for organizations that prefer to keep the evaluation findings confidential. Some consider publishing qualitative final reports as antithetical to their evaluation frameworks, as these miss the point of the whole effort.

In my view, when more attention is given to meta-analytic work on the quality of evaluations conducted using qualitative and mixed methodologies and social justice frameworks, fullest mutual confidence in the trustworthiness and convincingness of evaluations based on these frameworks may progress. I am particularly concerned that enthusiasm for new approaches such as application of appreciative inquiry in evaluation comes primarily, almost exclusively, from the evaluators' own statements. How do we know how and how well these approaches operate in the real world, the value of the results to the participants, and the applicability of the method? The evaluators promoting these approaches tell us how wonderful the approaches are. With a few exceptions, such as Rogers' (2004) keen and somewhat skeptical in-depth review and analyses of the appreciative inquiry model, there are few third-party reports; nor do we hear, in their own words, the views of the participants themselves on the strengths and limitations of evaluations conducted using a social justice ideology.

Synthesizing Qualitative and Social-Justice-Based Findings

Again, great progress has been made in the synthesis of more quantitative evaluations, so much so that evaluation synthesis in itself is seen as an independent methodology for reaching conclusions and as a strong partner in establishing causality. Such syntheses have long been recognized as among the ways to improve external or causal generalizability, and the robustness of recommendations.

In the qualitative and social justice areas, unfinished business is establishing similarly robust means of integrating the findings of many evaluations. Lack of published final reports, as mentioned above, is one barrier; lack of a clearing house, another; skepticism about the appropriateness of such an effort to begin with is an additional hurdle.

Some of the more difficult barriers may be methodological. One needs criteria for sorting out more and less trustworthy evaluations (see above), as well as methodologies for integrating the findings. The techniques for cross-site

analysis of case studies offer one excellent starting place. In principle, there is no reason the techniques of thematic analysis, of parallel and cross-tracks analyses, of computer-supported qualitative analyses, and similar approaches could not be applied to cross-evaluation syntheses. However, until we have published a sturdy amount of such syntheses, until these syntheses have been shown to have utility, and until the limitations and caveats are more firmly identified, qualitative and social justice frameworks may still be seen as methodologically less mature. (One needs to remember that for some qualitatively oriented evaluators, the less mature field is the quantitative, which can be seen as oversimplifying, missing, or misrepresenting what is happening in a program.)

A related area of unfinished business is using evaluations of programs that have similar deep structures to develop and test "big P" program theories. Examples include socio-ecological, dissemination, stage theories of development, empowerment, social marketing, and the effectiveness of different policy instruments (regulation, taxation, and incentives) as change strategies. Although evaluation could potentially contribute a lot here, only a few evaluators have ventured into this territory in practice. Datta & Grasso (1998) looked at evaluation of tax expenditures; Pawson & Tilley (1997) note that evaluation can best test the efficacy of underlying mechanisms across disparate contexts.

Evaluator Training

Progress has been made in developing training programs using formal academic settings, internships, pre-conference workshops, short sessions, the internet, journals, and a Niagara of evaluation texts. There is an extensive, but somewhat nervous literature on assessing the quality of these offerings, touching as these discussions must, on the raw nerves of accreditation and credentialing. A lot of talk is good;

a paucity of empirical study is not good. Even less progress has been made in examining the results of such training in terms of evaluator competencies. We have nothing like the Flexner report (1910) on medical education.

Such empirical studies of the results of evaluator training seem particularly urgent for several reasons. One reason is the emergent research on the dominant roles mentors and graduate experience play in evaluator practice (Christie, 2003). Another, and perhaps even more compelling, is that while systematic information is scant, most evaluations apparently are being carried out by non-evaluators as part of their overall program management responsibilities. These program directors are getting brief training through one- or two-day workshops, assisted by do-it-yourself guidebooks. The guidebooks can have many of the merits of an "Evaluation for Dummies" in delightful readability, coverage of frequently asked questions, concrete examples, and step-by-step guidance, yet stop where program directors may need the most help: actual indicators and measures. Yet another question is whether we are training for the past, rather than for the future as it is likely to be experienced by many evaluators in many countries: evaluation theory may lag behind evaluation practice.

Rist (2004), for example, has argued that evaluation practice is in its third generation whilst evaluation theory is in its second generation (if that far along). He sees the characteristics of the second generation (10 years ago from 2004) as characterized by:

- one study for multiple users
- reliance on large databases with computer support
- a focus on individual clients
- enlightenment rather than decision oriented
- multiple teams producing information
- shifting from quantitative versus qualitative methods to mixed methods

In contrast, Rist describes the third generation of evaluative studies as:

- multiple streams of evaluative information throughout the enterprise, rather than single isolated studies
- systems and partnerships, rather than individual evaluators or teams producing and sharing evaluative knowledge
- most evaluative information being produced by non-evaluators
- monitoring and evaluative streams that are beginning to merge
- databases that are continuous and virtual
- timeframes that are immediate
- analysis that is continuous
- virtual analysis of trends and conditions
- visual displays rather than hard-copy narratives
- data collection at multiple levels by multiple stakeholders
- internet as the new information glue
- increased transparency of evaluative knowledge
- emphasis on continuous organizational adaptation and improvement

Rist's perspective comes from many years of evaluator training and evaluation development in countries throughout the world. He does not intend this to be a description of evaluation in the United States or the "first world" only. Nonetheless, many of his observations seem close to home, with strong implications for evaluator training, or, more accurately, for training non-evaluators to include evaluation responsibilities in their work at high levels of evaluation competence. Here, evaluation practice may lag behind evaluation theory.

Turning in some depth to who is conducting evaluations, a sobering report by Christie (2003) shows that for at least one state (California) and at least one field (mental health), most of the people actually doing evaluations of the projects have little or no evaluation training, little or no knowledge of evaluation frameworks and theories, and little or no experience carrying out evaluations. Their evaluation responsibilities are marginal to their other tasks. This is consistent with Rist's observations, with experience from grant reviews, and may contribute to the emphasis on empowering stakeholders, coaching them, assisting them to do their own evaluations. That is, while mandates for evaluation often exist, the money to hire formally trained evaluators often doesn't exist.

The root causes and consequences of Christie's findings aren't examined in depth. What is the quality of evaluations her respondents are producing? If theory isn't used, are these evaluators-by-mandate just unfamiliar with various techniques and when to use them? Are they too close to the program and thus compromised in terms of doing quality work? Are we being too protective of our own field? Do we need to develop better, low-cost but smart ways to do evaluations without much expertise or money (see, e.g., Hatry & Wye, 1986)? Having reviewed evaluations produced through organizations such as the United Way, my sense is the consequences on the average are C– and at best, mixed. While a few evaluations are first-rate, most are misleadingly enthusiastic based on "evidence," such as "satisfaction" with services by those in the program until the end, even when over 90 percent of those originally referred have dropped out (not graduated, but left). Where the evaluations have been first-rate, the program directors have advanced degrees and some formal evaluation training. But this is anecdote; we lack systematic information.

Much of the information about evaluator training comes from surveys of the master's and doctoral-level courses in evaluation. Evaluator training is often integrated into departments such as health, education, welfare, and justice; stand-alone departments of evaluation, awarding their own professional degrees, are rarer. Debates on what such training should cover, and the best ways to combine scholarly knowledge with hands-on experience have been vigorous and continuing, as well they should be.

In addition to this formal training, as mentioned, pre-conference workshops such as those offered by the American Evaluation Association, special workshops on evaluation offered by international agencies such as the World Bank, and in-depth courses such as those provided through the Evaluation Institute and the Center for Evaluation at Western Michigan University are scaled for both formally trained evaluators and for "evaluators by default." These seem very well-attended, and may be a primary source of training.

Almost nothing is known systematically, however, about the content or quality of training offered to evaluation practitioners across these and other sources of evaluation knowledge, skills, and abilities. One could review the dozens of books now available on evaluation, perhaps obtain information on their sales, and possibly even conduct follow-up studies of those who rely on them as a significant source of guidance. One also could study the quality of training given to evaluation practitioners, and, quite usefully, review the quality of the evaluation proposals and the evaluation reports produced through such on-the-job training. Having done so on a small scale for a population of organizations over an approximately five-year period, I found that the vocabulary has changed (activities, outputs, immediate outcomes appear widely from the program logic templates) but little else, in terms of actual data collected, analysis, reporting, or evidence that the evaluations are used for program improvement or, despite the mandate, resource allocations.

As a field, unfinished business surely should include more extensive, rigorously empirical, and systematic attention to the content and quality of training for both academically based evaluators and evaluation practitioners. We need to examine the quality and the costs (direct and opportunity) of the evaluations produced, and continue the vigorous discussion of some form of training program accreditation, evaluator certification, and licensing.

Evaluation Research on Challenges in Evaluation Practice

To the credit of our field, in almost every area, experience is being shared, evaluations are being mined for the gold of knowledge about evaluation practice, assumptions are being challenged, and new ideas presented. Approaches with great intellectual appeal, such as stakeholder involvement or participatory democracy or appreciative inquiry, are being tried in diverse settings, their limitations better understood, and possible solutions developed. International cooperation and international collaboratives are speeding cross-national sharing of new ideas, effective strategies, and pitfalls. Of particular value are the *International Journal of Evaluation*, the swiftly spreading national evaluation associations (now in over 57 countries and regions), and international councils on evaluation. Evaluators now can access, via the net, other evaluations around the world. These efforts expand greatly access to exceptionally able evaluation theorists and practitioners. With the support of groups such as the Kellogg Foundation and the World Bank, we increasingly are learning together.

Yet, we still need considerable empirical work on evaluation practice, especially tests of ideas and propositions in our theories. Among the most central of such propositions is the claimed importance of stakeholder participation, and the related problem of unequal

opportunities to be the "participating stakeholder" in evaluations (Bryk, 1983). For the stakeholder involvement approach to be meaningful, not tokenistic, one presumably needs to have all the relevant stakeholder groups at the table, en masse, or through their representatives, and to have reasonably full and sustained engagement throughout the evaluative process. How does one adequately map relevant stakeholder groups, and develop processes with appropriate cultural sensitivity so the interactions will be on a level playing field? Where it is not possible, practically, to involve every single stakeholder in the decisions, how does one select representatives – or better, facilitate the selection by the stakeholder group of those they consider representatives – who truly "represent?" How can one adequately sustain meaningful participation, which takes a lot of time, for those who have many other responsibilities and who incur non-trivial expenses in attending? Particularly for large national studies, how "representative" are individuals such as the President or Chief Executive Officer of the many organizations formed to promote stakeholder interests? How much "better" at state or local levels is stakeholder representation? What are the ways evaluators have tried to deal with this challenge? Which ones have worked well, and which have not, in various circumstances? We need some criteria for deciding how wide to throw the net and when it is less appropriate or possibly damaging and counterproductive to have "all" stakeholders involved and full disclosure of all aspects of a report to all stakeholders. Such a nuanced understanding of stakeholder participation would be a useful elaboration of the discussion as it now stands.

One could say that almost anything one does to obtain stakeholder participation in an evaluation of a program such as one intended to decrease or delay drug use in pre-teens and teens is better than nothing. One could do one's best, report how many persons on the evaluation team are youth, and get on with the job without getting overly nice. There may be much to be said for such pragmatism – or it may be one among other instances of an attractive concept where evaluation research and practice has not yet caught up with evaluation theory.

New Challenges

Evaluation in contexts such as Rist identified (evaluation streams more than studies, rapid access to knowledge through the internet, organizational change and development) surely will be addressed in conferences, texts and eventually training. Two other challenges seem to me both fairly new and important for our field: the costs of success and evaluation misuse.

Too Much Evaluation?

Considered by criteria of ubiquity and infusion, evaluation has been rather a roaring success (Williams & Hawkes, 2003). Requirements for conducting evaluations both for program improvement and for accountability are found in grant application requirements from foundations such as the Kellogg Foundation and the Packard Foundation, from charitable organizations such as the United Way, from federal and state governments, and from international organizations such as the World Bank and International Monetary Fund. There are currently (2005) over 50 evaluation associations in countries around the world, many international as well as national journals of evaluation, and evaluation special interest groups embedded in scores of professional organizations.

This demand for evaluation may come at no small cost, in direct expenditures, in record

keeping and data requirements by service delivery organizations, and in opportunity costs, particularly at the level of the service delivery organizations. Almost all of this demand seems to be an unfunded mandate, with evaluation funds rather inversely related to distance between point-of-origin funder and the beneficiaries. The technical assistance centers for evaluation get funded, the evaluation consultants get funded, and perhaps very large organizations such as school districts will have a fairly well-staffed office for measurement, assessment and evaluation. The classroom teacher who has to keep all those records, who must allocate classroom time for testing and for observations, and who must report often and extensively usually is not funded directly for this work. Nor is the service provider for handicapped adults, the substance abuse treatment counselor, the "cop on the beat," and others. Indeed, they may be expected to donate their weekends for evaluation and record-keeping training.

Evaluations indeed can benefit programs, a result devoutly hoped for in theory, but unproven in practice. Demonstrably, however, the evaluation demands place unpaid burdens across a range of organizations, from the large agencies, who can afford a Director of Evaluation but at the cost of less direct services, to small groups, whose executive directors are already under stress trying to keep the organization financially afloat and those in need, served. Just one evaluation might be manageable; an agency receiving assistance from 15 different sources, however, may have to collect 15 different sets of data, organized around 15 different sets of reporting questions, to be delivered at 15 different times, and receive zero feedback on any of this.

Virtually nothing is known, systematically, about the full costs (direct and indirect, and opportunity costs), the actual documentable benefits, and the consequences, intended and unintended, of this orgy of evaluation mandates. We need to learn whether the benefits are high enough to be commensurate with the costs involved, and if not, to try out other strategies for helping organizations learn and be accountable in addition to, or besides, the current style of evaluation requirements.

The Politics of Methodology

Evaluation utilization and communication, as noted above, have been fairly well developed, with the accent rather on the positive with regard to program improvements, benefits and use. The analyses include, nonetheless, some useful discussions of the misuse of completed evaluations. Among the misuses are (1) citing only findings favorable to points the speaker or writer wishes to make; (2) failing adequately to report uncertainties, nuances, and caveats so the findings seem more certain than they are; (3) using data from the first implementation year of a multisite, multiyear program to make funding or program change decisions far beyond what the study permits; (4) citing only favorable studies whilst failing to discuss equally or more robust evaluations that are not consistent with the points the speaker/writer wishes to make; (5) keeping unfavorable evaluations in the limbo of eternal "in house" review so the findings are never made public; and (6) pressuring the evaluator to change the report submitted or actually changing a report already submitted. The Ethics Section in the *American Journal of Evaluation* is one source of instances (based on actual examples but with specific identities blurred); another, debates on Evaltalk about specific high-profile evaluations and their release, such as the first-year evaluation of the 21st Century Schools program.

Among the remedies, careful attention to expectations and to the evaluator's responsibilities and rights before the contract is signed are recommended, and may be helpful for relatively small evaluations. More broadly, Chelimsky and others remind us that evaluation of high-stakes programs, policies, and activities is inherently political; that evaluators need to be exceptionally scrupulous to have study designs reviewed by all stakeholders; and that, in the end, one needs courage, courage, and more courage.

Evaluation organizations have not played a systematic role in examining the evaluation designs before their funding, the reports before their release, and actions based on the findings before they become law. Scriven has pointed out that comparable professional groups have a presence in Washington, to alert their members to upcoming issues, to help educate decision-makers, and to represent the standards and views of the profession.

Critiques by individuals may be written after the fact on occasions such as the use of the "21st Century grant" first-year evaluation, which was released without prior review by evaluators and used, prematurely, to justify a decrease of $400,000,000 from the program budget. (The 21st Century Schools was a high-profile, fairly short-lived program intended to transform schools into educational centers for communities (version 1) or as an engine for academically oriented school change (version 2). It was supplanted by the No Child Left Behind Act, which focuses firmly and exclusively on academic achievement.) These evaluation critiques are often great, but late. We are not sufficiently skilled in becoming part of the initial decisions so that the millions badly used for certain evaluations are spent on better studies. Ethically, and as a matter of social justice, I do not see how we can continue to look the other way.

Such engagement requires finding meaningful common ground in our field. Some evaluators, who have written wisely and in great detail about the conditions of appropriate use, feel strongly that despite limitations, designs such as the randomized control group approach have more benefits than risk, and they have much experience to support this view. Other evaluators see the threats to validity in applied situations as notably restricting the utility of these designs, and urge guidance that best matches circumstances with evaluation designs to permit the most robust conclusions. They tend to have little positive experience with the "best match" approach to support their view, but can discuss instances of mono-method misuse.

The politics of methodology is an emerging area of concern with regard to evaluation use. We have a long history of identifying lessons learned from projects and programs (evaluation syntheses) and of recognizing program approaches that seem associated with exceptional results (best and promising practices, effective programs initiatives). Yet, perhaps the most reliable finding is that from an often huge body of relevant evaluations and reports, only about 10 percent of these reports, if that much, tend to survive reasonable screening for trustworthiness and evaluation quality.

The costs are too high to ignore this. Not-so-good programs with unusually robust evaluation designs may be selected for funding and recognition, while outstanding programs with feeble evaluations may be ignored. When the wastage comes from programs ostensibly funded as pilot tests or demonstrations, concerns rise even higher. The remedies have included providing evaluation technical assistance for grantees, requiring detailed information in the proposal on evaluation design and measures, with enough points for the section that a proposal could not be funded without an adequate evaluation, and upping the rewards for having a strong program vigorously evaluated.

At issue is how to do this while respecting the complexity of decisions regarding what measures and designs are both robust and appropriate for the situation. To some evaluators, there is a gold standard for designs where causality/attribution is important, and that is the randomized control test design. Federal agencies such as the US National Institutes of Health offer an extra 20 points for proposals promising to carry out the randomized control design, and give no extra points for a quasi-experimental, mixed method, or more qualitative design that might be more appropriate for the situation. There are some excellent texts detailing the threats to the feasibility and validity of the randomized control design (see, e.g., Shadish, Cook, & Campbell, 2002), which also suggest quasi-experimental or other approaches should the circumstances not permit randomization. Laudably, this quantitatively oriented text pays much needed attention to causal generalizability, or external validity, noting that more qualitative information may be most relevant to understanding these issues (see also Sechrest and Scott, 1993).

Relatively little is known about the quality of reviews of the evaluation designs in proposals, other than comments at some American Evaluation Association panel sessions by advocates of the randomized design expressing their concern that reviewers too often are not competent to appreciate the limitations and may not recognize when the supposed gold standard design is, in fact, lead. Similar concerns apply to the international collections of instances of randomized design use; it can be possible to use any design (qualitative, quantitative, and mixed) inappropriately. One wants to see not only that a certain design has been used, but whether the use is consistent with good evaluation practice.

As an illustrative example, the randomized design may be most appropriate when the intervention is well-bounded and when the time between initiation and completion relatively brief. At least in the education area, very swiftly my control group can become your experimental group, and vice versa, as schools apply for and win various grants for innovation and reform, and as federal and state mandates (also for innovation and reform) create stress and overlap the experimental innovations. This is not exactly "treatment contamination" nor can it easily be predicted or contained. Rather, the prudent evaluator may need to dedicate as much time to describing in detail the actual experiences of both treatment and non-treatment groups through the study, using the data to test such hypotheses as the effectiveness of treatment elements, regardless of the label under which they may be found.

This is not to suggest that evaluation practice is situated, rather like astronomy, at high altitudes above the political ebbs and flows of the real world. Where evaluation is embedded, who makes the decisions, what is of greatest focus, how much is invested in evaluation, as well as designs, methods, and measures follow these ebbs and flows. Administrations concerned with equity and social justice, historically, have sought to place the power of information in the hands of the beneficiaries of programs, found descriptive and process information particularly useful, and looked for outcomes such as community development, collaborations, and empowerment for local solutions to local understanding of problems. Administrations concerned with efficiency and effectiveness in achievement and more structured, quantifiable results have tended to support nationally developed criteria, emphasize causality, and want to know if programs work as intended, if they are cost-effective. And the relative influence of federal, state, and foundation/private sector concerns ebbs and flows too. Development of evaluation theory and practice has blended both reactions against the perceived limitations of these political stances and efforts to use the political

opportunity to advance evaluation practice and methods as the emphases emerged. These influences have been, are and will be part of evaluation practice. However, we need to be aware of them, and, where appropriate, seek to modulate them.

My concern, for example, is expressed in the context of the randomized control design, but it applies to any pendulum swing that would try to establish a single design as better than all others in all circumstances. I see this as an instance of the politics of methodology and would be just as concerned if the national gold standard switched to empowerment designs, fourth-generation approaches, or mixed-methods evaluations. For the present issue, for instance, we have an administration skeptical about the value of public schools and eager to promote charter schools and vouchers. The randomized design is said to be macro-negative. Requiring this design may create a body of ostensibly gold-standard evaluations showing relatively little benefit of interventions, thus providing a "scientific" basis for disenchantment with overall school improvement. This, in turn, can get transformed into enthusiasm for a less scientific default option, for charter schools, vouchers, and other changes that may be well-intentioned with regard to benefiting low-income children, but are based on inappropriate evaluation designs.

One would like to see the applicants and reviewers well-schooled in the analyses, speeches, and texts mentioned, which most thoroughly consider limitations on the randomized control design (or any other design selected as a gold standard) and which describe the value in different circumstances of alternative designs. One equally might wish to see more empirical, practice-based analyses of the specific instances where different designs are optimal for reaching certain benefits and minimizing certain threats to conclusions, a statement where perhaps all concerned with causal inferences could reach some agreement. And one would like to see also, for the future, continued efforts, with mutual respect, of bringing our field together before laws are passed and policies implemented with regard to evaluation, so our associations can speak for the field, so that various perspectives and value stances are fairly represented, and are fairly privileged in this grand and continuing discourse.

Making Evaluation More Consequential

All of the titles of chapters in this part refer to the interface between evaluation and political processes. Stake & Schwandt (Chapter 18) examine defining quality as values driven, and values as political process driven. Alkin, Christie & Rose (Chapter 17) assert that the very conduct of an evaluation is communication, of necessity involving stakeholders and other audiences, whose concerns are embedded in political processes. Walker & Wiseman's focus (Chapter 16) is on evaluations that operate in real time and concern policy processes; their analysis is strongly grounded in instances of how profoundly evaluation management requires an interplay of negotiations among many stakeholders, how much it is about managing relationships among policy actors. Mark & Henry's work (Chapter 14) makes the case that the changes they discuss evolved from policy debates, are applied in often highly charged political settings, and reverberate from a specific project or program into the larger policy space. To Whitmore et al., (Chapter 15), the beginning principles for an evaluation come from a social justice ideology: the principles of participation, of collective learning, of flexibility in working as a collective. Methods derived from these starting principles emphasize the lived experience of the more

marginalized groups, of assuring evaluators' cultural competencies, and analyses reflecting democratic processes of dialog and discourse.

One could reasonably conclude that evaluators, by and large, are now both awakened and mindful: evaluation is among the contemporary political strategies and it is inextricably rooted in political processes. Granted, there is variation in beliefs about what the methodological and ideological principles deriving from this awareness should be, as well as about how one best adjusts action to context in a specific situation. Stake & Schwandt and Whitmore et al., may not see eye to eye with Henry, for example. While the dialogs continue, it seems to me that many evaluators are getting exceptionally skillful in acting on the insights already reached, at least with regard to their individual practices.

Not so, however, with regard to our collective practice. By this, I mean influencing the political processes with regard to evaluation so we are helping lead the way to sound, beneficial practice, rather than reacting, accommodating, and sometimes wringing our hands after political decisions are made that affect many aspects of our field. The development by the international communities of evaluation organizations of standards and principles is a good step toward such collective practices. Gathering the professional will and the professional skill to speak evaluation truths to political power would be a fine next step. We do so already, again as individuals or through smaller international groups such as the Campbell collaborative. Perhaps fears such as Stake & Schwandt discuss, or Marianna's Trench-deep divergences would permit only a dumbing down of our positions to a very low common denominator. Perhaps, however, as these chapters suggest, as examinations of challenges well met, of unfinished business, and new challenges suggest, there can be meaningful common ground from which to move the political processes toward better collective practices.

Acknowledgments

Many thanks to the editor and reviewers of drafts of this chapter. In several instances, they said it so well, I have used their words, with deep appreciation for their thoughts and deep regrets I am unable to acknowledge the thinkers personally.

References

Alkin, M. (ed.) (2004). *Evaluation Roots: Tracing theorists' views and influences*. Thousand Oaks, CA: Sage.

Alkin, M., Daillak, R., & White, P. (1979). *Using Evaluations: Does evaluation make a difference?* Sage Library of Social Research, Vol. 76. Beverly Hills, CA: Sage.

Bamberger, M. (2000). *Integrating Quantitative and Qualitative Research in Development Projects*. Directions in Development Series. Washington, D.C.: The World Bank.

Boruch, R. F. (1997). *Randomized Experiments for Planning and Evaluation: A practical guide*. Thousand Oaks, CA: Sage

Bryk, A. S. (ed.) (1983). *Stakeholder-Based Evaluation. New Directions for Program Evaluation*, No. 17. San Francisco, CA: Jossey-Bass.

Campbell, D. T. & Erlebacher, A. E. (1970). How regression artifacts in evaluation mistakenly make compensatory education look harmful. In J. Hellmuth (ed.) *Compensatory Education: A national debate*, Vol. 3, *Disadvantaged Child*. New York: Brunner/Mazel.

Campbell, D. T. & Stanley, J. C. (1966). *Experimental and Quasi-experimental Design for Research*. Chicago: Rand McNally.

Chelimsky, E. & Shadish, W. (1997). *Evaluation for the 21st Century: A handbook*. Thousand Oaks, CA: Sage.

Chen, H-T. (1994). *Theory Driven Evaluation*. Newbury Park: Sage.

Christie, C. A. (2003). What guides evaluation? A study of how evaluation practice maps onto evaluation theory. In C. A. Christie (ed.) *The Practice-Theory Relationship in Evaluation. New Directions for Evaluation*, No. 97. San Francisco: Jossey-Bass.

Cook, T. & Campbell, D. (1978). *Quasi-experimentation: Design and analysis for field settings*. Chicago: Rand McNally.

Datta, L-E. & Grasso, P. (eds) (1998). *Evaluating Tax Expenditures. New Directions for Evaluation*, No. 79. San Francisco, CA: Jossey-Bass.

Donaldson, S. & Scriven, M. (eds) (2003). *Evaluating Social Programs and Problems: Visions for the new Millennium*. Mahwah, NJ: Lawrence Erlbaum Associates.

Fetterman, D. M. (1990). Ethnographic auditing. In Tierney, W. G. (ed.) *Assessing Academic Climates and Cultures. New Directions for Institution Research*. San Francisco, CA: Jossey-Bass.

Fetterman, D. M., Kaftarian, S. J., & Wandersman, A. (eds) (1996). *Empowerment Evaluation: Knowledge and tools for self-assessment and accountability*. Thousand Oaks, CA: Sage.

Flexner, A. (1910). *Medical Education in the United States and Canada*. New York: The Carnegie Foundation for the Advancement of Teaching.

Glass, G. (1976). Primary, secondary, and meta-analysis in research. *Educational Researcher*, 5, 3–8.

Glass, G. & Smith, M. L. (1981). *Meta-analysis in Social Research*. Beverly Hills: Sage.

Greene, J. C., Caracelli, V. J., & Graham, W. F. (1989). Towards a conceptual framework for mixed methods evaluation designs. *Educational Evaluation and Policy Analysis*, 11, 255–274.

Greene, J. P. (1998). A meta-analysis of the effectiveness of bilingual education. Report to the Tomas Rivera Policy Institute, University of Texas at Austin. http://www.ksg.harvard.edu/pepg/pdf/biling/pdf.

Hatry, H. & Wye, C. (1986). The uses of evaluation. In J. Wholey (ed.) *Organizational Excellence: Stimulating quality and communicating value*. Lexington, MA: D. C. Heath.

Henry, G. T. (1995). *Graphing Data: Techniques for description and analyses*. Thousand Oaks, CA: Sage.

Joint Committee on Standards for Educational Evaluation (1981). *Standards for Evaluation of Educational Programs, Projects, and Materials*. New York: McGraw Hill.

Joint Committee on Standards for Educational Evaluation (1994). *The Program Evaluation Standards: How to assess evaluations of educational programs*. Newbury Park, CA: Sage.

Kushner, S., Simons, H., Jones, K., & James, D. (2003). From evidence-based practice to practice-based evidence: The idea of situated generalization. *Research Papers in Education*, 18, 347–364.

Light, R. (1984). *Summing Up: The science of research review*. Cambridge, MA: Harvard University Press.

Light, R. & Smith, P. (1971). Accumulating evidence: Procedures for resolving contradictions among research studies. *Harvard Educational Review,* 41, 429–471.

Lipsey, M. & Wilson, D. B. (2001). *Practical Meta-analysis.* Thousand Oaks, CA.: Sage.

Mark, M., Henry, G., & Julnes, G. (2000). *Evaluation: An integrated framework for understanding, guiding, and improving policies and programs.* San Francisco, CA: Jossey-Bass.

Miles, M. & Huberman, M. (1994). *Qualitative Data Analysis,* 2nd edition. Thousand Oaks, CA: Sage.

Millsap, M. A., Chase, A., Obeidallah, D., Perez-Smith, A., Bringham, N., & Johnson, K. (2000). *Evaluation of Detroit's Comer School and Families Initiative.* Cambridge, MA: Abt Associates.

Mowbray, C. T., Holter, M. C., Teague, G. B., & Bybee, D. (2003). Fidelity criteria: Development, measurement, and evaluation. *The American Journal of Evaluation,* 24, 315–340.

Mosteller, F. & Boruch, R. F. (2002). *Evidence Matters: Randomized trials in education research.* Washington, DC: Brookings Institution Press.

Orwin, R. G., Sonnenfeld, L. J., Cordray, D. S., Pion, G. M. & Perl, H. I. (1998). Constructing quantitative implementation scales from categorical services data. *Evaluation Review,* 22, 245–288.

Orwin, R. G., Campbell, B., Campbell, K., & Krupski, A. (2004). Welfare reform and addiction: A priori hypotheses, post-hoc explorations, and assisted sense-making in evaluating the effects of terminating benefits for chronic substance abusers. *American Journal of Evaluation,* 25(4), 409–442.

Patton, M. Q. (1978). *Utilization-Focused Evaluation.* Beverly Hills, CA: Sage.

Pawson, R. & Tilley, N. (1997). *Realistic Evaluation.* London: Sage.

Pressman, J. L. & Wildavsky, A. (1974). *Implementation: How great expectations in Washington are dashed in Oakland.* Berkeley, CA: University of California Press.

Raudenbush, S. W. & Bryk, A. S. (2002). *Hierarchical Linear Models: Applications and data analysis methods,* 2nd edition. Thousand Oaks, CA: Sage.

Rist, R. (2004). Rethinking the utilization debate: From studies to streams. Paper presented at the Malaysian Evaluation Society Annual Conference. http://ww.danskevalueringssel-skab.dk/PowerPoint/slides_RayCRist.ppt.

Rogers, P. (ed.) (2000). *Program Theory in Evaluation: Challenges and Opportunities.* San Francisco: Jossey-Bass.

Rogers, P. (2004). Appreciating appreciative inquiry. In H. Preskill & A. T. Coghlan (eds) *Using Appreciative Inquiry in Evaluation. New Directions for Evaluation,* No. 100. San Francisco, CA: Jossey-Bass.

Rossi, P. H., Lipsey, M. W., & Freeman, H. E. (2004). *Evaluation: A systematic approach,* 7th edition. Thousand Oaks: Sage.

Schwandt, T. A. (1990). On judging trustworthiness in interpretivist methodologies. Paper presented at the Annual Meeting of the American Evaluation Association, Boston.

Sechrest, L., West, S. G., Philips, M. A., Redner, R., & Yeaton, W. (1979). Some neglected problems in evaluation research: Strength and integrity of treatments. In L. Sechrest, S. G. West, M. A. Philips. R. Redner & W. Yeaton (eds) *Evaluation Studies Review Annual,* Vol. 4 (pp. 15–35). Beverly Hills, CA: Sage.

Sechrest, L. & Scott, A. (eds) (1993). *Understanding Causes and Generalizing About Them. New Directions for Evaluation,* No. 57. San Francisco, CA: Jossey-Bass.

Shadish, W. R., Cook, T. D., & Campbell, D. T. (2002). *Experimental and Quasi-experimental Designs for Generalized Causal Inference.* New York: Houghton Mifflin.

Shadish, W. R., Newman, D. L., Schreirer, M. A., & Wye, C. (1995). *Guiding Principles for Evaluators. New Directions for Program Evaluation,* No. 66. San Francisco, CA: Jossey-Bass.

Stallings, J. (1975). Educational effects of teaching practices in follow through classrooms. *Monographs of the Society for Research in Child Development,* 40, 7–8.

Tashakkori, A. & Teddlie, C. (1998). *Mixed Methodology: Combining qualitative and quantitative approaches.* Thousand Oaks, CA: Sage.

Torres, R. T., Preskill, H. S., & Piontek, M. E. (1996). *Evaluation Strategies for Communicating and Enhancing Learning in Organizations.* Newbury Park: Sage.

Weiss, C. (1972). *Evaluation Research: Methods of assessing program effectiveness.* Englewood Cliffs, NJ: Prentice-Hall.

Weiss, C. (ed.) (1977). *Using Social Research in Public Policy Making.* Lexington, MA: D. C. Heath.

Williams, D. D. & Hawkes, M. L. (2003). Issues and practices related to mainstreaming evaluation: Where do we flow from here? In J. J. Barnette & J. R. Saunders, (eds) *The Mainstreaming of Evaluation. New Directions for Evaluation,* No. 99 (pp. 63–83). San Francisco, CA: Jossey Bass.

Yin, R. (2003). *Case Study Research: Design and methods,* 3rd edition. Thousand Oaks, CA: Sage.

PART FOUR

DOMAINS OF
EVALUATION PRACTICE

20

EVALUATION IN EDUCATION

David Nevo

Educational evaluation has come a long way since its initiation by Ralph Tyler more than half a century ago. It started with the assessment of student achievements, as part of the learning and teaching process, then came to be used later for curriculum development and review, but mainly still, at that early time, in conjunction with individual classrooms. Only in the mid-1960s and early 70s, with the increased demand for educational program and project evaluation coming from governmental organizations and other agencies, did educational evaluation expand beyond the classroom into the entire educational system.

Most of these early developments in program evaluation took place in the United States and were "exported" to other parts of the world some ten or twenty years later. In Europe, for instance, the major concern was – and in some countries still is – testing and student assessment. Gradually, timed tests and other achievement measures became not only assessments of individual student learning but also outcome measures for

other evaluation objects, such as programs, schools, teachers, and educational systems. Such evaluations now can be found around the world in many shapes and sizes reflecting the extensive relevance of educational evaluation.

Educational evaluation, while having much in common with other types of evaluation in areas such as social work, health services, and criminal justice, also has some unique features. First, the roots of evaluation in education are found in student testing and assessment, which has been conducted in schools around the world for centuries. Second, public involvement in the practice and use of educational evaluation is characteristically strong, since education is understood as a public good relevant to most members of a society, far beyond the relevance of social services, health, and criminal justice. Third, the role of teachers and their experience as evaluators (although mainly evaluators of students) cannot be ignored in designing and implementing educational evaluations that position teachers as evaluators, evaluation objects, and/or evaluation stake-holders. It often happens that promising evaluation approaches are rejected by teachers and other educators because they are not respectful of their own roles as educational evaluators or sensitive enough to the unique characteristics of local educational environments. These features are highlighted throughout the discussion of educational evaluation in this chapter.

Parallel to the rationale and structure of this Handbook, the chapter addresses the following topics and issues: (1) *defining educational evaluation* – measurement versus evaluation, description, and judgment, judgment versus understanding; (2) *roles and functions of educational evaluation* – decision making, improvement, accountability, professionalization, and certification; (3) *research methods and instruments* – experimental and non-experimental designs, traditional and alternative student assessment methods, qualitative and quantitative inquiry methods; and (4) *domains of practice* – student assessment, teacher evaluation, evaluation of instructional materials, program and project evaluation, and school evaluation. The main emphasis of the chapter is on the domains of practice in formal educational contexts. The discussion catalogs the various functions or purposes and forms or methods of evaluation in each of these educational domains.

The chapter concludes with a discussion of the future of educational evaluation in light of some expected developments in educational policy and practice around the world.[1]

Defining Educational Evaluation

What is educational evaluation? What does it mean? Is it a very complex concept or a simple one, in essence, but complicated by evaluation experts? Many attempts have been made in recent years to explain the meaning of evaluation and clarify the distinction between evaluation and other related concepts, such as measurement and research. The literature contains many approaches to the conceptualization of evaluation and the determination of its countenance in education. Many of those approaches have been unduly referred to as "models" (e.g., the CIPP Model, the Discrepancy Model, the Responsive Model, or the Goal-Free Model) even though none of them reaches a sufficient degree of complexity or completeness to justify the term "model." Stake (1981) rightly suggested that they be referred to as "persuasions" rather than "models."

Ralph Tyler's well-known definition asserts that evaluation is "The process of determining to what extent educational objectives are actually being realized" (Tyler, 1950, p. 69). Other leading evaluators, such as Cronbach (1963), Stufflebeam et al., (1971), and Alkin (1969), define evaluation as providing information for decision-making. In recent years there has been considerable consensus among evaluators that evaluation is the assessment of merit or worth (Joint Committee, 1994; Scriven, 1991), or an activity comprising both description and judgment. Following Stake (1967) and Guba & Lincoln (1981), Nevo has defined educational evaluation as an "act of collecting systematic information regarding the nature and quality of educational objects" (Nevo, 1995, p. 11). This definition combines description and judgment but distinguishes between them because of their different nature. Description can be based on systematic data collection and thus result in highly objective information. Judgment is based on criteria, which in most cases are determined by values, social norms, and personal preferences of stakeholders associated with the evaluation. Judgment may thus be very subjective in nature. Description and judgment, though coexisting in most evaluations, are used in different proportions for different purposes and by different types of evaluators.

Roles and Functions of Educational Evaluation

Scriven (1967) was the first to suggest the distinction between *formative evaluation* and *summative evaluation*. In its formative function, evaluation may be used for improvement and for the development of an ongoing activity (or of a program, person, product, and so forth). In its summative function, evaluation may be used for accountability, certification, or selection.

Other functions for educational evaluation have also been advanced. These include increasing awareness about certain activities, motivating desired behavior of evaluees, or promoting public relations. Evaluation can even serve the somewhat unpopular function of supporting the exercise of authority (Glasman & Heck, 2003). In formal organizations it is the privilege of the superior to evaluate his/her subordinates. And often the person in a management position does so in order to assert his/her authority. Although some evaluators (e.g., Cronbach, 1982; Stufflebeam et al., 1971) have expressed clear preference for the formative function of evaluation, the general perception seems to be that there are no "right" or "wrong" roles of evaluation, at least regarding the formative and summative roles of evaluation.

Educational evaluation can serve many needs at various levels of the educational system resulting in five major functions. They are related to decision-making, improvement, accountability, professionalism, and certification.

Decision-making is a very popular topic in the literature on educational administration where evaluation has featured under titles like *Educational Evaluation and Decision Making* (Stufflebeam et al., 1971), or *Evaluation in Decision Making* (Glasman & Nevo, 1988). Decisions are made by students, teachers, parents, and administrators about students, teachers, instructional materials, and the school as a whole. Information and facts are usually considered as beneficial to decision-making by decreasing the amount of uncertainty and increasing the degree of rationality in the process. Of course information, good as it might be, will never eliminate the uncertainty that is involved in choosing among alternatives, nor will it ever make decision- making a totally rational process. Nonetheless evaluation is useful for decision-making if it provides relevant information, when needed, and in a communicative form. Such information may not make the correct decision obvious, but it can improve our grasp of the problem at hand and the nature of the available alternatives.

Improvement is another ongoing need of educational systems that can be served by evaluation. Students have to improve their learning performance. Teachers have to improve their teaching and their teaching skills. Curricular materials have to be continuously updated and improved. Schools have to keep improving themselves in order to compete with other schools or in response to requests for innovation and modernization. In a world undergoing dramatic change even conservative institutions like schools must change rapidly, if not improve, just to keep up. An ongoing flow of various types of information to educational systems as well as to individual schools, teachers, and students seems crucial. Educational systems need information on changing student needs that have to be served, curricular opportunities that they can take advantage of, recommended instructional strategies to be followed, ongoing administrative processes that have to be improved, and a wide range of information on learning outcomes that have to be recycled.

School evaluation needs a wide perspective on formative evaluation to respond to such challenges.

To serve **accountability** is another well-known function of educational evaluation, a function of considerable purchase at this time around the world. The usefulness of evaluation as accountability in improving education, however, is not always clear, and simple solutions such as representing student achievement as a single indicator of accountability or basing accountability on external evaluation alone do not seem to work. Since the demand for accountability is not going to vanish in the near future, but rather may continue to gain momentum in many countries (as typified by the recent "No Child Left Behind" legislation in the USA), refinements of approaches to educational evaluation for accountability are needed. In particular, school stakeholders and external evaluators alike, instead of resisting the demand for accountability, may beneficially become active participants in accountability evaluation. Educational systems will have to develop wider perspectives on evaluation criteria for accountability. Schools and teachers will have to realize that instead of resisting the demand for accountability they will have to become active participants by developing their own evaluation portfolios for a dialog with external evaluation.

Professionalization of teachers, often positioned in opposition to the demand for accountability, is another need to be served by educational evaluation. While serving the needs of students is the main task of the school, the school is also a place for teachers, a place where they spend most of their working hours. Serving the professional needs of teachers would improve the way the students are served, since better teachers provide better service to students. When teaching is perceived as a profession, and teachers can be expected to plan, conduct and evaluate their work, rather than mechanically implementing a curriculum planned for them, then evaluation is an integral part of their work. It helps them analyze the needs of their students in conjunction with school goals, assess available resources and opportunities, choose instructional strategies and evaluate the quality of their work. Educational systems that believe in teacher professionalization must serve teachers' professional needs. Among other things, they have to provide teachers with necessary resources for self-evaluation and help them become involved in school evaluation as active participants rather than as passive objects.

Evaluation for **certification** is well-known in the educational system. Evaluation is widely used to certify teachers, school administrators, educational programs, or educational institutions seeking accreditation. At the school level, the major concern is for student certification, but occasionally the school is also involved in program certification when the school or some of its programs seek accreditation or other formal recognition. Although such accreditation is usually based on external evaluation, some schools aspire to be active partners in such evaluation activities rather than passive targets and destructive critics. Moreover, many accreditation systems require a strand of self-evaluation.

Society needs to know that its younger generation is ready to assume their social roles. Students, and their parents, need to translate their educational efforts and achievements into some documented "educational currency" that can be used later on for further education or for job procurement. Educational systems as well as individual schools use evaluation to fulfill their certification responsibility.

Specific examples and further discussion of the various roles and functions of educational evaluation are presented in the fourth section of the chapter ("Domains of Practice").

Research Methods and Instruments

In addition to traditional and still popular experimental and quasi-experimental designs, over the latter part of the twentieth century, other inquiry designs and methods have become legitimate for the conduct of educational evaluation. Among them are naturalistic approaches (Guba & Lincoln, 1981, 1989), jury trials, case studies, art criticism, and even journalistic methods. Some research methodologists still advocate the superiority of certain methods such as experimental design at one extreme (Boruch, 2003; Rossi, Freeman, & Lipsey, 1999), or naturalistic methods at the other (Guba & Lincoln, 1989; Mabry, 2003). Overall, however, there seems to be more support for an eclectic or mixed-methods approach to evaluation methodology (Datta, 1997; Greene, Caraelli, & Graham, 1989). At the present state of the art in educational evaluation it still appears, as it was a quarter century ago, that "the evaluator will be wise not to declare allegiance to either a quantitative-scientific-summative methodology or a qualitative-naturalistic-descriptive methodology" (Cronbach, 1982). It may well be true that for a complicated activity such as evaluation, the approach needed is one that seeks the best method or set of methods to answer the particular evaluation question at hand, rather than assuming that one method is best for all purposes.

Specific examples of instruments and further discussion of measurement and methodology issues are presented in the next section of the chapter in the context of the various domains of educational evaluation practice.

Domains of Practice

Students and their achievements have always been, and still are, the major focus of schooling.

Progressive educators view the student as central even when they do not like the way most schools do their jobs, or how they assess their impact on students. Conservative educators do not want the school to waste time on useless activities but rather direct its efforts toward the students' mastering basic skills and major assets of human culture.

As noted, the roots of educational evaluation are in the assessment of individual student learning. Such assessments continue to occupy center stage in most educational evaluation contexts, yet they have also considerably broadened to include projects, instructional materials, teachers, and the school as a whole. For these other evaluation objects, assessment of student achievement is often a major evaluative variable, but other evaluation measures and methods are also used. These are all discussed in this section, referring specifically to their **functions** and the **instruments** used for their conduct.

Student Evaluation

Student evaluation has been the major focus of education and of educational evaluation for so many years that one would expect it by now to have acquired solidly articulated principles and well-established procedures. Unfortunately this is not the case. Much headway has been made in recent years in conceptualizing major issues of student assessment and developing measurement procedures appropriate to student evaluation. But the more progress made, the more complex the issue of student evaluation has turned out to be. In a way we are now at a crossroads of various perspectives, some complementary, but some contradictory, which are to shape student assessment in the years to come. These perspectives reflect significant innovations in the field of student evaluation and relate mainly to the way it is used (*functions*) and the way it is done (*instruments*).

Functions of student evaluation: The distinction between *formative* or improvement-oriented and *summative* or accomplishment-oriented evaluation, which arose in the mid-1960s in the area of program evaluation (Scriven, 1967), emphasized that the various functions of evaluation are a basic consideration in any evaluation. The two new terms were soon applied to student evaluation (Bloom, Hastings, & Madaus, 1970) and are now widely used by teachers, although not always in their original meaning. Benjamin Bloom and his colleagues, in their early attempt to apply these concepts to student evaluation, added a third category of *diagnostic evaluation.*

Nevo (1995) suggested a distinction between *primary* and *secondary* functions of student evaluation. Primary functions of student evaluation are those in which the student is the object of the evaluation, which is intended to provide information for the improvement of learning or to certify individual educational accomplishments. Secondary functions of student evaluation are those where the object of evaluation is not the student, but rather the teacher or the school or some other object, and the results of the evaluation are used for school accountability, or to control students or motivate them. Nevo further suggested three primary functions of student evaluation (diagnosis, improvement, and certification) and three secondary ones (accountability, motivation, and discipline).

Tests and other instruments for student evaluation have a long tradition. First there were open-ended essay-type exams. They were composed of questions asked by teachers and answered by students in either written or oral form. Sometimes short questions were supposed to stimulate quite long answers. Sometimes students were asked to solve complex problems or discuss controversial issues in ways that would demonstrate their knowledge and understanding. They were also asked to work on projects or write papers outside the classroom using libraries and collecting data in laboratories or in the "real world." Examinations were usually conducted in conjunction with teaching, so nobody asked to what extent they actually represented the content of instruction. And just as teachers were trusted to teach their students, they were trusted to grade their examinations and mark their papers. Students were also tested by various kinds of examination boards, composed of educators and scholars, whose credibility was beyond doubt, and who were trusted, even more than individual teachers, to know how to ask the right questions and to determine how well they were answered. The whole evaluation process seemed quite simple and straightforward, but the questions given to students were in fact neither necessarily simple nor obvious. The evaluation process was based on the judgment of expert teachers and scholars and on the wisdom of their questions.

Then came "objective tests". These were usually long tests with a large number of questions, or *items* as they were called. Some of the items were questions that had to be answered in one sentence, or even one word or one number. Other items posed a question and also suggested four or five answers to choose from. These were called *multiple choice items*. And there were also other types, like *true/false items*, *matching items*, *sentence completion items*, and many more. The whole evaluation process, and especially the process of preparing the test, became quite sophisticated and usually too complicated for teachers. But the questions posed were quite simple, even simplistic, and detached from real life as well as from the learning process. No wonder that some educators referred to objective tests as an "insult to intelligence" (Smith, 1986).

But objective tests also had many advantages. Scoring was easy and most of it could be done by laypeople, with a high level of agreement among scorers. Testing was cheap and could be administered in a uniform way to a large group of students, in a relatively short period of time. Students' achievements were not contaminated by their ability to express themselves in written or oral form. And the fact that objective tests could cover a relatively large number of items in a short period of time created the presumption that they could yield valid inferences, since a single test seemed to offer a representative sample of a relatively large content area of instruction. All these seemed to be important in a mass production society and mass education systems. But, objective testing has also been the target of considerable controversy and criticism.[2]

The 1980s in particular constituted a decade of sweeping reforms in educational systems around the world, reminiscent of the progressive educational movements earlier in the century. Most of the basic assumptions and propositions in the areas of teaching, learning, school organization and teacher training were reexamined and reconsidered. Student evaluation was no exception, and objective tests were heavily criticized – for lack of authenticity because they were detached from real life problems and from school instruction; for valuing memorization and passive knowledge rather than active thinking; and for their simplistic nature and for trivializing student assessment.

But the trend of alternative assessment, moving away from traditional and objective tests, stemmed not only from new perspectives on education and schooling. It was also rooted in a new perception on evaluation, mainly program evaluation, which had been emerging since the mid-1960s. One aspect of this was the suggestion that evaluation should not limit itself to the evaluation of outcomes but look also at other aspects of the evaluation object such as goals and implementation processes (Stake, 1967; Stufflebeam et al., 1971). Another was the distinction between formative and summative evaluation, which supported the notion that student assessment should be used not only to certify accomplishments but also in a constructive/formative way as part of the process of teaching and learning. Somewhat later developments were the concepts of *participatory evaluation* (Cousins & Earl, 1995) and *empowerment evaluation* (Fetterman, 2001), which were aligned with commitments in alternative assessment (especially portfolios) to perceive students and teachers as active partners in the evaluation process.

Since "testing" had become a somewhat dirty word in the context of student evaluation, alternatives used the word "assessment." The most common labels were *performance assessment, authentic assessment, direct assessment*, or the more generic term *alternative assessment*. On the surface it looked like a return to the good old open-ended essay-type exam, but the various labels, which reflect nuances of emphasis, show that alternative assessment is much more than that (Gipps, 1994; Wiggins, 1998).

In alternative assessment, students are evaluated on the basis of their *active performance* in using knowledge in a creative way to solve worthy problems. The problems have to be *real problems*, i.e., non-routine multifaceted problems with no obvious solutions. These must be *authentic* representations of problems encountered in the field of study or in the real life of adults. Alternative assessment is based on the use of trained assessors, who are also experts in the field of study, at least at the level of expertise of a teacher who teaches the subject. Interaction between assessor and assessee is also strongly encouraged by alternative assessment.

Alternative assessment is receptive to various innovative methods of evaluation, which are very different from the typical paper and pencil examination. Two interesting methods, which have received special attention, are *portfolios* and *exhibitions*. A student portfolio is a collection of documents reflecting performance (e.g., test results, grades, awards), and products (e.g., papers, book reports, letters, tapes of oral presentations, drawings, physical models) produced by the student, inside or outside the school, during the process of learning. The student is free to choose the documents to be included in his or her portfolio, but the types of documents to be included may be specified. Teachers or other assessors review the portfolio and use it to evaluate the student, and the student is an important partner in this process. The student can decide what will be included in the portfolio, may also be invited to reflect on the selected documents, discuss their significance with the teacher, and thus affect the way the material is judged.

An exhibition is a demonstration of skill and competence in using knowledge for a defined purpose in a given task. The knowledge is part of the school's program, and the task may be chosen by the student or specified by the school. Typically, exhibitions are live performances of artistic or technical skill, competitions among individuals (for example, public debates), or demonstrations of projects developed over an extended period of time. Students are expected to exhibit the products of their learning and convince themselves and others that they can use knowledge. The school must be clear about what it expects of its students and how these qualities can be exhibited. It must also specify ahead of time the standards against which the exhibitions will be judged. The exhibition method is featured in Theodore Sizer's "Essential Schools" reform movement in the US (Sizer, 1984).

That is, both methods – portfolios and exhibitions – emphasize the importance of the student's participation in the evaluation process, and the interaction between the student and his or her assessor. In the portfolio method, students participate in choosing the documents to be included in their portfolio, and – especially if the portfolio is used for formative purposes – students are also expected to reflect on the meaning of the documents in an oral or written dialog with their teacher. In the exhibition method, students are partners in the evaluation process because they determine the nature of the exhibition, and because they interact with teachers and other audiences to convince them that the exhibition "proves" that they indeed can use knowledge and other resources which they are expected to acquire in school. In both methods some kind of *dialog* between two parties lies at the heart of the evaluation in spite of the fact that one party is a student and the other is a teacher; one is the evaluee and the other is the evaluator. The dialog does not deal with the results of an already completed evaluation; it is an intrinsic part of the evaluation process. In portfolios and exhibitions, the interaction between the teacher and the student is part of the evaluation process, in which both try to find out what the evaluation findings are in a dialog mode of evaluation.

Although alternative assessment methods present some inspiring ideas about student evaluation, which should be considered seriously by teachers and schools, they are not a panacea. Many issues relating to the validity and reliability of the various alternative assessment methods are still unresolved (Gipps, 1994; Moss, 1994), and most important, these methods are geared to a certain type of educational approach, which (unfortunately) is not common practice in every school. Alternative assessment presumes active learning, individualized instruction, cultivation of the student's mind, and a professional (rather than bureaucratic) conception of teaching, among other things. When a school is involved mainly in knowledge transmission, students are mainly concerned with memorizing, and teachers are perceived as executors of curricula preplanned for them by administrators and specialists, then alternative assessments will be like a golden ring in a pig's snout: irrelevant and an unjustified luxury. Thus, attractive as the ideas of authentic assessment, portfolios, exhibitions, and performance assessment might be, other evaluation methods can not be ignored. At least for the time being, traditional essay-type exams, as well as standardized objective tests, are still relevant for many schools and educational systems and should be considered as legitimate components of student evaluation.

Teacher Evaluation

Teachers have been evaluated for many years for various purposes, and teacher evaluation (or teacher appraisal) systems are part of many educational systems around the world (Campbell et al., 2004; Middlewood & Cardno, 2001). A review of teacher evaluation systems in the United States (Nevo, 1994) has suggested many uses of teacher evaluation, such as developing and ensuring teaching competence, certifying teachers, hiring new teachers, improving teaching performance, being accountable to parents and educational systems, and getting professional recognition and certification (National Board, 2002).

A fundamental distinction should be made between two major purposes of teacher evaluation (Fisher, 1994): professional development and accountability. These two functions are based on two different perspectives on the nature of teaching (Darling-Hammond, 2000; Haertel, 1991) and on opposing opinions regarding the potential benefits of accountability in education in general (Linn, 2000) and specifically in teacher evaluation (Campbell, et al., 2004). The first perspective

is based on a **professional** conception of teaching, assuming that teaching is a complex process which includes identifying needs, setting goals, choosing strategies, implementing plans, evaluating performance, reflection, and so forth. Such a conception of teaching would use formative/internal/self-evaluation for professional development. The other perspective is based on a **bureaucratic** conception of teaching, assuming that teaching is a simple process in which educational goals, curricula, and teaching methods are set by administrators and experts and the responsibility of the teacher is simply to implement a predetermined curriculum. This conception of teaching requires that summative/external evaluation be used for accountability and, usually, this is based on student achievement.

The various functions of teacher evaluation can be served by many **instruments and data collection procedures**.[3] Following are short descriptions of some of them. Usually, a combination of more than one instrument is recommended for any specific function of teacher evaluation.

Teacher competency tests are used to assess teachers' basic literacy and numeracy, their subject-matter knowledge in specific areas, and their pedagogical expertise. The tests employ multiple-choice items as well as open-ended questions and writing samples. The well-known National Teacher Examination (NTE) and the current Test for Teaching Knowledge (Educational Testing Service, 2000) are the best-known examples of such tests in the United States. Teacher competency tests, widely used in the US for various purposes, have been criticized for poor criterion-related validity, for not measuring many critical teaching skills, for not satisfactorily addressing the cutting score issue, and for treating pedagogy as generic rather than subject-matter specific (Haertel, 1991). Their main advantage seems to be in their standardization and suitability for large-scale use, thus providing a practical instrument for initial screening or statewide teacher evaluation programs.

Rating scales have long been popular in evaluating teachers, since they provide a quick judgment of a teacher's performance. Most rating forms include descriptors of job performance related to variables believed to apply to a wide range of teachers, and correlated with certain teacher behaviors and student test scores. While such rating scales are convenient, and in most cases have a certain amount of face validity, inevitably they are usually related to general characteristics of teaching, and therefore not adequately tailored to validly assess different teaching styles, job assignments, and school contexts.

Classroom observations are often considered by teachers and school administrators as the most "natural" way to evaluate teachers. How can one evaluate teachers without seeing them in action? Obviously, the omission of direct observation from any teacher evaluation program would be unthinkable, but its value should also not be exaggerated. Many important aspects of teaching, such as knowledge, understanding, and attitudes, are unobservable, and other aspects of many duties of teachers are observable but occur outside the classroom.

Clinical supervision: Systematic observations combined with other methods are used in "clinical supervision" of teaching practice. In this approach, a master teacher or specially trained administrator systematically observes and critiques the classroom practices of a teacher and provides feedback for improvement. In many applications, clinical supervision is strictly formative and is focused constructively on improving the teacher's classroom instruction performance. Sometimes, clinical supervision also includes a summative component and is designed not

only to improve performance but also to serve such decisions as tenure, promotion, merit pay, and termination.

Student ratings: Students are in a particularly advantageous position to observe and provide relevant information for evaluating their teacher's performance. Students experience their teacher's classroom performance on a regular basis, and their expectations of the teacher provide one important perspective for assessing performance and providing feedback for improvement. But students may also be biased in their ratings; those who are receiving high grades may give the teacher high ratings, even if they see the teaching as poor, and those who are receiving low grades might rate the teacher's performance as poor, even if they believe the teacher is doing a good job. Students in lower grades might also be too immature to assess their teachers in a significant way. And students in higher education are notoriously biased in rating the effectiveness of their instructors.

Student test scores, usually obtained from standardized achievement tests, have also been used to assess teacher effectiveness, especially for accountability purposes (as in the No Child Left Behind Act in the US). While most educators and parents agree that schools and educators should be judged on their contribution to student learning, attempts to incorporate indicators of student development into evaluations of an educator's services have repeatedly proved invalid and sometimes legally indefensible (Millman, 1997).

The teacher portfolio is an interesting recent addition to teacher evaluation methods (NBPTS, 2002; Supovitz & Brennan, 1997). This approach requires the teacher to maintain – in a folder or loose-leaf notebook ("portfolio") – evidence and exemplars of the teacher's performance in carrying out teaching responsibilities. A good portfolio will be grounded in the teacher's duties, the defined responsibilities from an up-to-date position description, and particular accountabilities established at the beginning of the school year. In addition to printed documentation, the portfolio may also include samples of self-developed instructional materials, evidence of student achievement, and video and audio tapes that record actual teaching episodes, or any other information that the teacher perceives as evidence of his/her professional performance.

Evaluating Instructional Materials[4]

Until not too long ago, textbooks were almost the only instructional materials available to teachers and students, and in many educational systems around the world this may still be the case. The textbooks were usually written by professional writers, school inspectors, or experienced teachers, and brought into the school by central educational authorities or by commercial agents. This situation has somewhat changed in the last four or five decades with the *New Curriculum Movement* of the late 1950s (Taba, 1962; Tyler, 1950) and the notion of *school-based curriculum*, a reaction to the "top-down" approaches in curriculum development of the 1970s and 1980s (Connelly, 1972; Skilbeck, 1984). The change was twofold. First, the New Curriculum Movement extended the definition of *instructional materials* from the narrow scope of *textbooks* to the broader scope of *instructional packages* or *instructional kits* containing, in addition to the traditional textbook, student worksheets and a teacher's guide, demonstration charts, audiovisual aids, enrichment materials, test items, data sets, and computer programs. Such instructional materials were usually developed by professional development teams, and accompanied by systematic evaluation. Second, the School-Based Curriculum Movement changed the top-down

approach to instructional materials by empowering schools and teachers to be active partners in curriculum development and design, and to develop their own instructional materials.

Evaluation can serve two functions in relation to instructional materials. In its summative function, it can help teachers and administrators assess the quality of available instructional materials so they can choose those that best meet the needs of their schools and students. In its formative function, evaluation can be an integral part of any attempt at developing curricular materials, combining materials or adapting available materials to the special needs of specific schools and students.

In its formative function evaluation is used in the process of **developing instructional materials**. Systematic development of instructional materials implies a relatively long process of coordinated effort. The process of developing an instructional unit usually includes the following stages: (1) planning the unit, (2) developing the first draft of the unit, (3) developing an experimental version, and (4) developing the final version of the unit. Each stage is accompanied by pertinent evaluation activities, which serve its specific information needs. The planning stage is served by context evaluation intended to identify the nature of the target population and assess the relevance of the unit's objectives. The first draft of the unit is evaluated through expert opinions. The implementation of the experimental edition is evaluated in a classroom trial, and the effectiveness of the unit is estimated by assessing the impact of its final version on student achievement.

Such a development process usually has a spiral structure, in which the transition from one stage to another is based on information provided by evaluation activities. Each stage includes development of curricular materials, evaluation, and revision of materials for the next stage of development. The spiral nature of this process also implies that in certain cases it is necessary to repeat the same stage several times until the materials are ripe for the next stage of development.

Certifying or choosing instructional materials for an individual school, a group of schools or an entire school system can be done in an intuitive way on the basis of personal preference. Materials can also be chosen in a more systematic way on the basis of relevant information on the quality of such materials provided by evaluation. In choosing instructional materials, several questions are usually addressed regarding the quality of the materials being considered for adoption. The questions relate to goals and rationale of the materials, their level of development, required resources, chances for proper implementation and chances for positive impacts if used.

The first group of questions relate to the *goals of the instructional materials and their rationale*, in order to identify the extent to which the materials are consonant with the school's goals and its educational vision. These questions can be addressed by reviewing documents that accompany the material, such as a teacher's manual or an evaluation report. Modern instructional materials are usually accompanied by such documents, and those that are not, have probably not been developed in a systematic way, something a school should know about when considering instructional materials.

When instructional materials are based on a sound rationale, and have objectives that meet the needs of identified students, then their *level of development* has to be assessed, by reviewing the content of the materials and their documentation. The *resources required* for implementation are an important consideration in choosing instructional materials. Some well-developed materials may be inappropriate

for a school that does not have the necessary resources for its implementation. The *chances for proper implementation* of instructional materials depend not only on the availability of resources but also on many other variables that can be identified only when actually using the materials. Therefore information is needed on previous experience in using the materials, information available from an evaluation report accompanying the instructional material, or by interviewing teachers who already used the material in their schools. Instructional materials now come with evaluation reports that contain, among other things, results of process evaluation as well product evaluation. If no evaluation report is available, and the material has not yet been used in any other school, the materials adopters should be aware of the risk involved in using such material, and take this into account when making their choice. The potential impacts and benefits of using the materials are usually related to expected student achievements as well as unexpected side-effects. Such information is obtained by means of tests and other student assessment instruments administered with appropriate evaluation designs.

Commercial as well as non-profit developers of instructional materials now tend to accompany their products by evaluation reports that attest to their quality when disseminating them in schools and educational systems. Teachers and administrators have learned to request such reports and review the findings that they present. The more such reports are requested by schools, the more they will become common practice for all instructional materials disseminated in the educational system. Developers of instructional materials realize now that when it comes to evaluation, no news is bad news, and if their materials do not come with evaluation reports, schools might prefer other materials that do.

Evaluating Educational Projects and Programs

Contemporary forms of program evaluation in education evolved in the mid-1960s. The major focus of program evaluation at that time was national and regional projects and programs, to which considerable resources were being allocated, and the public wanted to know the benefits of public investments in education. Only years later did program evaluation reach the school building, to evaluate localized programs and projects, joining the more traditional activities of student evaluation and teacher appraisal.

Projects are usually defined as short-term activities with specific objectives and allocated resources (e.g., a three-day workshop for teachers, or a two-year innovative project in individualized instruction). Programs, on the other hand, are ongoing activities representing coordinated efforts planned to achieve major educational goals (e.g., the school's science program for Grades 1 to 3, or the program for students with learning disabilities). Experimental educational projects created the need for formative evaluation, for monitoring and improvement, as well as for summative evaluation, to secure continuous funding and to respond to demands for accountability.

Educational projects/programs can be evaluated by external or internal evaluators, according to the function of the evaluation and the resources available for its implementation. The process of program evaluation tends to include the following components: (1) understanding the evaluation problem, (2) planning the evaluation, (3) data collection, (4) data analysis, and (5) reporting evaluation findings. There can be some flexibility in their order of application and/or they may overlap according to the theoretical conception guiding the evaluation. There could, for instance, be a certain overlap between understanding the evaluation problem and planning and initial data collection. Data collection and analysis can also sometimes be done simultaneously. Actually, an evaluation may quite well be conducted in short cycles, each of which includes the above mentioned components (Stake, 2004).

Contrary to what seems to be the common sense of novice evaluators, the first step in performing an evaluation is not major data collection or instrument development, but **understanding the evaluation problem and context**. This seems to be a crucial component in any evaluation, and has to be addressed before any major attempt is made at data collection, although some data might be useful for understanding the evaluation program. A good grasp of the evaluation problem requires understanding of (a) the nature of the project or program to be evaluated, (b) key evaluation audiences and stakeholders, (c) why the program is being evaluated, (d) what kinds of information should be collected, and (e) what criteria should be used to evaluate the program.

There are several tools evaluators can use to understand the evaluation problem in evaluating a program or a project. First, they can interact with stakeholders associated with the program, such as teachers, students, administrators, and parents, to find out what their needs, priorities, and concerns are, and learn as much as possible about the program. Second, they can observe some of the ongoing activities of the program and review its documentation and materials, to get acquainted with the way it operates. Third, they can learn more about the nature of the program and possible ways to evaluate it by reviewing available research and evaluation literature related to the program to be evaluated or other, similar programs.

The **planning** process for the evaluation can be simple or complex, but it will typically include several basic ingredients. These are: (a) evaluation questions in operational terms, (b) measurement instruments and data collection procedures, (c) samples and sampling procedures, (d) data analysis procedures, and (e) a timetable for implementation. Many evaluation texts provide guidelines for these processes (e.g., Rossi et al., 1999; Stake, 2004).

Evaluating Schools

Evaluating schools is important from two perspectives. On one hand, schools might be interested in an overall review of their educational and administrative activities in order to improve their overall functioning and performance (MacBeath, 1999; Nevo, 1995). On the other hand, a demand for accountability may require demonstration of the merit of the school and the extent that it fulfills its goals and meets the need of its "clients" (Linn, 2000; Carnoy, Elmore, & Siskin, 2003). These two perspectives are usually congruent with the distinction between internal and external evaluation, although both types of evaluation can be relevant to formative and summative evaluation. Both perspectives will be discussed to see how they can be combined into a dialog for school improvement. This is especially important in light of the growing demand for accountability in recent years, such as *No Child Left Behind* (Peterson & West, 2003) in the USA and OFSTED (Matthews & Sammons, 2004) in Britain. At the same time, there is an increase in the practice of internal school evaluation around the world (MacBeath & Sugimine, 2003; Nevo, 2002).

Many educational systems, especially in the US, use student achievement test scores to assess the quality of their schools (Carnoy et al., 2003). Student achievement is also the major criterion that parents and the public at large use in judging the quality of their children's schools. Clearly, student achievement

is a very important indicator of the quality of a school, and every school should do its best to enhance the progress of its students, but this should not be the **only** variable by which it should be evaluated, nor should achievement be only measured by standardized tests. Many authors have suggested a wide range of indicators for school effectiveness (e.g., Reynolds et al., 2002; Scheerens & Bosker, 1997) and OFSTED in Britain, as a major example of school evaluation, does not limit itself to student achievements, and inspects teaching methods, curriculum, school climate, and so forth.

The life of a school is far more complex than what can be reflected through student achievement. Representing the quality of a school solely by its students' performance is not only an injustice to the school and its personnel, it is also a very limited perspective on the complexity of the school and the schooling process. To assess the quality of a school and understand the nature of its problems, one should look into a wide array of issues related to the goals of the school, its educational philosophy, the characteristics of its students, the quality of its teachers, the variety of its educational programs, its physical resources, its social atmosphere, its educational accomplishments, and more. It is really hard to conceive how those who understand how complex education is, agree to judge the quality of a school by looking merely at the test scores of its students or other limited expressions of student performance. However, school administrators, parents, politicians, and others tend to believe that even though student achievement reflects only a small fraction of the quality of a school, schools that are held accountable for the achievements of their students will be motivated to improve their performance (Peterson & West, 2003).

And this is not the only negative wash-back effect that such school-level accountability evaluation has on the school. Schools evaluated only on the basis of outcomes may be inclined to refrain from innovations, since the introduction of innovative programs may result in a temporary decrease in student achievement during the period of adjustment to new programs and approaches. And an evaluation system interested solely in results might not even notice such innovations, let alone encourage the school to proceed with innovative programs.

From the perspective of school improvement, focusing on school outcomes is even less justified. Test scores may be useful in identifying problem areas in need of improvement but they do not provide guidance for the kind of improvement that the school should undertake. To cope with problems we need to understand their nature and roots. To explain unsatisfactory student performance, we need to understand the characteristics of the students and their teachers, and the nature of the educational philosophy of the school, as well as its social and organizational structure. A broad perspective on school evaluation is needed to provide a full range of information for such an understanding.

Based on the literature on educational indicators (op. cit.), a framework of **school quality indicators** can be delineated suggesting six groups of evaluation indicators that can be used to assess the quality of schools for summative and for formative purposes, for accountability as well as for school improvement (Nevo, 1995): (1) Community and students served by the school, (2) school vision, (3) school personnel, (4) material resources, (5) educational programs, and (6) school achievements.

The first group of school quality indicators relates to the *community and students served by the school*. The nature of the community in which the school is located, and the characteristics of its students are not merely variables that have to be taken into account in judging school achievements; they are important indicators of its quality. Sociologists studying school integration claim that the socioeconomic level of the pupils is a major determinant of student achievement. Many parents know that to find a good school for their children, they should look for one in a good neighborhood with good students. Yet, neighborhood quality is not a determining or causal factor of school quality; rather it is just a correlate. Schools are often over-rated because of the neighborhood in which they are located and the way they choose their students. Good schools are also expected to have a *vision*, a clear idea of where they want to go and how they want to get there. The school vision reflects the social and educational philosophy of the school and applies to pedagogy as well as to administration. It encompasses school perspectives regarding goals and objectives, instructional approaches, and policies for admission, retention and integration of students from different backgrounds. It also includes the school's evaluation policy, management style, and the authority it has to determine policies and ways of functioning, and the responsibility it bears to the students and to the community.

School personnel is a human factor which, in addition to students, has an impact on the quality of a school. However, while schools that use high standards to select their students may violate their commitment to their constituencies, this is not the case in the selection of school personnel. Good schools have high standards for selecting their principals and teachers, and are willing to invest in their continuous professional development and growth. The quality of teachers and principals is a critical indicator of school quality.

Material resources, such as budget, space, and equipment, are, like human resources, also indicators of school quality. Blackboard and chalk are no longer the only equipment teachers need to teach their students, and the traditional school building is also changing. Schools today use computers and other hi-tech equipment to develop new physical environments and change the school's educational environment and its ways of teaching and learning. Obviously, rich school facilities alone cannot ensure good education, and therefore the material resources of the school cannot be used as a single indicator of its quality. Cleanliness of the schoolyard and the level of noise in the corridors provide interesting clues to the school's management style and its educational priorities.

Educational programs and activities are a direct reflection of the schooling process, and thus important indicators of school quality, critical to understanding school achievements and attempting to improve them. In assessing the educational process of the school, one has to examine its major educational programs, its special programs for gifted students and for those with learning disabilities, its extracurricular and enrichment activities, and the provisions made for students with special needs. Good schools are usually more involved than others in innovative projects initiated by the school itself or by various organizations outside the school. Community and parent-involvement programs should are also relevant to these strands of school quality.

School achievement is clearly a major indicator of school quality, but it is not limited to student achievement as expressed by scores on standardized tests. The holding power of the school, parent satisfaction, judgments of school inspectors, accomplishments of school graduates, and awards earned by the school are also indicators of school achievement and should be considered when evaluating a school.

The above-mentioned list of indicators can be used as a framework for identifying the kinds of information a school needs in order to understand its strengths and weaknesses and

seek ways to improve its performance. No school can be expected to collect all the kinds of information identified, and each school should set priorities for data collection according to its needs and available resources. There are several ways in which a school could collect such data.

A school with its own evaluation team will be in a good position to collect most of the necessary information. Some of the information may have already been obtained by previous evaluation activities of the team, when looking into specific areas of interest, such as special programs and school projects. Other information can be retrieved from school files or formal reports and analyzed by means of data analysis procedures mastered by the team, or assisted by external technical advisors. For certain types of information, the internal evaluation team might have to collect new data by means of observations, interviews, or survey questionnaires involving students, parents, teachers, or school graduates. The evaluation team could also consider administering self-developed or standardized achievement tests to samples of students or classes. After data collection, the team would analyze the information, organize it according to the chosen scheme of school quality indicators, and draft an integrated document pointing out the strengths and weaknesses of the school, and the possible relationships among them. Such a document would also provide recommendations for improvement, to be further discussed by teachers and school administrators, and translated into a plan of action.

It is also possible to hire a team of professional evaluators and charge them with the responsibility of gathering available and new data to organize them into a comprehensive set of information describing the school. However, using an internal evaluation team, perhaps supported by (external) technical assistance, has the advantage of providing a good combination of familiarity with school needs and possession of methodological and organizational skills to conduct and utilize school evaluation. The ongoing activity of such a team will also eventually result in the establishment of a *school portfolio* consisting of information on the strengths and weaknesses of the school.

Schools in many countries are routinely reviewed by national or regional inspectors and supervisors; an example are Her Majesty's Inspectors (HMIs) within the framework of OFSTED in England and Wales. Such reviews are usually qualitative in nature, non-structured and based very much on intuition and personal impressions. Often, inspections or evaluations do provide invaluable insights regarding the quality of schools based on first-hand information and an ongoing association between the inspector and the school. But most such evaluations are not systematic enough and fail to meet standards of objectivity and reliability, and this has become more and more of an issue in recent years regarding both the evaluation of schools and evaluation in general.

In the United States, educational systems have tended to prefer more systematic ways of assessing their schools than inspector reviews. Student achievement, predominantly based on standardized multiple-choice tests, remains a major measure of school quality for American schools. State and local school district assessment programs evaluate (and sometimes rank) schools on the basis of their student achievement. Such school evaluation systems are structured and systematic and usually meet standards of reliability, but their validity and negative wash-back effects have been strongly criticized (Carnoy et al., 2003; Linn, 2000).

Internal evaluation and external evaluation are both important, but neither can exist by itself. External evaluation tends to bureaucratize, to become simplistic, and to be perceived by schools as a threat and as a basis for criticism from the educational system and the public at large. On the other hand, when internal evaluation operates without external evaluation it tends to deteriorate into a harmless non-judgmental activity, which schools perceive as an alternative to external evaluation and thus an excuse not to be evaluated externally. To avoid such pitfalls, external and internal evaluation of a school must be conducted simultaneously, independently of one another, but with significant interaction. Internal evaluation will protect external evaluation from becoming too simplistic, it will create a more positive attitude toward evaluation within the school, and thus make external evaluation less of a threat to teachers and other school educators. External evaluation will serve as an incentive to improve the quality of the school's internal evaluation activities, to suggest its own evaluation criteria as a challenge to external/national criteria, and thus to encourage *a dialog* with the external evaluation rather than rejecting it.[5] Such an approach to evaluation could actually serve as a basis for educational evaluation in its various domains rather than staying limited to the domain of school evaluation.

Conclusion

This chapter began with an analytical review of the major conceptions of educational evaluation as they have evolved in the evaluation literature from about the middle of the twentieth century and mainly in the United States. At the beginning the prevailing discourse of evaluation was *judgmental* in nature (Scriven, 1967; Tyler, 1950) and in line with the common dictionary definition of evaluation as "determining the value of some object." Cronbach (1963), Alkin (1969) and Stufflebeam (Stufflebeam et al., 1971) viewed it more as a *descriptive/narrative* discourse, defining evaluation as "providing information for decision making." Stake (1967), and later Guba & Lincoln (1981) tried to resolve the argument by combining both. They defined evaluation as an activity that comprises both description and judgment. But both, the descriptive as well as the judgmental, are coercive types of discourse since both assume an asymmetric relationship between the evaluator and his/her client or audience. In both cases, it is a relationship where the evaluator has something to "give" to a client or audience, but nothing to receive in return, besides acceptance and obedience, which we sometimes like to call *evaluation utilization.*

The descriptive/narrative discourse is coercive in nature by virtue of the power vested in the evaluator as the carrier of knowledge or information. Evaluators have many "good answers" to questions which they hope are relevant to their clients and will therefore be useful to them. The relationship between evaluators and their audiences is even more asymmetric in the judgmental discourse. Here the evaluator is not only telling the client what's going on, but also how good it is, and what is best in general, or for him or her specifically. Evaluation clients or audiences might lack the necessary technical evaluation skills but have an advantage over evaluators in setting priorities and interpreting findings. Therefore, the overall assessment of the evaluation object should be performed in close collaboration with clients and audiences in their specific contexts. And this is where dialog becomes crucial.

Like students who do not learn very much in a Freirian "banking" process (Freire, 1970), where teachers try to deposit knowledge in their students' heads, educators will not learn very much from evaluators who try to deposit their description of reality and judging its value. And like students, who are not motivated by teaching which is modeled on banking,

educators are not motivated to use evaluation that is presented in a one-way coercive discourse, whether it be descriptive or judgmental. Thus, in evaluation dialog is necessary for two reasons. First, to provide a better process for learning about reality, and second, to increase the motivation to use what has been learned. A dialog can make evaluation more insightful and increase evaluation utilization.

Dialog has drawn the attention of evaluators in recent years, especially in the context of democratic societies (Nevo, 1995; Ryan & DeStefano, 2000), providing new perceptions regarding the meaning of evaluation and its constructive use. This is also a time where democratic societies extensively practice coercive use of evaluation for accountability in their educational systems (e.g., No Child Left Behind in the US or OFSTED in the UK). Would it be naïve to suggest, in times like these, that dialog is the future of educational evaluation?

Notes

1. The structure of this chapter is based on a previously developed outline for the *International Handbook of Educational Evaluation,* published later by Kluwer Academic Publishers, co-edited by Kellaghan & Stufflebeam (2003).

2. See Norris (1990, Chapter 2), for a discussion of the influence of psychometrics on educational testing and evaluation in Britain and the USA.

3. Although the evaluation literature has described many teacher evaluation instruments over the years, the two teacher evaluation handbooks by Jason Millman and Linda Darling-Hammond (Millman, 1981; Millman & Darling-Hammond, 1990) are still very useful sources of information on such instruments and procedures.

4. I use the term *instructional materials,* rather than *curriculum* since there seems to be some confusion regarding the definition of curriculum. Sometimes it is defined as a selection from the culture of a society to be taught at school (e.g., National Curriculum) and sometimes it is referred to as a course of study or as a written prescription

of what should happen in the class, hence instructional materials.

5. Pertinent examples from ten countries around the world can be found in Nevo (2002).

References

Alkin, M. C. (1969). Evaluation theory development. *Evaluation Comment*, 2, 2–7.

Bloom, B. S., Hastings, J. T., & Madaus, G. F. (1970). *Handbook on Formative and Summative Evaluation of Student Learning*. New York: McGraw-Hill.

Boruch, R. F. (2003). Randomized field trials in education. In T. Kellaghan & D. L. Stufflebeam (eds) *International Handbook of Educational Evaluation*. Boston: Kluwer.

Carnoy, M., Elmore, R., & Siskin, L. S. (eds) (2003). *The New Accountability*. New York: RoutledgeFalmer.

Campbell, J., Kyriakides, L., Muijs, D. & Robinson, W. (2004). *Assessing Teacher Effectiveness*. London: RoutledgeFalmer.

Connelly, F. M. (1972). The functions of curriculum development. *Interchange*, 3, 161–177.

Cousins, B. J. & Earl, L. M. (eds) (1995). *Participatory Evaluation in Education: Studies in evaluation and organizational learning*. London: Falmer.

Cronbach, L. J. (1963). Course improvement through evaluation. *Teachers College Record*, 64, 672–683.

Cronbach, L. J. (1982). *Designing Evaluation of Educational and Social Programs*. San Francisco, CA: Jossey-Bass.

Darling-Hammond, L. (ed.) (2000). *Studies of Excellence in Teacher Education*. Washington, DC: AACTE Publications.

Datta, L. (1997). Multimethod evaluations: Using case studies together with other methods. In E. Chelimsky & W. W. Shadish (eds) *The Qualitative-Quantitative Debate. New Directions in Program Evaluation*, No. 61.

Educational Testing Service (2000). *Candidate information bulletin: Tests for teaching knowledge*. Princeton, NJ: Author.

Fetterman, D. M. (2001). *Foundations of Empowerment Evaluation*. Thousand Oaks, CA: Sage.

Fisher, C. M. (1994). The difference between appraisal schemes: Variation and accountability. *Personnel Review*, 23 (8), 33-49.

Freire, P. (1970). *Pedagogy of the Oppressed*. New York: Continuum.

Gipps, C. (1994). *Beyond Testing: Towards a theory of educational assessment*. London: Falmer Press.

Glasman, N. S. & Nevo, D. (1988). *Evaluation in Decision Making: The case of school administration*. Boston: Kluwer.

Glasman, N. S. & Heck, R. H. (2003). Principal evaluation in the United states. In T. Kellaghan & D.L. Stufflebeam (eds) *International Handbook of Educational Evaluation*. Boston: Kluwer.

Greene, J. C., Caracelli, V., & Graham, W. F. (1989). Toward a conceptual framework for multimethod evaluation designs. *Educational Evaluation and Policy Analysis*, 11, 255–274.

Guba, E. G. & Lincoln, Y. S. (1981). *Effective Evaluation*. San Francisco: Jossey-Bass.

Guba, E. G. & Lincoln, Y. S. (1989). *Fourth Generation Evaluation*. Newbury Park, CA: Sage.

Haertel, E. H. (1991). New forms of teacher assessment. *Review of Research in Education*, 17, 3–30.

Joint Committee on Standards for Educational Evaluation. (1994). *The Program Evaluation Standards*, 2nd edition. Thousand Oaks, CA: Sage.

Kellaghan, T. & Stufflebeam, D. L. (eds) (2003). *International Handbook of Educational Evaluation*. Boston: Kluwer.

Linn, R. (2000). Assessment and accountability. *Educational Researcher*, 25, 4–16.

Mabry, L. (2003). In living color: Qualitative methods in educational evaluation. In T. Kellaghan & D. L. Stufflebeam (eds) *International Handbook of Educational Evaluation*. Boston: Kluwer.

MacBeath, J. (1999). *Schools Must Speak for Themselves*. London: RoutledgeFalmer.

MacBeath, J. & Sugimine, H. (2003). *Self Evaluation in the Global Classroom*. London: RoutledgeFalmer.

Matthews, P. & Sammons, P. (2004). *Improvement Through Inspection: An evaluation of the impact of Ofsted's work*. London: Ofsted.

Middlewood, D. & Cardno, C. (eds) (2001). *Managing Teacher Appraisal and Performance*. London: RoutledgeFalmer.

Millman, J. (ed.) (1981). *Handbook of Teacher Evaluation*. Beverly Hills, CA: Sage.

Millman, J. (ed.) (1997). *Grading Teachers, Grading Schools. Is student achievement a valid evaluation measure?* Thousand Oaks: Corwin.

Millman, J. & Darling-Hammond, L. (eds) (1990). *The New Handbook of Teacher Evaluation: Assessing elementary and secondary school teachers*. Newbury Park, CA: Sage.

Moss, P. A. (1994). Can there be validity without reliability? *Educational Researcher*, 23(2), 5–12.

National Board for Professional Teaching Standards (2002). Standards and Certificate overviews. Retrieved from: www.nbpts.org.

Nevo, D. (1994). How can teachers benefit from teacher evaluation? *Journal of Personnel Evaluation*, 8, 109–117.

Nevo, D. (1995). *School-Based Evaluation: A dialogue for school improvement*. Oxford: Pergamon.

Nevo, D. (ed.) (2002). *School-based Evaluation: An international Perspective*. Amsterdam: JAI/Elsevier.

Norris, N. (1990). *Understanding Educational Evaluation*. London: Kogan Page.

Peterson, P. E. & West, M. R. (eds) (2003). *No Child Left Behind: The politics and practice of school accountability*. Washington, DC: Brookings Institute.

Reynolds, D., Creemers, B., Springfield, S., Teddlie, C., & Schaffer, G. (eds) (2002). *World Class Schools: International perspectives on school effectiveness*. London: RoutledgeFalmer.

Rossi, P. H., Freeman, H. E., & Lipsey, M. W. (1999). *Evaluation: A systematic approach*, 6th edition. Thousand Oaks, CA: Sage.

Ryan, K. E. & DeStefano, L. (eds) (2000). *Evaluation as a Democratic Process: Promoting inclusion, dialogue and deliberation*. San Francisco: Jossey-Bass.

Scheerens, J. & Bosker, R. (1997). *Foundational Studies in School Effectiveness*. Oxford: Pergamon.

Scriven, M. (1967). The methodology of evaluation. In R. E. Stake (ed.) *AERA Monograph Series on Curriculum Evaluation No. 1*. Chicago: Rand McNally.

Scriven, M. (1991). *Evaluation thesaurus*, 4th edition. Newbury Park, CA: Sage.

Sizer, T. R. (1984). *Horace's Compromise: The dilemma of the American high school*. Boston: Houghton Mifflin.

Skilbeck, M. (1984). *School-Based Curriculum Development*. London: Harper and Row.

Smith, F. (1986). *Insult to Intelligence: The bureaucratic invasion of our classrooms*. New York: Arbor House.

Stake, R. E. (1967). The Countenance of Educational Evaluation. *Teachers College Record*, 68, 523–540.

Stake, R. E. (1981). Setting standards for educational evaluators. *Evaluation News*, 2(2), 148–152.

Stake, R. E. (2004). *Standard-Based and Responsive Evaluation*. Thousand Oaks, CA: Sage.

Stufflebeam, D. L., Foley, W. J., Gephart, W. J., Guba, E. G., Hammond, R. L., Merriman, H. O., & Provus, M. M. (1971). *Educational Evaluation and Decision making*. Itasca, IL: Peacock.

Supovitz, J. A. & Brennan, R. T. (1997). Mirror, mirror on the wall, which is the fairest test of all? An examination of the equitability of portfolio assessment compared to standardized tests. *Harvard Educational Review*, 67, 472–506.

Taba, H. (1962). *Curriculum Development: Theory and practice*. New York: Harcourt Brace and World.

Tyler, R. W. (1950). *Basic Principles of Curriculum and Instruction*. Chicago: University of Chicago Press.

Wiggins, G. (1998). *Educative Assessment: Designing assessments to inform and improve student performance*. San Francisco, CA: Jossey-Bass.

EVALUATION OF HEALTH SERVICES: REFLECTIONS ON PRACTICE

Andrew Long

Evaluation in the health services sector has a long history. Classic examples range from the American surgeon Codman's suggestion in 1910, that all patients should be recalled after one year to see if their treatment had achieved its initial objective, to the fundamental questions posed by Cochrane (1972) about the effectiveness and efficiency of health services. Alongside have been continuing debates over the quality of medical care in the USA and beyond (Donabedian, 1966), and, more recently, the development and world-wide promulgation of evidence-based medicine (Sackett et al., 1996a). All are contextualized within wider policy concerns over health inequalities in the UK (Wanless, 2004) or health disparities in the USA (Smedley et al., 2002) and priority setting (Coast et al., 1996; Ham, 1997).

Four interconnecting themes can be identified within literature on health services evaluation:[1]

1. A *"what works?"* agenda. At its core lies evidence synthesis, pooling the results of, primarily, randomized controlled trials (RCTs), with a view to identify what works best and thus to inform practice and policy decisions. This is coupled with policy concerns over ensuring the efficient delivery of health services and cost containment.

2. An *empirical*, as opposed to a *theoretical*, perspective to evaluation. The predominant tendency is to evaluate a particular programme, intervention or service configuration, with lesser or no concern with an evaluation of the theory underpinning the programme or enhancing theory in a particular domain area.

3. The rise of a *consumer/citizen/user movement*. In the USA, this has a particularly high profile, associated with the campaigning activities of Ralph Nador, initially in relation to the car industry. Within the UK, this finds expression in an increasing policy interest in involving users in

research design (Baxter et al., 2001; Oliver et al., 2004), patient-centred care (Mead & Bower, 2000) and patient involvement in decision-making (Ford et al., 2003).

4. The purpose of evaluation, as including *evaluation for learning*. Evaluation becomes a means not just to see what worked where, how and for whom, but more substantially to identify and celebrate the learning arising from the implementation of new interventions or reconfigured services.

This chapter examines the nature and implications of each of these different themes in turn. Four case studies of evaluations of service interventions, illustrating the different themes, are then explored. Interest lies in drawing out the evaluation questions addressed, appropriateness of the methods used, insight into the way that the evaluations were done and wider questions arising. The chapter concludes by outlining promising and fruitful directions to shape future evaluation research in health services.

The Four Themes

The "What Works?" Debate

At a practice level, the "what works" agenda translates into a concern with demonstrating the value and benefit of current and possible service provision. Demonstrating effectiveness, measuring and monitoring achieved outcomes, and assuring the quality of the process of care, are essential components (Treurniert et al., 1997; Long, 2002). At a managerial and policy level, ensuring the provision of cost-effective treatment and care, value for money and minimizing costs are critical. Examples include health maintenance organizations in the USA and the work of the

National Institute for Health and Clinical Excellence in England and Wales. Their interests may encompass both process and outcome performance indicators, providing both a mechanism of accountability to wider funders and citizens and a means for others to judge the quality of service provision and guide decisions over access to services. Performance monitoring has also taken a wider remit, embracing not just aspects of process (quality of care) but also of outcome (symptom amelioration, quality of life and mortality).[2]

More generally, this agenda sits within the pursuit of evidence-based medicine (EBM) and evidence-based practice more generally, with its emphasis on clinical (and policy) decision-making being based on sound evidence (Sackett et al., 1996a; Macintyre et al., 2001). Sackett et al.,'s (1996b) classic elaboration of EBM talks in terms of integrating "clinical expertise" with "best (research) evidence". A later report from the US Institute of Medicine (2001) in a quality context extends this to "the integration of best research evidence with clinical expertise and patient preferences and values". The work of the Cochrane Collaboration, established in 1993 in the UK in the Cochrane Centre, and of the Campbell Collaboration, established in 2001, provides classic examples. Both aim to draw together the best evidence on, respectively, the effects of health care interventions and social, psychological, educational, and criminological interventions.

The power and influence of the EBM movement has led to a context wherein systematic reviews based on randomized controlled trials become a core source for the "best" evidence for policy and other decision-makers on what works. This approach has strong links with the "hierarchy of evidence" model, developed to assist the sifting of evidence for the periodic health examination (Canadian Task Force,

1979), and built around the notions of causation and control of bias. RCTs thus become the default evaluation approach to generate the required evidence base, and in consequence reduce the perceived credibility of other methods, and most particularly of qualitative research designs (Popay & Williams, 1998).

A Cochrane review typically takes the form of a systematic review of RCTs in the problem area with a view to identify which of a set of treatments work best and for whom. Other forms of evidence are commonly excluded (by definition, being of lesser quality). Where possible, a meta-analysis is undertaken to quantify the effect size of the intervention, using the measure of effect/outcome that is common across the retrieved studies. For example, in their review of the effectiveness of stroke units, the Stroke Unit Trialists' Collaboration (2001) had to use mortality, despite the fact that the focus of stroke units lies on rehabilitation (Gladman, Barer & Langhorne, 1996). A subtle shift in the "what works" question is evident, to "what works according to the chosen (or most researched) outcome criterion?"

The dominance of the RCT model is both understandable and problematic. The RCT has considerable strengths. Randomization avoids selection bias (chance dictates who is in the intervention and comparison groups) and in principle controls for possible confounding variables or alternative explanations for the findings. The RCT, like other research methods, also has its limitations. These include doubts over ethical feasibility of randomizing individuals to different treatment groups, a focus on short-term health (and other) benefits of an intervention (as the purity of the intervention group may become diluted over time) and the narrowness of the eligibility criteria which may limit generalization of the study's findings.[3] The latter is particularly germane in health services evaluation, with the common distinction between efficacy ("does it work in a controlled setting?") and effectiveness ("does it work in routine practice?").

RCTs work well where the effectiveness of a so-called "simple" intervention such as a new drug is being explored. However, the more complex the intervention, the more challenging the "what works" question becomes. For example, Thomson et al., (2004), describing their own attempts to develop a robust experimental design to evaluate the health gains of providing attendance allowances to older people,[4] argue for the need to match study designs to the level of knowledge about the effects of an intervention. Evidence from a pre-test, post-test design might be the first step. However, even the most seemingly simple interventions (e.g., a drug trial) are multifaceted; most commonly, interventions are complex, with the different components (for example, the actual drug and its use by the patient) closely inter-related. They may be better described as packages or programmes of care (cf. Pawson, 2003). In such complexity, the more simple "what works" question begs more elaborate phrasing as, "what part of 'it' works and in what way?"

Non-randomized and uncontrolled studies, for example, a pre-test/post-test design with no comparison group, may be appropriate where the purpose is to establish plausible outcomes or illustrate possible mechanisms of effect.[5] This is particularly germane where there is interest in addressing major policy (Coote, Allen & Woodhead, 2004) or public health questions. Indeed, Victora, Habicht & Bryce (2004) stress the need to move beyond RCTs in public health where the causal chains are more complex. Observational studies built on designs based on the plausibility of the theoretically predicted causal chain may be the only feasible option and provide valid evidence of impact. Similarly, policy relevant systematic reviews may need to include both quantitative and qualitative studies (Long, 2006) and/or adopt a different systematic review approach (Hammersley, 2001), for example, a theory-driven review (Pawson, 2002; Boaz & Pawson, 2005). Similarly, a qualitative research design would enable the generation of insight and understanding into how, and in what contexts, the intervention might work and achieve its outcomes.

Different types of question thus require different types of evidence and study designs. Even ardent exponents of EBM have reiterated this message within the clinical practice arena (Sackett & Wennberg, 1997; Guyatt et al., 2000). Glasziou, Vandenbroucke & Chalmers (2004, p. 30), while commenting favourably on the widespread use of hierarchies of evidence, point to misconceptions and abuses in application: "in particular, criteria designed to guide inferences about the main effects of treatment have been uncritically applied to questions about aetiology, diagnosis, prognosis or adverse effects". As the Institute of Medicine definition of EBM illustrates, the notion of "evidence" needs to embrace not just findings from research, but also judgment and patient values. All are central to the "what works" debate.

Empiricism, Theory and Evaluation

An alternative depiction of the "what works" agenda in health services evaluation is to characterize it as a dominance of methods over purpose. Pride of place has gone to sophisticated method development. Recent examples include efforts to develop ways to synthesize findings from qualitative studies (e.g., Britten et al., 2002) and, ways to combine evidence from both qualitative and quantitative studies (see EPPI-Centre, 2005).

Stame (2004, p. 59) points to the "original sin" of mainstream (positivist) evaluation, of "neither wanting to enter the 'value' problem

(thanks to a value-free stance), nor wanting to discuss the theoretical implications of programmes". The same criticism can be levelled against much of current clinical health services evaluation work. An empirically dominated, so-called "black box",[6] approach is followed through. In contrast, in other areas such as education or organizational analysis, approaches such as responsive evaluation (Stake, 1980) or fourth-generation evaluation (Guba & Lincoln, 1989) have taken to heart the "values" issue and recognized the importance of examining the different interests and views of stakeholders. Indeed, two decades ago, Smith & Cantley (1985) advocated a similar approach (pluralistic evaluation) within health services.

A drug trial provides a simple example. "Theory" (that is, how it might work) lies implicit within the hypothesis (this drug works better than the standard one or than a placebo) or is taken for granted as being grounded in an underlying biochemical or physiological framework. Context and person-related features surrounding the administration and taking of the drug (for example, the doctor–patient trust relationship, patient concordance or wider theories of health-seeking behaviour) are put to one side. However, for a breadth of understanding, the take-up of research findings into policy and the achievement of the expected outcomes in practice, theorizing and then evaluating these differing levels of effect (at a physiological and individual level, and/or onto wider impact at a societal level) becomes critical.

Three main approaches to enhance the role of theory in evaluation are evident in the literature (Stame, 2004, p. 61). For Chen & Rossi (1989), black box programmes are such because they have no theory; "the black box is an *empty box*". The task of the evaluator is thus to provide the missing theory. For Weiss (1987), programmes are necessarily confused because of the nature of decision- and policy-making and the influence of politics. "The black box is thus full of *many theories*", themselves depicted as theories of change (Weiss, 1995). All have to be brought to light in order to see which one should be tested. Finally, for Pawson & Tilley (1997) in their realist evaluation approach, it is people within their own contexts who, when exposed to programmes, do something which activates mechanisms, and thus change. Thus, *"people inhabit"* the black box.

Pawson (2003, p. 472) provides a simple explanation of the necessary role of theory. "Evaluation seeks to discover whether programmes work; programmes are theories; therefore, it follows that evaluation is theory-testing." Moreover, he continues, all programmes have a common core hypothesis, "if we provide these people with these resources it may change their behaviour". The task of the evaluator is thus to surface and articulate the theory prospectively (or attempt to reconstruct it retrospectively) and then to test it.

An approach with considerable popularity in the USA and Canada to assist in surfacing underlying theories and in testing them within evaluations is the use of "logic models" (McLaughlin & Jordan, 2004). It is based on exploring and making explicit the links between inputs, activities, outputs and outcomes.[7] The elements or links between them may be phrased, or become, testable hypotheses, for investigation using multi-variate methods and/or in-depth qualitative investigation.

Health service evaluation most commonly involves examination of complex programmes. Explicating what the complex intervention comprises, how it might in theory operate and the inter-relationship of this theory to wider knowledge, is a major challenge (Medical Research Council, 2000; Campbell et al., 2000). As Stame (2004, p. 64) remarks,

programmes ". . . often ignore the simplest propositions of social science, and treat each programme aspect separately". Or as Pawson (2003, p. 483) comments on the New Deal for Communities programme in the UK, "an assortment of hypotheses swarm through the intervention", waiting exploration through a theories of change or logic model approach.

The Consumer Movement

The role of the consumer within the evaluation of health services has become increasingly important in recent years. As Popay & Williams (1994, p. xiii) comment, "health and health care are no longer the preserves of specialists". The consumer's voice will form a significant part in evaluations of what works, and how (experiences of service provision and satisfaction in meeting needs), and provide a substantial input into the policy and practice of services delivery. Interest lies not just in recognizing the voice of citizens, their values and perspectives, but also hearing and involving users in evaluations (their focus, their methods and use of their results). Consultation and involvement form two major and contrasting strands.

Consultation may be taken forward *by* service organizers *with* stakeholders. While the latter may include service practitioners, in the current context interest lies in the consumer per se, that is, actual or potential users of health services and their informal (non-professional, non-practitioner) carers. Numerous examples of consultation are evident, ranging from the Oregon experiment in the USA on service priorities (Ham, 1997) to sentencing of offenders in child pornography (Court of Appeal, 2002) and user focus groups to consult on "best value" services (Cambridge & McCarthy, 2001).

Users can be consulted at any time in the policy process, from initial problem definition (what are appropriate needs?) to organizational improvement (how can the services be improved?) and policy performance (do they meet your needs?). A democratic strand is evident, in a need for accountability. Methods of consultation are multiple, from formal, and sometimes routine, surveys of client satisfaction or satisfaction with hospital stays to focus groups, citizen's juries, talk shops or consultation days (Mullen, 1999). "Listening to the people's voices" becomes a sine qua non. However, consultation as realized in this form can be described as "sponsor-driven and sponsor-designed"; most commonly, it is a unique or "one-off" activity, not a continuous process. Accordingly, it comes under criticism for being manipulative (are my views really taken heed of?), placatory and tokenistic (just to ask the consumer) (Ali, 2000).

Involvement entails a change of orientation: it is *by* users *within* health services policy, practice, theory generation (Beresford, 2000) and research and ranges from "increasing user participation" to "ceding to user control" (Arnstein, 1969) and enabling self-determination. Variations upon this theme arise both within health care services, though mostly in the less medically or technologically dominated areas, for example, mental health and learning disability, to the demands of the disenfranchised and marginalized groups, in particular, the disability movement (Barnes & Mercer 1996) and social care "survivors" (Wilson & Beresford, 2000).

Emancipatory and user-led approaches provide an illustrative example. These prioritize the standpoint of the user. Implications for evaluation take two forms. The first, user-led research, involves the user controlling all phases of the inquiry. The second, "emancipatory research" (Oliver, 1992; Barnes et al., 1999; Goodley, 2000), challenges the "expert", and, in its more radical form, argues that users are oppressed and thus as such they alone can understand and provide insight into the "oppressive reality" (Wilson & Beresford, 2000). A core dimension relates to the notion of accountability, that is, of the users to other users and the user organization from which they come.

Involvement may take a number of forms. Baxter, Thorne & Mitchell (2001) map out a number of levels of user participation (passive, consultative, active and ownership) against the various phases of the research process, from problem identification and design to writing-up, dissemination and action. A similar model is presented by Oliver et al., (2004, p. 8) in their review of involving consumers in the setting of NHS R&D agendas. Their matrix comprises different degrees of engagement for the researcher (minor partner or absent, responding to consumer action, inviting individual consumers and inviting consumer groups) against those of the consumer (consumer control, collaboration, consultation and minimal). For some, good practice would then be reflected in a partnership between users and practitioners or evaluators in which the majority of elements fall into the active and ownership types of participation (Fisher, 2002); for others, best practice involves user control (Morris, 1994). Yet other researchers, empathetic to the importance of the active consumer view and the need to articulate their under-recognized voice, pursue pro-active ways to involve service users, for example, through participatory action research.

The consumer movement has multiple implications for evaluations of health services, in relation to appropriate methods and the forms and levels of consultation and involvement. While research methods with emancipatory research initially tended to be qualitative (an emphasis on "giving a voice" to the user, Barnes, 1992), any approach is now increasingly seen as acceptable as long as it meets the principle of accountability (Barnes, 2003). Identifying what users value and outcomes that are of relevance to their lives and lifestyles become core objects of enquiry, and are needed to reflect the diversity of user views (Fisher, 2002). This extends across to recognizing the significance of all potential service users' views and participation of ethnic minorities in research studies (Hussain-Gambles et al., 2004). The "what works" question is thus broadened to ask at least, "what works for us, as users or potential users of services?"

Evaluation as/for Learning

Returning to the issue of the purpose of evaluation in health services might seem strange at this juncture. The purpose is surely clear. Drawing on the above, it is to address the "what works" question, suitably rephrased to embrace multiple stakeholder perspectives, especially those of the user or potential users, and informed or guided by relevant theory in order to also examine questions of "how" and "where". However, a further theme is slowly emerging in the health services field (most strongly within the area of community development and organizational change – for example, see Preskill & Torres, 1999; Fetterman, Kaftarian & Wandersman, 1996, Fetterman, 2001) of an additional or, sometimes, core purpose of evaluation as "evaluation for learning".

Perhaps the simplest defining purpose lies in the underlying rationale for doing an evaluation. Over and above exploring if something has worked, for whom and in what contexts, there is an implicit wider interest to learn from the implementation experience. As Eggers (Eggers & Chelimsky, 1999, p. 93) comments:

> If evaluations and their expected results are not conceived, from the outset, with a view to being used, they cannot be useful, so they are useless. Therefore, all evaluation designs have to specify how the evaluation is to be made useful and thus

who is to react to the evaluation's conclusions and recommendations.

Evaluation for learning is both more and not more than this. Two aspects are relevant: the under-use of research and evaluation findings in health services, and the issue of empowerment or engagement of evaluation stakeholders.

The Institute of Medicine (1990) estimates that it takes about 15–17 years from confirmed research findings to their adoption into standard clinical practice. To speed up this transfer, much energy and resources have been expended on mechanisms dedicated to transmit knowledge on "what works" into practice. Examples abound: short, pithy guidance summarizing research findings; journals dedicated to promoting evidence-based practice (*Evidence Based Medicine, Evidence Based Nursing*); guideline development; and dedicated research support units centred on "getting research into practice"[8]

Health services research (HSR) provides a different perspective on the way forward. A major part of the solution is seen to lie in a closer involvement of the decision-makers in the research process, that is, the research users who can make change happen (Brownlee, 1986; Long, 1996). The more the potential research user is involved, from the initial conceptualization to design and execution, the stronger will be the degree of ownership in the research and its outputs, thus leading to the (early) take-up of the research findings into practice.

These latter notions have again come to the fore within the UK clinical health services literature (Lomas, 2003; Dash, Gowman & Traynor, 2003; National Audit Office, 2003), this time lag itself providing an illustration of the research–practice divide (House of Lords, 1988; Hunter & Long, 1993). The joint Health

Foundation/Nuffield Trust study (Dash, 2003) advocates the need for a UK Academy of HSR, to mirror the long-established US and more recent Canadian HSR Foundations, the development of knowledge translators and the importance of building alliances between the NHS, academia and policy-makers. Similarly, drawing on the concept of "linkage and exchange" (Lomas, 2000), the National Audit Office (2003, p. 33) report concludes:

> The involvement of users throughout the research process helps to create a cadre of sophisticated research users who are not only able to make effective use of research, but can more clearly specify what their needs are. . . . The research providers, for their part, are better able to generate research targeted to the users' need. In this way the linkages amongst the three legs of the triangle – the procurer, provider and user – are tightened, and the resulting efficiency should produce value for money.

The second strand arises from an approach to evaluation which focuses on involving and engaging the multiple stakeholders in themselves doing the evaluation, for example, through the approach of participatory action research. Involving the target users of new initiatives in the evaluation, particularly those who are disengaged or marginalized (e.g., in a public health context, see Centres for Disease Control and Prevention, 2001), can transform an evaluation of "what works" into an empowering and engaging activity (Stern, 2004). Similarly, there is opportunity for substantial learning in all activities within any organization and within any programme or intervention. Within a learning organization (Senge, 1992), active processes will be established to share and exchange such learning and use evaluation inquiry as a mechanism to contribute to individual and team development (Preskill & Torres, 1999). The evaluation process itself may thus legitimate celebration of that learning.

Uncovering the learning experience may become either the dominant evaluation purpose or a critical element within a wider whole. While appreciative inquiry focuses on appreciating and exploring what is positive, for example, in an organizational change (Reed et al., 2002), others take a wider approach, drawing on identifying successes and what made them a success and examining things that did not go so well (the "failures"). At its essence is the key assumption that evaluation is for action and learning, to "improve and not (just) to prove".

Four Case Studies

So far this chapter has explored four major themes that are evident in the literature on health services evaluations. This section explores four evaluation studies, each chosen to illustrate two or more of the themes. The case studies include government initiatives (to reduce health inequalities) and organizational change (to promote inter-agency collaboration), clinical health behavioural change intervention for a chronic disease and an action research study to give older people a voice in decisions over their own lives. Particular interest lies in seeing how and why the evaluation was done in the way it was, to illustrate ways in which these themes are realized and addressed and to raise issues for further consideration.[9]

Health Sector Reforms

Given the range and quantity of organizational change and policy emphases, evaluating the effects and impacts of changing structures and models to deliver health care more efficiently and effectively is of considerable interest. While there are numerous examples,[10] Pollitt (1995) notes that there have been few broad-scope evaluations. To evaluate whether or not a particular set of reforms, such as a move to a market model of health care delivery (purchaser–provider arrangements and competition), will lead to the desired effects is, however, highly problematic. Simple experimental designs are not feasible and in principle are unable to cope with the complex interactions and effects that a reform within a wider health system comprises. In this context, van Eyk et al.,'s (2001a, 2001b) study of an evaluation of the health sector reform process in Adelaide, South Australia, is of considerable interest, in particular in terms of how the "what works" question was taken forward and whose perspectives were addressed (Exemplar 21.1).

EXEMPLAR 21.1

Evaluation of Health Sector Reforms in South Australia (van Eyk Baum & Blandford, 2001a; van Eyk, Baum & Houghton 2001b)

Background. In April 1996, four publicly funded health care agencies signed a memorandum of understanding to plan and implement a regional health service for the southern metropolitan area of Adelaide, South Australia. The four agencies comprised an acute care teaching hospital, a domiciliary care and rehabilitation service, a veterans' repatriation hospital and an integrated community health service including a community hospital. The evaluation, funded for three years, commenced mid-1998, soon after the agencies had determined their strategy. Shortly afterwards, it was evident that the strategy would not be implemented due to a change in the direction of State government policy, which was now to take forward integration across functional and clinical areas, rather than geographical ones.

Evaluation aim. Initially, this was to evaluate the strategy as it was implemented at a local level and as it affected and influenced organizational development. Following the change in State policy direction, the aim was revised to focus on the supports and barriers to achieving interagency collaboration.

Approach. Action research with evaluators' roles described as "intelligent observers", to provide "opportunities for the leaders in the system to reflect and enhance their understanding of what is happening" (van Eyk et al., 2001a, pp. 488–489).

Findings. At the individual's level, continuous change led to staff resistance with frustration over the lack of a clearly articulated direction and lower staff morale when change processes appeared to be rapid, unpredictable and confusing. Staff and cost cuts leading to perceived changes in the quality of service contributed to a lack of congruence of professional and organizational values. It was also very difficult for managers to plan and be pro-active. At an organizational level, a significant cultural shift was evident, resulting in increased collaboration and integration of services at a regional level. However, the efforts to take forward the change processes were made more difficult by the changing policy contexts in which each of the four agencies was operating. At a research level, the action research approach enabled the study to be sufficiently flexible to adapt to develop an understanding of the changing context and supported the agencies' capacities as developing learning organizations.

The "What Works?" Question

How can one uncover the effects and impacts of a complex organizational change and service as experienced by its users? The first step might involve finding out what "the change", and its potential multiple components, entailed (the need for interviews and observation, that is, to examine what people say and do), and then to think through how each could impact on users. A second step might involve adopting a theory-driven approach and/or use of logic models, to think through, clarify and make explicit possible mechanisms and implementation chains, and options for theory testing. Both focus on beginning to unpack the potential "black box" of the reform programme within a complex health system.

The evaluation team's emphasis here was on process. Interest lay in the "how" question and understanding the broader context. What were the motivations, concerns and potential benefits of the change, and what aspects of the reform might lead to an improved experience and outcome for service users (an emphasis on plausibility of links, rather than causality)? Methods were multiple, including analysis of documents, observation of meetings, staff postal questionnaire and in-depth interviews. The evaluation aimed to use the collected data to "tell a story of the complexity of the policy processes" (van Eyk et al., 2001a, p. 494) and perceived impact. It was thus important to gain the viewpoints of individuals with different roles and at different points and levels in the system. No single story will result, "but rather a range of perspectives from a number of different situations. . . . Each of these stories contributes something towards understanding the changes that have occurred and the decisions that have been made" (p. 500).

Evaluation for Learning

Learning was at the forefront of the adopted approach. An action research approach is ideally suited to a study of implementation and process and where interest lies in maximizing the likelihood of achieving the desired outcomes, or creating the (organizational and other) spaces where such outcomes could at least in theory be realized. It requires feedback to (key) participants at appropriate stages, which at a minimum provides a context in which further reflection and learning (about successes and failures) can take place. Here, the authors aimed to feed back information to the agencies involved and ". . . foster an organisational environment of continuous learning and reflection" (van Eyk et al., 2001a, p. 490). This result they seemingly achieved (van Eyk et al., 2001b), as their research approach proved to be both flexible and supportive of organizational learning.

The action research design was particularly apposite in light of the change in State policy direction. As the authors described, they faced a key choice soon after the evaluation's commencement – to curtail or refocus the evaluation? The fact that the latter choice was made (in a context of the agencies' strong wish for a continuation of the evaluation and the evaluators' recognizing the reality of (frequent) change in the health care environments) was enabled because of their choice of method. The method itself is oriented to support change whilst at the same time to generate knowledge. Whilst the refocus could still have occurred if a different, less fluid methodological approach had been taken, substantial alterations to what was measured, how and the like would have been required.

Being a participant in a complex organizational change may cloud the gaining of an overall perspective on the change, its experiences and effects. In this light, the authors described the evaluators themselves as "intelligent observers" and provide "opportunities for the leaders in the system to reflect and enhance their understanding of what is happening" (van Eyk et al., 2001a, pp. 488–489).

The feedback sessions were critical. These were taken forward via group discussions, structured around a discussion paper providing an overview of the wider changes in the health sector in Australia and world-wide and emerging findings. The paper became a dynamic object, being developed further following each discussion group. These meetings also provided a key mechanism to ensure the continued relevance of the evaluation to the partner agencies.

Issues Arising

This example illustrates an evaluation focused primarily on process and the challenge of evaluating an intervention within a complex "adaptive" and "reactive" health system (van Eyk et al., 2001b). Interest lay in in-depth understanding, on the role of the narrative(s) and multiple perspectives with evaluators acting as "intelligent observers" both within and above/outside the organizational change, thus contributing to development of a "learning organization" culture. A theory-driven approach, talking in the language of unpacking the implicit theory and use of logic models, would provide an additional dimension to the evaluation.

Health Action Zones

With the election of the New Labour government in the UK in 1997, there was an explosion of locally based initiatives aimed at local regeneration and reducing poverty and social exclusion. Each involved partnership and emphasized collaboration, at a health and social welfare level and with the local community. A high premium was also placed on reviewing and evaluating, and "where necessary, adapting policies to ensure they achieve maximum effect" (Secretary of State for Social Security, 1999). Health action zones (HAZs) are one such example (Exemplar 21.2). Their overall aim was to tackle health inequalities and modernize public services. Following an invitation to bid for HAZ status, 41 bids were received; 11 areas were successful in achieving HAZ status in April 1998 and a further 15 in April 1999. Each was initially offered a seven-year life span and provided with substantial core funding (e.g., the second-wave HAZs were allocated £74m in 1999) and opportunities to bid for additional innovations grants and development support. However, with the publication of the NHS Plan in 2000 (Department of Health, 2000), it became unlikely that the HAZs would continue in their original form for the full seven years. Other policy developments began to overshadow them.

EXEMPLAR 21.2

Evaluation of Health Action Zones (Judge, 2000; Barnes et al., 2003; Benzeval 2003; Mackenzie et al., 2003)

Background. Health Action Zones (HAZs) were established by the 1997 New Labour government as a partnership between the NHS, local authorities, the voluntary and private sector and community groups, to develop and implement local strategies to tackle health inequalities in some of the most needy parts of England. They initially had a seven-year life to take forward innovative and joined-up approaches addressing the interests of consumers and communities and respond to the needs of vulnerable groups and deprived communities. The national evaluation was commissioned in 1998, work begun in 1999 and substantive reports produced by 2003 (www.haznet.org.uk).

Evaluation aim. To undertake a national evaluation of the management and achievement of change of the HAZs in relation to the goals they have been set up to achieve.

Approach. The evaluation adopted a theories of change and realist evaluation approach. Focus lay on understanding about mechanisms (how things were done), contexts and outcomes. The evaluation comprised four components: a monitoring across all 26 local HAZs; a module on capacity for collaboration with a focus on five case study HAZs; a module exploring whole system change in eight case study HAZs; and a module of three HAZs focusing on progress in tackling health inequalities.

Findings. In the final report on the development of collaborative capacity, Barnes et al. (2003, p. 58) comment, "the 'HAZ' meant different things at different times in different places". The need is to understand how HAZs contributed to the changes ongoing in the area in which the local HAZ was a part. Achievements occurred through collaborations across organizational and sectoral boundaries. Examples included new models of service provision to previously excluded groups ("let's get serious", a project working with young men at risk of exclusion and being involved in criminal activity), closer links between health and community regeneration activities (the Sure Start programme for under-fives) and influencing mainstream health care organizations to work in collaborative ways. Evidence of the direct impact of HAZs on health inequalities was limited (Benzeval, 2003). However, the activities and existence of HAZs were felt to have pushed "reducing health inequalities" higher up the local agenda, broadened the understanding of the determinants of health, contributed to ongoing partnership structures and improved some mainstream services. The evidence from the integrated case studies on whole systems change pointed to the importance of a focus on mainstreaming (Mackenzie et al., 2003). Case studies which had a focus on the mainstream from the outset made most progress in effecting the new structures of the Primary Care Trusts and Local Strategic Partnerships.

The "What Works?" Question

As Judge (2000) comments, the HAZ initiative represented an "archetypal" comprehensive community-based initiative (Connell & Kubisch, 1995). The evaluators adopted a two-fold approach: a realist evaluation and a theory of change perspective. Interest lay in understanding why the programme might work, for whom and in what circumstances. Exploring the ways in which the new initiative was perceived by the local organizations and groups and reinterpreted became critically important.

The challenge posed by this approach is illustrated in the report on health inequalities (Benzeval, 2003). Ideally, the evaluators would be privy to debates on how any initiatives taken forward by the local HAZ might produce the desirable health changes. As the report outlines, this was not possible to do prospectively, at least in part because the national evaluation did not begin its in-depth work until mid-2000, a substantial time after the first-wave HAZs had begun and after implementation plans had been written. Chosen methods, however, retained a focus on understanding how the programme might work, that is, how the different mechanisms operated in different contexts. A two-fold strategy was adopted. The first involved a mapping of all the HAZs' strategies (via examination of high-level statements made by the HAZs and a survey of all health authorities conducted as part of a separate study, selecting out those which contained a HAZ partnership). The second comprised in-depth case studies of three HAZs, with data drawn from stakeholder interviews at two points in time and documentary sources.

User Involvement

The theories of change framework, as interpreted by the evaluation team (Sullivan, Barnes & Matka, 2002), involved a commitment to "co-research". The aim was to facilitate "dynamic exchange" (Barnes, Sullivan & Matka, 2003, p. 4) within available resources. Within the evaluation of capacity building, the co-research model was taken forward in two ways. The first involved working with the national HAZ network sponsored by the Department of Health. Members were invited to work with the evaluation team to develop and apply the evaluation framework, to refine the research questions and to undertake local data collection. Meetings were subsequently used to share progress. The second involved in-depth focus on five HAZ case studies. Discussion with HAZ workers in these sites and local evaluators led to the selection of different projects in each area that would reflect the diversity of population groups and ways of working.

These approaches show the strength of commitment by the evaluation team to user involvement. Users are interpreted here as evaluation participants, rather than users of the services which might arise from within the HAZ (other evidence is available on this in the various HAZ case study reports). For the approach to operate successfully, there needed to be a continued strength of commitment from the evaluation participants. However, in line with experience in the wider HAZ initiative, "a period of initial euphoria and enthusiasm (was) dampened by subsequent developments" (Barnes et al., 2003, p. 10). Moreover, "overall the HAZ became more of a top-down initiative ..." (p. 61), with

priorities set nationally, and more time spent locating the HAZ in the context of the statutory system than in establishing community objectives. There were multiple influencing factors, including the reorientation of the HAZ programme that lessened the impetus for community involvement. Success also depended on the level of trust between the evaluators and evaluated. The changed orientation of the HAZ initiative after 2001 led to reticence (participants not being as open as before for fear of misinterpretation) and a feeling of vulnerability (if judgements were made of the individual HAZ outside the national network).

Evaluation for Learning

A commitment to learning was central to the HAZ evaluation and is evident across all of the published reports. For example, as "pioneers" and "trailblazers" in tackling health inequalities (Benzeval, 2003), part of the task was to establish effective ways of learning from them. They were expected to disseminate good practice. Similarly, the co-research model within the capacity-building evaluation stream provided an opportunity both to identify things that worked well and to share those experiences.

While the learning gained by individual participants and from the experience of the HAZ itself is significant, additional interest lies in the potential for continued learning. At one level this might take the form of the commitment of individuals themselves to reflection and learning to inform their own work and, at another, commitment to ways of working and organizational processes to promote learning. A commitment to learning was indeed affirmed by participants in the five capacity-building case study sites. Individuals frequently referred to the HAZ as providing "a breathing space"; within the health inequalities evaluation, individuals pointed towards "creating a policy space". But the evaluators found it more difficult to find "systemised approaches that would help sustain learning over time and across HAZs" (Barnes et al., 2003, pp. 44–45). Rather the learning lay with individuals, from their experience of participating in the HAZ, learning which might then be passed on and carried with them into other jobs as they moved on their careers. Their potential as change agents, however, remained.

Issues Arising

This example illustrates again the major challenges posed in the evaluation of a complex initiative which itself is interpreted by its multiple participants in the context of their local area, other ongoing initiatives, relationships, etc. The theories of change model, while in principle offering considerable potential, proved difficult to apply. In evaluating impact on health inequalities, the team pointed to lack of knowledge about the specific causal pathways, difficulties in specifying in advance how the initiatives might achieve change and the interconnections with other ongoing initiatives in the HAZ. As Benzeval (2003, p. 73) comments, "[the HAZs] operated in a fast moving world with a range of different local contexts . . . [and] they adopted ever changing and multiple 'theories of change' in their rationale about how to proceed". Furthermore, the very complexity of the HAZ initiative challenged the use of the theories of change model.

Barnes et al., (2003, pp. 12–13) add further insight, drawing out seven dimensions of complexity, including those at a structural level (national, regional and local tiers, multiple health and local authorities and partnerships up and across) and layers of influence (persons with different levels of power and interests in the HAZ project). Perhaps of greatest significance and relevance to many evaluations is the change in commitment by the initial funder. Achieving measurable changes in health inequalities takes time. While initially accepted by government, short-term political imperatives led to a requirement for the HAZs to demonstrate their contribution to the achievement of nationally defined targets. "Time did not mark the linear development of HAZs towards long term outcomes; instead there was a break in the progression and a sense of people being shaken off course" (Barnes et al., 2003, p. 12). This finds echoes in other evaluations where changes in the local political environment and local priorities effect the situation being evaluated, in terms of the programme itself, and/or the timescale for the report and the deliverables.

Tele-care: a New Approach to Chronic Disease Treatment Management

Closer involvement of patients in decision-making over treatment and care in chronic disease has beneficial consequences. Increased patient involvement is associated with improved behavioural, biological and quality of life outcomes (Kaplan, Greenfield & Ware, 1989; Stewart, 1995). Interactions focused on patient concerns are consistently associated with increased patient satisfaction, reduction in anxiety and improved physiological status (Anderson, 1990; Roter, Hall & Merisca, 1998). For a chronic disease such as diabetes, policy recommendations (National Institute for Clinical Excellence 2003) favour structured patient education, available to all those with diabetes at diagnosis and then as required. However, achieving strict adherence/compliance is challenging for many patients and it is necessary for most diabetic patients to regularly depend on ongoing support from health care professionals (Fox & Kilvert, 2003). One approach that might successfully address these issues is the delivery of advice and support over the telephone (tele-care) (Exemplar 21.3). It offers a patient-centred approach and a way to overcome difficulties in access to conventional service provision.

EXEMPLAR 21.3

Evaluation of the Acceptability of a Tele-Care Approach to the Provision of Health Education for Type 2 Diabetes (Long et al., 2005)

Background. Good self-management of a chronic disease such as diabetes leads to improvement of health outcomes. Achieving strict adherence/compliance is challenging for many patients and most need to regularly depend on ongoing support from health care professionals. Care and support provided over the telephone may potentially be an efficient method to provide patient-centred diabetes care. A review of the literature (Blas & Jaffrey, 1997) concluded that telephone and computer communication improves the clinical health care process, patient outcome, compliance with medication and reduction of foot lesions. However, little research has been conducted on the acceptability of such systems to the patient and the effects and processes involved in changing behaviour.

Evaluation aim. To examine patients' views of the acceptability of and satisfaction with a proactive pro-active call-centre treatment support (PACCTS) system for blood glucose control treatment in type 2 diabetes.

Approach. A pre-test/post-test study was undertaken among the intervention group within a randomized controlled trial of 591 patients recruited and randomly assigned in a 2:1 ratio to the intervention and control group from 57 general practices in a deprived urban area in the North West of England. Acceptability was assessed in all 394 intervention patients after at least three pro-active calls from the call centre and at the end of the trial, via a purpose-designed instrument. This comprised 20 statements exploring different aspects of the call centre (each scored on a five-point scale) and four open-ended questions asking about advice and support provided, perceptions of control and additional follow-up advice required. At the end of the one-year study, a theoretically directed sample of 25 patients was chosen from the intervention group to take part in in-depth interviews to explore mechanisms of behaviour change.

Findings. More than 90% of respondents agreed or strongly agreed that the PACCTS approach was acceptable. Specific responses related to friendliness, helpfulness, convenient call scheduling and duration, knowledgeable staff, personally relevant call content and useful, personally tailored advice. More than 90% strongly agreed or agreed that the tele-care approach was acceptable and improved their knowledge of diabetes, control of diabetes and general well-being. Qualitative comments pointed to the importance of a personalized service, increased feelings of well-being, including confidence and self-control, help with problem-solving and patients developing rapport and a strong bond with the tele-carers.

The "What Works?" Question

The primary focus of the core study was to explore the effects of the tele-care intervention on the blood glucose control (HbA1c) of patients with type 2 diabetes over a one-year period (Young et al., 2005). With the ideal target level set at 7 percent or less, a random sample of patients with type 2 diabetes was selected from the local population and randomly allocated to the intervention group and a standard care group. The pro-active call-centre treatment support (PACCTS) system was delivered by two tele-carers, supported by a diabetes specialist nurse, who aimed to support and guide the patient as an individual towards achieving the best possible management of their diabetes. The patients received calls in a frequency inversely proportional to their level of blood glucose control; those with higher HbA1c levels (9 percent or more) received a call at monthly intervals, and those with lowest HbA1c levels (7 percent or less) every three months. Each scheduled call comprised protocol-based and computer software-supported sections about knowledge of diabetes, readiness to make changes, medication adherence and measurement of glucose control. The standard care group received their normal care, via a shared (GP-hospital clinic) care model, following the established local care protocol.

The appropriateness of an RCT to explore if the intervention works and is cost-effective is self-evident. It is the most powerful method to assess causality, feasible to undertake in this situation and one with greatest credibility in the clinical field. Interest lay in a definitive clinical, physiological outcome with a known relevance and action implication for longer-term ill-health and everyday treatment management.

The evaluation also needed to explore the acceptability of the tele-care approach. Both pre- and post-questionnaire measurement was undertaken and an in-depth substudy on a sub-sample of patients, choosing from among those whose control remained either "good" or "poor" and those whose control either improved or deteriorated. The open-ended questions in the pre-/post-questionnaire enabled respondents to write down things that they valued or changes in their own control and behaviour, and the sub-study more detailed insight into "how it worked"

from the service users" perspective. Combining the RCT with a qualitative component (a "mixed method" design) aimed to add depth and strength to the evaluation.

The Empirical/Theoretical Theme

While this RCT, again similar to others in the clinical field, is based on underlying physiological or clinical evidence and theory, wider issues of illness or health-seeking behaviour, learning theory or social networking are commonly, at best, left implicit. Alternatively, it may be that the patient is assumed to act rationally with the (objective) information provided to them and then make an informed choice. In addition, the psychological health behaviour change model is not always made explicit or studied to see if the expected effects are indeed realized (Ismail, Winkley & Rabe-Hesketh, 2004).

This study was initially no different. The protocol-driven computer support system was based on sound clinical evidence and the tele-carers well trained in its use and supported by a diabetes specialist nurse, herself supervised by the consulting physician. The "person"/tele-care dimension, that is, how the tele-carer put across the information to the individual patients in a motivational, or another supportive, interviewing style, its individual tailoring to their own personal situation, the building of rapport – all were implicit, yet central, to the intervention.

The addition of the acceptability study, undertaken by a research team with a social science background, and particularly the substudy using in-depth interviews, led to a re-examination and search for evidence of different behavioural change models and features of patient-centred care (Gambling and Long, 2006). For example, the patient interviews were reanalysed for evidence of core processes from within the trans-theoretical stages of change model of behavioural change (Prochaska & DiClemente, 1984; Prochaska, DiClemente & Norcros, 1992). This model, developed within the field of addiction (smoking, drug, alcohol), argues that the individual passes through a set of stages of (potential) change, running from pre-contemplation to preparation to action and maintenance. Alongside is a range of processes of change, in particular, experiential (for example, consciousness raising and self-evaluation) and behavioural (e.g., contingency management, stimulus control, helping relationship), the notion of decisional balance and self-efficacy. Such a reanalysis, in effect, exploration of the "how does it work?" question, aimed to surface elements of the underlying social learning model. This then raises the possibility of a future trial being informed and set to test a particular or mixture of behavioural change models.

Issues Arising

This example illustrates the common clinical evaluation situation where the workings and actual components of the intervention are not self-evident. In this health education and treatment management situation, at one level the intervention is based on a common-sense logic; giving people more information enables them to make more informed choices. However, it is necessary to go deeper than this and to explore how indeed patients respond to information provision. In the tele-care evaluation, such information provision is intertwined with its provision in a less familiar way, that is, via the telephone, especially important given the fact that the average age of the RCT sample was 67 years, ranging from 29 to 91 in the intervention group. It is interesting to reflect on the possible difference in the study results if the intervention itself had been directly guided by the stages of change model. An alternative evaluation approach would be to uncover the implicit learning model being taken forward by the tele-carers, following a theories of change approach. As Finch et al., (2003, p. 1208) comment from their overview of seven tele-health care studies, "accurately understanding the effects of a telehealthcare system is essential if the study results are to inform further service developments".

Giving Voices to Nursing Home Residents

Patient experiences and concerns are central to any evaluation of the quality of service provision. This is as important in acute hospital settings as institutional care. Indeed, the views of older people, their relatives and friends need to be at the core of attempts to develop appropriate care standards for older persons' residential and nursing homes (Raynes, 1998). The study reported by Mitchell & Koch (1997) provides insight into one attempt to elicit residents' views within a 32-bedded nursing home in Australia (Exemplar 21.4). This paper and a subsequent reflective article (Koch, 2000) covering a number of different studies using a similar evaluation approach provide insight into the challenges facing the evaluator.

EXEMPLAR 21.4

Giving Nursing Home Residents a Voice (Mitchell & Koch, 1997)

Background. Despite the large volume of research on older people, the voices of older people are rarely heard. Research suggests that the well-being of older people is enhanced if they

(Continued)

can exercise some control over their lives. Involving older people who are in nursing homes is, however, difficult in practice, not least due to their potential frailty or their admission to the home at a time of crisis.

Evaluation aim. To work with older people in the evaluation of care that they receive in a nursing home as part of a quality improvement process and, in general, to provide all stakeholders with a voice in the quality assurance process.

Approach. Fourth-generation evaluation involving negotiating quality issues with the care providers, the nursing home residents and their significant others. The evaluators took the role of facilitators for the negotiation process. Interviews were conducted with residents and significant others and evening stakeholder meetings held when the majority of staff could attend. As few residents were able to attend, their voices were heard through the reading aloud of excerpts from the interview transcripts.

Findings. Interviews were conducted with only seven residents who were able to articulate their views (the others all had varying degrees of dementia) and only two significant others were drawn into the study. Two themes came through: a lack of adequate space and privacy; and, the daily routines appearing to serve the interests of the staff rather than the residents.

User Consultation

Guided by the principles of fourth-generation evaluation (Guba & Lincoln, 1989), the evaluators set out to involve all the stakeholders in the quality assurance process. Ideally, involvement would extend from giving voice to their views and all the stakeholders meeting together to share and exchange views and ideas on the way forward. The actual evaluation process took the form of a consultation exercise, using a range of methods: participant observation (attending meetings, coffee breaks and resident gatherings); getting to know the residents and their regular visitors informally; interviews; and stakeholder meetings.

Perhaps unsurprisingly, involving frail people, many who had some degree of dementia, was only of limited success. Only seven out of the 32 residents were able to take part in an interview. To supplement this, the researchers tried to consult significant others who visited the older persons. Again this was of limited success (only two took part, though in a context

when few residents had regular visitors). Again, because of the timing of the stakeholder meetings, while only a small number of residents were able to attend (though most staff could) excerpts from the interviews were read out. As Mitchell & Koch (1997) noted, these meetings perhaps should have been scheduled when residents could attend.

Issues Arising

This study raises many important methodological challenges for evaluators (Mitchell & Koch, 1997; Koch, 2000). These range from gaining rapport with residents and seeking ways to include all of the residents to how to present the views of residents in a situation where anonymity cannot be assured or even offered, and in a context where the individuals are very vulnerable and could be victimized. While residents wanted their concerns heard, "they did not want to 'have a say' (Koch, 2000, p. 121); possible empowerment was leading to disclosure of their identity, adding to potential vulnerability. As Mitchell & Koch (1997, p. 459) provocatively query, "does this mean we should abandon resident involvement in nursing home decisions" and, by implication, attempts to seek their wider views and involvement in quality assurance and evaluation studies involving frail older people with some degree of dementia? The challenge for evaluators remains. Users' views, as expressed by users, are important. Only if necessary should the views of significant others as proxies be obtained instead. Most importantly, the perspectives of care providers and home managers may be biased and, at worse, misleading.

Conclusion

The context of health services evaluation is one wherein the need for evidence lies at its core, both to inform policy and practice, and major challenges centre on the issues of complexity, attribution and breadth of stakeholder perspective. What counts as evidence is, however, highly contested. While there is increasing recognition of the need to match study design to purpose, thus including the value of qualitative designs, this needs to be extended to embrace the philosophy or theory that underpins the programme being evaluated. Thus, for example, if the programme itself is centred on empowerment, an evaluative approach that enables participation and involvement by users is most appropriate to apply, with the evaluator acting more as a facilitator (Sullins, 2003).

Matching method to purpose leads to recognition of the use and search for "best evidence" (Slavin, 1986) and an approach to attribution that centres on the notion of plausibility. Unpacking the policy or practice decision-makers' theories, beliefs or assumptions about how the programme might work is

central. In this way, using the realist evaluator's language, interest lies in exploring the "context, mechanism, outcome" configurations, or in the language of logic models, examination of "how" the programme is delivered and "why" it leads to the observed results. Appropriate evaluation designs must be used to search for evidence on key parts of these chains or to test possible configurations.

One of the major challenges facing evaluators in the health sector is the complexity of the health systems. The greater the complexity the more problematic becomes the role of the RCT. The case studies provide a range of illustrations. At a macro level, evaluations of national or subnational policy initiatives (health sector reforms, HAZs) suggest the value and importance of theory-driven or theory-surfacing evaluation approaches. Options include theories of change approaches and use of logic models. At a micro level, the case study of a behavioural change strongly suggests the need for a mixed-method approach. In both instances, interest lies in knowing if X leads to Y (whatever the complexity) and in enhancing understanding of "how" the intervention or programme might work. More generally, the longer-term trend for evaluations in the health sector is towards a more "clear box" approach. The core "what works?" question is being continually phrased in a more extended form, "what works, for whom, when, where (in what circumstances) and why (it might work), and from whose perspectives?"

The phrasing of the "what works?" question in this way also refocuses attention on the "whose perspective" question. Again, there is an increasing trend to give primacy to the user's perspective, and perhaps to adopt an all-embracing approach such that all key stakeholders' perspectives are addressed, most especially in the context of a learning organization. The case studies again provide illustrations.

Involvement may be an ideal. In the HAZ evaluation the users were the participants in the organizations themselves, with the evaluators seeking their becoming co-researchers. In the nursing home, the users were service users (the home's residents) and consultation was the aim. In addition, the views of staff, themselves potentially key stakeholders, were explored. In the clinical evaluation study, patient experiences and opinions had appropriately to provide evidence on acceptability.

The potential of evaluation for and as learning is ripe for further development. This includes the participants in the evaluation (about what worked and how, and what could have worked), the commissioners of the evaluation (and thus their using the results of the evaluation), the evaluators themselves (about their modes of working, approach), as well as any wider contribution to knowledge. The HAZ and health sector reform case studies both illustrate the potential, even within situations where the wider or more local policy context was shifting around the participants. Finally, evaluation can be transformative. Indeed, some research design approaches, such as participatory action research or models of user involvement centred on user ownership, will be more facilitating than others.

Evaluation in the health (and other) sector(s) has a central role to play in assisting potential service users, practitioners and policy-makers to develop effective, cost-effective, efficient and acceptable models and mechanisms of health care delivery. As Coote et al., (2004, p. 1) comment, "understanding how knowledge is built and how evidence is gathered, interpreted and deployed is crucial to understanding the changes that would be needed to create such a system". The four themes that have guided this chapter reflect two underlying perspectives: a dominance of a pragmatic, summative and policy-driven tendency and an empowering, formative and process-focused tendency. The goal is a melding of "better" science, informed and/or driven by programme theory, with greater "user" involvement (be these service or knowledge users) to ensure exploration of the wider "what works?" question, namely, "what works, for whom, when, where and why, and from whose perspectives?".

Notes

1. For insight into the history of evaluation in the health sector and possible routes for some of the themes explored in this chapter, see: Long & Harrison (1985); Pollitt & Harrison (1992); Maynard & Chalmers (1997); and Wholey, Hatry & Newcomer (2004).

2. While a partial shift from process to outcome is evident at a monitoring/performance review level (e.g., see Long & Harrison, 1985; Davies, Nutley & Smith, 2000), this is not reflected in clinical practice. Research evidence suggests that outcome measures play little or no part. See Greenhalgh, Long & Flynn (2005) for a wider discussion of the use of patient reported outcome measures in routine practice.

3. For a discussion of the strengths and weaknesses of the experimental design approach (and alternatives), see Campbell & Stanley (1963) or Reichardt & Mark (2004). For a discussion of issues surrounding the use of RCTs in one domain area, that of complementary and alternative medicine where there is considerable debate over their appropriate use, see Mason, Tovey & Long (2002).

4. In the UK, an attendance allowance is payable by the State to people aged 65 or over who need frequent help or supervision and whose need has existed for at least six months. The actual rate depends on whether help is needed in or outside of the home and/or in the day or evening or both.

5. All of these arguments are quite familiar to those brought up within a tradition of classic epidemiology and research methods. For example, see Campbell & Stanley (1963) or Elwood (1988).

6. Stame (2004, p. 58) helpfully defines this as "the space between the actual input and the expected output of a programme". As Scriven (1994) notes, framing the evaluation question in terms of "does it work?" or "what works best?" may, however, be perfectly legitimate as long as this is the question in which the research commissioner is interested.

7. Examples of the approach and use of logic models can be seen in publications from the National Institute on Disability and Rehabilitation Research and its dissemination arm, the National Center for the Dissemination of Disability Research (NCDDR), for example, NCDDR (2004).

8. There are innumerable examples of such initiatives across the UK, Europe, Australia, the USA and Canada. For example, in the USA, the US Government Agency for Health Research and Quality has commissioned Evidence-Based Practice Centers to perform methodologically rigorous systematic reviews (see www.ahrq.gov). For a summary of evidence on what mechanisms work best, see Effective Health Care (2001) and the ongoing work of the Cochrane Effective Practice and Organisation of Care Group.

9. Coote et al., (2004) utilize a similar approach in their exploration of social programmes addressing issues of health inequalities, regeneration and social exclusion. They also identify similar themes to this chapter in their review of the evaluation literature.

10. Many examples of such complex national, policy initiatives, and their evaluations, can be found in the health and social care literature. Some include substantial budgets for evaluation. One such example from the USA is the Robert Johnson Foundation "Fighting Back" initiative against drug and alcohol use, with an investment of $88m over 12 years, including $14m set aside for independent evaluation (Sherwood, 2005). Critical reading of the evaluation reports (Saxe et al., 1997; Hallfors et al., 2002) and the overview of 12-year evaluation (Sherwood, 2005) is instructive both in terms of lessons, challenges and complexities of community trials for evaluation, and illustrations of the social interpretation of programmes by implementers (cf. Pawson, 2003).

References

Ali, R. (2000). Consultation: lip service or empowerment. *The Runnymede Bulletin*, March, 22–23.

Anderson, L. A. (1990). Healthcare communication and selected psychosocial correlates of adherence in diabetes management. *Diabetes Care*, 13, 66–76.

Arnstein, S. R. (1969). A ladder of citizen participation. *Journal of the American Institute of Planners*, 35(4), 216–224.

Barnes, C. (1992). Qualitative research: valuable or irrelevant. *Disability, Handicap and Society*, 7(2), 115–124.

Barnes, C. (2003). What a difference a decade makes: reflections on doing "emancipatory" disability research. *Disability and Society*, 18(1), 3–17.

Barnes, C. & Mercer, G. (1996). *Exploring the Divide. Illness and Disability*. Leeds: The Disability Press.

Barnes, M., Harrison, S. J., Mort, M., & Shardlow, P. (1999). *Unequal Partners: User groups and community care*. Bristol: Disability Policy Press.

Barnes, M., Sullivan, H., & Matka, E. (2003). *The Development of Collaborative Capacity in Health Action Zones*. Birmingham: University of Birmingham. http://www.haznet.org.uk/hazs/evidence/national.asp.

Baxter, L., Thorne, E., & Mitchell, E. (2001). *Small Voices Big Noises: Lay involvement in health research – lessons from other fields*. Washington Singer Press: Exeter. Available at http://www.conres.co.uk/pdf/small_voices.pdf.

Benzeval, M. (2003). *The Final Report of the Tackling Inequalities in Health Module*. London: Queen Mary, University of London, Department of Geography. http://www.haznet.org.uk/hazs/evidence/national.asp.

Beresford, P. (2000). Social users' knowledges and social work theory: conflict or collaboration? *British Journal of Social Work*, 29, 489–503.

Blas, E. A. & Jaffrey, F. (1997). Telephone and computer communication improves clinical health care process and patient outcomes. *Journal of the American Medical Association*, 278, 152–159.

Boaz, A. & Pawson, R. (2005). The perilous road from evidence to policy: five journeys compared. *Journal of Social Policy*, 34(2), 175–194.

Britten, N., Campbell, R., Pope, C., Donovan, J., Morgan, M., & Pill, R. (2002). Using meta-ethnography to synthesise qualitative research: a worked example. *Journal of Health Services Research and Policy*. 7(4), 209–215.

Brownlee, A. T. (1986). Applied research as a problem-solving tool: strengthening the interface between health management and research. *Journal of Health Administration Education*. 4, 31–43.

Cambridge, P. & McCarthy, M. (2001). User focus groups and best value in services for people with learning difficulties. *Health and Social Care in the Community*, 9, 476–489.

Campbell, D. T. & Stanley, J. C. (1963). *Experimental and Quasi-Experimental Designs for Research.* Chicago: Rand McNally College Publishing Company.

Campbell, M., Fitzpatrick, R., Haines, A., Kinmonth, A. L., Sandercock, P., Spiegelhalter, D., & Tyrer, P. (2000). Framework for design and evaluation of complex interventions to improve health. *British Medical Journal,* 321, 694–696.

Canadian Task Force on the Periodic Health Examination (1979). The periodic health examination. *Canadian Medical Association Journal,* 121(9), 1139–1154.

Centres for Disease Control and Prevention (2001). *Framework for Program Evaluation in Public Health.* http://www.cdc.gov/mmwr/preview/mmwrhtml/rr4811a1.htm.

Chen, H. & Rossi, P. (1989). Issues in the theory-driven perspective. *Evaluation and Program Planning,* 12(4), 299–306.

Coast, J., Donovan, J., & Frankel, S. (1996). *Priority Setting: The health care debate.* Chichester: Wiley.

Cochrane, A. L. (1972). *Effectiveness and Efficiency: Random reflections on health services.* London: Nuffield Provincial Hospitals Trust.

Connell, J. P. & Kubisch, C. (1995). Applying a theory of change approach to the evaluation of comprehensive community initiatives: progress, prospects and problems. In J. P. Connell (ed.) *New Approaches to Evaluating Community Initiatives*: *Concepts, methods and context.* Washington DC: The Aspen Institute.

Coote, A., Allen, J., & Woodhead, D. (2004). *Finding Out What Works. Building knowledge about complex community-based initiatives.* London: King's Fund Publications. For a summary, see: www.kingsfund.org.uk/pdf/FindingOutWhatWorks.pdf.

Court of Appeal (2002). Sentencing of young offenders involving child pornography: a consultation. *Justice of the Peace,* 19th January, 46–54.

Dash, P. (2003). *Increasing the Impact of Health Services Research on Health Service Improvement.* The Health Foundation and Nuffield Trust.

Dash, P., Gowman, N., & Traynor, M. (2003). Increasing the impact of health services research. *British Medical Journal,* 327, 1339–1341.

Davies, H. T. O., Nutley, S., & Smith, P. C. (eds) (2000). *What Works? Evidence-based policy and practice in public services.* Bristol: Policy Press.

Department of Health (2000). *The NHS Plan.* London: The Stationery Office.

Donabedian, A. (1966) Evaluating the quality of medical care. *Milbank Memorial Fund Quarterly,* 36(3), 166–206.

Effective Health Care (2001). *Getting Evidence into Practice.* York: Centre for Reviews and Dissemination, Effective Health Care Bulletins, 5(1).

Eggers, H. W., & Chelimsky, E. (1999). Purposes and use. What can we expect. *Evaluation,* 5(1), 92–96.

Elwood, M. (1988). *Causal Relationships in Medicine.* Oxford: Oxford University Press.

EPPI-Centre (2005). Recent EPPI-Centre systematic reviews. See http://eppi.ioe.ac.uk/EPPIWeb/home.aspx?&page=/hp/recent_reviews.htm.

Fetterman, D. M. (2001). *Foundations of Empowerment Evaluation.* Thousand Oaks, CA: Sage.

Fetterman, D. M., Kaftarian, S. J., & Wandersman, A. (eds) (1996). *Empowerment Evaluation: Knowledge and tools for self-assessment and accountability.* Thousand Oaks, CA: Sage.

Finch, T. L., May, C. R., Mair, F. S., Mort, M., & Gask, L. (2003). Integrating service development with evaluation in telehealthcare: an ethnographic study. *British Medical Journal,* 327, 205–1209.

Fisher, M. (2002). The role of service users in problem formulation and technical aspects of research. *Social Work Education,* 21(3), 305–312.

Ford, S., Schofield, T., & Hope, T. (2003). What are the ingredients for a successful evidence-based patient choice consultation? A qualitative study. *Social Science and Medicine,* 56(3), 589–602.

Fox, C., & Kilvert, A. (2003). Intensive education for lifestyle change in diabetes. *British Medical Journal,* 327, 1120–1121.

Gambling, T. S. & Long, A. F. (2006). Exploring patient perceptions of movement through the stages of change model within a diabetes telecare intervention. *Journal of Health Psychology,* 11(1), 117–128.

Gladman, J., Barer, D., & Langhorne, P. (1996). Specialist rehabilitation after stroke, *British Medical Journal,* 312, 1623–1624.

Glasziou, P., Vandenbroucke, J., & Chalmers, I. (2004). Assessing quality of research. *British Medical Journal,* 328, 39–41.

Goodley, D. (2000). *Self-Advocacy in the Lives of People with Learning Disabilities: The politics of resilience.* Buckingham: Open University Press.

Greenhalgh, J., Long, A. F., & Flynn, R. (2005). The use of patient reported outcome measures in routine clinical practice: lack of impact or lack of theory? *Social Science and Medicine*, 60(4), 833–843.

Guba, E. G. & Lincoln, Y. S. (1989). *Fourth Generation evaluation*. London: Sage.

Guyatt, G. H., Haynes, R. B., Jaeschke, R. Z., Cook, D. J., Green, L., Naylor, C. D., Wilson, M., & Richardson, W. S. (2000). Users' guides to the medical literature: XXV. Evidence-based medicine: principles for applying the users' guides to patient care. *Journal of the American Medical Association*, 284(10), 1290–1296.

Hallfors, D., Hyunsan, C., Livert, D., & Kadushin, C. (2002). Fighting back against substance abuse: are community coalitions winning? *American Journal of Preventive Medicine*, 23(4), 237–245.

Ham, C. (1997). Priority setting in health care: learning from international experience. *Health Policy*, 42(1), 49–66.

Hammersley, M. (2001). On "systematic" reviews of research literatures: a "narrative" response to Evans & Benefield. *British Educational Research Journal*, 27, 543–554.

House of Lords Select Committee on Science and Technology (1988). *Priorities in Medical Research. Vol. 1 1987–88 Session*. London: HMSO.

Hunter, D. J. & Long, A. F. (1993). Health Research. In W., Sykes, M. Bulmer & M. Schwerzel (eds) *Directory of Social Research Organisations in the United Kingdom* (pp. 41–47). London: Mansell.

Hussain-Gambles, M., Leese, B., Atkin, K., Brown, J., Mason, S. & Tovey, P (2004). Involving South Asian patients in clinical trials. *Health Technology Assessment*, 8(42), Available at: http://www.ncchta.org.

Institute of Medicine (1990). *Clinical Practice Guidelines: Directions for a new program*. Washington DC: National Academy Press.

Institute of Medicine (2001). *Crossing the quality Chasm: A new health system for the 21st century*. Washington DC: National Academy Press.

Ismail, K., Winkley, K., & Rabe-Hesketh, S. (2004). Systematic review and meta-analysis of randomised controlled trials of psychological interventions to improve glycaemic control in patients with type 2 diabetes. *The Lancet*, 363(9421), 1589–1597.

Judge, K. (2000). Testing evaluation to the limits: the case of English Health Action Zones.

Journal of Health Services Research and Policy, 5(1), 3–5.

Kaplan, S. H., Greenfield, S., & Ware, J. E. Jr. (1989). Assessing the effects of physician-patient interactions on the outcomes of chronic disease. *Medical Care*, 27(suppl), S110–S127.

Koch, T. (2000). "Having a say": negotiation in fourth-generation evaluation. *Journal of Advanced Nursing*, 31(1), 117–125.

Lomas, T. (2000). Using "linkage and exchange" to move research into policy at a Canadian foundation. *Health Affairs*, 19(3), 236–241.

Lomas, T. (2003). Health services research. *British Medical Journal*, 327, 1301–1302.

Long, A. F. (1996). Health services research – A radical approach to cross the research and development divide? In M. R. Baker & S. Kirk (eds) *Making Sense of Research and Development*. (pp. 51–63). Oxford: Radcliffe Medical Press,

Long, A. F. (2002). Outcome measurement in complementary and alternative medicine: unpicking the effects. *Journal of Alternative and Complementary Medicine*, 8(6), 777–786.

Long, A. F. (2006). Some methodological challenges in undertaking reviews in social care. In: J. Popay (ed.) *Moving Beyond Effectiveness in Evidence Synthesis: Methodological issues in the synthesis of diverse sources of evidence* (pp. 41–49). London: National Institute for Health and Clinical Excellence,

Long, A. F. & Harrison, S. (eds) (1985). *Health Services Performance: Effectiveness and efficiency*. London: Croom Helm.

Long, A. F., Gambling, T., Young, R. J., Taylor, J., & Mason, J. M. (2005). Acceptability and satisfaction with a telecarer approach to the management of type 2 diabetes. *Diabetes Care*, 28(2), 283–289.

Macintyre, S., Chalmers, I., Horton, R., & Smith, R. (2001). Using evidence to inform health policy: case study. *British Medical Journal*, 322, 222–225.

Mackenzie, M., Lawson, L., Mackinnon, J., Meth, F., & Truman, J. (2003). *National Evaluation of Health Action Zones. The integrated case studies. A Move towards whole systems change?* Glasgow: University of Glasgow, Health Promotion Unit. Available at: http://www.haznet.org.uk/hazs/evidence/national.asp.

Mason, S., Tovey, P., & Long, A. F. (2002). Evaluating complementary medicine: methodological challenges of randomised controlled trials. *British Medical Journal*, 325, 832–834.

Maynard, A., & Chalmers, I. (eds) (1997). *Non-Random Reflections on Health Services Research.* London: BMJ Publishing Group.

McLaughlin, J. A. & Jordan, G. B. (2004). Using logic models. In J., Wholey, H. P. Hatry & K. E. Newcomer (eds) *Handbook of Practice Program Evaluation* (pp. 7–32). San Francisco: Jossey-Bass.

Mead, N. & Bower, P. (2000). Patient centredness: a conceptual framework and review of the empirical literature. *Social Science and Medicine*, 51, 1087–1110.

Medical Research Council (2000). *A Framework for Development and Evaluation of RCTs for Complex Interventions to Improve Health.* London: Medical Research Council. Available at: www.mrc.ac.uk/complex_packages.html.

Mitchell, P. & Koch, T. (1997). An attempt to give nursing home residents a voice in the quality improvement process: the challenge of frailty. *Journal of Clinical Nursing*, 6, 453–461.

Morris, J. (1994). *The Shape of Things to Come? User led social services.* Social Services Forum Paper 3 London: National Institute for Social Work.

Mullen, P. M. (1999). Public involvement in health care priority setting: an overview of methods for eliciting values. *Health Expectations*, 2, 222–234.

National Audit Office (2003). *Getting the Evidence: Using research in policy making.* London: The Stationery Office.

National Center for the Dissemination of Disability Research (NCDDR) (2004). Shifting expectations: from activities to outcomes. *Research* 9(2). For other publications from the National Institute on Disability and Rehabilitation Research (NIDDR), see: http://www.ed.gov/rschstat/research/pubs/index.html.

National Institute for Clinical Excellence (2003). *Full Guidance on the Use of Patient Education Models for Diabetes.* Technology Appraisal No. 60. London: National Institute for Clinical Excellence. See: www.nice.org.uk.

Oliver, M. (1992). Changing the social relations of research production. *Disability, Handicap and Society*, 7(2), 101–114.

Oliver, S., Clarke-Jones, L., Rees, R., Milne, R., Buchanan, P., Gabbay, J., Gyte, G., Oakley, A., & Stein, K. (2004). Involving consumers in research and development agenda setting for the NHS: developing an evidence-based approach. *Health Technology Assessment* 8(15). Available at: http://www.ncchta.org.

Pawson, R. (2002). Does Megan's law work? A theory-driven systematic review. ESRC UK Centre for Evidence Based Policy and Practice. Working Paper 8. Available at: http://www.evidencenetwork.org/cgi-win/enet.exe/biblioview?780.

Pawson, R. (2003). Nothing as practical as a good theory. *Evaluation*, 9(3), 471–490.

Pawson, R. & Tilley, N. (1997). *Realistic Evaluation.* London: Sage.

Pollitt, C. (1995). Justification by works or by faith? Evaluating the new public management. *Evaluation*, 1(2), 133–154.

Pollitt, C. & Harrison, S. (eds) (1992). *Handbook of Public Sector Management.* Oxford: Blackwell.

Popay, J. & Williams, G. (1994). *Researching the People's Health.* London: Routledge.

Popay, J. & Williams, G. (1998). Qualitative research and evidence-based healthcare. *Journal of the Royal Society of Medicine* 901 (Suppl 35), 32–37.

Preskill, H. & Torres, R. T. (1999). *Evaluative Inquiry for Learning in Organizations.* Thousand Oaks, CA: Sage.

Prochaska, J. O. & DiClemente, C. C. (1984). *The Transtheoretical Approach. Crossing traditional boundaries of change.* Homewood, IL: Dorsey Press.

Prochaska, J. O., DiClemente, C. C., & Norcross, J. (1992). In search of how people change: Applications to addictive behaviours. *American Psychologist*, 47(9), 1102–1114.

Raynes, N. V. (1998). Involving residents in quality specification. *Ageing and Society*, 18, 65–78.

Reed, J., Pearson, P., Douglas, B., Swinburne, S., & Wilding, H. (2002). Going home from hospital – an appreciative inquiry study. *Health and Social Care in the Community*, 10(1), 36–45.

Reichardt, C. S. & Mark, M. E. (2004). Quasi-experimentation. In J. Wholey, H. P. Hatry & K. E. Newcomer (eds) *Handbook of Practice Program Evaluation* (pp. 126–149). San Francisco: Jossey-Bass.

Roter, D. L., Hall, J. A., & Merisca, R. (1998). Effectiveness of interventions to improve patient compliance. *Medical Care*, 36, 1138–1161.

Sackett, D. L. & Wennberg, J. E. (1997). Choosing the best research design for each question. *British Medical Journal*, 315, 1636.

Sackett, D. L., Richardson, W. S., Rosenberg, W., & Haynes, R. B. (1996a). *How to Practice and Teach Evidence Based Medicine.* Edinburgh: Churchill Livingstone.

Sackett, D. L., Rosenberg, W., Muir Gray, J. A., Haynes, R. B., & Richardson, W. S. (1996b). Evidence based medicine: what it is and what it isn't. *British Medical Journal*, 312, 71–72.

Saxe, E., Reber, E., Hallfors, D., Kadushin, C., Jones, D., Rindskopf, D., & Beveridge, A. (1997). Think globally, act locally: assessing the impact of community-based substance abuse prevention. *Evaluation and Program Planning*, 20(3), 357–366.

Scriven, M. (1994). The fine line between evaluation and explanation *Evaluation Practice*, 15(1), 75–77.

Secretary of State for Social Security (1999). *Opportunity for All: Tackling poverty and social exclusion*. London: The Stationery Office (Cmnd 4445).

Senge, P. M. (1992). *The Fifth Discipline: Art and practice of learning organization*. London: Century Business.

Sherwood, K. E. (2005). Evaluation of the fighting back initiative. *New Directions for Evaluation*, 105, 15–38.

Slavin, R. E. (1986). Best evidence synthesis: an alternative to meta-analytic and traditional reviews. *Educational Research*, 15, 5–11.

Slavin, R. E., (1986). Best evidence synthesis: an alternative to meta-analytic and traditional reviews. *Educational Research*, 15, 5–11.

Smedley, B. D., Stith, A. Y., & Nelson, A. R. (eds) (2002). *Unequal Treatment: Confronting racial and ethnic disparities in health care*. Washington, DC: National Academy Press.

Smith, G. & Cantley, C. (1985). *Assessing Health Care*. London: Croom Helm.

Stake, R. (1980). Program evaluation, particularly responsive evaluation. In W. B. Dockrell & D. Hamilton (eds) *Rethinking Educational Research*. London: Hodder and Stoughton.

Stame, N. (2004). Theory-based evaluation and types of complexity. *Evaluation*, 10(1), 58–76.

Stern, E. (2004). What shapes European evaluation? A personal reflection. *Evaluation*, 10(1), 7–15.

Stewart, M. A. (1995). Effective physician patient communication and health outcomes: A review. *Canadian Medical Association Journal*. 152, 1423–1433.

Stroke 'Unit Trialists' Collaboration (2001). Organised inpatient (stroke unit) care for stroke. *The Cochrane Database of Systematic Reviews*, Issue 3. London: John Wiley.

Sullins, C. D. (2003). Adapting the empowerment evaluation model: a mental health drop-in center case study. *American Journal of Evaluation*, 24(3), 387–398.

Sullivan, H., Barnes, M., & Matka, E. (2002). Building collaborative capacity through "theories of change": early lessons from the evaluation of Health Action Zones in England. *Evaluation*, 8(20), 205–226.

Thomson, H., Hoskins, R., Petticrew, M., Ogilvie, D., Craig, N., Quinn, T., & Lindsay, G. (2004). Evaluating the health effects of social interventions. *British Medical Journal*, 328, 282–285.

Treurniert, H. F., Essink-Bot, M-L., Mackenback, J. P., & van der Maas, P. J. (1997). Health-related quality of life: an indicator of quality of care. *Quality of Life Research*, 6, 363–369.

van Eyk, H., Baum, F., & Blandford, J. (2001a). Evaluating healthcare reform: the challenge of evaluating changing policy environments. *Evaluation*, 7(4), 487–503.

van Eyk, H., Baum, F., & Houghton, G. (2001b). Coping with health care reform. *Australian Health Review*, 24(2), 202–206.

Victora, C. G., Habicht, J-P., & Bryce, J. (2004). Evidence-based public health: moving beyond randomized trials. *American Journal of Public Health*, 94(3), 400–405.

Wanless, D. (2004). *Securing Good Health for the Whole Population*. London: HM Treasury HMSO. Available at: http://www.hm-treasury.gov.uk/consultations_and_legislation/wanless/consult_wanless04_final.cfm.

Weiss, C. (1987). Where politics and evaluation research meet. In D. Palumbo (ed.) *The Politics of Program Evaluation*. Newbury Park, CA: Sage.

Weiss, C. (1995). Nothing as practical as a good theory: exploring theory-based evaluation for comprehensive community initiatives for children and families. In J. P. Connell (ed.) *New Approaches to Evaluating Community Initiatives: Concepts, methods and contexts*. Washington DC: Aspen Institute.

Wholey, J., Hatry, H. P., & Newcomer, K. E. (eds) (2004). *Handbook of Practice Program Evaluation*. San Francisco: Jossey-Bass.

Wilson, A. & Beresford, P. (2000). "Anti-oppressive practice": emancipation or appropriation. *British Journal of Social Work*, 30(5), 553–573.

Young, R. J., Taylor, J., Friede, T., Hollis, S., Mason, J. M., Lee, P., Burns, E., Long, AF., Gambling, T., New, J. P., & Gibson, J. M. (2005). Pro-Active Call Centre Treatment Support (PACCTS) to improve glucose control in type 2 diabetes: a randomised controlled trial. *Diabetes Care*, 28(2), 278–282.

SOCIAL WORK AND THE HUMAN SERVICES

Ian Shaw with Carol T. Mowbray and Hazel Qureshi

Evaluative inquiry in social work and the human services[1] goes back at least as far as the parallel debates about whether social work is a profession, and if so, how should social workers be educated and trained for their task (Kirk & Reid, 2002). Evaluative inquiry in social work and the human services should contribute to the development and effectiveness of practice and services; enhance professional moral purpose; strengthen social work's disciplinary character and location; and promote human services evaluation marked by rigour, range, variety, depth and progression.

Human services evaluation can be divided for heuristic purposes into:

1. Programme, policy and practice evaluation designed to establish plausible *evidence* regarding best practice and the outcomes of policies

2. Services and intervention evaluation that aims to *understand* and learn about social problems, organisational responses, and direct practice

3. Evaluation seeking to promote *just* forms and outcomes of human services. I will review the field in terms of these three general purposes.

As with all evaluation domains in this part of the Handbook, there is a very extensive "body" of evaluation, and we would risk superficiality if we tried to assess evaluation of practice across various fields, such as children and families, learning disabilities, older people, mental health and so on. My[2] approach will be to review key themes, and illustrate them through occasional exemplars of evaluative programmes and projects. However, evaluation in these substantive areas of human services puts flesh on the skeleton of evaluative work. Carol Mowbray (Exemplar 22.1) illustrates this.

EXEMPLAR 22.1

Supported Education for Adults with Serious, Long-Term Mental Illnesses

Carol Mowbray

Background

Higher education is now considered a necessity for obtaining decent jobs with adequate salaries, career ladders, and benefits. Despite the importance of higher education, people with psychiatric disabilities are frequently unable to gain access to educational resources or maintain their involvement with educational institutions (Cheney, Martin, & Rodriguez, 2000; Unger, 1998). Main-line mental health treatments do not typically address a rehabilitation need like access to post-secondary education. Supported education (SEd) programs arose in response to requests from consumers and family members for services that could help individuals with serious mental illness begin or continue pursuit of higher education goals. Published reports on these SEd programs have been mainly descriptive, with only pre–post changes reported.

Aims and objectives

The Michigan Supported Education Research Program developed and implemented SEd services in the public mental health system, testing effectiveness through an experimental design. We recruited eligible participants from an urban area and randomly assigned them to one of two active conditions versus a control condition. The SEd program provided preparation, assistance and support, in a group format, to address higher education goals. The key features of the evaluation were measurement of service participation levels (not just assignment condition); use of program theory to specify underlying causal mechanisms through which outcomes would be achieved; utilization of quantitative and qualitative measures tapping proximal outcomes, reflecting the program theory, in addition to distal outcomes; a longitudinal design with five data collection points over 20 months; and multilevel modeling to optimize use of all available data.

Results, key issues, and likely future directions

The overall intervention effects were that 57% of those enrolled participated at least to a moderate extent, and 41% were engaged in some productive activity (higher education, vocational training, or work) at 12 months follow-up, compared to 27% at baseline. For the intervention conditions, the number of participants enrolled in college or vocational training increased significantly, from 6% to 28%; whereas in the control condition, enrolment over time did not change. Further, participants in the active intervention conditions had significantly higher levels of satisfaction and enjoyment than those in the control condition. In focus group sessions, the benefits frequently mentioned by participants were group support and encouragement, improved self-concept, gaining skills, and a renewed sense of hope (Bellamy & Mowbray, 1998; Collins, Bybee, & Mowbray, 1998; Mowbray, Bybee & Collins, 2002; Mowbray, Collins & Bybee, 1999).

In multilevel modeling analyses, significant intervention effects were found for three distal outcomes: more school or work activity, decreased social adjustment difficulties, and increased quality of life. The intervention also had significant effects on two proximal outcomes – increased SEd participation and more social support for educational/vocational goals. There were three specific mediation paths: (1) amount of SEd participation completely mediated condition effects on school or work activity; (2) social support for educational or vocational goals partially mediated the effect of the intervention on social adjustment difficulties; and (3) social support and its effect on social adjustment problems completely mediated the intervention effect quality of life.

In summary, the evaluation design not only demonstrated the effectiveness of supported education in multiple domains, but also suggested the mechanisms through which SEd achieves its positive results: more participation in the program directly affects school and work activities; SEd decreases social adjustment difficulties by enhancing social support for educational and vocational goals. Attention to program theory can enhance successful implementations in other sites, as well as resultant long-term outcomes associated with a program.

Supported education is now being disseminated and replicated throughout North America, as well as in Europe and Asia. More effectiveness studies are needed to demonstrate the settings, contexts, and participant characteristics which may optimize SEd success.

References

Bellamy, C. & Mowbray, C. T. (1998). Supported education as an empowerment intervention for people with mental illness. *Journal of Community Psychology*, 26(5), 401–414.

Cheney, D., Martin, J., & Rodriguez, E. (2000). Secondary and postsecondary education: New strategies for achieving positive outcomes. In H. B. Clark & M. Davis (eds) *Transition to Adulthood* (pp. 55–74). Baltimore: Paul H. Brookes.

Collins, M. E., Bybee, D., & Mowbray, C. T. (1998). Effectiveness of supported education for individuals with psychiatric disabilities: Results from an experimental study. *Community Mental Health Journal*, 34(6), 595–613.

Mowbray, C. T., Bybee, D., & Collins, M. E. (2002). Effectiveness of supported Education: Regression vs. multilevel modeling results. Washington, DC, NIMH Conference on Evidence-Based Practice.

Mowbray, C. T., Collins, M. E., & Bybee, D. (1999). Supported education for individuals with psychiatric disabilities: Long-term outcomes from an experimental study. *Social Work Research*, 23(2), 89–100.

Unger, K. V. (1998). *Handbook on Supported Education*. Baltimore: Brookes.

Evidence, Intervention, and Outcomes

The most pervasive – but by no means only – manifestations of evaluation concerns within the human services are with providing objective, impartial evidence for decision-making, providing public accountability, and generating or enhancing knowledge about social policy, social problems and how best to solve them. This particular set of commitments has been present in human services evaluation in three overlapping but distinguishable ways. First is an argument for evidence-based practice that, while shaped in parallel with developments in medicine and the health sciences, has developed some distinctive hallmarks. Second, a range of service and programme evaluations has been concerned with assembling evidence regarding human services outcomes, and also with fashioning ways of conceiving outcomes such that they are congruent with the special features of human services delivery. Third, there has been a dedication to a research and development model – sometimes referred to as intervention research – that seeks to develop empirically grounded practice strategies through an iterative process of inquiry and practice. We will review each of these three strands in this section of the chapter.

Evidence-Based Practice

Attention to the knowledge and evidence base within the human services has focused on both practice and policy. It is not agreed how far these linked concerns raise similar or different issues. It is also important to note that in social work and human services, the boundaries between evaluation and research (e.g., "intervention research") and also between evaluation/research and practice are somewhat blurred. This blurring is an interesting distinctive characteristic of the human services field and marks it off from applications of (for example) evidence-based practice (EBP) in health-related fields, criminal justice and, to some extent, education.

For the sake of manageability, I will focus on EBP in a USA context, where there has been limited attention to the boundaries of policy and practice. After briefly reviewing ways in which EBP has been defined and characterized, we will observe how its advocates have thought through the implications for human services intervention, management and training. We will observe recent and still emerging claims for modifications of EBP from within, and some probable future directions, before considering still-remaining criticisms that might be levelled against EBP.

Characterizing Evidence-Based Practice

Sackett's definition of EBP as "the conscientious, explicit and judicious use of current best evidence in making decisions about the care of individual patients" (Sackett et al., 1996, p. 71) is cited often enough in human services literature to leave the impression that discussion about definitional issues is redundant.[3] This would be unhelpful. Mullen (2004), for example, distinguishes between

1. A model of intervention that has been demonstrated effective.

2. A way of practising, using critical thinking.

The first of these sometimes has been disaggregated to include basing practice decisions on empirically based evidence as to the characteristics of intervention strategies that are likely to produce the desired outcomes, and evaluating the implementation of these interventions to ensure they are being implemented as intended (e.g. Roberts & Yeager, 2004, p. 5). The second characteristic, critical thinking, focuses more on professional judgment. It "denotes an approach to evidence, argument and decision-making which is closely related to scientific reasoning" (Macdonald, 2000a, p. 80) and has been said to include:

1. Assessing accurately the quality of evidence.

2. Recognizing and countering common fallacies of reasoning.

3. Recognizing how affective and cognitive biases can adversely influence professional judgment.

4. Establishing "a *modus operandi* which promotes accuracy or truth over winning the argument" (Macdonald, 2000a, p. 80).

Macdonald brings these various aspects together when she says that EBP represents "an approach to decision-making which is transparent, accountable, and based on a consideration of current best evidence about the effects of particular interventions on the welfare of individuals, groups and communities" (Macdonald, 2000b, p. 123).

EBP entails underlying claims regarding good practice that go beyond a plea for reason-based professional judgment and practice. For example, when Sackett writes of evidence-use as being "conscientious, judicious and explicit" this appears to entail three kinds of claim:

- A *moral* claim – "conscientious" suggests done according to conscience; as a moral duty.
- A *wisdom* claim – "Judicious" suggests sound judgment, and is a mark of practical wisdom and discretion.
- A claim to transparency and *openness* – "Explicit" appears to have the sense of leaving nothing merely implied.

EBP advocates often appear to distinguish hierarchies of evidence. Roberts & Yeager for example, refer to evidence levels from meta-analysis through single randomized control trials (RCTs) to "uncontrolled trials" and finally "anecdotal designs". In assessing EBP it is important to acknowledge that other factors, such as practice wisdom and values, *are* recognized by EBP protagonists. But there is still a general assumption that these should be subordinated to "rigorous consideration of current best evidence . . . of the *effects* of particular interventions" (Roberts & Yeager 2004, p. 6). It is not claimed by all advocates of EBP that only randomized control trials provide evidence about effects, but rather that RCTs give the most secure evidence about internal validity, and that internal validity is crucial. The net effect of this is that RCTs are often believed to be the "gold standard, the Rolls Royce of evaluation approaches" in the human services (Chelimsky, 1997, p. 101).

Commitments to certain ways of knowing typically bring with them, by their epistemological assumptions, constraints on the range of action and interventions that may follow (cf. Romm, 1995). This has been particularly clear in countries where supervision of criminal justice orders and youth justice orders is done by social workers or specialist trained professionals. The conclusions drawn by many from 1970s research on the effectiveness of intervention programmes in the criminal justice field that "Nothing Works" led to some demoralization of policy-makers and practitioners. There has been a shift since then, especially through increased confidence in cognitive and behavioural interventions. This has been given a major stimulus from work in Canada by Robert Ross and colleagues (Vanstone, 1999). Lipsey concludes that, assuming integrity of implementation, "[T]he more behaviourally oriented, skills-oriented, and multi-service programs tend to have larger effects" (Lipsey, 2002, p. 204). The general consensus on practice implications is that practitioners should:

- Target factors that have contributed to offending.

- Adopt methods that have structure and require active involvement in problem solving.
- Match degree of intervention to risk of offending.
- Have programme integrity, i.e. avoid drift, objective reversals or non-compliance (Davies, 2000).

Promoters of EBP within the human services are not unanimous on whether professional practice shows up positively as a result. Fischer was predicting that "by the year 2000, empirically based practice – the new social work – may be the norm, or well on the way to becoming so" (Fischer, 1993). That year has come and gone and Mullen laments that "for the most part social work practitioners are not engaged in evidence based practice" (Mullen, 2004, p. 208), and Kirk & Reid remark of social work that, "within the profession, science remains on the cultural margins, struggling for a voice and a following" (Kirk & Reid, 2002, p. x).

Practitioners may, of course, suspect they cannot win if they back an evidence-based approach. There may be some truth in this concern if Macdonald is correct when she claims that "we frequently overestimate social work's beneficial effects and underestimate social work's capacity for adverse effects. In general, the more rigorous the research design, the less dramatic the former and the more transparent the latter" (Macdonald, 2000b, p. 124).

EBP modifications, Directions and Reservations

The evaluative orientation of most evidence-based work in the human services owes most to accountability models of evaluation, and draws largely on quantitative and usually local, medium-scale inquiry projects. Typically, it makes little direct reference to the mainstream evaluation traditions or writers.

The original, fairly bullish versions of EBP in the human services have gradually been re-presented in terms that suggest a need to involve service users, and to take account of the local contexts in which services are delivered. General assertions that service users are – or at least ought to be – involved in EBP decision-making at the case level can be found in the recent literature. In the USA, writers who have not been strongly associated with stakeholder- or justice-based models of evaluation have added their voices to this claim (e.g. Corcoran & Vandiver, 2004; Gibbs & Gambrill, 2002; Howard, McMillen & Pollio, 2003; Mullen, 2004). Similarly, the need to take account of local contexts has gradually been acknowledged. In one of the most fully developed examples of this modification, Proctor & Rosen (2003) say that "Having a solid foundation of empirical support does not guarantee that a given intervention will meet the needs of a particular client" and, "although sometimes given short shrift, local knowledge is an important complement to research-based knowledge" (Proctor & Rosen, 2003, pp. 196, 197; cf Reid & Zettergren, 1999). They warn against the risk of over-committing to standardized interventions. They support modifying intervention systems to meet local contingencies in a careful and well-reasoned stepwise process. Practitioners should:

1. Locate evidence-based interventions relevant to the outcomes for pursuit.

2. Select the best-fitting intervention in view of the particular client problems, situation and outcomes.

3. Supplement and modify the most appropriate and best-supported treatments, drawing on practitioner experience and knowledge.

4. Monitor and evaluate the effectiveness of the intervention.

Lying just beneath the surface is an acknowledgement that EBP has to hold on to a tension between routinization of practice and professional judgement. While this is occasionally recognized, it is but fleetingly so (cf. Howard, McMillen, & Pollio, 2003).

These modifications are unlikely to persuade committed constructivist human services evaluators or those committed to alternative visions for human services evaluation reviewed later in this chapter, but they represent a significant shift of position away from a solely rational and relatively decontextualized model of evidence and intervention to one that takes cognizance of local context and professional judgement. This trend hopefully will be more extensively developed. There *is* a softening of strong versions of EBP. Munson, for example, pleads for a version of EBP that is "balanced with a relationship model" (Munson, 2004, p. 259). He argues that treatment "must have a developmental focus using a scientific perspective that relies on evidence that is grounded in a therapeutic relationship" (p. 252). Evidence alone and relationship alone do not produce change – both are needed.

It would be misleading, however, if we assumed that the only direction of EBP is towards a softening and accommodation with those who have hitherto been its critics. Considerable effort is being made to develop EBP standards (Proctor and Rosen, 2003; routinized guidelines (Mullen & Bacon, 2004; Okamato and LeCroy, 2004; Springer, Abell & Hudson, 2002a, 2002b), and strategies for learning and teaching EBP (Howard et al., 2003). Howard and colleagues tacitly acknowledge that EBP does not in practice provide a deliverable platform and are ready to allow that instructors "can teach interventions without compelling empirical support as long as . . . there is sufficient justification for the intervention" and the available "scientific support" for the intervention is also taught. They include "strong theoretical justification"

and "practice wisdom" as grounds for teaching non-empirical practice (p. 248).

It is beyond the scope of this chapter to review the achievements and limitations of EBP, except to say I am not convinced the problems it raises have been adequately resolved by the present generation of evidence-based evaluators. Rationalist ideas of efficiency do not sit comfortably with, for instance, ideas of democratic participation. Cronbach went as far as to say that, "Rationalism is dangerously close to totalitarianism" (Cronbach et al., 1980, p. 95). In response to arguments that quasi-experimental designs are convincing and plausible, he and his colleagues say tartly that

> The demand that an argument be "convincing" is nothing more than a rationalist attempt to define a category of conclusions that in no way rest on belief and values; in evaluation it is an attempt to place decisions outside politics by establishing an inescapable conclusion. (p. 292)

Too often the arguments of proponents of evidence-based human services suggest undue confidence in the power of science to solve human problems. EBP is presented as a continuation of the scientific revolution (Corcoran & Vandiver, 2004, p. 15), and "a paradigmatic [*sic*] break with the authority based and idiosyncratic practice methods that have historically characterized social services . . . interventions" (Howard et al., 2003, p. 239). Strong enthusiasts for EBP too often seem to place faith in a naïve falsificationism – a view that fallible theories can be tested with non-fallible facts (cf. Howard et al., 2003, p. 247), and to be premised on a simple correspondence assumption regarding the relationship between evaluation data and the real world. This on occasion tends to dogmatism, as when Howard and colleagues allude, in the context of teaching EBP, to the rise in malpractice actions against social workers, and the dangers of practising from alternative perspectives.

There is a further problem too little appreciated. The question, "Does it work?" is a sceptical question and "functions as an exclusionary gatekeeper" (Bogdan & Taylor, 1994, p. 296). Even assuming that design problems could be solved, the question still would not be helpful to practitioners. "Conscientious practitioners do not approach their work as sceptics; they believe in what they do" (p. 297). Bogdan & Taylor have worked to develop what they call "optimistic research", very similar in orientation to subsequent arguments for appreciative evaluation. "We have evolved an approach to research that has helped us bridge the gap between the activists, on the one hand, and empirically grounded sceptical researchers, on the other" (p. 295). The main focus of their research has been on questions of how people with severe disabilities can be integrated into the community. Rather than ask whether services are effective, they ask, "What does integration mean?" and "How can integration be accomplished?"

Outcomes and Interventions

If deliberations regarding evidence-based human services in the USA have concentrated on practice, parallel research and debate within the United Kingdom have more often crossed back and forth over the borders of policy and practice. It is, of course, possible to find tough-minded proponents of EBP represented for example in the work of Macdonald, Sheldon, Kazi, McGuire and others. But beside this there can be observed two rather different groupings; first, an intellectual alliance of feminist, post-modern, critical, and learning-oriented social work researchers who are only partly preoccupied with an evaluative agenda, and second, a coalition of service-focused evaluation researchers convinced of the need to develop a broader evidence base for their work. Add to this a mass of pragmatically

oriented evaluation and research practitioners and we have a mix of stances towards human services evaluation that can also be found in countries such as Sweden, Holland, Denmark, Switzerland, Finland, Norway, Spain, Australia, New Zealand, Canada and possibly in an emergent form in several eastern European countries.

Service Evaluation in Social Care

It is the service-focused evaluation researchers that have made the most direct challenge – from within and without – to the case for strong EBP. The orientation of those identified with this approach has been helpfully captured in a review by Qureshi, who premises much of what she says on the belief that

> Both policy and practice can be seen as occurring within multiple self-adjusting and interacting systems, characterized by non-linear relationships, uncertainty and fuzzy boundaries, giving rise to inherent unpredictability. (Qureshi, 2004, p. 19)

In situations of complexity "where uncertainty is high and agreement about action is low . . . professionals and policy-makers have more in common than might be supposed in terms of their best use of evidence" (p. 20).

Qureshi and her colleagues have developed this stance over some years through a programme of development-oriented research on outcomes with older people. Taking the example of domiciliary care she argues that the purpose of such care is not to *improve* health or quality of life, but to *maintain* quality of life. Put slightly differently she says that while health typically (not always) has "cure" as its aim, social work with older people has "care" as its aim. The outcome indicators will be different in each case. It leads to a focus on "success" in *maintenance*.

EXEMPLAR 22.2

Outcomes into Practice in Adult Social Care

Hazel Qureshi

Background

Social workers play key roles in relation to the care of older and disabled people in the UK. Their assessments are critical in controlling access to publicly funded residential services, and in designing and implementing packages of care which will keep disabled people (of all ages) in their own homes with an acceptable quality of life. However, there is criticism that the focus is too much on services actually available rather than desired objectives. At the same time, available statistical information from routine sources reveals little about outcomes for service users apart from whether or not they remain living at home.

Our initial scoping studies revealed that people at the front line in general did not practice in an outcome focused way, and indeed that people were confused by the prevailing health outcomes model, based on expectations of change and cure, which often did not seem to fit their work (Qureshi, 1999).

Aims and objectives

The program of research and development was designed to find ways to refocus both practice and information collection on broader outcomes for service users, thus enhancing the scope for a more explicitly evaluative ongoing approach in both of these areas.

What strategy was used in the evaluation/research/development described?

The program was conducted in two phases: first, widespread and inclusive consultation; second, collaborative research and development. The consultation was designed to investigate stakeholder concepts of outcome, and to identify realistic opportunities to incorporate a greater outcome focus in routine practice and agency information collection. In the research and development phase, researchers worked with local agencies (staff at all levels and service users) to attempt to implement five of the ideas generated during the first stage. The development process was researched to identify barriers and facilitators.

Results, key issues, and likely future directions

The consultations generated a new framework for understanding social care outcomes which recognized that although change is sometimes an objective of interventions, maintaining a situation or state unchanged may, equally, be a considerable achievement. In addition, objectives may relate to the way in which services are delivered (Qureshi, 2003). Staff seminars and the joint development of new documentation successfully underpinned the introduction of a focus on appropriate outcomes in assessment and care management, as well as in the collection of evaluative feedback from service users (Qureshi & Nicholas, 2001, Nicholas, 2003).

The work demonstrates the change issues involved in focusing on outcomes have to be actively addressed (Nicholas & Qureshi, 2004). One stream of work in a new program has been to collaboratively produce materials to assist managers and trainers in adult services to bring about the necessary changes (Nicholas, Qureshi & Bamford, 2003). If these innovations are to spread, the ideas must be implemented without researcher input. There are already examples where people in services have imaginatively integrated the ideas into their own independent developments.

References

Nicholas, E. (2003). An outcomes focus in carer assessment and review: value and challenge. *British Journal of Social Work*, 33(1), 31–47.

Nicholas, E., Qureshi, H., & Bamford, C. (2003). Outcomes into practice: Focusing practice and information on the outcomes people value – a resource pack for managers and trainers, York: University of York, Social Policy Research Unit.

Qureshi, H. (1999). Outcomes of social care for adults: attitudes towards collecting outcome information in practice. *Health and Social Care in the Community*, 7(4), 257–265.

Qureshi, H. (2003). A response to Dempster and Donnelly Outcome Measurement and Service Evaluation – a note on research design: The importance of understanding social care outcomes. *British Journal of Social Work*, 33(1), 117–120.

Qureshi, H. & Nicholas, E. (2001). A new conception of social care outcomes and its practical use in assessment with older people. *Research, Policy and Planning*, 19(2), 11–26.

This approach to practice, service and policy evaluation departs from a standard evidence-based model in four ways. First, it entails a criticism of any tendency to push for a hierarchy of evidence. "[T]here is no hierarchy of research methods that is independent of the question being asked" (Qureshi, 2004, p. 9). This is not a rejection or even criticism of randomized control trials as such, but rather a concern with "the tendency to slip imperceptibly from the existence of a hierarchy of designs suitable for research on clinical effectiveness, to the existence of a hierarchy of research methods per se" (p. 9). "Evidence is helpful, but rarely determines precisely what should be done to reach goals" (p. 20).

This language echoes House's early conclusion.

> Everyone agrees that information somehow informs decisions, but the relationship is not direct, not simple. Often the more important the decision, the more obscure the relationship seems to be. (House, 1980, p. 68)

House went as far as to say that, "subjected to serious scrutiny, evaluations always appear equivocal" (p. 72). He argued that evaluations can be no more than acts of persuasion. "Evaluation persuades rather than convinces, argues rather than demonstrates, is credible rather than certain, is variably accepted rather than compelling" (p. 73). Human services and social work evaluation researchers have generally plied their trade outside the evaluation community. While this has not always been to their disadvantage, the debate regarding service evaluation would have been enriched and pushed forward earlier, if there had been some mutual conversation on issues of evaluative judgment.

Second, there has been a push to accept a wider evidential base. Nicholas, for example in her work on carers, illustrates a growing recognition of the need to contextualize outcomes-based policies. To assess outcomes for caregivers, Nicholas stresses the need to understand "the complex, dynamic nature of care-giving which is interactive, contextual, temporal, based in relationships and on experience which changes over time" (Nicholas, 2003, p. 33). This leads to a wider acceptance of ways in which research findings may be useful for practice, without necessarily determining the form of intervention.

Sinclair & Wilson, in their discussions about effective fostering, make a central distinction between skilled performance in a particular situation (in this case "responsive parenting") and the prior conditions that make this likely – either conditions to do with the child, carer and their compatibility, or to do with the wider context (wider family, social worker, etc). They wanted to know why some cases were "successful" or not and what processes underlie changes as some cases worsen and other improve.

They adopted an analytic induction approach with elements of research and development tactics. Case interviews were followed by a review of the model. Further case interviews were succeeded by further modifications to the model. The case study they draw on confirms but also goes beyond the statistically derived model "in identifying

the processes involved in a way that is more precise and theoretically relevant" (Sinclair & Wilson, 2003: 1003. cf. Wilson, Petrie & Sinclair, 2003). This is an example of thoughtful, mixed-method development of good practice that develops the model from a large data set and utilizes a case study to check and deepen the conclusions (Wilson et al., 2003, p. 993).

Third, the gradual development of government standards for evaluation and research evidence begins to illuminate the different kinds of evidence that can be cited. This may be to:

- Demonstrate the necessity of action to support *values*.
- Support the promotion of certain *preventative interventions*.
- Demonstrate the *existence and nature of a problem* to be solved.

(Qureshi, 2004, p. 19)

Fourth and finally, service-focused evaluation in the UK and other countries gives greater emphasis to recognizing power dimensions of evaluation and developing some degree of inclusivity with service users. Qureshi argues that "One can simultaneously have a concern for democracy, or inclusiveness, and an attachment to a hierarchy of evidence for effectiveness" albeit they will each provoke different evaluative questions (Qureshi, 2004, p. 13). This illustrates ways in which values and knowledge are brought together in the post paradigm war era. Paradigm language unhelpfully polarized positions on the place of theory, values and world views in evaluation. The debate was too often cast as being between the advocacy of incommensurability of world views and thus of choices of methodology, ove against a position that, at its least, argued that differences of value, theory and world view will never have conflictual implications for choice of method. Either position has only to be stated to be seen to be implausible. Adherence to ethical principles – e.g. through the democratization of research – *may* prove detrimental to service effectiveness. Lewis some time ago aptly expressed the general point, "It is entirely possible that a manager who acts in an ethically commendable fashion may contribute to a less effective service for some and a more effective service for others" (Lewis, 1988, p. 282).

Intervention Research and Development

The broad stance on service evaluation remarked on in the previous paragraphs includes a thread of research and development, especially marked in American social work intervention research. Intervention research has been fundamentally shaped by Rothman & Thomas's (1994) engineering perspective for intervention development. There are a limited number of intervention studies – "about a dozen research reports a year (describe) an evaluated intervention in such detail that a practitioner might be able to replicate it" (Fraser, 2004, p. 212). A range of skills is needed:

> At once, intervention researchers must be clinical, substantive and methodological experts. They have to have good street sense. They have to be skilled in building partnerships with clinicians and agencies. Similar to good practitioners, they must be able to encode social cues, interpret social information, and regulate their own behavior to be effective in a variety of settings. (Fraser, 2004, p. 212)

A key bridging figure here is Bill Reid who died during the preparation of this Handbook (Shaw, 2004a). Reid first became widely known through Anne Shyne and his book, *Brief and Extended Casework*, which reported an experimental study comparing short- and long-term social work intervention (Reid & Shyne, 1969).

Planned short-term service provision yielded results at least as good as and possibly better than open-ended intervention. In the context of the time, when long-term casework was regarded as the ideal, "in this particular race (Planned Short Term Intervention) needed only a tie to win" (p. 175).

Reid took the lead in developing and testing task-centred practice – a short term, problem-solving approach to social work where the focus is on the problems that clients acknowledge as being of concern. Reid & Fortune describe the intervention as a "short-term problem solving approach to social work practice" that "fits well with current definitions of evidence-based practice" (Reid & Fortune, 2004, p. 226). With the cautious expansion of tested applications of task-centred intervention, it has latterly been presented as an "open pluralistic practice system" with "a core of values, theory and methods that could be augmented by compatible approaches" (pp. 226–227). It is especially congenial to cognitive-behavioural, cognitive, and family structural therapies – i.e. an empirically backed approach that focuses on client action as a means of change.[4]

The model has been research-informed throughout, and has a strong empirical orientation (e.g. Reid, 1997). This connecting strand running though Reid's career provides the context for a range of concerns. *First*, his outcome research and review work on other studies was one plank in the gradual renewal of confidence in evaluative research (Reid, 1988, 1997; Reid & Hanrahan, 1982). While he was convinced that the helping professions can demonstrate they are effective, he warned that the practical significance of identified effects was often slight, and their durability ambiguous. He sometimes appeared doubtful about the methodological criteria of such studies. In his chastening and memorable metaphor, "It is like trying to decide which horse won a race viewed at a bad angle from the grandstand during a cloudburst" (Reid, 1988, p. 48)!

In his observations on the direction of outcome research he commented favourably that "The researcher as evaluator is giving way to the researcher as developer of models" (Reid & Hanrahan, 1982, p. 338). This reflects his *second* cluster of concerns. He regards his task-centred practice research as a step-by-step process of development, testing and further development. He sought to develop unobtrusive and practitioner-friendly methods for field testing the early trial versions of specific practice interventions (Reid, 1994b).

Reid's *third* contribution recommended ways in which considerations of epistemology and methodology could be applied to social work. For example, he explored the potential of "change process research" (Reid, 1990). Practical and ethical constraints on experiments necessitate, in his view, the naturalistic study of process-outcome relations. A key notion about the process of change is that of understanding intermediate "micro-outcomes" depicted through intensive study of smaller elements of practice. This gives central importance to the immediate context of practice. Behind this careful steering was Reid's concern to reframe debate

> away from arguments about epistemological worldviews, and devote our energies instead to clarifying and resolving the specific issues embedded in these arguments. (Reid, 1994a, p. 465)

Reid is not the only significant figure in the intervention research field. Rothman & Thomas have made the most cited contribution (Rothman & Thomas, 1994), although a failing of British social work evaluation lies in the absence of a research and development model in the development of social work intervention.

Single-System Evaluation[5]

Human services evaluation has also proved a lively testing ground for the development of single-system approaches to practice evaluation. Reports of single-system evaluations have appeared in the social work literature, particularly in America, since the late 1960s. The strategy involves the intensive study of a one-client system, typically with before and after measures, as opposed to a more wide-ranging investigation of larger groups of service users. Single-system designs have clear attractions over more traditional group experimental designs. Apart from the obvious resource reasons for not undertaking large traditional experiments, grouped data hide the very information that individual practitioners and service users need if they are to act directly on it. Group measures reveal *net* change, not *gross*, individual change. Single-system designs avoid this problem. Unlike experimental, control-group designs which compare groups, single-system designs make comparisons between time periods for the same system, so that the individuals act as their own "control" over time. Advocates of quasi-experimental single-system designs believe that such methods have advantages of practical feasibility, encouraging a systematic approach, improving assessment and planning decisions, continuous feedback on performance outcomes, and, for more rigorous designs, the capacity to identify cause and effect.

There has been an interest in the extension of single-system designs to non-behavioural interventions, which will continue to be a central point of growth and discussion. If greater flexibility can be demonstrated for the application of empirical designs, then their attraction will spread, and the argument that such designs can be applied to everyday realities of practice will be more persuasive than it has been so far.

Additional Developments in Outcomes Evaluation

Before moving away from outcome-oriented evaluation, there are two contrasting areas of development that we have hinted at without comment. First, social work outcomes evaluation has played a part in the steady growth of research synthesis and meta-analysis. Second, the acceptance of the need for a wider evidential base, an interest in critical realism (Kazi, 2003a, 2003b; Pawson & Tilley, 1997), and sustained arguments from qualitative evaluators (e.g. Shaw, 2003) have led to a greater tolerance of the case for qualitative methods within outcomes research.

Synthesis and Meta-analysis

The launch of the Campbell Collaboration has brought together people from Europe, the USA and elsewhere in a collaborative effort that is unusual within the human services. The demand for knowledge synthesis and practice prescriptions has also been strengthened in Britain through the establishment of the Social Care Institute for Excellence (SCIE).[6] The mode of operation of SCIE in its early years has included a multiproject programme designed to establish ground rules for knowledge utilization (e.g. Pawson et al., 2003; Walter et al., 2004) and to develop the basis for standards of good practice (e.g. Crisp, 2003).

We synthesize in order to generalize. For those who claim a hierarchy of evidence, meta-analysis stands at the head of pyramid. But meta-analysis has an ambiguous relationship to the use of randomized control trials. Its advocates regard meta-analysis not as an adjunct to randomized control trials but as a more credible basis of evidence. Randomized control trials (or the component studies in meta-analysis) then become a means to an end. This is a paradox. We must have randomized control trials, and the more the better, otherwise no meta-analysis, so the argument goes. But we must treat the results of any given randomized control trial with, at best, caution. "We must be very cautious in interpreting a single set of results, even from a well-designed evaluation study" (Lipsey, 2002, p. 207).

Lipsey suggests five general conclusions from the application of meta-analysis to studies of programmes of intervention.

1. Many programmes are more effective than we thought.

2. Individual outcomes can easily produce erroneous results.

3. Method variations are related to outcome variations.

4. Programme effectiveness is a function of identifiable programme characteristics.

5. There is room for programme improvement.

His second point poses the problem of how do we reconcile the "fact" that meta-analysis produces positive effect size with an inability to conclude from any given study that X works? Lipsey's response is that Type II errors, from small sample sizes, are part of the answer. The relevance of this point is accentuated because human services evaluations often depend on small samples (Fraser, 2004). Lipsey also notes that the lack of statistically significant results only says that we have failed to reject null hypothesis, not that we have confirmed the absence of effects. But he admits that this subtle distinction is lost on policy-makers! He acknowledges that the sample size argument also counts against studies showing positive gains over against the control group. Treatment may be *worse* than we think.

His third point about the effect of method variations is also important for mixed-method human services evaluations. Meta-analysis has demonstrated that the neutrality of the typical range of methods for outcome evaluation cannot be taken for granted. "What we observe as program effects may reflect as much influence from the methods with which the program was studied, as the actual effects the program has on its intended beneficiaries" (Lipsey, 2002, p. 203). Fraser makes a similar point in his assessment of advances and challenges in intervention research. If outcome variance is due to in significant part to method, this may produce different results *between* methods, and, if unstable in its operation, may produce differences *within* the same method at different times. "The plurality of our methods leads to complicated findings and fuzzy plausibility" (Fraser, 2004, p. 218). This shows that human services practitioners will need to exercise continued caution about synthesized judgments of effect.

Qualitative Methods and Outcomes

Scepticism and even antagonism still surface from time to time when qualitative evaluation methods are under consideration. Thyer, for example, has not found reason to retreat from his comment some years ago that

> social work practitioner-researchers look in vain for qualitative research studies which have clearly demonstrated the effectiveness of social work intervention in solving problems of social importance. (Thyer, 1989, p. 312)

There is a range of positions among those who take a more accepting line towards qualitative evaluation. These extend from a pragmatic "horses for courses" position that sees method choice as epistemologically neutral and shaped simply by the practicalities of research planning and delivery (e.g. Cheetham et al., 1992), to the reverse of this in which qualitative strategies are seen in some cases to be the method of choice where previously they

would have been considered inappropriate (Patton, 2002; Shaw, 1999). In between lies a mixed-method approach that is ready to accept that no single design can provide complete evidence. The language of triangulation is often drawn on as a metaphor for this approach and is well represented by Qureshi's work reviewed above. Fraser is among those with an essentially quantitative orientation to human services evaluation who urge qualitative researchers to address outcomes issues. "If you are more oriented to qualitative research I ask you to study more than phenomena as they exist. Instead, devise a change strategy, implement it, and describe the processes leading to outcomes" (Fraser, 2004, p. 220). He accepts that it is impossible to develop culturally free methods. Culturally rooted concepts and categories "are the core elements of constructs" (p. 219). Thus, for example, the use of scales raises the problem of "scale equivalence" – alternate meanings may be given to items and response categories across people with different cultural backgrounds. This will be true both linguistically (meanings and nuances of words) and culturally (values attached to categories). The solution is *not* just greater sample size or sample diversity, but how we conceptualize. Conceptual differences (e.g. around race and ethnicity) may warrant separate activities within an intervention or even a separate culturally specific intervention.[7]

This should not be read as a plea to replace one uniformitarian orthodoxy with another. On the one hand, a notion that *only* qualitative methods can examine unique, complex cases is clearly not accurate, as there is an interesting history of idiographic and ipsative quantitative methods for individual case analysis in psychology in the work of people such as Rogers, Allport, Cattell and Kelly. Likewise, I am not convinced that all forms and traditions of qualitative methodology lend themselves equally or even directly to evaluative purposes in the human services. Stake probably had this in mind when he remarked that "to the qualitative scholar, the understanding of human experience is a matter of chronologies more than of cause and effect", and that "the function of research is not . . . to map and conquer the world but to sophisticate the beholding of it" (Stake, 1995, pp. 39, 43).

Understanding and Evaluating for Practice

This brief glance at ways in which qualitative methods contribute to understanding outcomes in human services has taken us some way from the strong versions of evidence-based practice and meta-analysis that have been nearer the core of the chapter. The final part of this chapter takes us further still from evidence-based practice and policy. We will consider the connections between professional practice and evaluation practice. We will also review the ways in which practitioners engage in disciplined inquiry. Finally, we will highlight the strong contribution that human services in general and social work in particular have made to the development of justice-based approaches to evaluation.

Qualitative Evaluation

Practitioners and evaluators may mutually benefit from considering how far the perspectives and methods of one provide a template for the other. The argument that qualitative research has a natural synergy with the processes of practice first strongly emerged in the writing of Jane Gilgun (1989, 1994) who proposed and elaborated the metaphor that practice fits qualitative research "like a hand fits a glove". Essentially, Gilgun's case is that practice and qualitative research in social work share a number of common features: the focus

on how informants construe their world is congruent with the social work injunction to start where the client is; the contextualization of data fits with the social work emphasis on understanding the person within his/her environment; "thick" description of individual case studies is parallel to the social work individualization of social work processes of assessment and intervention; and so on. Martin Bloom exemplifies those who have been equally forceful proponents of the view that the perspectives and methods of qualitatively oriented inquiry find their direct reflection in good social work practice (Bloom, 1999).

There is, of course, no unanimity on this. Padgett, a protagonist of qualitative research in social work, suggested that under closer scrutiny the glove really did not fit (1998, 1999). Padgett reasserts the value of the contribution of qualitative research to the knowledge base of social work, but draws out a number of criteria by which she asserts that practice and research are very different undertakings, and that there are both scientific and ethical reasons for ensuring that the two are not conflated. Primarily she argues that both are located in different paradigms (practice is irredeemably theory and model driven, located within normative views of social or individual functioning whereas qualitative research is concerned with theory generation and is non-normative), goals and practice/research relationships. Padgett's sting that provoked the strongest reaction was her argument that the conflation of research and practice was inherently unethical with compromises around standards of confidentiality, informed consent and withdrawal from research/treatment (Padgett, 1998, p. 376).

My own position is that there is a congruence at the level of logic between EBP and quasi-experimental evaluation. I am also persuaded that there is "a sympathetic connection" between certain kinds of social work and qualitative kinds of data – "talk, therapeutic conversation, agency records, narratives about experiences with organisations and macro systems" (Riessman, 1994, p. ix). The tie is proximate but neither universal and homogenous nor capable of straightforward transfer from one to the other. It requires methodological work, which I think can helpfully be described as involving "counter-colonizing" and "translating" (Shaw, 1996). Counter-colonizing requires practitioners to challenge the conventional donor–client relationship between practice and social science, and act upon evaluation research methods rather than simply apply them. "Translation" raises issues of language and culture, and underscores the interpretative character of the process. Social workers need to develop a dialogic practice, both within social work and with methodologists. For example, Janesick's "stretching" exercises for qualitative researchers are an example of work based on a learning rationale that provides a fertile basis for professional "counter-colonizing" and "translating" (Janesick, 1998). The quality of "methodological practice" will have an emergent, opportunistic and particularistic character. Whitmore's use of visual methods exemplifies this opportunist quality (Whitmore, 2001). To maximize the gains from this process social workers need to avoid remaining too much insiders. Above all, such "methodological practice" will have a participatory and collaborative character.

Viewed through these lenses, we can observe how differences between evidence-based practice and more hermeneutically inclined evaluation are not superficial. They are present-day manifestations of differences extending back more than three hundred years, between evaluation undergirded by empirical philosophy, in which the mind is viewed as essentially passive in perception, and idealist philosophy, which emphasizes the active powers of the mind to create and transform reality. The post-modern turn in social work has yielded a mistrust of evaluation, in the sense of a search for foundational truth. Derrida and Foucault's critical appraisals of knowledge have led to uncertainty and an emphasis on "the instability of meaning, the impossibility of arriving at foundational truths about the world, the myth of linearity and thus the impossibility of prediction, and the role of knowledge and technologies of cultural production in oppressive exercises of power and minority subjugation" (Penna, 2000, p. 262).

Practitioner Evaluation

Practitioner involvement in evaluation – research, development, or more general inquiry that is small-scale, local, grounded, and carried out by professionals who directly deliver those self-same services – is embraced across a wide range of professions as an essential ingredient of good practice.

McLeod has defined practitioner research as "research carried out by practitioners for the purpose of advancing their own practice" (McLeod, 1999, p. 8). This definition has much going for it, although it is incomplete. First, it includes a statement of purpose, and hence incorporates an implicit criterion for assessing the quality of practitioner research. It is not adequate to define practitioner research simply as research carried out by practitioners, without grounding it on a basis of purpose. Second, McLeod's definition makes explicit a practice rationale, rather than broader policy or academic rationales for research. Finally, it includes an implicit model of how practitioner research can be useful. McLeod seems to assume a fairly direct relationship between research and practice – or, as we may describe it, an "instrumental" model of information use.[8]

There have been several arguments in support of practitioner evaluation in social work, two of the most frequently heard being the professional obligation to be self-evaluating, and the belief that evaluation and practice draw on similar skills. McIvor aptly expresses these twin views when she says,

> The starting point . . . is the twofold belief that practitioners should be encouraged to engage in the evaluation of their own practice and that they possess many of the skills which are necessary to undertake the evaluative task. (McIvor, 1995, p. 210)

It is probably not helpful to search for the historical roots of practitioner research, although practitioners-as-researchers is no new idea. What is new is the range of arguments and exemplars offered for practitioner evaluation, its independent emergence in British and American education in the 1970s, in American social work in the 1970s, and in a different form in 1980s British social work, and in the gradual deepening and diversification of the influence of qualitative methodologies on social work.

Practitioner evaluation in social work is different in Britain and in America. In the USA there is a vigorous "scientific practitioner" movement based in general on outcome-oriented and quantitative methodology. We have already noted the importance of single-system designs in this context. The American social work journals have been the scene of continuing debate about the contribution of the empirical practice movement. Epstein has argued that both mainstream evaluation and social work practice have come to take "psychic determinism" positions,

> that locate the source of human trouble inside the individual person, in some non-empirical site such as the soul, the spirit, the psyche, the mind, personality structures and similar venues. (Epstein, 1996, p. 115)

In so doing, evaluators and practitioners are "concentrating on reading and changing the minds of poor people and those who are otherwise distressed and deviant" (p. 115). "The problem in both cases is that the context is missing" (p. 116). The implicit answer to Epstein's appeal appears to include a more sociologically informed and qualitative practitioner evaluation strategy. One approach to constructing such a strategy has been to analyse the differences and similarities in the data processing strategies of social work and qualitative research in order to assess ways in which they might be implemented (e.g. Lang, 1994; Ruckdeschel, Earnshaw & Firrek, 1994).

The limited empirical work on practitioner evaluation and research suggests it may be fruitful to consider its present character and future development in terms of the scheme shown in Figure 22.1 (Keane, Shaw & Faulkner, 2003). I have not presented this scheme as a normative framework – for example, it is *not* my view that the more complex the project the better it will be. But I am convinced that there is already great diversity in practitioner evaluation, and this diversity will be linked to variation in the relevance, value and impact of practitioner evaluation in human services. The typology does raise questions as to the possibilities for kinds of practitioner evaluation that are rarely on show at the moment. I have *italicized* some features of practitioner evaluation at the right-hand end of the two dimensions that – as far as I can judge – are rarely evident at present.

Visiting some of the origins and more recent directions in practitioner evaluation in social work prompts us to see it as a phenomenon that – rather than being special or narrowly associated with the place of social work in contemporary society – manifests a pervasive professional cluster of concerns about good professional practice. It is quite possible that the wider structures of which it is a part frequently hamstring the potential of such evaluation to operate as more than a fringe

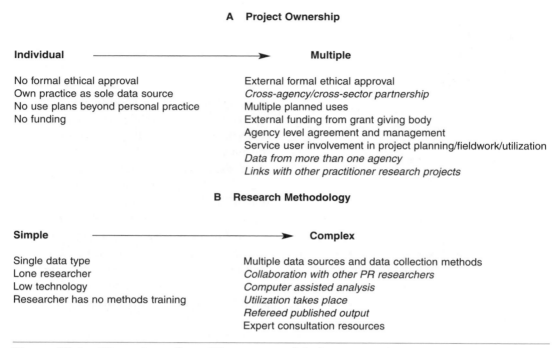

Figure 22.1   Dimensions of practitioner research in human services

operation – a "street market" version of mainstream evaluation. The probable volume of such evaluation simply serves to underscore the irony and significance of this situation. Human service stakeholders need to foster ways in which social workers, service users, agency managers, academics, government departments, and universities can work to a transformative agenda for practitioner evaluation – transformative for both practice and evaluation. This will involve refashioning the interface between the methodology and methods of practice and evaluation; generating practitioner evaluation capacity; recognizing the subtlety and critical potential of a genuinely "practical" agenda, and rescuing practitioner evaluation from a simply technical information-providing function, that bypasses the challenge to promoting diverse forms of social justice.

Justice and Human Service Evaluation

Evidence, understanding – and justice. This final section of the chapter focuses on the third of the evaluative purposes in human services identified in the opening paragraphs. Different strands can be identified in the development of the idea of empowerment in social work. These include self-help, liberational, professional, managerialist and market models.

> Empowerment has become the site of key struggles over the nature and purpose of politics, policy, services and professional intervention. That is why its meanings are heavily contested and it is important to recognize its *regulatory* as well as its *liberatory* potential. (Croft & Beresford, 2000, p. 117)

In social work practice and policy in western nations, professional and liberatory approaches

---

EXEMPLAR 22.1 Foundations of advocacy evaluation

Foundation	Key words
Political	Power; empowerment; standpoint; structures
Post-modernism	Interpretation; meaning; local relevance
Interpersonal learning	Understanding; reciprocity

---

have been most prominent, although considerable caution is necessary in generalizing, even across western countries and cultures.

> While professional approaches have focused on *personal* empowerment (bringing about change in the individual), the liberational approaches adopted by the disabled people's and service users' movements place equal emphasis on personal and *political* empowerment. (Croft & Beresford, 2000, p. 117)

Croft & Beresford are talking about practice and policy, but their distinctions and cautions apply in a very similar way to how concern about the oppressive potential of human services in relation to, for example, race, gender and disability, has emphasized the centrality of political, moral and human rights frameworks in shaping evaluative work. Evaluation is conventionally viewed as a relatively sophisticated means to a larger end. The problem focus, research design, fieldwork, analysis, reporting and dissemination of results are all seen as the work of experts seeking understanding that will be for the good of some present or future beneficiaries. One of the most far-reaching developments of recent years has been that practitioners within the human services increasingly have been challenged by forms of evaluation that are seen not as means to some external end but also (and for some advocates, solely) as ends in themselves. To borrow an apt phrase from Robert Stake, social workers have become "reluctant to separate epistemology from ideology, findings from yearnings" (Stake, 1997, p. 471).

The forms taken by this radical challenge are wider than evaluation and include feminist research, research within the disability movement, critical theory, justice-based commitments within research, participatory and reflective inquiry and qualitative evaluation as a dimension of direct practice. Advocacy positions cover a span of political stances. At one end is located *multipartisan* and multivocal research. This is well established in some American evaluation, for example, in Lee Cronbach and Robert Stake, and also in much interpretive research. More explicit advocacy positions are associated with much British *reformist* policy evaluation, and with some participatory evaluation. *Radical* positions of critical inquiry include the majority of feminist inquiry, research from the disability movement and among mental health "survivors", and the greater part of research that takes its primary impetus from neo-Marxist critical theory. These diverse positions stem largely from the different rationales that have been advanced for advocacy evaluation. There are three main rationales that parallel in some regards Croft & Beresford's ordering of empowerment positions (Table 22.1).

The foundation positions in Table 22.1 are, of course, abstractions. There *are* those who take one main position, perhaps particularly when associated with relatively radical political rationales. But it is equally common to encounter those who bridge more than one position – either on practical and opportunistic grounds or on the basis of more general arguments. For example, Reason has been strongly associated with the development of reflective inquiry approaches, but belongs to no single "camp". He firmly rejects post-modernism as nihilistic and does not major on any political rationale. However, he distances himself from conventional science (e.g. Reason, 1994). Fetterman – probably the best-known advocate of empowerment evaluation in the USA – sits closest to the third of these positions but has elements of the first. He regards empowerment evaluation as "designed to help people help themselves and improve their program using a form of self-evaluation and reflection" (Fetterman, 2004, p. 585). Two examples where social work has made a distinctive impact on critical, empowerment evaluation are participatory empowerment evaluation, and user-led evaluation.

Participatory Empowerment Evaluation

Whitmore's account of an evaluation of a pre-natal programme for single, pregnant mothers illustrates how positive outcomes may on balance be achieved. The evaluation was carried out over several months by four women who had themselves been through the programme, with Whitmore as consultant to the project. There were tensions in the group, and communication failures. One member left and another protested to Whitmore that

> Our world is different from yours. The fear is that people always want to humiliate you, put you down (for being on welfare) . . . We have a different lifestyle from you. We just don't trust people the way you do. (Whitmore, 1994, p. 92)

Whitmore concluded that she could never entirely share the worlds of the women with whom she worked. "My small words were often their big words. What I assumed was 'normal talk', they saw as "professor words" (p. 95). Martin arrived at similar conclusions

from her own feminist participative inquiry, concluding that it "places unrealistic expectations on the extent to which the researched can become involved in the research process", and that "even when problems are a major concern to people (the researched) they have work and private lives which usually take priority, whereas research IS work for the researcher" (Martin, 1994, p. 142). But the strength of their final achievements is evidence that participatory evaluation with oppressed groups goes beyond political rhetoric.

User-Led Evaluation

Whitmore concludes from a subsequent participatory project with young people that:

> We assumed that street involved youth were in the best position to evaluate their own services and we were right. They could not have done this alone, however. As much as we want to believe in "community control", this has to be seen in context, and the reality is that marginalized populations will need our professional support and commitment in working with them. (Whitmore, 2001, p. 98)

This captures the edges between participatory evaluation and user-led and controlled evaluation. Social work has to some extent led the way on exploring the possibilities for a full-blown user-led evaluation. In Britain, for instance, there are examples in the fields of mental health, older people, and learning disabilities. My own involvement in projects of this kind suggests there are at least three ways this makes for better practice in the human services.

First, it shifts the focus of what professionals and evaluators think are key questions to those that sufferers and survivors think are central. The likely priorities that mental health sufferers and survivors place at the centre will probably include coping, identity, information needs, support needs, self-help, carers, women's issues, rights and opportunities.

Second, it challenges a reappraisal of what human services practitioners think is good intervention. For example, user-led evaluation prioritizes:

- An emphasis on telling stories (hence narratives).
- Ground-level concerns of the disadvantaged. A comment from the floor in a UK consultation of user researchers mentioned a Ghana proverb – "A person who rides a donkey does not know the ground is hot".
- Experience. In the same consultation, someone cited Paulo Freire as saying, "Reading the world always precedes reading the word".

Third, user-led evaluation yields a powerful sense of what is stigmatizing. What does it mean to live on a locked ward? How do users experience language? The term "service user" may be rejected because it implies a one-way consumption. "Victim" carries similar passive connotations – as in "Victim Support" schemes. User evaluators may also wish to avoid terms that define the whole person in terms of the role, as in "carer". 'sufferer" – "because I *have* suffered" as one woman said – and 'survivor" may seem stronger words.

Fisher (2002) has claimed that user controlled evaluation may lead to methodologically stronger evidence. It may:

1. Ensure a problem focus is less reliant on perspectives on social issues held by the dominant group.

2. Lead to more representative samples because of lower refusal rates.

3. Guarantee better data quality because participants will be less defensive, e.g., in interviews.

4. Lead to the development of outcome measures that:

- Pay attention to the *processes* of service delivery.
- Understand people within their *social context*.
- Reflect the *diversity* of users' views on the quality of life.

5. Enable greater theoretical relevance and sensitivity to emerge during data analysis.

Possibly so, although the jury is still out. For the present, the benefits of user-led evaluation should not be treated as axiomatically better than other forms of evaluation. Nor should we slip into the solipsism of assuming only those who experience problems and services can understand them. It is not inevitable that evaluation that is justifiable on moral grounds will also be methodologically sounder. Also, there are ethical questions as to whether principles around informed consent, and confidentiality/privacy are especially at risk in user-controlled research. Finally, even when an alliance of service users and evaluation professionals is accepted as good practice, the role of independent academic judgement is not easily agreed. There are numerous methodological questions posed by empowerment evaluation. Are large dataset studies susceptible to empowerment evaluation? (Truman, 1999). More generally, does empowerment evaluation entail any prior methodological commitments, positively or negatively? (cf. Shaw & Gould, 2001, pp. 169–172). If human service providers *are* to be advocates, what implications does this have for debates about catalytic validity. (Lather, 1986).

Conclusion

We have reviewed three arenas of social work and human services evaluation in this chapter, namely, evaluation designed to establish plausible *evidence* regarding best practice and the outcomes of policies, services and intervention; evaluation that aims to *understand* and learn about social problems, organisational responses, and direct practice; and evaluation seeking to promote *just* forms and outcomes of human services.

> Historically, the influence of science on direct social work practice has taken two forms. One is the use of the scientific method to shape practice activities, for example, gathering evidence and forming hypotheses about a client's problem. The other form is the provision of scientific knowledge about human beings, their problems and ways of resolving them. (Reid, 1998, p. 3)

Reid's distinction is fundamental and too little appreciated. The parts of this chapter reviewing evidence-based practice and evaluation of service outcomes emphasize the second form of influence. The final section on matters of justice and understanding accentuate the first form of influence. Both fields of work are the scenes of lively and mobile inquiry, thinking and practice.

Notes

1. "Human services" is an American category, although it is increasingly adopted outside the USA. "Social care" (e.g. in Britain) and "community development" (e.g. in Africa and some Arab world countries) are other categories that condense a broad scope of formal and informal, state-regulated and independent, secular and faith-based, personal social services. The expression "human services" is used throughout this chapter as shorthand to refer to these coalescences of agencies, occupations and professions. Within these broad groupings are occupations that are typically a minority within the whole, although more or less professional, linked to higher education, subject to state or national regulatory frameworks, and research-based. Social work is an example of such an occupation.

2. The main thread of the chapter is the work of Shaw. Mowbray and Qureshi's work is contained within the exemplars. The use of the first person singular occurs in places where I do not want to commit all three authors to the view expressed.

3. See Sheldon for a straightforward adaptation of this definition to social work. (www.exac.uk/cebss @introduction.html)

4. There is a task centred practice website at www.task-centered.com.

5. The term *single system* has been widely adopted in social work and human services evaluation to indicate a less individualized meaning than that carried by the expressions single *case* or single subject, or even the term $N = 1$ research used in the field of psychology.

6. http://www.scie.org.uk.

7. Laird (2003) has offered a more radical critique of the cultural lacunae in much outcomes research.

8. The terms practitioner *research* and practitioner *evaluation* tend to be used interchangeably in the literature. However, what evidence we possess suggests that almost all practitioner inquiry includes an evaluative purpose (Shaw and Faulkner, 2006).

References

Bloom, M. (1999). Single system evaluation. In I. Shaw, & J. Lishman, (eds) *Evaluation and Social Work Practice*. London: Sage.

Bogdan, R. & Taylor, S. (1994). A positive approach to qualitative evaluation and policy research in social work. In E. Sherman, & W. Reid (eds) *Qualitative Research in Social Work*. New York: Columbia University Press.

Cheetham, J., Fuller, R., McIvor, G., & Petch, A. (1992). *Evaluating Social Work Effectiveness*. Buckingham: Open University Press.

Chelimsky, E. (1997). Thoughts for a new Evaluation Society. In *Evaluation*, 3(1), 97–118.

Corcoran, K. & Vandiver, V. L. (2004) Implementing best practice and expert consensus procedures. In A. R. Roberts & K. R. Yeager (eds) *Evidence-Based Practice Manual: Research and outcome measures in health and human services*. New York: Oxford UP.

Crisp B., Anderson, M., Orme, J., & Lister, P. (2003). *Learning and Teaching in Social Work Education: Assessment*. London: Social Care Institute for Excellence.

Croft, S. & Beresford, P. (2000). Empowerment. In M. Davies (ed.) *The Blackwell Encyclopaedia of Social Work*. Oxford: Blackwell.

Cronbach, L., Ambron, S., Dornbusch, S., Hess, R., Hornik, R., Phillips, D., Walker, D., & Weiner, S. (1980). *Toward Reform of Program Evaluation*. San Francisco: Jossey-Bass.

Davies, M. (2000). Nothing works. In M. Davies (ed.) *The Blackwell Encyclopaedia of Social Work*. Oxford: Blackwell.

Epstein, L. (1996). The trouble with the researcher-practitioner idea. *Social Work Research*, 20(2), 113–118.

Fetterman, D. (2004). Empowerment evaluation. In A. R. Roberts & K. R. Yeager (eds) *Evidence-Based Practice Manual: Research and outcome measures in health and human services*, New York: Oxford UP.

Fischer, J. (1993). Empirically based practice: the end of ideology? In M. Bloom, (ed.) *Single-System Designs in the Social Services*. New York: Haworth.

Fisher, M. (2002). The role of service users in problem formulation and technical aspects of social research. *Social Work Education*, 21(3), 305–312.

Fraser, M. W. (2004). Intervention research in social work: recent advances and continuing challenges. *Research on Social Work Practice*, 14(3), 210–222.

Gibbs, L. & Gambrill, E. (2002). Evidence based practice – counterarguments to objections. *Research on Social Work Practice*, 12(3), 452–476.

Gilgun, J. (1994). Hand in glove: the grounded theory approach and social work practice research. In E. Sherman & W. J. Reid (eds) *Qualitative Research in Social Work*. New York: Columbia University Press.

House, E. (1980). *Evaluating with Validity*. Beverley Hills: Sage.

Howard, M. O., McMillen, C. J., & Pollio, D. E. (2003). Teaching evidence based practice: towards a new paradigm for social work education. *Research on Social Work Practice* 13(2), 234–259.

Janesick, V. J. (1998). *"Stretching" Exercises for Qualitative Researchers*. Thousand Oaks: Sage.

Kazi, M. (2003a). Realist evaluation for practice. *British Journal of Social Work* 33(6), 803–818.

Kazi, M. (2003b) *Realist Evaluation in Practice*. London: Sage.

Keane, S., Shaw, I., & Faulkner, A. (2003). *Practitioner Research in Social Work and Social Care: An audit and case study analysis*. Cardiff: Wales Office for Research and Development.

Kirk, S. & Reid, W. (2002). *Science and Social Work*. New York: Columbia University Press.

Laird, S. E. (2003). Evaluating social work outcomes in Sub Saharan Africa. *Qualitative Social Work* 2(3), 251–270.

Lang, N. (1994). Integrating the data processing of qualitative research and social work practice to advance the practitioner as knowledge builder: tools for knowing and doing. In E. Sherman & W. Reid (eds) *Qualitative Research in Social Work*. New York: Columbia University Press.

Lather, P. (1986). Issues of validity in openly ideological research. *Interchange*, 17(4), 63–84 .

Lewis, H. (1988). Ethics and the Managing of Service Effectiveness in Social Welfare. In R. Patti, J. Poertner & C. Rapp (eds) *Managing for Service Effectiveness in Social Welfare Organisations*. Haworth.

Lipsey, M. W. (2002). Meta-analysis and program outcome evaluation. *Socialvetenskaplig Tidskrift*, 9(2–3), 194–208.

Macdonald, G. (2000a). Critical thinking. In M. Davies (ed.) *The Blackwell Encyclopaedia of Social Work*. Oxford: Blackwell.

Macdonald, G. (2000b). Evidence-based practice. In M. Davies (ed.) *The Blackwell Encyclopaedia of Social Work*. Oxford: Blackwell.

Martin, M. (1994). Developing a feminist participative research framework. In B. Humphries & C. Truman (eds) *Rethinking Social Research: Anti-discriminatory approaches in research methodology*. Avebury.

McIvor, G. (1995). Practitioner research in probation. In J. McGuire (ed.) *What Works? Reducing offending.* New York: Wiley.

McLeod, J. (1999). *Practitioner Research in Counselling*. London: Sage.

Mullen, E. (2004). Facilitating practitioner use of EBP. In A. R. Roberts & K. R. Yeager (eds) *Evidence-Based Practice Manual: Research and Outcome measures in health and human services*, New York: Oxford UP.

Mullen, E. & Bacon, W. (2004). Implementation of practice guidelines and evidence-based treatment. In A. R. Roberts & K. R. Yeager (eds) *Evidence-Based Practice Manual: Research and outcome measures in health and human services*, New York: Oxford UP.

Munson, C. E. (2004). Evidence-based treatment for traumatized and abused children. In A. R. Roberts, & K. R. Yeager, (eds) *Evidence-Based*

Practice Manual: Research and outcome measures in health and human services. New York: Oxford UP.

Nicholas, E. (2003). An outcomes focus in carer assessment and review: Value and challenge. *British Journal of Social Work,* 33(1), 31–47.

Okamato, S. K. & LeCroy, C. W. (2004). Evidence-based practice and manualized treatment with children. In A. R. Roberts & K. R. Yeager (eds) *Evidence-Based Practice Manual: Research and outcome measures in health and human services.* New York: Oxford UP.

Padgett, D. (1998). Does the glove really fit? Qualitative research and clinical social work practice. *Social Work,* 43(4), 373–381.

Padgett, D. K. (1999). The research-practice debate in a qualitative research context. *Social Work,* 43(4), 280–282.

Patton, M. Q. (2002). *Qualitative Research and Evaluation Methods.* Thousand Oaks: Sage.

Pawson, R. & Tilley, N. (1997). *Realistic Evaluation* London: Sage.

Pawson, R., Boaz, A., Grayson, L., Long, A., & Barnes, C. (2003). *Types and Quality of Knowledge in Social Care.* London: Social Care Institute for Excellence.

Penna, S. (2000). Post-structuralism. In M. Davies (ed.) *The Blackwell Encyclopaedia of Social Work.* Oxford: Blackwell.

Proctor, E. K. & Rosen, A. (2004). Concise standards for developing evidence-based practice guidelines. In A. R. Roberts & K. R. Yeager, (eds) *Evidence-Based Practice Manual: Research and outcome measures in health and human services,* New York: Oxford UP.

Qureshi, H. (2004). Evidence in policy and practice: what kind of research designs? In *Journal of Social Work,* 4(1), 7–23.

Reason, P. (ed.) (1994). *Participation in Human Inquiry.* London: Sage.

Reid, W. (1998). *Empirically-Supported Practice: Perennial myth or emerging reality?* Distinguished Professorship Lecture. New York: State University at Albany.

Reid, W. J. (1988). Service effectiveness and the social agency. In R. Patti, J. Poertner & C. Rapp, (eds) *Managing for Effectiveness in Social Welfare Organisations.* New York: Haworth.

Reid, W. J. (1990). Change-process research: a new paradigm? In L. Videka-Sherman & W. Reid, (eds) *Advances in Clinical Social Work Research.* Silver Spring, MD: NASW Press.

Reid, W. J. (1994a). Reframing the epistemological debate. In E. Sherman & W. Reid (eds), *Qualitative Research in Social Work.* New York: Columbia University Press.

Reid, W. J. (1994b). Field testing and data gathering on innovative practice interventions in early development. In J. Rothman & E. Thomas, (eds) *Intervention Research: Design and development of human service.* New York: Haworth Press.

Reid, W. J. (1997). Research on task-centred practice. In *Social Work Research,* 21(3), 132–137.

Reid, W. J. & Fortune, A. (2004). Task-centred practice: an exemplar of evidence-based practice. In A. R. Roberts & K. R. Yeager (eds) *Evidence-Based Practice Manual: Research and outcome measures in health and human services,* New York: Oxford UP.

Reid, W. J. & Hanrahan, P. (1982). Recent evaluations of social work: grounds for optimism. *Social Work,* 27, 328–340.

Reid, W. J. & Shyne, A. (1969) *Brief and Extended Casework.* New York: Columbia University Press.

Reid, W. J. & Zettergren, P. (1999). A Perspective on empirical practice. In I. Shaw & J. Lishman, (eds) *Evaluation and Social Work Practice.* London: Sage.

Riessman, C. K. (1994). Preface: Making room for diversity in social work research. In C. K. Riessman (ed.) *Qualitative Studies in Social Work Research,* Thousand Oaks: Sage.

Roberts, A. R. & Yeager, K. R. (eds) (2004). *Evidence-Based Practice Manual: Research and outcome measures in health and human services,* New York: Oxford UP.

Romm, N. (1995). Knowing as intervention: reflections on the application of systems ideas. *Systems Practice,* 8(2), 137–167.

Rothman, J. & Thomas, E. (eds) (1994). *Intervention Research: Design and development of human service.* New York: Haworth Press.

Ruckdeschel, R., Earnshaw, P., & Firrek, A. (1994). The qualitative case study and evaluation: Issues, methods and examples. In E. Sherman & Reid, W. (eds) *Qualitative Research in Social Work.* New York: Columbia University Press.

Sackett, D., Rosenberg, W., Gray, J., Haynes, R., & Richardson, W. (1996), Evidence-based medicine: What it is and what it isn't. *British Medical Journal.* 312(7023), 71–72 .

Shaw, I. (1996). *Evaluating in Practice.* Aldershot: Ashgate.

Shaw, I. (1999). *Qualitative Evaluation.* London: Sage.

Shaw, I. (2003). Qualitative research and outcomes in health, social work and education. *Qualitative Research,* 3(1), 57–77.

Shaw, I. (2004a). William J Reid: an appreciation. *Qualitative Social Work* 3(2), 109–115.

Shaw, I. (2005). Practitioner research: evidence or critique? *British Journal of Social Work,* 35(8), 1231–1248.

Shaw, I. & Faulkner, A. (2006). Practitioner evaluation at work. *American Journal of Evaluation,* 27(1), 1–20.

Sinclair, I. & Wilson, K (2003). Matches and mismatches: the contribution of carers and children to the success of foster placements. *British Journal of Social Work,* 33(7), 871–884.

Springer, D., Abell, N., & Hudson, W (2002a). Creating and validating rapid assessment instruments for practice and research: Part 1. *Research on Social Work Practice,* 12(3), 408–439.

Springer, D., Abell, N., & Hudson, W. (2002b). Creating and validating rapid assessment instruments for practice and research: Part 2. *Research on Social Work Practice,* 12(4), 768–795.

Stake, R. (1995). *The Art of Case Study Research.* Thousand Oaks: Sage.

Stake, R. (1997). Advocacy in evaluation: a necessary evil? In E. Chelimsky, & W. Shadish, (eds) *Evaluation for the 21st Century.* Thousand Oaks: Sage.

Thyer, B. (1989). First principles of practice research. *British Journal of Social Work,* 19(4), 309–323.

Truman, C. (1999). User involvement in large-scale research: bridging the gap between service users and service providers. In B. Broad (ed.) *The Politics of Social Work Research and Evaluation* (pp. 145–157). Birmingham: Venture Press.

Usher, C. L. (2004). Measuring and evaluating effectiveness of services to families and children. In A. R. Roberts & K. R. Yeager (eds) *Evidence-Based Practice Manual: Research and outcome measures in health and human services.* New York: Oxford UP.

Vanstone, M. (1999). Behavioural and cognitive interventions. In I. Shaw & J. Lishman (eds) *Evaluation and Social Work Practice.* London: Sage.

Walter, I., Nutley, S., Percy-Smith, J., McNeish, D., & Frost, S. (2004). *Improving the Use of Research in Social Care Practice.* London: Social Care Institute for Excellence.

Whitmore, E. (1994). To tell the truth: Working with oppressed groups in participatory approaches to inquiry. In P. Reason (ed.) *Participation in Human Inquiry.* London: Sage.

Whitmore, E. (2001). People listened to what we had to say. In I. Shaw & N. Gould *Qualitative Research in Social Work.* London: Sage.

Wilson, K., Petrie, S., & Sinclair, I (2003). A kind of loving: a model of effective foster care *British Journal of Social Work,* 33(8), 991–1003.

EVALUATION IN CRIMINAL JUSTICE

Nick Tilley and Alan Clarke

Introduction

The Focus of Evaluation Activity in Criminal Justice

Potentially there are a whole host of evaluation interests within the criminal justice system. For example, one could investigate the nature and level of victim satisfaction; explore issues of equity in criminal justice agency responses to victims and offenders according to age, ethnicity, gender or social class; study the quality of meals provided for prisoners; evaluate the effectiveness of execution methods; or examine the employment conditions and working practices of criminal justice personnel. However, as evaluation resources largely come from state agencies, both the scale and focus of evaluation activity tend to reflect their interests. Consequently, in practice, most evaluation efforts have been rather more sharply focused on the effectiveness of state-supported efforts at controlling crime and criminality. This preoccupation clearly reflects the major concerns of the state with social control and the preservation of order, albeit that this interest is often shared by the wider citizenry.

When the focus of evaluation is on justice this again tends to reflect state interests. The concept of "justice" is obviously a matter of philosophical debate. How it is understood can vary in practice with implications for criminal justice policies. At the time of writing, in Britain concerted efforts are being made to "close the justice gap" (Home Office, 2002). "Closing the justice gap" refers to an increase in the number of "crimes brought to justice", where "bringing a crime to justice" is understood to mean detecting it and applying a sanction, to wit holding someone formally to account for the incident. This way of construing justice is a rather particular one. Other senses – for instance non-conviction of the innocent, respect for citizen and offender rights, sentencing consistency and proportionality, even-handed application of the law to differing sections of the population, remedying inequitable social inequalities, and so on – are arguably just as, if not more, important but they are less pressing for the government in power. Evaluation resources are being devoted to means of "closing the justice gap", rather than to the achievement of other senses of justice, thus reflecting political priorities of the moment.

The current Scope of Evaluation Activity in Criminal Justice

Broadly construed, there is currently a wide range of types of evaluation activity directed at criminal justice agencies, only some of which comprise systematic studies by social scientists. In the United Kingdom, official inspectorates for the police, prisons and probation services all monitor, assess and report regularly on the activities of their constituent organizations, and the policies, programmes and practices operating within them. The modern movement towards performance management in public sector agencies has involved much target setting and use of performance indicators in efforts to track the chief outputs and outcomes of all criminal justice agencies. Much programme-related grant-giving in the UK is contingent on the production of evaluation reports, and many of these are fashioned by programme personnel themselves or those contracted by them. Treasuries concerned with maximizing the utility from public expenditure are requiring evaluation evidence of impact as a condition for new allocations and continued allocations of taxpayers' money. The Home Office in England and Wales, the National Institute of Justice in the United States and the Australian Institute of Criminology in Australia comprise government organizations conducting or contracting systematic evaluations in the field of criminal justice. Finally, there are evaluations of areas of criminal justice activity, funded, for example, by charitable foundations or national research bodies with some independence from the state.

Discourse about "evidence-based policy and practice", and new public management emphases on target setting and performance management in criminal justice, as in other areas of public policy, have respectively led to an explosion of evaluation-related activity in the interests of lesson learning and managerial accountability. In England and Wales, for example, the largest ever programme of research in criminology was initiated to evaluate projects associated with the Crime Reduction Programme, which ran from 1999 to 2002, with a view to improving the long-term evidence base (see Bullock & Tilley, 2003; Homel et al., 2004; Hope, 2004; Hough, 2004; Laycock & Webb, 2003; Maguire, 2004; Raynor, 2004; Tilley, 2004a). Initially the programme was granted £250 million, 10 percent of which was set aside for evaluation. Thereafter an additional £150 million was added specifically for the installation of CCTV systems.

The advent of problem-oriented policing, developed originally by Herman Goldstein in the United States but now widely adopted elsewhere also, has focused attention on evaluation as a routine activity (Goldstein, 1979, 1990; Read & Tilley, 2000; Scott, 2000). Eck & Spelman (1987) conducted an influential demonstration project in Newport News, Virginia, implementing problem-oriented policing. They devised "SARA" as an acronym to describe the processes gone through. SARA refers to Scanning, Analysis, Response and Assessment. Police officers are enjoined to identify recurrent problems, to analyze them, to devise strategies to remove or ameliorate them, and to assess their effectiveness. Evaluation activity is thereby built into problem-oriented policing.

The growing number of evaluation studies raises questions about syntheses of findings, and interest in this has been growing. The Campbell Collaboration, established for social policy in the wake of the counterpart Cochrane Collaboration for health and medicine, has a strong criminal justice presence (Farrington & Petrosino, 2001). The aim of the Campbell Collaboration is to capitalize on the findings from rigorous studies, to distil what has been learned.

The growth in evaluation has also drawn a wide range of persons and organizations into the conduct of evaluation in criminal justice. Those involved range from university departments, independent research consultancies, central government researchers, local agency researchers, past and present officials of various sorts, and practitioners. Most criminal justice agencies now devote resources to evaluating their own effectiveness, in part because this has become a condition for much funding.

Following the main emphasis in published findings, this chapter will focus on evaluations concerned with assessing the effectiveness of crime control measures. The next section briefly describes the broad types of policy, programme and practice that aspire to produce such control, and identifies some key issues of which the evaluator needs to be aware.

Evaluating Crime Control Policies, Programmes and Practices

Crime-control policies, programmes and practices fall into three main areas. These relate to *crime event* patterns and their futures, *potential offenders* and their future criminality, and *known offenders* and their future criminal behaviour. This categorization roughly follows Brantingham & Faust (1976) and their distinction between primary, secondary and tertiary crime prevention initiatives. Interventions that directly address crime events seek to reduce the opportunities for committing crime; many of the measures taken are "place-focused" and

involve improved security and surveillance (Eck, 1997). In contrast, policies and programmes directed at potential offenders and known offenders can be loosely described as "people-focused". In the case of potential offenders the aim is to target young people with a high probability of developing a criminal identity. Mentoring programmes for youth at risk fall into this category (Grossman & Tierney, 1998; Tarling, Burrows & Clarke, 2001). As regards programmes for known offenders, many of these are "treatment-oriented" and include cognitive-behavioural interventions, such as the well-established Reasoning and Rehabilitation Programme developed in Canada in the 1980s (Ross & Fabiano, 1985; Ross, Fabiano & Ewles, 1988), which aim to prevent reoffending.

While the aim of crime reduction interventions is generally a simple one, evaluating the success of programmes, policies and practices can be a fairly complex undertaking for a number of reasons. First, there are very substantial measurement difficulties. Crime is committed covertly. Recorded crime data are a function of reporting and recording decisions. These can change over time and place. Moreover, crime definitions are also liable to change and vary. Clear-up rates for most crimes are low, making it impossible to depend on official figures about participation in criminal behaviour and rates of offending by individuals or groups. Also, clear-up rates in local areas can change significantly over time (Burrows et al., 2005). Survey measures may be used instead of official data, but they are also not without problems. Victimization surveys are subject to the normal problems of non-response. Though they can often be technically sophisticated, they still depend on respondent memory, and only cover subsets of offences. Perhaps most significantly there has been relatively little survey measurement of crimes against organizations, such as businesses, hospitals, schools, or central and local government departments and agencies. Self-report studies of offending behaviour can comprise an alternative to official figures but clearly depend on the honesty of respondents. Where programmes are directed at reducing the fear of crime, measurement problems are legion. Question ordering and phrasing experiments have uncovered substantial instabilities in measurement findings (Ditton et al., 1999a; 1999b). Where there is an economic dimension to an evaluation this may involve cost-effectiveness analysis (assessment of costs per unit of output or outcome) or cost–benefit analysis (a comparison of the costs of a programme to its [normally monetarized] benefits) (Stockdale, Whitehead & Gresham, 1999; Roman & Farrell, 2002). Valuing non-monetary benefits in monetary terms creates huge problems, whether the method is rooted in "willingness to pay" or "willingness to accept" terms. The costing of inputs has in practice proved very difficult and quite arbitrary (for discussions see Adams, 1995; Stockdale & Whitehead, 2003; Farrell, Bowers & Johnson, 2005). So, whether the outcome of interest is crime events, criminal behaviour, victimization, costs and benefits, or impact of crime, measurement problems present significant and substantial problems.

A second issue is that interpreting observed changes in crime rates and patterns of criminal offending is also fraught with difficulties. Projects are often initiated in response to rising crime levels, raising the possibility of regression to the mean where rates are seen to fall. In local areas substantial pseudo-random year-on-year fluctuations in crime levels can occur, presumably due to local circumstances, though the nature of these is often unknown. Crime often follows seasonal patterns, creating some difficulties in interpreting short-term changes. Also, local areas are at the mercy of a whole host of external influences liable to affect criminality and crime patterns: these include transport changes, new commercial developments, alterations in economic conditions, and the migration of specific families and groups. These can all create problems in isolating specific intervention effects. Furthermore, low-dosage short-term programmes, such as national media campaigns about security behaviour, may create effects that prove very difficult to detect. Moreover, there are national and international crime trends which are at best only partially understood and add problems in discerning specific programme effects. For example, many western countries saw a fall in overall crime levels from the early to mid-1990s (Barclay & Tavares, 2003). Even understanding these in one country is fraught with difficulties (see the contributions to Blumstein & Wallman, 2000).

Thirdly, a particular crime prevention strategy may contain elements of more than one of the three broad approaches to crime control identified above. This could be part of a multi-modal, integrated strategy, where the efforts are implemented so as to complement one another. Take, for example, measures to address repeat victimization. Research findings across offence types and jurisdictions reveal that being a victim is a strong indicator of risk of revictimization (in particular in the short term), that repeat offences against the same target tend to be by the same offender, and that those same offenders tend to be prolific. Findings such as these can help to formulate a programme strategy that addresses both crime events and the identification and containment of high rate offenders (Chenery, Holt & Pease, 1997). Efforts to reduce subsequent crime events might include, in the case of domestic burglary, improvements to physical security or the mobilization of close neighbours to act as guardians. Efforts to inhibit prolific offending might involve the installation of CCTV and "forensic traps" to improve the prospects of detecting returning offenders. The simultaneous operation of measures liable to divert the offender and ones liable to catch those likely to return to a given address clearly potentially conflict with one another (see Tilley et al., 1999). Integrated strategies may involve stepped responses to an offence, beginning with efforts at diversion and then moving to efforts at detection, and/or they may involve case-by-case decisions about which approach to take. Identifying the patterns of interaction between the different elements of a programme and establishing which measures are responsible for any observed changes can cause enormous difficulties in evaluations.

Fourthly, as with other social interventions, consideration needs to be given to unintended as well as intended outcomes. One of the most frequently discussed side-effects is the displacement of crimes (see Hamilton-Smith, 2002). Where the aim is to reduce the number of crime events without addressing the criminality of those who would otherwise commit them, displacement of those offenders may occur in a number of directions. There may be geographic displacement of the same type of offence, displacement to a different type of crime, displacement to a different method of committing the same crime, displacement by time, displacement by target or a mix of these (Reppetto, 1976). Mirroring these potential (negative) displacement side-effects are potential (positive) diffusion of benefit effects (Clarke & Weisburd, 1994). These relate to crime prevention effects beyond the operational range of measures introduced. There may be temporal, spatial, target, tactic and offence-type diffusion of benefit effects or a mix of them. In any given programme, policy or practice, of course, displacement and diffusion of benefit may both occur at the same time. Net effects are a function of main effects and side-effects (Clarke & Eck, 2003).

Side-effects may equally be produced in criminal justice policies, programmes and practices designed to prevent the emergence of criminality or contain or treat the criminality of existing offenders. Labelling effects for those identified as offenders or likely offenders may create or confirm deviant identities or close opportunities for participation in legitimate activities (Wilkins, 1964; Young, 1971; Cohen, 1972). Techniques for committing crime may be transmitted where offenders are brought together (cf. Ekblom & Tilley, 2000). Similarly, offenders may learn how to justify their criminal behaviour through the application of "techniques of neutralization" (Matza, 1964).

Finally, initiatives to tackle crime and criminality can focus on individuals, groups or areas as targets for intervention. These targets can include people, households, properties, businesses, residential streets, neighbourhoods, cities or regions. Given such a diverse range of targets, the units of analysis for evaluation can vary in quite complex ways, which has methodological implications when it comes to assessing the overall effectiveness of a crime reduction scheme or series of schemes.

None of these difficulties is fatal for the conduct of outcome-focused evaluation studies but they require technical skills and fine judgment if findings are not going to be misleading. Few, if any, lay evaluations without the benefit of professional advice fail to fall into one or more serious technical traps. The British Safer Cities Programme, which ran in Britain from 1988 to about 1993, required evaluations of every individual initiative, of which there were some 3,500 in all. Almost every evaluation was conducted by local practitioners, with the result that little was produced that was capable of withstanding critical scrutiny. As Ekblom & Pease commented more generally, "Crime prevention has been dominated by two evaluative traditions and a great deal of self-serving unpublished and semi-published work that does not meet even the most elementary criteria of evaluative probity". (Ekblom & Pease, 1995, pp. 585–586). While there may be a great deal to commend participatory, community or practitioner evaluation, on the grounds of economy and self-learning, these approaches are unlikely to deliver robust outcome-focused findings.

Evaluation in Criminal Justice

What Works?

There are deep methodological divisions in relation to systematic criminal justice evaluations. For example, when it comes to establishing "what works" in terms of rehabilitative programmes, treatment initiatives and crime reduction strategies, there are enthusiastic advocates of experimental approaches (Feder & Boruch, 2000; Welsh & Farrington, 2001) and critics who maintain that "the experimental paradigm constitutes a heroic failure" (Pawson & Tilley, 1997, p. 8). The evaluation of criminal justice interventions using experimental methods has a long history in the United States, where randomized controlled field experiments have been used to study a range of topics including delinquency prevention programmes (Powers & Witmer, 1951; McCord & McCord, 1959), effectiveness of offender rehabilitation (Lipton, Martinson & Wilks, 1975), prevention of intimate partner violence (Sherman, 1992) and costs and benefits of intensive probation for drug offenders (Petersilia & Turner, 1993). Despite the support for experimental methods, randomized experiments in criminal justice are relatively uncommon (Weisburd, 2000) and only a small proportion of the published research in criminology involves studies where cases have been randomly assigned to treatment or control groups (Garner & Visher,

2003). As noted by one observer, "The history of the use of randomized experiments in criminology consists of feast and famine periods and a few oases [clusters of experiments] in a desert of nonrandomized research" (Farrington, 2003a, p. 219). Nevertheless, in the United States, the experimental approach has long been and continues to be the dominant methodological orthodoxy. There is a broad consensus that randomized experiments comprise the "gold standard" against which all other evaluation methods are to be judged. In a comprehensive report for the US Congress, published in 1997, on "what works, what doesn't, what's promising and what's unknown" in crime prevention, the lead author, Lawrence Sherman, presents the Maryland Scale of Scientific Methods against which individual studies can be judged:

1. Correlation between a crime prevention program and a measure of crime or crime risk factors.

2. Temporal sequence between program and the crime and risk outcome clearly observed, or a comparison group present without demonstrated comparability to the treatment group.

3. A comparison between two or more units of analysis, one with and one without the program.

4. Comparison between multiple units with and without the program, controlling for other factors, or a non-equivalent comparison group has only minor differences evident.

5. Random assignment and analysis of comparable units to program and comparison groups. (Sherman, 1997, p. 18)

The gold standard is the randomized control trial (RCT), which occupies Level 5 on the scale: the order of the methods that follow is basically shaped by the extent to which they approximate the RCT (Farrington et al., 2002). These five criteria also feature in other similar attempts at identifying a hierarchy of research evidence (Mihalic et al., 2001; US Department of Justice, 2004).

Outside the US, experimentalism in criminal justice evaluation has not been assumed to constitute an unequivocal gold standard in quite the same way, and there have been far fewer studies that would warrant a score of 5 on the Sherman scale (Harper & Chitty, 2005). Indeed, it has been noted by Farrington that the use of randomized experiments in Great Britain has actually "declined in the past twenty years" and "hardly any have been carried out since my review in 1983" (Farrington, 1983; Farrington, 2003b, p. 151). Several scholars have credited Ronald Clarke for this dearth of RCT experimental evaluations, and his influence is thought to have extended further afield (Farrington, 2003a; Nuttall, 2003; Weisburd, 2003). Clarke has been one of the half-dozen most influential criminologists in the world over the past 30 years, responsible both for a major paradigm shift in the discipline and for alterations in policy premises. He also headed the Home Office Research and Planning Unit for a period, the body that either conducts or funds most criminal-justice-related evaluation research in the UK. Both by status and by position Clarke has wielded enormous influence. He was committed to randomized experiments when he first arrived at the Home Office but his experience in an experiment at Kingswood training school led to him doubting the value of this methodological approach. The Kingswood experiment was conducted over a five-year period (1965–1970) and was designed to ascertain the relative effectiveness of two treatment regimes for delinquent boys aged between 10 and 17 years (Clarke & Cornish, 1972). The study raised some ethical concerns, caused difficulties in the management and

organization of the service facilities, and encountered problems regarding treatment complexity and change; all in all making it impossible to interpret any findings meaningfully. The authors concluded that:

> [T]he controlled trial would seem to have a more limited function in penal research than has sometimes been ascribed to it in the past and certainly much more limited than in medicine . . . [I]t is . . . unlikely that its widespread use at present would significantly advance knowledge about institutional treatment . . . This assessment accords well with recent views (Weiss 1970 . . .) concerning the limited value of experimental designs in evaluating social action projects. Even in clinical trials, Oldham (1968) has recently expressed disappointment with their achievements . . . . (Clarke & Cornish, 1972, p. 21)

The power of these conclusions and Clarke's influential position is deemed to explain why experimental evaluation studies in the UK failed to achieve methodological hegemony as they did in the US, and why they still do not comprise the taken-for-granted gold standard in criminal justice evaluation studies. Though ignorant of Clarke & Cornish's arguments, Pawson & Tilley (1994, 1997, 1998) have more recently elaborated and generalized still further on the Clarke–Cornish critique, as will be described later.

A watershed in the development of criminal justice responses to crime occurred with the publication in 1974 of an article by Robert Martinson, entitled "What Works: Questions and Answers about Prison Reform" (Martinson, 1974). This reported a review of experimental evaluations that had been conducted at the time and concluded that interventions were unlikely to be effective in reducing the probability that existing offenders would reoffend (Lipton, Martinson & Wilks, 1975). It ushered in the pessimistic phrase, "nothing works".

Despite recantation by Martinson (1979), and sundry critiques of Martinson's conclusions (e.g., Palmer, 1975; Glaser, 1977), the phrase and the conclusion stuck. Alongside other (non-experimental) research findings that seemed to show little crime control benefit from police patrols (Clarke & Hough, 1984; Kelling et al., 1974), a sense that crime could not be controlled through the conventional responses of the criminal justice system grew. The belief that "nothing works" found support in the UK (Brody, 1976) and once the idea that treatment did not work took hold, the need for experiments to evaluate treatment was quickly dispelled (Nuttall, 2003).

By the late 1980s the "nothing works" doctrine was being challenged and the idea that "something works" was gaining currency among both practitioners and researchers. For example, Gendreau & Ross (1987) re-reviewed the evidence about the effectiveness of efforts at rehabilitation and came to roughly the opposite conclusion from that of Martinson in 1974. They concluded that almost everything worked. This apparent paradox can be resolved when we note that Martinson found that "nothing works" *all of the time*, whereas Gendreau & Ross found that (almost) everything works *at least some of the time*. It is scarcely surprising that few if any measures work with all people in all conditions. Whilst some measures may never work under any conditions, it also seems likely that most seriously developed and properly implemented measures will work with at least some people, in some contexts, at least some of the time. The key evaluation question becomes not simply "what works?" but "what works for whom and in what circumstances?"

Experimental Evaluation

Although experimental evaluation involves a simple logic, the practical application can be very complex. The simple logic is this. Create two equivalent groups or areas and undertake a "before" measurement in each. Apply the intervention, that is the policy, programme or practice, to only one of the two groups or areas, and then take an "after" measurement. Any difference in the change from first to second measurement in the intervention (experimental) group compared to the non-intervention (control) group is deemed to be attributable to the intervention. Where cases are randomly assigned to each of the two groups, as in RCTs, the research design is referred to as a "true experiment". In contrast, where non-random methods are used to create experimental and control groups, or where a control group is absent, the design is a quasi-experimental one (Taylor, 1994). On account of the existence of experimenter bias, subject expectation and the effects of measurement per se, in practice experimental designs are often more elaborate than suggested above. Nevertheless, the logic remains the same.

Advocates of experimental studies in criminal justice advance a number of points in favour of this methodology. First and foremost, experimental evaluations are deemed to be very strong on "internal validity". They rule out many alternative explanations of change in the experimental group through the process of random allocation. They ensure that the expected and intended cause of change precedes the effect by experimental manipulation, and that various threats to internal validity are minimized, including those deriving from: "selection" (pre-existing differences between experimental and control groups); history (an event occurring at the same time as the intervention); maturation (the continuation of pre-existing trends); and regression to the mean (the tendency of extreme conditions to revert to the underlying mean) (see Farrington, 2003c, drawing on Shadish, Cook & Campbell, 2002). By creating equivalent groups, it is deemed possible to disentangle the effects of the treatment from the confounding effects of other factors that might influence desired outcomes.

Second, it is claimed that experimental studies are well-suited to estimating effect sizes. Thus, they are able not only to identify that a particular effect was produced, but they can also give some indication as to the magnitude of the observed effect. This clearly promises to inform cost–benefit analyses since the intervention measures can be costed, as can any benefits (or disbenefits), so as to determine the net benefit accruing from a programme. It is the aspiration of experimental evaluations to inform resource allocation to programmes and interventions not only by establishing which initiatives are successful but also by identifying those that have yielded most benefit per costed (normally a monetary valuation) unit of intervention (see Welsh & Farrington, 1999).

Third, supporters of RCTs in criminal justice argue that the charge that this form of experimentalism is unethical is misplaced, since the effects of most interventions are not known (Weisburd, 2003). Consequently, the control group or area cannot be said to be disadvantaged where the benefits (or disbenefits) to the experimental group are unknown. Moreover, experimental trials are believed not only to sort out ineffective programmes and practices from effective ones, but also and more importantly to identify harmful ones. Notwithstanding the fact that programmes are initiated with the best of intentions, they have been found in various experimental studies to do more harm than good (McCord, 2003). Examples include the Drug Abuse Resistance Education programme, which involves police officers going into schools to deliver a series of classes aimed at increasing the capacity of children to say no to narcotics (Rosenbaum & Hanson, 1998; Illinois State Police, 1999) and Scared Straight, which

entails taking early delinquent youths into prison to talk to offenders to scare them into lawful behaviour (Petrosino et al., 2000). Weisburd maintains that the failure to utilize experimental techniques constitutes a serious violation of professional standards when he asserts that: "The ethical problem is that when choosing nonexperimental methods we may be violating our basic professional obligation to provide the most valid answers we can to the questions that we are asked to answer" (Weisburd, 2003, p. 350).

Limitations of Experimentalism

Doubts have been expressed about the limitations of experimental approaches (Weiss, 1970; Eck, 2002). In the main, it is the methodological requirements of the experimental design that have been highlighted by critics. The nature and setting of some criminal justice interventions can be problematic when it comes to maintaining the integrity of an experimental research design. As discussed by Clarke & Cornish (1972), interventions are often pitched at the level of the institution. Here difficulties can be encountered when attempts are made to employ methods of random allocation and conduct double-blind experiments so as to eliminate the effects of the conscious or unconscious expectations of either the experimenter or the subject. The practical problems are exacerbated when interventions are targeted at neighbourhoods or whole cities. Here the orchestration of programmes requires the cooperation and collaboration of local stakeholders, who cannot be kept unaware of the programme. There is also the possibility that programme leakage from experimental to control areas may occur, thus undermining the validity of local comparison sites. What can count as equivalent areas for comparative purposes is fraught with problems, and choices are normally made on an ad hoc basis using any data that are to hand.

Using techniques such as blind trials in an attempt to rule out the effects of the ways in which programme recipients see interventions is not only impractical but also fails to appreciate how criminal justice interventions produce their impacts. Take, for example, the case of property marking to reduce crime. As a measure it does not directly stop crime. The most obvious causal explanation is that marked property is avoided as it will be hard to dispose of, and that offenders stealing it will be more easily caught. However, it turns out that property has not been recovered, nor offenders caught. Furthermore, reductions in theft of unmarkable property have been as great as markable property where effects have been found. This gives rise to the hypothesis that it was the publicity given to the property marking scheme and an increased sense of risk amongst local offenders that explained the fall in crime (Laycock, 1997). Thus the desired effect was produced as a result of a change in reasoning by prospective offenders.

Any change in the policy context or alteration to the structure, implementation or delivery of an intervention programme during the experimental period can invalidate the scientific integrity of the research design. For example, in the TARP evaluation the decision to shorten the lengths of sentences for some prisoners led to a change in the profile of prisoners recruited into the experiment (Rossi, Berk & Leniham, 1980). In a more general sense, the social world within which policies are implemented and programmes operate is a volatile environment and change is commonplace. Moreover, the social world varies a great deal by place. These are good reasons why an effect found amongst one spatio-temporally specific group from which samples have been allocated randomly, or amongst one specific area compared with its counterpart, cannot be generalized to other groups and areas. Findings about effects are not generalizable across time, place and subgroup: external

validity should not be assumed. Indeed, mixed impact findings are the norm in evaluations in criminal justice, and have been found, for example, for lighting upgrades (Painter, 1995), property marking (Laycock, 1997) and arrest for misdemeanour domestic violence (Sherman, 1992). These variations are to be expected given the variability of and changes occurring in the social world. The effect size found in any particular study is quite arbitrary. It cannot validly be used in economic models, as a basis for projecting expected utility. Averages across series of studies risk simply reflecting attributes of the particular sites selected for investigation.

The complexity of the social contexts in which criminal justice interventions are evaluated makes it difficult to establish internal validity and the situation is made more complex where multifaceted programmes incorporating a variety of potentially change-inducing initiatives are concerned. Drawing inferences from experimental findings is not a straightforward matter. Although results may indicate that the overall change in an experimental area is appreciably different from the change in a control area, it may not be possible to identify exactly what it was about the programme that brought about the observed effects. In area-based initiatives, where rates of crime fluctuate on a pseudo-random basis in the short timeframe on which most initiatives are measured, the difference in change between the experimental and control or comparison areas can be quite arbitrary (Marchant, 2004).

Clearly there are limitations to the use of experimental methods in criminal justice contexts. According to Eck (2002) the methodology adopted is critical to the nature of the intervention and the purpose of the evaluation. If what is contemplated is a standard response to be widely implemented, then raw estimates of net effects may make sense, since the variations in effect by subgroup are unimportant as there will be no scope for variations in the policy or practice by subgroup. In this context using experimental methods for looking at undifferentiated net effects may be appropriate. Where discretionary responses are counterproductive (as is evidently the case with some sentencing practices) a policy of standardized responses, with reduced net harm or increased net benefits, makes sense (cf. Tonry, 2004). Furthermore, if "uniformity of the social" across time comprises a reasonable assumption, past findings with internal validity may be reasonably dependable and make best sense. Even here, though, if refinements to the policy or practice are contemplated, some of the weaknesses in experimental methods may compromise the utility of evaluation findings. Where discretion is used or is on the cards, different approaches may be appropriate. Clarke & Eck (2003) have provided practical advice on how these may be conducted in relation to problem-solving efforts and local crime prevention.

Realist Evaluation

Realist evaluation endeavours to make good the shortcomings in "experimentalism" (Pawson & Tilley, 1992, 1997, 2004). Realists attempt to understand how interventions work by uncovering "context–mechanism–outcome pattern configurations". These assume a different meaning of causality from that taken for granted in experimental evaluation. Experimental evaluation assumes a "constant conjunction" or *successionist* account, in which causality is represented as an observable, sequenced association between events. In contrast, realist evaluation assumes a *generative* interpretation of causality, in which the activation of causal powers is required to produce patterned responses. Moreover, realist accounts acknowledge the importance of context by recognizing that the same measure may activate different causal powers in different settings and amongst different subgroups,

thereby producing different outcomes. Thus, programmes or interventions are not seen as externally imposed forces that simply elicit responses from subjects. Indeed, "it is not actual programmes which 'work' but the reasoning and opportunities of the people experiencing the programmes which make them work" (Pawson & Tilley, 1993, p. 2).

The primary objective of realist evaluations is to discern, test and refine context–mechanism–outcome pattern configurations. These comprise middle-range (neither locally specific nor unconditionally universal) testable theories linking types of condition and types of mechanism that generate specific outcome "footprints" (see Pawson, 2000; Pawson & Tilley, 2004).

The application of realist thinking can be illustrated with reference to an experimental evaluation designed to test the effectiveness of the use of arrest as a means of reducing misdemeanor domestic violence (Sherman, 1992). The study produced mixed findings and the variations in outcome were interpreted after the event as possibly due to some arrestees responding with anger rather than shame. Plausibly anger fuels violence, while shame may act as an inhibitor. It was conjectured that those perpetrators who were socially integrated, with jobs and membership of stable communities were more likely to respond by being shamed, whilst those who were socially detached, unemployed and living in fractured communities were more likely to display anger. This being the case, net effects in given cities will be a function of the balance of community characteristics and resident attributes. Such post hoc efforts to make sense of mixed findings and attempt to explain variations in the impact of a programme on particular subgroups are commonplace in many experimental studies.

From a realistic perspective such explanatory work, that is, identifying potential context–mechanism–outcome configurations, constitutes

EXEMPLAR 23.1 Context–mechanism–outcome conjectures from realistic evaluation workshop

Mechanism	Context	Data to test expected outcome pattern
Women's shame	Membership of "respectable" knowing community	Reduced levels of reporting of incidents amongst those with close attachments to communities valuing traditional family life
Women's fear of recrimination	History of violence; culturally supported violence; alcoholism of offender	Reduced levels of reporting incidents amongst chronically victimized
Women's fear of loss of Partner	Emotional or financial dependency on partner	Reduced level of reporting amongst poorer and emotionally weaker women
Women's fear of children being taken into care	Pattern of general domestic violence against whole family	Reduced level of reporting amongst families known to social services
Women's empowerment	Availability of refuges; support for women; financial resources of women	Increased levels of separation where support and alternative living arrangements available
Incapacitation of offender	Length of time held	Short-term reductions in repeat incidents
Offender shame	Membership of "respectable" knowing community	Reduced repeat violence within "respectable" communities
Offender anger	Cultural acceptability of male violence to women; what man has to lose from brushes with the law	Increased levels of violence amongst those violence-sanctioning communities marginal to mainstream society
Offender shock	Offender attachment to partner; self-image as law-abiding respectable person	Reduced levels of violence, and help-seeking behaviour amongst short-tempered "respectable" men
Changed norms about propriety of domestic violence	Positive publicity	Reduced levels of reported and unreported violence

Source: Tilley (2000a, p. 106)

theory-building and should precede the evaluation. In this way, ideas about how interventions might work, for whom and in what circumstances can be developed and used to identify what needs to be measured. These ideas can come from a myriad of sources. Table 23.1 summarizes the responses of participants in an evaluation workshop when asked to describe how various stakeholders might be expected to interact with or respond to mandatory arrest by police patrols in domestic violence incidents (Tilley, 2000a). A realist evaluation would build on this, or something like it, drawing on literature, social science theory and expert opinion, to develop a testable theory or set of theories of responses to mandatory arrest. This theory-driven approach is designed to identify what it is about an intervention that makes it work. This differs markedly from the more method-driven approach characteristic of randomized controlled experiments, where it is not considered necessary to understand how an intervention works in order to estimate its net effects (Chen & Rossi, 1983). However, it does not necessarily follow that experimental methods have no contribution to make as part of a theory-informed evaluation. As Tilley notes, "quasi-experimentation may be harnessed to realistic purposes, where theory development has reached a point where context and mechanism specification is possible" (2000a, p. 108).

Evaluation Review

The debate between experimental and realist approaches to evaluation extends beyond individual studies to reviews of research that capture what can be learned from combining the findings from a number of studies (Pawson, 2006). The two approaches are agreed that individual studies alone can be misleading and that more can be gleaned from a series of studies on a common topic. However, in practice replication proves very difficult. What is deemed to comprise the "same" from programme to programme always involves an element of selection. Even when an intervention is part of a regional or national policy initiative exact duplication across all programme sites is impossible, there will be variation among programme participants, differences in programme implementation and local conditions will vary between sites. For example, Tilley (1996) examined in detail three supposed replications of what had been found to be a highly successful burglary reduction project on the Kirkholt housing estate in Rochdale in North-West England (Forrester, Chatterton, & Pease 1988; Forrester et al., 1990). He found considerable differences in terms of a number of features including programme budgets, the size of the estates, the measures put in place and the personnel involved. They were also associated with very different outcomes. Each "replication" had made different choices. None could be considered "wrong". Making choices was necessary and inevitable and involved a taken-for-granted theory of the project. This applies both with replication studies and research reviews. Explicitly or otherwise, some theory of the programme lurks behind both the practice of replication and the selection of cases for inclusion in a review.

Systematic reviews of experimental studies, of the sort undertaken by the Campbell Collaboration, tend to take programme definitions at face value but to lay great store on finding, selecting and including all studies that fit their quality standards. It is deemed important not to omit studies that are methodologically adequate by experimentalists' criteria, even if they have not been published in journals. There is a risk otherwise of "publication bias", whereby studies reporting positive effects tend to be published more often than those producing negative findings. Campbell Collaboration reviews summarize the findings across all identified studies meeting threshold design standards, and draw conclusions accordingly. For example, in the field of crime prevention, they have found positive effects for street lighting improvements (Farrington & Welsh, 2002) and negative ones for the Scared Straight initiatives (Petrosino, Turpin-Petrosino & Finckenauer, 2000).

Meta-analytic evaluation research strategies aggregate findings of experimental studies in the interests of finding statistically significant small effects that might not be revealed in individual studies with relatively small samples. They have also been able to disaggregate effects in some cases by subsets, in the interests, like the realists, of identifying variations in effects between subgroups. In this type of analysis reference is made to "mediators and moderators", rather than "mechanisms and contexts" (Petrosino, 2000; Lipsey, 2003; Farrington, 2003c). There are important differences in the meanings of these terms, though both acknowledge that effects are often contingent and are produced in different ways, and both recognize that this is important in informing policy and practice. The differences in the meanings of the terms are these: mediators refer basically to steps between measure and effect (think dominoes), whilst mechanisms refer to the forces that lie behind the steps (think of the physics behind dominoes toppling and knocking one another over); moderators refer to contingencies that may affect the relationship (or apparent relationship) between variables (think publication bias), whilst context refers to the necessary, though again empirically contingent, conditions for mechanisms to be activated (think of the conditions for shared meanings between interviewer and interviewee to be generated).

Systematic reviews in realist evaluation do not privilege experimental studies. A "realist synthesis" methodology uses sets of studies, adequate by whatever standards are appropriate to the methods used, to develop and test theories linking context, mechanisms and outcomes (Pawson, 2002a; Pawson, 2002b; Pawson, 2006). They may begin with a mechanism, as does Pawson (2002c) in a review of "shame" programmes, or with a form of intervention, as, for example, in the realist overview of Neighbourhood Watch by Laycock & Tilley (1995). Some reviews are problem focused, for example, there are over 20 policing problem-specific guides published by the United States Department of Government that follow a realist logic and splice together evidence from whatever credible sources (see, e.g., Clarke (2002) on burglary of retail establishments and Weisel (2002) on burglary of single-family households). In all cases a patchwork of context–mechanism–outcome patterns emerges to inform policy and practice. It is, from a realist point of view, a little ironic that some outstanding examples of overviews with a realist logic, drawing on diverse literatures, have been produced by some of the strongest advocates of experimental methods within the Campbell Collaboration. These include a study of crackdowns (Sherman, 1990; Tilley, 2004b), a study of displacement and diffusion of benefits by Weisburd (Clarke & Weisburd, 1994), and an overview of criminality development and its inhibition by Farrington (1996).

Qualitative Evaluation

Qualitatively oriented forms of inquiry offer distinct but coherent perspectives on policy, programme and practice evaluation. While qualitative outcomes may be included as part of a summative evaluation strategy, such methods are of particular relevance when it comes to explaining *how* specific interventions or programmes actually achieve (or fail to achieve) their desired outcomes. Qualitative or naturalistic methods bring an important dimension to evaluation research design by making it possible to examine the nature of process–outcome relations, identify unintended consequences, establish causal mechanisms and map out the temporal dimension of critical events. From the perspective of crime prevention programmes it is important not only to know which forms of intervention are most likely to be successful, but also to have some understanding of the extent to which they are likely to produce the desired effect in different situational contexts. Knowledge of the social processes underlying the formulation and implementation of primary crime prevention efforts can best be obtained by the use of qualitative research techniques (Crawford & Jones, 1996).

With tertiary crime prevention programmes, understanding something about the processes through which certain interventions work with certain types of offender is essential. Where quantitatively oriented experimental or quasi-experimental methodologies have been used in isolation to measure treatment effects the findings have been inconclusive. The evaluation of cognitive behavioural treatment programmes for convicted offenders provides a good example. In the case of North America, while some early studies suggest statistically significant reductions in recidivism (Robinson, 1995) more recent findings illustrate no significant treatment effects (Van Voorhis et al., 2004). Systematic evaluations of the effectiveness of prison-based cognitive skills programmes in the UK have produced mixed results ranging from a modest positive impact to no observed treatment effect (Cann et al., 2003; Friendship et al., 2003; Falshaw et al., 2004). Many of these experimental studies focused on reconviction or recidivism as the sole outcome measure, thus ignoring differences between individual participants in their response to treatment. From a qualitative perspective the motivation of individual programme participants can be seen to be a key factor in explaining treatment impact. The motivation for change is influenced by a complex combination of factors including the personal circumstances of the participant, the institutional context in which the programme is delivered and the

degree to which the individual engages with the programme. In an analysis of motivational accounts of prisoners participating in cognitive skills training, Clarke, Simmonds & Wydall (2004) identified four types of participant: the hostile participant; the instrumentalist; the sceptic; and the self-developer. The nature and type of motivation to change was observed as a key to understanding successful programme participation. For some prisoners participation in the programme was found to produce intermediate, non-reconviction benefits.

Given that recidivism is an imprecise measure, there is a case for developing a wider range of intermediate measures of individual change and programme effectiveness in order to begin to explain why certain interventions work with certain types of offenders. This will necessitate combining quantitative and qualitative techniques (Matthews & Pitts, 2000).

Ethical and Accountability Issues in Criminal Justice Evaluations

Methodological issues are not the only considerations in criminal justice evaluation. As with any social science research or evaluation activity there are also ethical issues to consider. Ethical debates in mainstream social research concerning informed consent, the safety and well-being of participants, invasion of privacy and the use of deception are highly applicable in evaluative contexts. Furthermore, given that many criminal justice evaluations are commissioned by state agencies, and actions and decisions can follow from evaluation findings, the whole process of evaluation takes place within a politicized environment. Evaluators need both to have due regard to the welfare of those involved in an evaluation and those likely to be affected by the results, and to confront issues to do with their relationship with those commissioning studies. It is to this latter point that we now turn.

As Eleanor Chelimsky has observed, "Telling the truth to people who may not want to hear it is, after all, the chief purpose of evaluation" (quoted in Patton, 1997, p. 361). Truth-telling can cause conflict in the relationship between evaluators and clients. There can be pressures to massage findings in the interests of "proving" that a particular practice, measure or policy was a success. Those asking for evaluations frequently give as a rationale for the work they commission, a desire for proof that they are being effective in the face of sceptics. There can be indignation if the results are not as expected, and efforts can be made to negotiate changes in the text and/or substance of a report. One of the authors of this chapter has encountered this directly several times. On one occasion he refused to have a report published because the proposed changes did violence to the findings, and on many other occasions felt uncomfortable that the "spin" given to the findings was liable to mislead. If evaluations in criminal justice are to be of any value, it is imperative that they tell the truth as the researcher finds it (and as verified by competent independent referees). If publicized findings are known or suspected to be mere rhetoric they lose any meaning or credibility. Popper refers to "truth-telling" as the "regulative principle" in science (Popper, 1972). The ease with which it is possible to generate appearances of achievement in criminal justice interventions through selective use of evidence suggests that this principle may be useful in evaluation studies also. The power that commissioners of evaluation often have over which findings are and are not disseminated produces a risk of publication bias. The evaluator can then face a dilemma... The evaluator can face a dilemma between allowing a half-truth to be released and insisting that no findings at all are released. The one "refuse to publish at all" response referred to above did not stop the commissioners selectively quoting from the unpublished report. Evaluator dependency on future research contracts may incentivize collusion with pressure to adjust findings in line with commissioner preferences (Tilley, 2000b).

Given the wider political agenda, much evaluation research is conducted, ostensibly anyway, partly to hold those spending public money to account for what they are doing. The asymmetrical power relationship between evaluation stakeholders in criminal justice contexts adds an interesting dimension to the issue of accountability. In reporting findings, external evaluators are formally accountable to those commissioning the work and are responsible for delivering to their contract. If they do not like the terms of the contract, they presumably should not agree to the work in the first place. For many internal evaluators employed in criminal justice agencies, the situation is not so simple. They are dependent on their employers, are often relatively junior members of staff and are consequently in a weak position when it comes to choosing what to work on, what issues to address and what methods to employ. Evaluators have an ethical obligation to use research methods that will yield robust findings and to make clear any uncertainties in the findings they report. Again, internal evaluators are poorly placed to exert influence in this context. There are also ethical issues around accountability where practitioners who are directly involved in programme delivery are also responsible for measuring programme effectiveness. This can be a particularly sensitive issue where future programme funding is dependent upon a positive summative evaluation.

The Futures of Evaluation in Criminal Justice

As Marx put it, "Men make history, but not in conditions of their own choosing". A criminologist expressed the same sentiment in more gender-neutral terms, when he claimed, "People make choices, but they cannot choose the choices available to them" (Felson, 1986, p. 119). This section describes the choices we would like to see shaping the future evaluation culture in criminal justice. The chapter ends with a brief, tentative comment regarding the conditions that seem likely to face those who will actually make the choices.

A Preferred Future

1. Clearer evaluation questions and more differentiated evaluation activities. Evaluation activity needs to be more clearly oriented toward the specific purpose at hand. Were these purposes to be identified, future evaluations would be better commissioned and more appropriately designed, and debate across evaluators advocating different methods would be less acrimonious. This would encourage the greater use of multiple methods and multiple data sources as and when the need arose.

2. Fewer, better focused evaluations. In the past ten years there has been little short of an avalanche of evaluation activity. However, much evaluation in criminal justice is technically poor by any standards (Ekblom & Pease, 1995). Consequently, the dividend, in terms of providing sound evidence to inform policy and practice, has been disappointing. A smaller number of highly focused evaluations might be better suited to guiding policy and practice. This is not to suggest that local, small-scale evaluations are of no use. Such studies can be important for the improvement of local initiatives, as long as they observe the appropriate methodological protocol.

3. More theory-driven evaluation. Much evaluation in criminal justice is currently method-driven and preoccupied with dealing with threats to internal validity. Because programmes are theories, albeit often poorly articulated, complex, and changing, there is a need for evaluations to become more theory-driven.

As Weiss observed, citing Kurt Lewin, there is "nothing as practical as good theory" (Weiss, 1995). Well-tested theories are transferable within specified limits. Evaluation will best inform development in criminal justice policy and practice by explicating, testing, refuting or refining the theories underlying programmes, practices and planned interventions.

4. More formative evaluation. The disappointing results from evaluations of many programmes in criminal justice seem to derive from badly designed, loosely conceived and poorly implemented initiatives. Policy and practice-literate evaluators have an important part potentially to play in articulating and scrutinizing programme theories and plans in order to make them operational.

5. More systematic reviews and syntheses. Before commissioning a new evaluation study, it will generally make sense to review thoroughly what has gone before, partly to ensure that there is no simple duplication, but more particularly so that the evaluation can be designed to test and refine hypotheses about *how* the programme produces its effects, if any, and amongst whom. The Specific Problem Cops Guides, produced by the US Department of Justice, provide good examples of structured overviews designed to inform practice.

6. Evaluation in series. In criminal justice, evaluations are characteristically commissioned as individual pieces of work. This is one reason why retrospective reviews have an important part to play. But planned series of evaluations where successive studies can build on and refine findings of earlier ones may be preferable. The best example possibly relates to the sequence of Home Office funded studies relating to repeat victimization and its prevention. This began with the Kirkholt Burglary reduction project already mentioned, but was succeeded by further studies relating to racial attacks (Sampson & Phillips, 1992), domestic violence (Lloyd, Farrell & Pease, 1994; Hanmer, Griffiths & Jerwood, 1999), commercial burglary (Tilley, 1993), crime against schools (Burquest, Farrell & Pease, 1992), and further work on burglary and vehicle crime (Anderson, Chenery & Pease, 1995; Chenery et al., 1997). Refinements were achieved in understanding repeat patterns and working out how to make use of them for preventive purposes (Laycock, 2001). The British series has been followed by further research in other countries, adding to a cumulative body of policy and practice knowledge (Farrell & Pease, 2001; Pease, 1998). The series of studies, developing, testing and improving theory, has been helpful in achieving external validity for findings, thereby offering greater security in the transferability of lessons for policy and practice.

7. Focus on large effects. There may be some benefit in trying to identify marginal net effects in large, relatively cheap universal programmes, such as crime prevention publicity campaigns. However, as a general rule, future evaluation in criminal justice should try to find large positive and negative effects. In criminal justice, net effects are mostly a function of the balance between large positive effects, large negative effects, and nil effects, rather than a result of widely spread small effects. Any crime committed or not committed on account of the programme comprises a large individual effect. The more closely we can circumscribe the subsets within which these large effects occur, the better we will understand the programme, and the better informed and targeted future policy and practice will become.

8. Increased evaluator policy-literacy and policy-maker research literacy. Many evaluators have little experience or understanding of the complexities and realities of criminal justice practice and programme delivery. Few policy-makers grasp what is involved in conducting evaluations and have a tendency to formulate questions that cannot be answered at all, or cannot be answered within the given research budget and the designated time scale. Growth in both the policy literacy of evaluators and the research literacy of policy-makers is essential if more usable evaluations are to be conducted and appropriate use is to be made of evaluation findings. Moreover, many of the ethical problems that arise in commissioning and conducting criminal justice evaluations could be reduced once a better mutual understanding is achieved (Laycock, 2002).

9. More action research. "What works" knowledge in criminal justice is quite rudimentary. Few practitioners or policy-makers have a firm grasp of the potential knowledge. So far as the latter are concerned there are chronic temptations to follow public opinion, and public opinion is often held strongly even where mistaken and confused (Tilley & Laycock, 2000). There have also been enormous implementation difficulties in many projects and programmes. Evaluator involvement in action research can be useful in forming programme theories clearly, in tracing through the steps involved in creating the expected changes, and in informing adjustments to the programme as it unfolds by tracking the supposed processes (Eck & Spelman, 1987; Forrester et al., 1988; Clarke & Goldstein, 2002; Matassa & Newburn, 2003). At the same time evaluators have the skills to measure effects. The risk, of course, is that the involved action-researcher loses independence and biased findings follow. Though expensive, this might tell in favour of a second evaluation team responsible for tracking effects independently, as suggested in Connell et al., (1995).

10. More independently funded evaluation. Evaluations always and inevitably cast their spotlight on particular features of programmes and particular putative outcomes; invariably the focus tends to reflect the priorities and pre-occupations of the funding body. Criminal justice evaluations tend to be government and agency funded; consequently, other orientations and interests risk being overlooked (McConville & Shepherd, 1992; Hillyard et al., 2004; Tonry, 2004). In the interests of public debate over policy and practice, the development of systematic evaluations from perspectives other than those of formal agencies and government departments is crucial.

As outlined in this preferred future for evaluation, in order to understand "what works" in crime prevention and criminal justice, evaluations need to focus both on aspects of implementation and outcome. The ultimate aim is to ascertain what effects (intended or unintended) specific interventions do or do not have on particular people or places and then explain *how* the significant outcomes are achieved. This requires a theory-driven focus and a bringing together of a variety of forms of evidence, using both quantitative and qualitative methods of data collection and analysis. In such a theory-driven approach no single method constitutes a gold standard, "the only methodological gold standard is pluralism" (Pawson & Tilley, 2001, p. 323).

Future Conditions

The future will be shaped by the interests of those with powerful voices in the policy-making and evaluation research communities, and by the influence of existing self-reproducing practices. There are also powerful processes of globalization that are already seeing a widely found expansion in evaluation organization and activity, which may lead to more substantial convergence over methods of evaluation in criminal justice.

There are many evaluators whose practices and methodological predilections would steer evaluation in a different direction from the ten-point wish list outlined above. In particular, the burgeoning Campbell Collaboration comprises a strong international movement that prefers and enthusiastically advocates American-style experimentalism, and may effectively make it difficult to resist, especially if key gatekeepers to funding and access become persuaded that it really does provide a gold standard.

Policy-makers commissioning evaluations are unlikely in the near future to become more research literate and are unlikely to cease having the interests they currently have in either shaping the evaluation agenda or exerting their influence over the presentation of research findings. Moreover, evaluation research does not enjoy high prestige and as commonly practised is unlikely to lead to fresh discoveries. As such it will compete with difficulty for research monies to fund thorough independent evaluations in criminal justice. Series of studies are expensive and are unlikely to attract funding.

Notwithstanding these rather unpropitious conditions for the improvement of criminal justice evaluation, what actually happens will be partly a function of the persuasiveness of arguments such as those presented in this chapter.

References

Adams, J. (1995). *Risk*. London: UCL Press.

Anderson, D., Chenery, S., & Pease, K. (1995). *Biting Back: Tackling repeat burglary and car crime*. Crime Detection and Prevention Paper 58. London: Home Office.

Barclay, G. & Tavares, C. (2003). *International Comparisons of Criminal Justice Statistics 2001*. Home Office Statistical Bulletin 12/03. London: Home Office.

Blumstein, A. & Wallman, J. (eds) (2000). *The Crime Drop in America*. Cambridge: Cambridge University Press.

Brantingham, P. & Faust, F. (1976). A conceptual model of crime prevention. *Crime and Delinquency*, 22, 284–296.

Brody, S. R. (1976). *The Effectiveness of Sentencing.* Home Office Research Study 35. London: Her Majesty's Stationery Office.

Burrows, J., Hopkins, M., Hubbard, R., Robinson, A., Speed, M. & Tilley, N. (2005). *Understanding the Attrition Process in Volume Crime Investigations.* Home Office Research Study 295. London: Home Office.

Bullock, K. & Tilley, N. (eds) (2003). *Crime Reduction and Problem-Oriented Policing.* Cullompton, Devon: Willan.

Burquest, R., Farrell, G., & Pease, K. (1992). Lessons from schools. *Policing*, 8, 148–155.

Cann, J., Falshaw, L., Nugent, F., & Friendship, C. (2003). *Understanding What Works: Accredited cognitive skills programmes for adult men and young offenders.* London: Home Office Research Findings 226. London: Home Office.

Chen, H. & Rossi, P. (1983). Evaluating with sense; the theory-driven approach. *Evaluation Review* 7: 283–302.

Chenery, S., Holt, J., & Pease, K. (1997). *Biting Back II: Reducing repeat victimisation in Huddersfield.* Crime Detection and Prevention Paper 82. London: Home Office.

Clarke, A., Simmonds, R., & Wydall, S. (2004). *Delivering Cognitive Skills Programmes in Prison: A qualitative study.* Home Office Research Findings 242. London: Home Office.

Clarke, R. (2002). *Burglary of Retail Establishments.* Problem-Oriented Guides for Policing Series No. 15. Washington DC: US Department of Justice Office of Community Oriented Policing Services.

Clarke, R. & Cornish, D. (1972). *The Controlled Trial in Institutional Research: Paradigm or pitfall for penal evaluators.* Home Office Research Study 15. London: Her Majesty's Stationery Office.

Clarke, R. & Eck, J. (2003). *Become a Problem-Solving Crime Analyst.* London: Jill Dando Institute of Crime Science.

Clarke, R. & Goldstein, H. (2002). Reducing thefts at construction sites: lessons from a problem-oriented project. In N. Tilley (ed.) *Analysis for Crime Prevention.* Monsey, NY: Criminal Justice Press.

Clarke, R. & Hough, M. (1984). *Crime and Police Effectiveness.* Home Office Research Study 79. London: Her Majesty's Stationery Office.

Clarke, R. & Weisburd, D. (1994). Diffusion of crime control benefits: observations on the reverse of displacement. In R. Clarke (ed.) *Crime Prevention Studies*, Volume 2. Monsey, NY: Criminal Justice Press.

Cohen, S. (1972). *Folk Devils and Moral Panics.* London: MacGibbon and Kee.

Connell, J., Kubish, A., Schorr, L., & Weiss, C (eds) (1995). *New Approaches to Evaluating Community Initiatives.* New York: Aspen Institute.

Crawford, A. & Jones, M. (1996). Kirkholt revisited: some reflections on the transferability of crime prevention initiatives. *Howard Journal of Criminal Justice*, 35(1), 21–39.

Ditton, J., Bannister, J., Gilchrist, E., & Farrall, S. (1999a). Afraid or angry? Recalibrating the "fear" of crime. *International Review of Victimology*, 6, 83–99.

Ditton, J., Farrall, S., Bannister, J., Gilchrist, E., & Pease, K. (1999b). Reactions to victimisation: why has anger been ignored? *Crime Prevention and Community Safety: An International Journal*, 1, 37–54.

Eck, J. (1997). Preventing crime at places. In L. Sherman, D. Gottfredson, D. MacKenzie, J. Eck, P. Reuter & S. Bushway, *Preventing Crime: What works, what doesn't, what's promising.* A Report to the United States Congress, Washington, DC: US Department of Justice.

Eck, J. (2002). Learning from experience in problem-oriented policing and situational crime prevention: the positive functions of weak evaluations and the negative functions of strong ones. In N. Tilley (ed.) *Evaluation for Crime Prevention.* Crime Prevention Studies, Volume 14. Monsey, NY: Criminal Justice Press.

Eck, J. & Spelman, W. (1987). *Problem-Solving: Problem-oriented policing in Newport News.* Washington DC: Police Executive Research Forum.

Ekblom, P. & Pease, K. (1995). Evaluating crime prevention. In M. Tonry & D. Farrington (eds) *Building a Safer Society.* Crime and Justice, Vol. 19. Chicago: University of Chicago Press.

Ekblom, P. & Tilley, N. (2000). Going equipped: criminology, situational crime prevention and the resourceful offender. *British Journal of Criminology*, 40, 376–398.

Falshaw, L., Friendship, C., Travers, R., & Nugent, F. (2004). Searching for 'What Works': HM Prison Service accredited cognitive skills programmes. *British Journal of Forensic Practice*, 6(2), 3–13.

Farrell, G. & Pease, K. (2001). *Repeat Vicimization*. Crime Prevention Studies, Vol. 12. Monsey, NY: Criminal Justice Press.

Farrell, G., Bowers, K., & Johnson, S. (2005). Cost-benefit analysis for crime science: making cost-benefit analysis useful through a portfolio of outcomes. In M. Smith & N. Tilley (eds) *Crime Science: New approaches to preventing and detecting crime*. Cullompton, Devon: Willan.

Farrington, D. P. (1983). Randomized experiments on crime and justice. In M. Tonry & N. Morris (eds) *Crime and Justice*, Vol. 4. Chicago: University of Chicago Press.

Farrington, D. P. (1996). The explanation and prevention of youthful offending. In J. Hawkins (ed.) *Delinquency and Crime*. Cambridge: Cambridge University Press.

Farrington, D. P. (2003a). A short history of randomized experiments in criminology: a meagre feast. *Evaluation Review*, 27(3), 218–227.

Farrington, D. P. (2003b). British randomized experiments on crime and justice. *Annals of the American Academy of Political and Social Science*, 589, 150–167.

Farrington, D. P. (2003c). Methodological quality standards for evaluation research. *Annals of the American Academy of Political and Social Science*, 587, 49–68.

Farrington, D. P. & Petrosino, A. (2001). The Campbell Collaboration crime and justice group. *Annals of the American Academy of Political and Social Science*, 578, 35–49.

Farrington, D. P. & Welsh, B. (2002). *Effects of Improved Street Lighting on Crime: A systematic review*. Home Office Research Study 251. London: Home Office.

Farrington, D. P., Gottfredson, D. C., Sherman, L. W., & Welsh, B. C. (2002). The Maryland scientific methods scale. In L. W. Sherman, D. P. Farrington, B. C. Welsh & D. L. MacKenzie (eds) *Evidence-Based Crime Prevention*. London: Routledge.

Feder, L. & Boruch, R. (2000). The need for experiments in criminal justice settings. *Crime and Delinquency*, 46, 291–294.

Felson, M. (1986). Linking criminal choices, routine activities, information control, and criminal outcomes. In D. Cornish & R. Clarke (eds) *The Reasoning Criminal*. New York: Springer-Verlag.

Forrester, D., Chatterton, M., & Pease, K. (1988). *The Kirkholt Burglary Prevention Project, Rochdale*. Crime Prevention Unit Paper 13. London: Home Office.

Forrester, D., Frenz, S., O'Connell, M., & Pease, K. (1990). *The Kirkholt Burglary Prevention Project, Phase II*. Crime Prevention Unit Paper 23. London: Home Office.

Friendship, C., Blud, L., Erikson, M., Travers, R., & Thornton, D. (2003). Cognitive behavioural treatment for imprisoned offenders: An evaluation of HM Prison Service's Cognitive Skills Programme. *Legal and Criminological Psychology*, 8, 103–114.

Garner, J. H. & Visher, C. A. (2003). The production of criminological experiments. *Evaluation Review*, 27(3), 316–335.

Gendreau, P. & Ross, R. (1987). Revivification of rehabilitation. *Justice Quarterly*, 4, 349–408.

Glaser, D. (1977). Concern with theory and correctional evaluation research. *Crime and Delinquency*, 23, 173–179.

Goldstein, H. (1979). Improving policing: a problem-oriented approach. *Crime and Delinquency*, 25, 236–258.

Goldstein, H. (1990). *Problem-Oriented Policing*. New York: McGraw-Hill.

Grossman, J. B. & Tierney, J. P. (1998). Does mentoring work? An impact study of the Big Brothers Big Sisters Progam. *Evaluation Review*, 22(3), 403–426.

Hamilton-Smith, N. (2002). Anticipated consequences: developing a strategy for the targeted measurement of displacement and diffusion of benefits. In N. Tilley (ed.) *Evaluation for Crime Prevention*. Crime Prevention Studies, Vol. 14. Monsey, NY: Criminal Justice Press.

Hanmer, J., Griffiths, S., & Jerwood, D. (1999). *Arresting Evidence: Domestic violence and repeat victimisation*. Police Research Series Paper 104. London: Home Office.

Harper, G. & Chitty, C. (eds) (2005). *The Impact of Corrections on Re-offending: A review of "what works"*, 2nd edition. Home Office Research Study 291. London: Home Office.

Hillyard, P., Sim, J., Tombs, S., & Whyte, D. (2004). Leaving a "stain upon the silence": contemporary criminology and the politics of dissent.' *British Journal of Criminology*, 44, 369–390.

Home Office (2002). *Narrowing the Justice Gap Framework*. London: Home Office.

Homel, P., Nutley, S., Webb, B., & Tilley, N. (2004). *Investing to Deliver: Reviewing the implementation of the UK Crime Reduction Programme*.

Home Office Research Study 281. London: Home Office.

Hope, T. (2004). Pretend it works: evidence and governance in the evaluation of the Reducing Burglary Initiative. *Criminal Justice*, 4, 287–308.

Hough, M. (2004). Modernisation, scientific rationalism and the crime reduction programme. *Criminal Justice*, 4, 239–253.

Illinois State Police (1999). *D.A.R.E.: Drug abuse resistance education*. Springfield, IL: Illinois State Police.

Kelling, G., Pate, T., Dieckman, D., & Brown, C. (1974). *The Kansas City Preventive Patrol Experiment*. Washington DC: Police Foundation.

Laycock, G. (1997). Operation Identification, or the power of publicity? In R. Clarke (ed.) *Situational Crime Prevention: Successful case studies*, 2nd edition. New York. Harrow and Heston.

Laycock, G. (2001). Hypothesis based research. *Criminal Justice*, 1, 59–82.

Laycock, G. (2002). Methodological issues of working with policy advisers and politicians. In N. Tilley (ed.) *Analysis for Crime Prevention*. Crime Prevention Studies Vol. 13. Monsey, NY: Criminal Justice Press.

Laycock, G. & Tilley N. (1995). *Policing and Neighbourhood Watch: Strategic issues*. Crime Detection and Prevention Series Paper 60. London: Home Office.

Laycock, G. & Webb, B. (2003). Conclusion: the role of the centre. In K. Bullock & N. Tilley (eds) *Crime Reduction and Problem-Oriented Policing*. Cullompton, Devon: Willan.

Lipsey, M. (2003). Those confounded moderators in meta-analysis: good, bad and ugly. *Annals of the American Academy of Political and Social Science*, 587, 69–81.

Lipton, D., Martinson, R., & Wilks, J. (1975). *The Effectiveness of Correctional Treatment: A survey of treatment evaluation studies*. New York: Praeger.

Lloyd, S., Farrell, G., & Pease, K. (1994). *Preventing Repeated Domestic Violence: A demonstration project in Merseyside*. Crime Prevention Unit Paper 49. London: Home Office.

Maguire, M. (2004). The Crime Reduction Programme in England and Wales: reflections on the vision and the reality. *Criminal Justice*, 4, 213–237.

Marchant, P. (2004). A demonstration that the claim that brighter lighting reduces crime is unfounded. *British Journal of Criminology*, 44, 441–447.

Martinson, R. (1974). What works? Questions and answers about prison reform. *Public Interest*, 35, 22–54.

Martinson, R. (1979). New findings, new views: a note of caution about prison reform. *Hofstra Law Review*, 7, 243–258.

Matassa, M. & Newburn, T. (2003). Problem-oriented evaluation? Evaluating problem-oriented initiatives. In K. Bullock & N. Tilley (eds) *Crime Reduction and Problem-Oriented Policing*. Cullompton, Devon: Willan.

Matthews, R. & Pitts, J. (2000). Rehabilitation, recidivism and realism: evaluating violence reduction programmes in prison. In V. Jupp, P. Davies & P. Francis (eds) *Criminology in the Field: The practice of criminological research*. London: Sage.

Matza, D. (1964). *Delinquency and Drift*. New York: Wiley.

McConville, M. & Shepherd, D. (1992). *Watching Police, Watching Communities*. London: Routledge.

McCord, J. (2003). Cures that harm: unanticipated outcomes of crime prevention programs. *Annals of the American Academy of Political and Social Science*, 587, 16–30.

McCord, W. & McCord, J. (1959). *Origins of Crime: a new evaluation of the Cambridge-Somerville Youth Study*,. New York: Columbia University Press.

Mihalic, S., Irwin, K., Elliott, D., Fagan, A., & Hansen, D. (2001). *Blueprints for Violence Prevention*. Washington, DC: US Department of Justice.

Nuttall, C. (2003). The Home Office and random allocation experiments. *Evaluation Review*, 27(3), 267–289.

Oldham, P. (1968). *Measurement in medicine*. London: English Universities Press.

Painter, K. (1995). An evaluation of the impact of street lighting on crime, fear of crime and quality of life. Unpublished Ph.D. thesis, Cambridge University.

Palmer, T. (1975). Martinson revisited. *Journal of Research in Crime and Delinquency*, July, 133–152.

Patton, M. Q. (1997). *Utilization-Focused Evaluation: The new century text*, third edition. Thousand Oaks, CA: Sage.

Pawson R. (2000). Middle range realism. *Archives Européenes de Sociologie*, XLI, 283–325.

Pawson, R. (2002a). Evidence-based policy: in search of a method. *Evaluation*, 8, 157–181.

Pawson, R. (2002b). Evidence-based policy: the promise of "realist synthesis". *Evaluation*, 8, 340–358.

Pawson, R. (2002c). Evidence and policy and naming and shaming. *Policy Studies*, 23, 211–230.

Pawson, R. (2006). *Evidence-Based Policy: A Realist Perspective*. London: Sage.

Pawson, R. & Tilley, N. (1992). Re-evaluation: rethinking research on corrections and crime. In S. Duguid (ed.) *Yearbook of Correctional Education*. Burnaby, BC: Simon Fraser University.

Pawson, R. & Tilley, N. (1993). OXO, Tide, brand X and new improved evaluation. Paper presented at the British Sociological Association Annual Conference, University of Essex, UK.

Pawson, R. & Tilley, N. (1994). What works in evaluation research? *British Journal of Criminology*, 34, 291–306.

Pawson, R. & Tilley, N. (1997). *Realistic Evaluation*. London: Sage.

Pawson, R. & Tilley, N. (1998). Caring communities, paradigm polemics, design debates. *Evaluation*, 4, 73–90.

Pawson, R. & Tilley, N. (2001). Realistic evaluation bloodlines. *American Journal of Evaluation*, 22(3), 317–324.

Pawson, R. & Tilley, N. (2004). Realistic evaluation. In S. Mathison (ed.) *Encyclopedia of Evaluation*. London: Sage.

Pease, K. (1998). *Repeat Victimisation: Taking stock*. Crime Detection and Prevention Series Paper 90. London: Home Office.

Petersilia, J. & Turner, S. (1993). Intensive probation and parole. In M. Tonry (ed) *Crime and Justice: A review of research*, Vol. 17, (pp. 281–335). Chicago: University of Chicago Press.

Petrosino, A. (2000). Mediators and moderators in the evaluation of programs for children. *Evaluation Review*, 24, 47–72.

Petrosino, A., Turpin-Petrosino, C., & Finckenauer, J. (2000). Well-meaning programs can have harmful effects! Lessons from experiments such as Scared Straight. *Crime and Delinquency*, 46, 354–379.

Popper, K. (1972). *Objective Knowledge: An evolutionary approach*. Oxford: Clarendon Press.

Powers, E. & Witmer, H. (1951). *An Experiment in the Prevention of Juvenile Delinquency: the Cambridge-Somerville Youth Study*. New York: Columbia University Press.

Raynor, P. (2004). "The probation service 'Pathfinders': finding the path and losing the way." *Criminal Justice*, 4, 309–325.

Read, T. & Tilley, N. (2000). *Not Rocket Science? Problem-solving and crime reduction*. Crime Reduction Research Series Paper 6. London: Home Office.

Reppetto, T. (1976). Crime prevention and the displacement phenomenon. *Crime and Delinquency*, 22, 166–177.

Robinson, D. (1995). *The Impact of Cognitive Skills Training on Post-Release Recidivism among Canadian Federal Offenders*. Ottawa, Canada: Correctional Service of Canada Research Division.

Roman, J. & Farrell, G. (2002). Cost-benefit analysis for crime prevention: opportunity costs, routine savings and crime externalities. In N. Tilley (ed.) *Evaluation for Crime Prevention*. Crime Prevention Studies, Vol. 14. Monsey, NY: Criminal Justice Press.

Rosenbaum, D. P. & Hanson, G. S. (1998). Assessing the effects of school-based drug education: A six-year multilevel analysis of project D.A.R.E. *Journal of Research in Crime and Delinquency*, 35(4), 381–412.

Ross, R. R. & Fabiano, E. A. (1985). *Time to Think: A cognitive model of delinquency prevention and offender rehabilitation*. Johnson City, Tennessee: Institute of Social Science and Arts.

Ross, R. R., Fabiano, E. A., & Ewles, C. D. (1988). Reasoning and rehabilitation. *International Journal of Offender Therapy and Comparative Criminology*, 32, 29–35.

Rossi, P. H., Berk, R. A., & Leniham, K. J. (1980). *Money, Work and Crime: Experimental evidence*. New York: Academic Press.

Sampson, A. & Phillips, C. (1992). *Multiple Victimisation: Racial attacks on an East London estate*. Crime Prevention Unit Paper 21. London: Home Office.

Scott, M. (2000). *Problem-Oriented Policing: Reflection on the first 20 years*. Washington DC: US Department of Justice, Office of Community Oriented Policing Services.

Shadish, W., Cook, T D. & Campbell, D. T. (2002). *Experimental and Quasi-Experimental Designs for Generalised Causal Inference*. Boston: Houghton Mifflin.

Sherman, L. (1990). Police crackdowns: initial and residual deterrence. In M. Tonry & N. Morris (eds) *Crime and Justice: A review of research*, Vol, 12. Chicago: University of Chicago Press.

Sherman, L. (1992). *Policing Domestic Violence: Experiments and dilemmas*. New York: Free Press.

Sherman, L. (1997). Thinking about crime prevention. In L. Sherman, D. Gottfredson, D. MacKenzie, J. Eck, P. Reuter & S. Bushway, *Preventing Crime: What works, what doesn't, what's promising*. A Report to the United States Congress, Washington DC: US Department of Justice.

Stockdale, J. & Whitehead, C. (2003). Assessing cost-effectiveness. In K. Bullock & N. Tilley (eds) *Crime Reduction and Problem-Oriented Policing*. Cullompton, Devon: Willan.

Stockdale, J., Whitehead, C., & Gresham, P. (1999). *Applying Economic Evaluation to Policing Activity*. Police Research Series Paper 103. London: Home Office.

Tarling, R., Burrows, J., & Clarke, A. (2001). *Dalston Youth Project Part II (11–14): An Evaluation*. Home Office Research Study 232. London: Home Office.

Taylor, R. B. (1994). *Research Methods in Criminal Justice*. New York: McGraw-Hill.

Tilley, N. (1993). *The Prevention of Crime Against Small Businesses: The safer cities experience*. Crime Prevention Unit Paper 45. London: Home Office.

Tilley, N. (1996). Demonstration, exemplification, duplication and replication in evaluation research. *Evaluation*, 2, 35–50.

Tilley, N. (2000a). Doing realistic evaluation of criminal justice. In V. Jupp, P. Davies & P. Francis (eds) *Doing Criminological Research*. London: Sage.

Tilley, N. (2000b). The evaluation jungle. In S. Ballantyne, K. Pease & V. McLaren (eds) *Crime Prevention: What works?* (pp. 115–130) London: IPPR.

Tilley, N. (2004a). Applying theory-driven evaluation to the British Crime Reduction Programme: the theories of the programme and of its evaluations. *Criminal Justice*, 4, 255–276.

Tilley, N. (2004b). Using crackdowns constructively in crime reduction. In R. Burke (ed.) *Hard Cop, Soft Cop*. Cullompton, Devon: Willan.

Tilley, N. & Laycock, G. (2000). Joining up research, policy and practice about crime. *Policy Studies*, 21, 213–227.

Tilley, N., Pease, K., Hough, M., & Brown, R. (1999). *Burglary Prevention: Early lessons from the Crime Reduction Programme*. Crime Reduction Research Series Paper 1. London: Home Office.

Tonry, M. (2004). *Punishment and Politics: Evidence and emulation in the making of English crime control policy*. Cullompton, Devon: Willan.

US Department of Justice (2004). *Implementing Evidence-Based Practice in Community Corrections: The principles of effective intervention*. National Institute of Corrections, Community Corrections Division, US Department of Justice. www.nicic.org/pubs/2004/019342.pdf.

Van Voorhis, P., Spruance, L. M., Ritchey, P. N., Listwan, S. J., & Seabrook, R. (2004). The Georgia Cognitive Skills Experiment: A replication of reasoning and rehabilitation. *Criminal Justice and Behaviour*, 31(3), 282–305.

Weisburd, D. (2000). Randomized experiments in criminal justice policy: prospects and problems. *Crime and Delinquency*, 46, 181–193.

Weisburd, D. (2003). Ethical practice and evaluation of interventions in crime and justice: the moral imperative for randomized trials. *Evaluation Review*, 27(3), 336–354.

Weisel, D. (2002). *Burglary of Single-Family Households*. Problem-Oriented Guides for Policing Series, No. 18. Washington DC: US Department of Justice Office of Community Oriented Policing Services.

Weiss, C. (1970). The politicisation of evaluation research. *Journal of Social Issues*, 26, 57–68.

Weiss, C. (1995). Nothing as practical as good theory. In J. Connell, A. Kubish, L. Schorr & C. Weiss, C (eds) *New Approaches to Evaluating Community Initiatives*. New York: Aspen Institute.

Welsh, B. & Farrington, D. (1999). Value for money? *British Journal of Criminology*, 43, 345–368.

Welsh, B. & Farrington, D. (2001). Toward an evidence-based approach to preventing crime. *Annals of the American Academy of Political and Social Science*, 578, 158–173.

Wilkins, L. (1964). *Social Deviance: Social policy, action and research*. London: Tavistock.

Young, J. (1971). *The Drug-Takers*. London: Paladin.

24

EVALUATION OF DEVELOPMENT INTERVENTIONS AND HUMANITARIAN ACTION

Osvaldo Feinstein and Tony Beck[1]

Introduction

Development evaluation is the evaluation of interventions such as projects, programs, policies, and processes whose general objective is to promote development. Thus, the evaluation of aid projects funded by external donors (the type of development evaluation that dominated development evaluation during several decades) is a specific type of development evaluation, which also includes the non-aid dimension of development, such as trade.[2] There are also development evaluations focusing on clusters of projects/programs by sector or theme (e.g., agricultural projects). In addition, by the second half of the 1990s, development evaluations started to focus on country-level programs, and since 2000 there have been some new evaluation efforts addressing global programs.

Not surprisingly, whereas development evaluation has been a marginal topic for associations of evaluators based in developed countries, such as the American Evaluation Association, the *practice* of development evaluation is the main concern of national associations of evaluators based in developing countries (several of which were established in the late 1990s and at the beginning of the twenty-first century). However, the discussion on development evaluation as a discipline has been rather absent in the discussions of national and regional associations, and it became the main focus of the recently created "International Development Evaluation Association" (IDEAS).[3]

Every day large-scale international humanitarian action is taking place in at least 20 and sometimes as many as 40 locations around the world. Occasionally, this hits the headlines, in particular where there are western foreign policy interests involved. Evaluation of humanitarian action (EHA) has become the main means of accounting for the effects of humanitarian action – to donors, executive boards of international agencies, and western publics. For example, the international response to humanitarian needs created by the 1999 conflict in Kosovo led to 16 formal evaluations (Wood, Apthorpe, & Borton, 2001); and the response in Afghanistan after 2001 has led to at least 15 evaluations.

Evaluation of humanitarian action tends to mirror humanitarian practice – it is often rushed, heavily dependent on the skills of its key protagonists, ignores local capacity, is top-down, and keeps an eye to the media and public relations implications of findings. In some ways, in particular in relation to the context in which much EHA takes place, it differs radically from mainstream evaluation. In other ways it resembles mainstream evaluation, for example an earnest attempt to improve the quality of programming combined with lack of attention to use of evaluation findings. Its subject matter is usually controversial, and often sensationalized by the western media – famine in Southern and the Horn of Africa, Rwanda, Hurricane Mitch, Kosovo, and in the early twentieth-century Afghanistan and Iraq.

After a discussion on the differences and similarities between evaluation of development and humanitarian action, the first part of the chapter will review current practices of development evaluation, including its different types and the way in which its practitioners have organized themselves, concluding with the challenges faced by development evaluators. The second part of the chapter is organized as follows. First, a background section provides a general overview of both humanitarian action and EHA, pointing out main trends. In the following section findings of the successes and failings of humanitarian

action, as reported in 215 evaluations carried out since 2000, are elaborated. After this there is a discussion of the quality of EHA, drawing on a meta-evaluation carried out on 127 evaluation reports between 2001 and 2003. The final section examines some recent and likely future trends in EHA.

Differences and Similarities Between Development Evaluation (DE) and the Evaluation of Humanitarian Action (EHA)[4]

One important difference between DE and EHA is that whereas in development evaluation "sustainability" (i.e., the continuation of the effects of the development interventions after they are completed) matters, in humanitarian actions what is crucial is "effectiveness" or "efficacy" (the extent to which the objectives were achieved). Humanitarian actions have been more effective in achieving their short-term objectives, whereas longer-term objectives correspond more to development actions. EHA bears some similarities to development evaluation, in particular the use of procedures and tools such as document review, structured and semi-structured interviews, surveys and focus groups. While some agencies, for example, WFP and UNHCR, deal almost exclusively with emergencies, others such as UNICEF and many NGOs work in both emergencies and development situations, so that their evaluation offices cover both areas of work.

However, there are two substantial differences between EHA and DE. First, humanitarian agencies operate within a "humanitarian space" that may be constrained by deliberately restricted access (roadblocks, attacks on aid convoys and personnel) as well as access being restricted through poor infrastructure and seasonal climatic factors. The population being assisted may be subject to a range of human rights abuses and exclusion from accessing basic services by the armed forces and groups directly involved in the conflict or by others exploiting the breakdown of law and order. All of these areas need to be considered in EHA.

Second, key information on a range of matters of vital significance to evaluators is often unavailable. Whilst evaluators of development programs are also often faced with a lack of information on key indicators or decisions, such problems are considerably more serious in the case of EHA. Staff turnover, and the difficulties of accessing key data in areas such as mortality and morbidity, mean that EHA is at a considerable disadvantage when attempting to draw conclusions about interventions.

Current Practices of Development Evaluation

Purposes and Roles of Development Evaluation

There is a growing consensus[5] that development evaluation should serve both an accountability and a learning role. Though, early on, non-governmental organizations (NGOs) emphasized the learning role of evaluation, they have been under pressure to use evaluation also for accountability. To some extent this has also been the case with bilateral agencies (i.e., those corresponding to the aid agencies of developed countries' Ministries of Foreign Affairs), whereas the purposes of evaluation in international financial institutions evolved in a rather symmetric way, from an initial emphasis on accountability to a more balanced approach combining evaluation for accountability and for learning.

It is worthwhile to note that there are different views as to the relation between the learning and the accountability function of evaluation in the development evaluation context. Thus, whereas there is a widespread perception that there are trade-offs between the learning and the accountability function, an alternative conception has emerged by which learning and accountability are seen as complementary. In this view, accountability provides the incentive framework for learning, if there is an "accountability for learning,"[6] i.e., for using lessons learned from experience to improve the design and implementation of development interventions. An organizational solution to the "trade-off" (or dilemma) has been to leave the accountability function to auditors and the learning function to evaluators.

Different Types of Development Evaluations

For the purposes of learning and accountability different types of development evaluations are conducted. Development evaluations can be classified in terms of what is being evaluated (their "object") and how the evaluation is carried out (their "approach"). According to their object, it is possible to distinguish between project or program evaluations (evaluations of single interventions, such as the evaluation of rural development projects[7]), sector or thematic evaluations (i.e., evaluations of a cluster of interventions corresponding to a sector – e.g., transport – or a theme – for example, the environment), country evaluations (which can correspond either to the evaluation of the country program supported by a development agency, or, to all development interventions in a country. The latter is a type of evaluation that very seldom has been carried out, and it could be led by the recipient country. A more recent type is the of global public policies and/or programs, which are evaluations of partnerships (e.g., the evaluation of agricultural research programs supported by several donors).

In terms of evaluation approaches, a widely used approach in development evaluation is "objectives-based evaluation," which takes into account the objectives of development interventions as the basis for the evaluation. It assesses the degree to which the objectives were achieved (the "efficacy" or "effectiveness" of the intervention), the relevance of the objectives, the efficiency in the use of resources and the sustainability of the interventions.[8] A problem faced by this type of evaluation is that the objectives of interventions are not always appropriately defined, thus affecting their evaluability, i.e., the extent to which an activity or a program can be evaluated in a reliable and credible fashion. In order to cope with this problem, the logical framework or the results chain is sometimes reconstructed[9] in order to identify the "results chain" and key indicators.

Another approach that has been used, which also helps to increase the evaluability of interventions, and that complements "objectives-based" evaluation, is the so-called "theory-based evaluation" (TBE). It makes explicit the assumptions of the intervention or its implicit "theory of change"[10] The example shown in Table 24.1 corresponding to an evaluation of social funds, shows the way in which TBE was used to identify the main channels through which social fund projects are expected to influence institutional development, and possible side-effects. By making explicit the assumptions the process of learning from experience is facilitated, as the evaluation serves to test the hypothesis and, therefore, to contribute to the stock of knowledge.

An alternative approach, not based on the objectives of the interventions, is "goal free evaluation" (an approach introduced in 1972 by Michael Scriven). In fact, one of the most influential development evaluations, Hirschman (1995) corresponds to this approach,[12] which tries to identify patterns of critical success factors and hidden rationalities in sets of projects. Another approach, which sometimes complements those mentioned before, is "participatory evaluation," which in the development evaluation field has been particularly used in rural and health projects and programs, facilitating the incorporation of the views of those that are evaluated and/or of the population for which the interventions are intended;[13] furthermore, participatory evaluation facilitates the empowerment of participants (indeed, there is an emerging field of "empowerment evaluation"), increasing the ownership (and thus the use of evaluations) by those that participate in the evaluation.

It is also worthwhile to point out that an approach that was thought not to be applicable in development evaluation, randomized control trials (RCT), has recently been considered the "gold standard" for evaluation, including impact development evaluation. Though there is some scope for randomization in development evaluation, there are also limits to its application in this area.[14] It is at the micro or project level where this approach is best used, particularly in terms of generating knowledge on what does and does not work (but it does not addresses accountability). At this level there is a growing number of applications of RCT (see the chapter by Duflo & Kremer in Pitman et al., 2004). However, randomized designs face problems of external validity (given that the context of specific interventions are often critical for the outcomes, thus limiting the value of RCT for "scaling-up" (on this and on limitations to "internal validity," as well as on other rigorous methods, see the comments by Martin Ravallion in Pitman et al., 2004). Furthermore, it is unlikely that RCTs can be applied at the macro level, such as in the evaluation of national policies, and in the evaluation of complex development issues where there are multiple changing factors that influence the object of the evaluation.

EXEMPLAR 24.1   Application of theory-based evaluation: framework for analysis of institutional development impact

Theory	Assumptions	Data required to test the assumptions
Main channels		
Direct effects	The social fund project includes a well-designed and effective institutional development component	Extent and quality of capacity building activities; Observed changes in organizational behavior/capacities
Demonstration effects	There is knowledge about social fund approaches/procedures among government agencies	Evidence of government agencies embracing social fund procedures
Learning-by-doing effects	Social funds involve government agencies in decision making/planning	Extent of adoption of social fund approaches by government agencies
Demand effects	Communities increase their demand for government services	Level and nature of community demands
Side-effects		
Resource-allocation effects	Social funds and other agencies compete for staff/resources	Movement of staff from government to social fund agency
Systemic budget effects	Social fund resources are off-budget and undermine accountability, reduce fiscal prudence and distort the budgetary allocation process	Procedures for budget accountability
Decentralization effects	Social fund strengthens or undermines investment planning/resource allocation	Relationship between the social fund agency and local government

Source: Carvalho & White (2004), table 2.[11] This useful typology of effects could also be applied in other evaluation contexts.

Joint Evaluations

For several years developing agencies have been trying to carry out joint evaluations, in order to diminish transaction costs for developing countries and to gain additional insights in terms of what works and what doesn't, and the reasons for the observed results, from joint assessments. Furthermore, to the extent that the recipient country participates in the evaluation, it is more likely that there will be ownership of the evaluation by the recipient country, and, therefore, it is more likely that the recommendations and lessons learned will be applied.[15]

However, the practice of joint evaluations has shown some difficulties in applying this approach. Nevertheless, progress has been made in some recent joint evaluations, particularly those in the area of basic education (under the leadership of the Evaluation Department of the Dutch Ministry of Foreign Affairs) and the evaluation of the "Comprehensive Development Framework," which was modeled following the example of the 1996 joint Rwanda evaluation (described in Dabelstein & Rebien (2002) and by Borton & Eriksson (2004); see also subsequently in this chapter), involving in its design and implementation representatives of recipient countries, multilateral development banks, bilateral development agencies, international NGOs, and the private sector. A 30-member, multipartner steering committee and a five-member management group governed the evaluation.

Though joint evaluation efforts have focused on producing single evaluation reports, an approach that is emerging is to place emphasis on joint evaluation processes rather than only on its final product or outcome. In this way opportunities for valuable joint evaluation work can increase (e.g., joint case studies or joint surveys) even if a final single evaluation report cannot be produced (given, among other reasons, the different timeframes and audiences that evaluation partners have to take into account, which in some cases may not allow for the production of a timely single report).[16]

and promote the development of evaluation capacities in developing countries. These capacities, not only to conduct but also to manage evaluations, are crucial in order to promote ownership of evaluations and to facilitate their use. An interesting case is Chile, where during three decades a public sector evaluation system has evolved, outsourcing evaluations to the private sector and to universities (through a system of competitive bidding). The Chilean evaluation system takes into account the demands from the Parliament in establishing the evaluation program, and it has become a model that some countries in the developing world are using as a source of inspiration.

It is worthwhile to mention the four-week international program for development evaluation training (IPDET), launched in 2000, designed originally by the World Bank's Operations Evaluation Department, and since then delivered annually by an international faculty, at Carleton University, Canada. Furthermore, tools have been designed for systematic diagnosis of evaluation capacities at the country level, which are useful to identify suitable actions to address the critical constraints.[17] Finally, it should also be taken into account that, as in other areas, "learning-by-doing" plays an important role in developing evaluation capacities, and providing opportunities to do evaluations is therefore a way to provide opportunities to learn.

Capacity Building for Development Evaluation

One of the constraints for conducting joint evaluations that include recipient country representatives is the limited evaluation capacity available at the country level. Though in some cases there are potential evaluation capacities in developing countries that can be mobilized (a "potential supply"), generally there is need to level the playing field,

The Future of Development Evaluation

Challenges and New Directions

New modalities of development aid, such as those involving a common pool of resources by several donors ("basket funding," such as in "sector-wide approaches" or SWAPs, which instead of focusing on individual interventions in specific sectors deal with sectors – such as education – as a whole, with a comprehensive approach), pose new challenges for evaluators. Thus, the attribution of results to a program funded by a single donor, which is never an easy task, is made even more difficult when several donors fund jointly the same program. An approach that has been suggested to face this challenge, and which is gaining increasing support, is to focus on "contribution" rather than on "attribution," trying to identify the contribution of each development partner to the development results. However, this may be only a way to relabel the problem, as "contribution" may be equivalent to "marginal attribution," and it does not actually solve the attribution problem. Another approach is to "dissolve" the problem, focusing on other issues such as the governance of partnership programs, and/or to focus on the results of the development aid system as a whole. Of course, harmonization of evaluation practices would facilitate this type of evaluation.

An additional challenge is to find new ways of involving, in a significant way, developing-country evaluators in development evaluations. So far the role of developing-country evaluators in carrying out evaluations of development interventions has been quite limited. The most frequent arrangement (for their rather infrequent participation) is as consultants in missions of bilateral or multilateral agencies. One important reason for the lack of evaluations of development aid designed and carried out mainly by developing-country evaluators is the perception (and sometimes the reality) of a lack of sufficient capacities for evaluation at the country level. However, there is a vicious circle in that the lack of opportunities for designing and implementing evaluations deprives developing-country practitioners of opportunities to learn through a learning by doing process (as indicated above). One of the consequences of this

lack of opportunities is that the emergence of indigenous models of development evaluation becomes unlikely. An interesting and promising way of involving developing country evaluators has been tried in Tanzania, through an "independent monitoring/and evaluation/ group," composed of foreign and national experts (see Killick, 2004).

Furthermore, as indicated at the beginning of this chapter, development aid is only a subset of development interventions. There are other interventions and issues, such as trade and foreign direct investment, which have a significant impact on development, frequently being much more important than development aid, and therefore becoming very "relevant." Generating a demand for, and a capacity to carry out, evaluations of these crucial issues is one of the important challenges for development evaluators.[18] This type of evaluations would complement the more traditional evaluation of development focused on aid, requiring an adequate division of labor with researchers who had been working on these issues for several decades.

Finally, the implications of alternative views of development pose evaluation challenges that are not always acknowledged. Thus, Amartya Sen's conception of "development as freedom" and his "capabilities approach" has implications for the assessment of the relevance of development interventions, shifting the focus to the effects of development interventions on people's freedoms and capabilities. A more general challenge is to make explicit the implicit assumptions and values used in development evaluation. For example, economists conducting development evaluations frequently assume that the greater the removal of "distortions" to free trade, the better will be the development results in terms of increasing welfare; however, the economic "theory of the second best" shows that this is not necessarily the case and that when all distortions cannot be removed, then the removal of some distortions may increase or decrease welfare.[19] The importance of making explicit the values in development evaluation has been forcefully argued by Des Gasper (2004), complementing the emphasis on making theories explicit (characteristic of the "theory-based evaluation" approach). In fact, an "Assumptions Based Comprehensive Development Evaluation Framework" (ABCDEF) would allow development evaluators, and those that are evaluated, to become fully aware of the implicit and explicit assumptions made in the design of development interventions (including counterfactuals) and in their evaluations, thus facilitating a constructive and critical discussion that can facilitate the process of learning from experience.[20]

Development Evaluation as a Profession

Most development evaluation practitioners have a professional background in some social science discipline (such as economics, sociology, anthropology, political science, and history). However, through professional evaluation training such as that provided by the Master in Evaluation of the University of Costa Rica (which started in 1995) and the International Program for Development Evaluation Training (IPDET, at Carleton University, Canada,[21] as well as the formation of an association of development evaluation professionals, namely, the International Development Evaluation Association (IDEAS), development evaluation is becoming a profession with practitioners that are starting to consider themselves as development evaluation practitioners. Furthermore, there is a growing demand for this type of professionals, particularly for the evaluation of development aid interventions, thus creating opportunities for professionals trained in development evaluation. Another (complementary) way to cater

to this demand is through the mobilization of a potential supply of development evaluators whose background is research and/or development, and who may be able to carry out development evaluations with some guidance, thus developing as a by-product their competence as development evaluators. The involvement of locally based evaluators, who are fluent in local languages and fully familiar with the cultural, social, and political context, is one of the best ways to overcome the limitations of foreign evaluators.

It should be noted that the "development evaluation architecture" consists of a set of partially overlapping evaluation associations and networks: the OECD/Development Assistance Committee (DAC) Network on Development Evaluation, whose members are the evaluation departments of bilateral development agencies of the OECD countries (including as observers the Evaluation Cooperation Group (ECG) members and the chair of the United Nations Evaluation Group – UNEG); the ECG, composed by the evaluation units of the International Financial Institutions (including as observers the chair of the OECD/DAC Network and the Chair of the UNEG); the United Nations Evaluation Group (UNEG), which includes all the evaluation departments of the UN system (with the chair of the OECD/DAC Network as observer, and the World Bank representing the ECG); IDEAS and the national and regional associations of development evaluation practitioners based in developing countries (including their coalition or federation, the International Organization for Cooperation in Evaluation (IOCE), which was launched in 2003). Furthermore, NGOs are also active in development evaluation; for example, the International NGO Training and Research Center (INTRAC) provides support to NGOs in evaluation (and other areas) and is a useful source of information about NGOs' involvement in development evaluation.

Associations of Development Evaluation at the National, Regional and Global Level

Associations of evaluators in developing countries have been formed since 1990 at the national, regional, and global levels. The first of such associations was the Central American Evaluation Association, whose members have been mainly based in Costa Rica. It developed, jointly with the Canadian University of Hull, a masters program in evaluation, with several generations of graduates. Some of them have been participating in evaluations of program funded by the Central American Bank for Economic Integration. In the late 1990s national associations were formed in Asia, Latin America, and Africa. The African Evaluation Association was established in 1999 and held two regional conferences.[22]

A Latin American Program for Evaluation, PREVAL, was launched by the UN International Fund for Agricultural Development in 1995 (the program was designed in 1990). It has been organizing workshops on monitoring and evaluation, producing and disseminating evaluation documents, and it established a managed electronic network. Furthermore, the International Organization for Cooperation in Evaluation (IOCE), which is a federation of evaluation organizations, including those in developing countries, was created in 2003.[23] Finally, in August 2002 the International Development Evaluation Association (IDEAS) was launched, becoming the only global association whose main focus is development evaluation.

Thus, there has been an evolution from a period in which development evaluation was seen as a possible topic and/or "topical interest group" within established evaluation associations, such as the American Evaluation Association, to a situation in which the evaluation landscape has become populated with evaluation associations based in developing countries and with an international association, IDEAS, whose board includes a majority of members from developing countries. These associations are starting to play a role in promoting the demand for development evaluations, building an evaluation culture and, at the same time, are supporting the enhancement of capacities to undertake development evaluations with full involvement of developing-country practitioners and policy-makers. Thus, they are also promoting development through development evaluation.

The Evaluation of Humanitarian Action[24]

Background – the History of Evaluation of Humanitarian Action

Funding from international donors to humanitarian crises in the 1990s has averaged around US$5 billion a year. This is some 10 percent of all overseas development funding, although if all humanitarian funding is taken into account the figure is probably closer to US$10 billion a year.[25] Much of the actual work of humanitarian action is carried out by non-governmental organizations (NGOs) as implementing partners, with the UN, European Community Humanitarian Office (ECHO), and national donors as funders and monitors. The main UN actors are the World Food Program (WFP), the United Nations High Commissioner for Refugees (UNHCR), and the United Nations Children's Fund (UNICEF). A large number of NGOs are involved, in some high-profile emergencies more than 200, including internationally known organizations such as the International Federation of Red Cross and Red Crescent Societies (IFRC), the International Committee of the Red Cross (ICRC), Oxfam and Save the Children Fund. The multiple actors and funding mechanisms often make assessing humanitarian action complex.

Practitioners of humanitarian aid generally claim to anchor their work to the principles of neutrality and impartiality – for example, aid should be provided to those most in need, independent of political factors. As such it can be provided in any country or regime independent of its political or human rights record, and in this process is usually controlled by humanitarian agencies. In practice circumstances almost always intervene to problematize ethical approaches (IFRC, 2003), and the key humanitarian principles have been under increasing pressure with recent interventions in Kosovo, Afghanistan, and Iraq, where humanitarian responses are seen as being subsumed under western foreign policy priorities, or as part of the US led "war on terror" (see, among others, FIFC, 2004; Hansen, 2004; Slim, 2004; Vaux, 2004). However, the humanitarian–military interface is not well covered in EHA.

EHA is a relative newcomer in the evaluation field, occurring systematically across the humanitarian sector only from the mid-1990s. A few evaluations were carried out after the 1983–5 famine in the Horn of Africa, but numbers were limited until 1993 (Wood, et al., 2001). The catalysts for increased attention have been uptake in recipient governments, the UN, donor governments and NGOs of results based management (see below); increased funding to humanitarian action since 1991; and the Joint Evaluation of Emergency Assistance to Rwanda (JEEAR, 1996).

The JEEAR has been a touchstone of EHA since the mid-1990s. This has been because of its subject – the genocide in Rwanda – and its scope. Recently, the Danida Evaluation Secretariat commissioned a follow-up study to the JEEAR to determine the extent to which its recommendations have been carried out (see Exemplar 24.1).

EXEMPLAR 24.1

The Joint Evaluation of Emergency Assistance to Rwanda and Its Follow-Up

The Rwanda genocide in 1994 resulted in the killing of at least 800,000 people during a 10-week period. Those killed were predominantly members of the minority Tutsi ethnic group, but a significant number of politically moderate Hutus were also killed. Inaction by the "international community," including the US, and the evacuation of almost all non-Rwandan nationals, including the expatriate staff of most of the relief agencies, effectively cleared the way for the genocide. A massive refugee flow of over two million people to eastern Zaire (now the Democratic Republic of Congo – DRC) followed, provoking a large international relief effort and allocation of some US$1.4 billion between April and December 1994.

The enormity of these events led to an unprecedented collaboration to learn the lessons from the international response – the Joint Evaluation of Emergency Assistance to Rwanda (JEEAR). JEEAR consisted of four major studies: on historical perspective; early warning; the effects of humanitarian aid; and rebuilding Rwanda. It was managed by a 38-member steering committee, including all major actors in the humanitarian system, chaired by the well-respected head of the Evaluation Secretariat at Danida. In scope, size, and influence, it dwarfs all previous and subsequent EHA.

(Continued)

(Continued)

The main finding of the JEEAR was that humanitarian aid had been used as a substitute for effective political and military action. Only political or military intervention would have stopped the genocide, but instead the international community relied on a belated humanitarian response as its main intervention. An eight-year follow-up to the JEEAR – also unprecedented in EHA in terms of follow-up to evaluations, and unusual in any evaluation sphere – found that little had changed in this respect, for example in Sudan and DRC.

Study 3 of the JEEAR, focusing on the humanitarian response, was made up of a core team of three supported by 14 technical specialists, including anthropologists, and health and nutrition and logistic specialists. Interviews were carried out with 480 donor, UN, NGO, and government personnel, and some 140 beneficiaries of assistance. In terms of the humanitarian response, JEEAR found that shortcomings included response capacity, coordination, the monitoring of the effectiveness of overall efforts, the professionalism of some NGOs, and accountability mechanisms in the sector generally. While there has been some progress since 1994, many of these shortcomings still dog the sector.

Sources: JEEAR (1996); Rieff (2002); Borton & Eriksson (2004).

JEEAR established what was possible in EHA, although not as yet repeated, despite major emergencies such as Hurricane Mitch, Kosovo, East Timor, and Afghanistan, which led to the disbursements of substantial amounts of humanitarian aid from multiple donors.

How Evaluation of Humanitarian Action Has Been Structured and Carried Out

Evaluation of humanitarian action was marked through the 1990s by five main characteristics:

1. It tended to be atheoretical – that is, it did not during that period in general draw on conceptual thinking in mainstream evaluation, nor develop its own theory. This has meant that for the most part EHA has not been reflective as to the implications of methods selected, and the influence of these methods on evaluation findings (on which see Lipsey, 2000). The consideration of evaluator bias rarely arises.

2. Following from their atheoretical nature, EHA methods tend to be formalized and routine, with evaluation methods following much the same pattern: initial document review; an introductory round of meetings in national capitals; a two- or three-week visit to the affected country, with a focus on meetings at donor, the UN, and NGO offices in the capital and districts; usually somewhat rushed visits to refugee camps or project sites; and a debriefing in-country and back at the national capitals (ALNAP, 2003).

3. There are of course important exceptions. For example, much EHA is structured around the Development Assistance Committee evaluation criteria (OECD-DAC, 1999). These are standard evaluation criteria such as impact, effectiveness, and efficiency, adapted for the humanitarian field. For the most part the DAC evaluation criteria have not been used creatively and have tended to foster a focus on accountability-based evaluation as opposed to lesson learning (ALNAP, 2004b). In other words, EHA has concentrated until recently on what happened (e.g. how much food aid

was delivered, how many beneficiaries received aid, how many houses were built and for whom), rather than why things happened. This prioritizing of results over process has tended to hinder lesson-learning in the sector.

4. Much EHA consists of single-agency, single-sector evaluations, which tend to have a somewhat narrow focus on the effectiveness and impact of individual interventions (e.g. the WFP's food aid program in the Great Lakes of Africa, or Oxfam's water intervention in Angola). There have been very few joint evaluations and subsequently some of the wider political questions relating to human rights, protection, or the military-civilian interface, which could be better captured through joint evaluations, are inadequately evaluated.

5. The main purpose of EHA has been reporting to executive boards and donors. The impact of EHA is little understood, but in many cases evaluations are not changing practice in the ways intended. For example, a number of evaluations of housing programs in Bangladesh since 1988 have made similar recommendations, with little effect on practice (ALNAP, 2002).

However, partly because of concern regarding the lack of use of evaluation findings, and partly as a result of greater professionalization, over the last five years EHA has seen three encouraging trends:

- A move towards more experimental and participatory evaluation approaches, manifested mainly in real-time evaluation (see below for further details), now being used by a number of NGOs
- The move to more participatory evaluation is part of an attempt to achieve a better balance between accountability and lesson learning
- Again linked with the move to more participatory evaluation, many agencies have increased their focus on evaluation use,

stemming from dissatisfaction with lack of follow-up and interest in evaluations, and using Patton's work (1997).

EHA in Context

With much fanfare, most western government departments involved with aid and humanitarian action announced the introduction of results-based management (RBM) in the early 1990s. This was partly a result of cuts to aid budgets and the persistent accusation that aid does not work. Where donors went, recipients (NGOs, the UN, and developing-country governments) had followed by the late 1990s, and a substantial RBM industry had developed. While RBM consisted of window-dressing to a certain extent – so that results-based mismanagement may better describe it in some circumstances – it did shift the focus from development inputs to outputs and outcomes.

For the most part RBM led to the establishment or strengthening of evaluation offices; these were usually internal departments within organizations, but at the same time intended to be independent (OESP, 1997). The implications of this organizational set-up – the self-censorship, negotiation, and compromise so central to evaluation practice – is rarely discussed in evaluation reports. How far evaluation offices are in fact independent varies.

One of the results of the JEEAR was the formation of ALNAP (Active Learning Network for Accountability in Humanitarian Action) in 1997. The genesis behind ALNAP was the need for more coordination of evaluation and learning in the humanitarian sector. It is an international interagency forum with 51 full members representing the main humanitarian actors from within the UN, bilaterals, and NGOs. Among other activities it holds a six-monthly meeting of members and publishes an *Annual Review* on EHA findings and quality, and maintains an Evaluative Reports Database, which is an online database collection of EHA.

The majority of EHA is carried out by sectoral specialists (e.g. in water, food aid), working individually or in teams. Evaluators in many cases have a technical rather than a social science or evaluation background. One of the consequences of this is that EHA is often evaluation with affected people left out – in other words a focus on food aid "pipelines," nutritional data and operational agency staff opinions. This is perhaps the most problematic aspect of EHA as currently conducted. (In development evaluation this also happens to a considerable extent, though there is also an important set of practitioners of participatory development evaluation, and an increasing utilization of different ways to incorporate affected peoples' perceptions.)

EHA also tends to be carried out by expatriates, often from the country providing assistance. While this may ensure there is adequate technical expertise on the evaluation team, it also smacks of tied aid, that is, the requirement in many donor countries that aid money should to some extent provide employment or services to their own citizens. A good example is the spate of evaluations carried out on interventions in Kosovo; of 55 evaluators involved, only three were from the region (ALNAP, 2001). The flip side of this reliance on western evaluators is that little has been or is being done to support evaluation capacity in crisis hit countries, an exception being UNICEF's support to the African Evaluation Society (Nairobi M&E Network, 2002; AFREA is also supported in its development evaluation work by the African Development Bank, the World Bank, and other organizations such as the bilateral agencies of development assistance of Denmark, the Netherlands, and Norway). This despite the fact that there is evidence to suggest that EHA, which uses teams of national and expatriate specialists tends to be of higher quality, as this combines both local knowledge with international expertise (ALNAP, 2004a).

One of the ironies of this situation is that evaluation managers have noted that lack of well-qualified evaluators is probably the main constraint to improving the quality of EHA. Currently the "market" for evaluators operates like most markets with evaluation officers competing against each other. This means that those who have better knowledge, networks, and funds are at an advantage. While this may benefit individual agencies, it does not support improvement for the sector as a whole, particularly given there are so few joint evaluations.

Findings of Evaluation of Humanitarian Action

Part of ALNAP's work has been a synthesis of findings of EHA (ALNAP, 2001–2004). Over the last four years some 215 evaluations have been included, including 20 synthesis reports. This is probably the most systematic attempt to date to determine the strengths and weaknesses in the humanitarian sector. Several findings can be highlighted from this synthesis.

Humanitarian action is in general successful in meeting its short-term objectives of saving lives, feeding hungry populations, providing short-term health care, water and sanitation, and shelter. This in itself is a remarkable achievement given the often harsh operating environments. On the other hand, humanitarian action has failed to support livelihoods, or to establish a bridge between relief on the one hand and rehabilitation/reconstruction and development on the other. As such, humanitarian action is usually dealing with symptoms rather than causes. Part of this failure to build longer-term solutions has been a lack of attention to capacity development, although there have been pockets of success. The failure to hand decision-making and responsibility for humanitarian action to those who appear to do much of the work – that is, national organizations and staff – is an ongoing theme (e.g. Minear, 2002). Surprisingly little is known about what makes for positive capacity development, and much more is known about what undermines capacity, for example, competition between agencies and in-fighting about control of budgets.

Staff, and in particular national staff, are key to the success of humanitarian action. A large number of dedicated staff work in the sector, often on short-term contracts and in dangerous or stressful environments. At the same time these staff are often not supported or valued by reactive bureaucracies (People in Aid, 2004).

A number of commentators have claimed that humanitarian actors, in particular since the Kosovo conflict in 1999, have been co-opted by western foreign policy priorities (Rieff, 2002; FIFC, 2004; Duffield & Macrae, 2001). UN agencies and NGOs, in particular US NGOs, have been willing to follow their government policy and funding, despite the fact that their governments are belligerent, hence apparently going against the key humanitarian principles of impartiality and neutrality. For example, many humanitarian actors worked in Iraq because of pressure from their governments, the accessibility of funding, and the need for profile, despite the fact that only "pockets" of humanitarian need existed in Iraq. NGOs were also hesitant about criticizing human rights violations, for example by US and coalition Afghan partners in northern Afghanistan (ALNAP, 2004a).

Over the last decade increasing attention has been given to the development of needs assessments to improve aid effectiveness and impact. However, the lack of learning about and from affected populations when all agencies in their policies strive for a participatory approach seriously undermines the credibility of humanitarian action. And while more is known about livelihoods of beneficiaries and how these might be supported than 10 years ago, the mechanisms for translating this knowledge into practice are still underdeveloped (Hofmann et al.,

2004). At the same time there are several institutions which have taken learning from communities as a central feature of their work – for example, the Disaster Mitigation Institute in India, Groupe URD, and the Tufts University project on livelihoods in Afghanistan (e.g., Lautze et al., 2002). Constraints to learning from affected populations should not be underestimated, particularly in complex emergencies. Security considerations may make access difficult and curfews may keep contact brief. On the other hand, even in relatively stable situations such as refugee camps, learning from primary stakeholders is often limited.

A central finding from evaluations over the last four years, as well as much other literature (e.g., Minear, 2002; Rieff, 2002) is that the priorities of individual donors and agencies take precedence over a coordinated response, with subsequent loss of effectiveness. However, there has been some limited progress recently. A recent external review of the Inter-Agency Standing Committee concluded: "These [coordination] tools are significantly more developed than they were five years ago. There is evidence that field level coordination has improved, at least among the UN system of agencies and with a sub-set of the major international NGOs" (OCHA, 2003, pp. iii–iv). However, it also found: "much less evidence of progress on solving perennial problems of mandate gaps, capacity gaps, or system-wide problems, or in handling such issues as the 'transition from relief-to-development', IDPs, the military-humanitarian interface, etc."

The Quality of Evaluation of Humanitarian Action

A meta-evaluation of 127 evaluations of humanitarian action produced between 2000 and 2003 as part of the ALNAP *Annual Reviews* reveals that the overall quality of EHA, as measured against mainstream evaluation standards, is generally inadequate, undermining the

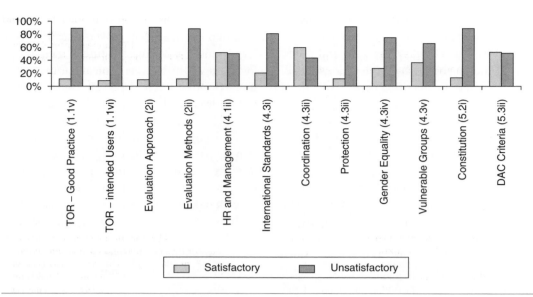

Figure 24.1 Three year totals of EHA report ratings, assessed using ALNAP's Evaluation Quality Proforma.

credibility of evaluation findings.[26] In addition, a considerable proportion – probably somewhere between 30 percent and 50 percent – of humanitarian aid is allocated not to the emergency or relief phase, but to rehabilitation and reconstruction. However, the most often used evaluation criteria relate to the emergency phase, in particular: the number of lives saved, nutritional and morbidity levels, and numbers who have received emergency shelter. If indicators relevant to rehabilitation were used the performance of humanitarian action would consequently be seen to decline.

Twelve areas key to EHA quality are covered in this section. The three-year averages of ratings for these areas are shown in Figure 24.1.

Overall EHA exhibits some strengths, in particular in evaluation of human resources, coordination, and the DAC criteria, but problematic areas remain. The main ones are opaqueness of evaluation methodologies; failure to meet good practice standards in use of methodologies; lack of systematic consultation with primary stakeholders; and failure to use agency policy to assess interventions. Insufficient attention to evaluation use and users remains common. A more detailed assessment of individual areas in the Quality Proforma follows.

Terms of Reference (TOR)

	Quality of TOR statement on expectation of good practice in approach and method	**Quality of TOR statement on intended use and users of evaluation outputs**
% satisfactory	11	8
% unsatisfactory	89	92

Evaluation reports were found to be weak in both of these areas. In general, reports did not specify adequately the key methodological tools that evaluators should use. It was also rare for terms of reference to outline clearly the intended use of evaluation reports, thus adding to the likelihood that the findings of reports will not be fully used.

Delineation of Methodology

	Appropriateness of the overall evaluation approach	**Appropriateness of the evaluation methods selected**
% satisfactory	10	12
% unsatisfactory	90	88

The first area refers to the theoretical approach drawn upon in the evaluation. As noted above, most EHA is atheoretical. For the second area a satisfactory or higher rating is given where a qualitative and quantitative multi-method approach has been used. To one of us (TB) this seems very controversial, as it appears to imply that mixed method evaluations will always be better quality. OF's interpretation of this point is that what is being argued here is that a multimethod approach is more satisfactory than one that relies only on one method. This does not seem controversial, as it is one way to "triangulate" in a complex reality. The following have all been adequately addressed: application of the DAC criteria; reference to international standards including international law; consultation with key stakeholders to inform findings, conclusions, and recommendations; triangulation for verification purposes; and gender analysis. As can be seen, a small minority of evaluations fulfill all of these requirements.

Quality of the Evaluation of Agency's Management and Human Resource Practices

% satisfactory	51
% unsatisfactory	49

This area is a strength in EHA, with over 50% of evaluations rated as at least "satisfactory" each year. Evaluators have consistently examined issues such as staff turnover, HQ–field communication, and security. However, other areas such as pre-departure briefing, training, and learning are less well covered.

Cross-Cutting Themes

	Evaluation of use of international standards	**Evaluation of co-ordination**	**Evaluation of protection**	**Evaluation of gender equality**	**Evaluation of consideration to vulnerable/ marginalized**
% satisfactory	20	58	10	26	36
% unsatisfactory	80	42	90	73	64

The cross-cutting theme that consistently scored well was coordination, which is related to the ability of evaluators to cover institutional factors. In the other four theme areas, reports performed consistently poorly except in the case of consideration to the vulnerable and marginalized where performance was somewhat better.

Much of the humanitarian system, including most of the UN operational agencies, and many NGOs, have been moving to what has been termed a human-rights-based approach to programming over the last few years. This means that human rights, as defined by international conventions such as the Convention on the Rights of the Child, provide an overarching framework for interventions. EHA, however, has not kept pace with changes in humanitarian programming, although it should also be mentioned that many agencies have adopted a rights-based approach as policy but this has yet to be turned into practice. The link between the cross-cutting themes of international standards, protection, and gender equality is that they deal with rights-based issues that are often controversial; these are the issues that are most often left out of evaluation terms of reference and with which evaluators appear to have the least skills. As noted, the single-agency, single-sector focus of much EHA tends to lead to a technical, apolitical focus. A good example is protection, referring to protection of the affected population from harm, which has been at the center of much discussion of humanitarian action in the last few years. The fact that this is so poorly covered in EHA is a central gap, and EHA is clearly a long way away from integrating a rights-based approach into a wider evaluative process.

Quality of Consultation with and Participation by Primary Stakeholders

% satisfactory	13
% unsatisfactory	87

Evaluation reports are expected to outline the nature and scope of consultation with, and participation by, beneficiaries and non-beneficiaries within the affected population in the evaluation process. This is a further area of weakness. Despite some good practice, EHA could rightfully be accused of systematically ignoring the views and perspectives of primary stakeholders in favor of those of institutional actors, particularly agency staff. This undermines its credibility and continues in the vein of humanitarian aid itself treating primary stakeholders as passive recipients of aid rather than active participants in their own recovery. This agency-centric perspective will only change if commissioning agencies insist on adequate primary stakeholder consultation and participation. But an equally important constraint would appear to be the structure of evaluation missions, which are usually short forays by foreign-based evaluators, with a focus on national capitals.

Application of the DAC Evaluation Criteria

% satisfactory	50
% unsatisfactory	50

Application of the DAC criteria is one of the stronger areas of EHA. Overall it is possible to conclude that evaluators have had reasonable success with their application and that they have become EHA's central evaluative tool. Some of the DAC criteria, in particular efficiency and coherence, have proven more problematic for evaluators.[27]

The Future of EHA

As noted, EHA has in the last few years been incorporating new methods to overcome some of its inherent problems. Real-time evaluation, pioneered by UNHCR (2002) and used as well by WFP, and UNICEF (2003), is increasingly being used to attempt to feed lessons learned into ongoing programs. As currently undertaken, real-time evaluation has some overlaps with monitoring, and some similarity to utilization-focused approaches in that it works with program stakeholders on assessment of key intervention issues during the course of the intervention, attempting to come up with evaluation recommendations which can be utilized immediately. This focus on iterative lesson learning is to be welcomed, and has had some immediate impact.[28] Exemplar 24.2 presents details of a real-time evaluation in Southern Africa undertaken by WFP.

EXEMPLAR 24.2

Real-Time Evaluation: Good Practice Case of WFP's Southern Africa Evaluation

Recent definitions of real-time evaluation (RTE) have stressed the importance of its timing, its interactivity, and participation of key users of information. As such it bears some similarity to utilization-focused evaluation, which emphasizes the evaluation process and the nature of the interaction between evaluation users and evaluator (Grob, 2003).

WFP piloted the RTE approach in impressive fashion in the evaluation of its response to the Southern Africa crisis (WFP, 2003). The evaluation included three missions between July 2002 and May 2003, with a summary and recommendations being submitted to the WFP Executive Board in October 2003.

In terms of staff time and committed resources, this was one of the most comprehensive evaluations undertaken by WFP, taking about 13 weeks in total. The core team for all three missions were a socio-economist, a nutritionist, and a needs assessment specialist. In addition, two separate logistics specialists were engaged for the second and third missions.

RTE was a new departure for WFP. Its previous evaluations were often of high quality, but used a mix of standard EHA techniques, with occasional reports being strong on consultation with primary stakeholders. The Southern Africa evaluation, on the other hand, organized its three missions to coincide with three phases of the project cycle: the inception period; the start of the most intensive implementation phase; and the closing stage of the Emergency Operation (EMOP), and preparation for the new EMOP. While experimenting with the RTE approach, however, the evaluation sometimes reads like a traditional *ex post* evaluation, and its focus appears at times to be as much on accountability as on feeding lessons back on an ongoing basis into the WFP system.

The longer evaluation period and the greater length of time spent in country appeared to facilitate more in-depth consultation with primary stakeholders. This took two forms:

- Focus group discussions with beneficiaries at Final Distribution Points in each country. This included observing distribution methods, discussions with distribution committees, and on-site briefings from NGOs.
- Household visits – at least two (in most countries) at each food distribution point visited–where in-depth semi-structured interviews with primary stakeholders were carried out. An ad hoc "sentinel site" study was also undertaken in Malawi and Zambia, where households were visited during each mission for an update on progress, and an insight into the impact of the operation.

(Continued)

(Continued)

The RTE (WFP, 2003, p. 3) notes that: "one great advantage of the RTE was being able to visit project sites as they were in full operation and with key staff still present," a point also emphasized in the UNICEF (2003) desk review of RTEs. This is particularly important given that many ex post evaluations are seriously constrained by key staff having moved on.

One other area of strength of the evaluation is its unusually detailed contextual analysis. Ex post evaluations sometimes have difficulty retracing key events. The WFP evaluation on the other hand, included a very detailed assessment of key events vis-à-vis the timing of the intervention. As the terms of reference note, RTE can help build a lasting description or chronicle of the intervention, which can later be used as a model for identifying lessons and good practice.

Agencies are in many cases already committed – through their policies and evaluation guidance – to covering adequately a number of the weaker areas in EHA identified above, and through its meta-evaluation ALNAP continues to support improvement in evaluation practice, including through ongoing dialogue with agencies. Some of the weaknesses in EHA may more easily be improved than others, for example, lack of transparency in detailing methodology. Other weaknesses are likely to be more intractable, for example: lack of analysis of social process and gender, and weak attention to rights-based issues such as protection; limited consultation with beneficiaries; and inadequate focus on utilization. EHA will need to be strengthened considerably both in its theoretical underpinnings and practice if its findings are to be considered credible.

Conclusion

The practice of evaluation of humanitarian action (EHA) and development evaluation (DE) initially focused almost exclusively on single agency, single sector/project evaluations; though this type of evaluation still dominates both EHA and DE, joint development evaluations involving several agencies started to become more frequent in the early twenty-first century.

Whereas EHA tended to be atheoretical, DE draws on social sciences and evaluation approaches, and both make use of procedures and tools such as document and literature reviews, surveys, focus groups, and structured and semi-structured interviews. Also both types of evaluations are structured around the DAC evaluation criteria.

The concern with the lack of sufficient use of evaluation findings led to innovations in the way in which these evaluations are conducted (with more emphasis on participatory evaluation, which promotes empowerment and capacity building), and new ways to communicate findings (e.g., through the press and through workshops).

Networks of evaluators in the north and in the south involved in EHA and/or DE were formed at the end of the twentieth century, and national and regional evaluation associations, most of whose members are involved in DE and/or EHA, emerged in developing countries. These "communities of practice," that are already playing a role in developing evaluation cultures in different countries and regions, and in building evaluation capacities, may also promote a further convergence (within the limits imposed by their different contexts) between the evaluation of humanitarian action and development evaluation.

Notes

1. Osvaldo Feinstein has been responsible for the part of the chapter on development evaluation and has completed some general revision work. Tony Beck has written the humanitarian evaluation parts of the chapter.

2. The use of the term "development" in this chapter corresponds to the broad field of practice and studies that focuses on poverty reduction in "developing countries"

3. IDEAS was launched in 2002, and its Board has a majority of developing-country members. See references for website.

4. This section is based on OECD-DAC (1999).

5. See DAC Working Party on Aid Evaluation (2001).

6. See DAC Working Party on Aid Evaluation (2001). This publication also includes a valuable discussion about feedback and the use of evaluations for learning and accountability.

7. For example, the ex-post impact study of the Noakhali Rural Development Project in Bangladesh, conducted by Danida (2002).

8. See DAC Working Party on Aid Evaluation (2002). This glossary was prepared by a task force which included evaluation experts of bilateral and multilateral development agencies. See also DAC (1998), Cracknell (2000) and Molund & Schill (2004).

9. The "logical framework" is a tool used to improve the design of interventions, most often at the project level. It involves identifying strategic elements (inputs, outputs, outcomes, impact) and their causal relationships (the "results chain"), indicators, and the assumptions or risks that may influence success failure. See DAC (2002).

10. See Feinstein & Picciotto (2001).

11. The original table in Carvalho & White (2004) includes "competition effects" among the "main channels," as well as some additional assumptions and types of data that for the sake of simplification were omitted here.

12. Albert Hirschman, one of the most eminent development economists, published two books that are goal-free evaluations (though he never considered himself an evaluator). In one of them he evaluated projects of the Inter-American Foundation (see Hirschman, 1984), and the other one (Hirschman, (1995) is an evaluation of projects supported by the World Bank.

13. Participatory methods in development (including participatory monitoring and evaluation) have been pioneered by Robert Chambers, (see, e.g., Chambers, 1994; Feuerstein, 1992. In this handbook Chapter 9 by Stevenson & Thomas also makes reference to participatory methods.

14. See the discussion of this approach in Pitman, Feinstein, & Ingram (2004), particularly the notion of "opportunistic randomization," for example where the resources of an intervention have to be rationed, and randomization/lotteries are used as a rationing device, thus allowing RCT without creating ethical issues that otherwise may arise. By the way, the use of the analogy with the "gold standard" by the strong supporters of randomization is rather ironic, given the acknowledged failures of the "gold standard."

15. See Dabelstein & Rebien (2002), which summarizes the different types of joint evaluation.

16. See Feinstein & Ingram (2003) for this sort of limited approach to joint evaluations (given the difficulties experienced in implementing full-fledged joint evaluations) emphasizing processes, including examples and a set of hypotheses on costs and benefits of joint evaluations.

17. For information on IPDET and on diagnostic tools for evaluation capacity development, see www.worldbank.org/evaluation/ecd, which also provides information on short evaluation courses.

18. See Picciotto & Weaving (2004).

19. See, for example, Sodersten & Reed (1990), p. 322.

20. The use of explicit counterfactuals in the evaluation of program aid is well presented in White & Dijkstra (2004). This book also includes an important and clear discussion of fungibility and its implications for the evaluation of aid, which due to space limitations cannot be treated in this chapter. On A. Sen's approach, see Sen (1999).

21. There are other evaluation training programs in Chile, Barbados, and Mexico. There are many more training programs that focus on "project appraisal," though frequently they are presented as courses on project evaluation (indeed, their focus is on ex-ante evaluation).

22. Details on the national and regional evaluation organizations that have been formed in the last years can be seen at www.mande.co.uk.

23. See http://www.internationalevaluation.com.

24. This section draws heavily on the work of TB for the Active Learning Network for Accountability and Performance in Humanitarian Action (ALNAP), and the four years of the ALNAP *Annual Review*. For further details see www.alnap.org. This section deals with humanitarian aid to developing countries; there is an extensive literature on evaluation of emergency aid in developed countries (e.g., Quarantelli 2000), which is not covered here.

25. Figures are taken from http;//www.global-humanitarianassistance.org/ghatrl.htm.

26. This section is drawn from ALNAP (2003). The meta-evaluation was performed using the ALNAP Quality Proforma, a meta-evaluation tool developed from good practice in EHA, the American Evaluation Association Program Evaluation Standards, and following Stufflebeam (2001). The Quality Proforma set out specific criteria against which evaluations are to be assessed on a four-point rating scale of: poor, unsatisfactory, satisfactory, and good. As slightly different rating systems were used over the three years covered, analysis has been carried out using "satisfactory" and "unsatisfactory" ratings only. A satisfactory or better rating was achieved when evaluations met good practice standards. For further details see ALNAP (2004b).

27. For definitions see ALNAP (2004b).

28. One example is the UNHCR Afghanistan real-time evaluation, where the evaluators had an audience with the UNHCR Executive Board immediately on return from Afghanistan.

References

ALNAP (2001). *Humanitarian Action: Learning from evaluation*. London: ALNAP.

ALNAP (2002). *Humanitarian Action: Improving performance through improved learning*. London: ALNAP.

ALNAP (2003). *Humanitarian Action: Improving monitoring to enhance accountability and learning*. London: ALNAP.

ALNAP (2004a) *Review of Humanitarian Action 2004*. London: ALNAP.

ALNAP (2004b). *Guide to the Evaluation of Humanitarian Action*. London: ALNAP.

Borton, J. & Eriksson, J. (2004). Assessment of the impact and influence of the 1996 joint evaluation of emergency assistance to Rwanda. Executive summary. Mimeo, 26th July.

Carvalho, S. & White, H. (2004). Theory-based evaluation: the case of social funds. *American Journal of Evaluation*, 25(2), 141–160.

Chambers, R. (1994). Participatory rural appraisal (PRA): Challenges, potentials and paradigm. *World Development*, 22 (10), 1437–1454.

Cracknell, B. E. (2000). *Evaluating Development Aid*. London: Sage.

Dabelstein, N. and Rebien, C. (2002). Evaluation of development assistance: Its start, progress and current challenges, In J.-E. Furubo, R. C. Rist & R. Sandahl, (eds) *International Atlas of Evaluation*. New Brunswick, NJ: Transaction Publishers.

DAC Working Party on Aid Evaluation (1998). *Review of the DAC Principles for Evaluation of Development Assistance*. Paris: OECD.

DAC Working Party on Aid Evaluation (2001). *Evaluation Feedback for Effective Learning and Accountability*, Paris: OECD.

DAC Working Party on Aid Evaluation (2002). *Glossary of Key Terms in Evaluation and Results Based Management*. Paris: OECD.

Danida (2002). *Evaluation in the Wake of a Flagship*. Copenhagen: Ministry of Foreign Affairs.

Duffield, M. & Macrae, J. (2001). Apples, pears and porridge: The origins and impact of the search for 'coherence' between humanitarian and political responses to chronic political emergencies. *Disasters*, 25(4), 290–307.

Feinstein, O. N. & Ingram, G. K. (2003). Lessons learned from World Bank experiences with joint evaluation. paper presented at the DAC Working Party on Aid Evaluation Workshop "Partners in Development Evaluation: Learning and Accountability," Paris. Available at http://www.minefi.gouv.fr/TRESOR/cicid/atelier/actes.pdf#proceedings.

Feinstein, O. N. & Picciotto, R. (eds) (2001) *Evaluation and Poverty Reduction*. New Brunswick, NJ: Transaction Publishers.

Feuerstein, M.-T. (1992) *Partners in Evaluation*. London: Macmillan.

FIFC (2004). *The Future of Humanitarian Action. Implications of Iraq and other recent crises*. Somerville: Tufts University, Feinstein International Famine Centre.

Gasper, D. (2004). *The Ethics of Development*. Edinburgh. Edinburgh University Press.

Grob, G. (2003). A truly useful bat is one found in the hands of a slugger. *American Journal of Evaluation*, 24(4), 499–506.

Hansen, G. (2004) Operational interaction between UN humanitarian agencies and belligerent forces: towards a code of conduct. *Humanitarian Exchange*, 26, 33–37.

Hirschman, A. O. (1984) *Getting Ahead Collectively*. New York: Pergamon Press.

Hirschman, A. O. (1995) *Development Projects Observed*. Washington D.C.: The Brookings Institution (first edition published in 1967).

Hofmann, C., Roberts, L., Shoham, J., & Harvey, P. (2004) *Measuring the Impact of Humanitarian Aid. A review of current practice*. London: ODI HPG Research Report 17.

http://www.minefi.gouv.fr/TRESOR/cicid/atelier/contrib/45.pdf.

IFRC (2003). *World Disasters Report*. Geneva: IFRC.

JEEAR (1996). *The International Response to Conflict and Genocide: Lessons from the Rwanda experience*. Copenhagen: Steering Committee of the Joint Evaluation of Emergency Assistance to Rwanda.

Kent, R. (2004). *Humanitarian Futures. Practical policy perspective*. London: ODI HPN Network Paper 46.

Killick, Tony (2004), Monitoring partnership-based aid relationships: A note. *Development Policy Review*, ODI, 22, 229–234.

Lautze, S., Stiles, E., Nojumi, N., & Najimi, F. (2002) Qaht-E-Pool: "A cash famine" food insecurity in Afghanistan 1999–2002. Somerville: Tufts University, mimeo.

Lipsey, M. (2000). Meta-analysis and the learning curve in evaluation practice. *American Journal of Evaluation*, 21(2), 207–213.

Minear, L. (2002). *The Humanitarian Enterprise: Dilemmas and Discoveries*. Bloomfield: Kumarian Press.

Molund, S. & Schill, G. (2004). *Looking Back, Moving Forward* (SIDA evaluation manual). Stockholm: SIDA.

Nairobi M&E Network (2002). The African Evaluation Guidelines: 2002. A checklist to assist in planning evaluations, negotiating clear contracts, reviewing progress and ensuring adequate completion of an evaluation. *Evaluation and Program Planning*, 25, 481–492.

OCHA (2003). *External Review of the Inter-Agency Standing Committee*. New York: UN Office of Coordination of Humanitarian Aid.

OECD-DAC (1999). *Guidance for Evaluating Humanitarian Assistance in Complex Emergencies*. Paris: OECD, Development Assistance Committee.

OESP (1997). *Measuring and Managing Results: Lessons for development cooperation*. New York: UNDP, Office of Evaluation and Strategic Planning.

Patton, M. (1997). *Utilization-Focused Evaluation: The new century text*. Thousand Oaks: Sage.

People in Aid (2004). *Understanding HR in the Humanitarian Sector – A baseline for enhancing quality in management. Handbook 1*. London: People in Aid.

Picciotto, R. & Weaving, R. (2004). *Impact of Rich Countries' Policies on Poor Countries: Towards a level playing field in development cooperation*. New Brunswick, NJ: Transaction Publishers

Pitman, G. K., Feinstein, O. N., & Ingram, G. K. (eds) (2004). *Assessing .Development Effectiveness*. New Brunswick, NJ: Transaction Publishers.

Quarantelli, E. (2000). The disaster recovery process: What we know and do not know from research. Newark: University of Delaware Disaster Research Centre, mimeo.

Rieff, D. (2002). *A Bed for the Night: Humanitarianism in crisis*. New York: Simon and Schuster.

Sen, A. (1999). *Development as Freedom*, New York: Oxford University Press.

Slim, H. (2004). *A Call to Alms. Humanitarian action and the art of war*. Geneva: Centre for Humanitarian Dialogue.

Sodersten, B. & Reed, G. (1990). *International Economics*. New York: St. Martin's Press.

Stufflebeam, D. (2001). Guiding principles checklist for evaluating evaluations.' http://www.wmich.edu/evalctr/checklists/guiding_principles.pdf.

UNHCR (2002). *Real-time Humanitarian Evaluations. Some frequently asked questions*. Geneva: UNHCR Evaluation and Policy Analysis Unit.

UNICEF (2003). *Desk Review of Real-Time Evaluation Experience*. New York: UNICEF Evaluation Working Paper.

Vaux, T. (2004). *Humanitarian Trends – a strategic review for CAFOD*. Oxford: Humanitarian Initiatives.

WFP (2003). *Full Report of the Real-Time Evaluation of WFP's Response to the Southern Africa Crisis 2002–2003*. Rome: World Food Programme.

White, H. N. & Dijkstra, A. G. (2004) *Programme Aid and Development*. London: Routledge.

Wood, A., Apthorpe, R., & Borton, J. (2001). *Evaluating International Humanitarian Action: Reflections from Practitioners*. London: Zed Books.

Relevant Websites

www.ecgnet.org
www.euforic.org
http://evaluation.wmich.edu/jmde/JMDE_Num001.html
www.ideas-int.org
www.intrac.org

www.mande.co.uk
www.oecd.org/dac/evaluation
www.undp.org/eo
www.worldbank.org/evaluation
www.alnap.org
http://www.unhcr.ch/cgi-bin/texis/vtx/research?id=3b850c744

EVIDENCE-BASED EVALUATION IN DIFFERENT PROFESSIONAL DOMAINS: SIMILARITIES, DIFFERENCES AND CHALLENGES

Alan Clarke

Introduction

The chapters in this part of the Handbook address a number of key issues relating to evaluation in a variety of policy contexts and professional domains. Some general themes to emerge include ways in which evaluative inquiry can produce evidence to ascertain the effectiveness of service provision and identify best practice; the role of multi-method research strategies in evaluation designs; the importance of a theory-driven approach in "what works" evaluations; and the contribution of participatory and collaborative forms of evaluation to the promotion of social justice. In North America and Europe these

issues have emerged within the context of both an explosion of interest in what has been termed "evidence-based policy and practice" and a growing debate about the use of randomized controlled trials for social intervention evaluation. Given this development, this chapter will consider whether the experimental model, which is predominant in evidence-based medicine, is transferable to other professional settings and policy contexts.

Evidence-Based Policy and Practice

In the closing decades of the last century many western democracies experienced significant changes in the administration, management and culture of public sector human service organizations. The shift towards "new public management" (Hood, 1991) or "new managerialism" (Pollitt, 1993) heralded the introduction of managerial reforms that were felt would produce rational, efficient and transparent decision-making with respect to the allocation of resources. This introduction of a business ethos gave rise to political, economic and managerial discourses around issues such as value-for-money, cost containment, accountability and effectiveness. As noted by Love, "the drive for increased accountability, effectiveness, and efficiency has sparked a measurement revolution" (2001, p. 437). Service providers are required to routinely monitor their activities and measure outcomes in order "to tell compelling 'performance' stories about how well their strategies have worked" (p. 438). The emphasis placed on results-oriented management and accountability has led to an "audit explosion" (Power, 1997, p. 67) and a growing demand for the systematic evaluation and monitoring of the impact of policies, programmes and practices. In the USA and the UK, for example, this intensification of performance monitoring has been characterized by an increasing emphasis on demonstrating the effectiveness of public services and conducting outcome-oriented evaluations of publicly funded bodies (US General Accounting Office, 1996; National Audit Office, 2000).

Chalmers identifies one major compelling reason for the rigorous evaluation of policy and practice when he asserts that "It is the business of policy makers and practitioners to intervene in other people's lives. Although they usually act with the best of intentions, however, their policies and practices sometimes have unintended, unwanted effects, and they occasionally do more harm than good" (Chalmers, 2003, p. 22). In this context, evaluative research

is seen as having the potential to produce reliable evidence to inform practice and policy interventions across a broad range of areas. At the policy-making level the growing interest in utilizing research evidence in the formulation and development of policies has given rise to what has been termed "evidence-based" or "evidence-led" policy-making (Young et al., 2002). In the UK, the idea that government policy should be informed by sound evidence and not guided by dogma is at the heart of the "modernizing government" agenda (Cabinet Office, 1999a; Parsons, 2001; Parsons, 2002). The belief is that policy decisions should be driven by evidence from research that illustrates what type of policy initiatives or interventions "work" (Cabinet Office, 1999b). This emphasis on the importance of research-based evidence and the adoption of a language of evidence-led policy is not restricted to the UK, but is in fact an international phenomenon. It is perhaps not surprising that the idea has attracted so much enthusiasm in policy-making circles, as it conveys such a simplistic and intuitive logic. As observed by Tilley & Laycock, "rooting policy in evidence has all the appeal of motherhood and apple pie" (2000, p. 13).

Since an evidence-based approach has considerable potential for transforming the organization, provision and delivery of a variety of public services, it is important that we gain an understanding of its origins and the extent to which it can be realistically applied across a diverse range of fields of professional activity. As noted by Marston & Watts (2003), "The term 'evidence-based policy' has evolved from the concept of evidence-based practice, both of which were preceded by evidence-based medicine" (p. 146). The nature of the disciplinary origins, epistemological leanings and methodological allegiances of the evidence-based model in medicine may have implications when it comes to transferring this approach to other professional settings such as social work and criminal justice. Thus, we need to identify the key defining characteristics of the evidence-based practice model in medicine before considering its potential as a generic cross disciplinary phenomenon.

Evidence-Based Medicine

As acknowledged by Mykhalovskiy & Weir (2004), evidence-based medicine has had a major impact on reasoning and practice in contemporary biomedicine and is now taught in medical schools across North America, the UK and parts of Western Europe. In the case of the UK, the evidence-based model of clinical practice was firmly established in the 1990s, with the growth of "health technology assessment" and evidence-based health care being described as "something of a revolution" (Stevens et al., 2001, p. 1). Its rapid expansion across the broad field of specialist areas in medicine and health care led to commentators referring to evidence-based medicine as developing from "an idea into a movement" (Trinder, 2000a, p. 211) and becoming "a cornerstone of UK health policy" (Reynolds, 2000, p. 17). Such was the nature and extent of its impact on health care policy and practice that it has been described as constituting a fundamental paradigmatic shift (Evidence-Based Medicine Working Group, 1992). However, while the term "evidence-based medicine" might be relatively new, the idea itself has a much longer history. For example, Sweeney (1996) suggests that its origins can be traced back to the 1830s when Louis, a French physician, introduced an epidemiological approach to clinical thinking when he compared clinical outcomes for two groups of patients that received different treatments.

Although an evidence-based perspective was a feature of the work of clinical epidemiologists throughout the twentieth century (Arenian & Lilienfield, 1994), it is only during the latter decades of that century that a new "science" of clinical decision-making began to take shape. Sackett et al. (1996) describe evidence-based medicine as "the conscientious, explicit, and judicious use of current best evidence in making decisions about the care of individual patients. The practice of evidence-based medicine means integrating individual clinical expertise with the best available clinical evidence from systematic research" (Sackett et al., 1996, p. 71). Clinicians are perceived as users and consumers of research. Ideally, when making clinical decisions and expressing medical opinions they should have recourse to the best available evidence rather than having to rely on professional intuition and unsystematic clinical experience. In this way, evidence-based medicine is viewed as an effective means of bridging the gap between research and practice. Advocates of this approach maintain that by identifying which treatments can be most usefully incorporated into practice, it offers the possibility of not only increasing the overall effectiveness of clinical interventions but also has the potential to ensure that maximum benefits are obtained from the health care resources available.

Evidence-based practice in this context is presented as incorporating five procedural steps or stages (Rosenberg & Donald, 1995; Sackett et al., 1996). First, the clinician formulates a clinical question concerning the treatment and care of a patient or group of patients. Second, the medical literature is consulted in order to identify the best evidence appropriate to the clinical problem in question. Third, a judgment is made regarding the validity and usefulness of the evidence. Four, where applicable, the information obtained is used to inform clinical practice. Finally, the outcome of the intervention is subjected to an evaluation.

The success of the application of this logical framework in guiding clinical decision-making depends on the quick and efficient dissemination of research findings and the ability of clinicians to critically appraise the evidence provided. In many areas of clinical endeavour the sheer volume of research findings can make the realization of evidence-based practice a daunting prospect for any clinician. Thus there is a strong case for undertaking systematic reviews of primary research evidence in a wide variety of clinical and health policy areas (Chalmers & Altman, 1995). The growing use of systematic reviews as a tool in the study of the effectiveness of health care interventions has led some observers to refer to the "systematic review revolution" (Stevens & Abrams, 2001). In medicine, this form of review is preferred to the traditional narrative review, on the grounds that the latter is by comparison a scientifically unsound and subjective technique (Light & Pillemer, 1984). From a methodological perspective, systematic reviews involve the synthesis of evidence obtained from numerous studies; a procedure that reflects an acknowledgement that science is a cumulative enterprise. By pooling the findings of comparable studies, systematic reviews help to both obtain an overview of the state of knowledge in a particular clinical setting and evaluate the extent to which generalizations can be made on the basis of findings from a number of independent clinical studies (Mulrow, 1994; Khan et al., 2003).

Meta-analysis, which is a form of systematic review, was developed as a technique to facilitate the combining of outcome data from a set of individual studies investigating a common intervention (Glass, McGaw & Smith, 1981; Wolf, 1986; Hunt, 1997). In clinical and health care settings it has been used extensively to evaluate treatment outcomes. It is characterized as a statistically objective technique that enables the recalculation of quantitative data from a large number of studies, thus effectively reducing the likelihood of random errors occurring in the evaluation of treatments as more patients are included in the meta-analysis than in any single study. As an analytic technique, a meta-analysis should be based on as fully a comprehensive collection of studies as possible (Clarke & Stewart, 1994). Given that studies with positive findings are more likely to be published than those that produce negative results (Egger & Davey-Smith, 1995), there is a potential for "publication bias" leading to an overestimation of treatment efficacy in systematic reviews (Dickersin, 1990). Consequently, systematic reviews need to be based upon both published and unpublished studies. The Cochrane Collaboration, an international network established in 1993, provides a repository for trial reports, and through The Cochrane Database of Systematic Reviews facilitates access to summaries of what is known about the effects of health care interventions in a variety of clinical and medical contexts (Clarke, 2002).

A key feature of the process of systematic review is that it judges the quality of the research evidence available. While this grading of evidence has led to the production of a number of "evidence hierarchies" (Woolf et al., 1990; Canadian Task Force on the Periodic Health Examination, 1994; Guyatt et al., 1995; NHS Centre for Reviews and Dissemination, 1996; NICE, 2004), they portray a similar rank ordering of methods of evaluating treatment efficacy. According to Stevens & Abrams (2001), randomized controlled trials (RCTs) are generally placed at the top of the hierarchy, with a typical scale adopting the following form:

    (i)   multiple RCTs, preferably large ones, suitably meta-analysed;

(ii) at least one properly designed RCT of appropriate size;

(iii) well-controlled trials without randomisation;

(iv) well-designed cohort or case control studies;

(v) multiple time series or dramatic results from uncontrolled experiments;

(vi) opinions of respected authorities based on clinical evidence, descriptive studies or expert committee;

(vii) small uncontrolled case series and samples. (p. 368)

From a methodological point of view, the RCT or clinical experiment has been described as "the most reliable scientific method in medicine" (Lilford et al., 2001, p. 11), "the archetypal primary research method" of health technology assessment (Lilford & Stevens, 2001, p. 7) and a "beautiful technique" that is the first choice research design for determining the effectiveness of medical interventions (Cochrane, 1972). Cochrane was an early, influential exponent of a research-orientated approach to the rigorous evaluation of health service provision and a champion of the view that RCTs were the best method for providing "hard evidence" of treatment efficacy. In its simplest form, the primary distinguishing feature of the RCT is that individual patients are randomly allocated to one of two types of groups; a "study" or "treatment" group, or a "control" or "comparison" group. Those patients assigned to the study group receive the new medication or therapeutic technique that is under evaluation, while patients in the control group receive an established intervention or an inactive treatment in the form of a placebo. The randomization procedure reduces selection bias and helps to ensure that both the study and control groups are similar in terms of their composition. This helps to increase internal validity by making it possible to disentangle intervention effects from the effects of contaminating or confounding factors that might

influence key outcomes. As long as the sample size is large enough to reduce sampling error, the potential for confounding factors is reduced as any patient characteristics likely to influence the response to treatment are evenly distributed between the different groups.

Providing the integrity of the randomization process is maintained, selection bias is unlikely to occur at the point of recruitment of subjects to clinical trials, as each patient has an equal chance of being allocated to a treatment group or a control group. However, there is a potential for bias occurring at the data collection stage. For example, if a patient is aware that they are in a particular treatment group this may influence their reporting and recording of perceived changes in their symptoms and general state of health. Also, where clinicians or investigators are optimistic about the potential positive impact of a new drug or treatment regimen, this may influence how they assess individual patient outcomes if they are aware of the group to which the patient has been assigned. There is a potential for experimenter or observer bias where the outcomes of interest have a subjective dimension, such as when measuring general health status or social well-being. The most effective way of reducing the likelihood of any systematic difference occurring in the ascertainment of outcomes between the different groups involved in an RCT is to conduct blind trials.

There are three main groups directly involved in the process of evaluating health care evaluations: the patients, the clinicians and other professional staff responsible for delivering treatment and the researchers (some of whom may also be practitioners) who are engaged in the technical task of evaluating the effectiveness of the treatment. Depending on the particular clinical setting, one or more of these groups may be "blinded" to some aspects of a treatment study. In this context it is possible to distinguish between "single", "double" and "triple" blind trials. The most common form of the single-blind trial is where the patients are the only ones who are unable to identify those who have received an active drug and those who have been given a placebo. In a double-blind trial, both patients and clinical practitioners are unaware as to which particular type of treatment has been administered to which group. In some cases patients, clinicians and researchers are unable to identify which of the study groups individual patients belong to until after the data have been analysed. These are known as triple-blind trials. Opportunities for introducing blinding into trial protocol vary depending on the nature of the healthcare context. In drug trials, placebos can be used to disguise the allocated treatment; however, this strategy is not possible when evaluating the relative effectiveness of different ways of organizing and delivering a particular type of health care.

Although RCTs and meta-analysis are well-established methodological procedures in health care evaluations, the weaknesses of these approaches have not escaped critical comment from medical researchers and practitioners. For example, it has been suggested that in some circumstances an over-reliance on RCTs may serve to mask the clinical complexity of cases, as there is a tendency to focus on only a small number of independent variables (Prescott et al., 1999). As regards meta-analysis, while there is evidence to suggest that sound meta-analytic studies can lead to improvements in clinical practice, there are situations in which meta-analyses have produced misleading information (Egger & Davey-Smith, 1995; Sweeney, 1996).

Nevertheless, there is no doubt that an evidence-based approach to policy and practice has captured the imagination of many health care professionals and that the randomized experimental approach to assessing the efficacy of interventions has become

established as the "gold standard" of evaluation evidence. This enthusiasm for applying the logic and method of experimental research designs to evaluation questions extends beyond the field of medicine. Evaluators have been encouraged to conduct more experiments in order to identify "what works" in a wide range of policy areas such as education (Fitz-Gibbon, 1999), social work (Macdonald, 2000; Sheldon & Chilvers, 2000) crime prevention (Sherman et al., 1998; Farrington et al., 2002b) and policing (Sherman, 1998). Indeed, there is evidence to suggest that social researchers are beginning to make more use of RCTs and experimental methods (Boruch, Snyder & DeMoya, 2000; Petrosino et al., 2000). However, outside of the health care field there is not the same level of consensus among practitioners and researchers over what qualifies as evidence of effectiveness and what methods and methodologies are best suited to generating and interpreting evaluative data. As described in the next section, the utilization of experimental research designs in these areas is strongly contested and methodological disputes are not uncommon.

Experimental Evaluation

As described above, the notion of experimentation is not only well-established in the evaluation of clinical interventions and medical procedures, but the RCT is placed at the very apex of a hierarchy of evidence. Alternative approaches to gathering evidence are judged as less than ideal by comparison and lacking in methodological rigour. While some commentators have expressed reservations concerning the heavy reliance on RCTs in medicine (Black, 1996; Sweeney, 1996; Britton et al., 1998), this has been very much against a backdrop of a research culture that extols the methodological virtues of the true experiment as an appropriate practical and ethical means of evaluating health care interventions. This is in marked contrast to the situation in other professional domains, where experimental methods and randomization procedures have received a less than enthusiastic response from some practitioners and researchers and consequently have featured less prominently in policy and programme evaluations. Experimental approaches have been criticized for being preoccupied with quantitative measurement, having a tendency to overlook contextual factors, being unsuitable for addressing process issues and having the potential to produce undesirable side-effects (Cronbach, 1982; Guba & Lincoln, 1989; Speller, Learmonth & Harrison, 1997).

While in medical science there has been a steady accumulation of evidence from randomized experiments, in other areas, such as social welfare, public policy and criminal justice, experimental designs have been employed much less frequently. For example, Shepherd (2003) observes that while medical research has witnessed a virtual "feast" of RCTs, there has been a comparative "famine" in the field of criminology. The dearth of experimental studies to investigate the impact of interventions designed to reduce offending behaviour has been well documented (Weisburd, 2000; Petrosino et al., 2001; Farrington, 2003a). In a brief history of randomized experiments in criminology in both the US and UK, Farrington describes how despite the overall famine in experimental research there have been "a few oases (cluster of experiments) in a desert of nonrandomized research" (Farrington, 2003b, p. 219). For example, in the US the California Youth Authority conducted a programme of experimental research on the effectiveness of correctional interventions from 1960 to 1975 and the National Institute of Justice supported a series of experimental studies in the 1980s. However, Garner & Visher (2002) report a

decrease in the number of experimental trials sponsored by the Institute from 1990 to 2000. As far as the UK is concerned, Farrington describes the period from 1965 to 1975 as the "'golden age' of British randomized experiments" in criminology (Farrington, 2003a, p. 164). Outside of these periods of sustained experimental research activity some RCTs were conducted but these tended to be small-scale, localized studies and relatively few in number.

The field of social care is another area where there is evidence of a veritable famine of experimental evaluation designs. This is perhaps somewhat surprising, given that social work was the first of the helping professions to attempt to measure the effectiveness of its work and some early studies in the US (Behling, 1961; Meyer, Borgatta & Jones, 1965) and the UK (Goldberg, 1970) adopted quasi-experimental methods. Various reviews of effectiveness studies in social work have identified small, episodic clusters of experimental and quasi-experimental designs (Sheldon, 1986; Macdonald & Sheldon, 1992). Furthermore, the trend appears to be towards a reduction in the number of such studies. According to Macdonald (2000), "in the last 15 years the number of trials of social work and social care per se has fallen; those conducted are generally smaller, and less methodologically secure than in earlier years" (p. 123).

In some areas of public policy there have been periods when experimental research designs have been utilized to evaluate the impact and effectiveness of policy initiatives and service provision. Take, for example, the evaluation of educational programmes in the US during what has been termed the "golden age of evaluation", that is, from the early 1960s to the early 1980s (Rossi & Wright, 1984). During this period systematic experimentation was a feature of many studies designed to test different approaches to welfare reform. However, support for prospective experimental studies using randomized designs gradually waned as only a few isolated studies revealed any evidence of change in the desired direction. The majority of studies recorded "zero effects". Consequently, this gave rise to a certain amount of pessimism regarding the ability of evaluation research to contribute to policy-making (Weiss, 1987). Commenting on the work of educational evaluators in the US, Cook (2003) notes that while randomized experiments are used in evaluating preschool education and school-based programmes designed to prevent negative behaviours (e.g., programmes designed to promote student health), they are rarely used to study strategies for improving scholastic performance. However, a few oases of RCTs designed to study factors influencing performance levels can be found. A notable example from the US is the Tennessee Experiment, which was conducted to ascertain the relationship between class size and educational achievement (Ritter & Boruch, 1999).

Although randomized experiments are considered by some evaluators to be "the flagships of evaluation" (Rossi and Freeman, 1993, p. 294), and the methodology is firmly established as being ideal for clinical investigations, not all members of the evaluation community support the idea of systematic experimentation as the principal strategy for evaluating social interventions. While in some quarters it is held that experimental studies are superior to non-experimental studies in providing valid answers to questions of policy (Shadish, Cook & Campbell, 2002), the observation that "a consensus has emerged within the professional evaluation community that random assignment is the method of choice for evaluating public programs" (Orr, 1999, p. 28) is open to question. Indeed, experimental designs are in the minority in many professional contexts. In the cases of education, criminal justice and human services and social welfare,

experimental approaches have given rise to fractious and divisive methodological disputes and philosophical arguments among evaluators. It would be wrong to interpret this as simply a feature of an ongoing battle in the paradigm wars. In each of these substantive areas of professional activity, there are advocates and critics of experimental design to be found within both the research and practitioner communities. The positions taken reflect not only a set of methodological preferences but are also influenced by organizational structures, prevailing research cultures and the extent to which evaluators and practitioners share a common understanding as to what evidence-based practice entails. Thus, in order to understand the reasons for the limited use of experimental techniques it is necessary to consider the criticisms levelled at this methodology and the extent to which the professional cultures in the different practice domains are supportive of, and responsive to, empirical evaluations of their work.

Commonly raised objections to the use of experimental techniques in social contexts refer to the complex nature of social interventions, the technical issues, practical problems and ethical dilemmas associated with random assignment procedures, and the methodological appropriateness of experimental designs. When questioning the feasibility of experimental evaluations of social programmes, critics often draw parallels with the situation in clinical settings.

The Nature of Social Interventions

A frequently expressed theme in criticisms of the use of experimental methods in "what works" evaluations concerns the nature and complexity of social interventions. For Mitroff (1983), in a general sense, the complex nature of social systems necessarily restricts the extent to which experimental designs can be applied in social settings. The social experiment is considered by some to be a fairly blunt instrument that is insufficiently sensitive to cope with the subtleties of human interactions and serves "to reduce complex influences to simple causal patterns" (Stecher & Davis, 1987, p. 25). Indeed, there are a number of reasons advanced as to why it is difficult to establish favourable experimental conditions in the case of social interventions. First, it may be difficult to isolate the intervention under investigation from wider social circumstances that may influence whether or not the intended outcomes are achieved. Second, in the case of some social programmes or interventions, it may be difficult to identify a specific set of objectives that can be tested by means of a randomized experiment. Finally, in some professional contexts, there may be a lack of consensus as to how the effectiveness of an intervention or service is conceptualized and measured.

One of the most damning criticisms of RCTs is that they are too rigid a tool in the context of social interventions. Critics who oppose the idea of transferring to human services and social welfare settings those experimental methods that are the hallmark of evidence-based practice in health care, often base their objections on the broad scope and diverse nature of social work activity. They maintain that there is something about the very nature of social work interventions that makes experimental evaluation inappropriate. Social work is not a "tidily delimited activity" (Cheetham et al., 1992, p. 13); the provision of social work support involves encounters that "are not straightforward or linear relationships, but multiple, multilayered, relational and complex" (Trinder, 2000b, p. 149). It is this apparent inherent complexity that is seen as preventing the adoption of classic experimental research designs to ascertain what works in social work practice.

The complexity of treatment situations has also been highlighted as a problem in the context of criminal justice interventions. For example, when Clarke & Cornish (1972) attempted to conduct a large-scale randomized trial in the UK, to evaluate a therapeutic community at the Kingswood Training School in Bristol, they ended up listing a number of objections to randomized experiments. One of these concerned the difficulties they encountered in ascertaining what actually constituted treatment. Their observations were made within a critique of the medical model, to the extent that penal treatments were viewed as being much more complex than medical treatments. The situation was further complicated by the fact that the treatments were not consistent but varied over time. Consequently, the "complexity of the treatments and the fact that they were changed significantly during the experiment meant that whatever results were obtained could not be explained" (Nuttall, 2003, p. 277).

Clearly there are qualitative differences between clinical treatments and the kind of interventions produced by social programmes. For example, in the case of the latter, programme participants or clients are not necessarily passive recipients of an intervention, but have the option of actively engaging with a programme. The level of commitment shown by an individual may be a function of a complex interaction of personal and social factors that are not entirely related to the treatment received, but nevertheless may influence programme outcomes. Take, for example, a criminal justice programme designed to reduce offending behaviour by providing cognitive skills training courses to change offenders' attitudes to crime and promote pro-social behaviour. In evaluating such a programme it is not possible to isolate recipients from their surroundings and create a controlled environment for the purpose of experimentation. The factors influencing offending behaviour are many and varied, and programme participants are embedded in a web of social relationships with family members and friends outside the context of the intervention. Given the complexity of attitude formation and change, these external factors may have a bearing on desistance from offending. However, to suggest that the inherent complexity of social interventions, and the difficulties of disentangling causes, warrants a universal rejection of RCTs as an evaluative strategy is perhaps overly hasty. True experiments have a valuable though limited role to play in evaluation. For example, randomized trials are designed to cope with external variations and confounding factors. While this does not necessarily mean that RCTs are appropriate in *all* situations where treatment efficacy is evaluated, they may constitute a viable option in certain contexts.

Technical Issues and Practical Problems

The nature of social interventions has implications when it comes to implementing experimental research designs. When highlighting the types of technical issues and practical problems encountered in this context, critics often draw a comparison with the conduct of clinical trials. In the case of the latter, the experimental context is one in which a clearly measurable treatment is delivered in a controlled situation and the physiological effect of the treatment dose is relatively predictable from one person to the next. In contrast, the situation facing social interventions is very different. Here the experimental situation is less easily controlled, the potential treatment effect is harder to predict and the exclusion of extraneous factors more difficult to achieve. Furthermore, given the form and nature of social interventions, double-blind trials, as used in the evaluation of pharmacological treatments, are not practicable.

Ethical Considerations

As Oakley (2000) asserts, "The modern use of RCTs in medicine and other fields carries with it substantial historical baggage" (p. 287). Examples of infamous cases of unethical medical experimentation, such as the Tuskegee syphilis study, can still influence resistance to experimental research designs (Jones, 1981). An objection commonly levelled at RCTs is that they are fundamentally unethical, on account of the fact that those people assigned to a control group are seen as being denied access to a service or treatment that would otherwise be of benefit to them. As Oakley et al., (1995) point out, this was an argument frequently expressed in the early days of evaluations of interventions in the field of HIV and AIDS. Whatever the professional context, where practitioners have a responsibility for providing clients with access to services, their views about the needs of individual clients may undermine their support for random allocation for the purposes of conducting an evaluation. In a controlled intervention study of social support in pregnancy, Oakley (1992) describes how the midwives responsible for delivering care expressed concern over the allocation of women to different treatment groups. In some instances they felt that women, who in their opinion were in need of additional support, were being allocated to the control group. Similarly, in the criminological field, Clarke & Cornish (1972) in their study of the Kingswood Training School, describe how practitioners expressed concern that random allocation could lead to some offenders receiving the "wrong" treatment or no treatment at all. As a result, practitioners referred a decreasing number of boys to the school, thus jeopardizing the integrity of the experimental design. From their experiences the authors concluded that "evaluation in the penal field poses particular ethical problems, of a complexity not usually encountered in medical research" (Clarke & Cornish, 1972, p. 8).

There is no doubt that practical and ethical problems are encountered when attempting to conduct randomized experiments in criminal justice settings. For example, Farrington et al., (2002a) describe how they had to abandon a randomized controlled research design and adopt a quasi-experimental approach in a study of the effectiveness of two intensive treatment regimes in young offender institutions. One of the main problems concerned the potential adverse consequences of the random assignment of young offenders to different regimes. In some cases, this could have led to young offenders being accommodated in institutions some distance from their homes, thus making it difficult for them to maintain contact with their families through regular visits. Thus, evaluators need to be aware of the possibility that controlled field experiments can have undesired consequences.

Whatever the programme or policy context, the ethical debate focuses heavily on the process of random assignment. Indeed, much of the criticism of experimental evaluation is directed not at experimental methods per se, but at the use of random allocation as a research technique. What is sometimes overlooked is that ethical issues are not confined to the implementation of experimental methodologies, but apply at all stages of the evaluation process irrespective of whether the research methods employed are experimental or non-experimental. It is just that the process of randomization confronts evaluators with some additional ethical dilemmas, such as the possibility of control group subjects being deprived of access to treatment. There is, however, an emerging literature describing how these ethical issues can be addressed and randomized experiments conducted in the criminal justice arena in accordance with ethical principles (Feder & Boruch, 2000; Weisburd, 2000).

A fundamental principle of experimental research is that experiments should only be undertaken in conditions where there is uncertainty surrounding the effects of a particular treatment. Where there is no knowledge that a treatment works, withholding the said treatment from control group participants is not necessarily unethical. In each evaluative context, the onus is placed on the experimental evaluator to demonstrate the feasibility of adopting an experimental approach and show how the advantages to be gained from conducting randomized experiments outweigh the disadvantages. Correspondingly, "the challenge to those opposed to experimentation is to show why experiments should *not* be used" (Farrington, 2003a, p. 164; emphasis in original). For those who consider RCTs to be the most powerful method available for assessing the effectiveness of a treatment or intervention, there is a moral imperative for conducting randomized experiments. As Weisburd (2003) argues:

> Traditionally, it has been assumed that the burden has been on the experimenter to explain why it is ethical to use experimental methods. My suggestion is that we must begin rather with a case for why experiments should not be used. The burden here is on the researcher to explain why a less valid method should be the basis for coming to conclusions about treatment or practice. The ethical problem is that when choosing nonexperimental methods we may be violating our basic professional obligation to provide the most valid answers we can to the questions that we are asked to answer. (p. 350)

Although his comments are made in the general context of crime and criminal justice evaluations, the argument is applicable to other policy areas and practice environments.

Despite the objections to RCTs, there is evidence of a growing interest in exploring the potential for using experimental methods for evaluating social interventions across a variety of policy and practice domains (Weiss, 1998; Fitz-Gibbon, 1999; Macdonald, 1999). Oakley et al., (2003) describe how they adopted randomization procedures and gained the informed consent of programme participants in three separate intervention studies. One study involved the evaluation of day care provision for mothers with young children, another compared two alternative strategies for providing support for mothers in deprived inner-city areas and one was an evaluation of peer-led sex education in secondary schools. The implementation of random allocation techniques was generally accepted by both service providers and potential recipients. Interestingly, the authors note that they ". . . found much less resistance among practitioners – teachers, local health and education authority staff, community organizations, health visitors – than among some of our academic social science colleagues" (Oakley et al., 2003, p. 185). On the basis of the experience gained in conducting randomized trials, they maintain that researchers wishing to apply such methods to the evaluation of social interventions need to invest time and effort in negotiating the use of random allocation. This requires much preparatory work and the research needs to be designed to ensure that it

1. addresses an important policy or practice question, which is considered a priority issue by trial participants;
2. has a clear scientific and policy rationale for using random allocation;
3. allows enough time for detailed discussions with the stakeholder groups that need to "sign" up to random allocation and is sensitive to stakeholder perspectives;
4. includes the careful piloting of recruitment and informed consent procedures and ways of explaining RCT design; and
5. gives particular consideration to the position of control groups, including how

best to encourage them to feel that it is worthwhile to make an active contribution to the research. (Oakley et al., 2003, p. 185)

The suggestion here is that experimental procedures form a legitimate part of the evaluators' methodological toolkit. This is far from arguing that RCTs represent a gold standard against which all other experimental and non-experimental designs can be found wanting.

Methodological Appropriateness

While there are some areas of policy and practice where evaluators have overcome ethical and practical problems and successfully conducted randomized experiments, there are still questions surrounding the transferability of this methodology from clinical settings and its application in the evaluation of social interventions. One issue concerns the type of evidence on effectiveness required to inform decision-making in the different practice environments. Basically, a distinction can be drawn between "pragmatic" and "explanatory" trials (Schwartz, Flamant & Lellouch, 1980). In the case of the former, the focus is on determining whether the group that received the intervention displayed, in aggregate terms, better outcomes than the non-intervention group. This pragmatic approach is characteristic of drug trials and the assessment of many healthcare initiatives, where the objective is to merely ascertain the net effect of an intervention as measured by aggregate outcomes. In contrast, explanatory studies seek to explore the causal connection between interventions and outcomes. In other words, the aim is not to simply establish if an intervention is effective, but to try and develop some understanding as to why it has the desired impact. This type of approach is of critical importance in contexts such as criminal justice and social work, where in the interests of more effective practice, practitioners need to know what works for whom and under what conditions. However, where experimental studies have been mounted they have tended to be of the pragmatic type, thus giving rise to the observation that ". . . experimentalists have pursued too single-mindedly the question of whether a program works at the expense of knowing why it works" (Pawson & Tilley, 1997, p. xv).

The pragmatic view that it is merely sufficient for professional practitioners to know if an intervention or treatment is effective, without also knowing *how* the positive results are achieved, is open to criticism. The successful transfer of evaluation evidence to policy or practice contexts is not an automatic process. The fact that experimental evidence might suggest that a particular course of action is effective does not guarantee that it will necessarily be acted upon by practitioners. As Simons (2004) indicates, motivation is of crucial importance. Professionals must not only want to make use of evaluation findings but they must also be able to perceive the relevance of such findings to their particular practice settings. The possibility of the successful application of evaluation evidence is therefore enhanced when professionals have knowledge and understanding of *how* certain treatments, programmes and interventions produce desired outcomes. It is the acquisition and application of such knowledge that helps to inform programme delivery and implementation.

While pragmatic evaluations are useful for either establishing the relative effectiveness of a number of different interventions or ascertaining whether a particular intervention is better than no intervention at all, they are of limited value when it comes to providing practitioners with evidence that will help them to identify what interventions might work with which types of client. Experimental studies generate evidence from aggregate populations in the form of averaged effects, which gives

rise to the question as to how applicable trial results are likely to be at the level of individual patients or clients. For example, in cases where interventions have diverse impacts on individuals, the randomization process aggregates these into mean scores for the different treatment groups. Thus, the positive effects experienced by some programme participants are cancelled out by the negative effects experienced by others. This is what is known as the aggregate net-effect problem and has implications when it comes to using evaluation findings to inform decision-making in professional practice. Whatever the occupational setting, the practitioner needs to establish the relevance of the research findings to her or his particular professional context. However, given the nature of social programmes, intervention effects can vary across diverse groups, thus casting doubt on the extent to which the aggregate results from a particular RCT can be expected to apply when translated to different individuals in different settings.

Evaluation research strategies that utilize randomized controls have been much criticized by scientific realists (Pawson & Tilley, 1997). Basically, experimental methods are seen as giving primacy to the generation of empirical evidence regarding programme effectiveness, at the expense of developing a theoretical understanding of how interventions work. In short, the suggestion is that the experimental method might be technically robust but it is not considered suitable for universal application. As Pawson & Tilley (1994) maintain: "Such an approach is a fine strategy for evaluating the relative performances of washing powders or crop fertilizers, but is a lousy means of expressing the nature of causality and change going on within social programmes" (p. 292). They assert that experimental methodology is underpinned by a successionist conceptualization of causality (Harré, 1972), which holds that causal inferences are founded on the observation of regularities in the occurrence and patterning of events. In other words, causes are not actually observed directly but inferred from the observation of outcomes. Consequently, if intervention and control groups are equivalent, apart from the fact that the former receives the treatment under evaluation, any difference in outcomes between the groups is attributed to the impact of the intervention. According to Pawson & Tilley, this notion of causality is not particularly helpful as far as evaluation research is concerned, as it does not offer any means of understanding the relationship between interventions and outcomes. The results of a RCT may suggest that an intervention has worked, but there is no way of deducing from the results what it is about the intervention that made it work.

From a realist perspective, adopting experimental controls and random allocation procedures in order to ensure group equivalence is seen as failing to appreciate the complex nature of social interventions. A social programme does not constitute a singular treatment or "dose", but consists of a complex series of interactions between people. In this context, interventions are not perceived as externally imposed forces to which subjects simply respond. According to the realist critique, " . . . it is not actual programmes which 'work' but the reasoning and opportunities of the people experiencing the programmes which makes them work" (Pawson & Tilley, 1993, p. 2); "programs 'work' if subjects choose to make them work and are placed in the right conditions to enable them to do so" (Pawson, 1997, p. 413). However, by randomly assigning subjects to intervention and control groups, to control for the influence of extraneous factors and cancel out the differences between groups, experimental evaluations are unable to explore those characteristics of individuals and groups that are associated with successful outcomes. Indeed, what is interesting about interventions in criminal justice is the important interaction that takes place between the nature of the intervention or treatment and the nature of the subjects involved. One of the aims of realist evaluation is to develop an understanding of this interaction by determining and investigating the mechanisms through which an intervention attempts to bring about change and also identifying the most favourable contextual conditions for such change. Adopting an explanatory perspective, Pawson & Tilley (1997) maintain that "outcomes follow from mechanisms acting in contexts" (p. 85), which they refer to as context–mechanism–outcome configurations (p. 77). This illustrates a "generative" conception of causality, in which causal powers are not seen as residing in specific programme events, but in the social relations and organizational structures which form part of a wider social system.

Whereas the traditional experimental approach to evaluation can be described as methods-driven, the realist approach, by comparison, is theory-driven. These have been referred to as "black box" and "white box" evaluations respectively (Scriven, 1994). The former is where the emphasis is placed on evaluating the overall effects of a programme without really investigating the individual components that constitute the programme. A "white box" evaluation studies the programme effects, but also examines how the individual components operate to produce programme outcomes. In the case of realistic evaluation, this entails evaluating specific mechanism–context interactions. This approach does not rule out the use of experimental methods entirely. As Tilley (2000) asserts, theory-driven quasi-experimentation may be possible in situations where a theory has been formulated to the extent that context-mechanism–outcome configurations can be clearly articulated.

While the realist paradigm has attracted a considerable amount of interest and generated much debate, there are as yet relatively few worked examples of studies where this perspective has been applied. In the area of crime and criminal justice, Pawson & Tilley (1997) describe how they used realist principles in evaluating the impact of closed-circuit television on criminal activity in car parks and Duguid & Pawson (1998) report a realist-oriented study of the rehabilitative effects of a prison-based education programme. In the field of social work, Kazi illustrates how adopting Pawson & Tilley's (1997) concept of the "realist evaluation cycle" (p. 85) helps to "penetrate into the realities of practice deeper than the traditionalist view of evidence-based practice" (Kazi, 2003, p. 816). This realist strategy involves the use of a broad repertoire of quantitative and qualitative methods to monitor context–mechanism–outcome configurations. As an approach it provides not only outcome data on programme effectiveness (i.e., what works), but also helps in the formulation of explanations as to why a programme may work for some clients but not others. Developing such a contextualized understanding of the effectiveness of an intervention is essential when it comes to making decisions about the practicalities and feasibility of making a particular programme available to a wider population.

As far as evaluation strategies for determining "what works" are concerned there is a place for both randomized experimental designs and theory-driven approaches. According to Davies, Nutley & Tilley (2000) ". . . a judicious mix of the two may provide rich evidence on which to devise interventions, inform policy and shape professional practice" (p. 271). Where a methodological choice has to be made, consideration needs to be given to the nature and complexity of the treatment or intervention and the circumstances in which it is

delivered. For example, RCTs are more appropriate in evaluative settings where there are only a small number of variables to consider, the treatment is relatively easy to administer, monitor and control, and human agency is of little consequence in terms of determining outcomes. In contrast, a theory-driven approach is best suited to policy and practice contexts where human agency is a critical factor and the relationship between treatment and outcomes is a complex one that requires some elaboration.

Mixed-Method Evaluation

As described above, in recent years the drive towards ensuring that policy and practice become "evidence-based" has led to an increasing demand for outcome-oriented evaluations that produce evidence of effectiveness. Alongside the development of a performance measurement culture in public sector organizations, there has been a growth in the number of experimental studies designed to determine the efficacy of various interventions and programmes. Given that it would be risky to base changes in practice on the findings of a single study, systematic reviews of multiple studies are undertaken to help build a wider knowledge base. It has been observed that "Making a decision about 'what works' based upon multiple RCTs is becoming as critical in the social, behavioural, and education sciences as it is in medicine" (Turner et al., 2003, p. 207). While this may be the case, the methodology is not without its limitations. Consequently, given the need for evaluative research to develop knowledge and understanding in order to answer "what works" questions, a wide range of methods and methodological techniques need to be drawn upon. As noted by Greene, Benjamin & Goodyear (2001), "We need to marshal *all* of our multiple ways of knowing, and their associated multiple ways of valuing, in the service of credible and useful understanding. We need to adopt a *mixed-method way of thinking* about evaluation, especially social and educational program evaluation" (p. 26, emphasis in original). In this context, RCTs are best seen as *one* of a number of methods capable of contributing to a comprehensive evaluative research strategy. It is the mixing of methods in a diverse range of professional settings that forms a major challenge for evaluators conducting "what works" studies.

The exhortation to include multiple ways of knowing and valuing in making evaluative judgments raises a question concerning the nature of evidence. While the idea that the decisions and actions of practitioners and policymakers should be based on evidence is not particularly contentious, controversy arises when it comes to establishing what actually counts as evidence and what kinds of knowledge are of value. Eraut (2000) distinguishes between three kinds of knowledge used by professionals: *codified* knowledge, *personal* knowledge and *cultural* knowledge. Evidence-based practice, in whatever professional domain, is not the simple, straightforward application of a body of codified knowledge produced by empirical research. Decision-making is informed by other factors, such as "practice-based evidence" (Eraut, 2003) "practical knowledge or wisdom" (Schwandt, 2000) and "tacit knowledge" (Polanyi, 1958). As Hargreaves notes, ". . . both education and medicine are profoundly people-centred professions. Neither believes that helping people is merely a matter of a simple and technical application but rather a highly skilled process in which a sophisticated judgment matches a professional decision to the unique needs of each client" (quoted in Hammersley, 2000, p. 170). This could also be said of other settings such as social work and probation. Thus, the knowledge on which practice decisions are based is not solely the product of the

application of scientific methods or the accumulation of evidence derived from formal and systematic evaluations. Indeed, " . . . judgments are discerned from experience and utilize wisdom – integrated experience and knowing – as much as specific knowledge or evaluation evidence" (Simons, 2004, p. 418). As such, professional practice generates its own evidence as well as making use of research-based evidence.

Critics of the evidence-based practice perspective claim that too much emphasis is placed on scientific evidence at the expense of professional experience and judgment. They maintain that many professions engage in practical rather than technical work. Hammersley (2000) argues that this is the situation with teaching, where the existence of multiple, diverse goals that are difficult to operationalize can mean that narrowly focused outcome evaluations can often fail to provide sound empirical evidence of the relative effectiveness of different interventions. Furthermore, he maintains that a focus on effectiveness can lead to too much emphasis being placed on those outcomes that can be easily measured, resulting in other educational goals being ignored. In the case of social work, Cheetham et al., (1992) argue that the processes and effects of social work interventions are so diverse that they cannot be incorporated in standardized outcome measures.

Whatever the professional context, when practitioners make decisions concerning the care and treatment of patients or clients they take a variety of factors and a number of different forms of evidence into account. For example, in commenting on the decision-making engaged in by general practitioners, Jacobson et al., (1997) illustrate the existence of different types of evidence, the limitations of RCTs and the need to use more than one research method when exploring physician–patient interactions in the delivery of health care.

Doctors also need evidence that is derived from a patient-centred paradigm and that recognises the personal and contextual elements to decision-making in practice. Examining these elements, another concern about EBM (evidence-based medicine) becomes apparent: the RCT is often unhelpful in these investigations even though it is promoted as the gold standard of research methodology. The research methods used to obtain data in the personal and contextual dimensions may require different strategies, allowing more for "circumstantial" evidence rather than the 'watertight' evidence of the RCT . . . (Jacobson et al., 1997, p. 450).

In health care evaluations, health is seen as a multidimensional concept; it is not defined by clinical criteria alone, but includes patient-provided assessments of physical functioning, general well-being and perceived quality of life. As clinically based measures of treatment outcomes do not always reflect the views and feelings of patients (Jenkinson, 1994), the increasing use of patient-assessed outcomes in the evaluation of care is to be welcomed, as these measures are sensitive to the positive and negative effects associated with the clinically defined treatment benefits (Jenkinson, 1995). Such subjective assessments of well-being can be used alongside RCTs in multimethod evaluations (Fitzpatrick, 1994).

A single-method evaluation research design, especially one based on random experimentation, is unlikely to reflect the everyday realities in which interventions operate and outcomes are generated. Although randomized experiments have a firmly established methodological pedigree, they also have their weaknesses. These are especially evident when dealing with complex and contextually diverse interventions. RCTs are more appropriate in situations where there are a small number of clearly identified, uncontested and easily measured outcomes; they are not particularly well-suited to natural settings in which

outcomes are conceptually ambiguous, ill-defined and not readily subject to quantitative measurement. The very nature of some social interventions can make it difficult for evaluators when it comes to identifying potential causal mechanisms. For example, Abrams (1984) noted how informal social care cannot be easily subjected to experimental evaluation on account of ". . . the problem of breaking down the intractable informality of the treatment; of reducing informal caring relationships to the sort of units, factors, events, variables, items needed if specifiable inputs are to be systematically related to specifiable outcomes" (p. 2). In circumstances such as these, qualitative methods can be applied to explore the experiences of programme participants and service users in order to identify what elements of a specific intervention they find beneficial in what contexts.

How the question of mixing methods is addressed within the domain of evaluation will to some extent be influenced by how professional practice is perceived as an activity. The dominant discourse of evidence-based policy and practice, as it currently stands, places considerable emphasis on the use of experimental methods for generating evidence to inform decision-making. According to this view, improving practice in any professional domain involves the technical application of knowledge generated by intervention studies. The status accorded to experimental techniques limits opportunities for mixed-method evaluative research designs. If professionals are to be encouraged to review practice, then evidence is needed that takes account of the reality of the practice worlds of professionals. In this context, Simons (2004) urges that we need to develop a conceptualization of practice as "an educational, moral, practical activity in which the agency of the person and the socio-political context are integral to the generation and use of evidence to inform practice" (p. 412). This broader conceptualization of professional practice calls for a wider range of evidence than can be provided by RCTs alone. Along with the growth in practitioner evaluation and the encouragement of participatory approaches, this will create a climate favourable to the adoption of multi-method evaluation strategies.

Developing more complex evaluations that combine and integrate different research methods is one of the major challenges in the foreseeable future. Compared to single method research designs, multimethod methodologies are more likely to provide a comprehensive understanding of programmes and their outcomes. Indeed, the very nature and complexity of interventions and practices in health, educational, criminal justice and social work settings makes combined methods evaluations essential in many contexts. However, in pursuing mixed and multiple methods evaluation designs, evaluators will no doubt face numerous philosophical, practical and political challenges. As is well documented in the evaluation literature, the merits and demerits of quantitative and qualitative approaches to data collection and analysis have been fiercely debated as part of the discussion of the "paradigm problem" (Chambers, Wedel & Rodwell, 1992). Consequently, introducing a combined methods approach may be more difficult in some contexts than others.

The philosophical differences characteristic of the major paradigmatic stances cannot be dismissed simply by choosing the most effective combination of methods in any given evaluative context. As Dingwall (1992) observes, the view that science is nothing more than a collection of techniques is a major methodological fallacy: "it is rather a state of mind or attitude and the organisational conditions which allow that attitude to be expressed" (p. 163). It is this state of mind or attitude that can be an obstacle when it comes to promoting the use of alternative methods and methodologies. For example, in medicine, the natural scientific paradigm has become the dominant discourse, which has resulted in the actual institutionalization of experimental methods. There are well-established administrative procedures and managerial processes for facilitating RCTs, which has to a certain degree led to the relative exclusion of some qualitative approaches (Greenhalgh, 1996). Shepherd (2003) explains the feast of RCTs in clinical medicine and the comparative dearth of such experimental designs in criminology in terms of cultural and structural factors. Clinicians not only treat patients and conduct research but they are also involved in the education and training of medical students and practitioners. This involvement facilitates the integration of theory, evaluation and practice at a professional level. In contrast, in criminology there is a marked disjuncture between academic criminology and professional practice. While there is an established research culture and a desire to understand what type of interventions are most effective, there is no universal acceptance of randomized experiments as the gold standard. Where randomized evaluations of crime and criminal justice programmes and practices have been undertaken, these have been the result of the influence of key individuals within the field, rather than a reflection of a broad-based acceptance of the randomized experiment as an ethically and practically appropriate means of evaluating criminal justice interventions (Farrington, 2003b).

Clearly, there is considerable diversity between the professional domains in the breadth, depth and quality of evidence that is available to inform decision-making. In part, this diversity may be attributed to a number of factors: the existence of differences in the attitudes of practitioners towards evidence-based practice; the extent to which there is support for evidence-based evaluation in different organizational contexts; the degree to which there is a research culture that actively fosters and facilitates rigorous, focused and systematic evaluations of programmes and policies; and the success with which closer working relationships or formal partnerships are established between evaluators and the users of evaluation research findings. The complex and diverse nature of social interventions presents a challenge to evaluators and no matter what the programme or practice context, producing credible evidence requires the use of both quantitative and qualitative methods as and when appropriate.

Conclusion

According to the evidence-based agenda, the prevailing view is that randomized experiments are required in order to generate an adequate body of scientific knowledge to inform policy and practice. However, as argued above, this "gold standard" model does not necessarily provide an adequate basis for professional practice in all contexts. The practice of evaluation is a multidisciplinary activity, which involves acquiring evidence and knowledge through the application of a broad range of methods and methodologies in diverse professional domains and policy settings. Within the various professional domains there is a need to encourage the accumulation of evidence from multiple evaluations, using a variety of methods, in order to produce generalizable findings regarding the principles of effective programming and thus ensure that the evaluation profession becomes "a reservoir for knowledge about generic patterns of program effectiveness" (Patton, 2001, p. 334). Furthermore, within the evaluation domain itself, much could be gained from accumulating knowledge

about the conduct of evaluation in the different policy and practice settings that would help to contribute to developments in the theory and practice of evaluation.

References

Abrams, P. (1984). Evaluating soft findings: some problems of measuring informal care. *Research, Policy and Planning*, 2(2), 1–8.

Arenian, H. K. & Lilienfield, D. E. (1994). Overview and historical perspective, *Epidemiology Review*, 16, 1–5.

Behling, J. H. (1961). *An Experimental Study to Measure the Effectiveness of Casework Service*. Colombus, Ohio: Ohio State University.

Black, N. (1996). Why we need observational studies to evaluate the effectiveness of health care. *British Medical Journal*, 312, 1215–1218.

Boruch, R., Snyder, B., & DeMoya, D. (2000). The importance of randomized field trials. *Crime and Delinquency*, 46, 156–180.

Britton, A., McKee, M., Black, N., McPherson, K., Sanderson, C., & Bain, C. (1998). Choosing between randomised and non-randomised studies: a systematic review *Health Technology Assessment*, 2(13), i–iv, 1–124.

Cabinet Office (1999a). *Modernising Government*. White Paper, Cmnd 4310. London: The Cabinet Office.

Cabinet Office (1999b). *Professional Policymaking in the 21st Century*. London: The Cabinet Office.

Canadian Task Force on the Periodic Health Examination (1994). *The Canadian Guide to Clinical Preventive Health Care*. Ottawa: Canada Communication Group.

Chalmers, I. (2003). Trying to do more good than harm in policy and practice: the role of rigorous, transparent, up-to-date evaluations. *The Annals of the American Academy of Political and Social Science*, 589, 22–40.

Chalmers, I. & Altman, D. (1995). *Systematic Reviews*. London: BMJ Publishing.

Chambers, D. E., Wedel, K. R., & Rodwell, M. K. (1992). *Evaluating Social Programs*. Boston: Allyn & Bacon.

Cheetham, J., Fuller, R., McIvor, G., & Petch, A. (1992). *Evaluating Social Work Effectiveness*. Buckingham: Open University Press.

Clarke, M. (ed.) (2002) The Cochrane Collaboration: preparing, maintaining, and promoting the accessibility of systematic reviews of health care interventions. *Evaluation and the Health Professions*, special edition, 25(1).

Clarke, M. J. & Stewart, L. A. (1994). Obtaining data from randomised controlled trials: how much do we need for reliable and informative meta-analyses? *British Medical Journal*, 309, 1007–1010.

Clarke, R. V. G. & Cornish, D. B. (1972). *The Controlled Trial in Institutional Research: Paradigm or pitfall for penal evaluators?* Home Office Research Study No. 16. London: Home Office.

Cochrane, A. (1972). *Effectiveness and Efficiency: Random Reflections on Health Services.* London: Nuffield Provincial Hospitals Trust.

Cook, T. D. (2003). Why have educational evaluators chosen not to do randomized experiments?. *The Annals of the American Academy of Political and Social Science*, 589, 114–149.

Cronbach, L. J. (1982). *Designing Evaluations of Educational and Social Programs.* San Francisco: Jossey-Bass.

Davies, H., Nutley, S. & Tilley, N. (2000). Debates on the role of experimentation. In H. T. O. Davies, S. M. Nutley, & P. C. Smith (eds) *What Works? Evidence-based policy and practice in public services.* Bristol: The Policy Press.

Dickersin, K. (1990). The existence of publication bias and risk factors for its occurrence. *Journal of the American Medical Association*, 263, 1385–1389.

Dingwall, R. (1992). Don't mind him – he's from Barcelona: qualitative methods in health studies. In J. Daly, I. McDonald & E. Willis (eds) *Researching Health Care: Designs, dilemmas. disciplines.* London: Tavistock/Routledge.

Duguid, S. & Pawson, R. (1998). Education, change and transformation: The prison experience. *Evaluation Review*, 22(4), 470–495.

Egger, M. & Davey-Smith, G. (1995). Misleading meta-analysis. *British Medical Journal*, 310, 752–754.

Eraut, M. (2000). The dangers of managing with an inadequate view of knowledge. Paper presented to the Third International Conference of Socio-Cultural Psychology, Brazil, July.

Eraut, M. (2003). Practice-based evidence. In G. Thomas & R. Pring (eds) *Evidence-Based Policy and Practice.* Milton Keynes: Open University Press.

Evidence-Based Medicine Working Group (1992). Evidence-based medicine: a new approach to teaching the practice of medicine. *Journal of the American Association*, 268, 2420–2425.

Farrington, D. P. (2003a). British randomized experiments on crime and justice. *The Annals of the American Academy of Political and Social Science*, 589, 150–167.

Farrington, D. P. (2003b). A short history of randomized experiments in criminology: a meagre feast. *Evaluation Review*, 27(3), 218–227.

Farrington, D. P., Ditchfield, J., Hancock, G., Howard, P., Jolliffe, D., Livingston, M. S., & Painter, K. A. (2002a). *Evaluation of Two Intensive Regimes for Young Offenders.* Home Office Research Study No. 239. London: Home Office.

Farrington, D. P., Gottfredson, D. C., Sherman, L. W., & Welsh, B. C. (2002b). The Maryland scientific methods scale. In L. W. Sherman, D. P. Farrington, B. C. Welsh & D. L. MacKenzie (eds) *Evidence-Based Crime Prevention* (pp. 13–21). London: Routledge.

Feder, L. & Boruch, R. (2000). The need for experiments in criminal justice settings. *Crime and Delinquency*, 46, 291–294.

Fitz-Gibbon, C. T. (1999). Education: High potential not yet realized. *Public Money and Management*, 19(1), 33–40.

Fitzpatrick, R. (1994). Applications of health status measures In C. Jenkinson (ed.) *Measuring Health and Medical Outcomes.* London: UCL Press, pp. 27–41.

Garner, J. H. & Visher, C. A. (2002). *The Co-production of Criminological Experiments.* Washington DC: The Urban Institute.

Glass, G. V., McGaw, B., & Smith, M. L. (1981). *Meta-analysis in Social Research*, Beverly Hills, CA: Sage Publications.

Goldberg, M. (1970). *Helping the Aged.* London: George Allen and Unwin.

Greene, J. C., Benjamin, L., & Goodyear, L. (2001). The merits of mixing methods in evaluation. *Evaluation*, 7(1), 25–44.

Greenhalgh, T. (1996). "Is my practice evidence-based?" Should be answered in qualitative, as well as quantitative terms. *British Medical Journal*, 313, 957–958.

Guba, E. G. & Lincoln, Y. S. (1989). *Fourth Generation Evaluation.* Newbury Park, CA: Sage.

Guyatt, G., Sackett, D., Sinclair, J., Hayward, R., Cook, D., & Cook, R. (1995). Users' Guides to the Medical Literature 9. A method for grading health-care recommendations. *Journal of the American Medical Association*, 274, 1800–1804.

Hammersley, M. (2000). Evidence-based practice in education and the contribution of educational research In L. Trinder with S. Reynolds (eds) *Evidence-Based Practice: A Critical Appraisal* (pp. 163–183). Oxford: Blackwell Science.

Harré, R. (1972). *The Philosophies of Science*, Oxford: Oxford University Press.

Hood, C. (1991). A public management for all seasons? *Public Administration*, 69(1), 3–19.

Hunt, M. (1997). *How Science Takes Stock: The story of meta-analysis*. New York: Russell Sage Foundation.

Jacobson, L. G., Edwards, A. G. K., Granier, S. K., & Butler, C. G. (1997). Evidence based medicine and general practice. *British Journal of General Practice*, 47(420), 449–452.

Jenkinson, C. (1994). Measuring health and medical outcomes: an overview In C. Jenkinson (ed.) *Measuring Health and Medical Outcomes*. London: UCL Press.

Jenkinson, C. (1995). Evaluating the efficacy of medical treatment: possibilities and limitations *Social Science and Medicine*, 41(10), 1395–1401.

Jones, J. H. (1981). *Bad Blood*, New York: Free Press.

Kazi, M. (2003). Realist evaluation practice. *British Journal of Social Work*, 33(6), 803–818.

Khan, K. S., Kunz, R., Kleijnen, J., & Antes, G. (2003). *Systematic Reviews to Support Evidence-Based Medicine: How to review and apply findings in healthcare research*. London: Royal Society of Medicine Press.

Light, R. J. & Pillemer, D. B. (1984). *Summing Up: The science of reviewing research*. Cambridge, MA: Harvard University Press.

Lilford, R. J. & Stevens, A. (2001). Introduction: Part I: Clinical Trials. In A. Stevens, K. Abrams, J. Brazier, R. Fitzpatrick & R. Lilford (eds) *The Advanced Handbook of Methods in Evidence Based Healthcare* (pp. 7–9) London: Sage.

Lilford, R. J., Edwards, S. J. L., Braunholtz, D. A., Jackson, J., Thornton, J., & Hewison, J. (2001). Ethical issues in the design and conduct of randomised controlled trials. In A. Stevens, K. Abrams, J. Brazier, R. Fitzpatrick & R. Lilford, (eds) *The Advanced Handbook of Methods in Evidence Based Healthcare* (pp. 11–24). London: Sage.

Love, A. J. (2001). The future of evaluation: catching rocks with cauldrons. *American Journal of Evaluation*, 22(3), 437–444.

Macdonald, G. (1999). Evidence-based social care: Wheels off the runway? *Public Money and Management*, 19(1), 25–32.

Macdonald, G. (2000). Social care: rhetoric and reality. In H. T. O. Davies, S. M. Nutley & P. C. Smith (eds) *What Works? Evidence-based policy and practice in public services.* (pp. 117–140). Bristol: The Policy Press.

Macdonald, G. M. & Sheldon, B. (1992). Contemporary studies of the effectiveness of social work. *British Journal of Social Work*, 22(6), 615–643.

Marston, G. and Watts, R. (2003). Tampering with the evidence: a critical appraisal of evidence-based policy-making. *The Drawing Board: An Australian Review of Public Affairs*, 3(3), 143–163.

Meyer, H., Borgatta, E., & Jones, W. (1965). *Girls at Vocational High: An experiment in social work intervention*. New York: Russell Sage Foundation.

Mitroff, I. (1983). Beyond experimentation. In E. Seidman (ed.) *Handbook of Social Intervention*, Beverly Hills, CA: Sage.

Mulrow, C. D. (1994). Rationale for systematic reviews. *British Medical Journal*, 309, 597–599.

Mykhalovskiy, E. & Weir, L. (2004). The problem of evidence-based medicine: directions for social science. *Social Science and Medicine*, 59(5), 1059–1069.

National Audit Office (2000). *Good Practice in Performance Reporting in Executive Agencies and Non-Departmental Public Bodies*. Report by the Comptroller and Auditor General.

NHS Centre for Reviews and Dissemination (1996). *Review of the Research on the Effectiveness of Health Service Interventions to Reduce Variations in Health:* Part I. York: NHS Centre for Reviews and Dissemination.

NICE (2004). *Guideline Development Methods: Information for national collaborating centres and guideline developers*. London: National Institute for Clinical Excellence.

Nuttall, C. (2003). The Home Office and random allocation experiments. *Evaluation Review*, 27(3), 267–289.

Oakley, A. (1992). *Social Support in Motherhood: The natural history of a research project*. Oxford: Blackwell.

Oakley, A. (2000). *Experiments in Knowing: Gender and method in the social sciences*. Cambridge: Polity Press.

Oakley, A., Fullerton, D., & Holland, J. (1995). Behavioural interventions for HIV/AIDS prevention. *AIDS*, 9(5), 479–486.

Oakley, A., Strange, V., Toroyan, T., Wiggins, M., Roberts, I., & Stephenson, J. (2003). Using random allocation to evaluate social interventions: three recent UK examples. *The Annals of the American Academy of Political* and *Social Science*, 589, 170–189.

Orr, L. L. (1999). *Social Experiments: Evaluating public programs with experimental methods*. Thousand Oaks, CA: Sage.

Parsons, W. (2001). Modernising policy making for the twenty first century: the professional model. *Public Policy and Administration*, 16(3), 93–110.

Parsons, W. (2002). From muddling through to muddling up: evidence based policy-making and the modernisation of British government. *Public Policy and Administration*, 17(3), 43–60.

Patton, M. Q. (2001). Evaluation, knowledge management, best practices, and high quality lessons learned. *American Journal of Evaluation*, 22(3), 329–336.

Pawson, R. (1997). An introduction to scientific realist evaluation. In E. Chelimsky & W. R. Shadish (eds). *Evaluation for the 21st Century: A handbook* (pp. 405–418). Thousand Oaks, CA: Sage,

Pawson, R. & Tilley, N. (1993). OXO, Tide, brand X and new improved evaluation. Paper presented at the British Sociological Association Annual Conference, University of Essex.

Pawson, R. & Tilley, N. (1994). What works in evaluation research?, *British Journal of Criminology*, 34(3), 291–306.

Pawson, R. & Tilley, N. (1997). *Realistic Evaluation*. London: Sage.

Petrosino, A., Boruch, R. F., Rounding, C., McDonald, S., & Chalmers, I. (2000). The Campbell Collaboration Social, Psychological, Educational and Criminological Trials Register (C2–SPECTR) to facilitate the preparation and maintenance of systematic reviews of social and educational interventions. *Evaluation and Research in Education*, 14(3/4), 206–219.

Petrosino, A., Boruch, R., Soydan, H., Duggan, L., & Sanchez-Meca, J. (2001). Meeting the challenge of evidence-based policy: The Campbell Collaboration. *Annals of the American Academy of Political and Social Sciences*, 578, 14–34.

Polanyi, M. (1958). *Personal Knowledge: Towards a post critical philosophy*. London: Routledge & Kegan Paul.

Pollitt, C. (1993). *Managerialism and the Public Services*, 2nd edition. Oxford: Blackwell.

Power, M. (1997). *The Audit Society: Rituals of Verification*. Oxford: Oxford University Press.

Prescott, R. J., Counsell, C. E., Gillespie, W. J., Grant, A. M., Russell, I. T., Kiauka, S., Colthart, I. E., Ross, S., Shepherd, S. M., & Russell, D. (1999). Factors that limit the quality, number and progress of randomised controlled trials. *Health Technology Assessment*, 3: 20, 1–143.

Reynolds, S. (2000). The anatomy of evidence-based practice: principles and methods. In L. Trinder with S. Reynolds (eds) *Evidence-Based Practice: A Critical appraisal*. (pp. 17–34). Oxford: Blackwell Science.

Ritter, G. W. & Boruch, R. F. (1999). The political and institutional origins of a randomized controlled trial on elementary school class size: Tennessee's Project STAR. *Educational Evaluation and Policy Analysis*, 21(2), 111–125.

Donald, A. (1995). Evidence based medicine: an approach to clinical problem solving. *British Medical Journal*, 310, 1122–1126.

Rossi, P. H. & Freeman, H. E. (1993). *Evaluation: A systematic approach*, 5th edition. Newbury Park, CA: Sage.

Rossi, P. H. & Wright, J. D. (1984). Evaluation research: an assessment. *Annual Review of Sociology*, 10, 331–352.

Sackett, D., Rosenberg, W., Gray, J., Haynes, R., & Richardson, W. (1996). Evidence based medicine: what it is and what it isn't. *British Medical Journal*, 312, 71–72.

Schwandt, T. A. (2000). Further diagnostic thoughts on what ails evaluation practice. *American Journal of Evaluation*, 21(2), 225–229.

Schwartz, D., Flamant, R., & Lellouch, J. (1980). *Clinical Trials*. London: Academic Press.

Scriven, M. (1994). The fine line between evaluation and explanation. *Evaluation Practice*, 15(1), 75–77.

Shadish, W., Cook, T., & Campbell, D. (2002). *Experimental and Quasi-experimental Designs for Generalized Causal Inference*. Boston: Houghton Mifflin Company.

Sheldon, B. (1986). Social work effectiveness experiments: reviews and implications. *British Journal of Social Work*, 16, 223–242.

Sheldon, B. & Chilvers, R. (2000). *Evidence-Based Social Care: A study of prospects and problems*. Lyme Regis, Dorset: Russell House Publishing.

Shepherd, J. P. (2003). Explaining feast or famine in randomized field trials: medical science and criminology compared. *Evaluation Review*, 27(3), 290–315.

Sherman, L. W. (1998). *Evidence-Based Policing*. Washington, DC: Police Foundation.

Sherman, L. W., Gottfredson, D. C., Mackenzie, D. L., Eck, J., Reuter, P., & Bushway, S. D. (1998). *Preventing Crime: What works, what doesn't, what's promising*. Washington, DC: U.S. National Institute of Justice.

Simons, H. (2004). Utilizing evaluation evidence to enhance professional practice. *Evaluation*, 10(4), 410–429.

Speller, V., Learmonth, A., & Harrison, D. (1997). The search for evidence of effective health promotion. *British Medical Journal*, 315, 361–363.

Stecher, B. M. & Davis, W. A. (1987). *How to Focus an Evaluation*. Newbury Park, CA: Sage.

Stevens, A. & Abrams, K. R. (2001). Consensus, reviews and meta-analysis: an introduction. In A. Stevens et al. (eds) ibid. (pp. 367–369).

Stevens, A., Fitzpatrick, R., Abrams, K., Brazier, J., & Lilford, R. (2001). Methods in evidence based healthcare and health technology assessment: an overview. In A. Stevens, K. Abrams, J. Brazier, R. Fitzpatrick & R. Lilford (eds) *The Advanced Handbook of Methods in Evidence Based Healthcare*. (pp. 1–5). London: Sage.

Sweeney, K. (1996). Evidence and uncertainty. In M. Marinker (ed.) *Sense and Sensibility in Health Care*. (pp. 59–86). London: BMJ Publishing Group.

Tilley, N. (2000). Doing realistic evaluation of criminal justice. In V. Jupp, P. Davies, & P. Francis (eds) *Doing Criminological Research*. London: Sage.

Tilley, N. & Laycock, G. (2000). Joining up research, policy and practice about crime. *Policy Studies*, 21(3), 213–227.

Trinder, L. (2000a). A critical appraisal of evidence-based practice. In L. Trinder with S. Reynolds (eds) *Evidence-Based Practice: A critical appraisal*, (pp. 211–238). Oxford: Blackwell Science.

Trinder, L. (2000b). Evidence-based practice in social work and probation. In L. Trinder with S. Reynolds (eds) ibid. (pp. 138–162).

Turner, H., Boruch, R., Petrosino, A., Lavenberg, J., de Moya, D., & Rothstein, H. (2003). Populating an international web-based randomized trials register in the social, behavioural, criminological and education sciences. *Annals of the American Academy of Political* and *Social Science*, 589, 203–223.

US General Accounting Office (1996). *Executive Guide: Effectively implementing the Government Performance and Results Act*. Washington DC: Author (GGD-96–118).

Weisburd, D. (2000). Randomized experiments in criminal justice policy: prospects and problems. *Crime and Delinquency*, 46, 181–193.

Weisburd, D. (2003). Ethical practice and evaluation of interventions in crime and justice: the moral imperative for randomized trials. *Evaluation Review*, 27(3), 336–354.

Weiss, C. H. (1987). Evaluating social programs: what have we learned?. *Society*, 25(1), 40–45.

Weiss, C. H. (1998). *Evaluation: Methods for studying programs and policies*, Upper Saddle River, NJ: Prentice Hall.

Wolf, F. M. (1986). *Meta-analysis: Quantitative methods for research synthesis*. Beverley Hills: Sage.

Woolf, S. H., Battista, R. N., Anderson, G. M. Logan, A. G., & Wang, E. (1990). Assessing the clinical effectiveness of preventive manoeuvres: analytic principles and systematic methods in reviewing evidence and developing clinical practice recommendations. *Journal of Clinical Epidemiology*, 43, 891–905.

Young, K., Ashby, D., Boaz, A., & Grayson, L. (2002). Social science and the evidence-based policy movement. *Social Policy and Society*, 1(3), 215–224.

AUTHOR INDEX

SUBJECT INDEX

Figures and Tables in italics. n, note